Mona Johnson
Brunel Us

Neuropsychology

Brain systems and psycho

✓ Neuropsychology
✓ Psychophysiology blasis - 15 ⇒ good / bad - v. much. Mona
✓ Psychobiology !   culturally determined.

at the innate level we are all born ⊂
1) a liking for the sweet
2) a dislike for the bitter
3) We don't like looming objects.
   Pain + tissue damage

The way we survive this the way the organism
has adapted.

         The brain is key adaptive.

approx
100 different chemicals ⊂ the brain
∴ Replacement therapy - ie dopamine for
   Parkinson pts.

Ocytolcoalhine = connects ⊂ memory.

Transplant cells into the brain (Sweden)
1) + supplying missing chemicals
2) Foetal transplants produce new nerve cells.

Brain systems and psychological concepts

John Boddy

Lecturer in Psychology
University of Manchester

John Wiley & Sons

Chichester New York Brisbane Toronto

Dendrites bring messages to cell

Library of Congress Cataloging in Publication Data:

Boddy, John.
   Brain systems and psychological concepts.

   Bibliography: p.
   Includes index.
   1. Neuropsychology. 2. Brain. I. Title.

QP360.B624 152 77-21203

ISBN 0 471 99601 7 (cloth)
ISBN 0 471 99600 9 (paper)

Typeset by Reproduction Drawings Ltd, Sutton, Surrey.

Printed in Great Britain by J. W. Arrowsmith Ltd.
Winterstoke Road, Bristol

The Head weighs approx 12 lbs × 10^{12}

There are more than 10,000 million cells in the human brain.

Each cubic inch of the cerebral cortex probably contains more than 10,000 miles of nerve fibres, connecting the cells together (The tangle within our heads make us what we are). If the cells & fibres in a brain were all stretched out end to end they would reach to the moon & back — yet the

To Bill and Betty
who gave me life and good values
to live by

fact that they are _not_ arranged end to end enabled man to go there himself.

35% of Communication is Verbal
The rest is body language.

Nuclear Acid = 4 Basic Units. — DNA

C
G
A
T

Acknowledgements

DNA can be extracted from the cell pour on some
washy up liquid & then some alcohol – stre-
um on UV light & can clearly see the
gluey DNA.
Basic Structure ⌐T A G C
⌐A T C G

always the code

DNA → RNA

→ Protein. Makes

The working Molecule
of the cell.

To begin at the beginning. I should first acknowledge the influence of Dr. G. Wallace who infected me with his enthusiasm for physiological psychology when he taught me as an undergraduate at Reading University. I hope that this book pleases him.

While writing this book I have gone through many trials and tribulations. The interest, encouragement, and support of many friends has given me the will to overcome bad times and complete it. I thank them all, particularly George Pavlidis.

Many students have read draft chapters of the book and I must thank them for their valuable critical comments.

My colleague, John Wearden, has an encyclopaedic knowledge of physiological psychology and I am indebted to him for guiding me to vital literature, particularly on the need for stimulation and the storage of information.

Most important, I must express my gratitude to the people who helped directly in the production of the finished typescript: to Terry Evans for his patience and for the precision of his exacting work on the preparation of the illustrations; to Leslie Robinson for typing the labels on the figures; to Marion Elms for undertaking the tedious job of typing the references.

Enzymes = 20 code

DNA to a protein is a 3 letter code

$4 \times \times 4 = 64$

Contents

Chapter three   Research techniques in psychobiology   79

PART 3   THE SPRINGS OF ACTION   105

Chapter four   Serving internal needs: hunger, thirst and body temperature   107

Chapter five   Sex and reproductive behaviour   137

Preface

I have been fascinated by the study of the brain mechanisms mediating behaviour since I was a psychology undergraduate in the early 1960s. It has since been the focus of my career in teaching and research at Manchester University. I have long wanted to write a wide ranging, not too specialist book on the subject, for my own education, if for nobody else's. I believe that scientists have an obligation to communicate their subjects vividly and intelligibly to as wide a public as possible. The public at large pays the scientist and so has a right to some return. This book is an attempt to expound psychobiology to an intelligent public without too much oversimplification or sacrifice of scholarship. Its primary target is students of psychology in their first and second years but it is hoped that there might be a wider readership from students of related disciplines and members of the public at large seeking an understanding of the natural phenomena which touch them most closely.

In the past the subject matter of this book would have been called physiological psychology, although I now think that the wide scope of the subject makes psychobiology a more appropriate term. Undergraduate students of psychology have often tended to find the physiological psychology component of their course an alien subject, whose relevance to the rest of psychology they have found difficult to see. Often their antagonism has been compounded by the difficulty which they have had in understanding the subject, particularly when they have lacked a good background in science subjects. In this book there is an effort to make physiological psychology (or psychobiology) relevant and intelligible to the student of psychology and to convey the excitement and challenge of attempts to understand the brain systems mediating our behaviour. To achieve these aims a radical departure from the traditional organization, emphasis, and style of physiological psychology books has been pursued.

It is my opinion that traditional books on physiological psychology contained too much physiology, particularly neurophysiology and sensory physiology, and not enough psychology. Thus, it is without apology that this book presents only the essentials of neuroanatomy, neurophysiology and sensory physiology. If the reader requires further details they can readily be found elsewhere. The emphasis in this work is on the study of brain systems mediating consciousness and behaviour, classified in a way which makes good sense to psychologists.

The perspective and tone of the book is set by an opening chapter on the evolution of the brain and some of its wider implications. There follows a section of the necessary groundwork on the nervous system and research methodology. The core of the book is in the sections: 'Springs of action' and 'Handling of information' (Parts III and IV), reflecting the two major approaches in contemporary psychology. Hopefully, the relevance of sensory physiology is more clearly demonstrated by its integration in the section on information handling. The final section, on the chemical basis of consciousness and behaviour dwells on issues brought into sharp focus by contemporary studies of the brain and which might now be considered to be an essential part of a psychologist's education, particularly because of their relevance to clinical psychology.

The neglect of central mechanisms in early works on physiological psychology quite reasonably reflected the fact that the brain was *terra incognita*. In recent years a great deal of research has been done on brain systems mediating consciousness and behaviour, much of it very exciting. However, writers have remained shy of including much of the data and theory because of its tentative nature. Many well publicized findings have subsequently been challenged by contradictory results. However, science progresses by a process of successive approximations. An understanding of this process may be as important to the student as acquiring knowledge of established facts, which can be remarkably elusive in a subject like psychobiology. This work does not claim to present only established facts. The incentive for a scientist's commitment is not solely the excitement of discovering facts. A stronger motivation may be the aesthetic attraction of seeking conceptually elegant solutions to the intellectual problems posed by phenomena demanding an explanation. In deference to my belief in the importance of this motivation many theories of a speculative nature are presented to the reader of this book. None of them is likely to be the whole truth and some of them may turn out to be quite wrong. However, the exposition of theories puts the empirical data of a subject within a logical framework which illuminates their significance and aids memory. Furthermore their elaboration will have served its purpose if it generates just a little intellectual excitement and creates a conceptual matrix on which the reader can build. Even the incorporation in the matrix of ideas which later prove to be wrong can still be valuable. The experience of their refutation helps to sharpen critical awareness and improve the flexibility of thought about a subject.

Inevitably, a great deal of data and theory is omitted. The contents of the book must reflect the particular interests and theoretical bias of the writer. This is the privilege of a writer who attempts to communicate his subject to a wider public. The possible penalty is the critical indignation which it arouses in colleagues. However, an attempt to be impartial bores with its shyness from the stimulation of theory and confuses with its equivocation. A book showing an honest bias, so long as it is made explicit, is more valuable if it stimulates interest and creates a perspective which can be enriched and modified by further study.

> The reader should note that, in lieu of a glossary, terms which
> are defined in the text appear in bold type in the index.

PART 1
PERSPECTIVE

Chapter one

Adapting to the environment

Introduction

The most distinctive and remarkable feature of man is his brain. Through the mediation of this organ man has made an infinitely greater impact on the planet earth than any other species living or dead. It is man's brain which is responsible for the range, diversity, and complexity of his behaviour, for his acute and finely detailed consciousness and for his unique capacity for reflection. These are more than sufficient reasons to study the relationship between man's brain and man's psychology.

Man is the culmination of a long, slow process of elaboration called evolution. The key to evolution is adaptation to the environment. Each evolutionary progression, from the dawn of life to man, occurred because it enhanced the ability of its possessor to adapt and thus, to survive. The multiplication and elaboration of the systems of the brain represents the most significant trend in evolution. An understanding of this process is therefore intrinsic to an understanding of the systems which operate in the evolved brain. Furthermore, a more general understanding of evolution and its ramifications creates a perspective against which the profound importance of the brain can be fully appreciated. With these arguments in mind we follow this preamble with an account of the most primitive forms of life, proceed to consider the basis of evolutionary progress, and then briefly survey the evolution of the brain through the evolutionary hierarchy of animal forms.

When unambiguous animal life first emerged from the 'organic soup' which is thought to have composed the seas of the cooling earth [Oparin, 1938; see also Jessop, 1970, Chapter 10] it took the form of a single cell. It was of the genus protazoa, often exemplified by the primitive amoeba. The boundary of this primordial cell was a semipermeable membrane enclosing a distinctive nucleus and a variety of other structures, supported by a complete matrix of internal membrane and fluid. These primordial cells were the ancestors of all cells, the basic structural units from which all living creatures are built.

Living organisms are distinguished from inorganic matter by being in a state of 'dynamic equilibrium'. This is a state in which the tendency of the organism to disintegrate into its inorganic constituents is constantly opposed by efforts to renew its spent energy resources and obtain materials to repair its structure.

For organisms to sustain the inner processes upon which their continued existence depends they must conduct appropriate transactions with their environment. They must ingest nutrients, organic substances necessary to power their activities, produce growth, and maintain their structure (see Chapter 4). The sum total of chemical reactions in which the nutrients are utilized is referred to as the organism's metabolism. The waste products residual from metabolic processes must be excreted. Organisms must avoid extreme environmental conditions (e.g. too hot or too cold) and toxic substances likely to damage their structure and disrupt their function.

In order to conduct these transactions with the environment the organism requires the functional properties of irritability, plasticity (implying information storage) and motility—properties which are possessed even by the most primitive members of the animal kingdom. Irritability implies that the organism is sensitive to environmental stimuli, and motility, that it can respond to internal or external stimuli with movement. Plasticity is the basis of information storage. It permits an organism to modify its responses to environmental stimuli according to their significance for its survival. In primitive organisms the store of information may be implicit in the differential sensitivity of receptors to foods and poisons. In the amoeba, for instance, chemical receptors which respond differentially to nutrients influence sluggish pseudopodia. These temporary motile projections of the cell mass enable the creature to approach and assimilate food.

The mechanisms described promote the survival of the organism and are therefore mechanisms for adapting to the environment. As will become apparent, the concept of adaptation is a primary one in considering the dynamics of evolution and the rationale of behaviour.

The nervous system

The basic mechanisms of adaptation to the environment in the most primitive organisms are precursors of elaborated forms of the same mechanisms in more highly evolved creatures. These higher animals are multi-celled with specialization of function among the cells. In these animals the functions of irritability and information storage are handled by specialized cells, called nerve cells or neurons (see Figure 2.1). These are collectively organized to form the nervous system (see Figure 1.1), which is the body's control and communication system. The neurones are highly specialized descendants of the original unicellular organisms. Neurones are distinguished by having a process, called the axon, which may be highly elongated so that information can be carried speedily between widely separated organs of the body.

As the nervous system developed in vertebrates (animals with a back-

Figure 1.1
The nervous system of
man: global view.

From Chandler Elliott,
H. (1970) *The shape of
intelligence*, New York,
Charles Scribner's Sons.
Reproduced by
permission of the artist,
Anthony Ravielli

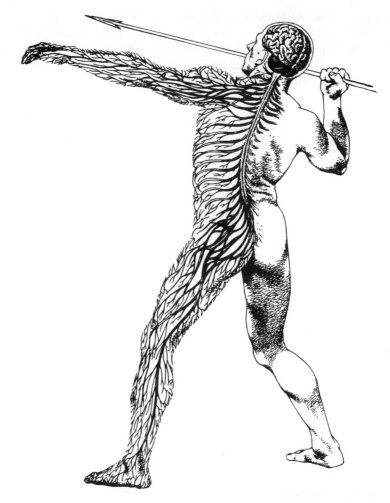

Figure 1.2
Lateral aspect of the
human brain

Courtesy of the
Department of
Anatomy, University
of Manchester

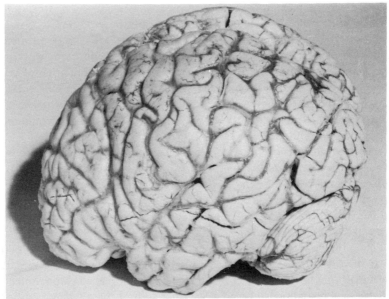

bone) it became organized around a concentrated mass of nervous tissue in the head, called the brain (Figure 1.2). The brain receives messages from the sense organs. These are extensions of the nervous system containing specialized receptor cells, which represent the most 'irritable' or sensitive of living cells. The different sense organs are constructed to respond selectively to different classes of environmental information. The senses are vision, audition, body senses (touch, pressure, pain, and temperature), smell, taste, orientation and proprioception (giving information about position and movement from receptors in the muscles).

Coming between the sensory and motor systems, the brain analyses, evaluates, and collates incoming information. It stores information when appropriate, and selects, initiates, monitors, and controls the organism's response patterns.

The elaboration of the brain and nervous system represents a line of development based on functional properties possessed by the earliest living creatures. It is a development which is subsumed under the general heading 'biological evolution'. We must appreciate the process of biological evolution in order to understand how the development of the brain and nervous system came about.

Biological evolution

The general nature of biological evolution has been the elaboration and diversification of life forms stemming from the common origin of the primeval cell. The suggestion that the earth's animal life was the result of 'descent with modification through variation and natural selection' or evolution, as the process is now called, was first put forward by Charles Darwin in his famous book *On the origin of species*, published in 1859. Darwin's hypothesis revolutionized biology and, although it has been modified in detail, its essence is now considered to be proven [Dobzhansky, 1962, p. 6, second edition].

The most general statement of the principle of evolution is that it proceeds by random mutation of the genes and the selection of adaptive mutations. This is a more precise version of Darwin's 'modification through variation and natural selection'. The understanding that mutation of the genes was the basis of 'variation' had to wait until Mendel's [1866] classic theory of the genetic basis of inheritance, not published until the end of the nineteenth century, had gained wide currency [for popular account see Dobzhansky, 1950].

The genes are analogous to a blueprint, collectively carrying the information which determines that a new life will inherit the characteristics of its parents. Every cell in the body carries the full complement of an organism's genes with two exceptions: the red blood cells, which carry no genetic material, and the sex cells in sexually reproducing animals, which carry half the complement of an organism's genes.

Primitive unicellular animals reproduce asexually by simple division into two, a process known as mitosis. When this happens the genetic material, after being organized into thread-like bodies called chromosomes, divides and reduplicates in such a way that each of the progeny resulting from mitosis inherits exactly the same complement of genes as its parent.

As a result each new organism is a carbon copy of both its twin and its parent. In turn it gives rise to further generations, each a copy of all preceding generations and each perpetuating the original configuration of genes.

Mutation of the genes

So long as the stability of the genes is preserved the reproductive process leads only to unending regeneration of identical organisms. The potential for evolution resides in the fact that the structure of the genes is not completely stable. Occasionally and at random a modification to this structure, called a mutation, spontaneously occurs. Radioactivity and certain chemical agents are sometimes responsible for gene mutation. The mutation of a gene in a parent implies that its progeny will be 'constructed' from a modified 'blueprint'. They will thus differ from their parent in some structural or functional characteristic. Any new mutation (the term refers to both the modification of the gene and the novel creature which results from this modification) is searchingly tested for fitness by the 'selective pressures' of the environment. Darwin hypothesized that evolution was governed by the law of 'survival of the fittest', an alternative expression to 'natural selection'. Fitness is an expression of the ability of an individual or a species to survive and perpetuate itself in its environment. The 'selective pressures' of the environment are the features of the environment requiring specific adaptive adjustments. These features include climate, terrain, vegetation, and other species, both predator and prey. For example in a cold climate the selective pressures would favour mutations improving the insulating qualities of an animal's coat.

If a mutation enhances or maintains the capacity of an organism to survive and reproduce then it will be preserved in future generations. No mutated gene reverts to its previous form but, if adaptive, it is perpetuated in its mutated form in subsequent generations unless further mutations occur.

Clearly a mutation reducing or destroying an organism's viability in its environment faces rapid extinction. This is the fate of most mutations. However, mutations which are successful may be the initial step in a chain of adaptive mutations. Extending over many generations, they may transform the organism beyond recognition into an altogether more elaborate and complex form. The process is immensely wasteful as mutation is always a random event and only a small fraction of the mutations which occur give the organism an adaptive advantage in its environment.

Direction in evolution

An outstanding characteristic of the evolutionary process is the fact that it has produced enormous diversity of life forms, representing many different directions in evolution. This diversification has been made possible by the way in which accidents of mutation have interacted with the multiplicity

of complex environments which have existed on this earth. In turn diversification has been encouraged by the way in which different species in the
same environment have established mutually dependent relationships. A
common example is the relationship between bees and flowers, in which
the flowers supply the bees with food, while the bees carry flower pollen
between the flowers for cross-fertilization.

Environmental complexity has implied many different evolutionary
routes to successful adaptation. This is reflected in the development of
many different themes, each offering adaptive advantages peculiar to
themselves. Examples of themes which have been the subject of a degree
of specialization are size (elephant), strength (lion), armour (rhinocerous),
camouflage (chameleon), speed (cheetah), insulation (polar bear) and
behavioural flexibility (man). Of course specialization has not meant that
a species has confined itself to developing one of these themes at the
expense of all the others. It has rather meant that a greater emphasis has
been placed on a theme or combination of themes relative to other adaptive features. For instance in the human species size, strength, speed,
armour, camouflage, and insulation have all been relatively neglected if we
are compared with other species. In our evolutionary development the
theme which has proved most profitable has been the elaboration of the
brain and nervous system in conjunction with manipulative apparatus,
the hands. This development has bestowed the outstandingly important
functional property of behavioural flexibility. This in turn has resulted in
an evolutionary breakthrough. Members of the human species have been
freed from the prison of their immediate environment because their
behavioural flexibility has enabled them to adapt to new environments
(or even modify their environment) without the need for slow metamorphosis by mutation of the genes and selection of mutations which are
adaptive to the environment.

Sexual reproduction

Despite random gene mutation, asexual reproduction could not produce
sufficient diversity and flexibility in evolution, it could only produce a
species in which each individual was a carbon copy of all other individuals,
who stood or fell together in the face of environmental adversity. Sexual
reproduction, which achieves segregation and recombination of the genes,
opens up new possibilities in evolution. Sexual reproduction has two
primary stages rather than the one of asexual reproduction. In the parent
of each sex the first stage is the formation of the sex cells or gametes (ova
in the female, sperm in the male). This is achieved by a form of cell
division known as meiosis. In meiosis the products of division inherit only
half of the complement of genes in the parent cell rather than the full
complement, as in mitosis.

The full complement of genes in sexually reproducing animals consists
of many thousands of genes organized in homologous (corresponding in
general structure) pairs (e.g. AA, BB, CC, DD etc.). The genes in each pair
may be identical (homozygous). However, each gene may have one or
more variants (alleles: e.g. $A_1, A_2, A_3 \ldots A_n$), which have occurred by

mutation, making pairs of non-identical alleles of a gene (heterozygous pairs) a possibility (e.g. A_1A_2, A_1A_3, A_2A_3). When meiosis occurs to produce the sex cells each product receives one gene from each of the homologous pairs, selection being on a random basis. Thus formation of the gametes produces segregation of the genes.

The second primary stage of sexual reproduction occurs following sexual union when, during fertilization, the sex cells contributed by each parent fuse to form the zygote. Each sex cell contributes a half set of genes, each gene destined to pair with its homologue, contributed by the other sex cell, to achieve recombination of the genes. Thus the zygote gains a full complement of genes properly organized in pairs. These genes programme the development of the new individual through its embryonic, foetal, infant, adolescent, and adult forms, with the details of development being modulated by the environment. The structural development of the organism from the zygote proceeds by the mitotic form of cell division.

The advantage of sexual reproduction becomes apparent when we consider the fact that each gene in any species may have one or more variants (known as polymorphism). The implication of this is that while the configuration of genes donated by the parents of an individual will endow him with the general characteristics of his species, the variants on particular genes will produce characteristics, such as red hair or blue eyes, specific to the individuals carrying those variants. We have seen that the particular combination of genes an individual receives is a matter of chance in the process of segregation and recombination, achieved by sexual reproduction. It follows that if many genes in a species have one or more variants (are heterozygous) then sexual reproduction opens up the possibility of a very large number of possible combinations of genes in individuals. It has been calculated that in the human species the number of possible genetic endowments is so great that it is extremely unlikely that any two individuals (apart from identical twins resulting from mitotic division of the zygote into two separate product cells) have ever had, or are ever likely to have the same constellation of genes [Dobzhansky, 1962, p. 30, second edition].

The transition to sexual reproduction greatly enhanced the potential for evolutionary progress implied by gene mutation. Differences in genetic make-up imply differences in structural and functional characteristics. Thus the constant manufacture of novelty effected by the segregation and recombination of the genes in sexual reproduction implies constant experiment, within a species, on the adaptive value of particular combinations of genes.

The totality of genes in a breeding population at any point in time constitutes the 'gene pool' from which the population draws to perpetuate itself. The structure of the gene pool can be specified in terms of the relative frequency with which specific alleles (variants) occur. The structure of the gene pool from which a population draws will be moulded to conform with the demands of its environment. More importantly, the gene pool will have a latent capacity to respond to changes in the selective pressures of the environment by changing its own structure appropriately.

A prominent example of the way in which the environment has acted upon the gene pools of different populations of the same species is genes for dark pigmentation of the skin which protect human populations living in hot regions, from the sun. These genes have not emerged in populations living in cooler, cloudier districts. Genetic variation within a species probably arises because the different mutations of a gene confer adaptive advantages which are different, but of equivalent value. Changes in the environment may reduce the adaptive value of a particular gene and either eliminate it from the gene pool or reduce its proportionate representation.

The prevalence of a particular gene may be mediated by more complex patterns of interdependence. For instance Allison [1954, 1955] has described a recessive gene (a gene whose effect is only felt when paired with the same allele), existing in human populations in west Africa, which if contributed by both parents (producing a homozygote) results in a severe anaemia (sickle cell anaemia) which is lethal for the sufferer. Clearly this gene is far from being adaptive. As the gene is recessive an individual receiving it from only one parent (a heterozygote) only suffers from a sub-clinical form of anaemia. However, in addition the heterozygote has higher resistance to certain virulent malarial fevers than persons in the population entirely lacking the sickle cell gene. Those who are heterozygous for the sickle cell anaemia gene are thus the fittest individuals in the population. This adaptive advantage, peculiar to the heterozygote, is called hybrid vigour. In the example cited above the potentially lethal mutation has been preserved in a particular proportion in the population gene pool because of its capacity to defend the other genes when it occurs in the heterozygote. The phenomenon is known as balanced polymorphism. This example also illustrates the way in which environmental factors act on the gene pool, the adaptive value of the recessive sickle cell anaemia gene being contingent on the prevalence of malaria. When individuals lacking the gene for sickle cell anaemia are not threatened by malaria the adaptive advantage of this gene in the heterozygote disappears so that the gene tends to disappear from the gene pool.

Particulate inheritance and unit characteristics

The idea that heredity is particulate, first proposed by the Russian monk, Mendel [1866], has been implicit in the preceding discussion. In contrast to the notion that heredity is determined by a 'blending' of the 'bloods' of the parents, this theory proposes that indivisible units of hereditary material, the genes, endow their possessors with a fixed potential for development along certain lines, in an 'all or none' fashion. The early supposition in the theory of particulate inheritance that unit characteristics, such as eye colour, coat colour, or even intelligence were determined by single genes has had to be abandoned [see Dobzhansky, 1962, pp. 33–37, second edition]. It appears that many or all of the genes may contribute to the development of any particular characteristic in an individual, in which case the characteristic is said to be polygenic. Conversely an individual gene may be pleiotropic and contribute to the development of several, possibly diverse characteristics. For instance it has been found that genes conferring particular coat colours in rodents are also partial determinants of body size [Connolly, 1971].

Genotype and phenotype

The configuration of genes which an individual carries has been characterized as his genotype [Johannsen, 1911]. Barring mutation, the genotype is fixed for the life of the organism. The genes determine the pattern of development of the organism and the general characteristics of its responses to its environment. However, the genes are not the sole determinants of these features, as the pattern of development programmed by the genes is modulated by the effects of the environment. Thus any individual is a product of the interaction of his genotype with the environment, and this product has been called the phenotype [Johannsen, 1911]. There are marked variations in the relative influence of genes and environment on different characteristics of the organism. The general morphology of our species (e.g. a head, a body, two arms, two legs, etc.) is fixed solely by our genes, as is eye colour and hair colour. Stature, once thought to be genetically determined, has been shown to be modulated by environmental influences, such as aspects of infant care and diet. On the other hand the language which we speak is determined solely by early experience (see Chapter 7), our genes only having provided us with the brain, nervous system, and muscle control that makes language possible. The relative contribution of genes and environment to such psychological dimensions as intelligence and personality is still the subject of vigorous debate, and there is undoubtedly a very complex gene–environment interaction in these cases. Behavioural geneticists have shown by techniques of 'inbreeding' and 'cross fostering' that traits such as maze learning ability and proneness to 'anxiety' (emotional reactivity) in rats are strongly influenced by the genes (see discussion in Chapter 9). If the phenotype of an adult creature is a complex function of gene–environment interaction, it follows that the adaptive value of a particular gene is not fixed, but varies with its mode of interaction with different environments.

The evolution of the brain

We have seen that evolution proceeded by mutation and selection aided, following the emergence of sexual reproduction, by segregation and recombination of the genes. The diversity, complexity, and changeability of earthbound environments made it inevitable that there would be diverse alternative strategies which evolving species could adopt to ensure at least some degree of evolutionary success: species survival. However, the degree of success which particular strategies permitted was variable. Primary emphasis on size, strength, armour, speed, camouflage, and other specific structural and functional features has proved to have its limitations. The evolutionary strategy which has proved most profitable has been the elaboration of the nervous system and brain in conjunction with manipulative ability. This has conferred the incomparable generalized functional

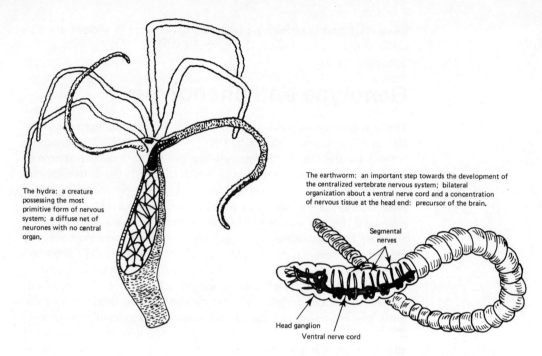

The hydra: a creature possessing the most primitive form of nervous system; a diffuse net of neurones with no central organ.

The earthworm: an important step towards the development of the centralized vertebrate nervous system; bilateral organization about a ventral nerve cord and a concentration of nervous tissue at the head end: precursor of the brain.

Segmental nerves

Head ganglion

Ventral nerve cord

Figure 1.3 Primitive nervous systems.

From Chandler Elliott, H. (1970) *The shape of intelligence*, New York, Charles Scribner's Sons. Reproduced by permission of the artist, Anthony Ravielli

advantage of behavioural flexibility. Evolution in this direction is seen at its apogee in man, a creature in which other qualities, for example speed and strength, have been neglected. In externals man is a puny and ill-protected being.

To gain a perspective on the adaptive value of man's brain it is educative to follow the evolution of the nervous system and brain in outline, and examine the functional properties conferred at different levels on the evolutionary scale.

Primitive nervous systems

The most primitive nervous systems (Figure 1.3) are found in aquatic coelenterates such as hydra, jelly fish, sea anemones, and coral. In hydra there are sensory cells, variously sensitive to chemical or mechanical stimuli, which are either directly connected to effectors (which comprise the organism's response system) or which feed into the organism's communication network. This comprises a web of nerve cells more or less uniformly distributed throughout the organism. As their nervous system is not organized around a co-ordinating central organ, isolated local responses often occur in these creatures. Over-all responses are slow and stereotyped because of the slow diffusion of impulses through the nerve network.

In the jelly fish, a radially symmetrical organism, the first step towards centralization of the nervous system is seen in the two nerve rings which occupy the 'bell' or 'umbrella' of the creature. The large upper ring receives fibres from sense organs and supplies the musculature which activates the bell. This arrangement facilitates speedy directional conduction of nerve impulses and promotes co-ordinated movement, such as is seen in the vigorous contractions of the bell by which the jelly fish propels itself along.

Radial nervous systems

The radial nervous system seen in its rudimentary form in the jelly fish, reaches the peak of its development in echinoderms such as sea urchins, sea cucumbers, and starfish. Connection between receptors and effectors is no longer direct, permitting isolated local activity, but is mediated by intermediate, internuncial, or associational neurones. In the starfish, for instance, radial nerves (the term nerve refers to a bundle of nerve fibres) serving each of the five arms are each connected to a circumoral ring of nerves which has a dominant controlling function. The circumoral ring is able to co-ordinate the creature's activities, for example providing the ordered sequence of arm movements used in 'walking'. These creatures are altogether more versatile in their behaviour than creatures with an indiscriminate nerve net. They display a variety of behaviours when feeding and even show temporary modification of behaviour following the application of aversive stimuli.

Bilateral nervous systems and encephalization

A momentous landmark in the evolution of nervous systems was the appearance of a bilaterally symmetrical organization of the body around

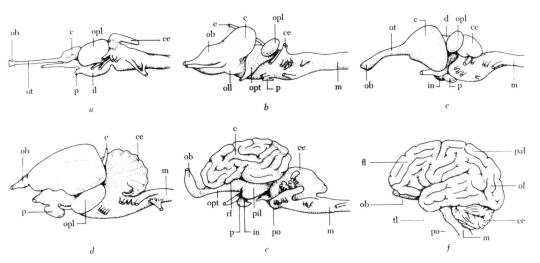

Figure 1.4

The process of encephalization: some stages in the evolutionary development of the vertebrate brain shown in representative species; (a) codfish, (b) frog, (c) alligator, (d) goose, (e) horse, (f) man. Sizes range from less than 1 cm in fish to 12–15 cm in man. Weights range from a few grams to 1200–1400 g. Key: c, cerebrum; ce, cerebellum; d, diencephalon; e, epiphysis; fl, frontal lobe; il, inferior lobe; in, infundibulum; m, medulla; ol, occipital lobe; ob, olfactory bulb; oll, olfactory lobe; opl, optic lobe; ot, olfactory tract; opt, optic tract; p, pituitary; pal, parietal lobe; pl, pyriform lobe; po, pons; rf, rhinal fissure; tl, temporal lobe.

From Rommer, A. S. (1962) *The vertebrate body*, London, W. B. Saunders and Co. Reproduced by permission of the publishers

a central axis, with a definite front and back. This is seen in the most primitive worms and is accompanied by the appearance of a central cord of nervous tissue coinciding with the central axis, and a perceptible accumulation of nervous tissue at the front. The central core of nervous tissue is called the notochord and is the precursor of the spinal cord. The accumulation of nervous tissue at the head end is called the head ganglion, and is the precursor of the brain. The body of the worm is divided into segments, each served by a corresponding segment of the nervous system. The segments of the nervous system are able to operate independently, as evidenced by the persistence of movement in the parts of a dismembered worm. Sensory nerves from external receptor organs travel to the notochord, where they connect with motor fibres destined for the musculature. This pattern of connection is a reflex arc. The notochord also provides a communication channel between segments, which facilitates co-ordinated patterns of movement by the whole body. The head ganglion evaluates information from primitive sense receptors (light sensitive and chemosensitive) in the head and initiates movements towards or away from stimuli, according to their significance. As one moves up the vertebrate subphylum (subsection of the animal kingdom) the development of the brain gathers momentum in a process which has been called 'encephalization' (Figure 1.4). As the brain or higher nervous system grows in size the greater the degree of control it exercises over the segments of the spinal cord and the less these segments are able to act independently. Thus, the brain comes to monitor input from all sense organs and to mediate all aspects of an animal's behaviour.

Homeostasis

The nervous system and the effector system which it controls have evolved because of their adaptive value in mediating the responses of an organism to its environment, in the interests of the survival of both itself and its species. For an organism to survive, its internal environment, chemical and fluid composition and temperature, must be maintained within very narrow limits. The American physiologist Cannon [1932] used the term homeostasis to express the process of maintaining a steady state of the internal environment (see Chapter 4). Cannon [1932] asserted that all motivation was subordinated to an animal's homeostatic requirements. Motivation is the generic term used in psychology when talking about the 'springs of action' or the genesis of behaviour. Feeding, drinking, and temperature regulating behaviour are obviously homeostatic when they meet their associated needs. Sexual, maternal, aggressive, and exploratory behaviour do not readily fit this conception unless the definition of homeostasis is broadened.

The behaviours listed above require that an organism is able to monitor its internal and external environment with reference to the survival needs of itself and its species. It should also be able to initiate the behaviour necessary to satisfy any current need. In many cases survival behaviour also requires the ability to discriminate potential satisfiers in the external environment, food and drink being obvious examples.

Innate behaviour patterns

In the early stages of evolution a creature's repertoire of adaptive behaviour emerged by the same process of mutation and selection of the genes as its other structural and functional characteristics (see Chapters 4, 5, and 6). The genes supplied a 'wiring diagram' for the nervous system which was little modified by experience. Thus, in existing species with rudimentary nervous systems, the pattern of connections determines that a circumscribed range of simple stimuli will each elicit a stereotyped and inflexible pattern of response.

To give an example, during the mating season the male three-spined stickleback displays aggressive behaviour towards other males making incursions on to its territory. It has been shown that, rather than responding to the total configuration of the invader, the defender's aggressive posture is evoked solely by the invader's red underbelly and nose down posture. Whereas the crudest models of a stickleback are successful in evoking aggression if they have red on them, a faithful model with no red on it is ignored [Tinbergen, 1951]. The aggressive behaviour itself is a ritualized sequence according to whether the fish is inside, at the bounds of, or outside its territory.

Stimuli (like the male stickleback's red underbelly) which creatures are genetically programmed to respond to are called sign stimuli. The stereotyped, stimulus bound patterns of behaviour which they evoke are called innate behaviour patterns.

Another example of slavish adherence to sign stimuli is seen in the mating behaviour of the male silkworm moth [Kellogg, 1907]. The male silkworm moth is able to locate females at distances of up to one mile purely by their scent, as they have very sensitive olfactory organs. However, if an experimenter removes the scent glands from a female moth and presents the male with both the scentless female and the severed scent glands, the male ignores the female and attempts to copulate with the severed scent glands.

There is a qualification to the apparent utter simplicity of the behaviour patterns described above. In the instances of mating behaviour mentioned the creatures will only respond to the sign stimuli when their nervous system is primed by internal hormonal influences. These in turn have been released by external stimuli arising from seasonal changes, such as warmer weather and longer days.

Towards the lower end of the phylogenetic scale (birds, fishes, insects) behaviour patterns can be classified as almost purely innate as they are automatically elicited by sign stimuli, invariant in pattern and sequence and uninfluenced by the creature's experience. As the phylogenetic scale is ascended complexity creeps in and the appearance of innate behaviour patterns, although stereotyped, may be a function of experience during the development of the animal. For instance a female rat reared in isolation will, on reaching maturity, build a nest characteristic of its species if given suitable materials. This strongly suggests that nest building in rats is an instinctive behaviour pattern. However, if a rat is reared, not only in isolation, but in a cage with a mesh floor which allows all solid materials, including the rat's own faeces, to drop through, the nest building behaviour does not appear. The appearance of the genetically programmed nest building appears to be contingent on the rat having had experience of manipulating solid objects [Riess, 1950].

The elaboration of innate behaviour patterns was a phase in evolution which reached its peak in insects and then declined. As the nervous system became larger and more centralized, the role of the genes in the precise programming of a creature's behaviour patterns declined. Larger brained animals have become more and more dependent on acquiring their behavioural repertoire by learning from experience. Larger brains enabled them to discriminate more complex patterns of stimuli in the environment and to develop a wider ranging and more flexible repertoire of behaviours in response. Both the discrimination of stimuli and the pattern of evoked behaviour came to be learned on the basis of the motivational state of the animal and the relevance of the stimuli to the animal's survival. The rigid patterns of innate behaviour allowing only one route to an adaptive goal are replaced by the flexible patterns of behaviour arising from drives and permitting a variety of adaptive strategies.

The drive state in higher animals is regulated by multiple rather than single factors. Whereas the sexual approach of the hormonally primed male silkworm moth is evoked solely by the female scent gland, the sexual arousal of even the rat, is a function of stimuli in all of the sensory modalities. Furthermore, by a process of learning new stimuli may become effective in arousing a drive state. The higher up the evolutionary scale one looks the more pervasive is the influence of acquired information (learning) on behaviour.

Information storage

The genes store information (see Chapter 13) by virtue of the fact that they constitute a set of instructions for the production of a new individual. Creatures with rudimentary nervous systems store information, in the sense that they are genetically programmed to produce specific responses to specific environmental stimuli. In creatures with simple nervous systems genetic programming with the information necessary for survival was the most efficient method of storage. However, innate behaviour patterns have the severe disadvantage that they are only adaptive to the specific environmental conditions which have selected them for perpetuation in the genes. The creature may fail to adapt to novel situations or may produce totally inappropriate response patterns if a sign stimulus is presented out of context. This is exemplified by the male silkworm moth's attempts to copulate with the isolated female scent glands.

Survival in the face of novel situations requires behavioural flexibility; the capacity to produce appropriate new behaviours. This capacity can only exist if the nervous system is able to store new information during the lifetime of the animal. In other words the genes must confer a nervous system whose configuration is plastic, amenable to modification, as a basis for changing patterns of response in the interests of adaptation.

Even the most primitive organisms possess a rudimentary capacity to modify their pattern of response; an amoeba will learn to avoid noxious stimuli. The capacity for information storage or learning increases as the brain grows in size and complexity; the one is a function of the other. The logic of information storage systems requires that they acquire more units and the appropriate connections between them if they are to increase their capacity, a fact which is reflected, for instance, in the construction of computers.

Information processing

In addition to greatly increasing the capacity for storing information the elaboration of the brain in evolution provided the mechanism for the development of a number of other powers which can be classified under the generic term 'information processing' (see Part IV). All information processing is dependent to a greater or lesser extent on information storage facilities, which are an essential ancillary.

The enhanced capacity for processing information arises, as that for information storage, out of the increase in the number of units (neurones) in the system and the increase in the extent and complexity of the connections between them. As in a computer this quantitative and organizational growth enhances the ability of the organism to analyse complex inputs of information, test logical relations and organize complex outputs, all in the interests of more subtle and ingenious adjustments to environmental pressures.

The first type of operation on information inputs to the nervous system, for which there is a need, is selection of relevant inputs for further processing. The complex environment of most species is the source of a massive barrage of environmental stimuli in which the majority are irrelevant to an organism's survival needs most of the time. Full processing of all incoming information would impose huge demands on central processing capacity. To solve this necessity the nervous system appears to have developed the capacity to discriminate between relevant and irrelevant incoming information before the central processor, which mediates conscious perception, is reached, and allow only relevant information to enter it for full processing. A filtering device *en route* to the central processor appears to select relevant information on the basis of physical characteristics, such as the tonal qualities of a voice being listened to, and block the further progress of information not possessing these characteristics. This is the phenomenon which psychologists call selective attention (see Chapter 12).

The process by which information, having entered the central processor, is analysed and integrated, to form what is consciously experienced as a meaningful whole, is called perception. The consciously experienced perceptual world of the human species is one of infinite complexity and subtlety. In contrast, we might infer that the perceptual world of lowly organisms is simple and limited as they respond only to a circumscribed range of undifferentiated stimuli. As the phylogenetic scale is ascended the perceptual world of species is enlarged as discriminative power increases. Perceptual abilities improve as a function of the elaboration of the neural substrate of perception and the increase in cerebral storage capacity. The perceptual world of higher organisms is not conferred by the genes but is largely acquired as a function of the organism's interaction with its environment, during which it learns to discriminate those patterns which are important to it. Higher creatures are so dependent on experiencing a 'normal' pattern-ed environment that an upbringing in an environment devoid of pattern results not only in a failure of the normal species perceptual abilities to develop but also measurable retardation in the physical development of the brain (see Chapter 7).

As the top of the phylogenetic scale is approached information proces-sing becomes even more sophisticated, manifest in the capacities for concept formation, problem solving, and abstract thinking which are largely the province of man. This class of information processing involves such things as symbolic representation, rule bound manipulation of symbols (in language) and discrimination of logical relations. Its adaptive function is manifest in man's extensive mastery of the environment. How-ever, elucidation of its neural basis, except in the most general terms, is an unsolved problem of the highest magnitude.

Selective pressures for brain development

Like all other features of terrestrial animal species the development of the brain must have been directed by gene mutation and selection. Thus, increased brain size, with its concomitant increase in capacity for inform-ation storage or learning, must have conferred adaptive advantage by enabling its possessors to respond more flexibly to the demands of the environment.

The elaboration of the brain implied, not only behavioural flexibility in the face of novel stimuli, but also a shedding of the stereotyped patterns of response endowed by the genes. The animal's behavioural repertoire is more and more programmed by the environment and less and less by the genes, but not without some cost to the organism. Whereas lower organisms are born with their behavioural repertoires more or less complete, higher organisms are born without the range of behaviours necessary for adapting to the environment. This repertoire has to be acquired and thus implies a period of dependence on the parents. This period of dependence of the off-spring on the parents, expressed as a proportion of lifespan, grows as the phylogenetic (evolutionary) scale is ascended. It is seen at its maximum in man where the period of dependence may be more than a quarter of the lifespan.

The benefits accruing from behavioural flexibility far outweigh the costs. It confers a more general adaptive ability than that given by particu-lar structures and specific stereotyped behaviour patterns. It enables a species to make a much more rapid response to changes in the environment than can be achieved by the slow process of mutation of the genes and selection of the fittest mutations. The infant member of a higher species can acquire a response repertoire which is adaptive to variants of the environment in which its predecessors evolved. The prime example of this is our own species which has proved capable of adapting to all terrestrial environments and is now adapting to extraterrestrial ones.

Behavioural flexibility and man

The phase of evolution which has led directly to man has been characterized by a primary emphasis on the interrelated development of the brain and behavioural flexibility. Together with this there has been an evolution of manipulative ability as a necessary vehicle for extending the scope of the behavioural flexibility promised by the degree of development of the brain.

When man's close predecessor assumed an upright stance his front limbs were freed for manipulative tasks. This permitted the extension of behavioural flexibility along a new dimension in the use of tools and active manipulation of the environment. The capacity to use progressively more sophisticated tools has greatly enhanced man's capacity to adapt to the environment. It has enabled him to supplement his own structural adaptive features when the need has arisen.

The evolution of the human brain and the evolution of the human manipulative apparatus appear to have fostered one another. The potential locked in the hands of prehuman man-apes could not be exploited without a powerful brain to conceive purposeful strategies, initiate complex manipulative activities and guide their skilful execution. Improved manipulative ability could not fail to enhance its possessors' capacity to adapt to their environment. Therefore any mutation improving the control mechanism, by incrementing the size of the brain, or refining its organization, on the one hand, or improving the manipulative apparatus—arms, hands, and fingers—on the other, could not fail to be successful. Genes endowing their possessors less generously with brain and manipulative apparatus probably suffered ever decreasing representation in the gene pool of the evolving prehominids because of their relatively poor adaptive value.

The evolution of the brain and manipulative ability, each complementing the other, could only occur if the adaptive value of this development became manifest at an early stage. This it appears to have done in the manufacture and use of tools. Discoveries of palaeontologists have indicated that man-apes, existing 500 000 to 1 000 000 years ago used tools of horn, bone and later stone [Washburn, 1960]. These man-apes were relatively small-brained, having cranial capacities of only 450–500 cm^3; half of the cranial capacity of modern man. They must have supplemented their puny 'natural' weapons, their hands, with crude manufactured weapons which made them both better hunters and better able to defend themselves. Tools used for digging probably enabled them to increase their supply of edible roots. The successful adoption of tool use by the man-apes must have altered the selective pressures on their progeny in favour of development of the brain and manipulative system, as these were developments which made tool use more effective. Progeny with mutations improving their 'brain power' and manipulative ability could enhance their own viability by improving on the tool-based adaptive strategies learned from their parents.

Once the interrelated trends of brain elaboration, refinement of manipulative apparatus and increasing tool use were under way, further developments could only improve an individual's adaptive potential, so that brain elaboration appears to have gathered a considerable momentum that rapidly led to the evolution of modern man. It took 10 000 000 years, from the time it diverged from the monkey line (phylum), for the hominid line to produce the tool-using man–apes. It took only a further 450 000 years for the man–ape to double his brain size and emerge as *homo sapiens*; modern man.

The development of language

The capacity to use tools was not the only consequence of brain elaboration of great importance for the evolutionary success of the hominid line. The emergence of language, in which people, objects, actions, and relations were given symbolic representation was a most important milestone in evolution. The use of language requires an elaborate coding mechanism which must clearly possess a large capacity for storing information. Only man appears to have the apparatus permitting the spontaneous emergence of language. Higher primates have been taught to communicate in a language consisting of visual shapes, but only on a limited scale and as a result of prolonged and intensive effort on the part of the experimenter [Premack, 1970]. It may be that the brain must achieve a 'critical mass' before language becomes possible. Also, although it is the case that the languages used by different human groups appear to differ enormously Chomsky [1968] has argued that there are underlying structural similarities which are a function of the organization of specific language areas in the brain. The fact that there appear to be circumscribed loci on the cerebral cortex concerned with language [Penfield and Roberts, 1959] is consistent with this theory.

The value of living in groups

Language interacts with other aspects of behavioural flexibility to establish its adaptive value. As man is a puny weakling when facing his environment naked and alone it has clearly always been to his advantage to co-operate with others of his species to promote their common survival. Some lower animals draw on the benefits of group living to promote their survival. However, co-operative activity in lower animals is very limited compared with that shown by humans. Some insect species have elaborate social systems [e.g. bees studies by von Frisch, 1967] but relations within them are governed by stereotyped, innate behaviour patterns.

Human groups are distinguished by the active co-operation which takes place within them and by the division of labour. As language emerged in evolution it must have greatly improved the precision with which co-operative activities could be carried out. Success in hunting or defence against an enemy is a function, not only of strength, but of strategy and proper deployment of resources. We must assume that developments giving rise to language were selected because they promoted survival by enhancing co-operative activities. Perhaps we should also note that to engage in co-operative activities of full human scope, requires a subordination of the immediate impulse of the individual to the requirements of the group. It appears that the capacity of the human group to impose such a discipline upon its members is itself a function of the development of the forebrain and its capacity to inhibit man from seeking immediate gratification of his needs (Figure 1.5).

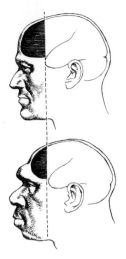

Figure 1.5
The brain of modern man compared with that of Neanderthal Man. The frontal lobes, supposedly associated with the capacity for planning and foresight, are more developed in modern man.

From Chandler Elliott, H. (1970) *The shape of intelligence*, New York, Charles Scribner's Sons. Reproduced by permission of the artist, Anthony Ravielli

Language and the transmission of adaptive strategies

The development of language has the more general role of transmission of adaptive strategies from one individual to another. The use of language removes the necessity of each new individual having to re-invent each tool and adaptive strategy developed by the previous generation. An inventor can describe his inventions to another man; parents and teachers can instruct children in the technology of their society. Furthermore, the utility of language goes far beyond improving the efficiency of immediate communication of technology from one man to another. It promotes a continuous process of refinement of the tools used by man, characterized as technological development. Existing technology can be communicated in much less time than it took to develop. Therefore, given suitable conditions, new generations have time to improve upon the technology of their fathers.

Cultural evolution

The emergence, in the biological evolution of man, of technological and linguistic abilities in a social setting, has paved the way for a novel and dramatic developmental process transcending the biological evolution which made it possible. This process has been called 'cultural evolution' [Dobzhansky, 1962, p. 8, second edition] and embraces technological and social evolution. Cultural evolution is the process by which man has progressed from Hobbes's 'state of nature' in which newly evolved modern man was supposed to have existed, to contemporary civilization in all its technological, economic, social, and cultural complexity. Cultural evolution has been an extraordinarily rapid process as the potential in man's brain has made it possible for dramatic progress to be made over a few generations, under favourable conditions. Adaptive modifications of the prevailing culture occur with much greater frequency than adaptive mutations occur in biological evolution, where many generations are required for beneficial gene mutations to emerge and establish themselves. It is estimated that the biological evolution of man from the first vertebrates to modern man took 500 000 000 years, whereas the cultural evolution from cave man to modern city dweller took only 50 000 years.

The latent potential in the brain of newly evolved man made the novel feature of cultural evolution possible. Conversely cultural evolution has enabled man to further realize the potential latent in his brain. The brain of man is unique among the adaptive features of terrestrial species insomuch as its full adaptive potential was not immediately realized following its evolution.

Twentieth-century man's cave-dwelling ancestors were probably not inherently less intelligent than himself (crudely measuring intelligence by brain size). However, twentieth-century man's proficiency in such things as high technology is based on an education which rapidly transmits a philosophy, skills, and knowledge laboriously accumulated and refined over many generations. We may speculate on whether further refinement of educational techniques will realize further untapped potential locked in man's brain.

The idea of the cultural evolution of man may be taken as a loose analogy for biological evolution. For instance it could be asserted that the strategies adopted by different human groups have been tested for 'fitness' by the selective pressures of the environment, with the result that only those with good adaptive value have been perpetuated. The study of social anthropology and history clearly shows that cultural evolution is not linear. Human societies have not only made rapid progress (as our own has in the last two centuries) but also have often stagnated, sometimes regressed and sometimes become extinct. Furthermore, it may be a mistake to suppose that cultural evolution occurs along a single dimension or several correlated dimensions. Civilizations have shown diversity in their forms and points of emphasis. Whereas it may not always be easy to analyse the rise and fall of civilizations within the conceptual framework of biological evolution, the extraordinary diversity of forms which human societies have taken powerfully illustrates the scope given by the behavioural flexibility, which has emerged as man's primary adaptive mechanism. In addition it illuminates the assertion that behavioural flexibility implies 'choice'. Man is not limited to a fixed set of adaptive strategies, ordained by his genes, but is given the opportunity to choose from alternative strategies, not necessarily differing in their adaptive value.

A universal adaptive strategy has been the use of tools and the manipulation of the environment—the development of technology. Indeed the adoption of these strategies appears to have provided the impetus for the final stages of the biological evolution of the brain. It follows from this that the vehicle through which behavioural flexibility has ensured man's survival has been the construction and use of artefacts; evolution has designed man to survive by his artefacts. Thus the criterion of 'naturalness', which is often used in judging man's activities and products, is not an appropriate criterion from an evolutionary point of view. 'Adaptive value' is the only criterion of judgement which can be derived from evolutionary imperatives.

Consciousness

A large part of this book is devoted to trying to understand the brain as a mechanism whose origins and workings will ultimately be understood in terms of physical laws. This approach ignores the most significant property of the brain from the standpoint of a person contemplating his own awareness of himself and his world, that it is the brain, the physical substrate underlying consciousness, which gives rise to this awareness. Consciousness cannot be investigated or understood in the mechanistic terms with which we account for other brain functions. Consciousness cannot be observed and measured in the way that overt behaviour and physical events can. Consciousness is private; known directly only to its possessor. The consciousness of others can only be inferred from external signs—expressions, gestures, and utterances—used in accord with accepted conventions.

Inferred states of consciousness are the basis for many statements about the role of the brain in generating consciousness. The most fundamental statement is that the nature and content of consciousness is totally dependent on the physical state of the brain. It appears to be impossible to alter the physical state of the brain, whether by accident, surgical intervention, administration of drugs or electrical stimulation without in some way modifying conscious experience. If the brain is severely damaged the gross nature of the behaviour that follows suggests that consciousness has been severely degraded. Psychoactive drugs have the capacity to modify the way in which we perceive the world, the way we feel about what we perceive and our over-all mood, by altering the physical state of the brain. The continuous flux of conscious experience which characterizes our waking lives is generated by internal and external physical stimuli which ultimately produce physical changes in the brain. Thus, whatever view philosophers may put forward concerning the relationship between the mind and the brain, they are constrained by the fact that manifestations of mind are inextricably linked with the physical state of the brain.

If the qualities of conscious experience are so dependent on the physical brain then we would expect that creatures with less developed brains than that of man would have a more limited capacity for conscious experience. As one descends the phylogenetic scale progressive limitations in the range of expressions, repertoire of behaviour and perceptual capacities leads us to infer that the scope for conscious experience becomes progressively more constricted. To express the converse we might quote from Teilhard de Chardin [1955] who said that 'a richer and better organized structure will correspond to the more developed consciousness [Teilhard de Chardin, 1955, p. 65, 1965 edition]. As we extrapolate back to the most primitive forms of life the only observable signs of a tentative, rudimentary consciousness are found in the emergent properties of irritability and motility. We might hypothesize that the dawn of consciousness occurs at this level. Teilhard de Chardin [1955, p. 65, 1965 edition] the famous Jesuit palaeontologist–biologist goes further and states that: 'refracted rearwards along the course of evolution, consciousness displays itself qualitatively as a spectrum of shifting shades whose lower terms are lost in the night'. He considered that even primitive matter had a 'within', a sort of rudimentary psychism, a hypothesis which is unprovable in the usually accepted terms. To account for the 'expansion and deepening of consciousness' in evolution, Teilhard de Chardin formulated the more acceptable 'law of complexity and consciousness' supposing that 'consciousness is that much more perfected according as it lines a richer and better organized material edifice', an oblique reference to the quantitative and organizational development of the nervous system. Teilhard de Chardin also asserted that in man, as a result of the process of cerebralization, a critical transformation has occurred whereby consciousness has been able to 'turn in upon itself' in the phenomena of reflection and self-consciousness.

Whereas it is philosophically interesting to speculate on the origins of consciousness and the relationship of concentration of consciousness to the complexity of the organized matter underlying it, it does not readily yield to analysis in terms of its adaptive value. Could we not all be as adaptive if we were complex but mindless automatons fulfilling all the functions of a human? The founder of behaviourism, Watson [1919] considered that consciousness is an epiphenomenon and that it is possible to treat humans as if they were automata because it has no significance from the point of view of adaptation to the environment. However, this view is not shared by all. To pursue this argument further is to go far into the realms of philosophy and outside the scope of this book. We must turn to the things man does to the world rather than his immediate experience of it.

Man's impact on the environment

Man evolved his brain, the specific apparatus by which he survives, in an environment formed by a multiplicity of natural forces. In the course of his technological evolution man, in turn, has had an ever increasing impact on his global environment through his. artefacts. However, man is now entering a phase where the long term costs of certain activities will have to be calculated if the edifice of his civilization is to be preserved, and possibly to ensure his long term survival.

The survival of the living things which are members of the global ecosystem is contingent on the preservation of a delicate balance in the relationships between the elements of that system. All species must have a breathable atmosphere (or clean oxygenated water) and enough to eat. The fertility of the soil must be sustained by the decay of organic matter. A balance must be maintained between predators and prey. Many other subsidiary equilibria must be preserved. The disturbance of any individual equilibrium may have repercussions throughout an ecosystem. Whereas the complex pattern of component ecosystems which comprise the global ecosystem are resilient enough to readjust to small perturbations, many of which occur apart from the intervention of man, they may be unable to adjust to large disturbances. Vicious processes may be initiated which will ultimately destroy the system. A prominent example of this is where the massive pollution of Lake Erie in North America has so depleted the water of life-sustaining oxygen that most organisms in the lake have died out or are about to do so [see Commoner, 1972]. The lake has been polluted by nitrates and phosphates, leached out of the soil, which have acted as a superfertilizer for blooms of algae. The rapid decay of the algae has depleted the water of oxygen while providing it with nourishment for ever more abundant blooms. This had led to ever greater demands on the water's oxygen supply by the processes of decay. The deterioration of this aqueous ecosystem has thus been brought about by a vicious circle or 'positive feedback' loop.

Paradoxically man's remarkable adaptive success is becoming a threat to his ultimate survival on a planet with finite resources. Adaptive technology has resulted in an enormous expansion of the human species which, in turn, threatens to outstrip the resources to feed it and sustain its technological activities. The problems of adaptation which man must now solve to promote his long-term survival are, of his own making, infinitely more complex than when he was a hunter and cave dweller. His latent potential for analysis and invention will have to be exploited to the full.

Selective pressures in man-made environments

Finally there is another aspect of man's impact on his environment which should be considered and that is the way in which environmental changes, engineered by man, feedback to the human gene pool. Only speculation exists on this topic at the moment, but classical theory leads one to expect that any change in the selective pressures of the environment would lead to a modification in the structure of the gene pool. We might speculate, as Dubos [1973, p. 52] has done, on the selective pressure exerted by the imposition of high-density living on human populations as the result of severe population pressure. Individuals with predisposing genes might develop stress symptoms resulting in early death or reduction of their reproductive capacity [a known result of stress; see Gray, 1971a, Chapter 6]. In this way the predisposing genes would be removed from the gene pool. Dubos [1973, p. 52] speculates on the Orwellian possibility that the people best adapted to social regimentation will have an advantage and that 'this will accelerate the movement of our societies towards the conditions of the ant hill'.

Summary

The brain and nervous system is the apparatus by which animal species conduct the transactions with their environment which keep them alive. This system monitors any changes in the internal or external environment, evaluates them and organizes appropriate responses by the organism's effector apparatus. It also stores information likely to be relevant to the creature's future needs. The nervous mechanisms by which more complex organisms support themselves are based on the fundamental precursor properties of irritability, plasticity, and motility, found in the single cells which are the most primitive forms of life.

The evolution of life forms from their common, primordial, unicellular ancestors has occurred by a process of mutation of the genes and selection of adaptive mutations. The genes are the hereditary material which determine that progeny will inherit parental characteristics. The scope of the evolutionary process was greatly increased by the emergence of sexual reproduction. This achieves segregation and recombination of the genes so that each of the progeny, in a species with genetic variation, has a unique configuration of them. Thus each act of reproduction is an experiment on the adaptive viability of a new genetic combination. Furthermore, the gene pool upon which a species draws can be modified, over a few generations, to meet changing environmental conditions.

The nervous system has evolved as a necessary adaptive mechanism in all animal species. In the line of evolution leading to man elaboration of the nervous system has been the dominant theme rather than emphasis on any other structural or functional feature with adaptive value.

Nerve cells (or neurones) and sensory cells, the units of the nervous system, are specialized derivatives of the primordial cells, in which the irritability property has been enhanced. The nervous system first appears in aquatic coelenterates (e.g. hydra, jelly fish) as a diffuse network capable only of initiating sluggish and amorphous responses to stimuli. Centralization is first seen in a radial organization of the nervous system, possessed by echinoderms such as starfish, and permitting execution of co-ordinated patterns of movement. The most critical development was of a bilateral body form symmetrically disposed about a head–tail axis. This configuration, first seen in the worm, favours the development of a central executive organ for the nervous system, located in the head. In the worm the head ganglion is precursor of the brain and the notochord precursor of the spinal cord which characterizes vertebrate species.

With ascent of the vertebrate phylum we see successive layers of neural tissue added to the brain in a process of encephalization. In higher animals independent control at the segmental level in the spinal cord progressively disappears in favour of over-all control of behaviour by the brain. As the brain is elaborated its capacity for both storing and processing information increases. There is less stereotyped innate behaviour and more learned behaviour of greater variety and flexibility. Perceptual and manipulative powers increase and become more dependent upon varied patterns of stimulation for their development.

The increase in behavioural flexibility which expansion of the brain brings in its train enables members of a species to survive under a greater range of environmental conditions. When members of the vertebrate phylum assumed an upright stance the front limbs became available as a manipulative apparatus. They complemented the developing brain to make a formidable adaptive combination leading to the use of tools and evolution of technology as powerful mechanisms of survival. Parallel and inter-related developments of language and complex social structures followed the accumulation of the necessary 'critical mass' by the brain. The biological evolution of the brain finally reached a point, in the human species, where a novel, superordinate process of cultural–technological–social evolution could take off. A concomitant of increase in size and complexity of the brain, and also a consequence of cultural evolution, has been a broadening and deeping of consciousness and the emergence of self-consciousness.

Man's brain has ensured his evolutionary success and enabled him to increasingly dominate his terrestrial environment by the manufacture of artefacts enhancing the prospects of individual and group survival. This very success has led to man threatening his own existence by overpopulation and the development of technologies disturbing ecological equilibria.

PART 2
FOUNDATIONS

Chapter two

The nervous system

Introduction

Early in Chapter 1 the concept of the cell was introduced. The cell is the fundamental biological unit from which all living creatures are constructed. It was observed that in multicellular creatures there is differentiation of cellular function and that a class of cells called neurones exist which are specialized for the transmission of information within the nervous system, the body's communication and control system. This book is concerned with the way in which the nervous system mediates the analysis of information from the internal and external environment and the organization of behaviour.

As a prelude to the introduction of the specific mechanisms discussed in the rest of the book it is necessary, as for any complex mechanism, to present an outline of the microstructure, gross structure, and general principles of operation of the nervous system as a foundation for the appreciation of later concepts.

The principal microstructural features of the nervous system are the neurones and the junctions between them which are called synapses. The study of neural and synaptic function produces basic insights into how information is coded, transmitted and integrated in the nervous system, and leads to an understanding of general principles of operation which apply to a range of specific mechanisms.

The nervous system as a whole (see Figure 1.1) is a differentiated structure in which the most obvious visible divisions are between the peripheral nervous system, serving sensory or motor functions, the spinal cord, and the brain. The brain itself can be divided into many component structures on the basis of either visible boundaries, such as surface fissures, or the more subtly defined borders of its many named nuclei. These are zones where there are high concentrations of cell bodies and their processes. Thus an account of the gross structure of the nervous system provides a map on which landmarks can be located and communicating pathways traced. Knowledge of the communicating nerve tracts connecting body organs and structures in the nervous system, and linking different structures in the nervous system, provides initial signposts to the functional importance of various specific nervous system structures.

Whereas the primary concern of this work is with the voluntary nervous system which organizes publicly observable behaviour, mediated by the skeletal musculature, the autonomic branch of the nervous system must be mentioned. This is the branch of the nervous system controlling the activity of internal organs vital to life, such as the heart, whose action is essentially involuntary. It should be noted, of course, that a creature's responses may have both voluntary and autonomic components. In the instance of emotional arousal, accelerated heart rate and respiration (among other things) help to supply the energy resources for fight or flight. Furthermore, in recent years it has been shown that the autonomic nervous system can be subject to a high degree of voluntary control [see Kamiya *et al.*, 1971], most dramatically illustrated in the case of yoga practitioners who can so attentuate heart rate and respiration as to achieve a state near to 'suspended animation'.

For some functions, notably reproduction, emotional arousal, and control of water balance, the nervous system works in conjunction with a slower communication system called the endocrine system. In this system the bloodstream transports substances called hormones from their site of manufacture in the endocrine glands to target organs where they perform some special function. For instance, luteinizing hormone is produced by the pituitary gland at the base of the brain, and travels to the ovary where it causes an egg to be released at the appropriate time.

In order to produce overt behaviour the nervous system must activate an effector system of muscles (controlling limbs) in a purposeful and co-ordinated manner. An outline of the motor system is given so that the reader's picture of the brain mechanisms underlying behaviour is completed by an idea of how their output is translated into action.

Microstructure and neural function

We may take the telephone system as an analogy for the nervous system. Our spoken messages are coded into patterns of electrical impulses by the receiver and are transmitted by wires to our selected destination. There the pattern of impluses is decoded into patterns of sound which are heard as a reproduction of our voice by the listener. The receivers of the nervous system are the sense organs which will be discussed in Chapter 11. The equivalent of the telephone wires in the nervous system are the neurones, or rather their elongated processes called axons. They are analogous in that they transmit information, coded into patterns of electrical impulses, between spatially separate locations. Beyond this the analogy breaks down as the neurone takes an active role in the transmission of information, whereas that of the telephone wire is purely passive.

Neurones are highly variable in their size and morphology, but most share the features illustrated in the schematic representation of a motor

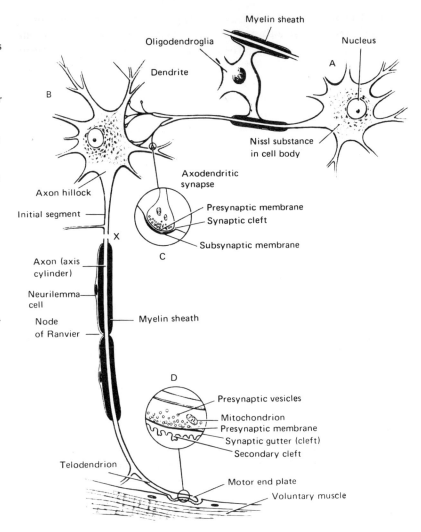

Figure 2.1
The primary microstructural features of the nervous system. A is a neurone located in the central nervous system and B is a motor neurone with its nucleus in the spinal cord and its termination in the peripheral NS at a neuromuscular junction. C is a synapse between two neurones and D a motor end plate, shown reconstructed from electronmicrographs.

From Noback, C. R., and Demarest, R. J. (1972) *The nervous system.* Copyright © 1972 McGraw-Hill, Inc. Reproduced by permission of the publishers

neurone of a mammalian spinal cord shown in Figure 2.1. In common with other types of cell the central feature of the neurone is the cell body (soma or perikaryon), which contains the nucleus and which in a typical motor neurone is about 70 µm across. The range of soma diameters is between 5 and 100 µm. The cell body is the location of the metabolic machinery which maintains the cell. The nucleus contains the DNA (deoxyribonucleic acid) molecules which encode instructions for the manufacture of protein within the cell. Proteins are both vital components of the cellular structure and essential for intracellular metabolic processes.

Axons

Emanating from the cell body is a specialized elongated process called the axon which is the basis for the neurone transmitting information over distance. This always occurs in a direction away from the cell body. Axons vary in length from a few micrometres in the brain to several metres in the peripheral nervous system, where they conduct information to or from the brain. The diameters of axons usually range between 1 and 20 μm, but in certain invertebrates, such as the squid, giant axons as much as a millimetre in diameter are found. These giant axons are ideal for experimental work involving recording of the electrical activity of neurones using microelectrodes. Axons may divide into branches along their course, and at the end divide into many terminal fibrils. At the end of these fibrils swellings about 1 μm across, called synaptic knobs (sometimes known as terminal boutons), make contact with other neurones—a purely functional contact as the synaptic knobs do not physically touch the next neurone.

Dendrites

Apart from the axon a neurone usually has a number of other multi-branching tapered processes called dendrites, which are about 5 μm in diameter and which break into many ultrafine terminal branches about 1 mm from the soma. The dendritic structure is referred to as the dendritic tree and the area of spatial extension of the dendrites as the dendritic field. The synaptic knobs of preceding neurones (presynaptic neurones) communicate with the dendrites, by making a functional contact, so that they act as receivers, collecting information from other cells and passing it to the cell body, as a precursor to transmission along the axon. The extension of the dendritic tree far beyond the boundaries of the cell body enormously widens the field from which any individual neurone can receive the converging influences of other neurones and can thus be seen as greatly enhancing the integrative properties of the nervous system.

The membrane

The interior of the neurone is composed largely of a viscous fluid called the cytoplasm. This is contained by an outer skin called the membrane which forms the boundary of the neurone. The membrane is a sandwich of fat between layers of protein, upon whose remarkable properties the capacity of the neurone to transmit information depends. Rather than forming an impenetrable barrier to all substances the membrane is semi-permeable, acting as a kind of sieve, which allows substances with small molecules to pass through it but blocks the passage of substances with large molecules. Part of the survival mechanism of the cell is its capacity to allow nutrients to enter through the membrane while denying access to toxic materials. Also it must allow the exit of the waste products from metabolic processes. As will be seen the information transmitting possibilities of the cell derive from the capacity of the membrane to temporarily change its permeability characteristics with a consequent change in the electrical potential between the inside and outside of the cell.

Neurones are bathed in an extracellular fluid containing salt (NaCl) in solution. The solute dissociates into sodium (Na) ions having a positive electrical charge and chloride (Cl) ions having a negative electrical charge. The intracellular fluid, on the other hand, has a relatively high concentration of potassium (K) ions with a positive charge. If the cellular membrane was freely permeable to all of these ions then random molecular movement would generate diffusion of ions across the membrane until, because of the concentration gradient, they were all in equal concentration on both sides of the membrane. However, when a neurone is 'resting' (i.e. not transmitting), although it is permeable to small chloride and potassium ions, it is almost impermeable to the sodium ions outside of the membrane, and to some other negative ions (large amino acid radicals or proteins) inside of the membrane. In addition a 'metabolic pump', exchanging sodium ions for potassium ions, counteracts a leakage of sodium ions from the outside of the cell in, and a leakage of potassium ions from the inside of the cell out. In these conditions the chloride and potassium ions, which are able to move freely through the membrane, are subject to countervailing forces. The positive sodium ions on the outside of the membrane exercise an electrical attraction on the negative chloride ions, tending to hold them on the outside, so that any potential difference between the inside and the outside of the cell is neutralized. In opposition to this there is a tendency for the chloride ions to move across the concentration gradient set up by the cell membrane and equalize the chloride concentrations on both sides of it. Similarly with potassium, the electrical attraction exercised by negatively charged protein ions operates to hold these positive ions inside the cell, in opposition to the tendency for them to diffuse out across the concentration gradient.

An equilibrium point is achieved where, although a greater concentration of chloride ions is held on the outside of the membrane, the inside of the cell is held at a net potential of −70 mV relative to the outside. (Figure 2.2) Thus the cell membrane can be said to be polarized. The measure-

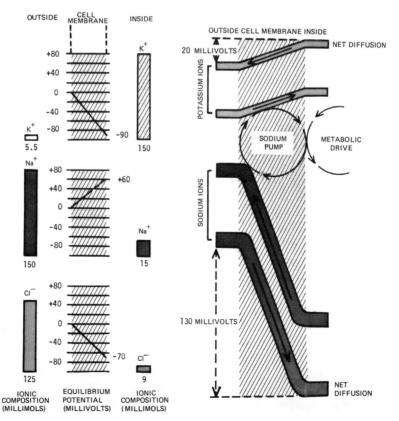

Figure 2.2
The ionic basis of the cell membrane potential. The left hand diagram shows the ionic compositions of potassium, sodium and chlorine outside and inside the cell membrane. The right hand diagram shows the diffusion fluxes across the cell membrane. Diffusion in one direction, down an electrochemical gradient, is countered by a metabolic pump driving the ions in the opposite direction.

From Eccles, J., *The synapse.* Copyright © January, 1965 Scientific American Inc. All rights reserved. Reproduced by permission of the publishers

ment of these transmembrane potentials, a major landmark in the investigation of cellular function, was first achieved by Hodgkin and Huxley [1939] and Curtis and Cole [1942]. It was accomplished by inserting microelectrodes, formed from long glass capillaries, and filled with saline solution or a metal, into the giant axons of squids, which are around 1 mm in diameter and are particularly suitable for this type of experiment.

The nerve impulse

A nerve impulse is propagated when there is a transient 'breakdown' of the cellular membrane resulting in a rapid influx of sodium ions. This leads to a disappearance of the potential difference between the inside and outside of the membrane and constitutes depolarization of the membrane. In fact there is an overshoot in which the interior of the cell goes from -70 mV to $+30$ mV, relative to the outside. This transient potential is referred to as the action potential or 'spike discharge', because of its appearance on oscilloscope screens used to monitor it. The negative resting potential of the neural membrane is restored by an outflow of positive potassium ions and rapid recovery of the membrane. The number of ions crossing the cell membrane during any one impulse is minute compared with the total number in the surrounding extracellular medium, so that the cell can fire many times in succession before exhaustion occurs. In resting periods following an impulse, sodium and potassium ions which have changed sides are subject to the relatively slow influence of the sodium-potassium pump, which trades these ions at the membrane until the normal balance is restored.

As the ion flow across the membrane of an active cell can be registered as a brief potential by recording between microelectrodes inside and outside of the cell and displaying the results on an oscilloscope (see Chapter 3), neural transmission can be characterized as an electrical event.

It is important to appreciate that the breakdown of the neural membrane which leads to generation of the nerve impulse does not take place over the entire cellular membrane simultaneously. An area of depolarization commences at the axon hillock, where the axon extrudes from the soma, and travels down the axon the way a flame travels down a fuse. The depolarization of one area generates electric current flows which have the effect of breaking down adjacent membrane further down the axon and thus giving momentum to the travelling wave of membrane depolarization. As the impulse travels down the axon, the area of membrane behind it is 'resealed' and the resting potential restored (see Figure 2.3). During any impulse there is an absolute refractory period when the neurone cannot be additionally excited by any further stimulus, however strong. This is followed by a very brief 'supernormal period' of heightened excitability and then in turn by a 'relative refractory period' when only an abnormally strong stimulus will generate an impulse. As the duration of the action potential of a nerve impulse is around 0.5 ms. the refractory properties of neurones place an upper limit on their rate of transmission of impulses at around $2000\,s^{-1}$.

The speed of transmission of impulses along an axon is highly variable, ranging from 1 to $100\,m\,s^{-1}$. Transmission is faster the larger the diameter

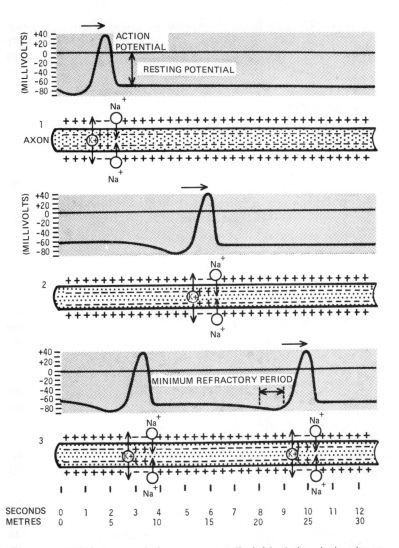

of an axon. This is because in larger axons a diminished electrical resistance accelerates the depolarizing effect of impulse generated current flows on adjacent membrane. The fastest rates of conduction are found in long axons carrying information from the periphery to the brain, or vice versa. Rapid conduction is achieved because they are clad in an insulating sheath of myelin (see Figures 2.1 and 3.1). The myelin sheath is formed from a type of satellite cell in the nervous system, called a Schwann cell. This winds itself around the axon in a spiral of many turns. The myelin sheath is interrupted every millimetre or so by gaps called 'nodes of Ranvier'. Because there is a gap in the insulation at these points current flows rapidly to them when an impulse reaches a previous node and, in turn, causes the spread of membrane depolarization associated with the progression of the impulse. Thus, rapid transmission is accomplished in myelinated neurones by impulses jumping from node to node in a manner known as saltatory conduction.

In addition to the Schwann cells, which form the myelin sheaths in the long conducting pathways, there are other types of satellite or glia cells which exist in profusion in the central nervous system, greatly outnumbering the neurones themselves. Their function is not well understood, but it appears to include that of mechanical support and protection. It also seems likely that a class of glia cells, called astrocytes, are responsible for transporting nutrient materials from blood vessels to neurones and removing waste products from neurones to the blood.

Synapses

Each neurone is just one unit among billions in a complex system. Until recently it was thought that each neurone made physical contact with others in its chain so that there was continuity throughout the nervous system. The brilliant histologist, Ramon Y Cajal [1934, 1954] was the first to argue convincingly that each neurone is a discrete unit. The advent of the electron microscope, making very high magnification possible, has shown that this is indeed true (see Figure 2.4). Each synaptic knob is

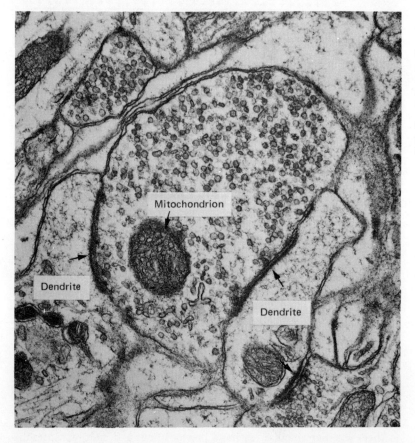

Mitochondrion

Dendrite

Dendrite

Figure 2.4
Electronmicrograph showing two presynaptic boutons making type 1 axodendritic contracts (arrows).

Courtesy of Dr. A. R. Lieberman, University College, London

separated from the postsynaptic membrane by a microscopic but distinct gap. These gaps are about 20 nm units wide and are usually referred to as synaptic clefts, the term synapse being the name for the junction between one neurone and another.

If information is to traverse chains of neurones then transmission must occur across the synaptic cleft. This is achieved by a switch from electrical to chemical conduction which is of great significance. When an impulse in a presynaptic neurone arrives at a synaptic knob it triggers the release of a transmitter substance, secreted in microscopic sacs, called synaptic vesicles, into the synaptic cleft. This transmitter substance is effective in increasing the permeability of the postsynaptic membrane and thus causing local depolarization. It should be noted that the membrane at these post-synaptic sites on the dendrites and soma of the cell differs in its properties from the axonal membrane in that it is specifically sensitive to chemical rather than electrical influences. The list of transmitter substances includes acetylcholine, serotonin, noradrenaline, and dopamine. Immediately following their release transmitters are degraded by enzymes such as acetylcholine esterase (or cholinesterase) so that their action is rapidly terminated, and the postsynaptic membrane depolarization occurs as a discrete event.

Excitatory and inhibitory post-synaptic potentials

The depolarization which occurs at the postsynaptic membrane following the release of the transmitter substance is initially slower, accompanied by a lesser change in potential and followed by a less rapid spread to neigh-bouring locations than that giving rise to the action potential which travels down the axon. The spread of depolarization affected by current flows at the postsynaptic locations rapidly diminishes with distance from the site of origin, in contrast to the non-decremental spread of depolarization as an impulse travels down an axon. The potentials generated at the post-synaptic membrane are known as excitatory postsynaptic potentials (EPSPs for short). These local potentials only produce impulse transmission when many of them summate, because of overlap in time and space, to a point where the threshold of the neurone is exceeded and a full blown action potential is generated at the axon hillock and transmitted down the axon. This threshold is usually reached when the inside of the cell becomes 10–20 mV less negative than normal.

In addition to excitatory transmitter substances there are also inhibi-tory substances, of which the best known example is γ-amino-butyric acid (GABA), which operates at inhibitory synapses. The effect of the inhibi-tory transmitter substance is to selectively increase the permeability of the postsynaptic membrane to potassium ions with a resulting outflow of these ions. This increases the negativity of the interior of the cell to as much as 80 mV so that the membrane can be considered to be hyper-polarized. The hyperpolarized potential is referred to as an inhibitory postsynaptic potential or IPSP. The hyperpolarization of a cellular mem-brane makes it harder to generate sufficient depolarization at excitatory synaptic locations on the same cell, to initiate the transmission of an impulse. The inhibitory synapse is thus a device for blocking the trans-mission of information along a particular neural pathway.

The chemical nature of transmission at synapses is profoundly import-ant when considering the neural basis for changes in psychological state and behaviour. There is circumstantial evidence that natural biological rhythms, particularly sleeping and waking, are produced by neural systems in which there is cyclical accumulation and dissipation of specific transmitter chemicals. The many drugs which man has developed to manipulate his psychological state appear to work by altering the transmission properties at the synapse; drugs reducing excitement or anxiety, or promoting sleep by blocking synaptic transmission; drugs elevating mood, promoting wakefulness, or sharpening perception acting by enhancing synaptic transmission.

Coding and integration in the nervous system

Having observed how transmission is achieved in the axon and at the synapse we should now examine how the nervous system fulfils its roles of coding and integrating information. Firstly it should be emphasized that the impulses which travel from the soma to the axon terminals are ungraded 'all or nothing' responses which only vary in amplitude in extreme circumstances. It is therefore the case that any variation in intensity of stimuli impinging on the nervous system can only be coded in terms of variation in the frequency of impulses generated and not in terms of their amplitude. The only other means of coding intensity in nerve tracts is by variation in the number of neurones activated. As the intensity of a stimulus increases, neurones with higher activation thresholds are recruited to increase the total number of neurones active.

It should be understood that in general the pervasive principle of coding by patterns of 'all or none' pulses is subordinate to a system of 'place coding'. The significance attributed to a pattern of impulses in a nerve tract is a function of the place of origin and the destination of that tract. Visual patterns are perceived as such because impulses are generated at receptors in the eye and travel, via the optic tract, to the visual cortex of the brain. If the optic tract was 'unplugged' and 'replugged' into the auditory receiving area of the brain then stimulation of the eye would result in auditory sensations and not visual sensations. Even information about the colour of a visual stimulus, which is a function of the wavelength of the incident light entering the eye, appears to be coded by the activation of receptors specifically sensitive to that wavelength and specific pathways by which they gain access to the brain. However, it should be remembered that this presentation of the principles of place coding represents a gross simplification and it should not be assumed that the problems of coding in the nervous system are anything like solved. In investigations of the detection of pattern by the visual system it is apparent that the notion of a one to one connection between a receptor site and its cortical projection cannot explain the observed phenomena. There are individual cells in the visual area of the brain which are activated when a specific visual pattern, such as a line slanted at 45°, is projected on to the retina (the light sensitive surface of the eye), irrespective of the retinal location at which the pattern is projected (see Chapter 12). This finding indicates that convergence and integration must occur in the visual pathway.

The integrative activities of the synapse
Whereas the neurone alone accomplishes basic transmission, it is at the synapse that we should look for the more subtle integrative properties of

the nervous system. Any individual neurone may be impinged upon by many presynaptic neurones—possibly running into thousands (see Figure 2.5). The determinants of whether a particular neurone will fire are a complex function of temporal summation, depending on the intensity of the activity in the presynaptic neurones, and spatial summation, depending on the number of excitatory and inhibitory synaptic locations which have been activated. This being so, one can readily appreciate that complex networks of neurones, such as exist in the brain, must offer extensive com-

Figure 2.5
Multiple synaptic endings on the cell body and dendrites of a neurone.

From Eccles, J. (1973) *Understanding the brain*. Reproduced by permission of the McGraw-Hill Book Co

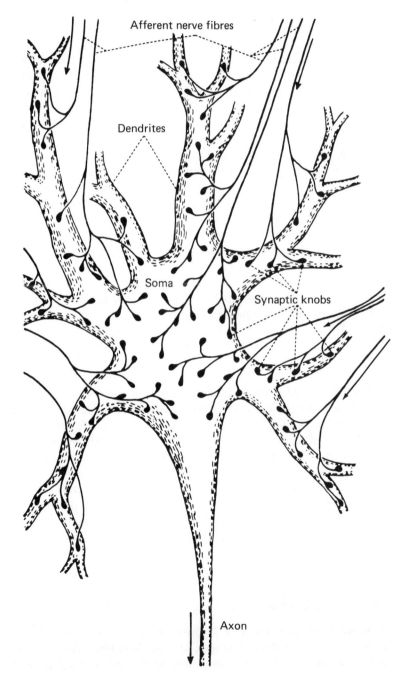

putational possibilities and be governed by a complex logic, as such complex choices are offered at each synapse.

The importance of inhibitory synapses as a source of negative feedback should also be grasped. The nervous system not only has to initiate behaviour but has to exercise precise control over the execution and termination of movements. It can readily be appreciated that a shift from excitation to inhibition in the nerve pathway innervating a muscle group could be of vital importance in the fine control of movement. Within the brain itself, inhibitory influences on the neural networks mediating drives, such as hunger, appear to be effective in terminating appetitive behaviour when a creature is satiated.

There is a qualification to the statement that all information in the nervous system is coded into patterns of 'all or none' nerve impulses. Whereas this may largely be true in the periphery it seems likely that slower graded potentials may be significant in information processing in the brain. It even seems possible that some neurones are able to influence one another through their slow potentials without the occurrence of a full blown impulse. Another point about slow potentials is that they may not necessarily be generated by stimuli impinging on the cell, but may arise spontaneously from within it, and may be modulated in a regular rhythm.

A final point which should be made concerning the functional significance of the synapse is its probable involvement in the storage of information, a primary capacity of nervous systems. The storage of new information implies that the organism is able to produce a novel response reflecting a plastic change in the nervous system. It appears likely that these plastic changes produce a modification of function at the synapse. This results in a modified resonse by the postsynaptic neurone to excitation by the presynaptic neurone (see Chapter 13).

Summary

To summarize; a neurone transmits information encoded in 'all or none' impulses. These travel along the axon by a process of constant regeneration produced by current flows which initiate membrane depolarisation ahead of the impulse. Activation of subsequent neurones is effected by the release of a transmitter chemical across the synaptic cleft which causes depolarization of the postsynaptic membrane, reflected in graded postsynaptic excitatory potentials. At an inhibitory synapse hyperpolarization is reflected in inhibitory postsynaptic potentials which raise the threshold for generation of an impulse in a neurone. When excitatory postsynaptic potentials reach a threshold level by temporal and spatial summation an 'all or none' impulse is initiated at the axon hillock and proceeds towards the axon terminals.

Gross structure

The study of the gross structure of the nervous system is called neuroanatomy. It is a very difficult subject to learn from the pages of a two-dimensional book because the structures of the nervous system have complex three-dimensional forms which have no intrinsic meaning for the student. Neuroanatomy is best learned by performing a brain dissection while referring to a suitable atlas of neuroanatomy. A particularly clear atlas of neuroanatomy from which non-medical students may learn neuro-anatomy without being overwhelmed by irrelevant detail is that produced by Netter [1953].

This section will present an outline of the human nervous system, the most elaborated of the vertebrate phylum. Lower vertebrates have nervous systems with strikingly similar basic configurations, but with higher structures absent or much less highly developed. Thus, the human nervous structures described in this section can be assumed to exist in similar locations and relations to other structures, in other species mentioned in this work.

The goal for the student attempting to learn neuroanatomy from a book of this type is to build a 'cognitive map' of the nervous system 'in his head'. This 'internal structure' can then be referred to when particular structures are mentioned during discussion of specific mechanisms in the nervous system. Initially it is useful to learn the terms which give the crude three-dimensional co-ordinates of locations in the nervous system (see Figure 2.6).

Figure 2.6
The use of some general terms in neuroanatomy

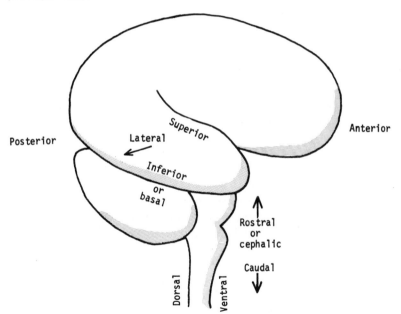

The terms rostral and caudal signify 'towards the head end' and 'towards the tail end' respectively.

The terms dorsal and ventral express 'towards the back' and 'towards the belly' respectively.

The terms medial and lateral refer to 'towards the middle' and 'towards the side'. Ipsilateral means 'on the same side' and contralateral, 'on the opposite side'.

There are complications in applying these terms to human neuro-anatomy. Because of man's upright stance the axis of his brain is turned at an angle of 90° to his spinal cord when compared with other vertebrates.

The consequence of this is that in the brain itself the terms anterior and posterior, for 'towards the front' and 'towards the back' respectively, are used instead of rostral and caudal. This peculiarity of man also means that in the brain dorsal and ventral refer to 'towards the top' and 'towards the base'. Alternatively, the term superior is often used to refer to 'towards the top' and the terms inferior and basal used to signify 'towards the bottom'.

Other useful terms are distal, expressing 'away from' the brain and proximal, expressing 'towards' the brain or body centre. The term afferent refers to nerve tracts conducting 'towards a particular structure', usually the spinal cord or the brain, and efferent refers to nerve tracts conducting 'away from a central structure', usually towards muscles which they innervate.

Finally, an important distinction which must be made between types of nervous tissue is that between grey matter and white matter, each named because of its characteristic appearance. Grey matter represents areas of concentration of nerve cell bodies and their processes while communicating tracts made up of long myelinated axons appear as white matter.

The peripheral nervous system

The peripheral nervous system is that aspect of the nervous system, lying outside the bony protection of the skull and spinal column, which forms a distribution network to the sense organs and muscles. The somatic division of the peripheral nervous system comprises the afferent pathways from the various receptor organs and receptor systems, and the efferent pathways innervating the skeletal muscles. These muscles (also known as striped muscles) are used to effect voluntary movements of the limbs and trunk. The autonomic branch of the peripheral nervous system (discussed in the next section, 'the autonomic nervous system') innervates the body's internal organs (known as the viscera), such as the heart and digestive system, whose functioning is largely independent of voluntary control. It includes afferent nerves from the sense organs in these structures and motor nerves to the smooth muscles controlling their function.

The central nervous system

The spinal cord
The peripheral nervous system is connected to the higher nervous system (the brain) either via the spinal cord or directly via the cranial nerves.

The evolutionary origin of the central nervous system was a network of nerves formed into a tube which ran from the front end to the back end of primitive chordates. The essence of this structure is preserved in the spinal cord of modern vertebrates. The spinal cord is an elongated nervous structure whose cross-section varies, but typically approximates to an ellipse with its minor axis in the dorsal–ventral direction. Its tubular aspect is preserved by the existence of a narrow canal running its length and connecting with the cavities (ventricles) in the brain. The spinal cord is protected by a bony enclosure consisting of the 33 vertebrae of the spinal column and their connecting ligaments and intervening cartilages.

The peripheral nervous system gains access to the spinal cord through 31 pairs of spinal nerves, each pair entering between two vertebrae, one on each side of the cord. Each spinal nerve, which contains unsegregated sensory and motor nerve fibres, divides and enters the spinal cord through a dorsal nerve root and a ventral nerve root. The dorsal nerve root is the entry for sensory nerves from the somatic receptors (touch, pressure, pain, heat, cold) and proprioceptors (sense organs within the muscles). The ventral nerve root is the exit for the motor neuron fibres which innervate the skeletal muscles.

The segmentation of the nerve supply to the spinal cord is reflected in the pattern of innervation of successive overlapping segments of the body. Each spinal segment innervates a band of skin, called a dermatome, at a corresponding level. Each dermatome half overlaps the dermatomes both above and below.

The study of a cross-section of the spinal cord reveals a central core of grey matter with an approximate 'H' or butterfly shaped configuration. The points of the 'H' projecting to the dorsal region of the cord are referred to as the dorsal horns of the central grey. The outer sheath of white matter contains the ascending and descending pathways projecting to the brain or other segments of the spinal cord. The grey matter of the spinal cord is the site where converging influences impinge on the motor neurones whose axons exit via the ventral nerve root (for details see the later section, 'The motor system').

The cranial nerves

In addition to the spinal nerves which handle communication between the central nervous system and the body there are twelve cranial nerves which enter the brain directly and handle sensory and motor functions in the head. The points of entry of these nerves are shown in Figure 2.7 and their functions are as follows:

1. *Olfactory* Mediating smell by transmitting from the chemoreceptors in the nose to the olfactory area of the brain.
2. *Optic* Carrying visual sensations from the light sensitive retina of the eye to the visual projection area at the occipital lobe of the brain.
3. *Oculomotor* Innervates muscles effecting adjustments of the lens and iris of the eye and some of the muscles responsible for eye movements.
4. *Trochlear* Innervates muscles which rotate the eyeball outwards and downwards.
5. *Trigeminal* Mediates sensation from the eye and face and innervates the muscles of mastication.
6. *Abducens* Supplies muscles which rotate the eyeball outwards.
7. *Facial* Innervates the facial muscles and salivary glands and mediates taste sensations.
8. *Acoustic* Mediates hearing and vestibular sensation used for the maintenance of balance.
9. *Glossopharyngeal* Mediates taste and sensation in the mouth and pharynx.

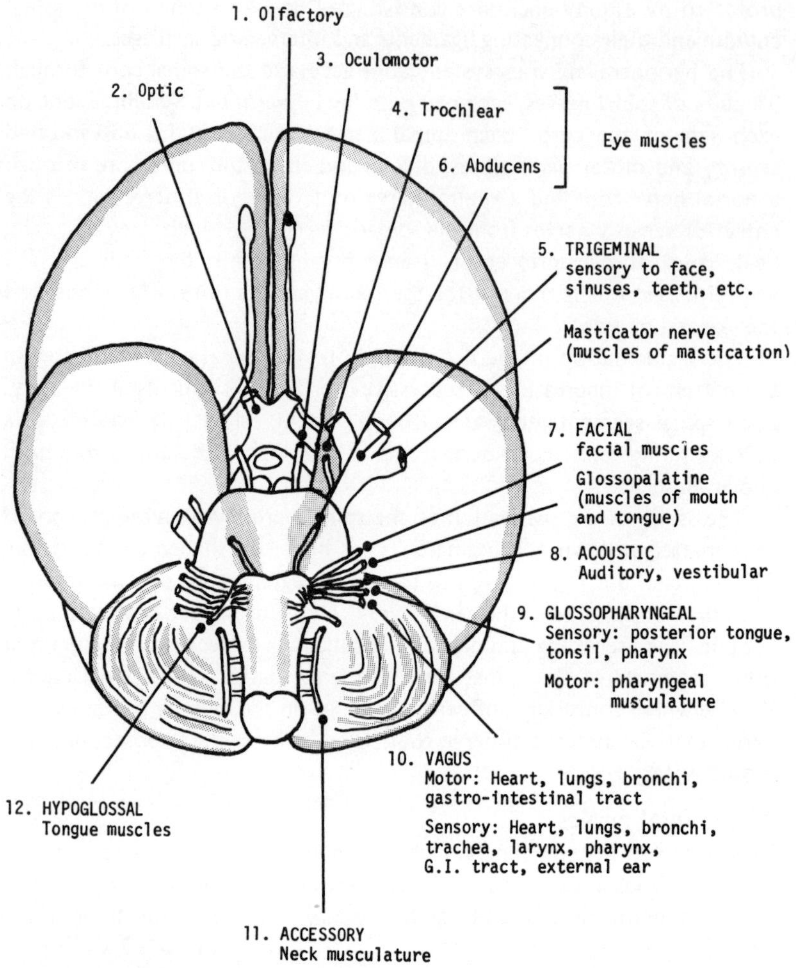

Figure 2.7
The twelve cranial
nerves

1. Olfactory

2. Optic

3. Oculomotor

4. Trochlear

6. Abducens

Eye muscles

5. TRIGEMINAL
sensory to face,
sinuses, teeth, etc.

Masticator nerve
(muscles of mastication)

7. FACIAL
facial muscles

Glossopalatine
(muscles of mouth
and tongue)

8. ACOUSTIC
Auditory, vestibular

9. GLOSSOPHARYNGEAL
Sensory: posterior tongue,
tonsil, pharynx

Motor: pharyngeal
musculature

10. VAGUS
Motor: Heart, lungs, bronchi,
gastro-intestinal tract

Sensory: Heart, lungs, bronchi,
trachea, larynx, pharynx,
G.I. tract, external ear

12. HYPOGLOSSAL
Tongue muscles

11. ACCESSORY
Neck musculature

10. *Vagus* Contain sensory and motor fibres serving the ears, pharynx, larynx, and viscera (heart, lungs, stomach, and intestines).
11. *Spinal accessory* Motor innervation to mouth structures and neck muscles.
12. *Hypoglossal* Motor supply to strap muscles of mouth and tongue.

The brain

The concentration of the important sense organs at the head end of the primitive chordates was accompanied by an increased concentration of nervous tissue at the head end of the neural tube. This was to allow the information gathered from these receptors to exercise control over behaviour. The development of the anterior segment of the neural tube was initially manifest as three bulges. In ascending order these were precursors of the hindbrain (rhombencephalon), midbrain (mesencephalon), and forebrain (prosencephalon (see Figure 2.8). The hindbrain and midbrain are collectively referred to as the brainstem as even in the highest vertebrates they form a stem like structure which merges with the spinal cord at its lower end.

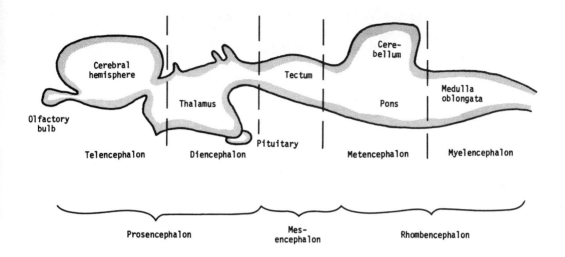

Telencephalon   Diencephalon   Metencephalon   Myelencephalon

Prosencephalon   Mes-encephalon   Rhombencephalon

Figure 2.8
The principle divisions
of the evolving brain.

From Romer, A. S.
(1962) *The vertebrate
body*, London, W. B.
Saunders and Co.
Reproduced by
permission of the
publishers

The brainstem

The hindbrain has become differentiated into the medulla oblongata (or myelencephalon) and the pons and cerebellum (collectively the metencephalon). The medulla oblongata (usually referred to simply as the medulla) is continuous with the spinal cord, the boundary between the two being taken as the decussation of the pyramids. This is the point where the pyramidal tract, containing the descending motor fibres, crosses from one side of the medulla to the other. The medulla contains ascending and descending fibre tracts and nuclei concerned with the regulation of vital functions, such as circulation and respiration, and relay nuclei in some of the tracts serving the special senses.

Rostral and dorsal to the medulla are the two highly fissured hemispheres of the cerebellum, a structure whose main concern appears to be with the fine control of motor activities (see the later section, 'The motor system'). In front of the cerebellum the central spinal canal widens to form a cavity known as the fourth ventricle. The ventral aspect of the brainstem is embraced by a prominent rounded structure called the pons which is composed of a band of fibres linking the two cerebellar hemispheres and also contains various nerve tracts and nuclei.

Rostral to the pons and cerebellum is a short final section of the brainstem called the midbrain. On the dorsal surface of the midbrain are two pairs of rounded protuberances called respectively the inferior and superior colliculi (alternatively the corpora quadrigemina inferior and superior). The lower inferior colliculus is a relay in the auditory pathway and the upper superior colliculus is concerned with visual functions, these structures being the archaic projection areas for these sensory modalities. The brainstem structures described are remarkably uniform across species from lower vertebrates, such as fish, to man. In fish, where there is little brain above the brainstem, the colliculi are the receiving areas for the auditory and visual sense modalities.

The medial portion of the midbrain is referred to as the tegmentum and contains ascending sensory fibre pathways from the spinal cord, *en route* to the thalamic relays. The ventral midbrain is called the cerebral peduncle and contains two large bundles of descending motor fibres originating from the pyramidal cells in the motor cortex.

The central core of the upper part of the spinal cord and the brainstem contain a diffuse multisynaptic network of short axoned neurones which is called the brainstem reticular formation. The segment in the medulla is sometimes referred to as the bulbar reticular formation and the upper part may be referred to as the tegmental reticular formation. The reticular formation extends rostrally and anteriorly into the hypothalamus and rostrally into the thalamus.

The cerebrum

Rostral to the brainstem (refer to Figure 2.9) are the two hemispheres of the cerebrum, the elaborated forebrain derived from the most anterior bulge of the neural tube. The pressure of the skull on the evolving brain has resulted in its formation into a series of folds. The folding of the forebrain has resulted in the contortion of the cavity in the neural tube to form the two symmetrically disposed lateral ventricles and below them the more medial third ventricle separating the right and left diencephalic structures.

Perhaps the most salient feature to note about the cerebral hemispheres is that there are two of them whose symmetrical disposition reflects the symmetrical disposition of the body structures about a central axis. Furthermore, each hemisphere controls the motor functions on the opposite side of the body, the dominance of the one hemisphere usually being reflected in a preference for using the hand on the opposite side of the body. Communication between the two hemispheres is achieved via the corpus callosum, a massive band of connecting fibres.

The diencephalon: (I) Hypothalamus

The forebrain is divided into the diencephalon, at the base of the cerebrum, with the more recently developed telencephalon above and partially enclosing the diencephalon. The diencephalon includes the thalamus and hypothalamus. The hypothalamus is a small but vital structure situated on the ventral surface of the cerebrum just anterior to the cerebral peduncles. The collection of small nuclei which form this structure appear to play a vital role in regulating activities, such as feeding, drinking, temperature control, and reproduction, which are essential for individual and species survival. They also appear to mediate emotional arousal. The hypothalamus is influenced from below by the ascending reticular formation, which merges into it, and by the sensory inflow to the brain, probably via the adjacent thalamus. It also has extensive connections with other diencephalic structures and with the cerebral cortex. One prominent afferent fibre tract which can be distinguished is the fornix. This arises in the hippocampus, a structure buried in the temporal lobe, and curves up and around the top of the thalamus. It then descends again to terminate in the mamillary bodies of the hypothalamus, which appear as protuberances from the ventral surface of the cerebrum (see Figure 2.11). Another major fibre tract which is often mentioned is the medial forebrain bundle (MFB) which projects from the anterior and lateral hypothalamus into forebrain areas anterior to this structure.

Beneath the hypothalamus the pituitary gland (or hypophysis) is

Figure 2.9
Medial sagittal section
of the human cerebral
hemispheres

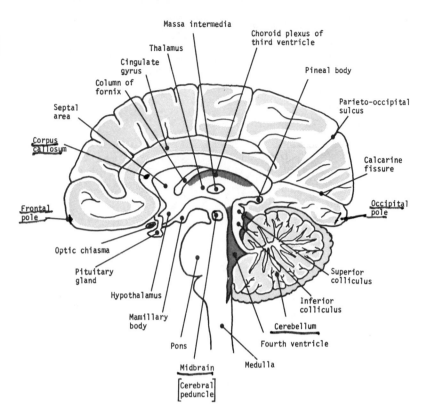

Figure 2.9
Medial sagittal section
of the human cerebral
hemispheres

suspended by its stalk, the infundibulum. The pituitary gland is the central gland of the endocrine system, secreting not only hormones controlling growth, reproduction, and water balance, but also hormones affecting the growth of subordinate glands, such as the thyroid and adrenal glands. The pituitary is in an intimate relation with the hypothalamus, which controls its secretions and is, in turn, regulated by feedback from hormones circulating in the blood.

The diencephalon: (II) Thalamus

Rostral and dorsal to the midbrain is the thalamus, a structure composed of two ovoid masses of ganglionic nuclei which are about 4 cm long in humans. The two halves of the thalamus are disposed on either side of the third ventricle which is bridged by a narrow band of tissue called the massa intermedia. The thalamus contains synaptic relays in the ascending sensory nerve tracts from the tegmentum of the midbrain. The postsynaptic fibres are distributed to the cortical projection areas for the sense modality whose signals they carry.

Two important thalamic relay nuclei appear as bumps under the posterior extremity of the thalamus. The lower more medial protuberance is the medial geniculate body, the final sensory relay in the auditory pathway, and the higher, more lateral one is the lateral geniculate body, the sole sensory relay in the visual system.

In addition to the specific thalamic nuclei, giving rise to fibres projecting only to the cortical receiving areas for the sensory systems which they

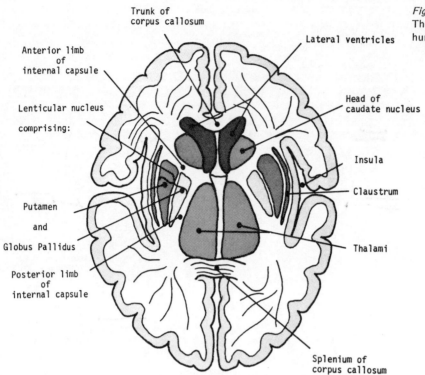

Trunk of
corpus callosum

Lateral ventricles

Anterior limb
of
internal capsule

Lenticular nucleus

comprising:

Putamen

and

Globus Pallidus

Posterior limb
of
internal capsule

Figure 2.10
The basal ganglia of the
human brain

Head of
caudate nucleus

Insula

Claustrum

Thalami

Splenium of
corpus callosum

belong to, there are non-specific thalamic nuclei with fibre projections to widely diffused cortical areas. These nuclei represent the rostral projection of the brainstem reticular formation and are sometimes referred to as the diffuse thalamic projection system (DTPS). This nonspecific system is intimately concerned with the generation of conscious awareness (see Chapters 6, 7, and 8). The thalamic nuclei belonging to this system are the midline nuclei, adjacent to the wall of the third ventricle, the internal medullary lamina and the ventro-lateral reticular nucleus.

The ventricular system

Within the cerebrum the cavity in the neural tube is contorted into the strange shapes of the lateral ventricles, one situated in the lower medial portion of each hemisphere. Roughly triangular in cross-section, the main cavity of each ventricle lies above the fornix and thalamus where the two are separated from each other by a thin layer of tissue called the septum pellucidum (or just septum). The septum is connected above with the corpus callosum, the massive band of fibres connecting the two hemispheres and forming the roof of the ventricles. The forward extensions of the ventricles, called the anterior horns, bend down slightly and terminate in the frontal lobe. The posterior horns of the lateral ventricles extend laterally and posteriorly into the occipital lobe. There are also inferior horns which curve around the posterior end of the thalamus and then curve laterally, downward and forward into the temporal lobes. The lateral ventricles communicate with the third ventricle via narrow canals called the foramina of Monroe, and the third ventricle communicates with the fourth ventricle in the brainstem, via the aqueduct of Sylvius. In turn the fourth ventricle communicates with the subarachnoid space, the space between the arachnoid and pia mater, two of the three membranes which cover the central nervous system. The outer membrane is called the dura mater. Within the ventricles tufts of small capillary vessels, called choroid plexuses, elaborate the cerebrospinal fluid which circulates in the ventricular system, the central spinal canal and the subarachnoid space.

The telencephalon: The basal ganglia

Enclosing the thalamus are the structures of the basal ganglia (Figure 2.10). Lateral to the thalamus and extending anteriorly is the white matter of the 'V' shaped internal capsule which is the route taken by the motor fibres as they descend from the motor cortex to the cerebral peduncle. Lateral to the internal capsule and within the 'V' lies the lens shaped lenticular nucleus which is subdivided into the inner globus pallidus and the outer putamen. Anterior to the thalamus and forming the anterior boundary of the internal capsule is the head of the caudate nucleus. This mass of grey matter has a long tail, from which the name is derived, which courses posteriorly across the top of the thalamus, becoming narrower and more lateral as it does so. It descends and curves round to terminate in the temporal lobe near the amygdaloid nucleus. These structures of the basal ganglia are sometimes collectively referred to as the corpus striatum or just the striatum.

The corpus striatum is part of the extrapyramidal motor system (see the later section, 'The motor system') and appears to be concerned with the fine control and co-ordination of movement as curious disabilities of movement control are associated with damage to its structures.

The rhinencephalon

The term rhinencephalon literally means 'smell brain', translating from the Greek (refer to Figures 2.9 and 2.11). In phylogenetically advanced animals it is a constellation of connected structures intimately concerned with the emotional intensity of responses to painful or pleasurable stimuli and with learning based on them. The principle structures are the septum pellucidum (or just septum), cingulate gyrus, hippocampus and amygdala. We have already learned that the septum is a layer of tissue separating the two lateral ventricles. It fills the area bounded above by the corpus callosum, and below by the fornix. The cingulate gyrus runs across the top of the corpus callosum, parallel to it, and can be seen in the medial view of the brain (Figure 2.9). If we follow the fornix in its curved trajectory rearwards, downwards, and then forwards we see that it runs into a structure called the hippocampus (Latin for sea horse). It is an elongated segment of cortex rolled into the temporal lobe and lying on the floor of the inferior horn of the lateral ventricle. The hippocampus appears to be important in either the entry of items into memory or the retrieval of items from it (see Chapter 13). Situated near the anterior extremity of the hippocampus and just above it is the amygdala which appears to be important in emotional behaviour (see Chapter 6). The cingulate gyrus and the amygdala are old cortical structures, sometimes referred to as being palaeocortical.

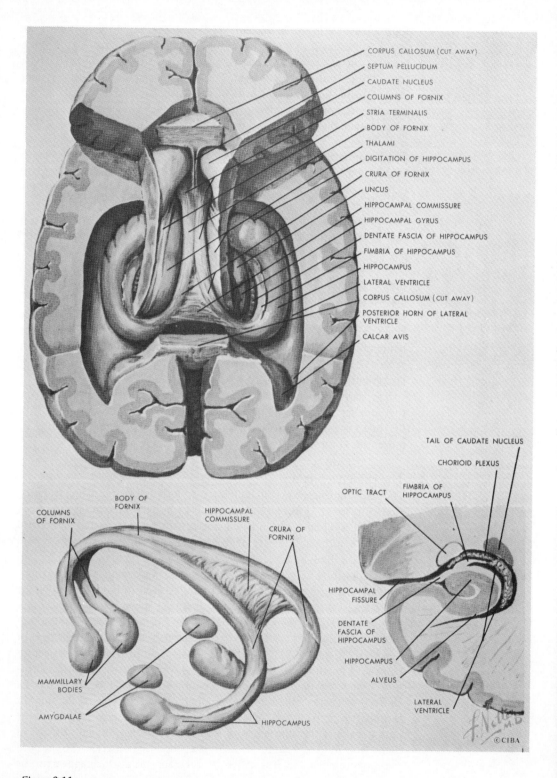

Figure 2.11
Human brain sectioned to show the hippocampus and other subcortical structures.

From *The CIBA Collection of Medical Illustrations*, Vol. 1.
Reproduced by courtesy of CIBA-GEIGY Ltd., Basle. All rights reserved

The cerebral cortex

The diencephalic and basal ganglia structures which have been described are subcortical structures. They are enclosed by the outermost and phylogenetically most recent layer of the brain, the cerebral cortex (see Figure 2.12). This layer is absent in the fish, rudimentary in amphibians and poorly developed in reptiles and birds. Figure 1.4 shows the progressive elaboration of the cerebral cortex from fish to man. The cerebral cortex is the brain's outer mantle of grey matter which consists of cell bodies, 50 to 100 deep, organized into six distinctive strata. Between the cortex and the subcortical structures there is white matter consisting of the myelinated fibres of cortical cells carrying inputs to and outputs from the cerebral cortex and forming interconnecting links between different cortical areas.

As the cell bodies are concentrated on the brain's surface in order to gain an adequate supply of nutrients from the blood capillaries which traverse it, an increase in the number of cortical cells could only be achieved by increasing the surface area of the brain. As increases in volume of the brain have been constrained by the bony cranium and the disadvantages of a greatly enlarged head, this increase in surface area has been achieved by the folding of the cortex into multiple convolutions (called gyri) with intervening fissures (called sulci) (see Figure 2.12). The increase in the number of convolutions of the cortex with evolution can be seen in the phylogenetic comparisons shown in Figure 1.4. By this device the human cerebral cortex is able to accommodate approximately ten billion neurones, three-quarters of the total number in the entire brain and four times the number found in the brain of the chimpanzee, man's most intelligent cousin.

Old or palaeocortical structures are hidden from view. We have already identified the cingulate gyrus and hippocampus. The newest part of the cortex is referred to as the neocortex and forms the visible exterior of the cerebral hemispheres. The lateral aspect is divided into four lobes by the major fissures of Sylvius and Rolando. The fissure of Rolando (or central sulcus) separates the frontal lobe from the parietal lobe posterior to it. Forward of the fissure is the anterior central gyrus which is the area of origin of the outgoing motor fibres and posterior to it is the postcentral gyrus which is the receiving or projection area for the afferent pathways from the body senses (touch, pressure, pain, heat, cold).

The fissure of Sylvius separates the temporal lobe below from the frontal and parietal lobes above. Also separation of the fissure of Sylvius reveals a hidden area of cortex called the island of Riel. The superior surface of the temporal lobe includes the projection area for the auditory system and the lobe appears to be important in memory. The rear portion of the cerebral hemisphere is called the occipital lobe. It is not clearly demarcated from the parietal and temporal lobes on its lateral aspect, but is bounded by the parietal–occipital sulcus on the medial aspect. The posterior extremity of the occipital lobe, the occipital pole, is the visual projection area.

The naming of the convolutions on the four lobes is according to a rational system of inferior, medial, or superior, according to location. In addition there is the supramarginal gyrus at the posterior extremity of the fissure of Sylvius, the angular gyrus of the posterior parietal lobe and the lateral occipital gyrus.

54

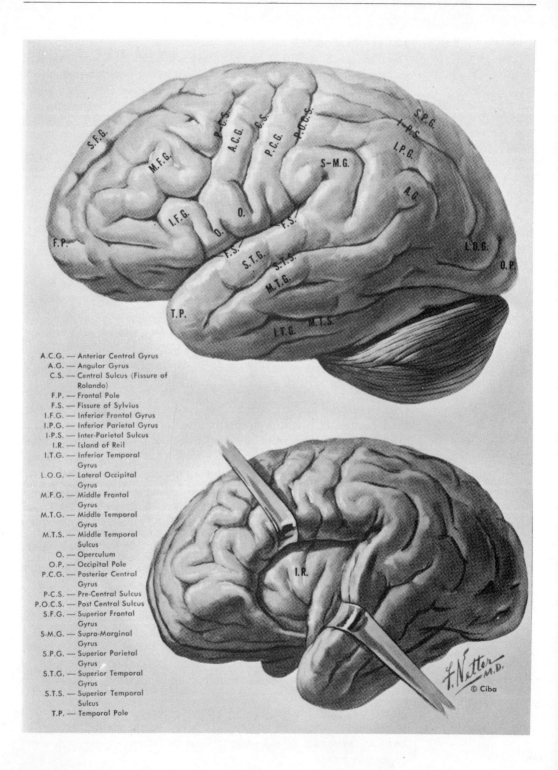

A.C.G. — Anterior Central Gyrus
A.G. — Angular Gyrus
C.S. — Central Sulcus (Fissure of Rolando)
F.P. — Frontal Pole
F.S. — Fissure of Sylvius
I.F.G. — Inferior Frontal Gyrus
I.P.G. — Inferior Parietal Gyrus
I.P.S. — Inter-Parietal Sulcus
I.R. — Island of Reil
I.T.G. — Inferior Temporal Gyrus
L.O.G. — Lateral Occipital Gyrus
M.F.G. — Middle Frontal Gyrus
M.T.G. — Middle Temporal Gyrus
M.T.S. — Middle Temporal Sulcus
O. — Operculum
O.P. — Occipital Pole
P.C.G. — Posterior Central Gyrus
P.C.S. — Pre-Central Sulcus
P.O.C.S. — Post Central Sulcus
S.F.G. — Superior Frontal Gyrus
S-M.G. — Supra-Marginal Gyrus
S.P.G. — Superior Parietal Gyrus
S.T.G. — Superior Temporal Gyrus
S.T.S. — Superior Temporal Sulcus
T.P. — Temporal Pole

Figure 2.12
Lateral aspect of the human brain. Artists impression with the principle sulci and gyri identified.

From *The CIBA Collection of Medical Illustrations*, Vol. 1.

The functions of the cerebral cortex are still very much a mystery, but it seems clear that the areas not committed to sensory or motor functions relate to learning ability and higher cognitive functioning. This seems to follow as the development of these areas in evolution is correlated with the evolution of intelligence, and because, logically, greater capacity for processing information must derive from a system which is quantitatively and qualitatively more complex.

The autonomic nervous system

The autonomic nervous system is differentiated from the somatic nervous system by both anatomical and functional criteria. However, it should be remembered that there is both some anatomical overlap and a pattern of interdependence between the systems.

The sensory side of the autonomic nervous system consists of afferent nerves from the sense organs in the viscera (internal organs such as the heart, lungs, stomach, intestines, blood vessels, etc.). However, afferent input along nerves not considered to be autonomic may evoke autonomic reflexes. An example is changes in pupil size elicited by changes in the level of ambient lighting transmitted via the optic nerve.

The motor side of the autonomic nervous system proceeds from its specific exits from the brain and spinal cord to innervate the glands, heart, and smooth muscle fibres which are found in the walls of blood vessels and hollow organs. This innervation produces such involuntary responses as 'gooseflesh' (piloerection) and changes in diameter of the pupil of the eye.

Whereas somatic motor fibres from the spinal nerve roots travel to the striped muscle which they innervate without synapsing, autonomic fibres from the central nervous system synapse in nuclei called the autonomic ganglia. Thus the fibres from the spinal cord to the ganglia, which are usually myelinated, are referred to as preganglionic fibres. The outgoing fibres from the ganglia innervate the smooth muscles and are usually unmyelinated. They are referred to as postganglionic fibres.

The motor segment of the autonomic nervous system is divided into a parasympathetic branch, which is concerned with the conservation of the body's resources, and a sympathetic branch which is concerned with the mobilization of the body's resources for action (see Chapter 6).

The preganglionic neurones of the parasympathetic branch have long fibres which terminate with few branching collaterals. The ganglia which they supply are in, or very near the organ innervated so that the postganglionic neurones have very short axons. The consequence of this arrangement is that any preganglionic parasympathetic discharge has a strictly localized effect on the organ adjacent to the ganglia activated.

There are four exits from the central nervous system for preganglionic parasympathetic nerve fibres (Figure 2.13).

1. *Hypothalamic* An outflow from the supraoptic nucleus of the hypothalamus innervates secretory cells in the pituitary gland.

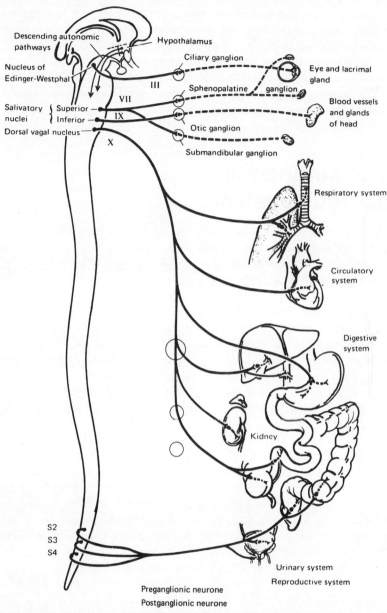

Figure 2.13
The parasympathetic branch of the autonomic nervous system.

From Noback, C. R., and Demarest, R. J. (1972) *The nervous system*. Copyright © 1972 by McGraw-Hill Inc. Reproduced by permission of the publishers.

2. *Tectal* Preganglionic fibres in the third cranial nerve (oculomotor) terminate in the ciliary ganglion which supplies the muscles adjusting the iris and lens of the eye.

3. *Bulbar* Preganglionic fibres in the facial nerve (see Figure 2.13 (VII)) and glossopharyngeal nerve supply ganglia controlling secretions in facial glands and dilation and constriction of facial blood vessels.

  Preganglionic fibres in the vagus nerve (see Figure 2.13 (X)) mediate parasympathetic control of the heart, lungs and alimentary canal.

4. *Sacral* Preganglionic fibres originating in the lateral grey matter of the spinal cord emerge from the second, third, and fourth sacral nerve roots of the spinal cord to supply parasympathetic ganglia in the colon, rectum, bladder, and reproductive organs.

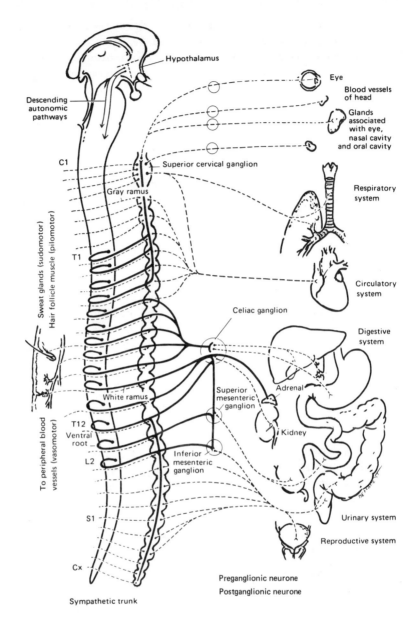

Figure 2.14
The sympathetic branch of the autonomic nervous system.

From Noback, C. R., and Demarest, R. J. (1972) *The nervous system.* Copyright © 1972 McGraw-Hill Inc. Reproduced by permission of the publishers

Hypothalamus

Descending autonomic pathways

Eye

Blood vessels of head

Glands associated with eye, nasal cavity and oral cavity

C1

Gray ramus

Superior cervical ganglion

Respiratory system

Sweat glands (sudomotor)
Hair follicle muscle (pilomotor)

T1

Circulatory system

Celiac ganglion

Digestive system

To peripheral blood vessels (vasomotor)

White ramus

Superior mesenteric ganglion

Adrenal

T12
Ventral root

Kidney

L2

Inferior mesenteric ganglion

S1

Urinary system

Reproductive system

Cx

Preganglionic neurone
Postganglionic neurone

Sympathetic trunk

In contrast to the parasympathetic branch, the sympathetic preganglionic fibres have short axons and terminate with many collaterals on postganglionic cell bodies in the sympathetic ganglia. These sympathetic preganglionic fibres emerge along the ventral spinal nerve roots of the thoracic and upper lumbar regions and enter their sympathetic ganglia, which are outside of the spinal cord, but adjacent to it (Figure 2.14).

These sympathetic ganglia are joined, by preganglionic fibres travelling upwards or downwards to synapse outside of their level of emergence from the cord. The resulting chain of ganglia forms a sympathetic nerve trunk, lateral to the spinal cord, extending from the base of the skull to the lower end of the spine.

The outflow of postganglionic fibres from the sympathetic nerve trunk innervates the lungs, heart, and peripheral blood vessels, sweat glands and erector pilorum muscles in the skin (which cause the hair to stand on end). The postganglionic outflow from another series of sympathetic ganglia in front of the spine (the coeliac and superior and inferior mesenteric) innervate the adrenal gland and smooth muscles in the walls of the blood vessels and lower intestine.

The consequence of the diffuse connections of the preganglionic sympathetic fibres in the sympathetic nerve trunk is that sympathetic activation is never selective, but is generalized to all of the organs innervated.

The importance of distinguishing between the parasympathetic and sympathetic nervous system can be appreciated when we consider their functions. The parasympathetic nervous system regulates the secretion of hormones by the posterior lobe of the pituitary gland, mediates the adjustments of the iris and the lens of the eye necessary for clear vision and causes lubrication of the cornea by the lacrimal glands. It promotes digestion by eliciting secretions from the salivary glands of the mouth, pancreas, and liver and by increasing peristaltic movement of the intestine. The heart beat is slowed and made shallower and lung function is inhibited by contraction of the small bronchioli by parasympathetic innervation. Thus, the over-all effect of the parasympathetic nervous system is to promote the 'preservation, accumulation, and storage of energies in the body'.

The sympathetic branch of the autonomic nervous system antagonizes the parasympathetic branch in the organs which they jointly innervate and in contrast acts as a 'spender of energies', priming the body for violent action. Sympathetic influences dilate the pupils and inhibit the intake and digestion of nutrients. They also speed and deepen the heart beat, promote exchange of gases in the lungs by dilating the bronchioli and cause constriction of the peripheral blood vessels. Finally sympathetic activation promotes secretion of adrenalin and noradrenalin by the medulla of the adrenal gland, the noradrenalin potentiating the effects of the sympathetic activation on the other organs of the body. This occurs because the postganglionic sympathetic nerve endings are noradrenergic. That is to say that noradrenalin is the transmitter substance by which they activate the organ innervated. The postganglionic parasympathetic nerve endings, on the other hand, produce acetylcholine as the transmitter substance so that they are said to be cholinergic.

The sympathetic nervous system thus mobilizes the body's energy resources in preparation for emergencies. It is a mediator of emotional arousal as a prelude to 'fight' or 'flight', a subject treated in detail in Chapter 6.

The division of function between the parasympathetic and sympathetic branches of the autonomic nervous system is not maintained with complete consistency. For instance stimuli provoking extremes of terror may cause slowing or even cessation of the heart, an increase rather than a decrease of intestinal peristalsis and a loss of sphincter action of bladder and rectum. However, in general, the parasympathetic nervous system promotes normal functioning and the sympathetic nervous system promotes emergency functioning in the internal organs whose regulation is normally independent of voluntary control.

The motor system

At the beginning of Chapter 1 it was observed that motility was one of the triad of interdependent properties by which an organism maintained itself in its environment. The processing of environmental information must lead to the production of an appropriate response by an effector system if the organism's information handling systems are to be of any adaptive value. In vertebrates the effector system, referred to as the motor system, is the configuration of muscles effecting body and limb movements and the neural circuitry controlling them. Clearly a knowledge of the principles of operation of this system is an important complement to the study of the neural and psychological processes mediating behaviour.

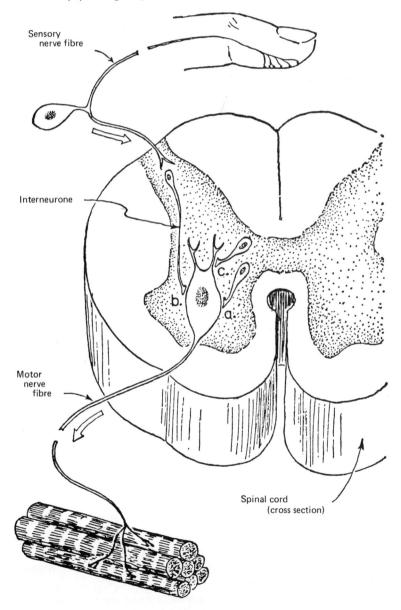

Figure 2.15
The spinal reflex arc.

From Galambos, R. (1962) *Nerves and muscles*. Copyright © 1962 Doubleday and Co. Inc. Reproduced by permission of the publishers

In primitive creatures there were relatively direct pathways between sense receptors and effectors in which simple responses were produced. As the central nervous system and the higher nervous system were elaborated in evolution the direct connections, found in lower creatures were preserved, while becoming subject to over-riding control by higher centres. Thus in higher vertebrates we find that the motor system is hierarchically organized. The simplest involuntary responses are organized at the lowest levels of the hierarchy, while more complex, finely co-ordinated and possibly novel responses are organized at higher levels.

The lowest level of integration of motor activity in vertebrates is at the segmental level in the spinal cord. Sensory fibres from receptors in the skin and muscles enter the dorsal nerve root. In the central grey matter of the spinal cord they synapse either directly, or via internuncial neurones, with motor neurones whose axons leave via the corresponding ventral nerve root to innervate striped muscle (see Figure 2.15). This pathway is the basis for spinal reflexes such as the 'flexion reflex' in which painful stimulation results in rapid withdrawal of a limb. In addition to direct connection from afferents at the same segmental level, the motor neurones in the ventral horns of the spinal grey matter are influenced by fibres from different segmental levels, and from the motor centres in the brain. Because the motor neurones are the focus of converging influences from different levels they are commonly referred to as 'the final common path', the terminology of Sherrington, the founder of modern neurophysiology.

The final common path and muscles

We should briefly look at the final common path and the muscles innervated before looking at the control system. The motor fibres of the somatic nervous system pursue an unbroken path from the motor neurone pool in the ventral horn of the spinal grey to the muscles which they innervate. These muscles are generally those which effect publicly observable movements and are called skeletal muscles, or alternatively striped muscles because of the regular sequence of dark striations along the fibres. Each muscle is made up of many cells called muscle fibres, which have some resemblance to nerve cells. The motor nerve fibres terminate on central sections of the muscle fibres at end plates (see Figure 2.1), each axon branching to innervate several fibres which collectively form a motor unit. In a similar manner to transmission at the synapse the muscle is excited by the release of the transmitter substance acetylcholine at the end plate. This causes an electrical impulse to travel down the muscle fibre in both directions. This releases calcium which allows the protein myosin to break down the energy rich substance adenosine triphosphate (ATP). This releases energy which hauls in filaments of the protein actin [Huxley, 1965] and so contracts the muscle. As muscles can only pull and cannot push, mobile limb joints are operated by two sets of muscles. The extensors attached to the outside of a joint pull it open, to straighten the limb. The flexors attached to the inside of a joint pull it closed, to flex the limb. These sets of muscles working in opposition are called antagonists, while muscles pulling together are called synergists.

There are actually two different types of muscle contraction. Movement of the limbs is effected by isotonic contraction in which the tension in the muscles remains constant while its length decreases. On the other hand posture is maintained against opposing forces by isometric contractions in which the tension in the muscle increases but there is no change in its total length.

Sense receptors in the muscles

Our motor system enables us to make patterns of movement which are complex, but precise and carried out in a smooth and orderly manner. These qualities of movement are only made possible because the muscles contain sense receptors which continually monitor their position and feed back the information to spinal and brain centres controlling movement. These receptors make it possible to apply continuous corrections to an evolving movement to ensure a high degree of precision. There are two types of sense receptors in the muscles; the golgi tendon organs and the muscle spindles. The golgi tendon organs are simply an afferent nerve fibre whose terminals lie in the tendons connecting muscle to bone. They have a relatively high activation threshold and are only likely to be excited when excessive muscular tension threatens to damage the tendons or even the bones. When they are activated the tendon organs deliver inhibitory volleys to the motor pools for the muscle which is contracting, thus causing it to relax, safeguarding the tendons and bones from damage. In a decerebrate animal whose limbs are rigid, because of the removal of higher inhibitory influences over-riding the stretch reflex, a strong force against a rigid muscle will cause a sudden relaxation of muscle tone and the assumption of a new position. This is because of the inhibitory effect of the golgi tendon organs which have been activated. This observation is known as the clasp knife phenomenon. More complex information about the degree, direction, and rate of change of muscle tension is given by the muscle spindles.

Muscle spindles

Muscle spindles (Figure 2.16) are small structures within the skeletal muscles formed by weak 'intrafusal' muscle fibres. These fibres, which make no direct contribution to the effort of the muscles they inhabit, are attached to the sheaths of the main 'extrafusal' fibres, so that they are stretched or contracted in tandem with them. The intrafusal muscle fibres are innervated by the small diameter axons of slow conducting motor neurones, called γ-motor neurones, which account for about 30% of the axons in the motor nerve. In the central region of the muscle spindle is an elastic non-muscular segment containing receptors sensitive to stretch, called annulospiral endings. These stretch receptors form the basis of a feedback loop which supplies spinal and higher control mechanisms with information about the degree, rate of change and direction of tension in the muscle. The results of such feedback in the spinal motor neurone pool can be seen in the stretch reflex (Figure 2.16) which occurs when a muscle is stretched by external forces. The muscle contracts to counteract this

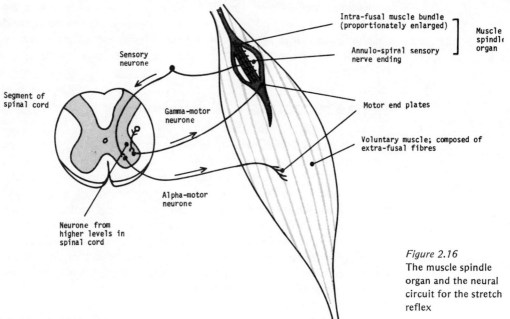

Figure 2.16
The muscle spindle
organ and the neural
circuit for the stretch
reflex

force and so maintain the position of the limb which it is attached to. This is a monosynaptic reflex in which the afferent fibres from the muscle spindle receptor enter the dorsal nerve root of a spinal segment and synapse directly with the α-motor neurones, which innervate the extrafusal muscles with their large diameter axons, and cause them to contract. This mono-synaptic reflex provides a very fast system for maintaining the position of a limb against a variable load and thus for resisting forces tending to throw an animal off balance.

The stretch reflex can be shown to be monosynaptic by stimulation of the afferent nerve from the muscle spindle. This produces a sharp wave recordable at the ventral (motor) nerve root with a latency of only just over 1 ms. As the transynaptic conduction time is about 0.8 ms, and conduction time through the nerve branches must be allowed for, a latency this short could only be achieved in a monosynaptic pathway. In contrast, the ventral root response, following stimulation of the cutaneous sensory nerve entering the dorsal root, is a series of waves with longer latencies, indicating multisynaptic connections.

Spindle bias

If muscles always resisted displacement from a fixed position then an animal would be immobilized. This condition is actually realized in the extreme rigidity of animals from which the cerebrum, and thus the over-riding control of the higher nervous system, has been removed. In the intact animal changes in the position of a limb are achieved without evok-ing the stretch reflex, by changing the 'bias' of the muscle spindles. This is effected by signals from central mechanisms exciting the γ-motor neurones which modify the tension in the intrafusal muscle fibres. The spindle bias system could be used in two ways in the production of movement. Merton [1950, 1951] has suggested that most voluntary movements are initiated by first exciting the γ-motor neurones causing the intrafusal muscle fibres to contract. The resulting increase in tension in the muscle spindle activates the annulospiral endings which transmit their discharges back to the motor pool to excite the α-motor neurones. Discharge of the α-motor neurones initiates a contraction of the extrafusal muscles and thus movement of the limb. The extrafusal muscles contract until the tension in the muscle spindles is relieved, when a new equilibrium state is reached. This new equilibrium is maintained by the operation of the stretch reflex until further adjustments of the tension in the intrafusal muscles again alters the 'bias' of the muscle spindle.

However, Valbo [1971] has shown that this sequence does not mediate the initiation of voluntary movements in man as records of extrafusal muscle activity precede discharges in the afferent nerve from the muscle spindle. Thus, we must presume that nerve fibres from the motor cortex of the brain synapse directly with the α-motor neurones and that parallel excitation of the γ-motor neurones produces a compensatory alteration in spindle bias so that the movement initiated can proceed unhindered.

Reciprocal innervation

It has already been observed that, as muscles can only pull and not push, articulated joints, such as those of the limbs, must have two antagonist muscles to operate them. As the contractions of one muscle group must always result in the extension of the antagonist this is another situation in which the stretch reflex must be suppressed if paralysis is to be avoided. Such embarrassment is avoided by a system of reciprocal innervation whereby feedback from the muscle spindles in a contracted muscle exercises an inhibitory influence on the motor pools for the antagonist muscle, thus preventing an opposing contraction. This inhibitory influence is mediated by inhibitory internuncial neurones, called Renshaw cells, in the spinal grey. When excited by the spindle afferents these give inhibitory outputs to the α- and γ-motor neurone pools for the antagonist muscle.

Recurrent collateral inhibition

Renshaw inhibitory cells are also incorporated in very short negative feed-back loops which effect recurrent collateral inhibition (Figure 2.17) on motor neurones. Collaterals branch from motor neurone axons before they leave the spinal grey and synapse with Renshaw cells. In turn, the axon terminals of the Renshaw cell synapse with a number of neurones in the motor pool, including the one giving rise to the collateral, which form a small 'field' over which it exercises its inhibitory influence. The motor neurones in the field of a Renshaw inhibitory cell cannot maintain a constant high rate of discharge. Periodically they cease to respond to excitatory influences because of the inhibitory potentials which build up due to collateral activation of the inhibitory Renshaw cells, which must be dissipated.

The utility of the system described is probably to allow the motor pools to effect graded muscular contraction, so important in the exercise of perceptual motor skills, rather than trigger massive muscular twitches upon receipt of any suprathreshold input. For a given level of sustained

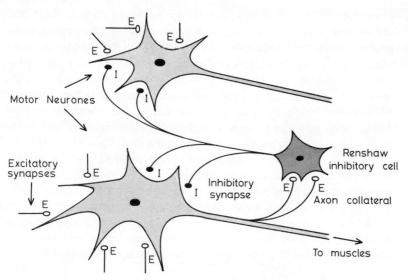

Figure 2.17
Diagram to illustrate
the principle of
recurrent collateral
inhibition by Renshaw
inhibitory cells

input to a motor pool, output is probably rotated among the fields of Renshaw cells as they asynchronously wax and wane in excitability under the influence of recurrent inhibition. Any change in input to the motor pool results in a change in the proportion of an excitatory cycle during which the thresholds of the motor neurones within any one field are exceeded. This implies a change in the total output from the motor pool and a corresponding increase in the vigour of muscular contraction.

Connectivity in the motor neurone pools

The rotation among motor neurone fields of Renshaw cells described above could only occur if the input to the motor neurone pool was distributed to all of the fields. The degree of interconnection in the motor neurone pool is very great. Incoming axons from both higher levels in the nervous system and from sense receptors at the segmental level have numerous terminal branches. In turn, the motor neurones themselves have wide dendritic fields. It seems likely that every afferent axon entering a motor pool has some influence on every motor neurone in it, and that every motor neurone is influenced by many incoming axons. The convergence of sensory inputs on the motor neurones is illustrated if the sensory nerve root of a spinal segment is divided. A stimulus intensity can be found which if applied to either of the resulting branches separately is insufficient to produce a response at the ventral nerve root, but if applied to both simultaneously results in a distinct response. Influences from both branches of the divided dorsal root converge on individual motor neurones where a process of spatial summation results in the discharge threshold being exceeded.

Reflexes

Examination of the mechanisms of motor control at the level of the spinal segment is educative because it presents us with a simplified picture of the operation of the nervous system. Input from sense receptors to a central mechanism initiates output to effectors. In the spinal reflexes (see Figure 2.15) we can actually observe adaptive behaviour at this level of organization. We are already acquainted with the simplest of these, the stretch reflex, which assists animals to maintain a chosen posture against opposing forces. Another prominent reflex is the 'flexion reflex' in which painful stimulation of the hindlimb results in immediate rapid flexion to remove the limb from the source of pain. This may be accompanied by extension of the opposite limb, tending to help support the animal, which is called the 'crossed extension reflex'. Unlike the stretch reflex the flexion and crossed extension reflexes are multisynaptic. Furthermore, while the stretch reflex and flexion reflex may occur at the level of one spinal segment the crossed extension reflex is suprasegmental, involving transmission from the segment at which afferent input occurs to the motor pool of another segment, from which action is initiated. Another example of a suprasegmental reflex is the scratch reflex in which an animal which is 'tickled' will scratch the stimulated region with the hindlimb on the same side.

The proof that these reflexes are spinal and not organized in the brain is seen in the fact that they are observed in animals in which the spinal cord has been transected below the brain—spinal preparations. These preparations, particularly of lower animals like frogs, will exhibit these reflexes in response to appropriate stimuli with all the appearance of purposive behaviour. The absence of connections to the brain is betrayed by the stereotyped and inflexible nature of the behaviour observed and by the organism's lack of spontaneity in the absence of evoking stimuli.

Many actions necessary for individual and species survival are of a reflex nature; respiration, heart beat, elimination and aspects of sexual behaviour. Some reflexes are organized at a spinal level and some in the brain stem or subcortical regions of the cerebrum, in which case they are said to be supraspinal. More flexible and highly patterned aspects of motor activity than reflexes are organized at higher levels in the nervous system.

The control of movement by the brain

The over-all control of movement patterns in vertebrates is by the brain, which even has a modulating influence on the sensitivity of spinal reflexes. The evolution of the brain is inextricably linked with the refinement of the systems of motor control in the interest of flexibility, complex patterning and precision in movements.

A number of brain structures, constituting a large proportion of its mass, are involved in the control of movement. Classically the motor system is divided into the pyramidal system and the extrapyramidal system on the basis of anatomical criteria, although the logic of this division is sometimes questioned in the light of recent knowledge.

The pyramidal system
The pyramidal system originates in the pyramidal cells of the pre-central gyrus—the motor cortex—and follows their long fibres which course down through the internal capsule to the cerebral peduncle and thence to the

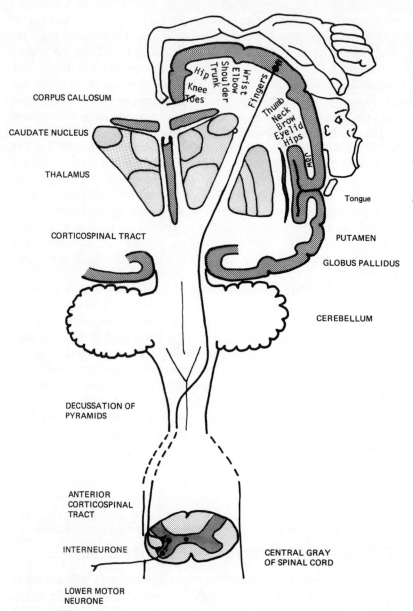

CORPUS CALLOSUM

CAUDATE NUCLEUS

THALAMUS

CORTICOSPINAL TRACT

Hip
Knee
Toes
Shoulder
Trunk
Elbow
Wrist
Fingers
Thumb
Neck
Brow
Eyelid
Hips
Jaw

Tongue

PUTAMEN

GLOBUS PALLIDUS

CEREBELLUM

DECUSSATION OF
PYRAMIDS

ANTERIOR
CORTICOSPINAL
TRACT

INTERNEURONE

CENTRAL GRAY
OF SPINAL CORD

LOWER MOTOR
NEURONE

Figure 2.18
The pyramidal motor system; the 'motor homunculus' gives an idea of the cortical area devoted to each particular motor organ.

Modified from Penfield, W., and Rasmussen, T. (1950), *Cerebral cortex of man.* Reproduced by permission of the Macmillan Publishing Co. Inc.

medulla. At the lower end of the medulla is the 'decussation of the pyramids' where about 80% of the fibres cross to the opposite side of the spinal cord and travel down it in a laterally situated tract until they terminate in the posterior horn of the spinal grey matter. The pyramidal fibres which do not decussate descend the spinal cord in a ventral tract, ending on motor neurones in the anterior horn of the spinal grey matter. About 10% of the pyramidal tract fibres synapse directly on motor neurones and the others synapse on internuncial neurones which mediate their influence on the motor neurones. The pyramidal fibres travel from their cell bodies in the motor cortex to the motor pools, without synapsing, and thus form the longest axons in the mammalian nervous system, achieving lengths as great as 10 m in the whale. The pyramidal tract takes its name from the medullary pyramids, the pyramidally shaped segment of the pyramidal tract as it descends in the medulla, and not from the pyramidal cells from which their fibres emanate, identically named because of their shape.

At one time it was thought that all the pyramidal fibres originated from the giant pyramidal cells (also called Betz cells) of the motor cortex. Now it appears that only about 20–40% of the fibres in the pyramidal tract originate from the motor cortex and only 2% from the giant Betz cells. Fibres originating in widely dispersed areas of the cortex converge on the pyramidal tract and thus must have some influence on the final common path of the motor system. However, recording the electrical responses of the pyramidal tract during stimulation of a variety of cortical locations indicates that by far the strongest influences on the pyramidal tract come from the pre- and postcentral gyri, the classical motor and somatosensory receiving areas respectively.

The motor cortex

Electrical stimulation of the motor area elicits muscle movements and is a technique which has been used to map the projection from the motor cortex to the various muscle systems of the body. The muscles are represented in an orderly fashion with the area of cortex devoted to particular muscle groups being proportionate to their importance to the organism and the precision of the movements which they are required to make (see Figure 2.18). Thus the large area of the human cortex devoted to the hands reflects their importance to the species for the execution of manipulative skills of high survival value.

Although the motor area is the only area of the cerebral cortex where electrical stimulation will evoke movement Eccles [1973] has argued that it is not the primary region for the initiation of movement but the final relay upon which widely dispersed cortical influences are focussed. Penfield and Roberts [1959] have observed that muscle movements elicited in conscious human patients by stimulation of the motor cortex are subjectively experienced as being beyond the control of the 'will', again suggesting that the initiation of voluntary movements involves other areas of the brain.

The intimate relationship between the discharges of pyramidal cells in the motor cortex and patterns of voluntary movement has been elegantly demonstrated in unit recording experiments performed by Evarts [1967, 1968]. Evarts recorded from single cells (using microelectrodes) in the area of motor cortex projecting to the arm in monkeys. When the previously trained monkeys rhythmically swung a control bar back and forth between stops, in order to obtain a grape juice reward, the discharge rate of the pyramidal cells varied synchronously with the animal's arm movements, increasing to a peak during flexion and decreasing during extension (see Figure 2.19). Furthermore, it was found that the peak rate of firing during flexion was proportional to the amount of force which the monkey had to exert to move the control bar against a load.

The functions of the motor cortex

The motor cortex has been associated with the initiation of voluntary movements and the control of rapid and precise movements in the exercise of a skill. Tower [1935, 1936] observed that in monkeys with bilateral section of the pyramidal tract, movements of the extremities lost their finer qualities of aim and precision and there was loss of the least stereo-typed and most discrete movements or elements of a movement. As the motor cortex is phylogenetically a recent addition to the brain the effects of destruction of the pyramidal system increase and the capacity to recover from it diminish as the phylogenetic scale is ascended.

There is contradictory evidence concerning the importance of the pyramidal system in the exercise of a skill as Ruch [1960] has reported that a human patient with bilateral destruction of the pyramidal tract has retained the capacity to play a Beethoven piano concerto. The explanation for this may be that this performance was a highly overlearned skill for which control had been handed to extrapyramidal mechanisms, such as the

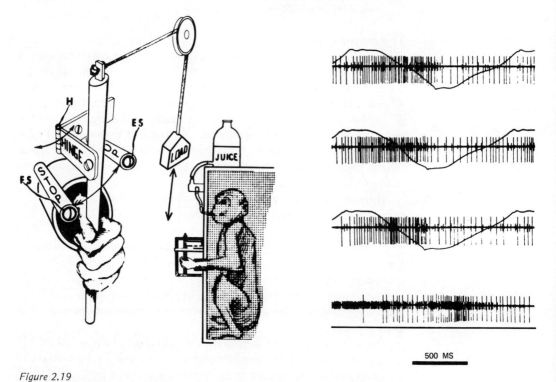

500 MS

Figure 2.19
Illustration of Evarts' experiment recording from individual pyramidal cells of the motor cortex in monkeys during rhythmic movement. A shows the apparatus in which a monkey had to make alternate flexion and extension movements under a variable load. A grape juice reward was given if the movements were made at the specified rate. B shows the activity, recorded from microelectrodes, of two units (one producing large spikes, the other small) in the motor cortex. By comparing with the superimposed trace of the movement (derived from a potentiometer output) it can be seen that the unit discharges are clearly correlated with each other and with the movement. In this case the unit discharges are maximal during the extension movement, represented by the descent of the movement trace. The bottom unit record shows the lack of correlation between the activity of the two units during a different movement pattern.

From Evarts, E. V. (1967) In M. D. Yahr and D. P. Purpura (eds.), *Neurophysiological basis of normal and abnormal motor activities.* Copyright © 1967 Raven Press, New York. Reproduced by permission of the publishers

cerebellum. The story might have been different if the patient had been required to make a sequence of precisely measured actions which were novel to him, or even play a piece of music which was unfamiliar.

It might be that the motor cortex handles the novel aspects of voluntary movement patterns, of which we are consciously aware, while other systems regulate overlearned movement patterns which are produced without any focal awareness on our part. Consideration of the extrapyramidal system offers more insight into the control of movement and regulation of posture, which occurs outside the focus of consciousness.

The extrapyramidal motor system

The extrapyramidal motor system consists of a number of brain structures which, among other connections, converge on the discrete extrapyramidal tracts which run parallel to the pyramidal tracts in the lateral and ventromedial portions of the spinal cord. The cerebral portion of the extrapyramidal system consists of a group of subcortical nuclei known collectively as the basal ganglia or corpus striatum. External to the cerebrum, behind and below, is the cerebellum. The basal ganglia structures which are members of the extrapyramidal system consist of the elongated caudate nucleus, arching over the thalamus, the globus pallidus and putamen (collectively forming the lenticular nucleus) flanking the thalamus, the intralaminar thalamic nuclei and the subthalamic nucleus and substantia nigra (black substance) below the thalamus.

The fibres of the pyramidal tract have branching collaterals which provide input to the extrapyramidal structures, particularly the caudate nucleus and putamen. In addition there is an extremely fast and reliable input, via pyramidal fibre collaterals and synapses in the brainstem nuclei, from the cerebral cortex to the cerebellar cortex. The pattern of connection from the pyramidal tract which has been outlined is consistent with the notion that the cortex provides an over-all plan of action and initiates it, while the subcortical structures supervise the details of its execution.

The basal ganglia

It has proved difficult to attribute precise functions to the basal ganglia (Figure 2.10). In the lower vertebrates such as birds and reptiles the basal ganglia are the highest brain structures, yet their ablation in the pigeon leaves flight and locomotion unimpaired, only eliminating the spontaneous appearance of these actions [discussed by Zeigler, 1964]. Tower [1936] found that stimulation of the motor cortex in the intact animal resulted in the movement of individual muscles. However, when the pyramidal tract was sectioned so that the effectors could only be accessed via the extrapyramidal system, stimulation of the motor cortex resulted in more complex movements, often resembling integrated acts. Waller [1940] has evoked walking movements by stimulation of the subthalamic nuclei in lightly anaesthetized animals. These findings possibly associate the extrapyramidal system with innate patterns of behaviour of a stereotyped nature. Alternatively it has been found that stimulation of various structures of the extrapyramidal system, using voltages too low to evoke movement, results in a global change in the excitability of the motor system. This is manifest in the changed amplitudes of tendon reflexes evoked during the experiment. This finding tends to support the proposition that the extrapyramidal motor system has a role in modifying the organism's over-all response tendency, perhaps adjusting excitability as a preparation for action.

Stimulation of the caudate nucleus has been found to have an inhibitory effect on cortical functions which may contribute to the ability of organisms to limit their reactions so that they are only evoked by restricted aspects of the environmental stimulus array.

A number of bizarre patterns of involuntary movement have been associated with lesions of the extrapyramidal system in man. In Parkinson's disease postural rigidity and incapacitating tremor appear to arise from lesions of the globus pallidus and substantia nigra. The symptoms have been relieved by making further lesions in the subthalamic nucleus and substantia nigra. A condition known as Huntingdon's chorea—characterized by rapid, involuntary, jerky movements—appears to stem from extensive lesions of the striatum. The slow repetitious, writhing movements of athetosis may result from lesions of the putamen. Lesions of the subthalamic nucleus appear to give rise to violent flailing movements of an involuntary nature known as hemiballismus. The associated fact that stimulation of the subthalamus results in rhythmic locomotor movements led Jung and Hassler [1960] to conclude that the subthalamic nucleus exercises over-all control over rhythmic movements of the limbs.

The tentative conclusion is that the cerebral section of the extrapyramidal system regulates the postural adjustments which are the background to our voluntary movements, and exercises a co-ordinating function which disciplines these movements.

The cerebellum

The cerebellum (Figure 2.20) is a very distinctive structure whose cortex is even more convoluted than that of the cerebrum in order to achieve a large surface area within a small volume. The folds are closer together than those of the cerebrum and the fissures go deep into the structure. Phylogenetically the cerebellum is an old structure which probably evolved in connection with the control of swimming in fishes. Eccles [1973] maintains that the cerebellum functions as a computer handling complex inputs both from the cerebrum and from the sense receptors, particularly those receptors monitoring the position of muscles and a creature's spatial orientation (the vestibular organs in the semicircular canals).

Some details about the connections of the cerebellum should precede further speculation about its functional significance. The neuronal structure of the cerebellar cortex is quite well understood. Input is achieved through two types of fibres, climbing fibres and mossy fibres. The principle type of cells in the cerebellar cortex are the Purkinje cells whose axons constitute the only output lines. They make inhibitory synapses in the cerebellar nuclei from which the results of cerebellar computations are distributed to other stations. The incoming climbing fibres twine around the dendrites of the Purkinje cells, thus synapsing directly with them. They exert an enormously powerful excitatory influence on the Purkinje cells, one climbing fibre impulse evoking several Purkinje cell impulses. The mossy

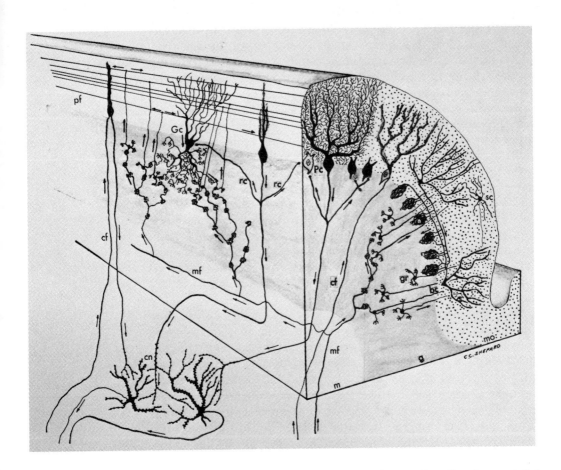

Figure 2.20
The neural 'wiring' of the cerebellum. bc, basket cell; cf, climbing fibre; Gc, granule cell; mf, mossy fibre; Pc, Purkinje cell; sc, stellate cell.

From Crosby, E. C., Humphrey, T., and Lauer, E. W. (1962), *Correlative anatomy of the nervous system*. © Macmillan Publishing Co. Inc. Reproduced by permission of the publishers

fibres branch enormously and synapse with granule cells whose parallel fibres either make direct contact with the dendritic trees of the Purkinje cells, or synapse with other internuncial cells (basket cells and stellate cells) which in turn influence the Purkinje cells. The mossy fibre inputs supply both excitatory and inhibitory influences to the Purkinje cells. There is enormous convergence between the mossy fibre input and Purkinje cell output as each mossy fibre contributes excitation to about 400 granule cells and about 80 000 granule cells contribute to the excitation of each Purkinje cell. Eccles [1973] speculates that the averaging of input achieved at the Purkinje cells, as a result of this convergence minimizes the influence of unreliability in individual units and, perhaps, adds subtlety and flexibility to performance in a way which we do not yet understand.

The climbing fibres and mossy fibres carry inputs to the cerebellar cortex which originate from both the motor cortex, where voluntary movements appear to be initiated, and from the sense organs, monitoring movement and orientation. Branching collaterals of the pyramidal fibres from the motor cortex synapse in subcortical nuclei, with cells giving rise to climbing fibres or mossy fibres. The Purkinje cells give an inhibitory output to the interpositus nucleus of the cerebellum, after which there is only one synapse, in the ventrolateral thalamus, in the fast return loop to the motor cortex. In addition the Purkinje cells also supply inhibitory influences to the fastigial and dieters nuclei of the cerebellum from which they influence the motor neurones either directly or via the brainstem reticular formation. Examination of the connections of the cerebellum clearly establish its focal position in the motor system and suggests that it has the capacity to exercise both 'feed-forward' and 'feedback' control over evolving movements.

We might illustrate the possible functions of the cerebellum with a speculative analysis. When the command signal for a limb movement—say hitting a tennis ball—is issued from the motor cortex a copy is transmitted to the cerebellar cortex via the collaterals of the pyramidal fibres. At the cerebellar cortex memory stores associated with the execution of skilled movements are accessed and, if necessary, the pyramidal tract discharge is modified by a correction signal delivered by the return loop to the cortex. This is feed-forward control. While the action is being executed the muscle spindles in the limb emit a continuous feedback of information about limb position and the rate and direction of movement, to the cerebellum. This is also the basis for a continuous series of corrections as the movement proceeds, so that the end product is a smooth, well integrated, and accurate movement.

Direct evidence that the cerebellar cortex receives copies of the command signals issued by the motor cortex has been found in unit recording experiments by Thach [1968]. It was found that the rate of discharge of Purkinje cells was modulated in phase with rhythmic arm movements made by monkeys in a similar way to cortical unit discharges in experiments by Evarts [1968]. Also the discharges of Purkinje cells brought about by movements were superimposed on a continuous background discharge, suggesting that the cerebro–cerebellar circuit is a dynamic loop whose continuous activity is modulated up or down by input of information.

The role of the cerebellum in producing smooth and accurate movements is documented by the effects of cerebellar damage in human patients whose attempts to touch a target, such as the end of their nose, with a finger are clumsy and irregular. The deficit is sometimes called intention tremor and bears a resemblance to the 'hunting' exhibited by servosystems in which feedback results in overcorrection. There is a loss of the ability to smoothly execute a movement involving the simultaneous use of several joints, a deficit called 'decomposition of movement'. Subjectively the patient reports a loss of the ability to delegate control of the details of movement to his subconscious; that every facet of movement has to be consciously thought out. This supports the supposition that the cerebellum is a vital control centre for manipulative skills, incorporating a store of information concerning the details of their execution. Perhaps this cerebellar store could be the basis for the patient, mentioned earlier, retaining his ability to play a Beethoven piano concerto following bilateral transection of the pyramidal tract.

The endocrine system

The endocrine system is an alternative system of communication within the body carrying messages which are usually less urgent, and concerned with longer term adjustments, than those carried by the nervous system. They are messages concerned with such functions as bodily growth, metabolism, reproduction, water and mineral balances and mobilization of body resources.

This system involves the production of specific chemical messengers, called hormones, within special secretory glands. The hormones are discharged into the bloodstream which transports them to their target organ which is primed to respond to their message.

The mediation of behaviour by the nervous system cannot be considered without reference to the endocrine system, because of the intimate relationship between the two in the genesis of adaptive behaviour. The nervous system controls the secretion of a number of hormones whose effects on the body are precursors for specific behaviour patterns, particularly in the case of sex hormones. Conversely the activity of the nervous system is itself influenced in some aspects by hormones, particularly those concerned with water balance, emotional arousal and, again, reproduction. It should also be noted in addition that chemical messengers, called pheromones, sometimes have a role in the communication between individuals of a species in integrating sexual or social behaviour.

This section provides a background and reference source whose relevance will become particularly apparent in Chapters 4, 5, and 6.

The pituitary gland

The pituitary gland (or hypophysis) is the master gland of the endocrine system (Figure 2.21). It is connected to the base of the hypothalamus by a short stalk, sometimes called the infundibulum.

The posterior lobe of the pituitary gland is called the neurohypophysis and is an outgrowth from the hypothalamus. Fibres from special neurosecretory cells in the supraoptic and paraventricular nuclei of the hypothalamus run into the sac which forms the neurohypophysis. The neurosecretory cells resemble nerve cells in every respect except that their axons terminate in swollen bulbs which deliver the hormone secreted within the cell, into the bloodstream. The evidence suggests that the hormones delivered into the bloodstream in the neurohypophysis are actually manufactured in the hypothalamus, in the bodies of the neurosecretory cells. [Ebling and Highnam, 1969, p. 4]. The hormones are transported to the neurohypophysis down the axons of these cells. The neurohypophysis produces two principle hormones:

1. Antidiuretic hormone which reduces the excretion of water from the body.
2. Oxytocic hormone which causes contraction of the smooth muscles of the uterus.

The intermediate and anterior lobes of the pituitary gland are collectively known as the adenohypophysis, which is derived from the epithelium of the mouth cavity. The intermediate lobe secretes a hormone which promotes the formation of pigment in the skin.

74

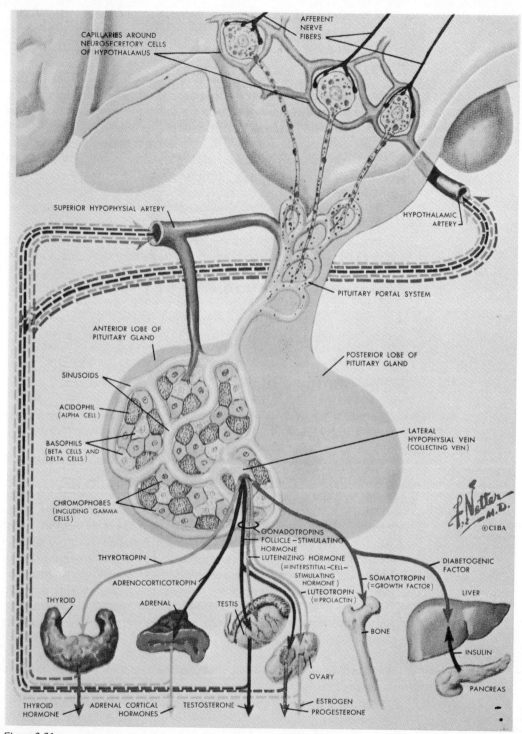

Figure 2.21
The pituitary gland: its control by the hypothalamus, its hormonal secretions and its relations with the rest of the endocrine system.

The anterior pituitary secretes many hormones:

1. *Somatotrophic hormone* (Somatotrophin STH) causes growth of skeleton and muscles. It also acts, through the pancreas, to elevate the blood sugar level.
2. *Thyrotrophic hormone* (thyrotrophin, thyroid stimulating hormone, (SHT) produces growth of the thyroid gland and secretion of thyroid hormones.
3. *Adrenocorticotrophic hormone* (adrenocorticotrophin, corticotrophin, ACTH) causes growth of the cortex of the adrenal gland the the production of glucocorticoid hormones (alternatively hydrocorticosteroids).
4. The three gonadotrophic hormones:
   a) *Follicle stimulating hormone* (FSH) stimulates the growth of the follicle, the sac in which the egg or ovum is formed, in the ovary of the female. It promotes maturation of the spermatozoa in the testicular tubules of the male.
   b) *Luteinizing hormone* (LH) induces the formation of the corpus luteum, a secretory body which produces progesterone, and ovulation in developed ovarian follicles.
   c) *Interstitial cell stimulating hormone* (ICSH) is identical or almost identical to LH but stimulates the production of testosterone by the interstitial cells in the male testis.
5. *Prolactin* (lactogenic hormone) stimulates milk secretion in conjunction with other hormones.

The hormones of the anterior pituitary are synthesized within the gland and released into the blood capillaries of the pituitary portal system. The secretory activities of the anterior pituitary are probably controlled from the hypothalamus. It is thought that neurosecretory cells deliver 'releasing factors' into a system of blood capillaries in the hypothalamus which drain, via a collecting vein in the pituitary stalk, into the anterior lobe of the pituitary. There the releasing factors trigger production of their hormones.

The release of gonadotrophic hormones from the anterior pituitary is subject to feedback control by the hormones oestrogen and progesterone secreted in the gonads. There are other factors, such as environmental stimuli, which influence pituitary activities, presumably through the mediation of the nervous system. In the rabbit the gonadotrophins producing ovulation are secreted following copulation. In other species, such as the ferret, whose mating is seasonal, the release of gonadotrophins is prompted as the period of daylight lengthens with the approach of spring.

The thyroid gland

In mammals the thyroid gland consists of a pair of lobes situated on either side of the larynx. The thyroid produces a hormone, containing iodine, which is called thyroxine. This hormone increases the metabolic rate as measured by oxygen consumption, and promotes bodily growth in conjunction with the pituitary hormone STH. Underactivity of the thyroid at birth, in humans leads to a condition known as cretinism in which there is stunted growth and mental retardation. Overactivity of the thyroid (hyperthyroidism) leads to an increase in the metabolic rate of up to 50%, increased heart rate, respiration, and heat production. Sufferers tend to be hot and emotionally hyperactive.

Thyroxine promotes metamorphosis in amphibians. When injected in young tadpoles they prematurely turn into tiny frogs. When administered to the Mexican axolotl, which normally lives and breeds in its larval state, it will metamorphose into a type of salamander.

The parathyroid glands

There are four parathyroid glands embedded in the thyroid gland. The parahormone produced maintains plasma calcium level.

The gonads (sex glands)

The gonads or sex glands are influenced by the gonadotrophic hormones from the pituitary and in turn produce their own hormones.

In the female the ovary secretes oestrogen which brings about the development of the secondary sexual characteristics; development of the breasts, female distribution of body hair, and fat. It is also responsible for the emotional and psychological changes associated with attaining womanhood. In lower animals oestrogen together with progesterone induce oestrus, the period of sexual receptivity in the female.

When the ovum is ejected from the follicle in which it develops in the ovary, the follicle is converted into a corpus luteum (yellow body) which releases the hormone progesterone. Progesterone helps oestrogen suppress further ovulation during that cycle and prepares the wall of the womb for pregnancy should fertilization occur.

The male sex hormone testosterone is formed by the interstitial cells of the testis under the influence of ICSH from the anterior pituitary. The production of this hormone leads to the production of male secondary sexual characteristics at puberty; the breaking of the voice, growth of facial hair, male distribution of body hair, growth of the reproductive organs, development of the characteristic male physique.

The adrenal glands

The two adrenal glands are located in front of and above the kidney. They are actually double glands in which the inner medulla and outer cortex have different endocrine functions.

We have already observed that the adrenal medulla is innervated by the sympathetic nervous system and secretes adrenalin and noradrenalin, transmitter substances which augment and prolong the effects of sympathetic activation. Sympathetic activation mobilizes the body's resources under stresses such as during anger, fear, cold, or low blood sugar. The effects of adrenalin and noradrenalin include increased output from the heart, constriction of surface blood vessels, dilation of blood vessels supplying muscles, enlargement of the airways in the lungs, pupil dilation, pilo-erection (seen as 'gooseflesh' in humans), inhibition of digestion and mobilization of sugar stored in the liver.

Unlike the adrenal medulla the adrenal cortex has no nerve supply. It produces hormones called corticoids of which there are two groups:

1. *Mineralocorticoids—Aldosterone* Regulates the level of sodium and other mineral salts in the body by reducing their secretion in the urine and sweat.

2. *Glucocorticoids—Cortisol* Regulates the general metabolism of carbohydrates, proteins and fats on a long term basis and modifies the metabolism in times of stress. Cortisol promotes the conversion of protein and fat to carbohydrate, which is used as a source of energy, with a concomitant increase in carbohydrate metabolism and an increased capacity for muscular work. It is also anti-inflammatory and anti-allergic.

The adrenal cortex is an alternative site of manufacture of the sex hormones—androgens, oestrogens and progesterone—although appearing to be of secondary importance. However, tumours of the adrenal gland may lead to the appearance of anomalous sexual characteristics. Also it is thought that the androgens manufactured in the adrenal cortex sustain the sex drive in women who have had their ovaries removed.

The pancreas

In this gland cells called the islets of Langerhans produce the hormones insulin and glucagon. Insulin is essential to the body's energy metabolism. It facilitates the entry of blood sugar (glucose) into the cells where it will be burnt as fuel and also acts to conserve the body's energy resources by promoting the conversion of blood glucose into its stored forms glycogen and fat. Glucagon, whose release is stimulated by adrenalin, promotes the conversion of glycogen back into its active form, glucose, when circumstances demand the mobilization of the body's energy resources.

Chapter three

Research techniques in psychobiology

Introduction

Progress in our understanding of the brain mechanisms mediating behaviour has depended very heavily on the development of research techniques which are ingenious and sophisticated, and which owe much to recent developments in electronics. The extreme complexity of the brain, the multitude of connections and the compacting of so many units into such a small space implies that any attempt to unravel its secrets will make enormous demands on the ingenuity and technological and methodological expertise of the researcher. Furthermore, there are likely to be many pitfalls awaiting the researcher, when attempting to interpret the results of an experiment using a particular technique and experimental design. Because of these considerations it was thought that the reader would find it useful to have a brief account of the main research techniques in psychobiology, together with details of the advantages and disadvantages associated with each of them.

Anatomical techniques

Anatomical techniques lay the foundations for research on brain function. They yield details of the hardware of the brain; the basic components and their arrangements and interconnections in the over-all structure. By revealing the complexity of the brain's structure anatomical techniques have indicated the scale of the task of trying to understand its functions.

The gross structure of the brain has been described and its parts named by gross dissection and study with the naked eye. This has provided agreed points of reference but limited cues to function.

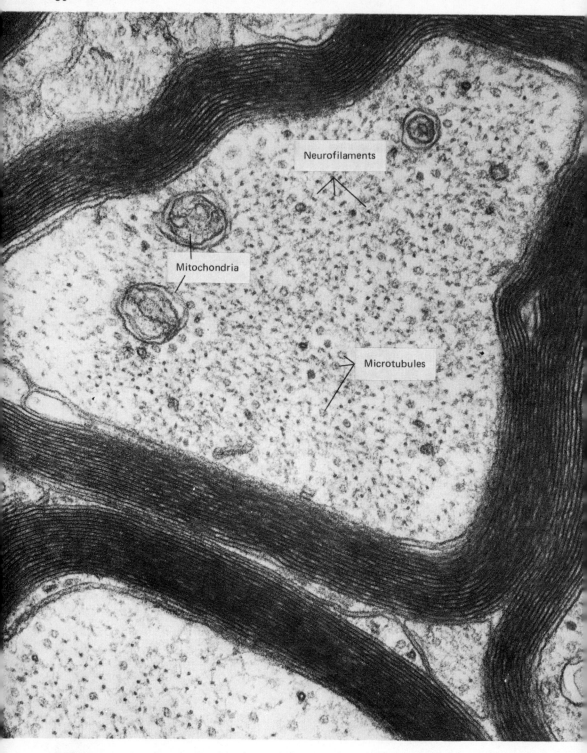

Figure 3.1
Histological techniques revealing the microstructure of the nervous system:
(i) Electronmicrographs giving cross-sectional views of myelinated axons in the CNS. The concentric layers of
the myelin sheath are readily seen.

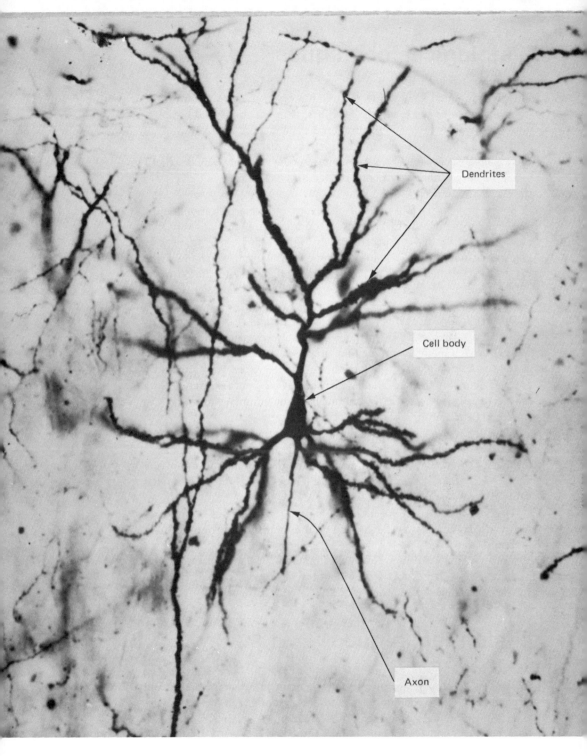

Dendrites

Cell body

Axon

(ii) The appearance of the cell body, dendritic processes, and initial part of the axon of a pyramidal cell from the cerebral (visual) cortex as shown in a light micrograph of a Golgi preparation.

Courtesy Dr. A. R. Lieberman of University College, London

Histological techniques

The study of thin slices of brain tissue under high-powered microscopes, and electron microscopes (Figure 3.1) has enabled us to describe the structural units of the brain, the neurones, their variability and organization in different sections of the brain and their patterns of connection, all of which are invisible to the naked eye. High magnification reveals connecting fibre pathways, otherwise invisible, whose existence may be crucial to the viability of theories of brain mechanisms which suppose that certain structures are connected.

Before brain tissue will reveal its structure under magnification it must be fixed and hardened, to prevent deterioration, and cut into very thin slices (20-100 μm thick) using a calibrated knife called a microtome. The preparation must then be stained with a chemical agent which highlights the features of the neural tissue which are of interest to the observer. Before staining the preparation appears as an undifferentiated mass of cellular elements.

Different chemical agents stain different structural features because of their special affinities. Nissl methods selectively reveal cell bodies while Weigart or Weil methods outline fibre processes and are valuable in tracing large fibre tracts. Reduced silver methods stain nerve cell bodies and their processes but not the surrounding glial cells. Colgi methods only stain a few nerve cells in the tissue treated but have the advantage that all of the structural details of those stained cells can be clearly seen.

Fibre tracts can also be traced using degeneration methods. If an area of brain tissue with cell bodies is damaged or destroyed, the fibres emanating from these cell bodies will progressively degenerate and die over a number of weeks. Selective staining techniques reveal the degenerated pathways and thus their destinations.

The knowledge of connections within the brain derived from histological studies provides a valuable test of the validity of theories of brain function which incorporate 'wiring diagrams'. However, it should be remembered that visible evidence that structural connections exist says nothing about their functional importance and does not differentiate whether they are excitatory or inhibitory.

Lesion techniques

A classical strategy in the investigation of brain function is to remove (ablate) or destroy (lesion) a part of the brain in a living creature and attempt to infer the function of the absent structure from changes in the animal's behaviour after the operation. A well known example of this is the inference that the lateral hypothalamus is the 'feeding centre' in the brain because following its destruction an animal completely ceases to eat.

In early ablation studies brain tissue was removed using scalpels or spoons. This technique had the major disadvantages that it was difficult or impossible to make small, precisely defined ablations, and that the operation left scar tissue which produced abnormal electrical activity. This made confident interpretation of the results impossible. A more satisfactory way of removing brain tissue is by suction which allows greater precision and leaves a cleaner wound.

The placement of small localized lesions in deep subcortical structures, such as the hypothalamus, has only been possible since the introduction of lesioning by implanted electrodes. A very fine stainless steel wire, insulated except at its very tip, is sunk into the brain and a current passed which destroys all of the tissue immediately surrounding the electrode tip, the area of damage being proportional to the level of the current. In order to accurately implant the electrodes in a deep brain structure which cannot be seen a stereotaxic machine, similar to that invented by Horsley and Clark in 1908, must be used. In this machine (see Figure 3.2) an animal's head is held rigidly in a fixed position, the animal first having been anaesthetized. Above the animal's head is an electrode holder attached to a system of steel runners which give it mobility in three directions at right angles to each other; anterior–posterior, lateral–lateral and up–down. Calibrated controls give fine adjustment along each of the axes so that the electrode tip can be accurately placed in any spatial location defined by three rectangular co-ordinates. An experimenter will usually obtain the co-ordinates of the brain structure which he wants to reach from a stereotaxic atlas for the species which he is working on, which contains this data for a 'standard' brain. Correction factors may be given to compensate for deviations from the dimensions of the standard brain. This is a very reliable method of reaching specific brain structures with an accuracy to within one millimetre. The co-ordinates in the horizontal plane are found first and the electrode is then lowered into the brain tissue to the depth required. A lesion is then made using either a direct current or an alternating current. Direct current, which is only suitable for making small lesions destroys tissue by a combination of heat and electrolysis. Reynolds [1965] has presented evidence that metal salts electrolytically deposited on the tissue surrounding the lesion have an irritative effect which prevents unequivocal interpretation of the behavioural effects of the lesion.

Radio frequency alternating currents destroy tissue by the heat produced and can be used to produce quite large lesions, apparently without causing any unwanted side effects. Because of the uncertainties associated with electrode placement and the extent of the lesion, lesion experiments are usually concluded with sacrifice of the experimental animals and histological verification that the lesions are where they were intended to be.

There are other methods of making accurate lesions involving the use of X-rays or high frequency sound waves beamed from diffuse sources in such a way that they converge at a focus in the area to be lesioned. The concentration of energy at the focus destroys the tissue, while outside the focus there is insufficient concentration of the waves to do any damage. These methods have the advantage that the damage is limited to the area of interest whereas the implantation of an electrode damages intervening tissue as it penetrates through to subcortical zones.

It is sometimes useful to make reversible lesions in which areas of the brain are temporarily put out of action. This can be achieved by using electric currents of a lower level than those which make lesions, by cooling areas of tissue below 25 °C or by placing small amounts of potassium salts on the cortex. Localized cooling of brain tissue can be achieved by circulat-

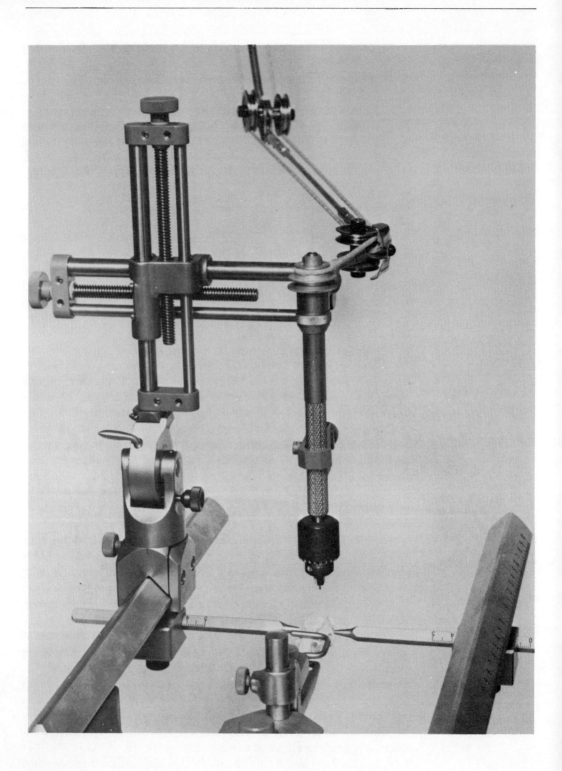

Figure 3.2
Two views of the apparatus for stereotaxic implantation of microcannulae:
(i) The stereotaxic frame: a dentist's drill, used for drilling the skull, is attached to
  the horizontal guide rail and poised to drill the skull which is held in the normal
  head position.

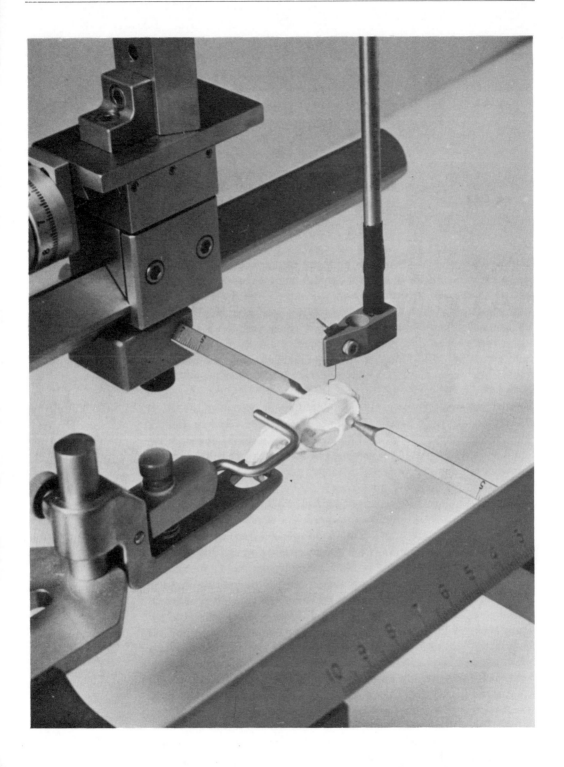

(ii) A close-up of the stereotaxic device to show a skull held firmly in position by the ear plugs, bite bar, and head clamp while the electrode holder is used to lower an electrode into the aperture in the skull.

Photographs by courtesy of D. O'Boyle of the University of Manchester

ing a cold fluid or gas through very fine concentric pipes (called cannulae), insulated to their tip and implanted in the brain in the manner described above for electrodes. This technique is sometimes used for exploratory investigations in human patients, in whom it is intended to destroy some brain tissue to obtain relief from distressing symptoms, such as the tremor of Parkinson's disease. Reversible lesions at the cortex can be made by using a cannula to place small quantities of potassium chloride on its surface. So long as it remains there it causes 'spreading depression' in which there is temporary inactivation of the neurones in the underlying cortical tissue. This technique can be used to depress an entire hemisphere of the brain.

Data on the effect of brain lesions in humans has been collected from people who have suffered brain damage in accidents (particularly high velocity missile wounds suffered during wars), who have some kind of brain pathology such as a tumour or an epileptogenic focus or who have been subjected to brain surgery for medical or psychiatric reasons. Interpretation is usually difficult as lesions are rarely strictly localized to a single structure to which a specific function can be attributed.

The implicit assumptions behind lesion experiments is that different brain structures have discrete functions which can be selectively eliminated independent of other functions. We cannot take these assumptions for granted. There are no *a priori* reasons for definitely excluding the possibility that the neural circuitry mediating specific functions is diffused through several brain structures or, conversely, that there is overlap of the neural systems serving several functions within one structure. That these are very real possibilities emerges from the results of a classical series of experiments conducted by Lashley [1950] in which he attempted to find the location of memory in the brain of the rat. He investigated the ability of his rats to learn mazes after selective ablation of different cortical areas. He was confronted with the perplexing finding that no one cortical area seemed more important than any other in memory. The deficit in the rats' maze learning ability appeared to be a function of the extent of the cortical destruction, not its location. One interpretation was that memory was everywhere, reduplicated many times throughout the entire cortex. Further experimental evidence suggests alternative interpretations. Functions which include perception, attention, motivation, or even motor control are essential for the process of storage and/or the demonstration of recall. Their disruption may therefore appear simply as a memory deficit if the tests used are insufficiently discriminative. This explanation introduces a further reservation about the investigation of brain function in lesion experiments by underlining the interdependence between neural systems. A creature's behavioural repertoire derives from the totality of its neural systems working together, not from independent contributions by each system. The growing realization that the brain is composed of subsystems which are blended in such a subtle way that they are spatially and functionally extremely difficult to separate, has led to the demand for new conceptual frameworks within which to understand its function.

Stimulation techniques

Stimulation techniques involve the short circuiting of complex and inacessible pathways from receptor organs to their target brain structures, by the artificial stimulation of those structures. The functional importance of the structures stimulated is tentatively inferred from the effect which it has on the animal's behaviour. Stimulation techniques are more consistent with the diffuse organization of the systems within the brain as they do not involve damage to subsystems contributing to the over-all performance of the brain, with its resulting interpretive difficulties.

The initial procedures for stimulating selected brain structures are similar to those for lesioning with an implanted electrode. Similar electrodes are implanted in the desired cerebral location using a stereotaxic machine. These electrodes are usually attached to a holder which is screwed and cemented to the animal's skull and which has sockets where the wires from the stimulator can be plugged in. This arrangement is called a chronic implantation and an animal thus equipped can lead a normal laboratory existence (see Figures 3.3 and 3.4) and be repeatedly subjected to brain stimulation over a long period depending on the objectives of the experimenter. At the termination of an experiment the location of the electrode tip is verified by histological examination (Figure 3.4 (ii)). Direct current stimulation of the brain has no discernible effect on behaviour except when it is switched on. Trains of pulses at rates between 50 and $300\,s^{-1}$ are usually used. The wires from the stimulator to the animal are flexible and extend from an articulated support so that the animal has as much freedom of movement as possible. In some experiments completely unrestricted movement has been achieved by attaching a miniaturized battery operated stimulator to the animal and activating it by remote control, using a radio transmitter.

Stimulation experiments have the advantage that the behaviour of a freely moving animal can be observed without the complications introduced by radical surgery or anaesthesia, with their profound and pervasive effects on many functions. By stimulating a range of locations within the brain the structures and pathways most strongly associated with specific functions, such as eating, have been mapped out. However, interpretation can be biased by neglecting the interaction between the effects of the brain stimulation and of environmental stimuli present. Stimulation which is found to elicit eating when food is present may elicit grooming or some other behaviour when food is absent [Valenstein et al, 1968]. The stimulating electrode may have access to neural systems mediating a range of behaviours from which selection is made by the environmental stimuli present.

The existence of spatially overlapping systems has been demonstrated by using chemical rather than electrical stimulation. Very fine cannulae have been implanted in the brain, using the techniques described, and have been used to deliver minute amounts of chemicals known to act on the nervous system. Grossman [1960] found that delivery of noradrenalin to

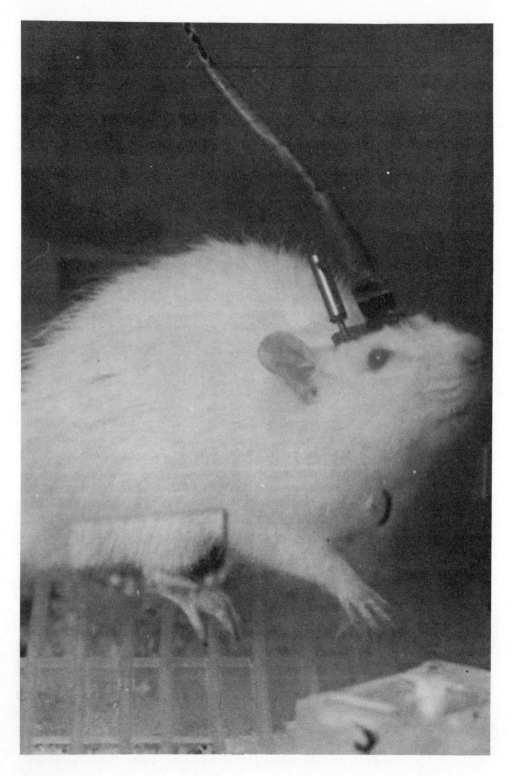

Figure 3.3
Brain stimulation/recording using chronically implanted electrodes in freely moving animals:
(i) Close-up of rat to show electrode mounting. The electrode on the left is depth adjustable.

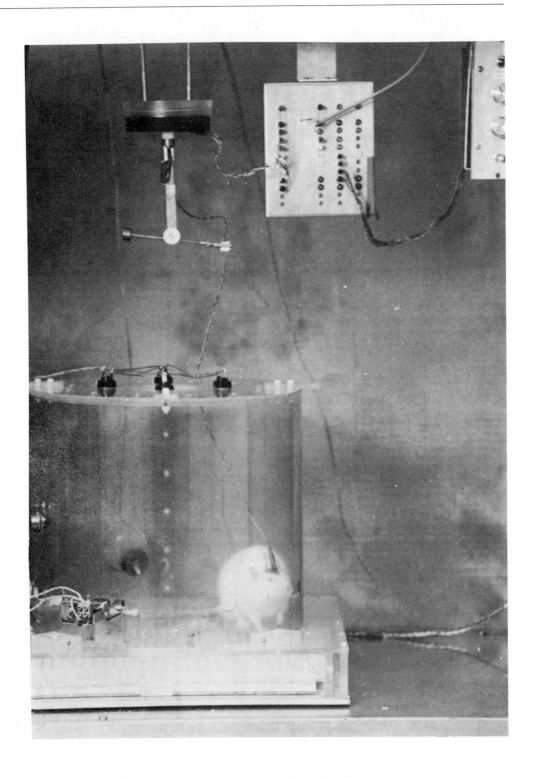

(ii) A chronically implanted rat seen in an experimental chamber. The rotating spring loaded gantry above the chamber enables the rat to move freely without entangling the electrode leads.

Photographs by courtesy of M. Belloum and D. O'Boyle of the University of Manchester

certain hypothalamic locations elicited eating behaviour, but that delivery of acetylcholine to the same locations elicited drinking. It appeared that the cannulae had access to spatially overlapping, but neurochemically separate systems, mediating different behaviours, which it was beyond the scope of the electrical probes to differentiate.

A further dimension to be considered in stimulation experiments is the parameters of stimulation. Clearly the strength of the stimulating pulses will determine whether the activation thresholds of the neural systems accessed will be reached and how far from the tip of the electrode the effect of stimulation will spread. In addition it has been found that the pattern of stimulating pulses is important. For instance locations have been found where a rapid train of pulses will make an animal more alert while a slow train of pulses will send it to sleep. Of course it should always be remembered that the pulses used in brain stimulation experiments are gross compared with the patterns of nerve impulses which provide the normal input to the structures stimulated; a further case for interpretive caution.

Recording techniques

In Chapter 2.1 it was observed that the transmission of information in the nervous system is accomplished by the propagation of impulses which can be characterized as electrical events.

This implies that the activity of the brain, as it processes information and organizes behaviour, will be a pattern of electrical events. This has been found to be so and it is possible, using suitable transducers, to monitor the electrical activity of different brain structures while the behaviour of the subject (animal or human) is manipulated by the experimenter. This procedure yields data, not only about the location of brain structures active during particular types of behaviour but also about the more dynamic spatial and temporal patterning of the brain's activity during a sequence of behaviour.

The electrical activity of the brain can be recorded from the scalp, from the cortical surface or, following stereotaxic implantation of electrodes, from deep structures (see Figure 3.4). Using macroelectrodes the summed voltages generated by many neurones in the region of the electrode are recorded while by using ultrafine microelectrodes it is possible to record the pulses produced by single cortical cells.

The electroencephalogram

The electrical activity of the human brain was first recorded from electrodes attached to the scalp by a German psychiatrist, Hans Berger, in 1925 [see Berger, 1929]. He called the record which he obtained the electroencephalogram (EEG for short), a name which has stuck. Once the authenticity of his records were accepted the technique gained wide popularity as a means of investigating brain function in both scientific and clinical contexts. It seemed to open a window on the brain's activities which could be used without the radical disturbance of its normal functioning caused by operative techniques.

The fluctuations in voltage at the scalp are very small, rarely exceeding 50 μV (10^{-6} V) during normal functioning. The high electrical resistance of the skin and bone between the electrode and the brain is partly responsible for this. The scalp signals are amplified by a factor of up to one million in order to drive a device such as an oscilloscope or a pen recorder, on which they are monitored.

The oscilloscope

The oscilloscope is a basic tool in electrophysiology, the monitoring of the electrical activity of the body. Its primary component is a cathode ray

Figure 3.4
(i) Medial sagittal section of a rat skull showing chronically implanted microelectrode *in situ*.

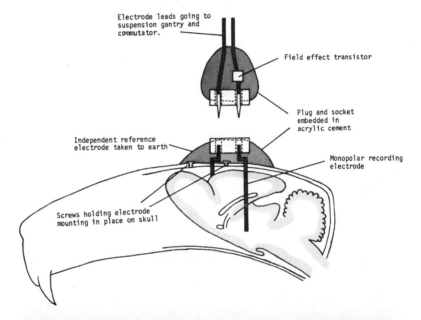

(ii) Photograph of a histology slide showing a cross-section of a rats brain with a microelectrode tract penetrating through to the substantia nigra, a subthalamic nucleus.

Courtesy H. Belloum and D. O'Boyle of the University of Manchester

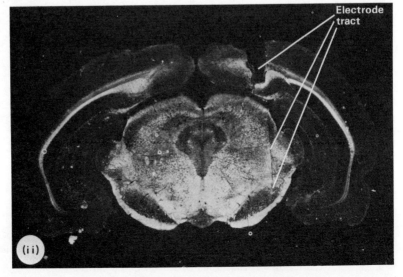

tube, similar to that used in a television set. An electron gun at the back of the tube issues a constant stream of electrons which cause the special coating on the screen to fluoresce at the point where they hit it, producing a clearly visible bright spot. The electron beam within the tube passes between two pairs of plates which deflect the beam by an electrostatic force proportional to any voltage applied to them. A signal source within

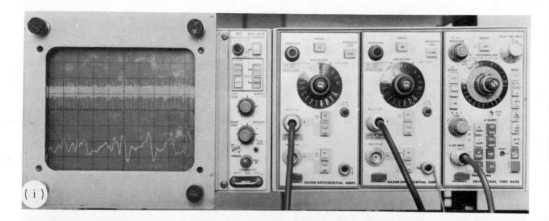

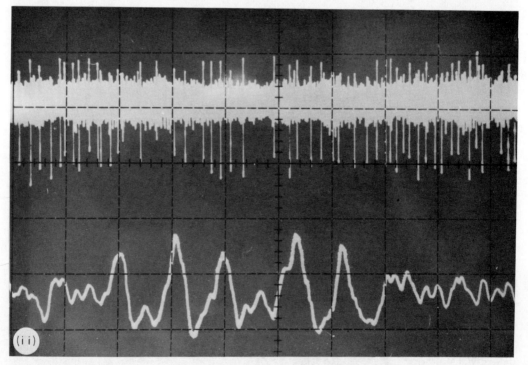

Figure 3.5
The oscilloscope: a basic tool of the electrophysiologist.
(i) Photograph of an oscilloscope front panel. On the screen is displayed the brain electrical activity of a rat with chronically implanted microelectrodes.
(ii) Close-up of the oscilloscope screen. The top trace is extracellularly recorded unit activity (neurone spikes or impulses) and the bottom trace is the gross record of brain electrical activity.

Photographs by courtesy of M. Belloum and D. O'Boyle of the University of Manchester

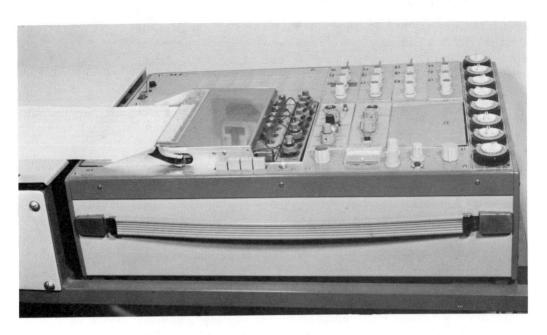

Figure 3.6
Six channel polygraph
for recording the
electroencephalogram
(EEG) and other
physiological variables.

Photograph taken in
the author's laboratory

the oscilloscope supplies a 'time base' by applying a regularly cycling voltage to plates which deflect the electron beam in a horizontal plane, so that it repetitively scans from left to right at a constant speed, instantaneously returning to the left of the screen at the end of each scan. The amplified voltage fluctuations from a signal source, such as the brain, are applied to plates which deflect the beam in the vertical plane, so that vertical excursions of the beam are superimposed on the regular horizontal scans provided by the time base. The complete picture which is traced on the oscilloscope screen (Figure 3.5) is thus a graph of variation in voltage over time. As this trace has only a transient existence on the oscilloscope screen it must be photographed with a special camera if a permanent record is to be obtained.

The oscilloscope has the advantage of a very high frequency response. It can respond to very rapid changes in voltage so that it is particularly suitable for recording fast transient patterns of activity generated by the nervous system. However, the procedure of photographing the tube is inclined to be cumbersome and expensive.

When a record of brain activity lasting longer than about a second is required and when a high frequency response is not so important a pen recorder (also known as an oscillograph; see Figure 3.6) is a cheaper and more convenient instrument to use. In a pen recorder the amplified signal from the scalp is applied to the terminals of a galvanometer which has a pen, usually writing in ink, attached to its coil. The signal applied to the galvanometer thus causes the pen to make excursions either side of its zero. These are permanently recorded on a band of paper which moves at a constant speed beneath the pen. The trace which the pen makes on the paper is once again a graph of fluctuations in voltage over time. Pen recorders often have a whole bank of pens, up to as many as 30, each being activated by the output from its own amplification system. Multi-channelled pen recorders are used to record the EEG from several different scalp locations simultaneously. Some channels may be used for recording other physiological variables such as eye movements, galvanic skin response (changes in the electrical conductance of the palm of the hand), or heart rate. The amplification required to drive a pen galvanometer is so great that two amplifiers are usually used, a preamplifier and a driver amplifier.

Because such high gain amplifiers are used for EEG recording great care has to be taken to avoid contamination of the record by signals generated by sources other than the brain. Spurious signals in the EEG record are referred to as artefacts. One potential source of artefact is from the electrodes which are made of a precious metal, usually silver. To obtain a good electrical contact these are fixed to the scalp over an intervening layer of conductive jelly or cream. Normally the conjunction of the metal and the salt generates a potential, as in a battery, by polarization effects. Such a voltage can swamp any signal generated by the brain. Polarization at the electrodes is counteracted by electrolytically coating the silver electrode with a layer of silver chloride. Movement of an electrode is another event which is liable to generate transient potentials which are picked up by the amplifiers.

Another external source of artefact is the mains electricity supply and other electrical apparatus which produce electromagnetic radiations. The electrode leads from the subject act as aerials which pick up these radiations and because the EEG amplifiers are so sensitive, they may appear on the oscillograph trace and obscure the record of authentic brain activity. This problem is avoided by a combination of amplifier design, good earthing and good electrode contacts.

Bodily organs other than the brain generate potentials which may be picked up by scalp electrodes; the skin, muscles, the eyes, and the heart, for instance. These are eliminated as far as possible by judicious placement of the electrodes, though rarely with 100% success. Experimenters must learn to recognize an artefact by its characteristic waveform and must be constantly vigilant for its presence in their records. Artefactual signals which are either slower or faster than the activity of the brain which interests the experimenter, are filtered out electronically in the amplification system.

Recording of the EEG may take place either between two 'active' electrodes attached to the scalp or between an active electrode on the scalp and an 'indifferent' electrode at a location such as an earlobe. In the former case the EEG is a record of the fluctuating difference in potential between two points, each of which is fluctuating in potential relative to zero. In the latter instance the indifferent electrode is assumed to be at zero (which may be incorrect) so that a record is obtained solely of the fluctuations in potential at the active electrode.

The patterns of activity seen in the EEG, and their interpretation, will be covered in more detail in Chapters 7, 8, 11, and 12. The frequency of the EEG signal, the number of fluctuations or cycles which occur in one second, varies over the range $\frac{1}{2}$-60 cycles (Hz), most of the activity being in the range 1–13 cycles. Discriminating between patterns and deciding what is meaningful in the EEG data, which initially appears as just a series of wavy lines, has presented researchers with some intractable problems. Rhythmic fluctuations in voltage at different central frequencies have been

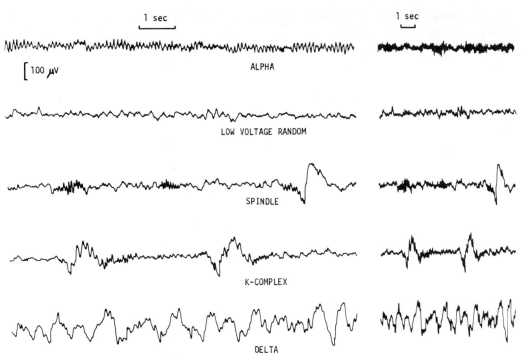

Figure 3.7
EEG records showing the patterns characteristic of different levels of sleeping and waking. On the left a recording speed of 25 mm s^{-1} has been used and on the right a rate of 10 mm s^{-1}, which is widely used in sleep research. At the top is the α-rhythm, which appears during relaxed wakefulness with the eyes closed. Below is the low voltage random activity seen at the onset of sleep. The next two EEG segments show patterns seen in the intermediate stages of sleep, 2 and 3. The first shows sleep spindles, brief waxing and waning bursts of waves in the range 13–15 Hz. The second shows K-complexes, prominent transients occurring spontaneously, or sometimes evoked by external stimuli. The bottom record is of slow, high voltage δ-activity signifying the deepest stage (4) of orthodox sleep (see Chapter 8 for further explanations).

From Snyder, F., and Scott, J. (1972). Reproduced by arrangement with Holt, Rinehart and Winston, New York, from *Handbook of Psychophysiology* by Greenfield/Sternbach 1972, © 1972

associated with different mental states on the sleeping–waking continuum (see Figure 3.7) and characteristic patterns have been associated with pathological states, particularly epilepsy. These patterns are usually recognized by visual inspection of the record which is not a very precise measurement technique.

Analysis of the frequencies present in a segment of EEG record is sometimes done by counting and measuring on the graph, a very tedious procedure. Today, automated frequency analysers or computers are often used.

In recent years there has been a great deal of interest in transient potentials evoked from the brain by briefly presented visual, auditory, or somatosensory stimuli. These potentials cannot easily be seen in the 'raw' EEG record because their amplitude is not greater than that of the background activity, unrelated to the evoking stimulus, which is present. Evoked potentials are extracted from the background 'noise', in which they are 'buried' by an analysis procedure known as averaging which is usually accomplished by a computer. This procedure and the experimental results which have stemmed from its use are outlined in Chapter 11.

Before leaving the EEG, future confusion should be avoided by a discussion of the generation of both the background EEG and evoked potentials in the brain. Not surprisingly it was originally supposed that the scalp EEG represented the massed discharges of many underlying cortical neurones summed together. However, from the start there was an obvious inconsistency between the 1 ms duration of a neural spike discharge and the 100 ms duration of a typical EEG wave. To cut a long story short it has subsequently been shown, with reasonable certainty, that the scalp EEG reflects, not neural action potentials, but synchronous slow fluctuations in membrane potential in the matrix of neurones from which it is derived. This finding does not at first sight look very favourable to the interpretation of scalp recorded brain activity in terms of cerebral information processing. However, there is further evidence, in the case of evoked potentials, that the firing patterns of cortical cells follow the oscillations in membrane potential, so that the notion that evoked potentials reflect cortical information processing retains its viability (see Chapters 11 and 12).

Perhaps a final point that should be made about the scalp EEG is that the fundamental assumption that it is generated in the brain is still not immune from attack. Lippold [1970] has presented evidence that the α-rhythm, a prominent rhythm with a frequency of around 10 Hz, recorded from relaxed subjects, may be generated by tremor of the eyes. He argued that when the eyes are not fixating a visual target a slight tremor occurs in the extraocular muscles which move the eyes. As there is a potential difference between the front and the back of the eye (the corneo–retinal potential) which sets up a potential field the tremor of the eye causes this potential field to oscillate. Lippold argued that this is broadcast along the extraocular muscles to the posterior regions of the scalp where it is picked up as α-rhythm. While this hypothesis is not considered proven [e.g. see Chapman *et al*, 1970] its plausibility does illustrate the difficulty in unambiguously interpreting gross electrical acitivity recorded external to the brain.

Even if we could be certain that all electrical activity recorded from the scalp was activity of cortical neurones, it is still very difficult to gain insights into brain function from the data collected. Use of the EEG to investigate brain function has been compared with using a mine detector to investigate the workings of a computer. As the EEG is the record of a massed response it is impossible to precisely define which aggregates of neurones are contributing to the signal recorded from any one point. It is also extremely difficult to determine whether the EEG signal represents a single pervasive pattern or two or more underlying patterns superimposed on each other.

Intra-cerebral recording

The electrical activity can be recorded from more precisely defined areas of the brain, with reduced attenuation and distortion of the signal by surrounding tissue, by placing electrodes on or in the cortex, or by implanting electrodes in subcortical structures. Clearly such recording requires the use of operative techniques with their attendant problems. Recording electrodes of stainless steel wire, insulated to their tip, are implanted in the brain, using the same procedures as for electrodes to be used for lesioning or stimulating. Indeed, the same electrode may be used, in turn, for all of these functions.

External to the brain, the amplifying and recording equipment used is very similar to that used for scalp EEG recording, except that the amplifier gains do not have to be set so high, as the signals picked up from within the brain are stronger than those picked up from the scalp.

When the recording electrode is implanted in a fibre pathway the potentials recorded represent the massed spike discharge of many axons adjacent to the recording electrode. On the other hand recordings obtained from grey matter where there are cell bodies, such as the cortex or subcortical nuclei, represent the massed effects of both spike discharges and slow graded potentials mixed up together. Filter circuits, which selectively eliminate either slow activity or fast activity, can be used to obtain recordings of either spike activity or graded potentials alone. The recording of the massed discharge pattern in a population of neurones reached by an electrode would seem to give direct access to the operations of the nervous system in processing and evaluating inputs or organizing outputs, depending on location. It can be argued that such gross recording neglects the discharge patterns of individual neurones which could make differing contributions to the over-all pattern. However, it does appear that it is the responses of populations of neurones which are important in coding information in the nervous system, the contribution of individual units being a function of statistical laws [see John, 1972]. It therefore seems likely that the recording of population responses will make a substantial contribution to our understanding of how information is processed in the central nervous system.

Unit recording

Techniques have been developed for recording from individual neurones in the brain, as has already been mentioned (Chapter 2.1). However, the acquisition of reliable recordings takes a great deal more skill and patience than the recording of population responses. The activity of single cells can be recorded from either the outside or the inside of the membrane using very fine microelectrodes. In the former case the tips must be less than $10\,\mu m$ in diameter and in the latter case less than $1\,\mu m$ in diameter. The electrodes are formed from either sharpened wire needles or finely drawn glass pipettes filled with a conducting solution (e.g. a salt solution). Such microelectrodes have a very high electrical resistance which means that a special type of preamplifier (cathode follower) must be used to obtain an artefact free record.

Recording the discharges of a unit extracellularly avoids having to impale the cell. The discharges, which are usually displayed on an oscilloscope (see Figure 3.5), appear as a series of 'spikes' of about 1 ms duration and perhaps $500\,\mu V$ in amplitude. The experimenter knows when his electrode tip is close enough to a particular cell to record its discharges alone by the fact that all the spikes are of the same amplitude. If there are two or more different spike heights then it is an indication that the electrode is recording from more than one cell.

Recording unit discharges intracellularly involves impaling the cell on the microelectrode tip. The membrane seals around the electrode so that it remains polarized. Spikes with an amplitude of about 100 mV are recorded between the intracellular electrode and an indifferent electrode, much greater than from extracellular electrodes. In addition a particular advantage of intracellular recording is that slow graded potentials can be picked up; potentials leading to a spike discharge, potentials with no resulting discharge and negative hyperpolarizing potentials resulting from inhibitory influences. Many of the fundamental discoveries concerning unit neural function, discussed in Chapter 2.1, have been made in intracellular recording experiments.

In classical unit recording experiments such as those on the giant axons of the squid [Hodgkin and Huxley, 1939] it has been possible to visually monitor the insertion of the electrode in the cell. In experiments involving recording from units in the brains of higher vertebrates it is impossible to make a visual selection of the cell to be recorded from. The usual procedure is to gently lower the microelectrode into the area of interest while monitoring any potentials which the electrode might pick up, on an oscilloscope. As the electrode tip approaches a cell its spikes will be recorded with progressively increasing amplitude, guiding the experimenter to an optimum position for recording. If a cell produces a rapid burst of spikes followed by silence it is an indication that the cell has been damaged. The ease with which a cell can be damaged underlines the sensitivity which must be achieved in adjustment of the electrode tip using a special micromanipulator.

A point of criticism about this method of gaining access to units in the brain is that it appears to introduce a bias towards recording from large cells, such as the Betz cells. This implies that the data which is available on unit activity in the brain is derived from an unrepresentative sample of its cells.

Another serious problem in unit recording is that because of the sensitivity required in the placement of the electrode, any slight displacement introduced by movement of the animal's head or brain relative to the electrode may ruin the recording. Even pulsations of the brain caused by the heartbeat can be responsible for such movement. This means that either the head must be held very rigidly in a massive head holder or that the electrode holder and micromanipulator must be cemented to the skull (see Figure 3.3 (i)). Usually in intracellular recording studies and sometimes in macroelectrode studies the experimental animal is anaesthetized. This is necessary if its head is being held rigidly and also has the advantage that it reduces the background 'noise', generated within the brain, from which the relevant signal must be discriminated. The disadvantage of anaesthetizing subjects is that it excludes the recording of brain activity in a conscious freely behaving animal. Also the responsiveness of the neural systems affected are grossly modified by the anaesthetic agent and the neural substrates of perception and consciousness would appear to be inactivated.

Behavioural techniques

So far we have discussed biological techniques for external intervention in the operations of the brain and for monitoring its activities. Research on the biological basis of behaviour, the theme of this book, also requires techniques and a methodology for studying the behavioural correlates of intervention in neural systems. In many studies of neural systems, particularly early ones, the sophistication of the biological techniques has not been matched by rigour in the study of associated behaviour. This occurred because the experimenters were primarily biologists. The increase in communication and co-operation between biological disciplines and psychology in recent years has led to the increasing adoption of rigorous techniques and methods, developed within psychology, in interdisciplinary research.

Typically, in early studies on the effects of lesioning or stimulating the brain casual observations of the animal's behaviour yielded qualitative descriptions of such phenomena as 'sham rage'. Following decortication, an animal seemed to exhibit the expressive signs of rage, but without directing it to an object and without its usual persistence. In some studies such as those of hunger and feeding the phenomena observed have lent themselves naturally to quantification in such terms as amount eaten.

It is proposed to make some brief observations on behavioural methods, with their emphasis on quantification and control, which have been fruitfully used in psychobiological research.

Many experiments in psychobiology involve learning or conditioning. The learning task may be central to an investigation on the biological basis of learning and information storage. Alternatively learning may be a prerequisite for, among other things, studies involving measurements of the strength of drives or assessment of the integrity of perceptual mechanisms.

A classical tool used for the investigation of learning abilities is the maze. The course of learning can be plotted quantitatively in terms of the lengths of time taken to reach the goal box, from the start, on successive trials, the number of errors (entries into blind alleys) made on successive trials and the number of trials required before the maze can be negotiated without error. Mazes were used to investigate the deficits in learning ability which followed ablation of different cortical areas in rats in the famous studies by Lashley [1950].

Another ubiquitous piece of laboratory equipment is the Skinner box in which an animal learns to press a lever in order to obtain a small quantity of food or some other reward (also known as reinforcement). The training procedure is called operant conditioning. Various experimental manipulations can be superimposed on the operant conditioning situation. One of the simplest is to require the animal to depress the lever several times before it receives each reward. When the number of lever presses required to obtain a reward remains constant from one reward to another the procedure is known as a fixed ratio operant conditioning schedule, when the number of lever presses required to obtain a reward varies then it is known as a variable ratio schedule. When an animal is on a 'low reward density' fixed ratio schedule (i.e. when many lever presses are required before each reinforcement is given) it has to work hard for its food so that its willingness to work hard, measured by the rate at which it will press the lever, is a good measure of strength of motivation. An interesting result was obtained when rats with lesions in the ventromedial nucleus of the hypothalamus were required to work for food on a low reward density fixed ratio schedule. Whereas they would gorge themselves into a state of extreme obesity when food was freely available, they would not work as hard as normals when required to lever press for their food. This result indicated that the hyperphagia (excess eating) resulting from the brain lesions could not be interpreted straightforwardly as being due to increased hunger.

Drive strength may be measured in a number of other ways which do not always give correlated results. Straightforward measures include speed of running down a runway to a goal box and strength of pull against a restraining harness, to obtain a reward. Alternatively an aversive drive may be pitted against another biological drive. For instance sex drive is sometimes measured by interposing an electrified grid between a male rat and a receptive female and recording the maximum shock which it will endure to cross the grid.

Aversive stimuli may be used in a learning situation. In passive avoidance learning, an animal (usually a rat) is placed on a small raised dais from which it will usually step down without much delay. When it steps down it receives an electric shock to its paws. The single experience is usually sufficient to teach it to stay put on the dais if placed there again. One trial learning of this type is invaluable in studies of the consolidation of the memory trace (see Chapter 13).

Active avoidance learning is also used. Typically an animal is shocked in the black compartment of a box which has a white compartment at the other end, into which the animal must escape. The animal may merely be required to run from the black to the white compartment or may be required to perform some operant response (such as pressing a lever) to open a communicating gate between the compartments.

Operant conditioning situations may be set up which exploit the discriminative or perceptual powers of the animal used. Having been given its 'basic operant training' the animal may then be required to learn that only levers with a particular sign on (such as a geometrical shape) will deliver a reward or that a reward will only be delivered when a light comes on over the lever. Learnt discriminations may be used when the neural structures mediating perception are being investigated by lesioning and/or stimulation. Discrimination tasks have also been used in experiments on the biochemical basis of memory in which attempts have been made to transfer memories from one animal to another in a brain extract. Training donor animals to approach a food tray only on presentation of a specific stimulus (such as a flashing light or tone), has been used to test whether brain extracts transfer a specific response, when injected in recipient animals, or whether they merely bring about a general improvement in learning ability.

Fuster [1958] has reported a particularly ingenious use of discrimination learning in an investigation of the role of the brainstem reticular formation in the regulation of arousal. Monkeys were trained to respond to briefly illuminated visual stimuli (geometrical shapes) by pushing a hand through a flap below the stimulus to obtain a food reward. Illumination of the stimulus started a timer and raising the flap activated a microswitch which stopped it, thus recording the monkey's reaction time. Decreased reaction time during stimulation of the reticular formation documented its role in mediating arousal. Also, as the monkeys had to discriminate between correct (rewarded) and incorrect (unrewarded) shapes Fuster was also able to use a discrimination error score as an index of arousal.

Reaction time is commonly used as a performance measure in experiments on humans involving the recording of the electrical activity of the brain.

Experimental controls

The quantification of behaviour is a simple aspect of psychobiological research compared with the problem of designing experiments which adequately control for confounding variables likely to vitiate the interpretation of the results. The complex way in which the subsystems of the brain interlock has already been described and the difficulty which this implies in the separation of variables can be appreciated. Some representative examples illustrate some of the problems and their tentative solutions.

Variations in the amplitude of evoked potentials recorded from the brain have been found to be correlated with variations in attention and attributed to brain mechanisms capable of blocking unwanted input. Alternatively it has been argued that the variations in evoked potential amplitude could be attributed to modulation of the amount of light entering the eye by the pupil, in the case of visual evoked potentials, or modulation of the effective intensity of sound at the cochlea by adjustments of the middle ear muscles, in the case of auditory evoked potentials. To control for pupil size one must either use subjects with congenital absence of the iris [Bergamini and Bergamasco, 1967], paralyse the pupillary muscles with atropine or use an artificial iris. To control for the effect of variations in tension of the middle ear muscles on the sound transducing apparatus, the muscles must be either paralysed or severed.

A problem which sometimes occurs in learning experiments using simple animals is to decide whether the behaviour observed is genuine learning, or merely 'sensitization'. For instance flatworms, which convulse when an electric current is passed through their water, can be conditioned to produce the convulsions when a previously neutral light is presented. The possibility that this reflects simply an increased sensitivity of the worm to light can be tested by subjecting a control group of worms to a random sequence of light and shock presentations. So long as this group develops no resonse to the light the sensitization hypothesis can be rejected.

The complexity of the subject of study is by no means the only source of error. Errors may be introduced by subjective biases on the part of the experimenter when scoring an animal's performance in tasks where there is some ambiguity about the nature of the response [e.g. see Rosenthal, 1966]. Such ambiguity exists in scoring blind alley entries in maze learning or approaches to a food tray upon presentation of a flashing light.

Biases in scoring may tend to support a hypothesis in which the experimenter has a vested interest.

The danger of experimenter bias is avoided by using 'blind' testing procedures in which an experimenter does not know which treatment the subject he is testing has received. The allocation of subjects to groups is decoded after completion of the testing. In experiments on humans a 'double blind' testing procedure may be adopted so that the possibility of subject bias as well as experimenter bias is avoided. For instance in studies on the effects of drugs one group of subjects will receive the drug and one group receive an inert substance (called a placebo), neither group knowing which they have received. The drugs are administered by experimenters who do not know whether they are administering the genuine article or the placebo and their effects are assessed by experimenters who do not know which treatment the subjects they are testing have received [see Rosenthal, 1966, pp. 388–400].

The design of experiments with adequate controls is of primary importance in psychobiology as failure to implement proper controls can nullify the interpretation of an experiment no matter how sophisticated the biological techniques which have been used. As an example the reader is referred to the experiment of Hernandez Peon *et al*. [1956] and the subsequent criticisms, discussed in Chapter 11.

Summary

Progress in psychobiology has followed the development of progressively more sophisticated investigative techniques and research methodology. Initially just the gross anatomy of the brain was described. High magnification using microscopes, and later electron microscopes, combined with staining techniques, later permitted description of the microstructure of the nervous system. Brain function was initially investigated by observing deficits in behaviour following lesions made with a scalpel or by suction. The use of stereotaxic machines together with electrical or cryogenic lesioning techniques greatly increased the precision with which lesions could be made. Reversible lesions can be made electrically or chemically. In humans there has been a great deal of study of behavioural changes in individuals who have suffered accidental brain damage.

By chronically implanting electrodes or microcannulae, using a stereotaxic machine, the brain can be electrically or chemically stimulated at different precisely defined locations. The functions of different structures can be inferred from the behaviour elicited. Inferences about brain function have also been attempted from records of its electrical activity in different situations. The gross electrical activity (electroencephalogram or EEG) can be recorded from scalp electrodes without surgical intervention, or from electrodes on or in the brain. Using microelectrodes implanted within the brain the spike discharges of individual neurones at various locations can be recorded.

Investigations in psychobiology cannot be reliably interpreted unless there is a rigorous approach to the behavioural aspects of experiments. Learning situations are used, not only to investigate learning itself, but also to study such topics as motivation and perception. Mazes and operant conditioning apparatus (Skinner boxes), active and passive avoidance learning are commonly used. In all experiments of such a multivariate nature adequate controls are vital and experimental designs must exclude the possibility of experimenter or even subject bias contaminating the results.

PART 3
THE SPRINGS
OF ACTION

Chapter four

Serving internal needs: hunger, thirst, and body temperature

Introduction

At the opening of Chapter 1 life was defined in terms of a dynamic equilibrium state which must be sustained by appropriate transactions with the environment. A living organism must periodically act to correct deficits, or shifts from equilibrium in its internal environment produced by depletion of essential nutrients, fluid, or changes in the external environment. The distinguished American physiologist Cannon [1932] has coined the term 'homeostasis' to refer to the maintenance of equilibrium in the internal environment. Richter [1942-3] has implied that homeostatic needs are the primary determinants of behaviour in man and animals. This chapter is concerned with those aspects of behaviour which are most clearly homeostatic.

A number of classical examples are usually quoted to support the assertion that behaviour can serve an organism's needs with precision. Rats which are 'cafeteria fed' by being allowed unlimited free access to supplies of different foods, regulate their feeding so that over all they take a balanced diet [Richter et al., 1938]. Rats which have had their adrenal glands removed, resulting in a deficit of salt owing to excessive excretion of the substance, prefer a weak salt solution to water. Normal rats do not appear to discriminate between the two solutions [Richter, 1939]. A clinical instance has been described in which a child was allowed to indulge a craving for salt while at home. When admitted to hospital for a minor operation the child suddenly died after a few days. At the post-mortem examination, it transpired that the child had died of a salt deficiency resulting from adrenal malfunction. In hospital the child had not been allowed to compensate for his excessive salt excretion by engaging in 'homeostatic' salt consumption, with tragic results.

Exceptions can be found to the principle that all behaviour is homeostatic. For instance not all humans with the opportunity to eat a balanced diet take that opportunity. Their culture may have such a strong influence on their hierarchy of motives that they will voluntarily suffer denial of their homeostatic needs for ideological or religious reasons. They may even put greater emphasis on purchasing consumer goods irrelevant to their homeostatic needs than on obtaining food. However, homeostasis is a good working principle, as a species whose behaviour did not predominantly serve its homeostatic needs would not survive for long.

Mechanisms mediating hunger and the regulation of food intake

In this context we are interested in the neurobehavioural mechanisms which mediate homeostatic behaviour. Let us consider the regulation of food intake. The following components of a regulatory mechanism, and the relations between them, have been investigated:

1. A feeding centre which:
   a) Monitors the internal environment for deviations from the equilibrium state.
   b) Initiates behaviour directed towards satisfaction of the hunger drive.
   c) Sustains consummatory behaviour once it has commenced.
2. A satiety centre which terminates consummatory behaviour when it receives signals that the creature is replete.

Cannon [e.g. 1934] put forward the influential 'local stimulation' theory of motivation, in which it was supposed that hunger was simply the sensation of contractions of an empty stomach. In turn it was asserted that the eating initiated by this peripherally determined hunger was terminated when the new sensations of a stomach distended with food were experienced. Cannon [1934] maintained that other motive states could be explained in the same way; that thirst was the sensation of a dry mouth and sexual arousal the sensation of genital irritation. The classical experiment of Cannon and Washburn [1912] was quoted to support the local stimulation theory of hunger. The stomach contractions of a hungry human subject were recorded using an inflated intragastric balloon connected to a pneumograph, a device which yields a graphical record of stomach contractions over time. It was found that there was a perfect correlation between contractions of the stomach and the subjective experience of hunger pangs.

Very soon after it was propagated serious flaws were found in the local stimulation theory of drives. Such a crude detector as stomach contractions could not account for specific hungers arising from a creature's need for a number of different nutrients in different proportions. The most conclusive refutation of Cannon's theory is the finding that denervation of the stomach does not abolish hunger [Morgan and Morgan, 1940; Grossman et al., 1947]. This finding suggests that the internal environment is monitored centrally, in the brain, rather than peripherally.

However, this does not mean that the contribution of the local stimulation theorists was worthless because contemporary theories are multi-factorial. They assign a contributory role to sensations from peripheral receptors in the oropharyngeal region (mouth and pharynx) and stomach, particularly in the termination of consummatory behaviour.

Central theories of hunger

To have monitors of the internal environment located in the brain is economical, makes for resilience and in particular is consistent with the functions of the circulatory system. The bloodstream is the body's transport system, distributing all the materials required by an organism's metabolism to the correct locations. Thus the shortage of any nutrient is likely to be quickly reflected in the depletion of that nutrient in the blood. The deficit will soon become apparent in the whole blood system as it is in continuous circulation.

The brain is an organ richly supplied by the bloodstream and is therefore in a position to monitor the qualities of the blood. It is particularly well suited to this function as one of the specialized properties of brain cells is irritability.

Central theories of hunger go back a long way. Magendie [1826] maintained that a brain centre is the source of the sensation of hunger and Bardier [1911] hypothesized that depletion of nutrients in the blood led to excitation of a hunger centre in the brain. At the time of their formulation central theories do not appear to have had much influence. Lately, modified forms of these theories have turned out to be the most fruitful.

Experimental support for a central theory of hunger

Of all the brain structures the diencephalon is particularly well supplied with blood vessels, so that it would appear to be a promising site to search for a 'feeding centre' activated by the qualities of the blood.

As far back as the early years of the nineteenth century there are reports in the clinical literature on man of an association between damage to the hypothalamus (usually tumours) and disturbances of eating; both aphagia—aversion for food—and hyperphagia—excessive eating (Figure 4.1).

Reports of hyperphagia following experimental lesions of the hypothalamus go back to the 1920s. The classic paper is considered to be that of Hetherington and Ransom [1940] who reported that bilateral electrolytic lesions of the ventromedial nucleus of the hypothalamus (VMH) in the rat resulted in hyperphagia leading to obesity. This finding has been confirmed by many other experimenters. Nevertheless, Reynolds [1963] and Dubuc and Reynolds [1973] have argued that the hyperphagia is an artefact of the electrolytic method of lesioning (where a direct current is used resulting in tissue destruction by migration of ions) and does not occur when other lesioning techniques, such as electrocauterization (lesioning with a radio frequency alternating current which generates

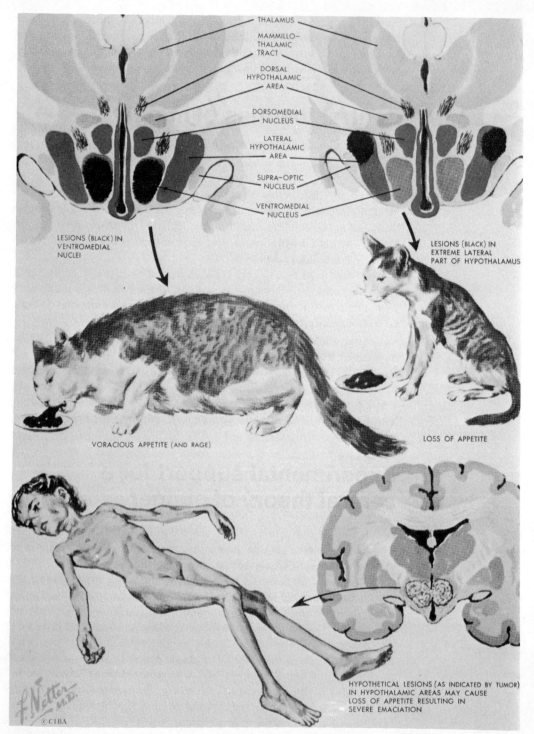

THALAMUS

MAMMILLO-
THALAMIC
TRACT

DORSAL
HYPOTHALAMIC
AREA

DORSOMEDIAL
NUCLEUS

LATERAL
HYPOTHALAMIC
AREA

SUPRA-OPTIC
NUCLEUS

VENTROMEDIAL
NUCLEUS

LESIONS (BLACK) IN
VENTROMEDIAL
NUCLEI

LESIONS (BLACK) IN
EXTREME LATERAL
PART OF HYPOTHALAMUS

VORACIOUS APPETITE (AND RAGE)

LOSS OF APPETITE

HYPOTHETICAL LESIONS (AS INDICATED BY TUMOR)
IN HYPOTHALAMIC AREAS MAY CAUSE
LOSS OF APPETITE RESULTING IN
SEVERE EMACIATION

Figure 4.1
Hypothalamic areas associated with the control of food intake; lesions which result
in hyperphagia and aphagia respectively.

From *The CIBA Collection of Medical Illustrations,* Vol. 1. Reproduced by courtesy
of CIBA-GEIGY Ltd., Basle. All rights reserved.

heat), are used. However, Hoebel [1965] has confirmed that hyperphagia occurs even when the VMH is lesioned by electrocauterization.

Brobeck *et al.* [1943] confirmed that the obesity following lesion of the VMH was due to accelerated fat synthesis resulting from overeating and not to disturbances of the animal's metabolism caused directly by lesioning the VMH.*

The fact that hyperphagia follows lesioning of the VMH suggests that a satiety centre responsible for terminating consummatory behaviour has been destroyed. Its discovery was the inspiration for a great deal of research interest in the hypothalamic systems underlying motivation.

The lateral hypothalamic feeding centre

Although historically the feeding centre was found after the satiety centre, it is more logical to discuss the feeding centre in detail first. Brugger [1943] discovered that electrical stimulation of the prefornical region of the hypothalamus, lateral to the VMH, elicited voracious eating, and sometimes drinking, in rats. This finding remained obscure until the publication of the classical finding of Anand and Brobeck [1951a, b] that bilateral lesions of the lateral hypothalamus (LH) in rats resulted in complete and permanent aphagia (failure to eat) and adipsia (failure to drink). Their experimental animals refused food freely available, ejected food placed in their mouths, removed food clinging to their face and paws and generally behaved as if food was an aversive stimulus. Such animals would starve themselves to death unless force fed. This finding of Anand and Borbeck suggested that the LH may be the feeding centre monitoring the internal environment, initiating drive behaviour and sustaining feeding. A number of other findings support this hypothesis. Epstein [1960] injected hypertonic saline, which is neuroexcitatory, into the lateral hypothalamus of rats, and by so doing induced previously satiated rats to start feeding again. Conversely he found that the injection of the neuroinhibitory drug procaine into the same region depressed feeding in hungry rats. The reverse findings were made when these two drugs were injected separately into the VMH; hypertonic saline suppressed and procaine induced feeding. This further supported the notion that the VMH was a satiety centre.

We might ask whether stimulation of the hypothalamus produces a drive state identical to hunger, or just the motor components of eating. Valenstein *et al.* [1968] found that electrical stimulation of the LH in sated animals produced not only eating when food was available, but searching behaviour when it was not. Such LH stimulation also produces hoarding behaviour similar to that seen in food deprived rats [Blundell and Herberg, 1973]. Furthermore rats motivated by electrically induced hunger will learn to press a bar for a food reward. All of these findings cumulatively strengthen the claim that 'electrically induced' hunger is equivalent to normal hunger.

Some other research reports suggest that we must pause before attributing one simple function to the lateral hypothalamus. Wayner and Carey

*This assertion has recently been challenged by Friedman and Stricker [1976] who present evidence that overeating in VMH lesioned animals is the result of increased fat synthesis rather than the cause of it.

[1973] and Valenstein *et al.* [1970] maintain that a wide range of activities can be evoked by stimulation of the lateral hypothalamus, depending on the environmental stimuli present. Wayner and Carey [1973] suggest that LH stimulation does not directly elicit the observed behaviour but increases the probability that certain behaviours will occur in the presence of appropriate stimuli (e.g. food). In addition to the findings that LH lesions lead to profound aphagia and adipsia Wayner and Carey [1973] have observed that there are a number of other consequences of this destruction, including impaired ability to avoid painful stimuli, impaired behavioural thermoregulation and a change in temperament towards apathy, indifference, and unsociability. These findings suggest that a number of motivational systems may overlap in the hypothalamus.

Grossman [1967, p. 363] has delivered minute quantities of neurochemicals to the lateral hypothalamus and other hypothalamic and extrahypothalamic locations through chronically implanted microcannulae. He found that different chemicals would elicit different drives from the same location. Whereas adrenalin would elicit the hunger drive, acetylcholine (or its synthetic analogue, carbachol) would elicit thirst. This finding led Grossman to assert that drive systems were composed of widely diffused parallel 'circuits' rather than discretely localized neural centres.

Another series of findings pose more serious interpretive problems for the lateral hypothalamic syndrome. Teitelbaum and Stellar [1954] and Teitelbaum and Epstein [1962] have demonstrated that rats with lateral hypothalamic lesions will recover from their aphagia. This occurs if they are force fed in the immediate postoperative period, and then literally weaned back on to their normal laboratory diet via wet palatable foods and then dry foods served with water. These rats recover their ability to match their food intake to their nutritional requirements, even when the food is diluted with a non-nutritional substance [usually cellulose; e.g. see Epstein, 1971]. However, in recovered LH lesioned rats water is only ever drunk with meals (called prandial drinking) to aid ingestion. Thus there is inadequate regulation of the animal's water balance.

Regulation of food intake is not normal under all circumstances in recovered LH lesioned rats. Hypersensitivity to bitter taste prevents the normal process of adjustment which leads to the maintenance of caloric intake when normal rats are fed a diet adulterated to have a bitter taste [Teitelbaum and Epstein, 1962]. Also there is a loss of 'glucoprivic' control, the ability to correct insulin induced low blood sugar (hypoglycemia) by compensatory eating, even when convulsions are imminent [Epstein and Teitelbaum, 1967; Epstein, 1971]. Thus the lateral hypothalamus does not lose all claim to be the feeding centre.

Extending the lesions in recovered lateral hypothalamic rats reinstates the aphagia [Teitelbaum and Epstein, 1962] suggesting that the areas round the lesion may have taken over the function of the destroyed area during recovery from aphagia. Another curious finding is that cortical spreading depression, induced by placing potassium chloride (KCl) on the cortex, will restore aphagia so effectively in a recovered LH lesioned rat that the recovery cycle has to be repeated over the same time scale [Teitelbaum and Cytawa, 1965]. Spreading depression involves a disruption of cortical function whose effects include abolition of recent memory (see Chapter 13). Teitelbaum [1971] has interpreted this and other findings to mean that normal cortical function is important for the recovery of sub-cortical function. He hypothesizes that in higher animals hunger is 'encephalized'. That is to say that patterns of learning mediated by cortical structures transform 'simple reflex oral ingestion patterns into motivated regulatory behaviour'. The recovery of feeding in LH lesioned rats precisely reiterates the pattern of development of feeding behaviour in infancy [evidence reviewed in Teitelbaum, 1971] which appears to reflect the fact that after LH destruction the 'encephalization' of the hunger drive achieved during development has to begin anew. Functional connections must be re-established between cortical structures concerned with the patterning of motivated behaviour, and the areas bounding the lesioned LH which take over its functions of monitoring the internal environment and mediating the aspects of consummatory behaviour which have a reflex nature.

Teitelbaum's [1971] theory of hunger bears a striking resemblance to Hebb's [1949] theory of drives in which it was supposed that specific drives, such as hunger, were not innate, in higher animals, but had to be differentiated by a process of learning.

The ventromedial hypothalamic satiety centre

We have already noted Hetherington and Ransom's [1940] classic finding that lesions of the ventromedial nucleus of the hypothalamus produces animals which are hyperphagic and become obese, suggesting that the structure would normally mediate termination of eating in sated animals.

Lesions of the VMH also produce heightened emotional reactivity, reflected in more 'fearful' behaviour and faster electric shock avoidance learning [Nisbett, 1972].

The hyperphagia observed in VMH lesioned rats has two phases [see, for example, Teitelbaum, 1955], an initial dynamic phase in which eating is voracious and weight gain rapid, and a subsequent static phase in which food intake decreases and weight is stabilized at a new high level. If an animal in the static phase is starved so that it loses weight the dynamic phase of hyperphagia is reinstated. These findings suggest that weight is regulated about a new 'set point' in VMH lesioned rats.

There is evidence for a reciprocal relationship between the VMH and LH through which the regulation of food intake is mediated. We have already seen that an excitatory substance (hypertonic saline) injected in the LH initiates feeding but in the VMH stops it. The reverse is observed with the anaesthetic procaine [Epstein, 1960]. Oomura and co-workers [1967] recorded the activity of single neurones in the VMH and LH and found that as discharge rates in the VMH increased those in the LH decreased (with a 3 s lag), and vice versa. Electrical stimulation of either the VMH or LH resulted in depression of the firing rates recorded from the opponent nucleus. The model suggested by these findings is outlined in Stellar's multifactor central neural theory of motivation [1954, 1959; see

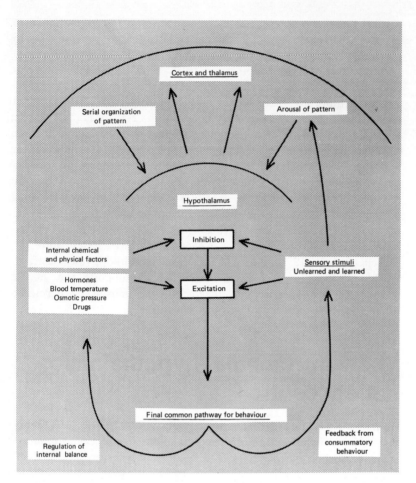

Figure 4.2
Schematic illustration
of Stellar's multifactor
centralneural theory of
motivation.

From Dethier, V. G.,
and Stellar, E. (1970),
Animal behaviour p.
104. Copyright © 1970
by Prentice-Hall, Inc.,
Englewood Cliffs.
Reproduced by
permission of the
publishers

Figure 4.2]. The LH is activated by nutrient depletion, inhibits VMH activity and promotes food seeking and subsequently feeding behaviour. In turn the VMH is activated by signals that repletion has been achieved, inhibits the LH and terminates feeding. The precise nature of the signals for depletion and repletion will be examined later.

There is another set of findings consistent with this model derived from experiments on intracranial self-stimulation. Olds and Milner [1954] accidentally found that rats would rapidly learn to deliver an electrical stimulus to their own brain via an implanted microelectrode by pressing a lever. Once the response had been learnt the rats would press the lever very vigorously, and among the brain areas from which the response could be elicited was included the lateral hypothalamus [Margules and Olds, 1962]. The phenomenon has been called intracranial self-stimulation.

The fact that rats and other animals gain some kind of satisfaction from self-stimulation of the LH appears at first sight to be paradoxical. Experimenter stimulation of this area elicits behavioural signs of hunger and we might think that hunger is dissatisfying. The paradox may be resolved if we suppose that self-stimulation simulates consummatory behaviour in which the activating effect of the olfactory and gustatory feedback on a feeding area generates the next feeding response (see below). The effects of self-stimulation must be equivalent to those of the sensory feedback. Hoebel and Teitelbaum [1962] have shown that while rats will self-stimulate faster in the LH when they are hungry, either satiety or concurrent stimulation of the VMH suppresses LH self-stimulation. If LH self-stimulation is taken to be a simulation of consummatory behaviour whose vigour is potentiated by higher drive states, then it appears that stimulation of the VMH produces the neural correlate of satiety and stops consummatory behaviour. Hoebel and Teitelbaum [1962] found that removal of the inhibitory influence of the VMH by either anaesthetization or ablation, when self-stimulation had been suppressed by feeding, allowed self-stimulation to recommence.

Paradoxes in VMH lesioned animals

Immediately following the discovery of the phenomenon it was assumed that animals with VMH lesions were hyperphagic because their hunger drive was greater and more persistent following the elimination of the inhibitory effects of the VMH. Paradoxically it has been found that on a number of behavioural measures of drive strength their hunger drive appears to be lower than that of normal animals deprived of food. The speed of traversing a runway to a food reward was slower and the strength of pull on a restraining harness to gain food was lower among VMH lesioned animals [Miller et al., 1950]. In addition rates of lever pressing for food on low reward density, fixed ratio, operant conditioning schedules (with delivery of reward only after several lever presses) were lower among VMH lesioned animals than normals [Miller et al., 1950]. Panksepp [1971a, b] found that, whereas normal rats allowed to feed for only one hour out of every 24 would speed up their feeding to achieve a normal caloric intake, VMH lesioned animals, similarly restricted, continued to eat at their normal speed, thus failing to compensate.

Nisbett [1972] has suggested that the failure of VMH lesioned rats to exhibit behavioural evidence of high drive levels is due to frustration potentiated by heightened emotional reactivity, which diminishes response vigour. Jaffe [1973] found that VMH lesioned rats were more sensitive than normals to changes in reinforcement contingencies (e.g. number of lever presses required for each reinforcement), their response rates going up more if reward density was increased, down further if reward density was reduced. This is consistent with heightened emotional reactivity. Peters et al. [1973] and Wampler [1973] found that rats trained to press levers for food on low reward density fixed ratio reinforcement schedules prior to VMH ablation did press the lever faster than normal animals postoperatively. This finding suggests that when the required operant behaviour is consistent with the animals' prior expectations frustration is not confounded with the hunger drive, whose true strength is revealed. Nisbett [1972] even quotes experiments comparing the performance of normal and obese humans at unwrapping awkwardly wrapped sweets. He claimed that obese humans, rather speculatively assumed to be the functional equivalent of VMH lesioned rats, would not work as hard as 'thin' people to obtain the sweets, unless 'prior training' had been given on unwrapping the sweets to enable them to bring their frustration under control.

If the 'frustration' hypothesis is incorrect and VMH lesioned rats really are not hungry, then we might ask what else might cause them to be hyperphagic.

Palatability and hyperphagia

Closer examination of the behaviour of VMH lesioned hyperphagic rats reveals that they are only hyperphagic when they are offered food which they like, that they will not eat food which they do not like, even if it is nutritious, and that they generally have an exaggerated sensitivity to taste.

Normal rats show a remarkable ability to maintain their caloric intake of food, following a short period of adjustment, when faced with positive or negative changes in the palatability of their diet by dilution, or adultera-tion of the taste [Teitelbaum, 1955]. Teitelbaum [1955] and Corbit and Stellar [1964] found that static hyperphagic rats reduced their caloric intake if presented with food diluted with non-nutritive cellulose, and refused to eat when presented with food adulterated with bitter quinine. Conversely static hyperphagics increased their caloric intake of food when it was sweetened with dextrose or non-nutritive saccharin. Furthermore, Epstein [1967a, b] found that normal rats would learn to feed themselves without tasting their food, by pressing a lever to deliver food directly to their stomachs, via an intragastric tube. Hyperphagic rats could not learn to do this unless saccharin was placed on their tongue simultaneously, as an incentive.

The interpretation of the findings above seems to be that the eating behaviour of the hyperphagic rat is regulated solely by the sensory qualities of the food without any reference to its nutritional requirements.

Corbit and Stellar [1964] claimed that taste sensitivity was maximal during the dynamic rather than the static phase of hyperphagia as asserted by Teitelbaum [1955]. This heightened taste sensitivity is not necessarily inconsistent with the presence of a strong hunger drive in hyperphagic rats as Valenstein [1967] and Gross [1968] have shown that food deprived animals have a stronger preference for sweet substances and a stronger aversion to taste degraded foods than non-deprived controls.

Role of the chemical senses in consummatory behaviour

Consummatory behaviour in hyperphagic animals appears to be primarily governed by taste,* a finding which underlines the importance of the chemical senses, olfaction (smell) and gustation (taste), in the adaptive functions of identifying food and sustaining consummatory behaviour (eating) until satiety intervenes. Whereas the hunger drive appears to be activated by depletion of nutrients in the bloodstream, the actual act of eating appears to be provoked and maintained by smell and taste. As

*Schachter [1971] has argued that overeating, obese humans resemble hyperphagic VMH lesioned rats in their tendency to let taste alone govern their eat-ing behaviour, without reference to actual nutrient need. For instance, in a study of hospitalized obese patients limited to a nutritionally adequate but totally bland diet of metracal, caloric in-put sunk to way below caloric output. Because of the consequent mobilization of fat stores to sustain energy metabolism they lost a lot of weight. In con-trast, a non-obese control group on the same metracal diet maintained a caloric input which matched their energy output.

Le Magnen [1971] says 'the pleasure of sensation reinforces the repetition of the consummatory response which provoked the pleasure', a statement defining the 'positive feedback' loop which sustains feeding until negative feedback intervenes in the form of satiety signals, and stops it. It almost appears as if taste generates a separate motivational state for the consummatory act. Morgane [1961a, b] has even claimed that hunger and feeding are mediated by different neural systems, the medial forebrain bundle and the lateral hypothalamus respectively. Whereas stimulation of the LH in normal animals produced both crossing of an electrified grid, taken as evidence of the hunger drive, and eating, stimulation of the LH, when the medial forebrain bundle was lesioned, failed to produce crossing of the electrified grid and only evoked eating if food was immediately available.

In VMH lesioned animals the positive feedback loop based on taste, which sustains eating, appears to be intact, but the complementary negative feedback appears to be missing. Thus so long as the food tastes good there is no mechanism to stop eating. It would appear that the VMH normally collects sensory signals registering satiety and exercises an inhibitory influence on the LH system mediating feeding behaviour sustained by taste.

There is experimental evidence that the chemical senses activate the feeding centre. Oomura *et al.* [1967] have shown that single cells in the LH discharge more rapidly when an animal is presented with an olfactory stimulus. Also exposure to food odours and the act of eating itself results in activation of the EEG recorded from the lateral hypothalamus [Sharma, 1967].

Intracranial self-stimulation in the lateral hypothalamus appears to have the same characteristics as consummatory behaviour. The latter is apparently sustained by the excitatory effect of taste on an LH system generating each consummatory response. In the absence of the VMH both taste maintained eating and self-stimulation continue *ad infinitum*. When the VMH is intact both behaviours can be attenuated when its inhibitory influence is activated by sensory feedback or electrical stimulation [Hoebel and Teitelbaum, 1962]. Phillips and Mogenson [1968] implanted electrodes in an area of the LH where stimulation would elicit drinking and where the animal (rat) would also learn to self-stimulate if given the opportunity. It was found that when the taste of water was improved by adding saccharin both the speed of drinking and the rate of concurrent self-stimulation increased. This appears to be clear evidence that both taste and self-stimulation have excitatory effects which summate in a common mechanism regulating the vigour of consummatory behaviour.

The evidence presented in this and preceding sections suggests that the LH feeding centre may have the primary function of regulating food consumption on the basis of its sensory qualities, while the monitoring of the internal environment occurs elsewhere.

Shifts in palatability accompanying satiety

Having tentatively established that consummatory behaviour is sustained

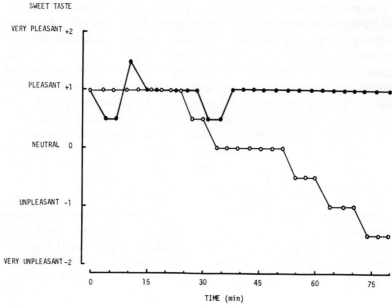

Figure 4.3
Graphical representation of Cabanac's results in his experiment on changes in the palatability of a constant taste (sucrose) with and without satiation. The closed circles represent the affective response of a fasting subject who repeatedly sampled sucrose (a sweet gustative stimulus), but expectorated after tasting. The open circles represent the responses of a subject who swallowed the test samples of sucrose.

From Cabanac, M. (1971) The physiological role of pleasure. *Science*, **173**, 1103–1107. © 1971 American Association for the Advancement of Science reproduced by permission of the author and the publisher

by an LH based system driven by taste, we might ask how the inhibitory effects of the VMH satiety centre affect this system. Le Magnen [1971] defines the palatability of food as the 'feeding response driven by the sensory stimulating effect (smell and taste)'. The palatability of a constant sensory stimulus may shift and in this fact we have a clue to how the satiety mechanism operates.

Cabanac [1971] has reported an experiment in which fasted human subjects had to make 'affective judgements' (a judgement on the pleasant–unpleasant continuum, using a five-point rating scale) of taste as they ingested successive samples of a sucrose solution. It was found that if subjects expectorated their sucrose after each tasting their judgements remained at the 'pleasant' end of the spectrum, across the series. However, if the subjects swallowed each sample of sucrose, their judgements shifted from 'pleasant' to 'unpleasant', showing that a constant taste lost its attractiveness as satiety approached (see Figure 4.3). Cabanac called the shift in affective judgement of a constant sensory stimulus 'alliesthesia' and suggested that it was the basis for establishing a 'set point' for body weight. As a corollary to this last point Cabanac suggested that overeating in obese persons occurs because alliesthesia intervenes too late to maintain an optimum body weight 'set point'. The taste of food remains attractive when dietary needs have been met.

Young [1940] and Le Magnen [1956] have shown that the decline in palatability, which is the evidence of satiety, is specific to the taste experienced, and that a new taste will still evoke a maximum palatability response. Le Magnen [1971] observes that the basis of human overeating, especially in France, may be the fact that traditional meals consists of a series of dishes of increasing palatability, which counteract the effects of satiation.

Le Magnen [1971] maintains that hunger potentiates palatability, citing as evidence the fact that animals deprived of specific foods, such as sucrose, increase the short term intake of these substances in solution. Alternatively foods adulterated with unpalatable substances, such as bitter quinine, become more acceptable to food deprived animals [Miller, 1955; Williams and Campbell, 1961]. Most people would agree that hunger sharpens the sense of taste and there are many stories of starving humans eating substances which were formerly unacceptable.

Stellar [1954], in his central neural multifactor theory of motivation, supposes that the intensity of a drive, such as hunger, is a function of the additive effect of internal environment factors and sensory factors, where it is implied that the sensory factors have a constant excitatory effect. Le Magnen's [1971] theory that hunger modulates the palatability of a given taste so that a constant sensory factor has a variable excitatory effect fits more closely to the data demonstrating shifts in palatability.

Giachetti et al. [1970] appear to have found the electrophysiological correlates of shifts in olfactory palatability. When deprived of food, the total discharges from the olfactory bulbs of rats were increased by presentation of the odour of the maintenance diet. When the rats were sated the discharges decreased. The current drive state had no effect on the olfactory bulb discharges evoked by odours not related to feeding.

Larue and Le Magnen [1972] found that removal of the olfactory bulb in rats resulted in a large increase in meal size, which may have been due to a failure to experience a shift in olfactory palatability when satiety was achieved. We can only suppose that the prolonged eating was sustained by high gustatory palatability, which did not shift, or other oropharyngeal sensations.

Food conditioning

Le Magnen [1971] has observed that although the palatability of certain flavours (e.g. sweet taste) are usually genetically determined there is considerable scope for learning which he has called 'food conditioning'. A classic refutation of the argument that all behaviour is homeostatic is the fact that saccharin, a taste analogue of sugar, is found to be rewarding and apparently highly palatable, although non-nutritive [Sheffield and Roby, 1950]. Le Magnen [1953] has even shown that short term intake of saccharin is increased in hypoglaecemic (low blood sugar) rats. However, Le Magnen [1954] also found that over five days hypoglaecemic rats learned that saccharin was non-repletive and consequently lowered their intake almost to zero. Otherwise similarly treated rats, given nutritious sucrose solution with the same 'taste value' as saccharin, progressively increased their intake over five days. This finding indicates that the palatability of a taste is modulated by the primary reinforcing effect of the nutritive value of the tasted substance. Taste itself would appear to be analogous to secondary reinforcement.

Roth *et al.* [1969, unpublished findings cited in Teitelbaum, 1971] have demonstrated that normal rats will learn to avoid a normally preferred-taste diet if it is repeatedly adulterated with a poison, a phenomenon known as 'bait shyness' because it tends to vitiate attempts to poison wild rats with adulterated food. It is another example of the modulating effect of 'food value' on palatability. These experimenters also found that recovered LH lesioned rats were unable to learn to avoid a taste associated with poison. Teitelbaum [1971] cites this and similar findings as further evidence for the 'encephalization' of hunger (see above) whereby the integrated patterns of behaviour associated with the regulation of food intake, are based on cortically mediated learning.*

Glucostatic monitoring of depletion – repletion

So far in this chapter we have tentatively established the existence of systems in the hypothalamus which mediate hunger, eating, and satiety. We have assumed that they operate by monitoring the level of nutrients in the blood, as it courses through the hypothalamus, and other relevant sensory signals. However, we have not established which specific nutrients have their level monitored and how an animal precisely regulates its food intake to meet its needs.

As hunger and eating behaviour occur relatively frequently the monitoring device must respond to a factor in the blood whose fluctuations are a large and immediate response to the organism's output and intake of energy. Carbohydrates, proteins, and fats are the three basic nutrients, and among these only carbohydrates seem to meet these criteria as the metabolisms of proteins and fats appear to be too slow. The carbohydrate metabolism is rapid and operates with minimal reserves stored in the blood. Carbohydrate circulates in the blood as glucose, alternatively known as blood sugar. These considerations have given rise to a glucostate theory to account for the monitoring of depletion–repletion, first put forward by Mayer [1953].

If the notion of a glucostat is taken to mean a mechanism which monitors the level of glucose in the blood and operates to maintain a certain level, then the glucostat theory runs into immediate difficulties. In both the pathological condition diabetes mellitus and in hunger diabetes, following fasting, there is ravenous eating despite abnormally high blood glucose levels, which should activate the 'stop' mechanism in a glucostat. Furthermore it has been found that neither intravenous nor intrahypothalamic injections of glucose depress feeding [Epstein, 1960].

Mayer [1953] overcame these objections by suggesting that the monitoring device responded to the rate of utilization of glucose, reflected in the

*Garcia *et al.* [1974] have argued that food conditioning is based on the concurrence of taste signals and gastric signals (e.g. in sickness) in a specialized brain-stem mechanism. Taste conditioning does not follow the normal laws of conditioning. It can occur when there is a long delay between the taste and the post-absorptive positive or negative reinforcing effects (e.g. sickness) of the substance tasted. Also taste aversion can only be conditioned by internal negative reinforcement. It cannot be induced by external punishment (e.g. electric shock).

rate at which glucose crossed cell membranes. As the rate of utilization of glucose is determined by the level of insulin in the bloodstream, it is not always correlated with the absolute concentration of glucose in the blood. In diabetes mellitus no insulin is secreted so that a low rate of utilization of glucose coexists with an abnormally high concentration of glucose in the blood.

Normally the depletion of glucose in the blood results in a diminishing rate of utilization, which Mayer asserts is the trigger for hunger. When the rate of utilization of glucose is high, large amounts of glucose are being taken from the blood as it circulates so that there tends to be a much higher concentration of glucose in arterial blood than venous blood. When this utilization rate is low, arterio-venous differences are small. Thus measurement of arterio-venous differences in glucose concentration is an indirect measure of the rate of utilization of glucose. Using this measure Mayer [1953] found that humans with low rates of utilization of glucose reported feeling hungry and increased their intake of food, while those with high rates of utilization did neither.

Grossman et al. [1947] used insulin injections to promote a transient ultrahigh rate of utilization of glucose, which lowered its level in the blood, and found that it increased hunger in humans. Insulin is sometimes administered to patients to improve their appetite when they are losing weight due to undereating. These findings show that low rates of utilization or low concentrations of glucose in the blood may trigger the hunger drive.

Stunkard et al. [1955] have elevated the blood glucose level in man by injecting the hormone glucagon which releases glucose from its storage depot in the liver (where it is stored in its inert form glycogen). This results in the reduction of hunger and of the gastric contractions associated with it. This supports the idea that there is a satiety mechanism which is activated by a set upper level of blood glucose utilization.

More specific evidence concerning the location of the glucostat comes from the work of Sandrew and Mayer [1973], and others previously [e.g. Marshall et al., 1955] who gave rats intravenous injections of poisonous compounds of glucose with either gold (gold thioglucose) or mercury (mercury thioglucose). It was found that these substances selectively damaged cells in the VMH, previously identified as a satiety centre, with the result that the experimental animals became hyperphagic. Further to this Anand and co-workers [1961, 1962] found that the discharge rates of single neurones in the VMH rose, as rates of glucose utilization rose, and vice versa. Oomura et al. [1969] complemented this evidence with the finding that 50% of single neurones monitored in the VMH increased their discharge rates when glucose was introduced into that location. Conversely decreased discharge rates were recorded from 25% of LH neurones monitored, following infusion of glucose into the VMH, giving some support to the theory that during satiety it is subject to a VMH inhibitory influence.

Sharma et al. [1961] found that when they elevated blood glucose utilization rates by glucagon injection in rats the electrical activity in the VMH satiety centre assumed an activation pattern and that gastric contractions, originally thought by Cannon to be the source of hunger, were inhibited. Lesion of the VMH under conditions of elevated blood sugar abolished the inhibitory effect of this condition on gastric contractions. Oomura *et al.* [1967] found that discharge rates of single neurones in the LH were depressed during hyperglaecemia (abnormally high blood sugar). When blood glucose was depleted such unit activity increased slightly in the LH feeding centre and decreased in the VMH satiety centre. Pfaff [1969] has shown that there is shrinkage of the nucleoli of VMH neurones in animals held to a low food intake, an indication of low cellular activity levels possibly due to a failure to attain satiety.*

Wayner and Cary [1973] have injected 2-deoxy-D-glucose (2DG), which antagonizes glucose utilization, either intravenously or directly into the LH via chronically implanted microcannulae, with the result that there was a prompt and sustained secretion of acid in the stomach and a small increase in eating. This finding, together with that of Wayner *et al.* [1971] that intravenous injection of 2DG in recovered LH lesioned rats failed to promote eating, supports the assertion that the LH is a feeding centre triggered by depletion of glucose. If they are confirmed these findings contradict the assertion by Panksepp [1971b, discussed later] that the LH is influenced only by the sensory qualities of food and not by the internal environment. However, they are not strong findings and the spread of effect of any chemical introduced intracranially by microinjection is difficult to assess.

Anand *et al.* [1961] have found that intravenous injections of blood proteins and blood lipids (fats) do not affect the activity of the hypothalamus, seemingly confirming the suspicion that these factors do not supply the signals which start and stop the feeding system. However, Panksepp and Booth [1971] have found that microinjections of amino acid solutions (amino acids are the constituents of proteins) into the LH of rats inhibits feeding behaviour suggesting that this factor may be monitored and furthermore that it registers satiety in the LH rather than the VMH.

Depletion – repletion and blood temperature

Brobeck [1947–8, 1960] has proposed a less obvious factor regulating food intake, the heat product of metabolism or 'specific dynamic action' as it is called. He maintained that the specific dynamic action resulted in a slight rise in the temperature of the blood which triggered the hypothalamic satiety centre. Stemming from this he suggested that the reason why high protein diets were less likely to cause obesity than high carbohydrate diets was because the heat product of protein metabolism was greater, so that satiety occurred earlier. Temperature may have some influence on eating as Andersson and Larsson [1961] have elicited eating by cooling the hypothalamus. However, Rampone and Shirasu [1964] found that hypothalamic temperature rose very soon after the commencement of eating and long before it ceased, so that it did not appear to be a factor in satiety. Grossman and Rechtschaffen [1967] showed that animals satiated as readily on cold food as hot despite a slight fall in hypothalamic temperature in the former instance. It appears to be rather unlikely that temperature

*Friedman and Stricker [1976] argue, in contradiction to the views advanced in this chapter, that the over-all level of oxidative metabolism (irrespective of which metabolic fuel is being used) is monitored in the liver, rather than the level of glucose utilization being monitored in the brain. However, this is as yet a tentative hypothesis which has only circumstantial evidence to support it.

has anything other than a minor influence on the regulation of food intake.

Three control systems for the regulation of food intake

It is intrinsically reasonable to suppose that hunger is initially generated by depleted nutrient levels in the blood, monitored by the hypothalamus. However, satiety cannot readily be accounted for in these terms. The relatively long process of digestion implies that the time lag between ingestion of food and consequent rise in blood sugar will considerably exceed the normal duration of a meal. This means that satiety and meal size must be mediated by a separate control system to that mediating hunger.

Le Magnen [1971] has elegantly demonstrated that there are, in all probability, three control systems regulating food intake. His basic studies involved merely the careful recording of meal sizes and intermeal intervals, over long periods, in free feeding rats. Firstly he found that the larger the meal the longer the interval before the commencement of the next meal. As the consumption of a larger meal implies that more time will elapse before nutrient depletion occurs again, this finding is consistent with the kind of hypothalamic blood sugar monitoring device which we have already discussed. This is Le Magnen's first control system.

The next finding was that meals were not necessarily larger, the longer the time elapsed since the last meal. The extent of a creature's nutrient deficit was not a precise determinant of meal size. An experiment by Davis *et al.* [1969] indicates that there is no mechanism for immediate metering of the nutritive value of food as it is ingested. If blood is taken from a donor rat immediately after a meal and transfused into a fasted animal, it does not suppress the food intake of the receiver. Transfused blood only suppresses food intake if it is taken between 45 min and 2 h after the donor has taken a meal. In other words the postabsorptive effect (i.e. elevation of blood nutrient levels) of ingested food does not become evident until some time after the end of the meal. Le Magnen concluded from these findings that there was a second control system based on oropharyngeal and gastric sensory feedback. It operates via the VMH to mediate satiety and regulate meal size.

The sensory feedback from the oropharyngeal system comprises olfactory and gustatory chemosensory feedback and tactile and proprioceptive mechanosensory feedback. The role of smell and taste in the maintenance of consummatory behaviour has already been discussed (see above). The relationship between the depletion monitoring system and the chemosensory feedback system is nicely illustrated in observations related by Le Magnen [1971], that the first control system makes a compensatory reduction in meal frequency when the second system is induced to increase meal size by the enhancement of the palatability of a diet.

The third control system integrates information from the other two systems to effect learned adjustments in intake over time. Le Magnen [1971] has called this 'food conditioning'. The experiments illustrating this phenomenon were related earlier in the chapter. It has been shown that rats and other animals will learn to regulate their caloric intake to meet their nutritional requirements in the face of change up or down in the palatability of their diet or restriction of their feeding schedules.

Sensory factors in satiety

We must now focus on the signals which cause Le Magnen's second control system to terminate food intake. We have already seen how immediate intake may be increased by palatability and how palatability shows a negative shift as a meal proceeds (see above). The chemical properties of food which determine taste remain constant and, as Cabanac [1971] has shown, the palatability of successive samples of food tasted but not ingested (it was expectorated) remains constant. The palatability of a taste merely reflects an organism's state of repletion–depletion. There must be sensory factors, other than taste, which 'meter' food intake and supply satiety signals.

The most immediate sensations derived from eating come from the tactile and proprioceptive sense organs in the oropharyngeal region (mouth and pharynx) and the stomach. Experimental work suggests that neither of these two locations is alone responsible for mediating satiety [Stellar, 1967].

Stellar [1967] has isolated the effects of gastric sensations from those of oropharyngeal sensations, in human subjects. He persuaded his subjects to feed themselves by operating an electric pump which delivered a liquid diet (Metracal) directly to their stomachs through an intragastric tube. In the absence of any external or oropharyngeal cues subjects were unable to estimate the quantity of Metracal consumed and failed to register any decrease in the subjective ratings of their hunger after quantities of Metracal which would have sated them if taken through the mouth. This suggests that humans are heavily dependent on oropharyngeal sensations for satiety.

On the other hand Epstein [1967] has shown that rats will learn to feed themselves and maintain a normal caloric intake by pressing a lever which causes food to be delivered directly to their stomachs through an intragastric tube. They will even respond to dilution of the caloric value of their food by ingesting more in this way. Presumably satiety is registered by stomach distension in this instance.

Finger and Mook [1971] have argued that the assumption that oropharyngeal sensations are absent during intragastric infusions of food may be false as thermal sensations from the food may be experienced as it passes through the intragastric tube. Holman [1969] has shown that intragastric feeding can only be sustained when the food is refrigerated, extinction occurring when it is warm.

Some support for the theory that satiety is at least partly registered by stomach distension comes from the work of Sharma et al. [1961] who showed that distending the stomach by inflation of an intragastric balloon caused activation of the electrical activity of the VMH, the supposed satiety centre. Furthermore, Hoebel and Thompson [1969] have shown that not only VMH stimulation but also gastric distension suppresses the self-stimulation of the LH feeding centre which can be observed in a hungry animal. Thus both gastric and oropharyngeal sensory factors appear to be important in the mediation of satiety.

There is some evidence that the amygdala may collect sensory feedback from eating and pass it on to the hypothalamus. Gloor *et al.* [1969] has shown that stimulation of the amygdala induces, via the stria terminals and the VMH, inhibition of the lateral hypothalamus.

It seems likely that as the sensory feedback from eating is relatively short lived its influence is likewise brief. Animals 'sham feeding' with an oesophagal fistula so that food is taken in through the mouth and then goes directly to the outside—not to the stomach—show only brief periods of satiation between meals [Stellar, 1967].

It seems that short term satiation mediated by the sensory concomitants of eating is replaced by long term satiation mediated by the postabsorbtive effects of ingested food on nutrient levels in the bloodstream. The experiments showing the effects of elevated blood glucose on the VMH (discussed earlier) are consistent with this notion. Further support comes from the finding of Davis *et al.* [1969] that a blood transfusion given to a hungry rat will only suppress eating if the blood is taken from the donor more than 45 min after completion of a meal.

Alternative hypotheses for the neural mechanisms controlling food intake

Panksepp [1971a, b] has shown that hyperphagic VMH lesioned rats depress their food intake, as do normal rats, when a preload of food is delivered directly to their stomachs shortly before a meal. Furthermore, hyperphagic rats do not eat continuously but eat meals which have a distinct beginning and end. This evidence suggests that some metering of food intake, based on postprandial sensory factors, must be occurring, even in the supposed absence of the satiety centre.

Panksepp has also observed that VMH lesioned rats do not speed up their eating, as normals do, if starved, or restricted to feeding for only one hour in 24. This indicated that VMH lesioned rats could not match their feeding behaviour to their immediate nutrient deficit, despite the fact that the supposed LH feeding centre was still intact.

These findings led Panksepp to advance a modified theory in which the LH mediates the short term sensory factors both starting and stopping eating, and the VMH mediates the operation of long term humoral factors (factors in the bloodstream) signalling depletion and repletion. Thus, the eating behaviour of VMH animals, under this theory, is influenced solely by the former system, which is why sensory factors have such an exaggerated effect on their food intake (see above). The evidence that the VMH is sensitive to blood glucose is consistent with the idea that it monitors humoral factors signifying depletion or repletion. However, the discovery by Sharma *et al.* [1961] that the electrical activity of the VMH is influenced by sensory feedback from the stomach can only be accommodated by supposing that the influence is mediated via the LH.

A ventromedial hypothalamus lipostatic mechanism

Le Magnen *et al*. [1973] have outlined another possible role of the hypothalamus (specifically the VMH) in the diurnal feeding cycle of the rat as the result of some subtle and elegant studies. These investigators have found that the normal rat is hyperphagic during the night and hypophagic (undereating) during the day, relative to their energy output. It appears that during the night increased secretion of insulin promotes the formation of fat (a process called lipogenesis) from food ingested, thus reducing the level of metabolites (nutrients) which might act on a glucosensitive system mediating satiety. Consequently hunger onset is more rapid and more meals are taken. During the day insulin secretion is suppressed and fat stored during the night is mobilized (lipolysis) and added to the available pool of metabolites circulating in the blood. The elevated level of nutrients delays the onset of hunger so that fewer meals are taken. This fat-feeding cycle may be an adaptive mechanism to provide an animal with reserves of energy during the day when it tends to sleep and does little foraging for food.

Le Magnen *et al*. [1973] note that in VMH lesioned animals insulin levels are elevated and formation of fat is promoted both day and night. They argue that this is because the VMH is responsible for the inhibition of insulin secretion which prevents hyperphagia during the day. Thus in the absence of the VMH there is a failure of this insulinosecretory inhibitory mechanism resulting in the normal night time hyperphagia persisting throughout the day. This function of the VMH is not necessarily inconsistent with the other functions ascribed to it. It could also be accommodated in the sort of theory put forward by Panksepp [1971a, b] and discussed in the last section.

We can see that although a general picture of the type of mechanisms regulating intake of food is being built up (Figure 4.4) there is still a lot of detail to be added to the picutre.

Thirst and water balance

Animal life on earth originated in the warm saline seas of the young planet, a benign aqueous environment which both served its inhabitants' hydrational needs and maintained them at a constant temperature favourable for the metabolic processes sustaining life.

When creatures first emerged from the sea they entered a gaseous environment with insufficient moisture to meet their hydrational needs and subject to large fluctuations in temperature inimical to the orderly maintenance of metabolic processes.

The members of the vertebrate subphylum who became adapted to a land habitat solved these adaptive problems by developing an internal substitute for their previous external marine environment. This is manifest as a circulatory system of blood, of identical salinity to the sea, its liquid volume and temperature being maintained by a variety of autonomic and behavioural mechanisms.

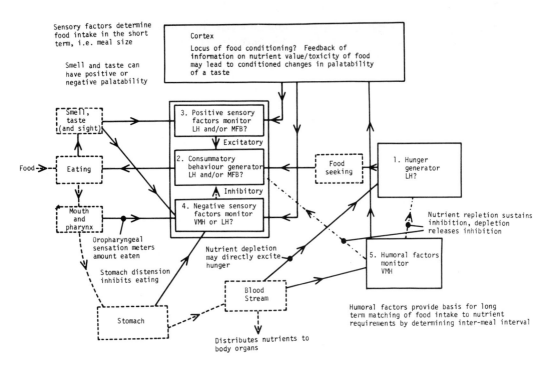

Sensory factors determine
food intake in the short
term, i.e. meal size

Smell and taste can
have positive or
negative palatability

Cortex

Locus of food conditioning? Feedback of
information on nutrient value/toxicity of food
may lead to conditioned changes in palatability
of a taste

Smell,
taste
(and sight)

Food → Eating

Mouth
and
pharynx

Oropharyngeal
sensation meters
amount eaten

Stomach distension
inhibits eating

Stomach

3. Positive sensory
factors monitor
LH and/or MFB?

↓ Excitatory

2. Consummatory
behaviour generator
LH and/or MFB?

↑ Inhibitory

4. Negative sensory
factors monitor
VMH or LH?

Food
seeking

1. Hunger
generator
LH?

Nutrient repletion sustains
inhibition, depletion
releases inhibition

Nutrient depletion
may directly excite
hunger

5. Humoral factors
monitor
VMH

Blood
Stream

Distributes nutrients to
body organs

Humoral factors provide basis for long
term matching of food intake to nutrient
requirements by determining inter-meal interval

Figure 4.4
Schema provisionally
summarizing our
knowledge of the
systems involved in the
control of food intake

The need for fluid is manifest as the thirst drive. Mammals are composed of 70-75% water by weight and a loss of water in excess of 0.5%
of body weight is sufficient to generate a thirst. Depletion of body fluids
occurs because water is continuously lost from the body by evaporation
from the skin and lungs, and excreted in the urine with the waste products.
In addition to replacing lost fluid by anticipatory drinking [Fitzsimons,
1971] and drinking occasioned by thirst, there is a hormonally controlled
mechanism with the capacity to conserve body fluid during a time of
hydrational need, by reducing the excretion of water from the kidneys.

The conservation of fluid during dehydration is activated by the release
of antidiuretic hormone (known as ADH), secreted by the posterior lobe
of the pituitary gland under the control of the supraoptic nucleus of the
hypothalamus [Verney, 1947; see also Netter, 1953, pp. 156-157]. ADH
is transported by the bloodstream, to the kidneys where it promotes
reabsorption of water from the tubules of the kidney. This results in the
reduction of diuresis, the discharge of urine, so that body fluid is conserv-
ed. Urine is formed in reduced volume but of greater concentration.

We are interested in the neural mechanisms regulating the body's water
balance and their trigger signals.

Cannon's [1918] 'local stimulation' theory supposed that thirst was
simply the sensation of a dry or parched mouth and a burning throat,
because water is drawn from the salivary glands during dehydration. However, Montgomery [1931a, b] has shown that extirpation of the salivary
glands in dogs does not increase water intake as the theory would predict.
Furthermore, Adolph [1947] has shown that drugs promoting salivation
in dehydrated human subjects do not abolish thirst. Teitelbaum [1971]
did find that LH lesioned rats, which had recovered from aphagia but not

from adipsia, would take water with their food (prandial drinking), apparently to aid ingestion through a dry mouth because of diminished salivary gland activity. Thus a dry mouth would only appear to be a stimulus to drink in certain circumstances.

The monitoring of body fluid levels appears to be mediated by very different mechanisms, responding separately to intracellular and extracellular dehydration.

The amount of intracellular fluid is a function of the osmotic pressure across the cell membrane. Osmotic pressure arises because there are solutes (substances which dissolve in water), such as salt, which are pervasive in body tissues, but which cannot freely cross the semipermeable cellular membranes. The consequence of this, if there is a greater concentration of the solute outside the cell than inside it, is that water is drawn from the inside of the cell to the outside in an attempt to equalize the concentration of the solutions on each side of the membrane. This process is called osmosis. The withdrawal of water causes the cells to become dehydrated and shrink, producing the kind of mechanical deformation likely to activate a nerve cell. Solutions with the solute at higher concentrations than in the body tissues are referred to as hypertonic, those at the same concentration are isotonic, and at a lower concentration, hypotonic. Because of their osmotic effect hypertonic solutions generate thirst, rather than quench it. This is readily illustrated if we drink a hypertonic salt solution (Figure 4.5).

Verney [1947] experimentally demonstrated the plausibility of the theory that thirst could be generated osmotically. He injected hypertonic saline solution into the carotid artery, which supplies blood to the basal diencephalon. This elicited a rapid and marked increase in ADH secretion consistent with a negative water balance. Holmes and Gregerson [1950a, b] found that intravenous injection of a variety of hypertonic solutions (NaCl, Na_2SO_4, CH_3COONa, sucrose, sorbital), whose solutes do not penetrate cell membranes, induced drinking in dogs. However, it was not necessarily sufficient to reduce the concentration of the solute in the blood to its preinjection level.

Andersson [1952] has elicited drinking in unanaesthetized goats by direct injection of hypertonic saline into the hypothalamus in the region of the paraventricular nucleus. As other neuroactive drugs injected in the same location and hypertonic saline in other locations failed to elicit drinking it appeared that Andersson had located the specific osmoreceptors in the hypothalamus.

In the section on hunger it was noted that destruction of the lateral hypothalamus in rats resulted not only in aphagia, but also in even more permanent adipsia [Teitelbaum, 1961], thus implicating the LH in regulation of water intake. Also Grossman [1960, 1962a, b] found that microinjections of acetylcholine, or its synthetic analogue carbachol, elicited drinking from the same LH locations in the rat where noradrenalin would elicit eating. Eating and drinking appeared to be mediated by anatomically overlapping, but neurochemically separated systems in the LH, and extending into other limbic structures. However, it seems possible that the overlap of feeding and drinking systems is peculiar to the rat as it is not found in goats and dogs. Andersson and McCann [1955] found that

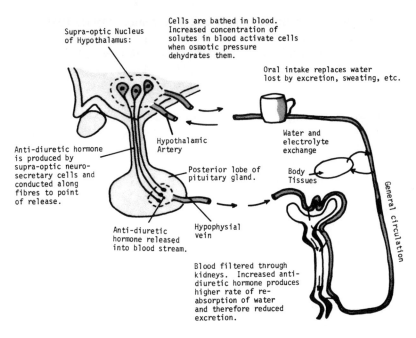

Figure 4.5
Neural and hormonal factors in the control of fluid balance. In this diagram only the detection of negative fluid balance by changes in osmotic pressure is represented

Supra-optic Nucleus of Hypothalamus:

Cells are bathed in blood. Increased concentration of solutes in blood activate cells when osmotic pressure dehydrates them.

Oral intake replaces water lost by excretion, sweating, etc.

Anti-diuretic hormone is produced by supra-optic neuro-secretary cells and conducted along fibres to point of release.

Hypothalamic Artery

Water and electrolyte exchange

Posterior lobe of pituitary gland.

Body Tissues

Anti-diuretic hormone released into blood stream.

Hypophysial vein

General circulation

Blood filtered through kidneys. Increased anti-diuretic hormone produces higher rate of re-absorption of water and therefore reduced excretion.

electrical stimulation of the paraventricular hypothalamic nucleus in the goat produces drinking and that lesion of this nucleus in goats and dogs produces adipsia without aphagia. Andersson and McCann also found that a slightly more anterior electrode placement produced both drinking and ADH secretion showing that the systems promoting ingestion and conservation of fluid are closely linked.

Volemic thirst

A monitor of water deficit operated by increases in osmotic pressure across cellular membranes (resulting in cellular dehydration and shrinkage) can only work if increases in the concentration of osmotically effective extracellular solutes is always correlated with the over-all degree of dehydration of the organism. In fact loss of fluid volume (extracellular dehydration) can occur without any change in osmotic pressure. This is referred to as an isotonic loss of fluid volume. A second system is required to monitor isotonic change in liquid volume. Adolph [1947] argues that water deprivation is a much better stimulus for drinking than cellular dehydration brought about by osmotically effective solutes. Fitzsimons [1971] argues that maintenance of extracellular volume is probably more important for short-term survival and he reviews the possible mechanisms for drinking caused by extracellular dehydration.

The earliest evidence that isotonic reduction of fluid volume results in thirst comes from the observation that haemorrhage produces thirst in man [Wettendorf, 1901; Gregerson and Bullock, 1933]. In rats both haemorrhage [Fitzsimons, 1961; Oatley, 1964] and haemorrhage following dehydration [Fitzsimons and Oatley, 1968; Fitzsimons, 1969] have been found to produce an increase in drinking. However, these results are not consistently found as Holmes and Montgomery [1951, 1953] were unable to obtain consistent reports of thirst experienced by blood donors and Schnieden [1962] was unable to obtain drinking in haemorrhaged rats. However, Fitzsimons [1971, p. 147] observed that haemorrhage is not the most satisfactory method of bringing about isotonic reduction of extracellular fluid.

Extracellular dehydration can also be brought about by sodium depletion which results in loss of water into the urine and into the intracellular space (by osmotic flow into rather than out of cells). McCance [1936] observed that sodium depletion in three healthy men resulted in copious drinking although the subjects experienced a sensation which subjectively differed from normal thirst. Excessive drinking resulting from sodium deficiency has also been observed in rats [Swanson et al., 1935; Radford, 1959] and dogs [Holmes and Cizek, 1951].

A simple and quick way of removing extracellular fluid is by peritoneal or subcutaneous injection of a substance called hyperoncotic colloid, in an isotonic saline solution. This induces a rapid accumulation of water and extracellular solute at the site of injection, resulting in acute isotonic depletion of fluid in the remaining extracellular space. Within an hour of injection there is a striking increase in the rate of drinking and a fall in urine flow [Fitzsimons, 1971, p. 148], further validating the assumption that loss of fluid volume is itself a stimulus for thirst.

Further evidence that there are two separate systems mediating drinking is supplied by the finding of Smith and Stricker [1969] that rats with a thirst induced by osmotic changes preferred water to an isotonic saline solution while rats with a thirst induced by loss of fluid volume preferred isotonic saline solution to water.

Detectors of
fluid volume change

The most obvious candidates for detectors of fluid volume change are the stretch receptors located in the walls of the blood vessels and heart, probably on the low pressure (venous) side as the veins, pulmonary vessels and atria contain about 80% of the blood and are between 100 and 200 times more distensible than the arteries [Gauer and Henry, 1963]. In support of this hypothesis Fitzsimons [1964, 1969a] has shown that obstruction of the blood flow on the venous side, which is assumed to cause the reduction in pressure usually occasioned by loss of fluid volume, results in drinking. However, obstruction of blood flow in nephrectomized (with their kidneys removed) rats is much less effective in promoting drinking [Fitzsimons, 1971]. Also obstruction of blood flow is much more effective in eliciting drinking if effected above the level of the renal arteries than below. These findings have led Fitzsimons to postulate that circulatory changes in the blood vessels of the kidneys have a special role to play in extracellular thirst.

Fitzsimons [1971] presents evidence that reduced arterial pressure stimulates the release of the substance renin from the kidneys, which in turn is responsible for generation of the substance angiotensin. Angiotensin is carried in the bloodstream to the hypothalamus where it stimulates thirst centres. Fitzsimons [1966] found that intravenous injections of angiotensin caused drinking in nephrectomized rats. Booth [1968] and Epstein *et al.* [1970] have found that minute injections of angiotensin into the septum, preoptic area or anterior hypothalamic region, via micro-cannulae, elicited drinking in rats in normal water balance. Much smaller amounts of angiotensin were found to be effective in promoting drinking than of carbachol, which Grossman [1960] and Fisher and Coury [1962] reported to selectively induce drinking when injected into the hypothalamus. Furthermore, carbachol had other complicating effects, not observed when angiotensin was used, so that it appeared that angiotensin had a direct and specific effect on a hypothalamic thirst system.

Satiety

The mechanisms mediating satiety in ingestion of fluid are poorly understood. Wayner and Carey [1973] note that lesions of the septal region result in excessive drinking and taste finickiness in rats so that this structure may be a counterpart of the VMH food satiety centre in the regulation of drinking.

In evidence of oropharyngeal stimuli for satiety Bellows [1939] found that dogs 'sham drinking', because of insertion of an oesophagal fistula, did cease drinking periodically despite the fact that no water was ingested into the stomach.

Gastric distension by direct placement of water in the stomach [Towbin, 1949; Adolph, 1950] has been found to reduce drinking in rats, hamsters, and guinea pigs, but not in dogs, showing that the stomach can be a source of satiety signals.

Milner [1970a, p. 315] has suggested that the amygdala may be a metering device for oropharyngeal sensation. If the amygdala is stimulated there is no output discharge until after a lapse of some time. This output will then outlast the stimulus evoking it by some further time. These properties are consistent with a mechanism which is activated by a cumulative input produced by drinking. It supposedly terminates drinking when a critical amount of fluid has been consumed, and continues to inhibit further consumption until the postabsorptive effects of ingested water are felt.

Finally we should take note of the argument of Fitzsimons [1971] that drinking when water is freely available is not a response to thirst but is an anticipatory behaviour regulated by a circadian rhythm and also modulated by eating. Free drinking rats actually consume more water than is absolutely necessary for their fluid economy, and consume most of it at night when they are most active, and when the greater proportion of their feeding occurs.

Temperature regulation

Not only must we maintain the volume of the surrogate primeval sea encapsulated in our bloodstream but, if we are to operate efficiently in a wide range of land environments, we must also maintain the temperature of both our blood and our body within certain narrow limits.

Warm-blooded animals (homoiotherms) maintain their core body temperature within the range 30–40 °C in a wide range of environmental temperatures. Cold-blooded animals (poikilotherms) adopt nearly the temperature of their surroundings and are consequently limited in the range of environments in which they can survive. They are inactive in the cold.

Body temperature is regulated by both involuntary and voluntary means. Body heat is kept down in high temperatures by perspiring, panting, and in some animals (e.g. rats) by spreading saliva on their fur. In each case the heat used to evaporate the moisture (latent heat of evaporation) on the body surface reduces its temperature. Excessive cold is countered by 'huddling', which reduces the surface area from which heat can be lost, shivering, which generates heat by muscular action and piloerection or hair fluffing which reduces heat loss by forming an insulating layer. Voluntary temperature regulating activities are well known in our own species (e.g. installing central heating) and others, many clearly being a function of learning in higher animals. For instance even rats will learn to operate a lever which switches on a heat lamp in a cold cage [Weiss and Laties, 1961] or a cold shower in a hot cage [Epstein and Milestone, 1968].

Clearly the regulatory mechanisms must be activated by temperature detectors. The body surface is the obvious place to monitor environmental temperature and temperature receptors there certainly do produce anticipatory behaviour for the regulation of temperature. The surface temperature receptors are most sensitive to the rate of temperature change in the external environment. However, changes in the body core temperature, whose regulation is most crucial for the organism's survival, follow external changes rather slowly.

Like other aspects of the internal environment, the body core temperature is reflected in the temperature of the blood, again this factor appears to be monitored in the hypothalamus. Stimulations of the preoptic region of the hypothalamus elicits panting, cutaneous vasodilation (which takes more blood to the body surface for cooling) and other cooling responses, in goats [Andersson et al., 1956]. More direct evidence for a hypothalamic 'thermostat' is that cooling the anterior hypothalamus (by circulating a cooling liquid through concentric microcannulae) causes huddling [Magoun et al., 1938], peripheral vasoconstriction (reducing heat loss from the blood at the body surface) and shivering [Hammel et al., 1960].

Single neurones have been located in the anterior hypothalamus which discharge when the area is heated [Nakayama et al., 1961, 1963; Hardy et al., 1964] and others, though far fewer, which discharge when it is cooled [Hardy et al., 1964]. None of these units responded when the skin on the face was cooled.

Benzinger [1962] has found a perfect correlation between the temperature of the blood flowing to the hypothalamus (measured at the ear drum) and heat loss through sweating in man. Furthermore if the anterior hypothalamus is cooled by holding a block of ice against the roof of the mouth the rate of perspiration is drastically reduced although skin temperature rises sharply as a result.

Generally speaking experimenters have found it more difficult to elicit regulatory responses to hypothalamic cooling than heating, suggesting that while the hypothalamus contains the primary monitor for overheating, the temperature receptors at the body surface are the main source of signals which elicit activities to conserve or gain heat.

In conclusion to this chapter we may say that the body's internal needs are generally reflected in the qualities of the blood. These qualities are monitored by special receptors in the hypothalamus which may be characterized as the sense organ for the internal environment. Hypothalamic mechanisms initiate, sustain, and finally terminate consummatory behaviour in response to a sequence of signals generated in the sensory systems of the hypothalamus itself and in the organs concerned with consummatory behaviour. In higher animals the cortex has an important role in patterning activities initiated by hypothalamic systems.

Summary

The term 'homeostasis' has been coined to refer to the maintenance of a 'steady-state' in the internal environment. To maintain homeostasis a creature must eat, drink, and keep its body temperature within a narrow range.

It appears that the primary monitoring of the internal environment occurs via the bloodstream as it traverses the neural systems of the hypothalamus. In the first instance lesion and stimulation studies suggested that the lateral hypothalamus (LH) responded to nutrient depletion and initiated hungry behaviour, while the ventromedial nucleus of the hypothalamus (VMH) responded to satiety signals and terminated feeding. It seemed that these two centres were in a reciprocal relationship with one another, heightened activity in the VMH inhibiting activity in the LH, and vice versa.

Later experiments have shown that overeating in VMH lesioned animals only occurs with highly palatable food, and that there is a hypersensitivity to taste which can over-ride nutritional need. This suggests that a primary role of the LH may be to sustain consummatory behaviour under the control of positive feedback provided by taste. This loop is only interrupted by negative feedback from the VMH when it receives satiety signals. There is a suggestion that obesity due to overeating, in humans, may be due to inadequate function of the VMH with the consequence that eating behaviour is regulated almost exclusively by the sensory qualities of available food and not by nutritional need. It seems that in normal humans the subjective correlate of negative feedback from satiety signals is a decline in palatability of food whose sensory qualities remain constant. This may be due to reduced responsiveness of the systems mediating 'pleasure' or the activation of antagonistic systems mediating displeasure.

The palatability of food is also subject to change by learning, based on its nutritional value. Thus initially palatable tastes may become unattractive if they are associated with a non-nutritive substance (e.g. saccharin) or a poison.

Diverse studies indicate that the VMH monitors the rate of utilization of blood sugar, normally a correlate of blood sugar level. There is also some evidence that amino acid levels may be monitored in the hypothalamus. As VMH lesioned animals cease to respond appropriately to either elevation or depletion of nutrient levels in the bloodstream, Panksepp has suggested that this structure has an over-all monitoring function for the internal environment. Panksepp attributes to the LH the function of monitoring both positive and negative sensory feedback, but not the internal environment.

While a raised blood sugar level inhibits eating by its effects on the VMH, there is a considerable delay between eating and elevation of blood sugar and nutrient levels following digestion. It would appear that in the short term satiety is mediated by sensory feedback from receptors in the mouth, pharynx and stomach. It seems that in humans oropharyngeal metering is of primary importance. However, rats can learn to regulate the intake of food delivered via an intragastric tube, suggesting that good use can be made of gastric sensory feedback.

Le Magnen has summarized the evidence and outlined the three control systems which regulate food intake to meet a creature's homeostatic needs. The first system, based on monitoring nutrient levels in the blood, determines when hunger will arise and its satisfaction be pursued. This system compensates for variations in meal size from meal to meal, so that in the long term intake matches nutrient needs. The second system, based on positive or negative responses to the sensory qualities of food (i.e. palatability) and sensory feedback from eating, determines meal size. In the short term there is no precise matching of food intake to need. The third system involves feedback from the nutrient value of digested food to the mechanism evaluating palatability. It permits learning so that substances which are initially palatable, but are non-nutritive or even poisonous, become unpalatable.

Living organisms require water for a variety of bodily functions. Regulation of water balance is achieved by a dual system. In addition to initiating drinking depletion of body fluid is communicated to the supraoptic nucleus of the hypothalamus, which triggers the release of antidiuretic hormone from the posterior pituitary gland. This conserves body fluid by reducing the excretion of water via the kidneys. There are two types of thirst, osmotic and volemic, produced by intracellular and extracellular dehydration respectively. The former is produced by osmotic pressure when extracellular solute concentration rises due to fluid loss. The latter arises when there is isotonic depletion of extracellular fluid. Osmotic thirst appears to be detected in the paraventricular and adjacent regions of the hypothalamus. Volemic thirst appears to be detected by pressure receptors in the arteries supplying the kidneys. There is evidence that reduction in blood pressure triggers the release of renin, which is instrumental in the production of a substance called angiotensin. Angiotensin is carried by the bloodstream to the preoptic and anterior hypothalamus where its detection elicits drinking.

It is essential for the survival of warm blooded animals that they maintain their body temperature within narrow limits. Changes in external and internal temperature must be compensated for by involuntary and voluntary responses to gain or lose heat, as appropriate. The principal detectors of overheating would appear to be in the anterior hypothalamus, where the temperature of the blood is monitored. External thermoreceptors appear to be more important as a source of information about excessive cold.

A recurrent theme in discussion of serving internal needs is the central role of the hypothalamus, which appears to be the sense organ for the internal environment.

Chapter five

Sex and reproductive behaviour

Introduction

The importance of sexual reproduction in adaptation to the environment and evolution has been outlined in an earlier chapter. Sexual reproduction achieves segregation and recombination of the genes, which promotes constant experiment on the adaptive value of different combinations of genes within a species. This experimentation is a basis for improvement of the gene pool and for a rapid response of the gene pool to any change in the environmental pressures demanding an adaptive response.

All but the most primitive creatures reproduce sexually. The details of sexual reproduction and its controlling mechanisms vary enormously from species to species, but certain basic features are common to all species. In all species hormones play a central role in the whole chain of events leading to the appearance of sexual behaviour, right from differential development of the sexual organs to the priming of an animal for sexual arousal. Nowhere do we see a closer and more complex integration of hormonal and neural mechanisms than in the mechanisms of reproduction. In addition to there being several different hormones, each with different functions, there are individual hormones which serve more than one function. This depends on the phase of a creature's development in which it is active and the target organ on which it is acting.

The existence of two sexes is a prerequisite for sexual reproduction. The development of either male or female gonads and genitalia in the embryo is determined by the type of hormone circulating in the embryo. The subsequent organization of neural structures to serve either a male or female function is similarly determined by the nature of the hormones present at a critical developmental period. In the developing organism the achievement of sexual maturity is brought about by hormones and in the adult periodic or seasonal changes in fertility and sexual activity are programmed by the hormones. In the female the integrated sequence of events which constitute the fertility cycle is organized by the hormones. Hormones prime neural mechanisms in the brain and possibly also in the spinal cord which mediate sexual arousal and copulatory behaviour. In addition, a creature's hormonal balance appears to predispose it towards sex specific patterns of behaviour, such as territorial aggression, which are not directly concerned with reproduction. In the female maternal behaviour is hormonally triggered.

It should be understood that the behaviour which is under hormonal influence is not actually initiated by the hormones. The hormones prime the organism for patterns of behaviour whose appearance and part of whose intensity is determined by the attractiveness of a prospective mate and the stimulation received from this consort. Furthermore, the secretion of sex hormones is itself influenced by external stimuli and the behaviour of the animal, particularly in some species. It should also be noted that the degree of dependence on hormones for sexual arousal and consummation decreases as the phylogenetic scale is ascended.

Sexual differentiation

The classical genetic difference between the sexes is that whereas the last of the 23 pairs of chromosomes in the female are identical (XX), those in the male are non-identical (XY). Despite this conspicuous difference in the hereditary material the genes do not determine sexual differentiation directly. In the early embryo there is no differentiation of sexual characteristics, but common structures from which either male or female sex organs can develop. Duct systems are present which are the precursors of the sex organs of both the female (mullerian duct) and the male (wolffian duct) (see Figure 5.1).

Whether these rudimentary sexual structures develop into those of a male or a female is determined by hormones secreted by these sex organs. It appears that 'nature's first choice, or primal impulse is to differentiate a female' [Money, 1970] as a female will develop in the absence of male sex hormones (androgens, most prominently testosterone) irrespective of genetic sex. It is hypothesized by Jost [1970] that the male Y chromosome may confer maleness on an embryo by determining the production of a local hormone which promotes early and rapid development of the testes in the undeveloped sex organs. The testes produce the androgens which promote the full development of male sex organs.

It has been shown that if male foetal rabbits are surgically castrated [Jost, 1962] or if the action of androgen is blocked by the injection of the hormone cyproterone [Neumann and Elgar, 1966] then they will be born with a perfect facsimile of female external genitalia, including a vagina large enough for copulation when mature. However, the gonads are testes and the uterus and fallopian tubes are absent. If the hormonal influence of the testes is continually suppressed and female hormones are administered, the feminized male rabbit matures to exhibit patterns of sexual receptivity and sexual behaviour indistinguishable from that of other females.

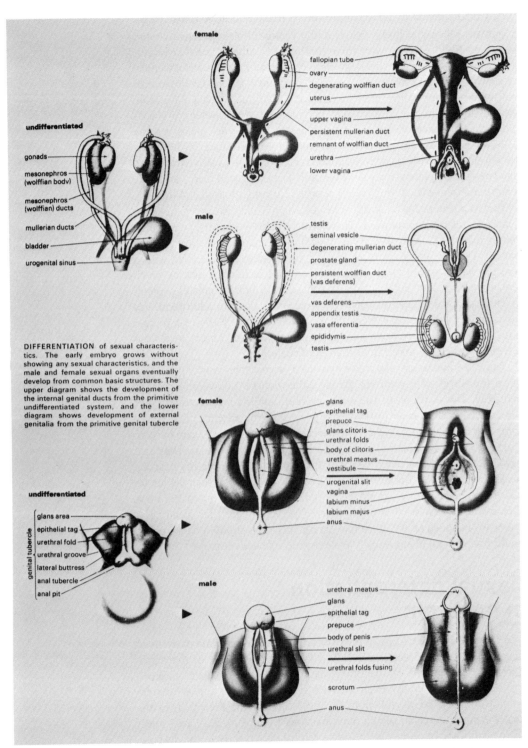

Figure 5.1
The differentiation of sexual characteristics in humans.

From Jost, A. D. (1970) Development of sexual characteristics. *Science J.*, 6(6), 67–72.
Reproduced by permission of Syndication International Ltd

This phenomenon of feminization of a genetic male sometimes occurs in humans when the body tissue of the foetus displays insensitivity to androgens. Children born with this syndrome have the external apparatus of a female, but only a vestigial uterus and instead of ovaries, undescended testes which produce no sperm. Invariably assigned as females because of their external appearance, their feminization continues during maturation because the androgen insensitivity persists and development proceeds under the influence of oestrogen produced, as in normal males, by the testes. It is not always realized that males always produce some female sex hormone and vice versa. As adults these androgen insensitive feminized males pass as completely acceptable females. They may well marry and have been found to display strong maternal drives towards adopted children.

Just as a genetically male foetus can be feminized, so can a genetically female foetus be masculinized. This has been achieved in rats, guinea pigs, and monkeys [Money, 1965] by injecting pregnant mothers with androgens. This produces an offspring equipped with a penis, but with a scrotum which is empty as the gonads are not testes, but ovaries which remain internal. The adult behaviour of these masculinized females depends on the hormonal regime on which they are maintained in adulthood, but tends towards that of the male. In masculinized female rhesus monkeys both explicit sex behaviour and patterns of play and threat behaviour resemble that of the male rather than the female.

The masculinization of genetic females is sometimes found in humans when the cortex of the adrenal gland in the foetus produces an excess of androgen. The secretion of the male sex hormone is a normal function of the adrenal cortex, even in females. Babies with the adrenogenital symptom, as it is called, develop a penis instead of a clitoris but again have an empty scrotum and, instead of testes, internally located ovaries. They also have a uterus and shortened vagina, which opens into the urethra near the neck of the bladder. Because of their external appearance such babies are usually assigned as boys. If subject to an appropriate regime of hormone therapy and given surgical treatment to prevent menstrual bleeding at puberty (a sequel to the hormone treatment) such children can grow to adulthood with an unequivocally male psychosexual identity.

Sexual differentiation in the brain

The characteristic sexual rhythms of the body and appropriate patterns of behaviour do not automatically follow from the possession of the reproductive organs of one or the other sex. Like the sex organs themselves, the centres in the brain which mediate sexual behaviour appear to stem from a common neural substrate in both sexes. If these centres, in the anterior preoptic region of the hypothalamus (see Figure 5.2), are subject to the influence of androgens during a critical period early in the development of the young, a strong bias towards male patterns of behaviour is seen in the developing animal. If the influence of androgens is eliminated by castration a female pattern of behaviour develops.

If testosterone is administered to female rats within a critical period

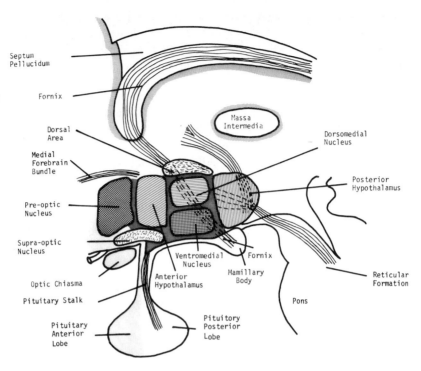

Figure 5.2
Schematic
reconstruction of the
hypothalamus, medial
view, showing major
nuclei including those
of the anterior preoptic
region involved in
sexual behaviour

Septum
Pellucidum

Fornix

Dorsal
Area

Medial
Forebrain
Bundle

Pre-optic
Nucleus

Supra-optic
Nucleus

Optic Chiasma

Pituitary Stalk

Pituitary
Anterior
Lobe

Massa
Intermedia

Dorsomedial
Nucleus

Posterior
Hypothalamus

Ventromedial
Nucleus

Fornix

Anterior
Hypothalamus

Mamillary
Body

Reticular
Formation

Pons

Pituitory
Posterior
Lobe

just after their birth [Harris and Levine, 1965] or to foetal guinea pigs
during a critical period just before birth [Phoenix *et al.*, 1969; Young *et
al.*, 1964], the resulting animals at maturity will fail to exhibit the female
oestrous cycle, in which oestrus or sexual readiness is only manifest during
the fertile period following ovulation. Instead their sexual readiness is
uncyclical, like that of the male, and they are in a constant state of oestrus
(in the physiological sense) though without ovulation. In addition their
sexual behaviour is disorientated and disorganized and they repulse any
male who approaches them. Money [1970] argues that the abolition of
the oestrous cycle occurs because the hypothalamic nuclei which would
normally control the cyclic release of hormones from the pituitary gland
are masculinized by the testosterone and lose this capacity. The nuclei
regulating sexual behaviour suffer a similar fate. The sensitivity of hypothalamic cells to testosterone has been documented by the fact that they
take up large amounts of radioactively labelled male hormone [Money,
1970].

In the converse to these experiments male animals have been castrated
before the critical period in which androgen masculinizes the hypothalamus. The 'sex' of the hypothalamus has been tested by grafting an ovary
behind the lens of the castrate's eye, where it is subject to the hormonal
influences of the pituitary gland. An ovary thus placed has been found to
exhibit the cycles of activity characteristic of the female, showing that in
the absence of androgens the male animal's hypothalamus has been feminized and is influencing the secretory activity of the pituitary gland in a
cyclical fashion [cited in Money, 1970].

Early castrated male animals, which have become feminized, are sexually
apathetic unless primed with the female hormones oestrogen and proges-

terone, when they display a feminine response pattern. It should be emphasized that these hormonal manipulations in critical periods just before, or just after birth have masculinizing or feminizing effects which are irreversible. For instance testosterone injections administered to an adult male rat, castrated at birth, fail to elicit ejaculatory behaviour or intromission behaviour [Phoenix et al., 1959; Harris and Levine, 1965].

The behavioural effects of using hormonal manipulations to modify sexual differentiation of brain structures extends beyond purely sexual behaviour to other aspects of social behaviour. Young et al. [1964] observed that masculinized (pseudohermaphroditic) female rhesus monkeys exhibited typically male behaviours such as the issuing of threats, initiation of play and 'rough and tumble' play significantly more frequently than normal female controls. Even in humans it has been claimed that females, masculinized by excess adrenal androgen, but surgically corrected and reared as girls, exhibit a high incidence of 'tomboyism' with a lack of interest in play reflecting 'rehearsal for motherhood' and a heightened interest in sport and other boyish activities [Ehrhardt et al., 1968].

We should note that the commitment to the behaviour pattern of one sex is never complete. The females of many species will occasionally display the mounting behaviour appropriate to males [Beach, 1968]. Lordosis, the flattening of the back which the female rat exhibits to facilitate the entry of the male, is rare in males but can be elicited by the administration of high doses of the female sex hormone oestrogen [Davidson, 1969]. It appears that a feminized hypothalamus retains some capacity to produce male behaviour and a masculinized hypothalamus some capacity to produce female behaviour. Fisher [1956] accidentally showed that microinjections of the male hormone testosterone into certain hypothalamic areas in male rats elicited, not typical male behaviour, but rather a facsimile of the maternal behaviour shown by the female rat towards its young. Testosterone is chemically a close relation of the female hormone and it appears that, taking the role of progesterone, it activated normally dormant neural structures, mediating feminine patterns of behaviour, in the male.

Gender identity

The foregoing discussion establishes that the assignment of an individual as male or female is not always as straightforward as it superficially seems and that maleness and femaleness are not mutually exclusive attributes. It is possible for a genetic female to have both masculinized genitalia and brain structures or just masculinized brain structures and vice versa for the male. Furthermore, normally masculinized or feminized brain structures retain some potential for mediating the behaviour of the other gender. Indeed it seems possible that the male-female balance within the brain structures is variable so that, notwithstanding the anatomical differences between the sexes there is a continuum between complete maleness and complete femaleness, with few individuals at the extremes. This appears to be subjectively reasonable among humans as individuals differ in the extent to which they exhibit the demeanour and behaviour of the opposite sex.

It appears that the male–female balance in the brain structures is 'fixed' by the hormonal balance at the critical phase of development during which sexual differentiation in the brain occurs. The enduring structural influence which this fixing of the brain structure has, even on human behaviour, is shown by the boyish behaviour exhibited by girls with the adrenogenital syndrome. The critical point is that this boyish behaviour persists even though any masculinization of the genitals has been surgically reversed, any later manifestations of masculinity hormonally corrected and all the pressures of their upbringing have been such as to inculcate a female gender identity [Ehrhardt et al., 1968].

The fact that the girls with the adrenogenital syndrome mentioned above, have displayed some boyish behaviour does not mean that they have not accepted their assignment to the female gender. Also they do not show explicit or latent inclination to lesbian behaviour. Structurally determined tendencies to display the behaviour of the opposite sex are an undercurrent beneath a gender identity accepted by the self and others, which is determined by social influences in a person's upbringing. Money [1970] observed that genetic females with the adrenogenital syndrome unequivocally accepted assignment as either girls or boys according to whether their upbringing was that which was culturally approved for a boy or a girl. When the gender assignment of such children has been provisional and their upbringing has shown ambivalence concerning their gender identity, this has resulted in adults with ambivalent desires to be changed to the other sex.

The increasing knowledge of the hormonal basis of sex differentiation in anatomical and neural structures has not greatly clarified the basis of homosexuality. The frequency of cases of contradictory sexual different-iation, such as those discussed above, is not high among homosexuals. Also there is no clear evidence of an anomalous hormone balance in adulthood being responsible for homosexual behaviour. The administration of testosterone to either male or female homosexuals leads to an increase in homosexual activity in both cases. Androgens appear to be libido enhancing hormones for both sexes [Everitt and Herbert, 1969; Herbert, 1970; Money, 1961a]. In contrast oestrogen has the effect of reducing male sex drive, apparently being an erotic tranquillizer.

One plausible clue to a possible physiological basis for homosexuality is the existence of a critical period for the hormonally guided organization of neural structures in the hypothalamus. Incorrect hormone balances at the critical period may have an anomalous feminizing or masculinizing effect on these structures which results in a predisposition towards homo-sexuality. However, it still seems likely that influences in a child's upbring-ing play a large part in the emergence of homosexual behaviour. Also homosexuality should be viewed against the perspective that most individ-uals retain some behaviour tendencies of the opposite sex which can be translated into overt homosexual behaviour in certain circumstances. Many animals engage in homosexual behaviour some of the time and in some human cultures overt homosexuality or bisexuality is considered to be the norm [e.g. see Ford and Beach, 1952].

Reproductive cycles

Following the sequence in which hormones stimulate the development of sex specific reproductive organs and organize sex specific neural structures in the brain there is a period of relative dormancy in the sexual history of the organism while it grows to maturity. Sexual maturity is attained following a further hormonally stimulated developmental spurt at puberty, which occurs during the early teens in humans. In the male human androgens secreted in the testes are responsible for the well known signs of puberty. The penis, scrotum, and testes quickly attain their adult appearance, sperm are produced and the capacity for erection and ejaculation is gained. The secondary sexual characteristics appear. The voice breaks, changing from treble or alto to tenor or bass, and adult patterns of body hair grow, showing most prominently around the sex organs and under the armpits. The body becomes more muscular.

In the female ovarian oestrogens promote characteristic body changes, the development of the breasts due to the fat mobilizing effect of oestrogen, the appearance of subcutaneous fat and generally rounded contours. The vagina, labia, and uterus become enlarged and the clitoris becomes erectile. The most momentous event is the menarche, the first occurrence of menstrual bleeding from the vagina, resulting from a breakdown of the endometrial lining of the womb. This event heralds the beginning of the menstrual cycle, the fertility cycle which is continuously repeated, except during pregnancy, until loss of fertility at the menopause.

Following puberty the pattern of variation in sexual drive and readiness for reproduction varies from species to species. In male humans the elevated production of androgens at puberty is maintained in adulthood until an eventual slow decline occurs in middle and old age. Consequently the genitalia retain the appearance attained at puberty and the sex drive remains relatively constant, except that it diminishes in strength with advancing years. In some animals, such as deer and sheep, breeding only occurs at certain seasons of the year so that the young are born at a time when the weather and food supplies are favourable for their survival. Seasonal changes, such as length of daylight, appear to trigger the secretion of gonadotrophic hormones by the anterior pituitary gland via its hypothalamic control mechanisms. In the male, interstitial cell stimulating hormone promotes the secretion of testosterone in the testes, which in turn brings about the growth of the genitals and also excites the appearance of territorial aggression and other behaviour related to mating. During the mating season the males are sexually insatiable, but towards the end of the season the production of testosterone diminishes, the genitals regress and the sex drive and its associated behaviour disappears.

The females of most species have a fertility cycle, the menstrual cycle in primates, the oestrous cycle in subprimate mammals. Each female human is born with a lifetime's supply of several hundred thousand primordial eggs, or ova, in her ovaries. These mature, one at a time, in successive cycles. As only about 500 are brought to maturity in a woman's lifetime many are wasted. Each cycle is initiated by the release of the gonadotrophin follicle stimulating hormone (FSH) from the anterior pituitary. This promotes the growth of one ovarian follicle, the 'shell' which encloses the ovum. The follicle produces the female hormone oestrogen, which feeds back to the hypothalamic mechanism controlling the pituitary, causing reduction of FSH output, but inducing the production of luteinizing hormone (LH). LH brings about the terminal ripening and final rupture of the follicle, resulting in the release of the egg—ovulation. The egg enters the fallopian tube where it awaits fertilization. At ovulation LH transforms the ruptured follicle into a gland called the corpus luteum (yellow body) which commences the production of progesterone. In subprimate mammals the combined secretion of oestrogen, which peaks at ovulation, and progesterone brings the animal into heat (oestrus), the only period when the female is sexually receptive and directs its behaviour towards soliciting the sexual attentions of the male. Meanwhile, while the follicle is ripening oestrogen promotes the building of the lining of the uterus. Then following ovulation progesterone completes the preparation of the thick, vascular (well supplied with blood vessels) lining of the womb for implantation of a fertilized egg.

If the egg is not fertilized it eventually starts to degenerate (after about 10 days in humans) and the corpus luteum to regress, terminating the production of progesterone. The endometrial lining of the womb breaks down and is shed, carrying with it the degenerated egg. It appears as the menstrual flow. Towards the end of the cycle the production of oestrogen is reduced. This removes inhibition on the production of FSH which recommences, stimulating the growth of another follicle and thus initiating another cycle in a self-perpetuating sequence.

If an egg is fertilized it produces its own hormone, chorionic gonadotrophin, which prevents regression of the corpus luteum. Thus progesterone production is continued and the uterine lining is sustained for later implantation of the egg so that pregnancy can take its normal course.

Primate females, subject to the menstrual cycle, tend to have a higher sexual drive during their fertile period, but do not have an exclusive period of sexual receptivity as with creatures subject to the oestrous cycle. Oestrous cycles are much more variable than menstrual cycles in length and their appearance may be governed by external stimuli. In seasonally breeding animals the production of FSH by the pituitary may be triggered by such stimuli as rise in ambient temperature and changes in daylight hours, as mentioned previously. Also in some creatures, such as rabbits, ovulation is triggered by the actual act of copulation, or the excitement associated with it. The stimuli activate hypothalamic control mechanisms which cause LH to be secreted [for discussion see Davidson, 1972, pp. 75-78].

The role of hormones in sexual arousal

Mating behaviour in mammals usually consists of a period of courtship whose end product is the sexual arousal of both parties. In the male the special tissue of the penis becomes engorged with blood resulting in the achievement of an erection. In the female the vagina is lubricated, its walls become engorged with blood and it dilates in preparation for penetration. Intromission is achieved when the erect penis is inserted in the vagina. During the copulation which follows a series of pelvic thrusts on the part of the male produce intense stimulation of the glans penis from the moist vaginal wall which eventually produces reflex ejaculation, when sperm-bearing seminal fluid is discharged into the vagina in a series of spurts. The sperm are thus favourably placed high in the vagina, from which they can swim, via the cervix and uterus to the fallopian tubes. The duration and character of courtship behaviour and the number of intromissions and pelvic thrusts required to produce ejaculation varies greatly from species to species, and among humans, from society to society and even individual to individual [see Ford and Beach, 1952 for review].

In order to investigate the degree of control which the hormones have over courtship, arousal, and copulation the sources of hormones have been removed by extirpating the gonads in animals of both sexes. Castration of the male, which results in the rapid disappearance of androgens from the system has effects on sexual behaviour which vary from species to species and to a surprising extent from individual to individual. There is usually some decline in the sexual responsiveness of the male, but copulatory activity may be sustained for a long period of time or even indefinitely. Stone [1927] castrated adult male rats, both with and without copulatory experience and found that whereas copulatory behaviour declined rather rapidly in some animals it persisted for many months in others. Preoperative copulatory experience did not significantly enhance postoperative sexual performance. He found that the first sexual response to be eliminated was ejaculation. Significant reductions in frequency of ejaculation followed removal of the testes after one week in cats [Rosenblatt and Aronson, 1958] and in rhesus monkeys after five weeks [Phoenix et al., 1973]. Hart [1968a] found that after three weeks the frequency of mating in dogs dropped to about half its preoperative level. It has been suggested that the persistence of mating behaviour in castrated animals, even if reduced, is maintained by adrenal androgens. This possibility has been ruled out by the finding that copulatory activity persists, even in animals which have been castrated and adrenalectomized [Beach, 1970; Bloch and Davidson, 1968].

A tentative explanation which has been advanced for the gradual decline of sexual activity following castration is that it is secondary to impairment of an animal's capacity for erection and ejaculation. It has been observed that castrated males in several species, including rats, guinea pigs, cats, and dogs exhibit intense pelvic thrusting but are unable to achieve intromission and ejaculation [Beach, 1970; Young, 1961]. Erection, intromission and ejaculation may be sources of sensory feedback which have a reinforcing effect on the voluntary components of copulatory behaviour, such that in the absence of this sensory feedback from the penis extinction of the behaviour occurs. In support of this hypothesis it has been found that section of the nerve tracts mediating sensory feedback from the penis is alone capable of reducing mating behaviour in cats [Aronson and Cooper, 1966, 1967, 1968] and rhesus monkeys [Herbert, 1973]. However, it has little effect on rats [Larsson and Sodersten, 1973].

Castration of the male before puberty in all mammalian species, includ-

ing man, severely impairs adult sexual responsiveness. This fact was capitalized on in some eastern cultures where eunuchs were used to guard the
harems of their rulers. However, Ford and Beach [1952] have observed
that animals castrated before puberty may display immature patterns of
sexual behaviour in adulthood although they do not show the full adult
mating pattern. It has been suggested that the experience of copulation
'marks' the neural tissue mediating sexual behaviour in such a way as to
free it from a dependence on the exciting effects of androgen. Rosenblatt
and Aronson [1958] found that very few castrated cats with no preoperative sexual experience achieved intromission with receptive females
but cats with prior experience continued mating for at least two weeks
following castration. However, as previously observed, Bloch and Davidson
[1968] found no such difference in postcastration sexual behaviour
between previously experienced and previously inexperienced rats.

Verification that any decline of sexual responsiveness following castration in adult guinea pigs is due to the absence of the priming effect of
androgens is shown by the finding that daily injections of testosterone
propionate (testosterone in a crystalline form) restores sexual activity to
its preoperative level in castrated guinea pigs.

It is very difficult to determine the degree of dependence of the sex
drive on hormonal levels in the human male as manipulations of the internal
hormonal environment by castration or hormone injection are confounded
with the psychological effect of these manipulations. It is probably because
of different expectancies that men who have been castrated for either
medical reasons or because they have committed sex crimes, report effects
ranging from rapid 'asexualization' to retention of sexual interest and
capacity over many years [Bremer, 1959].

In support of the proposition that testosterone influences arousability
in man it has been observed that there is a diminished incidence of spontaneous erection following castration or regression of the gonads, which is
restored by injections of testosterone [Yamamato and Seeman, 1960;
Bremer, 1959]. In clinical practice it is generally accepted that androgen
treatment increases potency in hypogonadal or castrated men [Lloyd,
1968]. However, it has been found that differences of as much as 100%
in blood plasma testosterone levels are not correlated with differences in
sexual activity [Kobayashi et al., 1966]. Also Ford and Beach [1952,
p. 48] cite a report by Tauber of men who were impotent, and supposed
themselves to be so because of a testosterone deficiency. When, following
assay, they were informed that their testosterone levels were quite normal
they promptly recovered their sexual competence.

With the exception of humans, removal of the ovaries in the female
almost invariably results in an immediate complete loss of sexual responsiveness. Species exhibiting this loss include mice [Wiesner and Mirskaia,
1930], rats [Nissen, 1929], guinea pigs [Hertz et al., 1937], and monkeys
[Ball, 1936]. That the change in sexual responsiveness is due to the
ceased production of sex hormones is indicated by the fact that subsequent
administration of oestrogen to ovariectomized animals restores sexual
behaviour. A complex synergistic relationship between oestrogen and
progesterone appears to exist. Injections of oestrogen alone have been
found to produce activity levels characteristic of the oestrous phase

[Young and Fish, 1945] and other signs of sexual arousal in the rat [Beach, 1942b], and an inclination to assume the mating posture in the cat [Whalen, 1963]. However, in neither case is receptivity to the male complete and it has been found that only when oestrogen injections are followed by progesterone injections is oestrous behaviour indistinguishable from that of a normal rat. Whalen [1966] hypothesizes that oestrogen merely acts to facilitate postural adjustments for copulation, having no effect on arousability *per se*, as oestrogen levels have no discernable effect on 'arousability' in species such as higher primates and humans which do not have special sexual postures. In contrast to the apparent complementary effects of oestrogen and progesterone acting together, in producing sexual receptivity, other observations have associated progesterone with the suppression of sexual receptivity in guinea pigs and macaques [Davidson, 1973] and have suggested that oestrogen is an erotic tranquillizer in humans [Money, 1970]. Tentative evidence that contraceptive pills with a high dosage of progesterone are associated with loss of libido in women taking them is suggestive that this agent reduces sexual arousability in humans [Grant and Mears, 1967]. Also Udry and Morris [1968] have raised the possibility that an apparent decrease in women's sex drive during the late luteal phase of the menstrual cycle is the result of progesterone secretion peaking at that time.

The reduced dependence of more highly evolved species on hormones is indicated by the fact that removal of the ovaries in humans does not usually result in loss of libido. Women given oestrogen, supposedly to maintain sexual desire following ovariectomy, have sometimes discontinued the treatment because it made no difference to their sexual drive and capacity for orgasm [Money, 1961a]. It has been suggested that testosterone is the libidinal hormone, even in women, and that testosterone secreted by the adrenal gland is the basis for the persistence of arousability in ovariectomized women. Loss of sexual drive has been reported following removal of the adrenal gland in women [Waxenburg *et al*., 1959]. However, these cases represent radical surgery on persons seriously ill with cancer so that there must be serious reservations about attributing the loss of libido to elimination of circulating testosterone alone. It has been claimed that administration of testosterone increases sexual responsiveness in women [Foss, 1951; Salmon and Leist, 1943], but Davidson [1973] surmises that this effect may have been secondary to testosterone induced growth of the clitoris with concomitant increase in sensitivity of the organ.

The neural control
of sexual behaviour

The direct control of sexual behaviour, influenced by the hormones, is mediated by the nervous system. It therefore follows that the critical hormones must exercise their influence by sensitizing the neural structures which organize sexual behaviour and its preliminaries.

We have already seen that early in development the hormones organize neural structures in the brain to give behaviour either a male or female bias and that these structures are in the anterior preoptic region of the hypothalamus (Figure 5.2). It appears that it is precisely these structures which are primed by circulating hormones in the adult animals, so that the appearance of a suitable mate triggers the pattern of behaviour which culminates in copulation.

The indispensability of the anterior preoptic region of the hypothalamus for the production of an integrated pattern of sexual behaviour is clearly established by lesion studies. Lesions of the area in male rats [Giantonio et al., 1970; Heimer and Larsson, 1966; Lisk, 1968], cats [Hart et al., 1973] or dogs [Hart, 1974a] either abolishes or markedly reduces copulatory attempts. Similarly placed lesions in female guinea pigs [Dey et al., 1940; Brookhart et al., 1940, 1941], cats and rabbits [Sawyer and Robinson, 1956; Sawyer, 1956, 1957] resulted in permanent anoestrus (failure to come on heat) and complete lack of sexual responsiveness.

It is a plausible suggestion that the disappearance of sexual activity following hypothalamic lesions is secondary to the disruption of hypothalamic control of sex hormone secretion by the pituitary gland. This possibility has been ruled out by the observation that oestrogen treatment fails to restore sexual responsiveness in lesioned females [Brookhart et al., 1940, 1941; Sawyer and Robinson, 1956], and that the lesions are not followed by any impairment of pituitary function [Sawyer and Robinson, 1956] or testicular atrophy [Soulairac and Soulairac, 1956]. Indeed Sawyer and Robinson [1956] found evidence that a more medial and posterior hypothalamic region regulated pituitary secretion of gonadotrophins as stimulation of this area in even anterior hypothalamus lesioned animals resulted in ovulation, while lesion of the same region resulted in permanent anoestrus which was reversible by oestrogen treatment.

Hart [1974a] observed that in male dogs, while castration only produced a gradual diminution of mating activity, despite the elimination of testosterone from the circulation within 24 h, anterior preoptic hypothalamus lesions produce an immediate abolition of copulatory behaviour. This finding seems to clearly support the assertion that the anterior preoptic hypothalamus has a vital direct role in the mediation of sexual behaviour.

Further supporting evidence comes from experiments in which electrical stimulation of the anterior preoptic hypothalamus has been found to dramatically facilitate mating behaviour in the male rat [Malsbury, 1971; Vaughan and Fisher, 1962; van Dis and Larsson, 1971]. Increased frequency of mounting oestrus females and a dramatically reduced period of refractoriness after ejaculation (from 5 min to 27 s) has been found. It has also been found that circumscribed lesions in the rostral midbrain reduce the inhibitory period following ejaculation, indicating that sexual refractoriness in the male may be imposed by inhibitory neural processes [Clark et al., 1975].

Finally the injection or implantation of sex hormones into the relevant hypothalamic regions confirms that the anterior preoptic hypothalamus is the location where hormones activate the neural structures organizing mating behaviour. The specific sensitivity of neurones in the anterior preoptic hypothalamus to testosterone is indicated by the fact that they show a high uptake of radioactively labelled testosterone [Pfaff, 1968; Sar and Stumpf, 1973]. The implantation of crystalline androgen (which diffuses

into the surrounding tissue over a long period] into the anterior hypothalamic region of castrated and sexually inactive male rats has been found
to evoke copulatory activity [see Davidson, 1972, pp. 83–87]. The possibility that the appearance of sexual activity is secondary to the growth
stimulating effect of the hormone on penile spines, mediating the sensitivity
of the organ, is discounted by the findings that ejaculatory patterns persist
for months or years after the disappearance of these spines [Aronson and
Cooper, 1967]. Hormonal treatment reinstating spine growth in castrated
animals, without activation of the brain, does nothing to restore sexual
behaviour [Beach and Westbrook, 1968].

Implantation of oestrogen in the anterior preoptic hypothalamic region
in the female produces oestrus behaviour in cats [Harris et al., 1958],
rats [Lisk, 1962] and rabbits [Palka and Sawyer, 1966], findings which
complete this documentation of the neuroendocrinological systems of the
brain which mediate sexual behaviour.

Spinal reflexes
in sexual behaviour

Whereas the anterior preoptic hypothalamus appears to be necessary for
the evocation of the full physiological and psychic concomitants of arousal
and of integrated patterns of sexual behaviour, some components of the
sexual response are organized at a spinal level. As early as 1900 Sherrington
observed that erection and ejaculation seemed to be mediated by spinal
reflexes. Since then the retention of reflexes involving erection and ejaculation following transection of the spinal cord have been reported in guinea
pigs [Bacq, 1931], cats [Dusser de Barenne and Koskoff, 1932], rats
[Hart, 1968b], dogs [Hart, 1967] and humans [Monro et al., 1948;
Talbot, 1955; Zeitlin et al., 1957]. Riddoch [1917] reported that after
recovery from spinal shock genital stimulation produced a coitus reflex
(erection and ejaculation) in human patients with completely transected
spinal cords. Money [1961a] found that 66% of a group of 500 patients
with section of the spinal cord were capable of erection and 20% capable
of coitus.

Hart [1974a] has presented evidence that even the sexual reflexes
organized at a spinal level are influenced by the level of circulating androgens. Following the elimination of androgen by castration there was a
decrease in the number of erections which could be evoked from male rats
with transected spinal cords. Administration of androgen to the same
animals restores their capacity to produce erection in response to genital
stimulation. The observation that the cutaneous sensitivity of the penis
was no less in castrated animals than normals [Cooper and Aronson,
1974] refuted the suggestion that the androgen promoted the appearance
of the spinal reflexes by enhancing the sensitivity of the penis. Furthermore, Hart and Haugen [1968] reported that spinal implantations of
testosterone propionate in male cats with transected spinal cords increased
sexual reflex activity without any evidence of androgenic stimulation of
sexual accessory organs.

Sensory stimuli and sexual arousal

So far emphasis has been placed on internal mechanisms mediating sexual receptivity, sexual arousal and the performance of the sexual act. For successful mating to occur the sexual arousal of a male and a female in proximity must be synchronized. This means that the readiness of prospective partners for sexual behaviour, achieved by hormonal priming, must be translated into mutual action via the external stimuli which each presents to the other. These stimuli permit mutual identification and promote mutual arousal.

In species low on the phylogenetic scale identification may occur solely on the basis of simple characteristics monitored through a single sensory channel. For instance, the courtship behaviour of the male three-spined stickleback is triggered solely by the swollen underbelly of a gravid female [Tinbergen, 1951]. The rigid dependence on this 'sign stimulus' means that another male stickleback that is fat from overfeeding, may be the target for sexual advances.

The mating behaviour of the male silkworm moth is regulated by the sense of smell. It can detect the scent exuded by the females at very great distances and the influence of this sensory channel is so dominant that the male will attempt to copulate with scent glands severed from their owner, in preference to a scentless but otherwise intact female [Kellogg, 1907].

Olfactory stimuli are employed to announce sexual readiness and attract members of the opposite sex at all levels on the phylogenetic scale, the chemicals upon which they are based being a variety of hormone called pheromones. A bitch on heat excretes a substance in her urine which is attractive to males. In human cultures natural odours are supplemented by manufactured perfumes intended to enhance the sexual attractiveness of both females and males.

More sensory stimuli come into play in the regulation of sexual behaviour as the phylogenetic scale is ascended. For instance in some species of frog the male will grasp any other male or female, receptive or unreceptive, on the basis of visual cues. Then auditory and tactile cues become important as other males and unresponsive females utter a warning croak which advises the aggressor to desist. A receptive female silently acquiesces in the male's grasp, and, being full of eggs ready for fertilization, presents a much fatter profile to encompass, which encourages the male to persist with his advances [Noble and Aronson, 1942].

Auditory stimuli in the form of mating calls are widely employed by male animals to announce their presence to nearby females and to excite them. Bull alligators bellow, porcupines whine, howler monkeys howl, baboons click, and birds sing. In the case of the macaque monkey the receptive female makes characteristic noises to arouse the male [see Ford and Beach, 1952, pp. 102-104].

In many species the visual stimulus pattern presented by one sex to the other may serve, not only for identification, but also as a 'sexual display' in competing with others for the attention of a member of the opposite sex. The male peacock competes for the attention of a female by displaying his extravagant plumage. Even in species which do not engage in conspicuous sexual displays, such as laboratory rats, dogs, and primates it has been observed that members of one sex differ considerably in their attractiveness to the other. It is hardly news to state that individual members of the human species differ in their sexual attractiveness, but it is interesting to note that the defining characteristics of female beauty, for instance, differ considerably from culture to culture [Ford and Beach, 1952, pp. 90–98] and even between different historical epochs.

In addition to responding to 'attractiveness' in the opposite sex the males of many species also respond to novelty. It has been observed in monkeys that with increasing familiarity the male requires increasing periods of foreplay before ejaculation is achieved. The visual, and possibly auditory stimuli which effect the initial attraction lose their arousing power and tactile contact becomes necessary for arousal to occur. However, if a new female partner is introduced the male proceeds quickly to ejaculation. In many mammalian species including monkeys, bulls, sheep, pigs, rats, and guinea pigs it has been observed that the introduction of a new partner or an increase in the number of partners freely available produces a reduction in the period of refractoriness between ejaculations [for review see Schein and Hale, 1965].

We have seen that for animals in the wild the distance receptors, vision, audition, and olfaction are important for males and females to identify and attract each other. However, when held in the close confines of a laboratory cage it has been shown that abolition of these senses is no impediment to mating in rabbits [Brooks, 1937] and rats [Beach, 1942a]. Beach concluded that no one modality was essential for the elicitation of sexual behaviour and that any modality conveying relevant information could sustain mating behaviour. In the albino rat he found that mating behaviour persisted even when all sensation had been abolished except tactile sensations from the face.

Surprisingly it has been found that elimination of sensation from the female genitalia does not change apparent sexual receptivity, or abolish copulatory behaviour in the female rabbit [Fee and Parks, 1930; Brooks, 1937], cat or rat [Ball, 1934]. These results should be interpreted cautiously as Whalen [1966] has presented evidence for a possible dissociation between the mechanisms mediating arousal and oestrogen primed mechanisms mediating postural adjustments for copulation, in the female. The operation of the latter mechanism alone may have been responsible for the copulation observed following the abolition of genital sensations, especially as degree of sexual arousal is more difficult to assess in the passive female. We have already noted that the elimination of sensory feedback from the penis in male cats [Aronson and Cooper, 1966, 1968] and rhesus monkeys [Herbert, 1973] leads to disorientated sexual behaviour and ultimately to reduced sexual activity.

Although copulation can occur in the absence of genital sensation, it appears that mutual genital stimulation is normally important for synchronizing sexual arousal in many primate and subprimate mammalian species. In primate species the male may engage in manual and oral investigation of the female genitalia and sometimes the female may manually stimulate the male. In subprimate mammals the male may engage in oral investigation and stimulation of the female's genitals, an act which has an important synchronizing function. The stimulation experienced by the female increases her sexual arousal, while simultaneously her sexual odours, experienced more intensely by the male during his investigations, increase his arousal.

In human societies there is a great deal of variation in the duration and type of sexual foreplay. In a few societies there is a bare minimum of sexual preliminaries. However, in most societies there is foreplay which may commence with grooming and proceed via stimulation of the female's breast to mutual genital stimulation for which both the hands and the mouth may be used [see Ford and Beach, 1952, Chapter 3]. This variety in human sexual behaviour underlines the supposition that the expression of the human sex drive occurs almost entirely through learned patterns of behaviour.

In addition to hormonal systems priming an animal for sexual activity we should note that the arousing stimuli presented by mates and the stimulation resulting from copulation, in turn feed back to the hormonal mechanisms regulating their operation [see Davidson, 1972 for discussion]. We have already seen that in a number of species, including cats, rabbits, ferrets, ground squirrels, and many birds, copulation or even just sexual arousal precipitates ovulation. Sexual arousal activates the hypothalamic mechanisms which command the anterior pituitary gland to produce LH, the hormone which brings about ovulation. Female pigeons may be induced to ovulate solely by observing a reflection of themselves in a mirror; the only known case of narcissism in endocrinology. Even in species where the female is considered to ovulate spontaneously, coming into heat may be hastened by the presence of a male, as when ewes are penned with a 'teaser' ram or vixens are continuously heckled by a dog fox.

In addition it has been shown that in male rats [Taleisnik *et al*., 1966] and rabbits [Saginor and Horton, 1968] copulation appears to stimulate the secretion of LH in the pituitary which leads to increased testosterone production. This sustains the sex drive and the appearance of the sexual organs. In ageing male rats copulation with ejaculation appears to reduce spontaneous atrophy of the reproductive system [Thomas and Neiman, 1968] thus supporting the assertion that 'sex is good for you'.

The neocortex, learning, and sexual behaviour

Beach [1947, 1952] has propagated the widely accepted doctrine that as mammalian brains become more highly evolved sexual behaviour is subject to progressively greater cortical control, with an accompanying reduction in dependence on hormones. In many less evolved mammalian species including rats, rabbits, guinea pigs, cats, and dogs the female continues to exhibit mating behaviour even after complete removal of the cerebral cortex [Beach, 1952, p. 257, 1970 edition]. However, in male cats [Beach *et al*., 1955] and male rats [Larsson, 1962, 1964] even ablation of restricted areas of the neocortex produces severe impairment of sexual behaviour. Some of the differences between the sexes may be due to the fact that the more active male is more affected by disruption of cortically located mechanisms concerned with perception and motor control.

In more highly evolved species than those mentioned survival is not possible in the absence of the cerebral cortex. Thus the degree of cortical control over sexual behaviour must be inferred from its apparent degree of freedom from dependence on hormones, and the extent to which it appears to be learned. In fact [Hart 1974b] presents some comparisons of the persistence of ejaculatory ability, following castration, which do not always support Beach's doctrine. The neocortex of the cat is more developed than that of the rat and that of the rhesus monkey is more developed than that of the cat. Consistent with Beach's doctrine it was observed that following elimination of the sex hormones by castration, retention of the ability to ejaculate persisted longer in cats than in rats and longer in monkeys than in cats. However, in the dog, whose neocortex is less developed than that of a rhesus monkey or even a cat, ejaculatory capacity survived castration longer than in either of these two supposedly more highly evolved species. Hart suggests that the sensitivity of neural tissue to androgens may vary from species to species independent of degree of brain development, in response to different selective pressures. He speculates that it is in the interest of social animals, such as dogs, for sexual behaviour and its con-comitant aggressive and scent marking behaviour to be maintained all the year round, independent of seasonal variation in hormone levels, in order to maintain the group structure. The feral relative of the domestic cat, on the other hand, is asocial and thus has no need of the accompaniments of sexual behaviour outside of the breeding season.

Circumscribed cortical lesions may increase sexual activity when made in certain locations, although abolishing or reducing it in others. The classical Kluver–Bucy syndrome [Kluver and Bucy, 1939], following destruction of the temporal lobe in monkeys and other animals, includes increased sexual activity and indiscriminate choice of sexual partners, which extends to partners of the same sex and of different species. This effect has since been more precisely associated with destruction of the amygdala [Schreiner and Kling, 1953]. In human patients it has been observed that a reduced sexual drive is associated with epilepsy stemming from a focus in the temporal lobe [Gastaut and Collomb, 1954], while hypersexuality follows removal of the temporal lobe [Terzian and Dalle Oré, 1955; Blumer and Walker, 1967]. It has been suggested [Gloor, 1960] that the amygdaloid nucleus in the temporal lobe is a funnel for neocortical influences on subcortical mechanisms mediating the arousal of drives. The evidence that both hypo- and hypersexual behaviour can be produced by differently located cortical lesions suggests that different cortical structures have the capacity for either exciting or inhibiting the lower mechanisms mediating sexual arousal. Which occurs depends on other influences, such as learning.

The degree of development of the neocortex is considered to be associa-ted with the contribution which learning makes to an animal's behaviour repertoire. The dependence of the appearance of competent patterns of adult sexual behaviour on learning derived from social contact has been investigated in several different species. Beach [1958] found that rearing rats in isolation had no obvious effects on their postpubertal ability to copulate, although Zimbarbo [1958] found that isolation reared male rats were slower to mount a receptive female and achieved fewer intromissions and ejaculations. It should be remembered that isolation rearing has been shown to have a general retarding effect on behaviour and even on the development of the brain [Rosenzweig et al., 1968], which is confounded with any specific effects on sexual behaviour. Isolation reared male guinea pigs show excitement when presented with receptive females, but their attempts to mount them are disorientated, often being made at the side or head end [Valenstein and Young, 1955; Valenstein et al., 1955]. Rosenblatt [1965] reported that isolation reared male cats do not even attempt to mate. Harlow [1962] observed that while isolation reared male monkeys made disorientated and incompetent attempts to mount receptive females, isolation reared females tended to aggressively repulse the advances of an experienced male and failed to mate. Both Harlow and Rosenblatt observe that the young of commonly studied mammalian species engage in activity that is clearly a precursor for adult sexual behaviour. The evidence suggests that although some of the components of sexual behaviour may be innate, their rehearsal in a social context is necessary to produce an integrated pattern in adulthood.

In human cultures preadolescent children sometimes engage in play which can be construed as rehearsal for adult sexual behaviour, when such play is not taboo. Anecdotal evidence affirms that humans who have received no instruction in the mechanics of coitus may be unable to accomplish it until they have been told how it is done. The great variety of human sexual behaviour, both between and within cultures, testifies to the strong influence of learning on its pattern, usually based on cultural norms. Apart from being the only species which copulates face-to-face—in all other mammalian species the male approaches the female from behind—humans are almost alone in using a variety of different coital positions. Only higher primates, such as chimpanzees, are comparable to man in exhibiting individualistic patterns of mating and these are species which also appear to have to learn the appropriate pattern of adult sexual behaviour in a social context.

Aspects of sexuality peculiar to man

We have seen that human sexuality is differentiated from that of lower animals by its greater independence from hormonal control and by the fact that it is greatly influenced by experience. Both of these differences suggest a greater involvement of the cerebral cortex in sexual arousal and sexual action. Some researchers postulate a clearly demarcated cognitive component to human sexuality [e.g. Money, 1965]. This is evident in autonomously generated fantasies which produce sexual arousal. Such fantasies may be initiated or supplemented by pictorial or narrative material with a strong sexual content, a form of stimulus which has been found to be more effective in producing arousal in men than in women

[Money, 1970]. Money [1965] has observed that sexual fantasies, complete with all the concomitant feelings of sexual arousal, have been reported by human patients with severed spinal cords and thus complete absence of sensation from the genitals. Furthermore male patients who have had to have their penes removed and a female patient who had to have her vulva, labia and clitoris removed all reported the retention of the capacity for both sexual arousal and orgasm [Money, 1965]. These cases indicate that erotic cognitions can occur independently of sensations from the primary erogenous zones and supports the argument that human eroticism is to a large extent located in the cerebral cortex.

Money [1965] argues that sexual fantasies are cognitive rehearsals for sexual behaviour. In the child and adolescent he suggests that they play an important part in the development of the individual's gender role, as a male or female, and the individual's sexual predilection as a heterosexual or homosexual.

The sexuality of the human female is perhaps more sharply differentiated from that of lower animals than that of the human male. The undiminished persistence of the sex drive after ovariectomy, in the human female, is unique amongst mammalian species. The human female also appears to be unique in her capacity to experience orgasm, an event which is experienced by the males of all mammalian species, for whom it is clearly signalled by the occurrence of ejaculation. Ejaculation is not a part of a woman's orgasmic response but a number of other physiological responses which occur during coitus reach one or more distinct peaks to corroborate the subjective report of orgasm or orgasms [Masters and Johnson, 1965]. These responses which peak during orgasm include increased respiration, acceleration of the heart rate (see Figure 5.3 (i)) and spasmodic muscle contractions which include contractions of the uterus in a manner analogous to those during childbirth. In lower species, such as the dog, it has been found that the heart rate of the female increases and reaches a plateau during intromission (see Figure 5.3 (ii)), indicating the achievement of a 'plateau' of sexual arousal, but that there is no distinct peak to indicate the achievement of an orgasm [Ford and Beach, 1952, pp. 261-262]. Masters and Johnson [1965] observe that the human female's orgasmic response is highly variable and Ford and Beach [1952] claim that many women actually have to learn to recognize their orgasmic peak because it is not always so clearly demarcated as that of the male; further evidence for cortical involvement in sexual cognitions. Ford and Beach [1952, p. 33] observe that some women never experience orgasm. The repressive mores of certain societies and the deficient technique of the male may conspire against a woman achieving orgasm. On the other hand Masters and Johnson [1965] note that if a woman receives prolonged sexual stimulation she may be able to achieve a series of orgasms without ever descending from the 'plateau' stage of sexual arousal. Men experience a distinct refractory phase following orgasm which denies them the benefit of multiple orgasms. Ford and Beach [1952, p. 32] have speculated that the occurrence of a distinct orgasm in the human female, alone among species, is a result of the face-to-face coital position, unique to humans, with its consequent stimulation of the highly sensitive clitoris.

The large topic of human sexuality has been treated in detail elsewhere

Figure 5.3
Physiological changes
during copulation in
humans and dogs:

(i) Graphs of changes in
pulse rate in a man
and a woman during
sexual intercourse.

From Boas, E. P., and
Goldschmidt, E. F.
(1932) *The heart rate.*
Reproduced by
permission of Charles
C. Thomas, publisher,
Springfield, Illinois.

(ii) Graphs of changes
in blood pressure in a
male and female dog
just before, during
and after copulation.

From Ford, C. S., and
Beach, F. A. (1951)
*Patterns of sexual
behaviour.* © 1951
Clellan Stearns Ford
and Frank Ambrose
Beach. Reproduced
by permission of
Harper and Row,
publishers

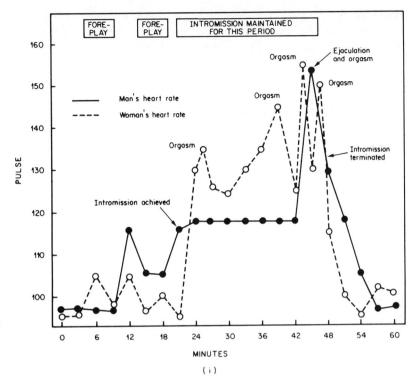

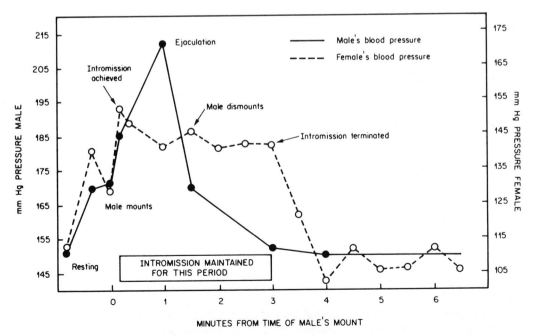

[Ford and Beach, 1952; Kinsey *et al.*, 1948, 1953; Masters and Johnson, 1966] and the brief comments in this chapter are only intended to give some signposts to the breadth, subtlety, and complexity of this enigmatic topic.

Maternal behaviour

As the phylogenetic scale is ascended the young of species are dependent on one or both parents for an increasing proportion of their lifespan. This dependence requires that the mother exhibit maternal behaviour as a follow through from courtship and mating. Aspects of maternal behaviour would appear to be sensitized by hormonal influences but not as dependent on them as mating behaviour. Rosenblatt [1967] observed that female rats with their ovaries or even pituitary glands removed would still exhibit maternal behaviour, though with a two week latency, after being presented with pups. Whereas only about 50% of primiparous (giving birth for the first time) rats which have had their ovaries removed just prior to giving birth will accept and rear their pups, 100% of similarly ovariectomized rats with previous maternal experience will satisfactorily rear their pups. Thus, as in the case of mating, experience of maternal behaviour reduces its dependence on hormones. It has been demonstrated that hormones can trigger neural circuits which organize maternal behaviour. Fisher [1964] claims that injection of female sex hormones into the medial preoptic nucleus of the hypothalamus produces nest building, retrieval of scattered pups and other aspects of maternal behaviour, not just in females, but in males as well. Also the implantation of progesterone in the preoptic nuclei or supraoptic decussation in either female or male ring doves produces incubation behaviour if the creatures are presented with eggs and a nest. Evidence from lesion experiments concerning the hypothalamic circuits organizing maternal behaviour does not appear to be available.

The cortex appears to be important for maternal behaviour as medial cortical lesions in rats impair nest building, suckling, and retrieval of the young [Stamm, 1955]. Similar findings have been made following lesions of the dorsal hippocampus [Kimble *et al.*, 1967], suggesting that limbic structures may have a role in organizing maternal behaviour.

Whereas the components of parental behaviour appear to be innate in lower mammalian species, more highly evolved creatures, such as monkeys, seem to require an appropriate pattern of infant social experience for adequate parental behaviour to emerge in adulthood. Harlow [1962] has observed that isolation reared female monkeys, when they can be persuaded to mate, neglect their offspring and treat them cruelly. It has been asserted that in human societies maternal deprivation, which is one step away from isolation rearing, is part of a vicious process whereby poor social adjustment and incapacity to show normal parental care and affection perpetuates itself from generation to generation within families [Bowlby, 1951; Rutter, 1972].

For parental behaviour to be successful the young must show a positive valence towards their parents. The behaviourists have always supposed that the attachment of the young to their parents arises because the parents acquire secondary reinforcing properties by virtue of their role in satisfying the child's primary needs. Lorenz [1952] and other ethologists maintain that maternal attachment is innate and have elaborated on the phenomenon of 'imprinting', seen in lower animals, in which newly born or hatched animals attach themselves to the first moving object which they see and thenceforth regard it as mother. In this manner ethologists themselves have come to be regarded as mother by broods of ducklings! Harlow [1962] demonstrated that when infant monkeys were given a choice between two surrogate mothers, both inanimate, they preferred to cling to one covered in soft terry towlling to one constructed of hard wire but yielding a supply of food. Thus it appears that affection between mother and child may be an emotion which is uncontaminated by the expectation of a material pay off.

Summary and conclusions

We have seen that in all species the foundation of reproductive behaviour is hormonal. Hormones initiate the anatomical differentiation of the sexes into male and female, each with their characteristic and complementary generative organs. Hormones organize the neural structures destined to mediate sexual behaviour so that they produce the appropriate sex specific behaviour pattern. Hormones bring the individual to sexual maturity, organize the fertility cycle in the female and prime both sexes for arousal by the appropriate stimuli. Hormones stimulate the patterns of behaviour associated with the feeding care and shelter of the young. The hormones are not alone responsible for all of these phenomena. In the instance of the fertility cycle, the sequence in which the hormones are released is a function of the control of the secretion of pituitary hormones by the hypothalamus and feedback control of the hypothalamus by ovarian hormones. In courting behaviour, mating behaviour and maternal behaviour hormones sensitize the neural structures which mediate the behaviour when the animal is presented with the appropriate stimuli from a member of the opposite sex.

Hormonal control of reproductive behaviour is rigid in less highly evolved species. However, in more highly evolved species the capacity for sexual arousal and copulation attains some autonomy from hormonal influences in adulthood, particularly following some initial sexual experience. In the most highly evolved species, particularly man, the primitive motivational systems at the base of the brain would appear to provide only an initial impetus to sexual behaviour. Not only does adult sexual capacity achieve partial independence from hormonal influences but the circumstances and techniques for inducing sexual arousal and the manner of copulation appear to be almost totally a function of learning and thus a reflection of the practice of specific cultures.

160

Chapter
six

Responding
to emergencies:
emotion

Introduction

In addition to the routine maintenance of its internal equilibrium, survival requires that an animal periodically mobilizes its adaptive resources to cope with an emergency. The many and varied emergencies which species face include attacks by predators, combative competition with their own species for mates, territory, or leadership, exposure to painful stimuli, and dangers such as those of fire or drowning. To deal with such emergencies the brain must be able to make a rapid evaulation of a dangerous situation and quickly organize an adaptive response, usually 'fight' or 'flight'. Concomitantly a creature's energy resources must be fully mobilized in order to sustain the intense muscular effort likely to be required.

An organism's response to emergencies has four primary aspects. Firstly, there is the experiential aspect which, from the common usage of the term, leads us to label our response to an emergency and its associated subjective experience as an emotion. In emergencies we may label our experiences as fear or rage. Experientially human emotions encompass, not only the acute tensions of fear and anger, but also the euphoria of pleasurable excitement, the motive paralysis of depression, the pleasurable tensionlessness of relaxation and many other states of emotion. Thus one-dimension upon which emotions appear to be distributed is active–passive. Some theories of emotion postulate reciprocally opposing mechanisms mediating the balance between activity and passivity in emotional tone [e.g. Gellhorn, 1968].

Secondly, intense emotion is quickly communicated, both within and between species by its expressive aspects, characteristic facial expressions, posture and vocalizations. The enraged cat bares its teeth, flattens its ears, arches its back, erects its fur and hisses. Thirdly, the outward expression of an animal's emotional state is accompanied or followed by emotional behaviour which may simply be running away, or may be fight. Fighting, particularly between members of the same species, in suprimate mammals often involves the production of relatively stereotyped innate response patterns which have the appearance of a ritual [Lorenz, 1966]. This is particularly evident in lowly creatures, such as the stickleback, whose territorial aggression is evoked by the sign stimulus presented by the red underbelly of another male intruding on his patch. At the boundary of his domaine the defending male stickleback challenges any intending intruder with a nose-down threat posture. When stags fight during the rutting season they meet head-on and lock antlers, but never attack the flanks of their antagonists, where their antlers would cause mortal wounds. This illustrates the restrained, ritualistic nature of fighting between con-species. Even in inter-species predatory aggression it has been observed both that cats kill rats, and rats kill mice with a stereotyped bite through the back of the neck [quoted in Moyer, 1971].

The occurrence and intensity of our experience and expression of emotion is a function of an underlying pattern or arousal of brain and body, the fourth aspect of emotion. This primes the organism to make a fast and vigorous response in an emergency. The somatic response has many components, several of them generating sensations which are an integral part of our experience of an emotion. We feel a dry mouth, our heart 'pounds', we breathe hard, we feel 'butterflies in the stomach' and our limbs may tremble. In the classical James–Lange theory of emotion [James, 1884] it was supposed that emotion was simply and solely the feeling of the bodily changes which followed the perception of an exciting fact and that without these feelings there would be no emotion.

As arousal of the brain and body is such a fundamental characteristic of an organism's response to emergencies its nature and significance should be understood before proceeding to the discussion of mechanisms mediating specific patterns of behaviour in emotion.

Arousal of the brain

All information about the external environment (and much about the internal environment is transmitted to the brain along the afferent nerve tracts from the sense receptors. Some of this information is of no significance to the animal and is filtered out before it reaches the central information processor (see Chapter 11). Other information is either novel, therefore requiring evaluation for its possible significance, or may indicate that a known danger is present. In these instances it is essential that the information processing mechanisms in the brain are operating at maximum efficiency and that the relevant signals are given priority in the allocation of information processing capacity to different signal sources (see Chapter 11).

The efficiency with which our brain can process information is clearly a function of our state of arousal; whether we are asleep, awake but drowsy or wide awake and alert. Our state of behavioural arousal and alertness is a function of the responsiveness of our cerebral cortex to incoming sensory information. This is usually reflected in the degree of activation of the scalp EEG (electrical activity of the brain; see Chapter 3) which is measured in terms of the extent to which slow, high voltage activity is replaced by fast, low voltage activity. The level of cortical arousal is continuously regulated by a structure in the brainstem called the brainstem reticular formation (BSRF) or reticular arousal system (RAS) (see Chapters 7 and 8; Figure 7.1). This structure has neural projections to all parts of the cortex and is indispensable for the maintenance of wakefulness, which it achieves by sending a continuous 'tonic' barrage of impulses to the cortex during waking hours. In addition all of the sensory pathways have branching fibres which synapse in the RAS so that a signal in any one sensory modality can activate this mechanism. Thus, if cortical arousal is below its optimum a danger signal, or novel or intense stimulus in any one sense modality will activate the RAS which will, in turn, 'ring alarm bells' throughout the cerebral cortex whose operational efficiency in all departments is rapidly raised to a high level. The efficacy of the RAS in improving the efficiency of our cortical information processing mechanisms is clearly documented in an experiment by Fuster [1958] on monkeys. He trained monkeys to discriminate between tachistoscopically displayed geometrical shapes which announced the availability of a food reward and ones which did not. They had to respond by reaching for the food reward through a flap beneath the correct shape. Opening the flap operated a microswitch which stopped a timer, started when the stimulus was tachistoscopically displayed. When he stimulated the RAS of monkeys through chronically implanted electrodes during performance of the task, Fuster found that their response times were faster and their percentage of incorrect responses fewer than when the monkeys performed without the stimulation.

Lindsley [1951, 1970] has advanced an 'activation' theory of emotion in which the RAS plays a central role. He argued that the organism is in a continuous state of emotional flux, in contrast to the view that emotions are states which are either 'on' or 'off'. Intense emotion merely reflects the highest levels of arousal. Not only does the RAS produce the cortical activation seen in emotion, but also the somatic arousal, whose neural mechanisms are located in the zone where the RAS merges with the hypothalamus. While Lindsley's activation theory fails to account for the diversity of emotions and may have overemphasized the importance of the RAS, there is no doubt that display of emotion is impossible without activation of the system described by Lindsley. We will see later in the chapter that it seems likely that the RAS modulates the sensitivity of mechanisms mediating the patterns of response peculiar to specific emotions.

Somatic arousal

Once cortical arousal has led to assessment of the arousing stimulus as dangerous, vigorous muscular action, 'fight' or 'flight', is likely to be required as a sequel to cope with the 'emergency'. The somatic arousal observed in emotion would appear to be an adaptive preparation for intense muscular effort. This suggestion was first made by Cannon [1915] in his 'emergency function' theory of emotion, which, despite attempts to refute it, has survived and is still being elaborated on [see Mason, 1972].

Somatic arousal is mediated by the sympathetic branch of the autonomic nervous system. Its influence on body organs innervated is generally to antagonize the influence of the parasympathetic nervous system and by so doing generate increased function in those organs.

The fuel (blood sugar) and oxygen necessary for energy metabolism in the muscles is carried in the bloodstream. Thus one of the primary manifestations of somatic arousal is an increase in heart rate, together with a deeper heart beat. This results in blood being pumped to the muscles at a greater rate. The distribution of blood to the muscles and to the brain is further assisted by dilation of the blood vessels within these organs, as well as by withdrawal of blood from other irrelevant organs, such as the stomach, by constriction of the blood vessels supplying them. Oxygenation of the blood is improved by deeper and faster respiration and by dilation of the bronchioli of the lungs.

Explicit evidence of preparation for action in emotional arousal is seen in increased muscle tone, which may be so great as to produce tremor.

Digestion is concerned with long term homeostatic regulation of the body and is not relevant to short-lived periods of intense activity. Thus, in fear the digestive functions cease, reflected in reduced secretion of saliva and of digestive juices. The former is responsible for the sensation of a dry mouth. Blood is withdrawn from the stomach wall and stomach motility ceases, with a complete loss of muscle tone in the stomach walls, which may lead to a sensation of 'butterflies' or nausea, or may result in actual vomiting. However, in the lower intestine fear produces increased motility which may be reflected in diarrhoea or, in extreme cases, involuntary voiding of the bowels.

In anger, paradoxically, the stomach shows the opposite response of hyperfunction, with increased secretion of digestive juices, increased supply of blood to the stomach wall and increased motility. This response has been noted in a few individuals who have had to have stomach fistulas (direct openings into the stomach), following accidents, which have permitted direct observation of the stomach wall. Prolonged hyperfunction of the stomach leads to bleeding, increased pain sensitivity of the stomach wall and eventually to ulceration [Wolf and Wolf, 1947].

Graham [1972] reviews the evidence that suppressed hostility is an important factor in the genesis of stomach ulcers. The functional significance of increased stomach activity in aggressive states is an enigma, unless one supposes that overlapping neural substrate mediates both non-predatory and predatory aggression, in which case the stomach hyperfunction can be seen as a preparation for the eating which normally follows predation.

Piloerection, erection of the body hair or fur, is a universal response in emotional arousal and in longer haired animals deters antagonists by enhancing the apparent size and ferocity of the responder. Dilation of the pupil of the eye is another response which is observed and may be effective in improving the efficiency of vision. Of great interest to psychologists is the easily recorded electrodermal response, a change in the electrical properties of the skin, usually recorded as a change in resistance. Although the question of its origin is still controversial, the evidence favours the hypothesis that the lowering of skin resistance seen in emotional arousal is largely attributable to sudomotor (sweat gland) activity [Edelberg, 1972]. Sweating may occur as a concomitant of emotional arousal to dissipate the heat likely to be generated in the event of intense muscular activity.

Arousal of the pituitary – adrenal axis

In addition to the bodily changes outlined, alarming situations provoke marked endocrine arousal reflected in a radically changed pattern of secretory activity by the pituitary–adrenal axis (see Figure 2.21). The best known response is the secretion of adrenalin and noradrenalin by the medulla of the adrenal gland under the excitatory influence of its sympathetic innervation. Noradrenalin is the neurotransmitter substance active at the neuromuscular junctions where postganglionic sympathetic fibres excite the organs which they innervate. Therefore the consequence of these junctions being bathed in the noradrenalin which has been released into the bloodstream is to potentiate and prolong the effects of sympathetic activation.

Adrenalin promotes the conversion of glycogen, an inert form of sugar stored in the liver, into its active form, glucose. This is the classical concomitant of emotional arousal which Cannon [1915, 1920] underlined as a fundamental component of the preparation for muscular action, stating that 'since the fear emotion and the anger emotion are, in wild life, likely to be followed by activities (running or fighting) which require contraction of great muscular masses in supreme and prolonged struggle, a mobilization of sugar in the blood might be of signal service to the labouring muscles'. Cannon [1915, 1920] actually inferred the release of adrenalin in emotional arousal from the glycosuria (high level of sugar in the urine) which he observed variously in frightened cats, football players excited about an important match and medical students anxious about impending examinations. Another effect of adrenalin which Cannon noted was an increase in the coagulative properties of the blood, an effect likely to be useful in the event of injury.

Mason [1972] has reviewed more recent studies in which the elevation of adrenalin has been measured directly in the urine or the blood, during or following emotional arousal. Elevated adrenalin and noradrenalin levels have been found in men following acrobatic flight in an aircraft and in viewers of arousing films, irrespective of whether arousal was aggressive, anxious, or sexual. Women filing clerks were found to secrete more adrenalin and noradrenalin under the pressure of piece work than when paid an hourly rate. Adrenalin secretion was found to be correlated with work load in operators at a telephone exchange. In students about to take an examination adrenalin secretion was found to be correlated with self-rated anxiety.

Ax [1953] and Funkenstein [1955] have argued that fear and anger are differentiated by the secretion of adrenalin in the former case and noradrenalin in the latter case. Funkenstein [1955] cites observations that aggressive animals, such as the lion, have a predominance of noradrenalin in their adrenal gland, while animals, such as the rabbit, which depend on flight for survival, and animals living very social lives, have a high ratio of adrenalin to noradrenalin. In a study of sportsmen, just prior to competition, cited by Mason [1972], individuals who showed active, aggressive emotional arousal had elevated noradrenalin levels, while those whose emotional arousal was tense and anxious, but passive, had elevated adrenalin levels. Reis and Gunne [1965] found that amygdaloid stimulation producing rage also produced a significant rise in endogenous levels of noradrenalin in the forebrain. Furthermore, Reis and Fuxe [1969] found that whereas drugs which inhibited noradrenalin blocked rage, those that potentiated it facilitated rage. These two findings not only document the association of noradrenalin and rage but further suggest that it may be a specific transmitter substance in neural circuits mediating aggression.

However, in many experiments it has been found that emotional arousal results in the elevation of both adrenalin and noradrenalin levels, a finding which is inconsistent with the idea of a differential response, unless one supposes that in many cases of emotional arousal the emotions aroused are 'mixed'.

A further prominent psychoendocrine response in emotional arousal is the conjoint response of the anterior pituitary gland and adrenal cortex, under the control of the hypothalamus. Arousing stimuli activate a pre-optic hypothalamic centre to secrete a releasing substance. This is carried in the hypophyseal–portal blood system to the anterior pituitary, where it triggers the secretion of adrenocorticotrophic hormone (ACTH). ACTH is transported in the bloodstream to the adrenal cortex where it promotes growth and stimulates the secretion of hydrocorticosteroid hormones such as 17-OHCS. The effects of frequent or sustained activation of this system are seen in enlargement of the adrenal gland such as is found in animals subject to population stress, and in wild animals compared with those kept in a laboratory.

Among the functions of the hydrocorticosteroid hormones are the release of sugar from stores in free fatty acids and the promotion of anaerobic (without oxygen) energy metabolism, which is necessary to maintain vigorous muscular effort, functions which are clearly consistent with the 'emergency function' theory of emotion.

Again, Mason [1972] has reviewed studies of hydrocorticosteroid release during emotional arousal. In animals, elevation of 17-OHCS levels has been found during avoidance conditioning, exposure to novel stimuli, handling by experimenters, constriction in a restraining chair, and inter-cage transfer. In humans increased 17-OHCS secretion has been found in test pilots during flight, in drivers in the Indianapolis 500 motor race, in soldiers before a battle, in students before an examination, and in patients before an operation. It has even been shown that puncture of a vein to obtain a blood sample on which to make 17-OHCS measurements, itself causes elevated 17-OHCS, an indication of the sensitivity of the response and of the methodological rigour required in experiments in which changes in levels of secretion are measured.

Generally the hydrocorticosteroid response is found to be greater during the anticipation of painful or unpleasant stimuli than during their actual occurrence. This seems to be consistent with the subjective experience of greater psychological discomfort while uncertain about, or waiting for an unpleasant event. Also the 17-OHCS response is particularly intense when a subject is stressed by having to work hard at a difficult task to forestall aversive stimuli. In the laboratory a typical example would be to require an animal to press a lever to forestall frequent electric shocks. In human society the social and economic pressure to climb up or retain one's position in the managerial hierarchy of a highly competitive organization might be considered such a situation.

17-OHCS levels have been studied in psychiatric patients and found to be persistently elevated in anxiety neurotics. They are elevated in schizophrenics during periods of intense affective arousal, but not during periods of profound psychotic withdrawal. In depressive patients elevated 17-OHCS only appears to occur when there is intense awareness of the illness and an attempt to struggle against the symptoms.

Mason [1972] argues that the psychoendocrine response in emotional arousal is a coherent pattern with interaction between all the elements. The hormones appear to work together rather than independently. Each hormone affects more than one function (multipotency) and each function is regulated by more than one hormone. Adrenalin releases glucose from the liver and releases sugar from free fatty acids as well as the other effects discussed. Hydrocorticosteroids and growth hormone act synergistically with adrenalin to potentiate the release of free fatty acids, while insulin antagonizes the effect of adrenalin by promoting the conversion of sugar to fats and glycogen.

Mason has conducted a multiple hormone assay in monkeys during a shock avoidance task (lever pressing to avoid periodic electric shocks) prolonged over three days and during a three day recovery period. He has characterized the pattern of psychoendocrine activity as a catabolic-anabolic sequence. During the catabolic phase hormones are produced which release energy sources from store and promote rapid energy metabolism for periods of intense effort. During the succeeding anabolic phase, after the emergency has passed, the pattern of hormone release changes to one which promotes replenishment of depleted energy stores while regulating energy metabolism to the optimum required for survival in a non-aroused state.

During the catabolic phase, in addition to the release of adrenalin, noradrenalin and the corticosteroids there is release of thyroid hormone, which increases oxidative metabolism, and growth hormone which further potentiates the release of sugar from glycogen and fat. Conversely there is depressed secretion of the anabolic hormones insulin, testosterone and oestrogen, which promote the conversion of energy sources from their active to their stored forms. In the recovery phase the elevated catabolic hormones return to their normal levels, though at different rates, while the anabolic hormone levels are elevated. Insulin facilitates the entry of glucose into the cells, promotes the formation of fat and glycogen and stimulates protein synthesis. Testosterone promotes the synthesis of protein in the muscles and oestrogen probably promotes the synthesis of fat. Thus this co-ordinated pattern of endocrine activity nicely regulates the relationship between the varying demands of the environment on the organism and the organism's preparedness to meet these demands.

Objections to the 'emergency function' theory of emotion

The psychoendocrine response in emotional arousal, on which Mason [1972] has elaborated in some detail is entirely consistent with Cannon's 'emergency function' theory of emotion, advanced more than half a century earlier. Mason re-affirms its essential validity. However, there are some challenges to the theory which should be dealt with. The first objection is that in contemporary human societies intense muscular activity in 'fight' or 'flight' is a relatively rare sequel to emotional arousal. However, the theory has never supposed that violent muscular activity is an inevitable consequence of emotional arousal, merely that such arousal is a preparation for muscular activity, should it be required. Unlike other need serving mechanisms such as hunger, somatic arousal is a response to anticipated need, rather than a need which already exists. In our evolution the adaptive value of emotional arousal stemmed from the high probability that vigorous action would be required following the evoking stimulus. In contemporary human societies social and cultural evolution has reduced the appropriateness of a violent response to stimuli evoking emotional arousal. Thus for humans, the adaptive value of the response has been devalued by environmental changes, although without detracting from its original functional significance.

Another objection to the 'emergency function' theory of emotion is that extremes of arousal lead to a disorganization of behaviour patterns, which is the opposite of adaptive. Thus the relationship between arousal and efficiency of behaviour is represented graphically as an inverted U-shaped curve on which best performance can be seen to occur at an optimum level of arousal, not at a maximum [see Broadhurst, 1957]. The disorganizing effect of extreme arousal may merely reflect the fact that the mechanism is overfunctioning because it is experiencing operating conditions outside the range of those which occurred sufficiently frequently to influence its evolution. Individual differences in proneness to disorganizing arousal may reflect a combination of genetic predisposition modulated by pattern of life experience (see Chapter 9). The logic of evolution leads one to expect that each evolved mechanism will have limits, drawn by the circumstances of its evolution, and outside of which it will break down.

Objections to the notion of generalized arousal

In the discussion so far it has been implied, with only a few exceptions, that there is a pattern of arousal which is common to all emotions, and within which all the indices are correlated. Thus, arousal theorists have relied on single measures, such as the galvanic skin response, as an indication of the general level of arousal, likely to be reflected in all other measures [e.g. see Lindsley, 1951]. Lacy [1967; see also Lacy and Lacey,

1970] has challenged this assumption, observing that arousal can be partitioned into three major components, cortical, autonomic, and behavioural, and that these are not invariably correlated. He reviews the evidence that pharmacological manipulations and lesions can produce animals in which cortical arousal coexists with behavioural sleep or vice versa. This may be due to the artificial separation of systems which normally act in concert. There still remains the perfectly natural instance of paradoxical sleep. In other respects the deepest phase of sleep, this is accompanied by an EEG characteristic of alert wakefulness. In Chapter 8 it is argued that during this period there exists the endogenously generated consciousness of dreams, which is consistent with cortical arousal.

In addition Lacey [1967] observes that increased blood pressure (an inevitable concomitant of the increased cardiovascular activity in emotional arousal) actually antagonizes cortical arousal. Pressure receptors in the carotid sinus, a distended segment of the carotid artery in the neck, discharge into a section of the reticular formation which inhibits cortical arousal. Intense activation of the pressure receptors of the carotid sinus by strong pressure on the neck has such a powerful inhibitory influence on the cortex as to rapidly render a person unconscious. Lacey suggests that this pressure receptive system may provide negative feedback, which prevents a runaway arousal response that might ultimately be counterproductive to survival.

Lacey [1967] reports that during close attention to the environment for an expected stimulus there is a deceleration, rather than an acceleration, of heart rate, which is associated with increased cortical arousal. The heart rate accelerates when action follows evaluation of the stimulus. This effect may reflect a hitherto unreported phase in the pattern of response to emergencies. An initial brief phase of high cortical arousal may serve for identification and evaluation of threatening stimuli, while a succeeding phase of high somatic arousal, with reduced cortical arousal, may facilitate a vigorous response requiring little further cortical involvement.

Lacey's observations provide a caution against adopting an over simplified view of the brain's response systems but do not detract from the essential validity of the hypothesis concerning the functional significance of arousal. Furthermore, Lacey's findings provide only a very limited picture of the differentiation of emotions by specific arousal patterns.

Differentiation of the emotions

The approach to emotion through the study of generalized cortical and somatic arousal has given us little data bearing on the clear differentiation of emotions by behaviour and subjective experience. Those who argue, following the tradition of James [1884] and Lange [1885], that the visceral sensations generated during emotional arousal are a primary feature in the subjective experience, maintain that the emotions are differentiated by our cognitions of the external events responsible for our arousal. If our arousal follows an insult we label it anger, if it follows a suspicious noise in the night we label it fear. The implication of this view is that the neural substrate underlying the differentiation of our emotions is largely cortical. It occurs in the locations where environmental data is probably evaluated, and integrated with any data about visceral events. Prominent protagonists of 'cognitive theories' of emotion are Schachter and Singer [1962] and Gellhorn [1968], whose views will be discussed later in the chapter.

The contrary view to that of the cognitive theorists, following in the tradition of Cannon's 'thalamic process' theory, is that different emotions are mediated by separate and distinct subcortical neural circuits which organize a pattern of expression and behaviour, if not somatic arousal, peculiar to themselves and which generate the characteristic subjective experience. We have seen that an armoury of techniques is available for the investigation of possible localization of function in neural masses and we will now look at their application to delineating the neural structures mediating emotion.

The neural structures mediating emotion

The earliest evidence suggested that the mechanisms mediating rage were located in the brainstem as Goltz [1892] observed that decerebrate dogs would exhibit rage responses to stimuli which failed to elicit such responses in intact animals. This finding was confirmed by Woodworth and Sherrington [1904], at Liverpool University, who described a 'pseudoaffective reflex', elicited by normally painful stimuli, in cats with their cerebral hemispheres removed (all neural tissue above the midbrain). The elements of this reaction included mouth opening, retraction of the lips and tongue, snapping of the jaws, lowering of the head, opening of the eyelids, dilation of the pupils, increased blood pressure, and vocalizations which could be either angry or plaintive. The reactions were vigorous and could occur singly or in combination, but were invariably brief and never amounted to an effective attempt to attack or escape.

More convincing outbursts of rage, more complete, better integrated, and more readily elicited, were later found to occur in decorticate animals with the diencephalon still intact [Dusser de Barenne, 1920; Cannon and Britton, 1925; Cannon, 1927; Bard, 1928]. This decorticate rage was still described as 'pseudoaffective' or 'sham rage' because it lacked direction, not surprising in view of the absence of the sensory, perceptual, and motor mechanisms of the cerebral cortex, and because it occurred spontaneously or was evoked by the slightest and most innocuous stimulus. It was argued by Lashley [1938] that decorticate sham rage was due to postoperative irritability of the remaining neural tissue. Bromiley [1948] claimed to refute this explanation by the report that sham rage had persisted over three years of survival of a decorticate dog. However, cortical lesions can give rise to irritative foci whose effect is very long lived.

Decorticate sham rage was an experimental finding which inspired Cannon [1927] to put forward a 'thalamic process' theory of emotion (Figure 6.1) to challenge the James-Lange theory which had held sway

Figure 6.1
Schematic illustration
of the Cannon-Bard
theory of emotion.

From Cannon, W. B.
(1931) Again the
James–Lange and the
thalamic theories of
emotion. *Psychol Rev.*,
38, 281–195. © 1931
American Psychological
Association.
Reproduced by
permission of the
publishers

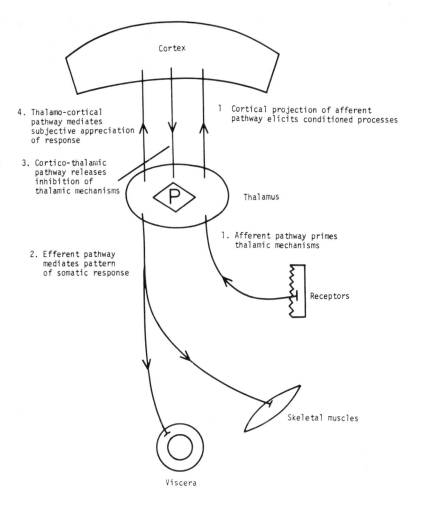

Cortex

4. Thalamo-cortical
   pathway mediates
   subjective appreciation
   of response

1 Cortical projection of afferent
   pathway elicits conditioned processes

3. Cortico-thalamic
   pathway releases
   inhibition of
   thalamic mechanisms

P

Thalamus

1. Afferent pathway primes
   thalamic mechanisms

2. Efferent pathway
   mediates pattern
   of somatic response

Receptors

Skeletal muscles

Viscera

since the 1880s. James [1884] had asserted that emotion was simply the feeling of the bodily changes as they occurred following the perception of an exciting fact. Firstly, Cannon criticized this view on the grounds that visceral changes were too slow, that the viscera were too insensitive and that visceral changes could be dissociated from the expression and feeling of emotion. Elimination of visceral sensation by section of the spinal cord failed to diminish expression of emotion in animals [Sherrington, 1900] or reported experience of emotions in humans [Dana, 1921]. The artificial induction of visceral changes by injection of adrenalin in humans failed to produce reports of full emotional experience in the absence of appropriate conditions [Maranon, 1924]. Subjects experienced 'cold emotions' in which they felt 'as if afraid'. These facts, together with decorticate sham rage suggested to Cannon that the expression and experience of emotion was produced by the arousal of thalamic processes. He supposed that the very low rage threshold in decorticate animals arose because of the removal of cortical inhibitory influences on the thalamus, which would normally only be released following the elicitation of 'conditioned processes' in the cortex, by an external situation. The release of the thalamus from cortical constraint led the thalamic neurones to 'then discharge precipitately and intensely', exciting downward paths innervating the viscera and muscles and also exciting afferent paths to the cortex, as a basis for emotional experience. Cannon stated that 'the peculiar quality of the emotion is added to simple sensation when the thalamic processes are roused'. Cannon's thesis appeared to be particularly well documented from human experience by the facts of a strange complaint called pseudobulbar palsy which appears to stem from lesions of the neural pathways linking the thalamus and cortex in both directions. This condition is characterized on the one hand by paralysis of voluntary movement of the facial muscles, but on the other by a liability to spontaneously produce involuntary and usually inappropriate, prolonged displays of the facial expressive signs of emotions such as laughing or crying. This is consistent with the release of thalamic processes due to damage to corticothalamic inhibitory pathways. Furthermore these bouts of emotional expression are not accompanied by the inner feelings usually associated with the emotion, a fact which is consistent with failure to report thalamic processes to the cortex due to damaged pathways.

The location of the neural substrate which co-ordinated the reaction pattern seen in emotional arousal quickly shifted from the thalamus to the hypothalamus as in 1928 Bard demonstrated that the sham rage response occurred just as readily in cats in which not only the cortex but also the thalamus had been removed so that no cerebral tissue remained rostral, lateral, or dorsal to the caudal hypothalamus. Bard acknowledged the older evidence that we have discussed, indicating that affective reactions can be obtained from decerebrate animals [see review by Bard and Mount-castle, 1948]. However, he observes that in these and his own experiments the threshold for eliciting these responses is much higher (only nociceptive stimuli) than for decorticate animals. Also items of the response are missing and those that do occur are not integrated to produce the sort of 'attack with claws and teeth directed forward and downward and supported by an appropriate stance', seen in decorticate hypothalamic cats. Bard therefore concluded that the hypothalamus had an executive and integrating function in the management of rage behaviour, largely exercised by a facilitatory influence on brainstem mechanisms.

The hypothalamus and emotion

The intimate involvement of the hypothalamus in the organization of affective behaviour is well documented by many other experiments (refer to Figures 5.2 and 6.2). In 1934 Ransom reported that by electrical stimulation of the hypothalamus in cats he could evoke 'behaviour fully expressive of rage' in which the cat 'behaved as if it had been threatened by a barking dog'. Later Grinker and Serota [1938] evoked profuse expression of emotion, together with massive sympathetic discharge, by electrical stimulation of the hypothalamus in human patients. This was accomplished via electrodes inserted up through the nose and embedded in the sphenoidal bone beneath the hypothalamus. In contrast White [1940] reported that stimulation of the hypothalamus in human patients produced sympathetic and parasympathetic discharge but no strange feelings or subjective ex-

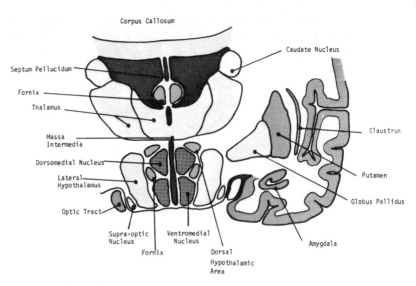

Figure 6.2
Cross-sectional diagram of the hypothalamus to show the major nuclei, including those (the dorsomedial and ventromedial) involved in the arousal of emotion. Figure 5.2., a medial view of the hypothalamus should be referred to for the location of other hypothalamic nuclei

perience of emotion.

Masserman [1941] stimulated the hypothalamus in cats and claimed that this produced a 'pseudoaffective' response which was 'mechanical, stereotyped and stimulus bound'. In no sense could it be interpreted as an emotion that was fully expressed and experienced. However, in many later experiments, which we shall discuss, aggression and other emotions elicited by hypothalamic stimulation have appeared to be fully expressive of the emotion. Where appropriate targets have been present, rage has been focussed in an accurately directed and co-ordinated attack [e.g. Egger and Flynn, 1963]. Thus Masserman's degraded affective responses must have been a function of the absence of appropriate targets for rage, or the placement of the stimulating electrodes outside of the critical area of the hypothalamus.

Later experiments have suggested some degree of localization of different emotions in the hypothalamus. Hess and his co-workers conducted extensive investigations of the behavioural and autonomic consequences of stimulating a multitude of diencephalic locations [for review see Hess, 1954]. They found that defensive behaviour could be elicited by stimulation of the prefornical region (anterior-medial) of the hypothalamus, while motor activity going over to flight could be elicited by stimulation of the posterior hypothalamus. Other experimenters have elicited aggression by stimulation of the medial hypothalamus [Egger and Flynn, 1963], the dorsomedial nucleus of the hypothalamus [Ingram, 1952] and the ventromedial nucleus of the hypothalamus [Glusman and Roizon, 1960]. However, in man Heath [1963] produced pain and intense feelings of rage by stimulation of the posterior hypothalamus. Flight responses have been produced by stimulation of the posterior hypothalamus [e.g. Roberts, 1958] and also by stimulation of the anterior [Yasukochi, 1960] and dorsomedial hypothalamus [Glussman and Roizin, 1960]. De Molina and Hunsperger [1962] have associated aggression with an inner prefornical region of the hypothalamus and escape with an outer region of this structure. This confusing picture may have been compounded by experimenters failing to distinguish between aggression uncontaminated by fear, and the defensive aggression displayed by a fearful animal unable to escape. Strong links might be expected between the circuits mediating escape and defensive aggression, with consequent equivocation between the alternative behaviours when their neural substrate is stimulated, depending upon the perceived opportunities to escape.

Lesions of the ventromedial nucleus of the hypothalamus have been found to produce 'extremely, chronically, and incurably savage behaviour in cats' [Wheatley, 1944]. This finding is consistent with the ventromedial hypothalamus having an inhibitory influence on adjacent neural structures mediating specific behaviour patterns, such as we have seen it to have in relation to consummatory behaviour (see Chapter 4). However, the lesion finding is not easily reconciled with the discovery that stimulation of the ventromedial hypothalamus produces rage [Glussman and Roizin, 1960]. These contradictory results can only be readily explained if we suppose that electrolytic lesioning of the ventromedial hypothalamus produced irritative zones at the boundary which excited adjacent structures. Dubuc and Reynolds [1973] claimed that electrolytic lesioning leaves irritative metal deposits at the borders of the lesioned area.

Apart from the behavioural consequences of hypothalamic stimulation we should note, following their extensive discussion earlier in the chapter, that characteristic endocrine responses have also been produced. Mason [1958] found that stimulation of locations in the anterior-medial hypothalamus resuled in elevated ACTH and consequently increased hydrocorticosteroid hormone secretion.

Cortical control
of emotion centres

The studies of the diencephalic mechanisms mediating the reaction patterns seen in emotional arousal are made under the implicit assumption that these mechanisms are controlled by and interactive with higher structures, particularly the cerebral cortex. We have seen Cannon's [1927] suggestion that the cortex exercises inhibitory control over the subcortical mechanisms and is also the recipient of impulses giving rise to emotional experience.

There has been a considerable elaboration of ideas about the forebrain structures implicated in emotional behaviour and emotional experience. Inspired guesswork led Papez [1937] to propose a hypothetical circuit for emotion which included the hippocampus (Figure 2.11) and cingulate gyrus (Figure 2.9), structures of the rhinencephalon (literally 'smell brain'; sometimes referred to collectively with other old cortical structures as the 'limbic system'). Papez supposed that the hippocampus was a collector for 'incitations of cortical origin', presumably derived from cortical processes representing the generation of memory images or the appraisal of external events. These incitations were carried, via the fornix, to the mamillary body of the hypothalamus where emotional expression was generated. Impulses from the hypothalamus travelled, via the anterior thalamus, to the cingulate gyrus, which Papez conceived to be the receptive region for the experience of emotion. In addition, Papez stated, 'radiation of the emotive processes from the gyrus cinguli to other regions in the cerebral cortex would add emotional colouring to psychic processes occurring elesewhere'. In a revised version of Papez's theory, Maclean [1949] attributed the experience of emotion to the hippocampus and de-emphasized the role of the cingulate gyrus. The evidence which Papez presented in support of his theory was largely anatomical evidence concerning the connectedness of the structures involved. However, he does observe that lesions of the brain, called negri bodies, which occur in rabies tend to be concentrated in the region of the hippocampus and that consistent with his notion of an excitatory role for the hippocampus the symptoms of rabies include intense emotion, 'intense fright and mingled terror and rage'.

Evidence in support of rhinencephalic involvement in the mechanisms of emotion quickly followed Papez's theory with the finding, by Kluver and Bucy [1939], that ablation of the temporal lobes (including the hippocampus and amygdala) in monkeys rendered the animals emotionally unreactive, docile and fearless as well as producing tendencies to put objects in their mouth and indiscriminately and hypersexuality. More detailed evidence on the role of the rhinencephalon in emotion has come from the work of Bard and Mountcastle [1948] who removed the neocortex in cats, while sparing rhinencephalic structures, including the cingulate gyrus, hippocampus, amygdala, and piriform lobe. The result of this operation was quite the reverse of the sham rage exhibited by totally decorticate animals, the neodecorticate creatures remaining extremely placid and failing to display anger to even the gross provocation of cruel and painful treatment. Instead of the usual anger they produced only plaintive cries and attempts to escape. Subsequent removal of either the cingulate gyrus or the piriform lobe, hippocampus, and amygdala in the neodecorticate cats converted the excessively placid state to one of extreme ferocity, thus confirming the restraining influence of rhinencephalic structures on subcortical mechanisms mediating aggression. Bard and Mountcastle also found that, while bilateral extirpation of the cingulate gyrus had no effect on the rage threshold, bilateral destruction of the amygdala led to the gradual development of a very low threshold for the exhibition of intense rage, with calculated and accurate attacks on the source of stimulation.

As rage was completely inhibited following neocortical removal Bard and Mountcastle reasoned that the cingulate gyrus must exercise a strong inhibitory influence on subcortical mechanisms, which is funnelled through the amygdala, itself capable of inhibition. The raised rage threshold following removal of the neocortex suggested removal of an excitatory influence and the lowered rage threshold following removal of the amygdala, in the inhibitory pathway, suggested that the neocortical excitatory influence on subcortical structures bypassed the amygdala. Thus Bard and Mountcastle radically revised Cannon's [1927] conception of purely inhibitory control of the subcortical mechanisms by the cortex and introduced the more flexible notion of control by both inhibitory and excitatory influences (see Figure 6.3).

Arnold [1950] has also presented an excitatory theory of emotion. Like Lashley [1938] she argued that the sham rage phenomenon in decorticate animals was not a release phenomenon, but was the result of excita-

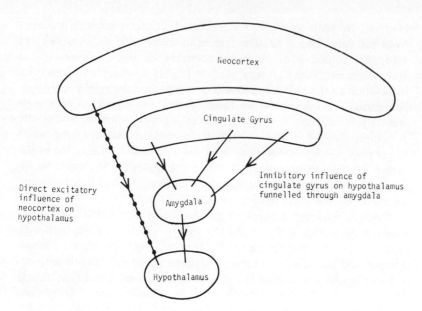

Figure 6.3
Bard and Mountcastle's
theory of emotion
shown in schematic
form

tory irritation by scar tissue. Arnold observed that prefrontal leucotomy, interrupting the fibre connections between the frontal cortex and the subcortical regions, resulted in a reduction in emotional reactivity in humans and animals, consistent with the removal of an excitatory influence. Fulton and Jacobsen [1935] observed that following frontal lobotomy, (the functional equivalent of leucotomy) chimpanzees no longer displayed temper tantrums when frustrated by non-reward of a learned response. Furthermore alcohol and other drugs (e.g. tranquillizers) which appear to have their greatest depressant effect on neocortical structures (see Chapter 15) are effective in reducing anxiety, again suggestive of removal of an excitatory influence. In contrast alcohol appears to lower the threshold for aggression, suggesting either that aggression is mediated by clearly separate structures, or possibly that reduction of anxiety has diminished an antagonistic influence on the mechanisms mediating aggression. In human socialization indiscriminate aggressive responses are suppressed by techniques which include fear of punishment.

The enigmatic amygdala

To return to the rhinencephalon we note that there is a contradiction between the observation of Kluver and Bucy [1939] that rhinencephalic ablation produces placidity and that of Bard and Mountcastle [1948] that amygdalectomy produces ferocity. Later work by Schreiner and Kling [1953] indicated that bilateral amygdalectomy in animals including cats and ferocious wild lynxes produced placidity. Gloor [1960] in a review of studies of the amygdala (see Figure 2.11), acknowledged the contradictory results from ablation experiments and claimed that there was no evidence for spatially separated inhibitory and excitatory areas within the amygdala which might have explained them. He was constrained to put forward the rather imprecise hypothesis that the amygdala has a general role in the modulation of subcortical activity, selecting the pattern of behaviour appropriate to the situation. Contradictory behaviours in amygdalectomized animals arose from damage to the selection mechanism so that behaviours were selected without reference to their appropriateness to the situation.

In a more recent review Moyer [1971] presents evidence that there is localization of excitatory and inhibitory functions for different categories of aggression in discrete amygdaloid nuclei. This will be discussed in the next section. De Molina and Hunsperger [1962] have used an elegant series of experiments to demonstrate the organization of emotion mechanisms in a hierarchy of increasing importance, in the amygdala, hypothalamus, and midbrain. They observed that defensive behaviour could be produced by stimulation of any of these areas alone in the intact animal. However, electrocoagulation of the midbrain affective behaviour zones suppressed affective behaviour normally elicited by stimulation of the amygdala or hypothalamus; electrocoagulation of the critical areas of the hypothalamus suppressed affective reactions produced by stimulation of the amygdala but not those produced by stimulation of the midbrain; and interruption of the stria terminalis tract, connecting the amygdala to the hypothalamus, abolished defensive reactions evoked by amygdaloid stimulation, but did not affect those produced by stimulation of the hypothalamus or midbrain.

Moyer's specific circuit theory of aggression

Moyer [1971] has advanced a contemporary theory of the neural basis of aggression based on a survey of research in this area. He argues that aggression falls into a number of clearly separate categories; predatory, inter-male, fear induced, irritable, territorial, defensive, maternal, and instrumental. These are distinctions whose systematic investigation has been neglected by other experimenters. Each of these categories is outwardly distinguishable by the specific evoking stimuli and/or the characteristic behaviour pattern. Predatory aggression is only directed against a natural prey and it is manifest in stalking behaviour, quiet, efficient, and deadly, contrasting with the noise and drama of other forms of aggression. In stags, whereas inter-male aggression is expressed by clashing antlers, defence against attackers from other species is conducted with the front hooves. Fear induced aggression can be inferred from the fact that it follows attempts to escape which are frustrated. Irritable aggression is true rage, provoked by pain or frustration, and territorial and maternal aggression have clear situational determinants. Instrumental aggression is aggression which is learnt on the basis of prior patterns of reinforcement.

In addition to being outwardly distinguishable, Moyer asserts that each category of aggression is mediated by its own separate neural circuit, the aggression circuits being distributed in the hypothalamus and rhinencephalon. He concedes that there may be some overlap of the circuits. Each aggression circuit has a trigger threshold which is a function of both the specificity and intensity of the stimulus. The trigger threshold of the aggression circuits is variable, both between and within individuals. Inter-individual differences in threshold arise because of inherited differences in neuronal and hormonal systems and possibly because of inherited over sensitivity of these circuits. Moyer suggests that the inheritance of patho-logically low aggression thresholds may be analogous to the inheritance of epilepsy, a complaint that is sometimes accompanied by aggressive tenden-cies. In extreme cases of pathological aggression ultrasensitive circuits trigger spontaneously without the normal evoking stimulus. Aggression circuits may also respond to abnormal excitation generated by brain lesions such as epileptic foci and irritative tumours. Differences between individ-uals, and within the same individuals at different times, arise because of variation in hormonal and biochemical influences. Testosterone appears to selectively sensitize the circuits for inter-male aggression during the mating season, in seasonally breeding animals and may influence assertiveness in humans. There is also evidence that the circuit for irritable aggression is made more sensitive by hypoglycaemia (low blood sugar). In addition the aggression circuits are supposedly subject to both facilitatory and inhibitory influences from other neural systems. For instance predatory attack by a cat on a rat, initiated by hypothalamic stimulation, is potentiated by stimulation of the brainstem reticular formation [Sheard and Flynn, 1967]. Conversely Heath [1963] has demonstrated that when rage is blocked by stimulation of the septum in pathologically hostile human patients, it is replaced by happiness and mild euphoria, suggesting that the aggression circuits may have been blocked by excitation of an incompatible neural system.

Moyer presents some neurophysiological evidence for differentiation of the aggression circuits. If the lateral hypothalamus of a cat is stimulated it will ignore the experimenter and quietly and efficiently stalk and kill a rat [Wasman and Flynn, 1962]. On the other hand, following stimulation of the medial hypothalamus it will exhibit pronounced sympathetic arousal, utter angry cries and with claws unsheathed launch a well directed attack on a nearby person, while ignoring an available rat [Egger and Flynn, 1963]. The stimulus bound nature of the predatory behaviour evoked by stimulation of the lateral hypothalamus is demonstrated by a stimulated cat's reduced tendency to attack a stuffed rat and even slighter inclination to attack a foam rubber block. It has also been shown that the predatory aggression circuit of the lateral hypothalamus is cholinergic as Smith *et al.* [1970a] have provoked mouse killing in normally non-killing rats by the injection of carbachol (synthetic acetylcholine) into that area. Conversely injection of the cholinergic blocking agent methyl atropine into the same lateral hypothalamic site stops killing behaviour by rats which normally kill mice spontaneously. Although the lateral hypothalamus has also been associated with eating (see Chapter 5), the usual sequel to predatory aggres-sion, the two classes of behaviour appear to have separate substrates. Lesions which abolish eating only temporarily inhibit predatory aggression [Karli, 1956].

There is a lack of clear cut evidence concerning the localization of other types of aggression in the hypothalamus. There have been suggestions that fear induced aggression in cornered animals stems from the anterior hypo-thalamus [Yasukochi, 1960] and the dorsal hypothalamus [Romaniuk,

1965]. A number of studies have identified the ventromedial nucleus of the hypothalamus with irritable aggression [see review by Moyer, 1971, pp. 40–41] which has been evoked by both stimulation and lesion of this area.

The amygdala appears to be involved in the circuits for predatory, fear induced, and irritable aggression. Amygdalectomy has been found to eliminate predatory aggression in the cat [Summers and Kaelber, 1962] and the rat [Wood, 1958]. Amygdalectomy also reduces fear induced aggression in monkeys, rats and cats [Kluver and Bucy, 1939; Schreiner and Kling, 1953; Shealy and Peale, 1957], but on the other hand appears to increase irritable aggression [Bard and Mountcastle, 1948; Schreiner and Kling, 1953], a combination of findings which has been a source of great confusion. Among a number of neurosurgical operations which have been performed to reduce unmanageable aggression in humans the most promising is bilateral amygdalectomy [see Moyer, 1971, pp. 87–92]. Stimulation of the human amygdala produces aggression. King [1961] was the target of angry, verbally hostile, and threatening behaviour when he stimulated the amygdala of a female patient with a 5 mA current. The patient became mild mannered and apologetic when the current was turned off. In another case [Ervin et al., 1969] amygdaloid stimulation used in an attempt to relieve intractable pain produced rage and indiscriminate assaultive behaviour in a patient whose conduct was usually 'courtly and dignified'. In another patient stimulation of the right amygdala produced outbursts of rage and assaultive behaviour similar to that seen in the spontaneous episodes which he exhibited. Violent aggressive behaviour has also been observed following stimulation of the hippocampus [Sweet et al., 1969].

Moyer [1971, pp. 42–45] reviews studies suggesting localization of function in the amygdala, which has eight identifiable nuclei. The following effects were evoked by stimulation of its different zones: predatory facilitation from the dorsal portion and predatory inhibition from the medial portion of the lateral nucleus; fear induced facilitation from the central and basal nuclei and fear induced inhibition from the ventral portions of the lateral and basal nuclei; irritable facilitation from the medial nuclei and irritable inhibition from the central nuclei which it shares with fear induced facilitation (see Figure 6.4).

Figure 6.4
Schematic diagram to show the role of different nuclei of the amygdala associated with different kinds of aggression.

From Moyer, K. (1971) *The physiology of hostility*, Chicago, Markham Publishing Co. Reproduced by permission of the author

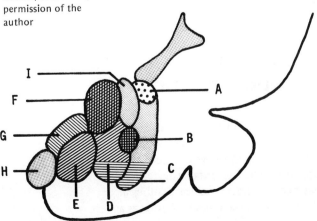

The rhinencephalic structures, the hippocampus and cingulate gyrus, to which Papez [1937] attributed great importance in his circuit for emotion, remain implicated in emotion. Hippocampal lesions appear to increase irritable aggression in cats [Green *et al*., 1957], as does cholinergic stimulation of the hippocampus [Maclean and Delgardo, 1953]. Irritable aggression has been observed to increase in cats [Kennard, 1955] and dogs [Brutkowski *et al*., 1961] following destruction of the cingulate gyrus. In contrast cingulectomy in monkeys has been observed to render them less fearful and more docile [Kennard, 1955]. Cingulectomy has been used to treat uncontrollable violence in men in whom, subsequent to the operation, outbursts are milder and less sustained, although more easily provoked [Le Beau, 1952; Tow and Whitty, 1953].

Irritable lesions and pathological aggression

Pathological aggression in man appears to have a consistent association with abnormal discharges in rhinencephalic structures, originating from either irritative tumours or epileptic foci [see Moyer, 1971, pp. 87–89]. Gibbs [1951] has estimated that around 50% of epileptics with an anterior temporal lobe focus have psychiatric disorders between fits which Gloor [1960] characterizes as a propensity 'to be provoked into explosive and violent anger, often for causes of a trifling nature'. Several studies have indicated that aggressive behaviour including pyromania, violent sex behaviour, murder, and other acts of violence are associated with 14 per second and 6 per second positive spikes in the EEG record [see Moyer, 1971, pp. 60–61, 88]. Even in individuals exhibiting uncontrollable aggressive outbursts who have no surface EEG abnormalities, disturbed behaviour appears to be accompanied by hypersynchronous activity recorded from depth electrodes implanted in rhinencephalic structures [Ervin *et al*., 1969; Heath, 1962; Monroe, 1959]. Like epilepsy itself, many inter-ictal (between fits) aggressive dyscontrol symptoms are episodic with the individuals behaving quite normally in between episodes. Periods of abnormal discharge produce aggressive outbursts beyond the voluntary control of the individual and thus with a similar status to an epileptic fit.

Hormonal and biochemical influences on aggression circuits

An account of the neural circuitry mediating aggression would be incomplete without a further discussion of the hormonal and biochemical influences modulating their thresholds. We have seen that the circuit for predatory aggression is triggered by acetylcholine. We have also seen that androgens sensitize the circuits initiating inter-male and irritable aggression. Androgen reduction by castration has been found to reduce fighting in animals [Beeman, 1947; Seward, 1945; Sigg, 1969] and has been used as a rather drastic measure to control violent sex crimes in man [Hawke, 1950; Lemaire, 1956]. Oestrogens appear to antagonize androgen and have been found to reduce aggression, even in chimpanzees which have already been castrated. Oestrogen may be more effective in blocking androgens than castration because castration does not affect the production of androgens by the adrenal gland. Oestrogen has been used to control violent behaviour in man [Sands, 1954; Dunn, 1941]. Dunn [1941] has described the case of a 27 year old male, imprisoned for sexual assaults on young girls, who was a persistent trouble maker and constantly preoccupied with sex. His urine contained abnormally high concentrations of gonadotrophic hormone and testosterone. Following stilboestrol (synthetic oestrogen) treatment his sexual responsiveness diminished and his behaviour became more tractable.

Perhaps the most common instance of proneness to irritable aggression in humans occurs during the premenstrual phase in women. In several studies it has been found that crimes of violence committed by women are heavily concentrated in the week prior to menstruation [e.g. see Dalton, 1961, 1964]. Three tentative explanations have been advanced to explain this premenstrual irritability. The first is that it is due to a fall in the level of progesterone [Hamburg et al., 1968; Dalton, 1964]. The second is that it is due to an increase in the secretion of aldosterone from the adrenal cortex resulting in the retention of sodium and water, with increased neuronal irritability as a possible consequence [Janowsky et al., 1967]. Lastly it has been suggested that it is due to a cyclic hypoglycemic reaction [Morton et al., 1953]. Improvement has been claimed following treatment for all of these conditions during the premenstruum so that in an individual the premenstrual syndrome may be due to any one of these conditions, or to a combination of them.

Hypoglycemia has been implicated in the genesis of irritable aggression apart from in the premenstrual syndrome. Frederichs and Goodman [1969] have reviewed studies which strongly linked hyperirritability with hypoglycemia. Gloor [1967] observed that patients who become hypoglycemic due to islet cell tumours in the pancreas are extremely aggressive, but become 'quite civilized' when their blood sugar is raised. Wilder [1947] has compiled evidence that hypoglycemia is a causal factor in many instances of antisocial aggressive behaviour including matrimonial strife, threats and acts of murder, destructiveness, and cruelty to children and he suggested that hypoglycemia may represent a temporary state of 'moral insanity'.

It is interesting to observe that the link between hypoglycemia and aggression can be accounted for by the coincidence of the neural monitor of blood glucose and part of the circuit for irritable aggression in the ventromedial nucleus of the hypothalamus. If it could also be shown that hypoglycemia lowers the threshold for triggering the predatory aggression circuit then we could see the adaptive value of the association.

Gellhorn [1968] asserts that the hypothalamic mechanisms mediating emotional arousal are activated by adrenalin, observing that the introduction of minute quantities of adrenalin into the posterior hypothalamus produces cortical arousal. He also observes that emotional responsiveness to such external stimuli as slapstick films or provocation is potentiated by adrenalin injections. Also in this context we have already seen the evidence of Reis and Fuxe [1969] that noradrenalin may be an energizing agent in the aggression circuits.

The control of aggression

Moyer's specific circuit theory of aggression implies that aggression is amenable to control, either by selective ablation of segments of the aggression circuits, by activation of antagonistic circuits or by chemical modification of the threshold of the aggression circuits. The reduction of pathological aggression in humans by amygdalectomy or cingulectomy has already been mentioned. Following partial amygdalectomy by cryosurgery (tissue destruction by very low temperature liquids or gases) patients who were formerly constantly enraged and assaultive, have been released from solitary confinement into open wards and observed to smile for the first time [Heimburger *et al.*, 1966].

Heath [1963] has blocked violent aggression in a psychomotor epileptic by stimulation of the septal region. This appears to activate antagonistic systems as the patient's experience changes from one of rage to one of happiness, mild euphoria, and incipient sexual arousal. Heath has evoked the possibility of patients terminating their own uncontrollable aggression by pressing an 'anti-hostility button' on a transistorized, self-contained brain stimulator worn by the patient.

There is less risk of irreversible damage to functions other than the disordered ones being treated when chemical agents, rather than neurosurgery, are used to modify the sensitivity of aggression circuits. Valzelli [1967] has reviewed studies indicating that as many as 74 different drugs reduce aggression. Kline [1962] claims that the reason 'wards formerly filled with screaming, denudative, assaultive patients now have window curtains and flowers on the table' is due to the effectiveness of phenothiazines in reducing psychotic hostility. The phenothiazines and tranquillizers appear to have a 'taming' effect over and above their sedative action. Perphenazine and thioridazine have both proved useful in aggression reduction in a wide variety of patients and the anticonvulsant Dilantin has also been successful in controlling hyperexcitability in non-epileptic patients. Hyperactivity in children with restlessness, aggressiveness, temper tantrums, disobedience, impulsivity, and poor concentration has been effectively treated by the stimulant amphetamine, presumably by selective activation of inhibitory mechanisms in the forebrain. Other classes of drug which effectively reduce irritability are the so called minor tranquillizers propanediols (meprobamate and tybamate) and the benzodiazepines (including chlordiazepoxide, diazepam and oxazepam). Diazepam has been remarkably successful in eliminating destructive rampages in psychotic criminals [see review of aggression control by drugs in Moyer, 1971, pp. 101-105].

The development of techniques for controlling aggression raise some profound ethical problems and evoke sinister visions of their use by unscrupulous and totalitarian governments. It is difficult to argue that it is wrong to bring relief to a person who suffers constant uncontrollable outbursts of rage, as unwelcome to himself as to others, because of some focal brain malfunction. Even the drastic measure of brain surgery might seem justified in some such instances. However, surgery has attendant risks of infection and there is always the possibility that brain surgery will have effects beyond those intended, diminishing the intellectual powers and degrading the level of awareness of the patient in subtle ways. The use of brain surgery becomes even more problematical around the decision threshold where the judgement of what constitutes antisocial behaviour is subjective and perhaps influenced by 'ideological' biases on the part of the doctor.

Whereas practical considerations impose fairly severe constraints on even the most ruthless totalitarian regime making wholesale use of brain surgery or brain stimulation to achieve rigid social control, this is not so with aggression controlling drugs. The possibility is evoked that the propensity of a home or foreign population to resist oppression or aggression could be reduced by introducing aggression controlling drugs into the water supply or even the milk. Moyer [1971, p. 106] quotes an instance where a colony of vicious and untameable squirrel monkeys were rendered friendly and manageable by administering tiny amounts of diazepam to their milk supply. The control of aggression is a subject for study where it must be difficult for scientists to stand aloof from the wider implications of their activities.

Ergotropic and trophotropic systems and emotion

Gellhorn [1968] has advanced a quite different conception of the neural substrate of emotion to that which has just been expounded. We have seen that it has been difficult to establish a precise hypothalamic location for different patterns of emotional behaviour. Gellhorn has interpreted the results of the many experiments involving lesion or stimulation of different hypothalamic locations to indicate that it contains only two major subdivisions; an 'ergotropic' posterior division and a 'trophotropic' anterior division. Activity of the ergotropic system gives rise to states of arousal marked by cortical activation and increased sympathetic activity. Activity of the trophotropic system lowers the state of cortical and somatic arousal, giving rise to synchronous EEG waves, slowed heart rate and a tendency to sleep. It is supposed that the two systems are in a reciprocal relationship so that excitation of the ergotropic system is associated with diminished responsiveness of the trophotropic system and vice versa.

Gellhorn supposed that quite heterogeneous emotions of an aroused nature, including both joy and rage, were associated with discharge of the ergotropic system. Similarly trophotropic activity is associated with emotions as diverse as 'postprandial happiness' (after meals), sorrow and despair. Although Gellhorn observes that highly specific patterns of contraction occur in the facial muscles during particular emotions, he does not appear to consider that there is any subcortical differentiation of neural circuitry which accounts for the differences between individual emotions. He contrasts the paucity of different types of ergotropic and trophotropic downward discharges with the 'enormous variety of emotional patterns in civilized man' [Gellhorn, 1968, p. 149] and suggests that neocortical development with associated cognitive processes accounts for this variety. Gellhorn suggests that the prevailing balance between the ergotropic and trophotropic systems determines the group character of the emotions, while cognitive factors determine the specific emotion. Thus, if the responsiveness of the ergotropic system is intensified by stimulation of the amygdala, petting a cat will evoke a rage response, while during trophotropic dominance a painful stimulus will induce sleep.

Gellhorn considers that the ergotropic-trophotropic balance is modulated by other brain structures. He interprets the rage evoked by stimulation of the amygdala to indicate activation of the ergotropic system, while reduced emotional responsiveness produced by stimulation of the caudate nucleus or septum is attributed to activation of the trophotropic system.

Prevailing mood, as well as transient emotion, is claimed to be a function of the ergotropic-trophotropic balance so that depression, for instance, is associated with trophotropic dominance. ECT (electroconvulsive therapy) and excitatory drugs such as amphetamines and mescalin, which elevate mood, are considered to act by stimulating the ergotropic division of the hypothalamus. The ergotropic-trophotropic balance is also considered to be a function of the biochemical environment of the brain, so that the depression which is induced by administration of reserpine is attributed to the depletion of noradrenalin (an ergotropic substance) which it brings about. Conversely the depression relieving effects of monoamine oxidase inhibitors is due to the increase in noradrenalin in the brain occasioned by blocking the enzyme which destroys it. The relationship between brain catecholamine (of which noradrenalin is an example) concentration and mood is documented elsewhere [see review by Kety, 1970 and Chapters 14 and 15]. Kety observes that amphetamines and imiprimine (which blocks reuptake of noradrenalin from the synapse) effectively increases the availability of noradrenalin at the synapse and also that the administration of electroconvulsive shock to rats twice per day for a week appears to stimulate increased noradrenalin synthesis in the brain. This latter finding gives a clue to the mechanism by which ECT relieves depression.

Gellhorn places an unusual degree of emphasis on muscle tone and posture, remarking that not only does ergotropic activation result in increased muscle tone, but also that the feedback of proprioceptive impulses produces further activation of the ergotropic system. From this fact he makes the curious assertion that 'sadness, which is associated with muscular relaxation, is prevented or inhibited by assuming a military posture'.

To account for the diversity of emotional states, in spite of there being such undifferentiated subcortical mechanisms, Gellhorn adopts Schachter and Singer's theory [1962] that 'cognitive processes play a major role in the development of emotional states'.

Schachter and Singer [1962] tested their cognitive theory of emotion in a complicated and ingenious experiment. After inducing somatic arousal in unsuspecting subjects, by a prior injection of adrenalin, the cognitions available to them were manipulated to favour interpretation of the arousal as being due to either euphoria or anger. Subjects were misled into thinking that they were participating in an experiment on the effect of 'vitamin injections' (which were in fact adrenalin) on vision. While waiting for a fictitious test of their vision they were kept in a waiting room with an experimenter's stooge. In the 'euphoria' condition the stooge fooled around, did zany things and initiated various amusing games. In the 'anger' condition both the subject and the stooge were given a questionnaire which contained progressively more outrageous questions about such matters as the respondents' sex life. The stooge expressed progressively more vigorous signs of anger and annoyance. The somatic arousal of subjects was assessed by measures such as heart rate. During the sessions in the waiting room behavioural arousal was assessed by hidden observers, and after the experiment subjects registered their subjective feelings of arousal on rating scales. All subjects were given injections, but one group was given an inert placebo and among those injected with adrenalin, one group was not informed of any side effects, one group was given a list of fictitious side effects and a control group was told the real effects. It was found that those subjects who had been injected with adrenalin, and had not been able to associate their bodily symptoms with the injection, displayed higher levels of emotional arousal (observer and self-rated), in both the 'euphoria' and 'anger' conditions, than subjects who had either been injected with the placebo or who had been able to attribute their bodily symptoms to the injection. This result seemed to verify Schachter and Singer's hypothesis that a general pattern of sympathetic activation was characteristic of emotional states and that 'one labels, interprets and identifies this stirred up state in terms of the characteristics of the precipitating situation and one's apperceptive mass'. The range of sympathetic activation situations was extended in an experiment by Schachter and Wheeler [1962] who injected not only adrenalin and a placebo, but also and inhibitor of sympathetic activation, chlorpromazine. Laughter and amusement was then rated while subjects viewed a slapstick film, and was found to be in proportion to the degree of sympathetic activation, being greater with adrenalin than with the placebo and greater with the placebo than with chlorpromazine. Again the intensity of emotion was a function of general sympathetic arousal, while the type was a function of available cognitions.

Reconciling the theories

There would appear to be a profound contradiction between the theories supposing that specific subcortical circuits mediate different emotions and those supposing that a general pattern of activation underlies all emotions, while differentiation is purely cognitive. However, even if there is no clear differentiation of the pattern of sympathetic activation, it is difficult to deny the specificity of some of the more stereotyped aspects of expression and behaviour in emotion. Even in humans we have noted that the lesions of pseudobulbar palsy result in the uncontrolled involuntary production of the facial expressions of specific emotions. Also abnormal patterns of electrical activity in rhinencephalic structures result in easily provoked, uncontrolled outbursts of specifically aggressive behaviour. These observations and other similar ones strongly suggest that specific subcortical mechanisms have been released. Even Gellhorn does not deny the specificity of facial expressions in emotion.

It is quite feasible to incorporate the notion of general arousal in a specific circuit theory of emotion. Moyer [1971] has gone some way towards doing this by postulating that the sensitivity of the aggression circuits is modulated by both chemical and neural influences from elsewhere. Thus he observes that stimulation of the reticular formation, with its general arousing effect, intensifies aggression evoked by stimulation of specific circuits. Moyer's theory accounts for the observations of Schachter and Singer [1962] that adrenalin injected subjects showed more anger than placebo injected subjects, if one supposes that the adrenalin sensitized the aggression circuits. The finding that the subjects who were informed of the effects of the injections did not display such high emotional arousal is more difficult to account for. However, we might expect that the triggering and control of the aggression circuits would be at least partially effected by cortical mechanisms mediating cognitions of somatic arousal and external events. The coexistence of convincing evidence for both general arousal and specific circuits strongly suggests that any theory of emotion must account for both of these factors, whose interaction appears to determine the threshold, intensity, pattern and direction of emotional arousal.

A final caveat is to remind the reader that the experimental support for theories of emotion is generally rather weak. Both lesion and stimulation of specific brain structures may produce gross disturbances of function which obscure the subtleties of the circuits affected. Emotional behaviour has often been observed in a rather casual manner with no systematic attempt to either classify it properly or to quantify it. Theories of emotion are therefore often excessively speculative and should be approached with a critical attitude.

Summary

The organism responds to emergencies with arousal of the brain, which increases the efficiency of information processing, and arousal of the body, which prepares it for vigorous muscular effort. Arousal of the brain is mediated by the brainstem reticular formation which receives afferent inputs from all of the sensory pathways. Arousal of the body is mediated jointly by activation of the sympathetic branch of the autonomic nervous system and by the hormonal secretions of the pituitary–adrenal axis, both under the executive control of the hypothalamus. Somatic arousal consists of increased activity in the cardiovascular and respiratory systems which increases the supply of well oxygenated blood to the muscles. In fear this is accompanied by reduced activity, and, in hostility, by increased activity of the digestive system.

Psychoendocrine arousal of the pituitary–adrenal axis results in the release of hormones such as adrenalin, noradrenalin, hydrocorticosteroids and thyroxin which contribute to both the release of energy from the body's stores and the increase in energy metabolism.

Lesion and stimulation studies indicate that there is a hierarchy of levels of control of the patterns of emotional reaction exhibited in emerg-encies. The individual components of emotional expression appear to be organized in the midbrain. The midbrain centres appear to be facilitated by hypothalamic mechanisms which organize and integrate the over-all pattern of emotional expression. Selection of the appropriate hypothalamic mechanism appears to be achieved by rhinencephalic structures, particular-ly the amygdala. The forebrain appears to have both inhibitory and excitatory control over the subcortical emotion centres, the exercise of this control presumably being a function of cognitive processes occurring in the forebrain. There is controversy over the specificity of the subcortical mechanisms mediating emotion, but there is considerable evidence for specific circuits, particularly for different types of aggression. The sensitiv-ity of emotion circuits is modulated by neural influences from other structures and by biochemical and hormonal influences. The emotion circuits are triggered, except in pathological instances, by specific environ-mental stimuli.

Chapter
seven

The need
for
stimulation

Introduction

A species' most obvious survival needs are met by the systems, already discussed, which maintain an organism's internal equilibrium, generate reproductive behaviour and mediate adaptive responses to threatening situations. The classical doctrines of both the analytical and behaviourist schools of psychology supposed that once these primary needs had been met, the organism achieved a tensionless state which rendered it motiveless and immobile until disequilibrating changes in the internal or external environment produced new impulses to action [e.g. see Hebb, 1955].

This theory was severely embarrassed by the prevalence of apparently spontaneous 'stimulus seeking' behaviour, such as curiosity, exploration, manipulation and play, which occurred when all the primary needs were clearly satisfied. This was originally dealt with by postulating secondary, or derived, drives, which arose from the repeated association of a neutral stimulus with a primary reinforcer. A rat may acquire a secondary drive to turn on a light. Because the light has previously been flashed on during the delivery of a food reinforcement for an operant response, the light becomes a drive object in its own right. The animal will make old responses, or learn new responses, to turn the light on. Other findings cast serious doubts on the secondary drive explanation of curiosity behaviour. Responses which are made to gain a neutral stimulus, quite rapidly extinguish in the absence of a primary reward. Furthermore, it is difficult to see how a secondary drive can lead an animal to seek stimuli which have never before been experienced.

There are compelling arguments to counter the doctrine that a creature free from internal tensions must necessarily be inert. The doctrine is inconsistent with the rational needs of a behavioural economy, which the inexorable forces shaping evolution must have designed for survival. A satiated and inert creature which ignores the intrusion of a novel stimulus may imperil its life. One which becomes aroused, orientates itself and investigates the stimulus may consequently avoid a danger, or, if it is not dangerous, file away the information for future reference. A satiated creature which, during its freedom from internal tensions, spontaneously investigates and explores novel features of its environment, will acquire knowledge relevant to its future survival needs; the whereabouts of food and shelter; routes of escape from danger; places to hide from predators.

The acquisition of useful knowledge of the environment requires the perceptual abilities to differentiate and identify its important features. Phylogenetically primitive creatures have an innate capacity to produce stereotyped response patterns to a few simple, but crucial features of their environment. The triggering of territorial aggression in the stickleback, by the red underbelly of an intruding male, is an example. In creatures with more highly developed brains, particularly man, only rudimentary perceptual abilities are possessed at birth. These must be elaborated by a process of learning if the creature is to exploit its behavioural potential and cope adequately with its environment, when it achieves independence from its parents. It appears that the human infant must learn to perceive such crucial features as the depth and distance of objects. It seems likely that such perceptual learning will require repeated exposure to a wide range of stimulus patterns normally occurring in the creature's environment. An autonomous drive for varied patterns of stimulation seems necessary to serve the need for this experience.

The varied patterns of stimulation which an organism seeks for the purpose of perceptual learning and environmental knowledge are ultimately registered in brain structures. There they must be responsible for plastic changes in the neural networks which carry the substrate for perceptual and other forms of learning. We might also surmise that this stimulation of neural structures is important for promoting their full development and functional efficiency, as use appears to be a prerequisite for the maintenance of health in biological systems. Muscles respond to exercise by increasing their strength and stamina, but atrophy as the result of inactivity.

In this chapter it is proposed to examine the evidence for autonomous drives under the general heading of 'stimulus seeking'. The role of the reticular activating system in mediating these drives will be outlined. The general need of the nervous system for varied patterns of stimulation will be discussed.

Orientation and investigation

When an unfamiliar noise occurs in the vicinity of a cat it pricks up its ears, raises its head, turns towards the source of the noise and tenses its muscles for action. Psychophysiological variables (e.g. heart rate, respiration, EEG) show patterns of arousal (see Chapter 6). This pattern of activation is the 'orientation reaction', by which a creature seeks to know the significance of a novel stimulus [for reviews see Berlyne, 1960, Chapter 4; Lynn, 1966].

The continuum of behaviours, by which animals gain knowledge of the unfamiliar in their environment, extends from the orientation reaction (OR), an evoked response to a sudden novel stimulus, to spontaneous

Figure 7.1
The ascending reticular
arousal system (ARAS
or RAS), showing its
collateral inputs from
the incoming sensory
pathways and its wide
cortical projections.

From Magoun, H.
(1963) *The waking
brain*. Reproduced by
permission of Charles
C. Thomas, publisher,
Springfield, Illinois

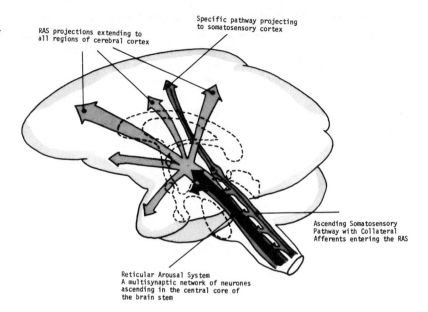

RAS projections extending to
all regions of cerebral cortex

Specific pathway projecting
to somatosensory cortex

Ascending Somatosensory
Pathway with Collateral
Afferents entering the RAS

Reticular Arousal System
A multisynaptic network of neurones
ascending in the central core of
the brain stem

forays into' unknown terrain. Our description of the OR introduces conceptual frameworks which deal with this class of behaviours and an organism's response to different levels of stimulation in general. This conceptual
framework is an offshoot of arousal theory (see Chapter 6).

The influx of environmental stimuli received by an organism appears to
be regulated by the reticular arousal system (RAS; see Figure 7.1) of the
brainstem (discussed in detail in Chapters 6 and 8). It monitors all sensory
inputs via collateral fibres from the sensory nerve tracts. A novel stimulus,
a signal that a reward is about to be delivered or a warning of impending
danger all activate the RAS. Upward discharges from the RAS produce
arousal of the entire cerebral cortex (seen as activation of the EEG),
increasing its functional efficiency. Downward discharges produce arousal
patterns in the neuroendocrine system, viscera, and musculature. The
behavioural concomitants of this arousal response include direction of
head, eyes, and ears towards the source of stimulation and a posture of
readiness for action. The total pattern of arousal defines the orientation
reaction. Arousal may culminate in emotional behaviour when a stimulus
has fear or aggression provoking properties. If a stimulus which triggers an
arousal response is evaluated as having no significance, arousal subsides to
its normal levels.

The ultimate aim of the orientation response appears to be reduction of
the arousal engendered by a novel stimulus to an equilibrium level. Its
arousing properties are eliminated by either escaping from its presence or
reducing uncertainty about its significance. We can discern a homeostatic
system closely analogous to those we have seen which act to reduce
deviations from the equilibrium level in the internal environment.

Arousal theorists such as Lindsley [1951], Duffy [1957, 1962], Malmo
[1957] and Hebb [1955] have argued that the RAS produces non-specific
arousal of the nervous system which underlies all motive states. The goal
of behaviour is to restore this arousal to an optimum level. Arousal may

fall below the optimum, as well as being raised above it. Exploratory activity and attempts to relieve the monotony of restricted sensory environments appear to reflect the operation of a drive to raise the level of arousal in the NS. The organism seems to seek a level of environmental stimulation, set by the RAS, that will sustain its arousal at the optimum level. Stimulus dimensions include intensity, information value, temporal, and spatial fluctuation. The optimum level of stimulation sought by an individual will vary according to such factors as phase of the sleeping-waking cycle and level of stimulation in the immediately preceding period. Inter-individual differences in optimum levels of stimulation appear to arise as a function of both experience and genetic predisposition (see Chapter 9).

Evidence for autonomous stimulus seeking drives

To the non-psychologist curiosity, exploration and play appear to be conspicuous examples of innate behaviour. Many experimenters have provided necessary scientific proof by demonstrating that animals will engage in these classes of behaviour when all other drives are satiated [see Berlyne, 1960]. For instance, rats will explore a novel grid iron patterned maze [Dashiell, 1925] and will even cross an electrified grid to gain access to it [Nissen, 1930]. The fact that they would more willingly overcome an aversive drive to explore than to reach food and water, indicated that the urge to explore had the force and direction to be accorded the status of an independent drive itself.

Exploration only has adaptive value if it produces increased knowledge of the environment. Thistlethwaite [1951] demonstrated experimentally that exploration resulted in the learning of a maze, even when no conventional reward was given. 'Latent learning' was inferred from the rapidity with which hungry rats, which had previously explored the maze, learned to reach the goal box to gain a food reward.

Welker [1961] has observed that animal play and exploration increases as one ascends the phylogenetic scale and peaks at some point in childhood. These observations are consistent with the greater dependence of more highly evolved animals on learning in infancy. Play can be seen as the context for the acquisition of skills necessary for both survival and social interaction.

Sensory and perceptual deprivation

Interest in the effects of isolation, in the very different circumstances of 'brain washing' and long space flights, has given a great deal of impetus to research on human 'stimulus needs'. Human volunteers have been subjected to either sensory or perceptual deprivation [original work by Bexton et al.,

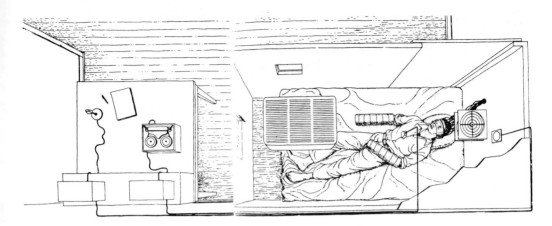

Figure 7.2
Sensory deprivation
chamber and associated
apparatus.

From Heron, W., The
pathology of boredom.
Sci. Amer., **196**, 52–56.
Copyright © January,
1957 by Scientific
American Inc. All rights
reserved. Reproduced
by permission of the
publishers

1954]. In the former instance sensory stimulation is minimized by confining subjects on a bed, in a dark sound-proofed room (see Figure 7.2). They may also wear large cuffs to reduce tactile stimulation. In the latter instance stimulation is limited to diffuse, unpatterned light and sound by the wearing of translucent goggles and headphones broadcasting only white noise [for a review of methods see Rossi, 1969].

Individuals subject to conditions of sensory deprivation (SD) find it a rather exquisite form of torture. This is despite the prediction of earlier psychological theories that, given satisfaction of all other bodily needs, such a tensionless state should result in total contentment. Highly paid subjects press the 'panic button', to secure release from its excruciating monotony, long before their allotted time of sensory isolation has passed. Tolerance of sensory deprivation varies, between individuals, from a few hours to a few days.

SD and PD (perceptual deprivation) not only produce an intense drive to restore normal patterns of stimulation, but also effect changes in cognitive functioning, motivation, and physiological variables. Subjects report that during SD they lose the ability to concentrate and think coherently, and in some cases experience hallucinations [alternatively claimed to be hypnogogic imagery by Cohen, 1967]. While the capacity to memorize is unimpaired, SD and PD produce deterioration in the ability to solve problems involving reflection and active manipulation of ideas [Suedfeld, 1969]. After release from SD subjects experience 'motivational inertia', manifest in such effects as reduction in the length of invented stories and slower rates of speech [Suedfeld, 1969, pp. 142–143].

Physiological changes found during SD and PD include over-all slowing of the EEG, attributable to slowing of the α-rhythm and an increase in activity in lower frequency bands [see Zubeck, 1969; Heron *et al.*, 1972].

Generally there is a correlation between the slowing of the EEG and the decline in cognitive performance, and both of these measures have similar post-deprivation recovery periods [Zubeck, 1969]. The decline in cognitive performance might follow from a reduction in the capacity of the NS to sustain its own arousal, reflected in the slowed EEG. Over all, the detrimental effects of SD and PD on the NS and cognitive functioning appears to reflect the nervous system's need for patterned stimulation to maintain its efficiency.

We should pause to observe the need for caution in the interpretation of findings made in SD and PD experiments. Contradictory findings have been reported which might be attributable to differences in the severity of the conditions, inter-individual differences in tolerance of SD and the effects of unintentional suggestion or prior knowledge (SD experiments have received wide publicity in the mass media) on the subjects' verbal reports and test performance [see Solomon, 1972].

The sensory deprivation paradigm has been utilized to explore the defining features of 'stimulus need'. Consistent with the postulation of a stimulus seeking drive, it has been found that increasing time of stimulus deprivation produces higher rates of button pressing, to earn brief visual or auditory presentations of boring stimulus material, such as stock market reports [see review by Jones, 1969]. Jones [1969, pp. 186-189] found that informationally rich stimulus sequences were a greater incentive for response than ones with high complexity, or high fluctuation, when presented to SD subjects responding for relieving stimulation. He argued that SD activates a homeostatic drive seeking an optimum level of information input from the environment. Information is defined in terms of the degree of statistical uncertainty in the stimulus configuration. The current optimum is a function of the point in the sleeping–waking cycle and other factors.

Schultz [1965] maintains that 'level of sensory variation' is the superordinate stimulus dimension. Findings cited by Jones and Schultz emphasize that the level of arousal of the RAS is not adjusted around the optimum simply by the crude level of sensory stimulation, but by meaningful patterns of variation in the level of stimulation. These patterns of variation are implicit in the unpredictable changes in energy levels, in the temporal and spatial dimensions, which demarcate significant events in time and space (see Introduction to Part IV).

Optimal levels of stimulation for optimal arousal

Most of the evidence which we have surveyed is consistent with the hypothesis that the organism strives to attain a degree of variability in its sensory input which approximates to a current optimal value set by the RAS. This sensory input sustains a concomitant optimal level of arousal. Changes in input variability which result in shifts away from the optimal level of arousal are registered by the RAS which consequently generates a drive to restore input variability to this optimum. The organism may seek more or less stimulation according to whether the shift is above or below the optimum. The optimum itself is modulated according to such factors as phase of the sleeping–waking cycle and prior patterns of input; shifting up when the organism has been deprived, down when it has been satiated. If the organism is unable to attain a sensory input within its optimum range on the relevant dimensions then there appears to be an increasing deterioration in the functional efficiency of its information processing mechanisms, whose period of recovery is a function of the period of deprivation.

Both the findings and the theory have important implications for human activities in an epoch of industrialization and high technology, in which many people are exposed to conditions of both under and overstimulation. The most pervasive instance of perceptual deprivation may be on production line working characteristic of modern industry. The combined monotony of a repetitive task performed under conditions of unvarying mechanical noise may induce slowness and decrements in cognitive performance which leads to errors and accidents in the work task and lethargy and passivity outside of it [see Solomon, 1972]. Driving lorries long distances across featureless landscapes (e.g. the desert areas of Australia) is another instance where lowered arousal, consequent on effective perceptual deprivation, may lead to accidents. Another area in which the detrimental effects of sensory and perceptual deprivation have been neglected is in medicine where conditions of severe deprivation may occur in intensive care units, postoperative care and eye surgery [Solomon, 1972] and may result in psychological disturbances in the patient.

Need for sensory input for neural development and health

During a creature's waking hours a level of stimulation around the optimum sustains a level of cortical arousal, mediated by the RAS, which, in turn, ensures that the cortical neuronal networks which process information are sensitized to respond to the inputs arriving from the sense receptors. Evidence has accumulated that the cortical neuronal networks need this input to promote their normal development and to sustain their functional efficiency. This need is reflected in the changed structural and functional characteristics of the neuronal networks affected, and in the impoverishment of the behavioural repertoire mediated via these systems when an animal is reared or maintained in restricted sensory environments.

The majority of experiments on the degenerative effects of sensory deprivation on neuronal networks have involved elimination or restriction of visual input alone. As long ago as 1890 Donaldson observed in a post-mortem examination on a woman of 60 who had been blind and deaf since the age of two, that the cerebral cortex was abnormally thin in the occipital and temporal areas, and that cell diameters and numbers of cells were reduced in these regions. These observations have been replicated in more recent studies of common laboratory animals. Matthews [1964] found that there was extensive loss of cells from all lamina of the visual cortex in monkeys whose eyes had been enucleated at birth. When reared in darkness from birth both rats and kittens have been found to have less cortical volume than usual [Fifkova, 1967; Gyllensten et al., 1965, 1966; Globus and Scheibel, 1967] although the experimenters have not been able to attribute this reduction to changes in neurone type and number. Gyllensten et al., [1967] have found a reduction in the diameter of cell nuclei following dark rearing in kittens.

Many authors have found degenerative changes in the apical dendrites of visual cortex cells following elimination of vision at birth or later. These changes include reduction in branching and over-all length of dendrites in kittens [Coleman and Reisen, 1968] and deformation of dendritic spines in rabbits [Globus and Scheibel, 1967]. The number of spines on the apical dendrites have been found to be reduced by 22–35% in mice [Valverde, 1968], 35% in rabbits [Globus and Scheibel, 1967] and 25% in rats [Fifkova, 1968]. Fifkova [1970] has observed that when visual input, which has been excluded by eyelid suturing at birth in kittens, is restored within 10-30 days then the number of spines on the apical dendrites is restored to normal. If restoration of visual input is delayed for two months or more then the number of dendritic spines remains permanently depleted.

The particular significance of changes in the apical dendrites is that these are the locations at which the incoming sensory fibres synapse with the neurones of the cortical networks. The degenerative structural changes observed must be a consequence of insufficient levels of synaptic activity for development and sustenance of the structural basis of neural connectivity. The functional result of this structural deficiency must be an effective degradation of information seeking access to the cortical neuronal networks. This should be reflected in a deterioration of the ability of an animal to make perceptual discriminations in the modality concerned. It might additionally, or possibly alternatively, be the case that structural changes at the synapse are the substrate of perceptual learning generated by varied sensory experience, and that structural deficits at this location reflect a failure of perceptual learning due to lack of the necessary experience.

Electrophysiological evidence of the need for varied sensory input

Wiesel and Hubel [1963] have provided electrophysiological evidence of functional deterioration following visual deprivation, in an extension of their classical studies of the receptive fields of cortical neurones [Hubel and Wiesel, 1962; see Chapter 12]. They found that single cells in the visual cortex of cats, which were specifically responsive to slits of light in a particular orientation, were much more sluggish in their response to stimulation when kittens had had their eyelids sutured from birth. This result was associated with reduced diameters of the cortical cells involved.

Hubel and Wiesel's [1962] original finding that single cells within the visual cortex respond to features in the visual environment as specific as a slit of light at a particular angular orientation, suggests that there is a physical substrate mediating visual perception which achieves its results by feature analysis. The results of Barlow and Pettigrew [1971] suggest that the structure which effects this analysis is set up by visual experience, as single cells in the visual cortex of the dark reared cats tend to respond to slits of light at any orientation, rather than at specific orientations, as in normally reared animals.

Further interesting evidence concerning the influence of visual input on the functional characteristics of the feature analysing system comes from

Figure 7.3
Kitten in the restricted
visual environment used
by Blakemore (1970)
to investigate the effect
of visual experience on
the development of
feature analysing cells
in the visual cortex.
The ruff around the
kitten's neck prevents it
from seeing even its
own body.

From Blakemore, C.
(1971), Why we see
what we see. *New
Scientist*, **51** 614–617.
Reproduced by
permission of the
author and *New
Scientist*

studies in which patterned visual input is allowed, but is restricted to a single unchanging feature. Blakemore and Cooper [1970] reared kittens in the dark, except that for five hours each day they were placed in a cylinder marked with either horizontal or vertical black and white stripes (see Figure 7.3). In addition they wore a black collar which restricted vision of their own bodies. When investigated at five months of age they found that the majority of cells in the visual cortex of these animals responded exclusively to lines at angles which were distributed closely about either the vertical or the horizontal, according to their visual experience. The fact that they were unable to detect any silent areas of the visual cortex suggested that the visual environment had induced cells to assume an orientation sensitivity reflecting its predominant characteristics, rather than producing selective maturation of innate structures. The kittens in this experiment showed permanent behavioural deficits consistent with the functional abnormalities in the range of responses shown by the cortical units. They showed clumsiness when attempting to follow moving objects, failed to avoid obstructions such as table legs and in particular appeared to be blind to contours perpendicular to those experienced in the cylindrical world of their infancy.

Muir and Mitchell [1973] have confirmed the visual ineptitude of cats reared in single feature environments in measurable terms. They showed that such animals are deficient in their ability to discriminate between striped patterns (gratings) of different spatial frequencies (number of stripes per unit angular width) which are at right angles to the stripes which have constituted the animal's sole experience of the visual world.

The influence of early experience on the orientation specificity of cells in the visual cortex has been confirmed by other investigators working with cats [Hirsch and Spinelli, 1970; Pettigrew et al., 1973] but not with rabbits [Mize and Murphy, 1973] in which there is probably more visual processing at the retina.

In addition to striped environments, kittens have also been reared in environments consisting solely of point sources of light, with a resulting deficiency in the number of cortical cells responding to contours in different orientations, but a superabundance of cells responding to point sources of light [Pettigrew and Freeman, 1973; van Sluyters and Blakemore, 1973].

In a sequel to their 1970 paper Blakemore and Mitchell [1973] make the rather surprising claim that at 28 days of age, in dark-reared kittens, as little as one hour of exposure to an environment with horizontal or vertical stripes induces a corresponding predominance in orientation specificity of cortical neurones, which does not appear to be significantly augmented by any further experience. However, Hubel and Wiesel [1970] observe that the period of physiological sensitivity to the effects of unilateral eye closure in kittens does not commence until 28 days of age and lasts for 2-4 weeks. Monocular visual deprivation during this period results in a reduction in number of binocularly driven single cells and of cells driven by the deprived eye, in the visual cortex. In addition there is atrophy of lateral geniculate body cells receiving input from the deprived eye. Opening of the deprived eye up to five years after the critical period produces only limited physiological recovery and no detectable reversal of the geniculate atrophy. In behavioural studies Dews and Wiesel [1970] showed that the only permanent effect of monocular visual deprivation during the critical period was a reduction in acuity, visual control of motor behaviour showing recovery to normal levels. This evidence for a limited period of susceptibility to the detrimental effects of visual deprivation suggests that innately determined mechanisms of visual analysis require priming by appropriate patterns of stimulation, a phenomenon analogous to that of 'imprinting' described by Lorenz [1952].

The studies described represent a tentative approach to elucidating the neurophysiological correlates of the development of perceptual abilities, showing how the formation of the physical substrate of perception is influenced by differences in the degree and character of the stimulation experienced in different environments. The behavioural evidence for differences in perceptual abilities induced by different environments is also documented.

Perceptual abilities in different cultures

Figure 7.4
Visual ecology and perceptual development:

(i) The Muller-Lyer illusion which is only strongly experienced by people who live in a 'carpentered' environment with many verticals and horizontals and where there is extensive use of line drawings to represent three-dimensional scenes.

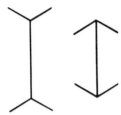

(ii) The Zulu hut provides a domestic environment which is not dominated by verticals and horizontals. The Zulus are not so susceptible to visual illusions.

From Gregory, R. L. (1966) *Eye and brain* © R. L. Gregory Reproduced by permission of the author and Weidenfield and Nicolson Ltd., publishers

The visual environment in western, urban, industrialized societies contains many manmade artefacts, such as buildings, with a profusion of vertical and horizontal contours which, because of the three-dimensionality of visual space, recede to a vanishing point. This has been characterized as a 'carpentered' environment and is contrasted with the visual environments experienced in less technologically advanced cultures in which there is a greater range of contours at all orientations and a much reduced frequency of horizontal and vertical contours.

The differential effect of these different visual environments on perceptual development is reflected, among the latter cultures, in a reduced susceptibility to visual illusions which incorporate cues for depth represented on a flat surface. Segall *et al.*, [1963] compared 15 societies, including urban American, white South African, non-European students, Dahomeans, Zulus, and Bushmen on susceptibility to the Muller–Lyer, Sander parallelogram, and two versions of the horizontal–vertical illusion. Groups remote from an urban industrialized setting showed little or no susceptibility to the illusions and the authors concluded that those who experienced the illusion did so because of a combination of rectangularity in their visual environment and familiarity with the conventions for representing a three-dimensional carpentered environment on a flat surface (i.e. in pictures) (see Figure 7.4). Leibowitz and Pick [1973] found that uneducated Ugandan villagers were much less likely to experience the Ponzo illusion than Ugandan students. This was despite the fact that both lived in similar environments with many carpentered features. The difference between the

Figure 7.5
Drawings by an
operated cataract
patient at various times
after his operation.
They suggest that a
process of perceptual
learning is necessary
when a sense modality
is newly given to an
individual, even in
adulthood.

From Gregory, R. L.,
Eye and brain. © R. L.
Gregory Reproduced
by permission of the
author and Weidenfield
and Nicolson Ltd.,
publishers

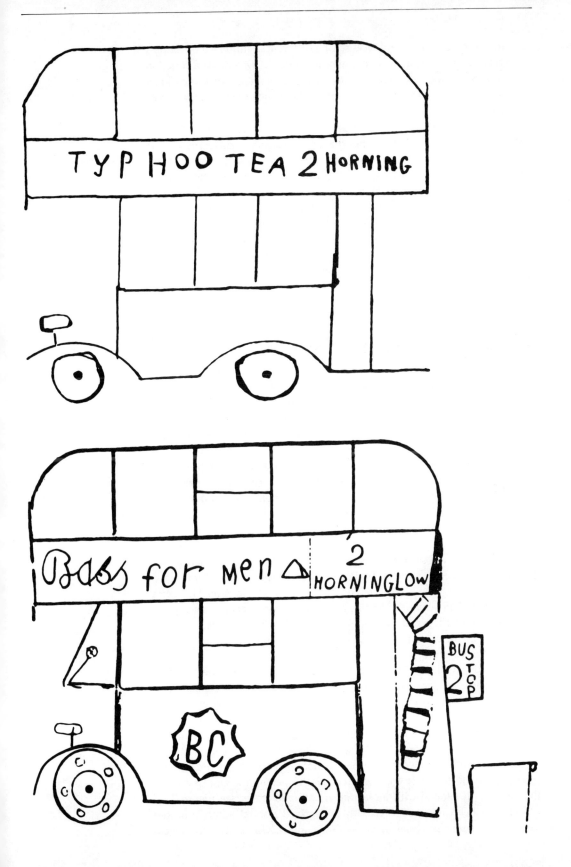

two groups must have arisen because of a differential influence of flatness cues versus depth cues, in the two-dimensional figure, which was a function of education. Failure to respond to depth cues in a two-dimensional figure may be a function of the amount of experience of representation of three-dimensional objects on a flat surface.

We have seen in the work of Blakemore and Cooper [1970] that the visual experience of a cat determines the representation of different angular orientations among orientation specific cells in the visual cortex. Annis and Frost [1973] suggest that the predominance of verticals and horizontals in urban settings enhances the number of human visual cortex cells sensitive to these orientations, relative to others, and that this is reflected in the fact that visual acuity was at its highest for these orientations in a sample of urban Canadians which they tested. In contrast they found that a sample of Cree Indians who have contours at all orientations equally represented in their environment, showed no differences in acuity as a function of orientation.

Sensory preconditioning

Riesen [1961] has characterized the process by which organisms acquire the capacity to recognize recurring stimulus patterns, and respond to them in a predictable manner, as sensory preconditioning. Sensory preconditioning involves the formation of sensory–sensory associations between the elements of a stimulus configuration which occur contiguously in time and/or space. These associations may be within a sensory modality or between sensory modalities. The substrate of these associations is postulated to be a modification of neural structures by contiguous inputs which occurs independently of any instrumental response or an observable, specifiable, experimentally controlled, reinforcement. The lack of opportunity to form visual–visual associations is reflected in the difficulty which cats, reared in the dark or diffuse light, have in learning to discriminate between geometric figures, a finding which is replicated in birds, rats, chimpanzees and man [see Riesen, 1961, p. 69]. However, it seems possible that deprivation of visual input does not preclude perceptual learning later in life as Chow and Stewart [1972] have claimed that kittens reared in darkness for two years are able to perform visual pattern discriminations after only moderate training.

It has been possible to investigate the retardation of dark reared humans in cases where persons, blind from birth with congenital cataract, have been given sight by an operation in their adult years [von Senden, 1932]. Immediately after the operation these patients show gross deficits in their ability to perceive form, three-dimensionality and distance, thus confirming the detrimental effects of visual deprivation on the appearance of perceptual abilities. However, the persistence of plasticity of the nervous system into adulthood is corroborated by the perceptual abilities which the patients developed with increasing visual experience (see Figure 7.5). It has even been reported that with undeprived normal adults repeated exposure of complex visual forms, without any reinforcement contingencies, leads to progressive improvement in the ability to recognize these forms [Franz and Layman, 1933]. Similar exposure to complex sound patterns leads to acquired distinctiveness in the subject [Forgus, 1958].

Kendall and Thompson [1960] have reported a very rigorous demonstration of sensory preconditioning which involved exposing cats to two second bursts of 250 Hz and 2000 Hz pure tones in immediate succession. After 20 preconditioning trials the cats were trained to make an instrumental response to avoid an electric shock when the lower frequency tone was presented. In subsequent tests of the generalization of the response to other tones between 250 and 8000 Hz clear evidence of an association was manifest in the sharp peak of responding which was found following presentation of the 2000 Hz tone.

Riesen [1961] has emphasized the importance of sensory-motor and motor-sensory preconditioning as a requisite for successful orientation in space and perception of movement. Any movement of an animal potentially generates visual and proprioceptive feedback, yielding information about position and motion in the environment relative to position and motion of the organism. Failure to make these sensory-motor and motor-sensory associations results in deficits such as failure to discriminate between moving and stationary objects. This occurs in cats which have been allowed patterned light stimulation but restrained from making any body movement [Riesen and Aarons, 1959].

Held [1965; see also Held and Bossom, 1961; Held and Freedman, 1963; Held and Hein, 1963] has presented evidence that learning to appreciate the spatial co-ordinates of different facets of the visual field only occurs when the visual and proprioceptive feedback from self-produced movements can be correlated with the command signals which initiated them. In experiments on humans Held [1965] and his coworkers capitalized on the fact that subjects can adapt to distortions of their visual field produced by wearing goggles with prism lenses. Presumably a process of perceptual relearning results in increasing accuracy in co-ordinating movements with the new disposition of the visual field. If subjects are denied the opportunity of making self-produced movements while they are wearing their distorting prisms then they fail to exhibit adaptation to their changed visual field, persistently making the same errors in such tasks as placing dots at the corners of a square.

In an experiment on the role of active movement in original perceptual learning [Held and Hein, 1963] each of two littermate kittens were attached to opposite ends of a 'carousel' device (see Figure 7.6). One kitten had its legs free and had its harness attached to a pivot so that it could tow the device round in a circle, or turn around on the spot. The other kitten was constrained in a gondola which allowed it identical visual experience to the other kitten but prevented it from making any active movement. The kittens were placed in this device three hours per day for ten days, between the ages of eight and twelve weeks. The rest of their existence was spent in darkness. At the end of this period the active kitten showed normal behaviour in visually guided tasks such as warding off a collision or avoiding a sharp drop (visual cliff), while the passive kitten was unable to cope with such situations. These experiments are vivid illustrations of the need for sensory stimulation correlated with movement if a

Figure 7.6
The carousel device used by Held and Hein to demonstrate that adequate perceptual development depends on the integration of visual and proprioceptive information.

From Held, R., Plasticity in sensory motor systems. *Sci. Amer.*, **213**, 85. Copyright © November, 1965 Scientific American Inc. All rights reserved. Reproduced by permission of the publishers

creature is to learn to perceive the three-dimensionality of the visual world and make accurate movements within it.

The effects of enriched and impoverished environments

In the experiments which have been described so far significant changes in structure and function in the nervous system and, concomitantly, in perceptual ability, have been attributed to stimulus deprivation. However, it has been stimulus deprivation of an extreme kind, outside of the range of environmental conditions which the different individuals of a species might be expected to encounter. In view of the argument concerning the relative importance of genetic inheritance versus environment in the determination of the capacities of individuals it is of great scientific and practical interest to know whether less extreme variations in the qualities of the environment produce differences in behavioural capacities which are reflected in the structure, physiology and chemistry of the brain. If such differences attributable to environmental conditions do exist then there are important implications for methods of rearing and educating the human species to attain maximum exploitation of their inherent potential.

In a well known series of experiments Bennett *et al.* [1964; and see

Figure 7.7
The three environments, impoverished, normal and enriched, which Rosenzweig's group used to investigate the effect of environment on measures of brain development.

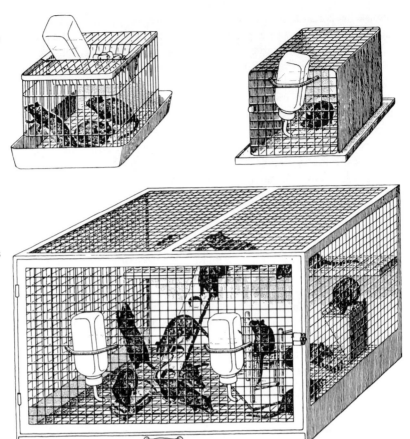

review in Rosenzweig *et al.*, 1972] reared rats in environments characterized as enriched, normal and impoverished (see Figure 7.7), littermates being allocated to each of the three conditions to achieve matching of genotypes. The rats in the enriched environment enjoyed the facilities of a large cage, which they shared with 10–12 other rats and which was equipped with 'toys' such as ladders, wheels, boxes and platforms. In addition these rats were given daily 30 min of exploring an area three foot by three foot with a changing pattern of barriers, were frequently handled by experimenters and also received some formal training in mazes. In the normal environment rats were subject to standard laboratory conditions of confinement in groups of three, in plain cages, without any special handling or training. The impoverished environment consisted of solitary confinement in cages with plain, solid walls, preventing any view outside, and with the minimum of handling and general stimulation consistent with satisfying their primary physical needs. Animals were kept in these environments from weaning (25 days of age) up to 80 days of age when they were killed and their brains removed for analysis.

It was found that the rats which had experienced the enriched environments had cerebral cortices which were thicker and heavier, and in which there was a greater concentration of the enzyme acetylcholine esterase (AChE), than those of the rats kept in the impoverished environments. The increase in cortical mass could not be attributed to an increase in the number of neurones and appeared to stem from an increase in the number of glia cells. It is reasonable to suppose that increased functional activity in cortical neurones might stimulate the multiplication of glia cells as such activity would increase the demand for nutrients for which glia is the transport medium. In addition an increase in glia cells might be an accompaniment of increased growth and branching of neurones as a type of glia forms the sheath around the neuronal processes.

It is the enzyme acetylcholine esterase which neutralizes the transmitter substance acetylcholine after the trans-synaptic propagation of each impulse. This ensures that each postsynaptic impulse is a discrete event. It is therefore to be expected that AChE will be found in increased concentration following increased synaptic activity.

To complement the study cited, Krech et al. [1962] found that there were differences in learning ability correlated with the structural and biochemical differences induced in the cerebral cortex by manipulating parameters of environmental complexity.

It is valuable to know whether the apparently beneficial effects of environmental complexity are only felt by the young of the species. It appears that it is not as adult rats given the privilege of an enriched environment for 80 days show an elaboration of brain structure over and above that attained during a youth spent in a normal laboratory environment. [Rosenzweig, 1966].

The environmental complexity described by Rosenzweig's research group is clearly a multifaceted concept. Some attempt has been made to tease out the relative importance of some of the different elements of environmental complexity. Rosenzweig et al [1972] cite experiments indicating that variation in the structure and chemistry of the brain cannot be correlated with differences in the frequency of handling by experimenters or with the amount of stress, reflected in activation of the pituitary–adrenal axis, experienced by the animals in different environments. It might be supposed that the impoverished environment produces 'isolation stress' or the enriched environment stress due to 'information overload'. Furthermore, Rosenzweig and Bennett [1972] showed that social stimulation from other rats was not a significant feature of the enriched environment in producing changes in the brain. Rosenzweig et al. [1972] believe that the changes which they have observed are the physical substrate of learning and memory which has occurred because of a greater variety of stimulus patterns in the environment.

In a fine analysis of changes in thickness of the cerebral cortex it was found that the greatest increase occurred in the occipital region, suggesting that complexity in the visual environment made the greatest contribution to the over-all gain in cortical weight [Rosenzweig et al., 1972]. However, there was evidence of interaction between the effects of input in different sensory modalities as there was still some increase in thickness of the occipital cortex when rats were subjected to the enriched environment in darkness. Globus et al. [1973] observed that an enriched environment led to an increase in the number of dendritic spines on the basal dendrites of cortical neurones, but not on the apical dendrites. The basal dendrites principally receive intracortical connections so that the enhanced connectivity between cortical areas implied by increased spine density may reflect an increased demand on intracortical systems to integrate complex multi-sensory information. This cortical function is very much consistent with the ideas expressed earlier in this chapter that perceptual and perceptual-motor skills develop as a function of repeated association of data within senses, across senses and between motor systems and the senses, a process characterized as sensory preconditioning. We should note in passing that the restriction of the change in dendritic spine density to the basal dendrites is in contrast to the earlier findings of Globus *et al.* [1967] and Valverde [1968] that total visual deprivation leads to a reduction in spine density on the apical dendrites, which handle afferent inputs from the senses. Thus it appears that changes in the morphology of cortical cells differentiate between a failure of the environment to provide any sensory input at all and a failure of the environment to provide the type of complex, multi-sensory input which stimulates integrative activity within cortical information handling systems.

The effects of different environments on human brain development

The environmentally induced differences in various parameters of brain development found by Rosenzweig's research group, although statistically significant and often replicated, were small and should be treated with some caution when considering their wider implications. It is tempting to extrapolate from the findings made on rats to humans, yet it is difficult to verify the influence of experience on brain development in humans because of the unacceptability of the relevant experiments. The only evidence which we have is from the post-mortem examination of the brains of persons who have lacked one or more senses from an early age. In a study by Donaldson [1890], cited previously, a blind deaf mute was found to have atrophied visual and auditory areas.

It is relatively easy to study the behavioural effects of differences in the amount and variety of stimulation during infancy. Comparisons have been made between children reared at home and children reared in institutions where they receive little stimulation, and between children reared in cultures showing patterns of child rearing which are divergent in terms of the amount and variety of stimulation given.

In his now famous monograph Bowlby [1951] documented the intellectual and social impairment of children raised in institutions compared with those raised in a normal family environment. Bowlby attributed this impairment to the emotional effects of the absence of a stable mother figure, but later researchers [particularly Casler, 1961, 1968] have considered the possibility that it might be at least partially attributable to stimulus deprivation [for review see Rutter, 1972, Chapter 5]. Many reports have claimed that institutionally reared children are intellectually and linguistically retarded [Haywood, 1967; Tizard, 1969] and more likely to exhibit mental subnormality than children brought up in normal homes [Goldfarb, 1945a, 1945b; Pringle and Tanner, 1958; Provence and Lipton,

1962]. Francis [1971] has claimed that children with Down's syndrome ('mongolism') show slower development in institutional settings than in normal family settings. Both Francis [1971] and Rutter [1972, p. 83] observe that in institutions which give a good level of care and intellectual stimulation children need suffer no impairment of their cognitive skills. Studies in which the factor of disruption of child-parent bonds is separated from that of stimulus deprivation indicates that it is the latter which is responsible for any retardation of language and intellect observed [Rutter, 1972, pp. 82-85].

Brossard and Decarie [1971] subjected two and three month old babies, who were living in an institution, to the human equivalent of Rosenzweig and coworkers' [1972] enriched environment for rats. They were bombarded with taped sound patterns, interesting visual stimuli (e.g. mobiles) and increased periods of being talked to and played with by adults. The authors claimed that in consequence there was superior developmental progress up to the age of five months (the limit of the study to date) compared with controls who were given levels of stimulation which were normal for the institution. However, in this study they were unable to differentiate between the beneficial effects of perceptual and social stimulation.

The results of such experiments as these pose many interpretive problems as the different elements of a complex programme of stimulation may make different contributions to any improvements in performance observed. There is probably a long way to go before we can outline the characteristics of programmes of stimulation in infancy, and education in childhood and youth which will maximize an individual's cognitive growth.

Permanence of deprivation induced deficits

It is both scientifically and socially important to know whether the deficits induced by stimulus deprivation are permanent and irreparable. The ethologists' notion that the external stimuli for many crucial events in development must occur within 'critical periods' [Nash, 1970, Chapters 8 and 9] has won wide support among psychologists. Consequently it has popularly been supposed that the detrimental effects of early stimulus deprivation could never be restored. However, we have seen in the work of Rosenzweig et al. [1972] that an enriched environment experienced during adulthood can augment brain development beyond that produced by a youth spent in a normal laboratory environment.

Kagan and Klein [1973] have presented some impressive evidence for recovery from stimulus deprivation among human children, from an intercultural study. In certain remote Guatemalen villages infants suffer from considerable stimulus deprivation during the first two years of their life as they are kept in dark huts, rarely played with or spoken to and only given the attention necessary to fulfil their physical needs. At 18 months to two years of age these children resemble institutional children observed in urbanised settings, showing fearfulness, lack of responsiveness to stimulation and retardation of speech. They are several months behind a comparison group of children from the USA on a series of developmental tests. However, once the Guatemalen children become mobile the freedom with which they are allowed to wander, play, and associate with other children permits them to optimize the amount of stimulation which they experience. This shows when they are later tested at the age of ten and no longer exhibit any retardation when compared with United States children of the same age. The effects of early deprivation appear to have been repaired by high levels of stimulation in a subsequent period. However, in interpreting this data we should remember that it is an untested hypothesis that the level of stimulation of the Guatemalen children in the supposed recovery period is closer to the optimal than that for United States children and it is this rather than specifically recovery which brings about the observed return to parity.

Summary and conclusions

It appears that higher organisms experience a need for patterned stimulation maintained at an optimum level. This optimum level is set by the reticular arousal system and shifts over time as a function of such factors as phase of the sleeping–waking cycle and the level of stimulation in the organism's immediate history. The level of stimulation experienced by an organism governs the degree of arousal which the RAS produces in the cerebral cortex, and thus the efficiency with which the cortex can process incoming information.

The need for stimulation is manifest in spontaneous activities such as investigation, exploration, play, and manipulation which occur independently of any other primary physiological need. It is also shown in the inability of humans to tolerate prolonged sensory or perceptual deprivation.

The physical basis of the stimulus need is to promote the full development and sustain the structure and functional efficiency of neuronal networks which external stimuli impinge upon. Prolonged stimulus deprivation produces measurable decrements in the structure, function, and chemistry of the brain and concomitant deficits in cognitive function. In particular varied patterns of stimulation, including stimulation correlated between modalities and stimulation correlated with command signals for motor acts, are required to develop the perceptual abilities which enable a creature to adequately evaluate stimuli, manipulate objects and move around safely in its environment. There is controversy about the amount of experience required for normal development. It may be relatively little. Furthermore it appears that an enriched environment in later developmental stages or even adulthood will repair the structural and behavioural deficits of early deprivation.

In the final analysis it appears that the coherence of man's conscious mind is dependent on ever changing stimulus patterns in the outside world. 'Sensory variety is not just the spice of life, it is the bread of life' [Zuckerman, 1969b].

Chapter eight **Sleep**

Introduction

The need for the survival promoting activities, whose neural basis has been discussed in the preceding five chapters, is easily understood. It is much more difficult to comprehend why we need cyclically recurring periods of sleep which alternate with these activities and stand in sharp contrast to them. Sleep is characterized by a reduction of activity and reactivity which appears to render the sleeper defenceless against predators and other dangers, and thus to reduce, rather than enhance his survival prospects.

Early theories concerning the function of sleep [see Kleitman, 1963, Chapters 33 and 34] appear to be derived from its phenomenology. As we approach our sleep period we are aware of a general decline in our drive level and inclination to activity and of subjective feelings of fatigue and drowsiness. Following a satisfactory period of sleep we feel refreshed, alert, and active. These observations suggest that our active waking life involves exhaustive processes in the body tissues which give rise to a need for periods of inactivity during which restorative processes can occur. Typical theories of this type maintain that sleep results directly or indirectly from the accumulation of toxic products; 'hypnotoxin' [Legendre and Pieron, 1911-12, cited in Kleitman, 1963] or 'fatigue toxin' [Cabitto, 1923, cited in Kleitman, 1963]. The sleep–wakefulness cycle suggests that the body is like a battery which requires periodic recharging by reversing the processes which occur when it is supplying energy.

The expectations generated by our subjective appreciation of sleep are confounded by the evidence from a high volume of research sustained over a number of years. No researcher has been able to conclusively demonstrate the existence of either a fatigue toxin which is dispersed by sleep, or a restorative process which occurs only during sleep. There is evidence of a simple nature which is inconsistent with the progressive accumulation of a fatigue product. Firstly the quantity of sleep does not increase as a function of amount of waking activity. A baby is less active than an adult but sleeps much more. Furthermore, there is enormous variation between individuals in the amount of sleep taken which appears to be independent of amount of waking activity [e.g. see Jones and Oswald, 1968; Rechtschaffen and Monroe, 1969; Webb, 1971]. Perhaps a more important observation is the enormous inter-species variation in the length of sleep, ranging from 6.2 h per 24 h in the tapir to 19.4 in the opossum [Zepelin and Rechtschaffen, 1970, cited in Webb, 1971]. Also deprivation of sleep does not produce sleepiness which increases in a linear progression. When subjectively assessed or objectively measured, peaks of sleepiness occur during the period when the individual would normally be asleep and reduced sleepiness is experienced during the day. Shiftworkers changing to the nightshift find that the sleep which they obtain during the day is briefer and more disturbed than sleep taken at night [cited by Snyder and Scott, 1972, p. 681]. All the evidence indicates that the sleeping–waking cycle is regulated by a stable internal clock, with characteristics peculiar to the individual, and resistant to modification by such factors as enforced wakefulness. Why such an internal clock should exist, if not to disperse the products of fatigue, is a taxing problem. One recent theory of the function of sleep [Webb, 1971, p. 171], rather than emphasizing the defencelessness of the sleeping animal, suggests that it could have a protective and conservative function in the ecology of behaviour. Webb suggests that in man sleep not only conserves energy, but prevents him from blundering around in the dark 'falling off cliffs, drowning in bogs, being consumed by effective night predators—very poor returns relative to his energy expenditure'.

Not only have initially plausible theories about the function of sleep proved difficult to sustain in the face of experimental evidence, but so have apparently self evident conceptions about the nature of sleep. Sleep appears to both the observer and the sleeper, in retrospect, to be a period of profoundly reduced reactivity to external events, near total immobility and absence of mentation or consciousness. It appears to involve a shutting down of the brain systems mediating information processing, consciousness and organization of motor responses. The fact that we remember dreams is a hint that sleep is not a period of total internal quiescence. Furthermore, the activity of some individual brain cells is found to increase during sleep [evidence reviewed in Williams et al., 1973, pp. 286-287]. During the phase of sleep in which we dream, in particular, there is clear evidence that although muscular responsiveness is actively suppressed, the brain is highly active. It gives rise to vivid conscious experiences, distinguishable from those of waking by the fact that their content is primarily generated internally, rather than by external stimuli, and that it rarely results in an enduring memory trace.

Even during the phases of sleep when we do not dream it appears that although the state of the brain is profoundly changed, it is a change in pattern of activity, rather than a change from activity to passivity [Williams et al., 1973].

In order to understand sleep as a process it is first necessary to describe the observable characteristics of sleep more fully as a preliminary to discussion of the neural structures, neurophysiological processes and neurochemical events which appear to generate the sleeping–waking cycle.

The stages of sleep

Sleep is largely characterized by the absence of overt behaviour, which limits the possibility of its study by traditional psychological methods. It is true that there is some movement during sleep, but this is composed mainly of changes in posture which occur with greater frequency as the night progresses [see Kleitman, 1963, Chapter 10]. It has proved possible to condition subjects to make limited muscular responses, such as moving their hand. This has proved useful in the investigation of reactivity to external stimuli occurring during sleep [e.g. Oswald, 1962, pp. 47–48]. However, the only instance of fully developed, apparently purposive behaviour patterns occurs in the 'zombie-like' behaviour of sleep walking which is relatively unusual.

In the absence of overt behavioural measures the sleep researcher has had to rely heavily on the recording of physiological and neurophysiological variables to obtain a picture of the progression of inner events occurring during sleep.

A great deal of impetus was given to sleep research by the development of EEG recording techniques which yield an over-all picture of the electrical activity of the brain (see Figure 3.7). The all night recording of the EEG from sleeping subjects has led to the description of five different patterns of EEG, characterizing five different stages of sleep. The first classification scheme was put forward by Loomis and coworkers [1937, 1938]. In stage A an interrupted α-rhythm was associated with the drowsiness occurring at the onset of sleep. Stages B to E were stages of definite sleep with a general trend to higher voltage and slower waves as stage E, supposedly the deepest phase of sleep, was approached. Loomis's scheme has subsequently been replaced by a modified scheme, now generally accepted, which was suggested by Dement and Kleitman [1957]. This followed the epoch making discovery of the additional stage of rapid eye movement sleep (REM) by Aserinsky and Kleitman [1953]. Dement and Kleitman collapsed the five stages of what is now called non-REM (or NREM or orthodox or slow wave or SWS) sleep into stages 1–4. In stage 1 the EEG is low voltage, mixed frequency with slowed and irregular α-activity and sometimes activity in the 4–6 cycle range. In stage 2 sleep the low voltage, mixed frequency activity of stage 1 is interrupted by 'sleep spindles', waxing and waning bursts of 12–14 cycles activity, and 'K' complexes, complex high amplitude waveforms exceeding 0.5 s in duration. Stage 3 is marked by the appearance of slow, high amplitude δ-waves in the frequency band 1–2 Hz which occupy up to 50% of the record, and the persistence of intermittent sleep spindles. In stage 4 spindles no longer occur and the record is dominated by δ-activity. The progression from stage 1 to stage 4 usually occurs in an invariant sequence following the onset of sleep, each succeeding stage appearing to represent a deeper phase of sleep than the last.

Perhaps the most prominent milestone and stimulant to sleep research was Aserinsky and Kleitman's [1953] discovery of REM sleep. In addition to recording the EEG they recorded eye movements during sleep and observed that there were recurring phases during which there were rapid conjugate eye movements of variable direction and amplitude, which resemble the jerky fixational shifts occurring during waking (see Figure

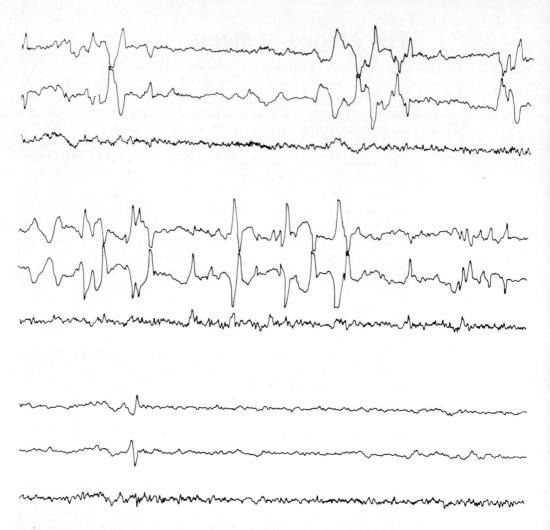

Figure 8.1
Electro-oculographic and EEG patterns during REM (paradoxical) sleep. Each group
of three traces represents a 15 s sample. The first trace in each group is the parietal
EEG; the second and third represent lateral movement of the right and left eyes
respectively. The mirror image form of the right and left eye movement patterns
indicates that they are the conjugate movements which, during sleep, only occur
during the REM phase.

From Snyder, F., and Scott, J. (1972). Reproduced by arrangement with Holt,
Rinehart and Winston, New York, from *Handbook of Psychophysiology* by
Greenfield/Sternbach 1972, © 1972

8.1). In fact two Russian sleep researchers Denisova and Figurin [cited in
Snyder and Scott, 1972, pp. 655–656] had, 25 years earlier, reported a
phase of sleep in children, in which rapid eye movements and irregular
breathing occurred, but the observation was never followed up. Aserinsky
and Kleitman's rediscovery of rapid eye movement sleep has led to the
detailed investigation of its many facets and the revelation of its paradoxical nature.

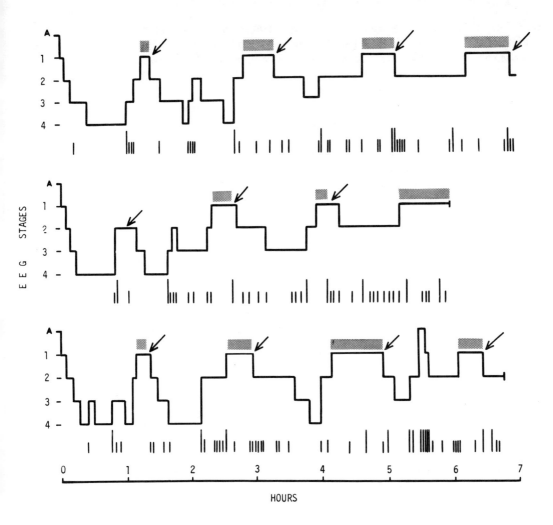

Figure 8.2
The profile of three successive nights' sleep when the sleep is broken down into its different EEG stages. The REM periods are shown by the heavy bars on the graph. The arrows indicate the commencement of cycles which run from the end of one REM period to the end of the next. The vertical strokes indicate the occurrence and intensity of body movements.

From Dement, D., and Kleitman, N. (1957) Cyclic variations in the EEG during sleep and their relations to eye movements, body motility and dreaming. *Electroenceph. clin. Neurophysiol.*, **9**, 673–690. Reproduced by permission of Elsevier/North Holland Publishing Co

   REM sleep is a recurring pattern which usually makes its first appearance 90 min after the onset of sleep, following the progression from stages 1 to 4 and back again to stage 2. Thereafter periods of REM sleep recur at approximately 90 min intervals, the periods lengthening from 5–10 min early in the night to 20–30 min towards the end of the night's sleep. Four REM periods occur in the typical night's sleep of a human adult and occupy about 20% of total sleep time (see Figure 8.2).

REM sleep has been given the alternative name of paradoxical sleep, and for good reason. The EEG pattern which accompanies the rapid eye movements is fast low voltage activity, without spindles or 'K' complexes (see Figure 8.1). It is more like that recorded from a person who is awake and alert. Direct recordings from midbrain, reticular formation and diencephalon structures also indicate intense arousal, as does the appearance of hippocampal θ-activity (regular waves at about 6 Hz). Unit recordings during REM sleep further document a state of intense excitement in the brain, as groups of neurones throughout the brain show integrated burst patterns with very high discharge rates. Also there is a dramatic acceleration of discharges in the pyramidal tract which account for the phasic muscle twitches that are another feature of REM sleep [see Williams *et al.*, 1973 for review of unit recording studies].

A further 'phasic' aspect of REM sleep indicating a concomitant high level of brain electrical activity are characteristic 'spikes' which may be recorded from macroelectrodes implanted in the pons, lateral geniculate body of the thalamus and occipital lobes. These appear to be co-ordinated with eye movements and have been named PGO (pontine–geniculate–occipital) spikes. While autonomic activity during REM sleep does not show a consistent pattern of arousal, heart rate and respiration show an enormous increase in moment to moment variability suggestive of intermittent arousal [e.g. see Snyder and Scott, 1972, pp. 669-673].

In sharp contrast to the persistent highly aroused state of the brain and the intermittent arousal of the autonomic nervous system, the body musculature is at its most relaxed. Muscle tonus, as measured by electromyogram activity, is lower than during any other phase of sleep. There is a profound tonic inhibitory influence from the pontine region of the brainstem [Pompeiano, 1967] which effectively paralyses the body, so that the only results of intense discharges in the pyramidal tract are occasional muscle twitches of small extent.

Depth of sleep

The contrasting aspects of REM sleep bring into focus the problem of defining the depth of sleep. As sleep is usually thought of as defining the lower segment of an arousal continuum the most obvious way to define depth of sleep would seem to be in terms of difficulty of awakening. According to this criterion stages 1-4 of orthodox sleep represent progressively deepening phases and, despite the manifold evidence of intense cortical arousal, REM represents the deepest phase of sleep. However, this relationship between the stage of sleep and the minimum intensity required to awaken the sleeper only holds when the awakening stimulus is a stimulus of no special significance to the sleeper. Casual observation suggests that a significant stimulus is more likely to awaken a sleeping person than one that is familiar and insignificant. People living in towns habituate to quite loud traffic noise, and sleep through it, while an unfamiliar noise will awaken them. Sharpless and Jasper [1956] showed that while habituated tones failed to arouse cats, slightly changed tones woke them immediately. Rowland [1957] and Christake [1957] showed that stimuli acquired arousing properties after they had been paired with electric shocks.

The differential responsiveness of a sleeping person can be investigated without actually awakening them, as they will sometimes follow instructions, given prior to sleep, to make a limited muscular response, such as squeezing a hand, to specified stimuli occurring during sleep. Also the registration of transient stimuli by the sleeping brain is revealed by the appearance of 'K' complexes in the EEG. Oswald [1962, p. 47] reports that when played over a tape recorder, a sleeping subject's name elicits muscular and EEG responses, which names with no special significance to the sleeper do not elicit. Williams *et al.* [1964, 1966] have deepened the paradox of REM sleep by showing that tone stimuli, initially less often responded to during REM sleep than the other stages, are more often responded to during the REM phase of sleep after they have been established as a warning of impending punishment. Okuma *et al.* [1966] required human subjects to make button presses to photic flashes during sleep, with subsequent awakening for questioning. During stage 4 (δ-wave) sleep stimuli were rarely perceived and never responded to. While both reported perception and muscular responses occurred duing other phases of sleep, there was a much higher frequency of correct perception, without a muscular response, during REM sleep. It appears that despite the lack of external signs of consciousness, significant external stimuli are registered in the brain and in consciousness more readily during REM sleep than during its other stages.

Dream consciousness

It seems contradictory to suggest that stimuli enter consciousness during sleep, as sleep is generally thought of as being synonymous with unconsciousness. Yet there is strong evidence that the substrate of consciousness functions at a high level during REM sleep. As we emerge from sleep into wakefulness our memory often informs us of a bizarre form of consciousness occurring during sleep—the dream. We clearly separate our dream consciousness from that of waking because the images of the dream clearly do not arise from objects currently present in the real world and because the sequence of events and images in the dream is judged, in retrospect, to be disordered and bizarre. A great weight of evidence suggests that most dreams occur during REM sleep. Many researchers have monitored the progression of sleep stages by recording the EEG and eye movements and have woken subjects up during selected stages. Different researchers have reported that following between 60 and 88% of awakenings during REM sleep, subjects have been able to recall dreams. Few investigators report dream recall on more than 20% of awakenings from NREM sleep, and when they are reported they are usually less vivid, less bizarre and less emotional than dreams reported following awakening from REM sleep [for review see Hartmann, 1967, p. 12].

Knowledge of the phenomenological correlate of REM sleep has given rise to speculation about the significance of the rapid eye movements, autonomic variability and unexpected activation of the brain which characterizes it. Snyder and Scott [1972, p. 691] cite findings associating the direction and timing of eye movements with the following of images which the subject has reported as occurring during their dream. They have similarly reviewed evidence associating respiratory changes with the emotional content of dreams and with activity involving the respiratory system (e.g. speech, laughter, choking) occurring during a dream [Snyder and Scott, 1972, p. 692]. The intense cortical activity indicated by the activated EEG pattern and high level of single cell discharges is clearly consistent with the generation of a stream of consciousness.

The peculiarity of dream consciousness is that its content is determined largely by internally generated activity, presumably involving access to stores of past events, rather than by external stimuli. This domination of consciousness by an internally generated input must clearly be facilitated by the restriction on sensory input usually achieved during sleep. However, it is interesting to note that stimuli below the threshold for arousal, presented during REM sleep, are often incorporated into dreams whose content is reported on subsequent awakening [e.g. see Hartmann, 1967, pp. 137-8]. This incorporation of external stimuli into the content of dream consciousness is further evidence that dream consciousness is generated by the same substrate as that of waking but is based on input from an internal source.

The mystery and uniqueness of dream consciousness is accentuated by the fact that it is only known through verbal report of an evanescent memory image, and that it occurs during periods of bodily relaxation so complete that its persistence during awakening from a dream sometimes gives rise to a feeling of paralysis. During dreaming there is almost complete suppression of the overt behaviour from which the conscious state of an individual is usually inferred, making that consciousness almost invisible. However, we shall see that following various experimental manipulations, sleep deprivation, certain drug treatments and brain lesions, the internally generated dream images may break through into consciousness without paralysis of the musculature occurring. Then the behavioural concomitants of dream consciousness are quite visible.

The neural mechanisms of sleep

Contemporary investigations of the neural mechanisms of sleep stem from classical transections of the brainstem of cats performed by Bremer [1935] in the 1930s. Bremer was testing the hypothesis that sleep was a passive phenomenon, a reduction of brain activity due to elimination of sensory input. In his first preparation, the *encephalé isolé*, Bremer severed the entire brain and brainstem from the spinal cord, thus isolating the brain from all somatosensory input. Using the newly developed technique of EEG recording and observation of pupil dilation, as the spinal transection abolished most other overt signs of wakefulness, Bremer observed that this preparation continued to show the sequence of changes characteristic of the normal sleeping–waking cycle. From the standpoint of the passive 'deafferentation' theory of sleep this can be accounted for by the fact that all of the sensory systems in the head have uninterrupted access to the brain. In Bremer's second preparation, called the *cerveau isolé*, the brainstem was transected high in the midbrain, leaving only the visual and olfactory inputs to the brain intact. This preparation persistently displayed the immobility of the eyes, constriction of the pupils and synchrony of the EEG characteristic of a sleeping cat, with no interruption by signs of wakefulness. Bremer concluded that this endless state of sleep arose because of a profound reduction in afferent input.

The brainstem reticular formation and sleep – wakefulness

Bremer's discoveries have subsequently been taken as the foundation for a rather different theory; that there is an autonomous mechanism in the brainstem regulating the periodic alternation between sleeping and waking. The activating functions of the brainstem reticular formation (BSRF) have already been mentioned in Chapters 6 and 7 (see Figure 7.1). An early anatomical description of this diffuse multisynaptic network of neurones, ascending from the medulla to the diencephalon in the central core of the brainstem, was given by Ramon y Cajal [1909]. Intense interest in its functional significance was generated much later by the now classical experiments of Moruzzi and Magoun [1949]. They showed that stimulation of this structure in *encephalé isolé* cats translated the cortical EEG from that of sleep to that of wakefulness. The functions of the BSRF or RAS (reticular activating system) have been reviewed by Lindsley [1960] and Magoun [1963]. The RAS has diffuse projections to all cortical locations by which it can produce generalized cortical arousal. Arousal can be produced by a signal in any sensory modality, as all of the sensory systems have branching inputs into the non-specific RAS. The RAS will also produce the periodic cortical activation, characteristic of the sleeping-waking cycle, independent of the sensory inputs to the brain (i.e. when they have all been interrupted). This suggests that the cycle arises from competing mechanisms in the brainstem, alternating in dominance as they exhaust and recharge.

Batini *et al.* [1959a, b, c] have shown that if the brainstem is transected between the two classical cuts of Bremer, in mid pons prior to the entry of the trigeminal nerve (the midpontine pretrigeminal preparation), then the cat thus treated will show persistent patterns of wakefulness which will continue even if all remaining sensory inputs are interrupted. This finding suggests that the periodic sleep observed in the *encephalé isolé* must be initiated by a mechanism in the lower brainstem and that wakefulness must be promoted by a mechanism in the upper brainstem. Furthermore, as the wakefulness promoted by the upper brainstem is sustained quite independently of sensory input, sleep cannot be passive, but must be promoted by a mechanism actively anatagonizing the influence of the wakefulness mechanism.

At first sight a relatively simple picture seems to be emerging in which the alternation between sleeping and waking is regulated by two clearly differentiated centres in the brainstem. The model is complicated by the evidence that there are other sleep promoting structures in the diencephalon and basal forebrain. As early as 1944 Hess showed that electrical stimulation of the massa intermedia of the thalamus produced all of the behavioural characteristics of spontaneous drowsiness and sleep. Clear evidence documents the role of the non-specific nuclei of the thalamus in inducing the widespread synchronization of cortical electrical activity which is characteristic of sleep. Monnier et al. [1960] confirmed that sleep followed low frequency stimulation of the medial thalamic nuclei. However, this does not prove that this structure is the origin of sleep promoting influences. It may be a relay in a cortically directed projection system originating from a sleep centre in the brainstem. The fact that insomnia does not follow from destruction of the medial thalamus [Anderson and Anderson, 1968; Angeleri et al., 1969; cited in Bremer, 1974] supports the latter interpretation. Furthermore, the persistent wakefulness of the midpontine pretrigeminal preparations of Batini's group, with their thalami quite intact, tends to refute the theory that the medial thalamus is the origin of impulses promoting sleep.

It could be maintained that the persistent sleep patterns of the *cerveau isolé*, which occur despite the elimination of the sleep promoting mechanisms of the lower brainstem, is evidence of the domination of a forebrain sleep centre. The postulation of such a mechanism is only necessary if sleep can only occur by the intercession of an active mechanism. If sleep can occur as a passive phenomenon, following the removal of a tonic activating influence, then the sleep of the *cerveau isolé* is simply explained by the disconnection of the midbrain arousal mechanism. An active mechanism might still be necessary to promote sleep in a fully intact brain by antagonizing the influence of an arousal system which would otherwise be continually active. We should observe however, that some experimenters question the classical observation that the *cerveau isolé* displays only persistent sleep. Moruzzi [1974] claimed that chronic decerebrate cats displayed physiological changes clearly related to the alternation of sleep and wakefulness and Adametz [1959] has presented evidence that when the midbrain reticular formation is lesioned in stages, with intervening periods of postoperative recovery, then the sleeping–waking cycle survives, and is not replaced by the persistent somnolence of Bremer's *cerveau isolé*. It may be that forebrain structures, normally fulfilling a subsidiary role, are able to take over the functions of the brainstem mechanisms which normally regulate the sleeping–waking cycle.

Forebrain structures promoting sleep

Other forebrain structures have been clearly implicated in sleep. The destruction of the posterior portion of the hypothalamus, which is continuous with the brainstem reticular formation, results in a persistent pattern of somnolence. This class of evidence is the basis for Gellhorn's [1968] division of the hypothalamus into an activating posterior ergotropic region and a deactivating anterior trophotropic region (discussed in Chapter 6). Sterman and Clemente [1974] observe that both low and high frequency stimulation of the anterior hypothalamus or adjacent structures of the basal forebrain (the orbitofrontal cortex) elicits sleep, which follows all of the normal preparatory behavioural adjustments such as finding a corner, lying down, and assuming a sleeping posture. Bilateral destruction of the basal forebrain was found to be followed by the suppression of sleep and an increase in wakefulness. In single cell discharge studies [Sterman and Clemente, 1974, pp. 90–92] many cells of the preoptic area of the hypothalamus showed irregular activity with intense bursting patterns, during the onset of sleep. Sterman and Clemente suggested that the targets of these discharges were the nuclei of raphe, a system of nuclei in the lower pontine area of the brainstem which we will see is associated with the onset of sleep.

Not only does stimulation of the basal forebrain elicit neuroelectric potentials from the raphe nuclei, but stimulation of the raphe nuclei produces subtle alteration in the discharge pattern of basal forebrain units. These observations led Sterman and Clemente [1974, p. 92] to postulate that the basal forebrain was the initiator of sleep, and that its influence on the rest of the brain was mediated by the raphe system, with which it was in a reciprocal relation. There is further evidence consistent with this view as Kogan [1969; cited in Williams *et al.*, 1973] has shown that in the cat the slow waves of NREM sleep originate in the deeper layers of the frontal cortex, then spreading, as sleep develops, to the more superificial layers of the frontal cortex, the remainder of the cortical mantle, the diencephalon, and finally the brainstem reticular formation.

The indispensability of the cerebral cortex to NREM sleep has been shown by Jouvet [1962, 1965] who found a complete and permanent absence of the spindles and slow waves characteristic of this phase of sleep during three months survival of neodecorticate cats. However, in these preparations all the signs of REM sleep appeared with clockwork regularity. This indicated that the mechanisms promoting REM sleep were more clearly focussed in the brainstem. It also suggested that the REM to REM cycle was the manifestation of a more primitive rhythm than the diurnal sleeping–waking rhythm. Kleitman has called this faster rhythm the basic rest activity cycle [BRAC; see Kleitman, 1963, Part 3].

Although there is strong evidence that the presence of the cortex is necessary for the appearance of the slow waves of NREM sleep this does not necessarily mean that the cortex is the initiator. It could be that the brainstem and/or thalamic structures initiate sleep, but are dependent on reciprocal discharges through corticothalamic feedback loops to intensify and sustain synchronization in both structures.

Specific brainstem structures promoting NREM and REM sleep

In recent years the mapping of the brainstem structures promoting sleep has become more precise. The raphe nuclei (see Figure 8.3) have already been mentioned as a target for impulses from a basal forebrain centre, tentatively proposed as the initiator of sleep. The raphe nuclei extend, in

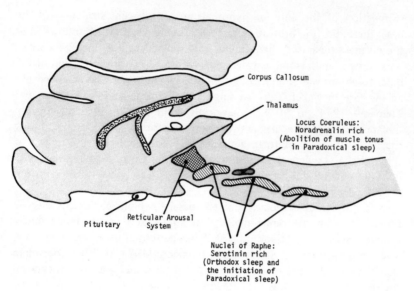

Corpus Callosum

Thalamus

Locus Coeruleus:
Noradrenalin rich
(Abolition of muscle tonus
in Paradoxical sleep)

Pituitary

Reticular Arousal
System

Nuclei of Raphe:
Serotinin rich
(Orthodox sleep and
the initiation of
Paradoxical sleep)

Figure 8.3
Schematic cross-section of a cat's brain to show the neural structures and active neurochemicals involved in the induction of orthodox and REM sleep.

From Jouvet, M. (1967), The sleeping brain. *Science J.*, 3, 105–111. Reproduced by permission of Syndication International Ltd

the midline of the brainstem, from the medulla to the lower midbrain. Thus the sleep abolishing midpontine transection of Batini *et al.* [1959a, b, c] severed two-thirds of the raphe system from the wakefulness promoting system of the midbrain. Jouvet [1974] has shown that the destruction of 80–90% of the raphe system produces complete insomnia for 3–4 days with only 10% of time occupied in slow wave sleep during the following 10 days.

REM sleep appears to be more unequivocally located in the brainstem than NREM sleep. Animals with all of the brain above the pons removed, except for a hypothalamic island, show periodic alternation between waking and the muscle atonia characteristic of REM sleep, without any intervening signs of NREM sleep [Jouvet, 1962, 1965]. Lesions of pontine nuclei (caudal aspects of the nucleus reticularis pontis oralis and the rostral segment of the nucleus reticularis pontis caudalis [Jouvet and Delorme, 1965; cited in Williams *et al.*, 1973] suppress signs of REM sleep in cats. Lesions of another pontine nucleus, the locus coerulus (see Figure 8.3), reduce the tonic muscle atonia associated with REM sleep, with dramatic effects [Jouvet and Delorme, 1965]. It appears, that in the absence of the normal inhibitory influences on the intense motor output which are normally present, the animal exhibits complete and fully developed behaviour patterns during REM sleep. These seem to occur without reference to environmental stimuli and rather as if the creature were responding to hallucinations. Without the tonic inhibition of muscular activity an animal would appear to act out its dreams.

Recent unit recording studies by McCarley and Hobson [1975] have implicated giant neurones in the tegmentum of the pons in the genesis of REM sleep. They are quiescent during wakefulness and NREM sleep, but precede the onset of REM sleep with burst patterns of discharges, which appear to be correlated with the PGO spikes and rapid eye movements constituting the primary phasic aspects of REM sleep.

The biochemical basis of sleep

We have seen that the history of ideas of the origins of sleep includes a number of theories supposing that there are specific sleep inducing substances which accumulate in the body. In recent research the biogenic amines, serotonin and noradrenaline have been found to be implicated in the genesis and maintenance of sleep, and their manifest importance has led recent reviewers to assert that 'neurochemistry is the basic science of sleep' [Williams *et al.*, 1973].

The recent development of histofluorescent techniques in biochemistry has facilitated the mapping of the differential distribution of amines in different brain structures. Falk *et al.* [1962] and Dahlstrom and Fuxe [1964] have shown that the raphe system is rich in serotonin containing neurones which show a bright yellow fluorescence. Dahlstrom and Fuxe [1964] have traced the terminals of these serotoninergic neurones to widespread regions of the brain and spinal cord. Jouvet [1974] has destroyed the major part of the raphe system in cats and, as we have seen, produced insomnia which persisted wholly, and then partially for 10–13 days. Following sacrifice, biochemical analysis of the brains of the insomniac preparations indicated that there was a significant decrease in cerebral serotonin. A significant correlation was shown to exist between the extent of destruction of the raphe system, the intensity of the insomnia produced, and the selective decrease of cerebral serotonin.

The levels of brain serotonin have been manipulated by other means than lesioning. The most important method has been pharmacological, using PCPA (*p*-chlorophenylalanine), a substance which depletes brain and peripheral serotonin in a graded manner, without significantly affecting the levels of other brain amines. Koella [1974] has shown that intraperitoneal injections of PCPA result in a period of insomnia proportional to the dose. Loss of all phases of sleep commences 24 hours after injection, peaks after three to four days, and recovers to control levels after eight days to two weeks, depending on dose. The attribution of this loss of sleep to depletion of serotonin, was confirmed by the fact that an injection of the serotonin precursor 5-hydroxytryptophan produced an almost immediate return of slow wave sleep to control levels, or above.

Koella [1974] also plottted the time course of changing serotonin levels in various brain structures, following injections of PCPA, and found that they lagged behind the return of sleep to normal levels. Koella offers alternative explanations for this discrepancy. One possibility mooted is that serotonin available at receptor sites in the brain returns more rapidly than total brain serotonin. Alternatively, Koella suggests that there may be a negative feedback system, with a delay, which builds up a pressure for sleep, in spite of there being low levels of serotonin. This hypothesis also explains the 'rebound' (transient increase in percentage of sleep time above control levels) which occurs after lower doses of PCPA, in spite of the fact that serotonin is not elevated above control levels during this rebound period.

Koella [1974] also presents evidence that there is another mechanism through which serotonin exercises its antiwaking influence, in addition to that exercised via the directly acting, hypnogenic, serotoninergic raphe system. Koella observed that the injection of 5-HT (i.e. 5-hydroxytrypta-mine, another name for serotonin) into the carotid artery produced, after initial arousal, up to 20 min of slow waves and spindles in the EEG. As 5-HT does not normally cross the blood–brain barrier, except in small amounts Koella looked for a possible 'hole' in this barrier. He found evidence for such an entry point at the lower end of the floor of the fourth ventricle, in the area postrema. Cauterization of this area, or local application of the serotonin blocking agents LSD-25, or methysergide, reduced or eliminated the synchronizing effects of intra-carotid serotonin. Conversely, the topical application of serotonin to this area produced the appearance of, or increase in, spindle bursts and slow wave output. Koella argued that the 5-HT induced activity, in the area postrema, is translated into hypnogenic influences on the brain, via the nucleus tractus solitarius, with which it has demonstrable connections. Stimulation of this nucleus induces synchronization of the EEG. Koella advances argument and evidence that it constitutes a variable gain mechanism in a negative feed-back connection with the reticular formation, to check excessive arousal. When the gain is increased by serotoninergic activity in the area postrema, it exercises a marked antiwaking influence on the reticular formation. This complements the directly acting serotoninergic hynotic mechanism of the raphe system.

An interesting experimental observation cited by Koella [1974] is that intracarotid injection of serotonin in an animal, in which the sleep promot-ing zone of the lower brainstem had been transected, produced only the signs of cortical arousal characteristic of an excitatory drug. Hartmann [1967, p. 69] notes that serotonin has paradoxical effects, having excitat-ory or inhibitory effects according to the levels of the drug administered, and sometimes being associated with sedated and excited states following each other in sequence. These findings underline the assertion that sleep is not simply a reduction in the level of cortical activity by inhibitory influences, but rather a radical change in its pattern of activity, effected by brainstem and diencephalic mechanisms with the power to impose a pervasive synchrony on the firing patterns of cortical neurones.

There is general agreement that a serotoninergic system in the brain-stem initiates sleep, probably by both exercising a restraining influence on the upper brainstem arousal system, and by a more direct synchronizing influence on cerebral structures. It is implicit in the ideas of Jouvet, the leading protagonist of the serotoninergic theory of sleep, that sleep is sustained by these serotoninergic mechanisms, and also that serotonin triggers REM sleep. The only evidence which appears to embarrass the serotoninergic theory of sleep is the finding that single cells in the raphe system show reduced discharge rates during NREM sleep relative to during waking [Harper and McGinty, 1972]. The authors argue that the role of the raphe cells may be limited to constraining activities which interfere with sleep at sleep onset.

Biochemical mechanisms of REM sleep

Both serotonin and noradrenaline are implicated in the triggering and maintenance of REM sleep. Lesions of the raphe system, which produce partial insomnia by depleting cerebral serotonin, eliminate REM sleep completely, if NREM sleep falls below 15% of a 24 h record in cats [Jouvet, 1972]. Both PCPA, which depletes cerebral serotonin, and reserpine, which interferes with the storage of serotonin and other biogenic amines, eliminate NREM sleep and the tonic inhibitory aspects (tonic inhibition of the motor system) of REM sleep [e.g. see Williams et al., 1973]. Brain serotonin levels have been manipulated by regulating the body's intake of the 5-HT precursor 5-HTP (5-hydroxytryptophan) or the 5-HTP precursor L-tryptophan. While 5-HTP increases NREM sleep but decreases REM sleep, in cats, L-tryptophan increases both NREM and REM sleep in man [findings cited in Williams et al., 1973]. In dietary manipulation experiments Hartmann [1967, p. 71] found that while tryptophan free diets reduced REM sleep, tryptophan loaded diets increased it. In these experiments on manipulation of serotonin levels by injection or diet, increases in REM time occurred because REM sleep was triggered more often, decreases, because it was triggered less often. This indicated that serotonin was specifically involved in the triggering of REM sleep.

The familiar categories of evidence indicate that a noradrenergic mechanism sustains REM sleep after it has been triggered by serotonin. Histochemical mapping shows that the locus coerulus, which we have seen is strongly implicated in REM sleep, is rich in noradrenaline (NA) containing neurones, although there are some acetylcholine containing neurones as well. Reduction of cerebral NA synthesis by the blocking action of α-methyl-p-tyrosine [Torda, 1969, cited in Williams et al., 1973], or by dietary depletion of the NA precursors phenylalanine and tyrosine [Lester et al., 1969, cited in Williams et al., 1973], reduces the amount of REM sleep. Torda [1969] claimed that intracerebral NA injections restored the REM sleep levels reduced by α-methyl-p-tyrosine. However, Jouvet [1972] cites the quite contradictory finding that α-methyl-p-tyrosine has no effect on REM sleep.

Warburton has reviewed studies suggesting that REM sleep is mediated by cholinergic systems rather than noradrenergic. Jouvet [1967] has shown that the cholinergic blocker atropine prevents REM sleep in normal and REM sleep deprived cats. On the other hand REM sleep is increased by the anticholinesterase physostigmine [Jouvet, 1962]. Hernandez-Peon [1963] claimed that the introduction of acetylcholine into crucial diencephalic regions produced orthodox sleep closely followed by REM sleep. As the phenomenological, behavioural and electrophysiological components of REM sleep are complex it would not be surprising if it were produced by a complex mechanism depending on multiple chemical agents.

In other studies the administration of NA, or its precursors, in intact animals or humans, produces arousal and tends to suppress stage REM. Furthermore, we have seen that NA is implicated in the activation of aggression circuits clearly associated with arousal (see Chapter 6). This evidence is not necessarily inconsistent with an important NA involvement in REM sleep as cortical activity during REM is, as we have seen, characteristic of arousal. The curious coexistence during REM sleep, of insensitivity to external stimuli, muscular atonia, and intense cortical activity suggests a mechanism of some subtlety and precision, whose properties may not be readily revealed by gross biochemical manipulations.

There is evidence that the mechanisms responsible for the different aspects of REM sleep can be dissociated. For instance the drug reserpine releases the substances serotonin and noradrenaline from storage, but blocks their further synthesis. In small doses reserpine increases both NREM and REM sleep [see Hartmann, 1967, pp. 69-72], presumably because of a temporary increase in serotonin and noradrenaline. In larger doses it produces apparently complete insomnia [e.g. see Dement, 1969] which might be attributed to its blocking effect on serotonin synthesis. However, although the muscle atonia of REM sleep does not occur in the reserpinized animal and the cortical activity is typical of wakefulness, the animal is behaviourally comatose and produces an uninterrupted discharge of PGO spikes, which are a prominent phasic manifestation of REM sleep [Dement, 1969, p. 252]. Administration of the serotonin precursor 5-hydroxytryptophan restores NREM sleep, and subsequent administration of the noradrenaline precursor, dopa, restores the tonic components of REM sleep [Dement, 1969, pp. 250-252]. This suggested to Hartmann [1967, p. 68] that noradrenergic neurones in the locus coerulus were primarily responsible for the tonic descending inhibitory discharge producing the muscular 'paralysis' of REM sleep. However, the effect of reserpine on brain amines is so pervasive that unequivocal interpretation of its effects is impossible, so that a noradrenergic influence on the intense cortical activation seen in REM sleep cannot be ruled out.

The possible interaction between serotonin and noradrenaline in generating the phenomena peculiar to REM sleep deserves further consideration. We have already seen that, although the serotoninergic raphe system promotes sleep, serotonin itself can act as an excitatory transmitter substance at the cortex. The well known hallucinogenic drug, lysergic acid diethylamide (LSD), which has been shown to mimic serotonin's synaptic effects [Aghajanian et al., 1970], produces hallucinations and intensifies perception by its excitatory effects. It has been observed that schizophrenics, whose consciousness is also strongly influenced by internally generated events, have a serotonin synergist in their body tissue consistent with excess production of this substance [Woolley, 1967]. It may be that the role of serotonin in REM sleep is to activate the generators of internal events, which perhaps involves accessing the organism's memory banks, and is possibly manifest in the PGO spikes. These internal events are processed by the normal mechanisms of conscious awareness (see Chapters 11 and 12) and emerge as dreams. Noradrenaline may be effective in both maintaining the level of cerebral activation necessary for conscious awareness and the suppression of motor activity necessary to prevent dreams being acted out. Alternatively, acetylcholine may be responsible for the cortical activation, and noradrenaline for the motor suppression in REM sleep. During schizophrenic hallucinations, and also following prolonged sleep deprivation, the hallucinations and disordered behaviour observed (also seen following lesions of the locus coerulus) might be a sign that the usual co-ordination of the different mechanisms, restricting dream experience to periods of motor inhibition and isolation from external stimuli, has broken down. Consequently the material of dreams breaks through into waking life. In the schizophrenic it has been observed that the deprivation of REM sleep does not result in the rebound which is usually observed in normal subjects [Dement *et al.*, 1970, p. 108], suggesting that the pressure for REM sleep has been discharged while the individual has been behaviourally awake.

Theoretical considerations

Despite the fact that nearly one-third of our life is spent asleep the explanation of our need for sleep remains elusive. In recent years it has been assumed that NREM sleep and REM sleep must serve different needs because they are so different in character. Oswald [1969] and Baekeland and Lasky [1966], claimed that large amounts of physical exercise resulted in an increase in slow wave sleep and Oswald [1969] claimed that increased quantities of the body repair and growth hormone, somatotrophin, was found in the blood plasma during slow wave sleep. From these findings Oswald [1969] derived the eminently plausible theory that slow wave sleep is a time for bodily restitution following exhaustive processes during waking. Other experiments have claimed that physical exercise has no clear-cut effect on slow wave sleep [Hauri, 1966; unpublished finding cited in Snyder and Scott, 1972] and Horne and Porter [1975] have shown that vigorous exercise early in the day has less effect on the sleep profile than such exercise late in the day, indicating that recuperative processes can just as well occur during periods of less active wakefulness. In response to this evidence Oswald and Adams [personal communication] assert that sleep is permissive, rather than necessary, for restorative processes to occur. They cite more recent evidence that protein synthesis is increased during sleep. We examined other arguments against the theory that sleep is necessary for the occurrence of restorative processes early in the chapter. We have also discussed Webb's [1971] theory that periods of inactivity and low energy expenditure may have evolved to serve a protective and conservative function in survival.

REM sleep is clearly more eventful than NREM sleep and in recent years a very diverse selection of theories have appeared attempting to explain its significance. One constellation of data, including the fact that the young of species spend a far greater proportion of their sleep time in REM than adults, has produced the theory that REM is a time for processing and sorting data accumulated during the day [Evans, 1968]. This hypothesis is not amenable to empirical testing of a very precise and critical nature.

Another observation from cross-species comparisons is that there is a correlation between REM time and the amount of binocularly co-ordinated eye movements. Berger [1969] has argued from this data that REM sleep may therefore have an essential role in the establishment and maintenance of the binocularly co-ordinated eye movments, necessary for accurate depth perception. While this possibility is not clearly refuted by existing knowledge, it cannot accommodate all of the data which has been collected concerning REM sleep.

Jouvet [1974] has advanced a theory that the phasic events and arousal of REM sleep reflects the processing, not of information received from the external world, but of genetically coded information which organizes the neural substrate of learning. It is difficult to grasp the precise meaning and implications of the theory as it is rather diffusely formulated. Jouvet observes that there are much higher levels of REM sleep *in utero* and in the immediate postnatal period. This suggests to him that the endogenous stimulation, represented by the PGO spikes, might be essential to genetically programmed maturational processes, particularly those concerned with the development of the capacity to learn. Jouvet also reviews the evidence that noradrenergic neurones, supposedly active during REM sleep, have plastic and regenerative properties, manifest at the synapse, and consistent with genetically instructed organizational change in the neural network. Jouvet suggests that the hallucinatory behaviour (usually involving rage or defence), which follows removal of the inhibition of motor output during REM sleep, by lesion of the caudal locus coerulus, is the 'motor expression of the PGO code transmitted by noradrenergic neurones'.

Dement and his coworkers [Dement, 1969; Dement *et al.*, 1970] emphasize the operation of two distinct mechanisms during REM sleep and focus on the significance of the phasic events, particularly the PGO spike discharges. PGO spikes precede the full development of REM sleep by some time and Dement [1969, pp. 250–252] observed that if animals were persistently woken at the appearance of the first PGO spike, and thus denied the opportunity of any PGO spike discharge, then there was a greater rebound of REM sleep–PGO spike discharge than following simple REM sleep deprivation. Furthermore, in the rebound period following REM sleep deprivation, there was increased intensity of PGO spike phasic activities, offsetting the fact that REM rebound never fully replays the debt of REM sleep time lost. On the other hand when animals are aroused so gently from REM, that although fully developed REM sleep is prevented, a full quota of PGO spikes occurs, no REM rebound occurs [Dement, 1969, p. 252]. Similarly, there is no rebound after animals have recovered from the effects of reserpine and PCPA, which suppress NREM and REM sleep but permit the continuous production of PGO spikes. Dement and his colleagues build a convincing argument that the 'necessary' aspect of REM sleep is the discharge of PGO spikes which arise from some kind of accumulation of energy making progressively greater demands for release.

If an animal is deprived of REM sleep there is evidence of greater excitability and particularly augmented sex and hunger drives. Also we have seen that REM deprivation arising from denial of sleep, lesions and antagonistic drugs (e.g. PCPA) may lead to hallucinatory behaviour in which aggression and defence are prominent. Schizophrenics who suffer from hallucinations show no rebound from REM sleep deprivation. The enhanced excitability of neural tissue following REM sleep deprivation is documented by the lowered threshold for the appearance of convulsions in cats and rats.

From these facts Dement argues [Dement, 1969, pp. 259–261] that the phasic aspects of REM sleep represent the discharge of metabolic energy, which has accumulated in drive systems in the brainstem. This energy normally serves as a reservoir ready to initiate and sustain drive behaviour when it is needed. During REM sleep excess of drive energy is discharged via the phasic events, particularly the PGO spikes, as if by a safety valve, while the behavioural concomitants are normally suppressed by the tonic inhibitory mechanism. During NREM sleep drive systems are actively suppressed by the serotoninergic neurones. Evidence which would seem to be crucial to this theory, but which is missing from Dement's writings, is that increased output of drive energy during waking is followed by decreased REM sleep. It is interesting to observe that Dement's theory of the significance of REM, the dreaming phase of sleep, is similar to the psychoanalytical theory of dreams [e.g. Freud, 1900, or see Fisher, 1970] in which it is supposed that dreams are the expression of undischarged drive energy resulting from socially conditioned inhibition.

Summary

Sleep is a period of behavioural quiescence and reduced reactivity to external stimuli. There are four discernable stages of orthodox or NREM sleep in which apparently increasing depth is accompanied by increasing synchrony and decreasing frequency in the EEG. This progression in the stages of sleep does not reflect a reduction in brain activity, but a radical change in the pattern of activity towards a pervasive rhythm. Structures in the basal forebrain, lower brainstem and medial thalamus all appear to have a role in promoting NREM sleep. The most crucial mechanism would appear to be the raphe system of the lower brainstem in which the pressure for sleep arises from the synthesis of serotonin, which is released at widely distributed terminals within the cerebral cortex.

The stages of orthodox sleep appear in a cycle which is punctuated approximately every 90 min (in humans) by the appearance of REM sleep (rapid eye movement sleep, paradoxical sleep, dream sleep). In this phase tonic inhibition of muscle tone is coexistent with electrocortical arousal, phasic spikes in the pons, geniculate body and occiput, rapid eye movements, muscle twitches and autonomic irregularities. The threshold of arousal from this stage of sleep depends on the significance rather than the intensity of the awakening stimulus, and following awakening dreams are usually reported by the sleeper. The tonic and phasic aspects of the REM stage of sleep can be dissociated by sleep deprivation, lesions, or certain drugs. Loss of tonic inhibition of motor activity results in the appearance of stereotyped behaviour patterns apparently representing the behavioural expression of the phasic aspects of REM sleep. REM sleep appears to be a phase of intense cortical activity and, in effect, consciousness in which the bizarre and disordered images of our dreams are generated by endogenous stimuli. Behaviour relevant to this synthetic inner world is normally suppressed. REM sleep appears to be sustained by mechanisms in the region of the pons. The locus coerulus seems to be clearly associated with the tonic inhibition of motor activity. Serotonin appears to be implicated in the genesis of REM sleep and noradrenaline in its maintenance.

Although sleep deprivation generates an intense pressure for sleep no physiological need, which can only be served by sleep, has been conclusively established. Tentative theories concerning the significance of orthodox sleep and REM sleep have been discussed.

Chapter nine

Individual differences in reactivity

Introduction

In Chapters 4-7 we have reviewed the basic mechanisms concerned with the survival of individual organisms and of species. Clearly the fundamental characteristics of the mechanisms for regulating the internal environment, reproduction, responding to emergencies and so forth, are endowed by genetic configurations, which are the product of a long process of evolution, by mutation and selection of adaptive mutations. We have seen in Chapter 1 that within sexually reproducing species, there is genetic variation which is the basis for constant experiment on the survival value of different genetic combinations, in new individuals. The most obvious manifestations of genetic variation are seen in external features such as morphology, colouring and stature. There is genetically based variation in such a wide range of 'visible' features that we might reasonably go on to conjecture that there is also genetically based variation in behavioural characteristics, arising from structural and functional differences in the neural substrates underlying basic survival mechanisms. Our subjective observations certainly support the proposition that our fellow humans vary on such dimensions as intelligence, drive, and emotionality. Since the last century psychologists have been developing measuring instruments which clearly differentiate between individuals on a number of behavioural dimensions, and thus validate our subjective impressions.

Whereas there is general agreement that individual differences in characteristic behaviour do exist, there are two major areas of controversy. One is over the question of whether dimensions, such as intelligence, along which behavioural capabilities are measured, have any real existence. The other is over the source of individual differences. Are they inherited, are they derived from the effect of different environmental experiences or are they a function of interaction between genes and environment. So far our inference that behavioural propensities are inherited has been based solely on the supposition that genetically based variation in distinctive external features of a species, generalizes to all structural and functional features. We are in need of solid empirical evidence for our assertion. We have already examined some rather convincing evidence that the development of the nervous system is modulated by experience (Chapter 7) so that a hypothesis attributing all inter-individual differences to genetic variation would appear to be untenable.

There is no intention in this chapter to scan the vast psychological literature on individual differences and their basis. The chapter is an attempt to tentatively show how the subject of individual differences may be incorporated in a perspective on behaviour, based on the assessment of evolutionary adaptive value and an understanding of underlying brain and nervous system mechanisms. It is proposed to examine genetic and environmental sources of variation in the illustrative behavioural trait of 'emotional reactivity', and to consider how they might be 'teased' apart. Inherited sex differences in emotional reactivity and other aspects of behaviour will be discussed in the context of their evolutionary adaptive significance. The dimensions of human personality will be outlined and two accounts of possible neural substrates for these dimensions will be discussed, one in terms of differential sensitivity of the reticular activating system, the other in terms of differential sensitivities of positive and negative reinforcement systems. As a preface to the latter theory there will be an outline review of research on the neural substrate of reinforcement. The theory and data will be related to issues in human psychopathology.

Inherited differences in reactivity

The separation of genetic from environmental sources of individual variation is very difficult in normal circumstances. As each creature, at least among higher species, is reared by its own parent or parents, one cannot distinguish which aspects of its behaviour may be attributed to the environment its parents have provided and which to its genes. The development of a methodology for analysing out the inherited components of behaviour has led to the birth of a distinct new science called behavioural genetics.

A behaviour trait which experimenters claim to have isolated in rats, and which has been subjected to extensive analysis for its heritability, has been named 'emotional reactivity', a term which is used synonymously with 'fearfulness'. The trait has been isolated on the basis of the inter-correlation found between different measures which might intuitively be supposed to reflect fearfulness. Fearfulness has been most frequently measured in an apparatus standardized by Broadhurst [1960] called an 'open field'. Designed for rats, it consists quite simply of a circular arena, about three feet in diameter, in which a rat is placed and exposed to the glare of photoflood lamps and loud noise played over a speaker. As rats defecate when they are afraid, the fearfulness which they display in this situation is measured by counting the number of faecal boluses which they drop. A further measure, called the 'ambulation score' is derived from a record of the rats' movement. This is obtained with the aid of markings on the floor of the open field which divide it into compartments. Ambulation

Figure 9.1
Graphs to show the separation of defecation scores (as indices of emotional reactivity) of rats over successive generations of selective breeding, in studies by Hall (1951; top graph) and Broadhurst (1960; bottom graph).

From Gray, J. (1971), *The psychology of fear and stress.* Reproduced by permission of Weidenfield and Nicolson Ltd., publishers

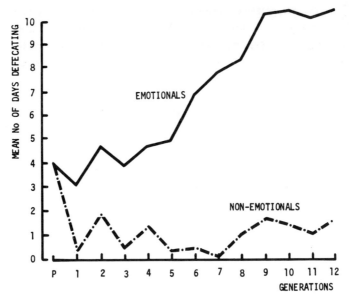

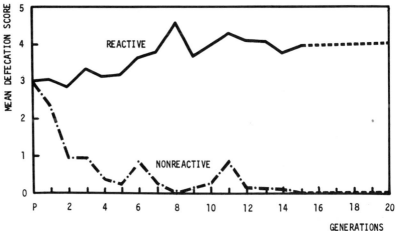

might be supposed to represent level of exploratory behaviour, which you would expect to be reduced in a fearful rat.

Defecation has been found to be a general response of rats in a variety of situations, which might reasonably be construed as frightening [Parker, 1939]. Furthermore open field defecation scores have been found to be correlated with other presumed measures of fearfulness in different situations. An example of this is the emergence test [Anderson, 1938] in which the speed with which an animal will emerge from its home cage into an unfamiliar open space is measured; fearful animals being slower to emerge. Thus the defecation and ambulation scores in the open field seem to reliably locate a rat's position on a continuum of fearfulness. Using the open field test Hall [1951], and later Broadhurst [1960], have pursued programmes of 'selective breeding' to produce distinctive strains of high scoring 'Maudsley reactive' (highly emotional or fearful) rats and low scoring 'Maudsley non-reactive' (non-emotional or non-fearful) rats (see Figure 9.1). The work was done at the Maudsley hospital in London. Selective breeding was achieved by consistently mating high scoring females with high scoring males and vice versa. The progressive separation in open field scores which is obtained over successive generations is some evidence that differences are due to genetic inheritance. However, this fact alone is not sufficient evidence for the heritability of the trait, as a 'fearful' mother might provide either pre or postnatal environment which engenders the development of post or even prenatal fearfulness in her offspring. The possibility of the postnatal environment being a major determinant of an individual's fearfulness is quite simply controlled for by the technique of 'cross-fostering', in which reactive mothers are allocated non-reactive pups to rear, and vice versa. Rats reared with mothers of the opposite strain exhibit the emotional reacitivity characteristics of their genetic mother, rather than their foster mother, when tested in the open field in adulthood.

Prenatal environment is controlled for by the technique of 'reciprocal cross' in which reactive males are mated with non-reactive females and vice versa. On average the progeny of both sets of matings should receive the same genetic configurations. Any differences between the two groups of progeny would be attributable to differences between the reactive and non-reactive interuterine environments provided by their respective mothers. As no differences were found between the open field scores for the two sets of rats, in adulthood, prenatal environment can be ruled out as a source of variation in reactivity during the selective breeding programme.

The experiments discussed were designed explicitly to expose the genetic influence on the selected behaviour trait. They do not exclude the possibility that inherited differences in reactivity are modulated by the environment. Environmental influences on nervous system structure and function and concomitant behaviour are discussed at several points in this book (particularly Chapter 7) and later in this chapter. Experiments in Broadhurst's laboratory [Broadhurst, 1960] indicated that genetic factors account for about 50% of the variance in defecation scores and 75% of the variance in ambulation scores of rats in the open field. Clearly the proportionate contributions of genetic and environmental factors will be a function of the range of environmental variation encountered by different members of a specific strain.

The behaviour traits exhibited by the Maudsley reactive and non-reactive strains of rats have been found to be generalized to a range of behaviours beyond those in the open field, which were measured as the basis of the selective breeding programme. Indications of greater fearfulness in the reactive strain compared with the non-reactive strain included higher rates of grooming, faster escape responses from shock and confinement under water and slower emergence into an unfamiliar environment. When bar pressing for food is disrupted by an electric shock, response suppression is greater among reactive than non-reactive rats. Exploratory behaviour is greater in non-reactive than reactive rats.

This section serves to show that generalized behavioural propensities may be inherited genetically. From this work on animals we might tentatively extrapolate to humans and surmise differences in personality and susceptibility to neurotic disorders which are based on inherited factors. This possibility is explored later in the chapter. Clearly genetically based differences in behaviour must reflect structural and functional differences in the underlying neural substrate, another topic to be explored later.

Acquired differences in reactivity

We have attempted to show that genetic factors account for a substantial proportion of the inter-individual variation in emotional reactivity. It has only been remarked in passing that differential environments are the source of any remaining variance. In Chapter 7 evidence was produced that inter-animal differences in learning ability and perceptuomotor skills could arise from differences in the patterns of stimulation experienced during development. It is also demonstrable that a creature's emotional reactivity is a function of the presence or absence of certain types of stimuli during infancy.

The nature of the environmental influences on the emotional development of the rat are a little surprising. It might be expected that the experience of painful or unpleasant stimuli in infancy would lead to greater fearfulness in adulthood. Levine [see review by Levine and Mullins, 1966] and Denenberg [1964] have shown that, following repeated exposure (usually daily) to mildly noxious stimuli in infancy, the contrary is true, and it results in reduced fearfulness displayed in adulthood. The 'noxious' stimuli which have been used are 'handling' (removal from the home cage, brief placement in another container and subsequent replacement in the home cage) and electric shocks of various intensities. In adulthood handled or shocked animals defecate less and ambulate more in the open field test, emerge faster in the emergence test and explore more in novel environments, than rats which were unstimulated in infancy. Also stimulated rats are more resistant to ulceration in conflict situations, achieve higher body-weights and survive longer than unstimulated rats. In general the infant stimulated rats appear to be less fearful. However, it should be noted that there is an optimum level of infant stimulation which produces the minimum adult fearfulness so that too much stimulation results in as higher levels of adult fearfulness as too little.

If the adult adrenal corticosteroid response (see Chapter 6) is monitored in infant stimulated and unstimulated rats a rather more complex picture emerges of the effects on adult emotional responsiveness. In the open field the handled rats produce a more rapid, but less sustained, corticosteroid response, so that over a period the total response of the unhandled rats is greater. The handled rats appear to have the capacity to make a graded corticosteroid response, which is small for innocuous stimuli, but large for intense stimuli or danger signals. The unhandled rats, on the other hand, produce a near maximal response to even the slightest stimulus. The enhanced capacity of the stimulated animals to match their emotional response to the demands of the situation is reflected in the greater speed and efficiency of shock avoidance learning compared with unstimulated animals. Denenberg [1964] presents evidence that the adult emotional reactivity of an animal is a function of emotionally arousing experiences during a critical period in infancy. If the right responses do not occur at the right time, then there is irrevocable reduction in the flexibility of the animal's response system. It could be that the hormones produced during infant emotional arousal 'organize' the neural substrate for emotion in an analogous way to that in which hormones set-up the circuits for producing the behaviour of male or female (see Chapter 5).

We might tentatively extrapolate from the effects of mild noxious stimulation on animals, to humans. The findings cited would predict that an individual who was over protected from stresses during infancy and childhood, would grow up unable to match his emotional responses appropriately to the particular demands of a stressful situation. Anecdotal observations of persons who were over protected as children fit these predictions.

The attempts by the behavioural geneticists to tease out environmental influences from genetic influences, on emotional development, are comprehensive enough to include the prenatal interuterine environment, an environment whose effects are altogether more difficult to assess. In a typical experiment on the effects of prenatal environment, by Joffe [1969], using a technique developed by Thompson [1957], fear was induced purely psychologically. Pregnant rats were presented with stimuli which they had been trained to associate with an imminent shock, by repeated stimulus–shock pairings, prior to conception. To avoid any effect of the prenatal environment of the mother on the postnatal environment which she might provide for her offspring, the pups were fostered by non-reactive mothers who had experienced no stress during pregnancy. Meanwhile, the offspring of the unstressed mothers were fostered by the mothers which had been stressed during pregnancy. This was to provide information on how stress during pregnancy affects the offspring, through the postnatal environment which that mother provides. Repetition of this procedure for each of the four mating combinations possible with a reactive and non-reactive strain of rats, permitted an analysis of the interaction between genes and environment. Two control groups were used in the experiment; one in which mothers were not stressed either before or during pregnancy and one in which intended mothers were conditioned by pairing of a neutral stimulus with a shock before conception, but in whom the resulting conditioned fear was never elicited during pregnancy.

Only the most important findings yielded by this experimental design are outlined. Offspring whose mothers had been frightened during pregnancy were better at avoidance conditioning than either of the control groups. This suggested that a mother stressed during pregnancy produced offspring whose emotional reactivity was better adapted to the avoidance of dangerous situations. Analysis of open field ambulation scores reveals some surprising results in which the pups of mothers frightened before conception, but not during pregnancy appeared to have been affected by their mothers environment prior to conception. Furthermore the nature of the effect depended upon the genetic makeup of the pups. The offspring of the mothers frightened prior to conception showed lower ambulation scores if their fathers were from the non-reactive strain, but higher ambulation scores if their fathers were reactive. What is even more surprising is that the rats whose mother had been frightened both before and during pregnancy did not differ from normal controls in the ambulation scores. It appeared that stress after conception counteracted the effects of stress prior to conception. Extension of the experiment to include the effects of different classes of offspring on the behaviour of their foster mothers, rather than vice versa, adds further complexity. The progeny of mothers stressed either before, or both before and during pregnancy, affected their foster mothers in such a way that they failed to show the normal postrearing decline in ambulation scores. Not only does the environment provided by the mother affect the infant, but the environment provided by the infant influences the mother's behaviour, which might in turn react on the infant, and so on. No one variable is held steady so that the effects on dependent variables can be observed. Cause and effect are inextricably confused and final outcomes are a function of 'the dynamic interplay of forces exerted by all variables' [Gray, 1971a, p. 106]. We can see that the emotional makeup of an individual is a function of the complex interaction between the genetic endowment and the pre and postnatal environment.

Individual differences and social organization

Inter-individual differences in emotional reactivity and other behavioural traits arise because of genetic variation in a sexually reproducing species and because of accidents of environment. The functional significance of genetic variation is that it provides a basis for experiment with different genetic combinations, and for a rapid response to changes in the environment (see Chapter 1). In more highly evolved, and particularly social species, genetic variation may serve additional, more complex functions. In a social species, whose survival is dependent upon co-operation within a group, genetically induced variation in behavioural characteristics may be a basis for 'division of labour'. Different individuals might perform different tasks, each essential to group survival, according to how well their inherited capabilities fit them for these tasks. In addition to genetic factors we have seen in Levine's [Levine and Mullins, 1966] infant handled rats the 'tuning' of each individual's emotional response mechanism by his infant environment, serves to adapt him to that particular type of environment. One could argue that in the human species the facility for both genetically and environmentally based variation in behavioural characteristics encourages the establishment of division of labour in the interests of group survival. In our society it is a fundamental assumption that different individuals are suited to different occupations by their ability and temperament. The hierarchically organized class structure of our society, which is one reflection of the division of labour, may be particularly resistant to change because of strong genetically and environmentally determined predispositions of individuals to accept membership of the class into which they are born. In industrialized societies, where the majority of the population are working class, the frustration of the aims of both democratic and revolutionary socialist parties must be attributed to their failure to convince sufficient of the working class that their class membership denies them social and economic justice[1]. Partly because of this fact socialists are inclined to argue that the emotional and intellectual characteristics of working class people are imposed purely by their environment and are part of the pattern of suppression by the ruling class[2]. At the opposite extreme adherents of the extreme right of politics argue that class differences (under which racial differences might be subsumed) reflect purely genetic differences between groups which morally justifies the power relationships which exist, or which they think should exist. The fact that psychologists and biologists can be found who lean towards one or other of these positions is an indication of the intensity of the academic controversy over the relative contribution of genes and environment to individual differences. The social and political implications of the issue tend to arouse strong emotions. The polarization of opinion is also evidence for the difficulty of achieving a complete academic detachment, divorced from all value judgements.

Sometimes the level of argument on the genes versus environment issue is little more than a slanging match. At its best the argument reaches a high level of sophistication in which both the behavioural dimensions, which are defined and measured (e.g. intelligence), and the nature and status of possible gene–environment interaction, are subject to keen critical analysis. In considering this issue two points should be remembered. One is that two groups differing in their mean score on some behavioural dimension (e.g. intelligence) usually have a large overlap of the distribution of scores, which precludes a 'clean' separation of the two groups. It is virtually never possible to clearly separate two populations on biological or psychological criteria, except trivial or morally neutral ones such as skin colour or language. The second point is that a statement that a genetically based difference exists, on average, between two groups, in no way implies scientific endorsement of a claimed moral superiority that justifies one group subordinating another to its will. The supposition that it does is a deplorable departure from scientific objectivity which we have seen lead to a totally degenerate barbarism in such cases as the Nazis' treatment of the Jews and the Slavs. The social and political implications of assertions about inter-race and intergroup genetic differences make the topic a minefield which psychologists and biologists should cross with the greatest of care.

Sex differences

At least, few people would challenge the assertion that the human species divides clearly into two major groups; males and females. However, there is considerable argument about how different the two sexes are, apart from

---

1.The difficulties experienced by a class-conscious activist in trying to convince his fellow workers that they are unjustly oppressed and should seek redress through united political action is vividly portrayed in Robert Tressell's famous novel *The ragged trousered philanthropists*.

2.In his work *One dimensional man* the left-wing theorist Herbert Marcuse outlines the 'environmental machinery' by which the forces of capitalism supposedly shape the consciousness of both workers and managers to serve its own purposes.

the obvious biological differences. The different biological roles of men and women in reproduction dictate a division of labour which must have commenced long before we evolved into our human form. However, in most societies this division of labour and roles, between men and women, goes far beyond the minimum implied by the biology of reproduction. In this present era there is a great deal of argument over the question of whether the allegedly subordinate and restricted roles of women is justified by innate characteristics of women which suit them exclusively to their traditional role. At one polar extreme in this debate are militant feminists who maintain that all apparent behavioural differences between men and women are culturally induced and can be eliminated by changes in child rearing methods and education. At the other extreme it is asserted that a woman's instincts and abilities suit her to care for children, husband, home, and little else.

The question of genetic differences in behavioural disposition between the sexes has been empirically investigated and hypotheses have been put forward concerning the functional significance of such differences. In Chapter 5, we saw that the intersexual behavioural differences determined by the perinatal sexual differentiation of the brain, and the adult sex hormone levels went beyond the act of copulation itself. In monkeys the prenatal masculinization of a genetic female produced a creature with distinctly male patterns of active play and assertiveness [Harlow, 1953]. In male deer the rise in testosterone levels initiated by seasonal changes produces inter-male aggression as an adjunct to courtship behaviour.

Gray [1971b] and Gray and Buffery [1971] have explored sex differences in emotional and cognitive behaviour in mammals, including man, and have looked at their neural and endocrine basis and evolutionary adaptive significance. Considerable attention has been given to sex differences in emotional reactivity, the focus of this chapter, along the dimensions of both fearfulness and aggressiveness. In the rat and other rodents commonly used in psychological laboratories it appears that the female is less fearful than the male. In the open field it defecates less and ambulates more. The female emerges faster from familiar into novel ground and engages in more exploration of a novel environment. It is better at active avoidance learning, presumably because its behaviour is not subject to the disorganizing effect of intense fearful arousal. There are also differences in the psychoendocrine response. Consistent with previous observations on less fearful animals, the adrenal corticosteroid response of the female is initially more rapid and intense but subsides much more quickly than that of the male, paralleling the difference between the handled and non-handled rats in Levine's experiments [see Levine, 1962]. When kept in overcrowded conditions male rats exhibit a greater increase in weight of the adrenal glands (an accepted index of stress) than females. In conflict situations male rats exhibit greater proneness to the development of ulcers than females, but in enforced immobilization the relationship is reversed.

In primates and man the rodent sex differences in fearfulness appear to be reversed. Girls report more fears than boys and Gray [1971a] observes that among women there is a greater incidence of crippling phobic disorders, neurotic anxiety, and psychosomatic disease, in all of which inappropriate, prolonged, and intense 'fearful' arousal is a dominant feature. Women are also more prone to reactive depression than men. Gray [1972] maintains that reactive depression stems from frustration, equated with fear, following removal of 'accustomed rewards'. Examples are such events as desertion by a spouse or loss of a job. When tested on Eysenck's 'Maudsley Personality Inventory' women emerge with higher scores on the introversion and neuroticism dimensions, than men [Eysenck and Eysenck, 1969], indicating personality characteristics predicting 'fearfulness' and related psychiatric disorders. Men, however, are more prone to psychogenic ulcers than women. As males appear to be more aggressive than females, this lends credence to the suggestion, advanced in Chapter 6, that suppressed aggression, rather than anxiety, produces the gastrointestinal changes which can lead to ulceration.

The sex difference in fearfulness of mammals appears to be modulated by oestrogen, which antagonizes this characteristic. Female rats are even less fearful than normal (indicated by open field defecation and ambulation scores), when endogenous oestrogen levels are high during oestrus, and oestrogen injections lead to decreased open field fearfulness in both males and females. However, reduction of circulating oestrogen by ovariectomy does not appear to increase fearfulness in the female, so that the basal level of fearfulness would appear to be determined by the underlying functional characteristics of some neural substrate. Manipulation of androgen levels, which modulate the aggression threshold has no effect on the behavioural fearfulness of male or female rats, but it does appear to modify the adrenal corticosteroid stress response. An oestrogenic reduction in fearfulness in female chimpanzees is suggested by their increased dominance during oestrus [Van Lawick-Goodall, 1968], and it is tentatively suggested by Gray [1971b] that premenstrual depression in women is a reflection of increased fearfulness due to depleted circulating oestrogen.

In rodents, primates and humans there is considerable evidence that the male is more inclined to active and aggressive behaviour. Among humans many more males than females are convicted of violent crimes and it has been observed that from an early age [3–5 years; cited by Blurton-Jones, 1967] boys engage in more rough and tumble play than girls. The role of testosterone in sex differences in aggressiveness is documented in Chapters 5 and 6.

Gray and Buffery [1971] also present evidence that in both rats and man, males are superior to females in tasks involving spatial ability, while human females have superior linguistic ability to males.

Gray and Buffery [1971] argue that the sex differences, which appear to exist, have evolved to serve the specialization of roles of males and females in mammalian social organization. This specialization of roles arises, in the first instance, from the much heavier burden which the females bear in reproduction itself. Gray and Buffery [1971] derive their arguments from those of Wynne-Edwards [1962] who maintains that a dominant purpose of social behaviour is to homeostatically regulate the population density of a species, so that the resources to support it are not outstripped. The aggressiveness of the male, observed in all of the species discussed, is the basis of sexual competition and territorial activity. This ensures perpetuation of the most viable genes in the gene pool, and limits the reproductive rate in a particular habitat, by either psychologically emasculating, or dispersing, unsuccessful males. The greater fearfulness of male rodents may also, paradoxically, facilitate the dominance based system by ensuring that dominance conflicts are not unduly prolonged and that the victorious male can proceed with his reproductive activities unhindered. In rodents the females have no part in any competition for dominance so that enhanced aggressiveness and fearfulness are not traits which are required of them. The stress which male rodents experience in an overcrowded habitat clearly serves the population control function as it antagonizes the sex drive and leads to a reduced rate of reproduction [see Gray, 1971a, Chapter 6].

Primates and humans contrast with rodents in maintaining 'sexually interdigitated' dominance hierarchies in which both sexes engage in dominance activity, but in which males are, on average, more dominant than females. In primate and human societies male dominance can be viewed as an aid to group cohesiveness and adaptive co-operative activity, while the females are preoccupied with child rearing.

Buffery and Gray argue that the better spatial ability of the male is related to its needs in dominance interactions (sometimes involving combat), exploratory and territorial activity and group protection. On the other hand the greater linguistic ability of the human female is visualized as a vital adjunct to her child-rearing role in which she has a heavy responsibility for passing language skills on to the child.

There is always a caution against attributing sex differences in behaviour to innate factors. Unless a creature is reared in isolation, which in mammals leads to widespread behavioural disturbance, it can always be argued that its sex specific behaviour pattern is due to differential treatment of male and female offspring. This argument is most vigorously evoked for human sex differences by the protagonists of women's equality with men. The human infant has a long period of dependence on its parents, when its behaviour is moulded by their influence. Thus, it is very difficult to control for the effects of differential environment in human sex difference studies. One point to observe about sex differences in behaviour patterns is that even if they are not environmental, they are not determined directly by the genes, but are secondary to the pattern of hormone secretion at a critical perinatal stage (see Chapter 5). The dormant neural substrate for both male and female behaviour exists in all foetuses, whatever their genetic sex. The presence or absence of androgens determines whether it is the male or female substrate which is sensitized (see Chapter 5). In one study, in which genetic females had had the external features of anomalous masculinization surgically and hormonally corrected, and who had been reared as females, it was claimed that they nevertheless showed a greater inclination to tomboyish behaviour and athletic activity, than a control group of normal females (see Chapter 5). This study seems to represent an instance of innate tendencies resisting cultural pressures tending to oppose them.

As in any other attempts to find intergroup differences in behaviour traits it should be remembered that the sex differences are differences between the means of overlapping populations and do not logically imply moral superiority or divine rights to power for one or the other sex. The differences which do exist presumably evolved to subserve division of labour, when other aspects of our biological evolution were still progressing, and when social structures were still at a simple and primitive stage. Sex differences are therefore of a vestigial nature and do not support an argument for the rigid division of roles and the subordination of one sex by the other, in the complex structure of contemporary society. The important fact is not that there are mean differences in personality and abilities between races or sexes, but that there are differences between individuals. There is only one superordinate goal of social and educational policy which the empirical data logically justifies, in a society based on humanitarian ethics. This is to give each individual, whatever their race or sex, the opportunity to realize their potential and find the occupation and lifestyle which best suits their temperament and talents.

The biological basis of personality

So far in this chapter we have explored some interindividual differences, the question of whether they are due to genetic or environmental variation and their evolutionary adaptive significance. My brief in writing this book now leads me to search tentatively for functional differences in the nervous system which might be the basis for individual differences. A psychologist who has stimulated extensive exploration of dimensions of personality, whose basis might be represented in terms of structure and function in the nervous system, is Eysenck [see Eysenck, 1967]. Eysenck argues that the conceptual framework for personality which is best supported by the empirical data is one with two orthogonal dimensions; one introversion-extroversion, the other stability–neuroticism. Eysenck and his colleagues have developed a personality test, the 'Maudsley Personality Inventory', which locates the position of the individual on these dimensions. As with other dimensions of behaviour, the testing of a representative sample of the population yields a normal distribution of scores on both dimensions, in which the majority of individuals are grouped around the middle point, between the polar extremes. Only a few people are completely introverted or completely extroverted. To say that the introversion–extroversion and stability-neuroticism dimensions are orthogonal means that an individual's position on one dimension is completely independent of his position on the other. For instance you can be either a stable or a neurotic extrovert. Eysenck [1967, p. 5] acknowledges his debt to personality theorists going back as far as the Greek physician Galen, who lived in the second century A.D. Galen's postulated dimensions of changeable–unchangeable and non-emotional–emotional, which determined whether the individual was of melancholic, choleric, sanguine, or phlegmatic temperament, are cited as the precursors of Eysenck's dimensions. The characterization of the dimensions is well known and has been given in detail elsewhere [Eysenck, 1967, pp. 34–40]. Adjectives which describe the extrovert are: sociable, active, lively, excitable, and impulsive. Adjectives describing the introvert are: unsociable, thoughtful, and serious. The stability–neuroticism continuum closely resembles the dimension of emotional reactivity which has been focused on in the discussion of the genesis of individual differences.

The neurotic end of the dimension presupposes high emotional reactivity, whether fearful or aggressive. Individuals at the extreme of the neuroticism dimension show traits which are considered pathological by the rest of society and whose nature varies according to their position on the introversion–extroversion dimension. The neurotic introvert is likely to suffer from persistent irrational anxiety, phobias, obsessive–compulsive symptoms, or reactive depression. They are pathological because of their 'internal unease' and their inability to face the ordinary demands of life. The neurotic extrovert is the psychopath, governed by the impulse of the moment, and without thought of any suffering he might inflict on others, or the consequences of his actions to himself. Society cannot accept him because he flagrantly disregards its rules. According to Eysenck, while the population of a mental hospital is likely to contain a high proportion of neurotic introverts, the population of a prison is likely to contain a high proportion of neurotic extroverts.

Eysenck [1967] reviews the behavioural and physiological measures which relate to his personality dimensions. He then examines current notions of nervous system function which are complemented by the behavioural data in order to produce a theory of the biological basis of personality. Eysenck argues that the introvert has a more excitable reticular arousal system (RAS; see Chapters 6, 7, and 8) than the extrovert and consequently a higher level of cortical arousal. This is reflected, in the introvert, in the facilitation of learning, conditioning, memory, perception, and cognitive processes generally. Because the endogenously generated level of activity in the RAS is high the introvert has reduced needs for external stimulation to attain his optimal level of arousal. Thus his high level of internal excitation accounts for the introvert's relative aversion for stimulating activities, exciting events, and social contact.

In contrast, the extrovert is postulated to have a relatively inexcitable RAS and a relatively active system in the non-specific thalamus inhibiting cortical arousal, so that this factor is generally lower. Consequently he shows inferior performance to the introvert in sensory discriminations, conditioning, and other cognitive tasks. Furthermore, the relatively low level of endogenous excitation and the rapid habituation to external stimulation produced by the thalamo-cortical inhibitory system leads to a search for external stimuli in order to achieve the optimum level of arousal. Thus it is the lack of internal stimulation which supposedly impels the extrovert to seek noise, excitement, new experiences and social contact.

It is only possible to mention a few of the many experiments whose results are consistent with the predictions of Eysenck's theory. It is well documented that the RAS modulates cortical arousal (see Chapters 6, 7, 8, and 12) and that activation of the RAS increases cortical arousal. This is manifest at the physiological level by desynchronization of the EEG, increased amplitude and briefer refractory periods of primary evoked potentials in the classical projection areas, an increase in single cell responses to sensory input and an increase in the rate of flicker of a visual stimulus, which single cells are able to follow. At the behavioural level stimulation of the RAS has been found to speed choice reaction times and improve discrimination performance [Fuster, 1958]. There is some evidence that introverts have higher amplitude sensory evoked potentials (EPs) and faster EP recovery functions (minimum interstimulus interval at which a second stimulus will evoke a response of the same amplitude as that to the first stimulus) than extroverts [see Eysenck, 1967, pp. 257-261]. At the behavioural level it has been found that the auditory thresholds of intro-verts are lower than those of extroverts, again indicating their higher sensitivity [see Eysenck, 1967, pp. 101-102]. Several experimenters have found that critical flicker fusion (CFF) threshold is higher in introverts than extroverts, which is consistent with the prediction that the introvert cortex should have better resolving power for temporally patterned stimuli.

A further important fulfilment of Eysenck's predictions is the finding that introverts condition more easily than extroverts, supposedly because of their higher levels of cortical excitation. This has been shown when the eyeblink reflex, elicited by a puff of air, has been conditioned to a neutral stimulus [see Eysenck, 1967, pp. 118-119]. However, we should observe that there is evidence that conditioning of this nature is not a cortical phenomenon (see Chapter 13). Its substrate may be established in the brainstem. Differences in conditionability are used to explain the different psychopathologies associated with the extremes of the introvert–extrovert dimension. The anxieties, fears, and over strict conscience of the neurotic introvert arise because he has conditioned so strongly to stimuli associated with punishments and painful experiences during his formative years. The impulsiveness, delinquency, lack of conscience, and oblivious disregard of the consequences of his actions, which characterize the psychopathic, neurotic extrovert arise because his unconditionability is reflected in insensitivity to punishment and a consequent failure of socialization.

Eysenck postulates that cortical inhibition is more readily induced in the extrovert by the non-specific thalamic nuclei. The physiological evidence for this is that slow stimulation of these areas induces slow waves in the EEG and behavioural sleep (see Chapter 8). Evidence which is inconsistent with the theory is that rapid trains of pulses to the non-specific thalamus produce cortical arousal (see Chapter 8). Also the non-specific thalamus is implicated in the generation of the secondary components of the cortical sensory evoked potential, which appear to reflect the processes underlying the conscious perception of external stimuli. This is hardly consistent with an inhibitory function of the non-specific thalamus, and Eysenck's theory could only be sustained if it could be shown that there was differentiation of function in this area.

An attempt has been made to demonstrate the more rapid accumulation of inhibition in extroverts by investigating reminiscence effects. In percep-tual or perceptual–motor tasks demanding sustained attention, a rest period results in a stepwise improvement in performance, which has been attributed to dissipation of inhibition. Using a pursuit rotor task, in which the subject has to follow a moving spot of light with a stylus, the improve-ment in 'time-on-target' score, was found to be greater in extroverts than in introverts, after a rest period [Eysenck, 1967, p. 133].

Another prediction which is derived from Eysenck's theory is that because of lower excitability and more rapid habituation, due to more powerful inhibitory influences, extroverts will seek higher levels of stimula-tion from the external environment. Conversely they will be less tolerant of sensory and perceptual deprivation. There is an underlying assumption that both extroverts and introverts make differential demands upon their external environment to achieve an optimum level of arousal (see discussion in Chapter 7). Consistent with these predictions it has been shown that extroverts will push buttons to punctuate quiet and darkness, with loud music and bright lights, more frequently than introverts, while introverts will more frequently seek quiet and darkness to bring relief from loud music and bright lights [Eysenck, 1967, pp. 111-113). We seem to be approaching an understanding of why extroverts like noisy parties and introverts do not.

While Eysenck visualized that the sensitivity of a system, embracing the RAS, its cortical projections and the cortico-reticular return loops, is the neural basis of the introversion–extroversion dimension of personality he hypothesises that the basis of the stability–neuroticism dimension is an RAS–visceral brain circuit. He borrows MacLean's [1949] concept of the visceral brain, whose constituent structures are the hypothalamus, cingulate gyrus, septum, hippocampus, and amygdala. The involvement of these structures in emotional behaviour is well proven (see Chapter 6). It has also been shown that their activity is modulated by the RAS [e.g. Sheard and Flynn, 1967]. The specific involvement of the hypothalamus in the patterning of emotional behaviour is indicated by its dominant responsibility in the production of autonomic arousal. Eysenck [1967, p. 232] dissents from the view of the arousal theorists [e.g. Lindsley, 1951; Duffy, 1962] that there is a single dimension for which the terms arousal or activation can be used interchangeably. He suggests that the term arousal should refer to increased activity of the reticulo-cortical system and activation to increased activity of the reticulo-visceral brain system. The only individuals in which the activity of these two systems is correlated are in the neurotic introvert, in which both systems are highly excitable, and the stable extrovert, in whom neither are.

The neural basis of reinforcement

Accepting as his premise that personality can be reduced to the two fundamental dimensions of introversion–extroversion and stability-neuroticism, Gray [1971a, 1972] has outlined a modified theory of their neural basis. Rather than considering that the location of an individual on these dimensions is a function of the excitability of an arousal system and a system for emotional activation, Gray considers that personality is a function of the sensitivity of systems mediating positive and negative reinforcement. Therefore, before examining Gray's thesis in more detail, it is necessary to introduce the topic of the neural basis of reinforcement.

Reinforcement is a central concept in many theories of learning and its genealogy can be traced to Thorndike's 'Law of effect' [1913]. It is defined as that process which will increase the probability that a given behaviour will be evoked by a given stimulus. In the ubiquitous paradigm of the Skinner box the probability that a lever pressing response will be elicited by the sight of a lever increases every time that the lever press is reinforced by the delivery of food. We must add the qualification that for the reinforcement to be effective the hunger drive must be aroused.

Food, which satisfies the hunger drive, is seen as a positive reinforcement, or reward. Behaviour is also influenced by negative reinforcements, or punishments. A rat in a Skinner box may be presented with a light signal which informs it that, unless it presses a lever, it will receive an electric shock through the floor of its cage. The shock is a negative reinforcement, or punishment, which increases the probability that the warning signal will elicit a lever press. The lever pressing behaviour in this instance is active avoidance behaviour, in which the response forestalls the punishment. The reluctant schoolboy does his homework in order to avoid the punishment which he will receive if he does not do it. Negative reinforcement may also be used to inhibit rather than to evoke a response. This would normally occur when the prospects of both positive and negative reinforcement are present, producing an approach–avoidance conflict. A rat may learn to inhibit a response of approaching a food tray, because it receives an electric shock for doing so. When inhibition of a response is learnt by negative reinforcement it is known as passive avoidance. The child learns to inhibit its inclination to plunge its hand into an attractively flickering fire because of the negatively reinforcing pain which it experiences when it does so.

To say that reinforcement increases the probability of certain behaviours reveals nothing about the process of reinforcement itself. Hull [1943] maintained that reinforcement was produced by 'drive reduction'. A rat's lever pressing response is reinforced because the food delivered reduces the hunger drive. Negative reinforcement is effective because the escape response reduces the drive for pain avoidance. This theory, which is very attractive at first sight, turns out to have some severe difficulties. The consumption of food does not result in the immediate restoration of the internal deficits which were the origin of the hunger drive as digestion is a relatively lengthy process. Furthermore, it has been found that the more immediate reduction of drive by intravenous injection of glucose, which raises blood sugar much more rapidly than eating, is much less effective as a reinforcement than food presented for normal oral intake. We saw in Chapter 4 that smell and taste have an important part to play in the short term regulation of food intake. It seems that there are qualities of reinforcing agents, other than their drive reducing properties, which are effective in increasing the probability of occurrence of instrumental behaviour. Our consummatory behaviour, eating, drinking, and sex is subjectively the source of pleasurable experience. In Cabanac's [1971] experiment, reported in Chapter 4, we saw that the pleasure (measured by a rating scale of affective judgements) derived from a constant stimulus varied according to a person's current need state. A spoonful of glucose which tasted pleasant to a hungry individual, tasted unpleasant to a satiated one. Water which was painful for an already hot person to plunge his hand into, was pleasantly hot to a cold person. Olds and Milner [1956; also Olds, 1962; Olds and Olds, 1965] have argued the case for a hedonic theory of reinforcement in which 'pleasant' stimuli are positively reinforcing while 'unpleasant' stimuli are negatively reinforcing.

Olds and Milner [1954; see also Olds, 1956a] claim to have located the neural substrate of reward in an observation which owed more to serendipity than design. During an experiment on the behavioural effects of

Figure 9.2
Medial sagittal sections
of the rat's brain
showing reward areas
(medial forebrain
bundle) and punishment
areas (periventricular
system), mapped from
self-stimulation
experiments.

From Levitt, R. A.
(Ed.),
*Psychopharmacology:
a biological approach.*
Reproduced by
permission of John
Wiley and Sons,
publishers

MEDIAL FOREBRAIN BUNDLE (REWARD)

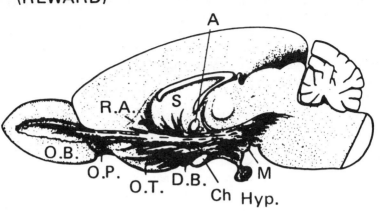

PERIVENTRICULAR SYSTEM (PUNISHMENT)

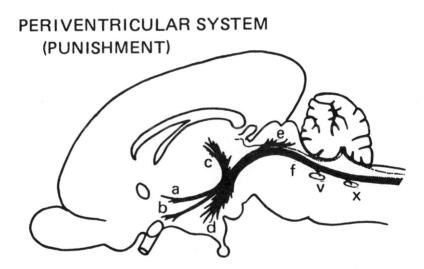

brain stimulation they noticed that, when electrodes were implanted in the septal area, their experimental rats developed a strong tendency to move towards, or stay within, the area of their cage where they received the stimulation, as if it had pleasurable qualities. The desirability of the brain stimulation was confirmed when the rats were supplied with levers connected to suitable circuitry so that they could press and deliver a stimulus to their own brains. With electrodes implanted in quite widely distributed diencephalic and palaeocortical areas, rats would lever press vigorously to deliver trains of electrical impulses to their brains. Electrodes implanted in the medial forebrain bundle elicited the most energetic responses (see Figure 9.2). One possible explanation of this behaviour was that the electrical stimulation was energizing a 'motor loop', which merely reproduced the lever pressing response in a stereotyped manner, bypassing systems mediating drive and pleasure. This possibility has been ruled out by the demonstration that a rat will make a variety of responses, including running a maze [Olds, 1956b] and crossing an electrified grid in an obstruction box [Olds, 1960], to attain a brain stimulation reward. It seemed that the brain stimulation had reinforcing properties and Olds [1956a] maintained that the subjective correlate of this stimulation was pleasure. Electrodes have even been implanted in the human brain during the investigation of the therapeutic possibilities of brain stimulation, and individuals to whom this has been done have reported that they experienced pleasurable sensations, including those of sexual arousal [e.g. see Heath, 1963].

In addition to the discovery of positively reinforcing areas, other areas, such as the medial hypothalamus, have been found where a behavioural response which switches on stimulation is never repeated. The stimulus appears to be unpleasant and negatively reinforcing, or punishing (see Figure 9.2). The positive and negative reinforcing areas often run close together so that stimulation through the same electrode may activate both systems at different times [Olds and Olds, 1961, 1965; Roberts, 1958]. There appears to be a reciprocal inhibitory relationship between the positive and negative reinforcement areas as Valenstein [1965] has shown that rewarding brain stimulation can counteract the effect of punishing brain stimulation. Also Heath [1963] has observed that stimulation of the septal reward area in humans will block uncontrollable rage, attributable to excitation of the medial hypothalamic punishment areas, and replace it with euphoria.

There has been argument over the issues of whether the drive to obtain self-stimulation is analogous to the classical physiological drives, and whether the stimulation received reproduces the neural events normally generated by sensory feedback from consummatory activity. The hypothesis that self-stimulation is acting upon normal drive areas is supported by the finding that self-stimulation rates in the lateral hypothalamic feeding area are elevated in a hungry rat and depressed in a satiated one, and that experimenter initiated stimulation in the same region will elicit eating [Hoebel and Teitelbaum, 1962]. Similar findings have been made when electrodes have been implanted in a zone concerned with thirst [Phillips and Mogenson, 1968]. It has already been argued in Chapter 4 that self-stimulation in these instances must generate neural events equivalent to those generated by sensory feedback, such as taste and smell, from consummatory behaviour. Objections to the theory that self-stimulation behaviour is based upon the same positive reward system which produces normal instrumental behaviour, such as lever pressing for food, comes from the observation that the effects of self-stimulation decay much more rapidly than those due to natural rewards. In an extinction situation, when the current is turned off, there is a very rapid fall-off in lever pressing and the self-stimulation behaviour can usually only be restored by 'priming' the animal with a 'free' reinforcement [Olds and Milner, 1954]. In contrast to rats running mazes for food reward, when the first runs on a new day are faster than the last runs on the previous day, Olds [1956b] found that, with brain stimulation as a reward, rats tended to run through the maze much more slowly at the beginning of a day. Furthermore, it has been found difficult to train rats to self-stimulate when the intervals between reinforcements have been increased, as in ratio and interval schedules [Sidman et al., 1955].

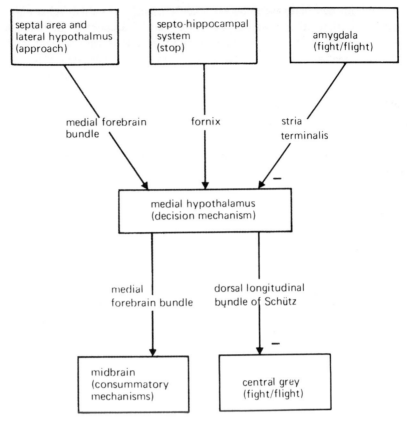

Figure 9.3
Block diagram to illustrate some aspects of Gray's theory concerning the production of approach, passive avoidance and active avoidance behaviour by different brain systems.

From Gray, J. (1971), *The psychology of fear and stress.* Reproduced by permission of Weidenfield and Nicolson Ltd., publishers

Deutsch [1960] has suggested that brain stimulation in rewarding areas produces a rapidly decaying drive state which motivates the next response. In support, Howarth and Deutsch [1962] found that in rats trained to self-stimulate, decrements in responding, following a period of removal of the response lever, were a function of time of removal of the lever, and not of the number of previously rewarded responses. Herberg [1963] has argued that if self-stimulation generates a fast decaying drive state, then summation with an existent natural drive, like hunger, should delay extinction of a self-stimulation response. Whereas Herberg found that hunger level had no effect upon self-stimulation, Deutsch and DiCara [1967] found that hunger retarded extinction briefly.

Gibson *et al.* [1965] have argued that extinction of self-stimulation is more rapid than under normal reinforcements because the reward from self-stimulation is coincident with the response. Some resistance to extinction arises with conventional reinforcements because of the normal delay between the instrumental act and the consummatory response. Gibson *et al.* [1965] and Pliskoff *et al.* [1965] set up an experimental paradigm in which an 'instrumental' lever pressing response gave the rat access to a second lever, for which the depression constituted a 'consummatory response', delivering brain stimulation to the rat. In this situation, when the time relations between the instrumental response and the eventual feedback from the consummatory response were closer to those obtained when conventional rewards are used, extinction followed a more normal pattern.

Some of the discrepancies between conventionally rewarded behaviour and brain stimulation rewarded behaviour can be accounted for if one assumes that brain stimulation mimics only the effects of sensory feedback from consummation, and not the longer term deficit restoring effects of conventional reinforcements. The persistence and durability of operant behaviour might normally be an additive function of short-term sensory and long term deficit restoring effects. It has certainly been shown that behaviour is influenced by both. Although it has been shown that in the short term hungry rats will respond to obtain the purely sensory reward of non-nutritive saccharin, in the longer term their response rates will decrease, reflecting the failure of the saccharin to restore blood sugar [Le Magnen, 1954]. It has also been shown that if preferred taste food is poisoned just sufficiently to produce illness, then even though the illness follows the consumption by a considerable delay, an animal develops an aversion to that taste [see Chapter 4; Teitelbaum, 1971, 1969; Garcia et al., 1974]. Again an influence of the long term consequences of behaviour is clearly implied. It appears that the reinforcement of behaviour could be a complex function of both hedonic sensory feedback and drive reduction.

Gray [1970, 1971a, 1972] has elaborated upon the precise location of the positive and negative reinforcing areas, the processes involved in their activation, the nature of their influence on different classes of behaviour (see Figure 9.3) and their relationship to the dimensions of personality. Gray accepts Olds' work locating the reward mechanism in the septal area, lateral hypothalamus and medial forebrain bundle. He claims that this system operates to maximize its own input (which is rewarding, or, in subjective terms, pleasurable) via connections to the motor system which executes approach responses to rewarding stimuli. Gray [1970, 1971a, 1972] embodies the novel principle that in addition to active approach to rewards, active escape from punishments is mediated by the same positively reinforcing system. Active escape or avoidance is usually initiated by a warning signal which stimulates the organism to instrumental action forestalling an unpleasant stimulus. Typical instances in the laboratory might be where a rat in a shuttle box runs from the black to the white compartment, because it had previously been shocked in the black compartment, or where a rat presses a lever in response to a light coming on, which warns of an impending electric shock. Gray calls his hypothesis, that active avoidance is based on the reward system, the 'hope=relief' hypothesis. The warning signal elicits conditioned fear of the impending punishment, which is mediated by a mechanism in the central grey of the midbrain. Implicit in an animal's attempts to escape is a state of 'hope', which is justified when the attempt is successful, and the resulting 'relief' reflects activation of the reward mechanism. Consistent with this hypothesis Stein [1965] has shown that stimulation of the reward mechanism facilitates avoidance behaviour.

Olds and Olds [1965] have found that stimulation of the central grey of the midbrain is aversive. It is also an area where fight or flight can be elicited. The initial response to aversive stimulation of this area is an 'unskilled' unconditioned escape response. However, when given the opportunity, the rat would learn the 'skilled' escape response of pressing a lever to obtain 'time-out' from aversive stimulation which would otherwise be continuous. When the forebrain (supposedly including the reward areas)

of skilled escapers was depressed, using chlorpromazine or spreading depression (see Chapter 13), they would revert to their previous unskilled escape behaviour in response to aversive midbrain stimulation. Predictably, self-stimulation of these forebrain rewarding areas was also eliminated when they were depressed. Gray [1971a] asserts that these findings show that skilled escape learning is mediated by 'relieving non-punishment', involving activation of the reward areas when the escape attempt is successful.

As a complement to the 'go' mechanism of the reward system, which energizes approach or avoidance behaviour, Gray also postulates a 'stop' mechanism which inhibits punished responses, and also responses which were previously rewarded, but are now unrewarded. In other words the 'stop' system is the origin of passive avoidance and extinction. In order to sustain this model Gray equates fear, which is the basis of passive avoidance, with frustration, the effect of the non-appearance of an expected reward. Gray not only locates the neural substrate of this mechanism in a system which includes the RAS, medial septal nucleus, hippocampus and basal forebrain, but also identifies a specific pattern of activity, the hippocampal θ-rhythm, with activation of the stop system. The medial septal nucleus and the hippocampus appear to be the most important structures, the medial septum apparently driving the 7.5–8.5 Hz hippocampal θ-rhythm. This system for behavioural inhibition has been put out of action by lesioning, administration of small doses of sodium amylobarbital (which selectively depresses the septum and hippocampus and blocks hippocampal θ) or blocking the hippocampal θ-rhythm by stimulating the septum at a high frequency. In all of these instances there is a failure of both passive avoidance learning and of extinction of responses to non-rewarded stimuli. In contrast active avoidance learning is actually improved and rewarded approach learning unimpaired following these treatments. This suggests that normally active avoidance learning is partially antagonized by competition of the stop system commanding that the animal 'freeze' in response to fear provoking stimuli.

Gray [1970, 1971a, 1972] reports a number of ingenious experiments involving driving of the hippocampal θ-rhythm, by stimulation of the medial septal nucleus at frequencies within the narrowly defined θ range, or blocking of the hippocampal θ-rhythm using either high frequency stimulation, or amylobarbital. θ Driving during extinction actually speeded up the process, consistent with enhanced activity of the stop system. In contrast θ driving during 50% of acquisition trials when a thirsty rat is being rewarded with water on 100% of lever presses actually retards subsequent extinction. This apparent paradox is resolved by recalling that extinction is normally slower when a response has only been partially reinforced (i.e. on less than 100% of trials) during acquisition training. θ Driving has falsely activated the frustrative non-reward system during rewarded trials so that the effects of partial reinforcement have been mimicked. This interpretation was supported by the results of the converse experiment in which θ blocking was applied during non-rewarded trials, in a partial reinforcement acquisition condition, with the result that extinction, instead of being slowed, was as rapid as following 100% reinforcement. The θ blocking falsely suppressed activation of the 'frustrative non-reward' system which is normally responsible for the build up of resistance to

extinction during partial reinforcement. Similarly if hippocampal θ-rhythm is abolished by medial septal lesions then the partial reinforcement retarded extinction effect disappears, whether the lesions are made before acquisition, or after acquisition and before extinction.

Personality and sensitivity to rewards and punishments

Following from his elaboration of the mechanisms of reinforcement Gray [1971a, 1972] presents a modification of Eysenck's [1967] view that introversion–extroversion is determined by the level of activity in the RAS. Gray argues that it is the activity of his fear=frustration system embracing the RAS, medial septal nuclei, hippocampus and orbital frontal cortex which determines the degree of introversion. He observes both, that certain levels of RAS activity supply an input which drives hippocampal θ [Stumpf, 1965], and that there is a negative feedback loop by which the hippocampus 'turns down' RAS activity.

The neurophysiological correlate of introversion is a high level of activity in the hippocampal stop system, giving rise to fearfulness and strong tendencies to inhibit behaviour followed by punishment or frustrative non-reward. There is an over sensitivity to punishment, which leads to a proneness to develop neurotic disorders in the group which Eysenck [1967] calls dysthymic; anxiety neurosis, phobias, obsessive–compulsive symptoms, and reactive depression. The three former instances can clearly be related to inhibition of behaviour to avoid punishment. Reactive depression, which may follow such events as bereavement, desertion by a lover or loss of a job, can be seen as stemming from loss of an accustomed source of reward, in other words 'frustrative non-reward' in Gray's terminology. We might refer back to the observation [Gray, 1971a] that because of their greater genetic endowment with fearfulness women are more prone to dysthymic disorders than men. In line with our hypothesis it is found that females are more introverted than males [Eysenck and Eysenck, 1969]. Eysenck [1967] observes that the introvert is easier to condition than the extrovert, but his human conditioning experiments, such as eyeblink conditioning, almost invariably involve punishment. Thus Gray maintains that the greater conditionability of the introvert stems specifically from the greater sensitivity of the punishment system. Eysenck [1967, Chapter 6] observes that drugs, such as barbiturates and alcohol have an extroverting effect on behaviour due to their depressive effects on forebrain function. As we have seen, Gray has shown that small doses of the barbiturate, sodium amylobarbital, selectively depresses the septo-hippocampal system with effects which are limited to passive avoidance and extinction and do not extend to approach or active avoidance learning. Gray [1972] observed that in addition to motor acts, the septo-hippocampal system appeared to have the capacity to inhibit sensory input, as stimulation of this area apparently attenuated evoked potentials in the

RAS, hypothalamus, and sensory systems. This phenomenon may be related to the capacity to exclude irrelevant inputs in selective attention. Eysenck [1967, pp. 87–89] has reported that introverts have a greater capacity to sustain vigilant attention for occasional faint signals than extroverts. This represents a capacity to focus on one signal source and exclude other sensory inputs, the latter function apparently being one of the capabilities of the septo-hippocampal system.

The extrovert, in contrast to the introvert is not readily conditionable, a lack which Gray attributes to him being 'bad on fear'. The septo-hippo-campal system which inhibits responses that have been punished or have failed to elicit a reward is relatively insensitive. Gray goes further and maintains that in the neurotic extrovert the reward system is, if anything, over sensitive so that the behaviour of the neurotic extrovert is almost entirely governed by reward. The consequence of this particular balance can be disastrous for society as these appear to be the ingredients which make up a psychopath. Such an individual fails to become socialized, and lacks the attributes of a conscience, guilt, and remorse, because of his insensitivity to punishment. Consequently the psychopath 'lives in the present only. His immediate wishes, affections, disgruntlements rule him competely, and he is indifferent about the future and never considers the past' [Mayer-Gross et al., 1960].

Because the psychopath is especially sensitive to reward he seeks immediate fulfilment of his desires which leads to impulsive, delinquent, and feckless behaviour. It is interesting to observe that in delinquent behaviour there is usually some attempt to avoid detection, which can perhaps be seen as reflecting 'active avoidance' in which the 'hope=relief' principle is operating. Because of the insensitivity of the punishment system relative to the reward system there is an 'excess of hope' that punishment will be avoided with the consequent positively rewarding effect of both relief and the spoils of crime. The event of either failure to avoid punishment or failure to gain a reward (frustrative non-reward; as in gambling for example) will have no effect because of the insensitivity of the septo-hippocampal system mediating inhibition of behaviour on this basis. It is interesting to observe in this context that Broadhurst's [1960] non-reactive, 'extroverted' strain of rats were better at active avoidance learning than his reactive rats, perhaps once again reflecting greater activation of the 'hope=relief' reward system by successful escape and reduced sensitivity of the septo-hippocampal system tending to inhibit behaviour.

The relative sensitivities of the reward and punishment mechanisms can account for both the introvert–extrovert and stability–neuroticism dimensions of personality. The stable introvert is more susceptible to punishment than reward, but is of relatively low sensitivity in both areas. In the stable extrovert there is a greater susceptibility to reward than punishment, but again no over sensitivity in either mechanism. Neurotics have a generalized over sensitivity to both rewards and punishments, but in the introverted neurotic this is relatively much greater for punishment, and in the extroverted neurotic relatively much greater for reward.

This theory of the physical basis of personality is, of course, highly tentative. It does have two major virtues. One is that it points to viable and realistic approaches to this difficult topic and thus stimulates research which has benefits for clinical psychology. The other is that the theory attempts to deal with objectively measurable dimensions of behaviour, and generates predictions which are amenable to experimental testing at the pharmacological, neurophysiological, and behavioural levels.

Summary and conclusions

This chapter ranges widely across different facets of the topic of individual differences. In the first section we saw that the employment of selective breeding techniques, with cross-fostering controls, showed that differences in emotional reactivity were genetically determined to a large degree. Nevertheless, experiments involving variation of type and intensity of stimulation in infancy, showed that the range of adult emotional responses, and the matching of emotional responses to the external situation, were both functions of 'tuning' of the systems mediating patterns of emotional response, during critical periods in development.

There appeared to be genetically inherited differences in emotionality, aggressiveness and other behavioural characteristics which separated males and females. The appearances of these differences in evolution could be attributed to the division of labour between the sexes in reproduction and its effects on the pattern of social organization.

Proceeding to human personality differences we find that they tentatively resolve into two-dimensions of reactivity; one of general reactivity to external stimuli called introversion–extroversion, and one of emotional reactivity called stability–neuroticism. One account of the neural basis of these dimensions aligns the introversion–extroversion continuum with the reactivity of an RAS-cortex loop, and the stability–neuroticism dimension with an RAS-visceral brain loop.

A prominent difference separating introverts from extroverts is their relative susceptibility to rewards and punishments. We have seen that there is a system in the medial forebrain bundle, lateral hypothalamus, and septal area which mediates reinforcement of behaviour rewarded by either pleasurable sensory feedback, with subsequent drive reduction, or by relieving escape from punishment. While there is a midbrain area which mediates unconditioned flight or fight responses, there is a medial septal–hippocampal–basal forebrain system mediating the reinforcement of inhibition of responses which have evoked either fear-inducing punishment or frustrative non-reward. This system for the regulation of behaviour by rewards and punishments suggests an alternative basis for the introvert–extrovert and stability–neuroticism dimensions in the relative sensitivities of the reward and punishment mechanisms.

PART 4
INFORMATION
SYSTEMS

Introduction

In the preceding chapters we have considered how the various behaviours of organisms are generated and how they arise out of the survival needs of the individual and the species. All of the behaviours discussed represent transactions with the environment which are regulated by the monitoring of information from both the external and internal environment. Information concerning such factors as internal deficit or external threat initiates behaviour. In turn the behaviour brings about changes in the internal or external environment, as in satiety or successful escape, generating information which exercises feedback control of behaviour.

The regulation of behaviour by information presupposes a number of different functions. The first is the reception of information. All environmental events can be represented as changes in the level or distribution of energy. Thus the first requirement of a biological information handling system is to have receptors which are sensitive to different forms of energy and which can translate intensity and pattern into coded representation in the nervous system. From the receptors one might expect 'raw data' from the environment to be forwarded to information processing mechanisms for analysis and evaluation of their significance. However, our terrestrial environment is usually the source of a vast barrage of information incident upon an organism's sense receptors, much of which is irrelevant to the organism's immediate needs. Consequently organisms appear to have developed the capacity to select information which is relevant to their needs and exclude that which is irrelevant, at some locus in the channel from receptor organ to a central information processor giving rise to conscious perception.

The analysis of information, the attribution of meaning and the generation of relevant responses are functions requiring that the organism has stored information as their basis. In higher animals most of the information which is the basis of their perceptual abilities and response repertoire is acquired during the animal's lifetime. It is based on the reiteration in the animal's experience of characteristic features of its environment and the rewarding or punishing consequences of events and its own actions. Stored information is retrieved by the recurrence of significant stimulus patterns, or parts of these patterns which serve as retrieval cues.

It is proposed to examine the neural basis of the reception, selection, analysis and storage of information. As in other nervous system functions, information handling occurs as an integrated pattern of events whose elements are not readily separable when the 'hardware' of the system is investigated. Aspects of both selection and analysis of information, and by implication, storage, can be found at all levels in the system from receptor organ to cerebral cortex. In this section each chapter focuses on one discernible function and the principal mechanisms underlying it, while admitting that there is a considerable overlap.

The concept of information

Before proceeding to examine the substrate of biological information handling systems it is valuable to attain a better understanding of the concept of information in the structural sense. As far as we as organisms are concerned, information arises because matter and therefore energy is not uniformly distributed in the universe, and because there is uncertainty about future events, which can be defined in terms of rapid changes in the distribution of matter and energy. Information implies unpredictable change or discontinuity, as space or time is scanned. There is, of course, a continuum between totally predictable events, such as the tick of a clock, and highly unpredictable events such as an earthquake. There is variation in the likelihood or probability that events will occur. An event or signal which has a high probability of occurrence, such as the word 'the' in a written message, conveys little information. A signal which has a low probability of occurrence, such as the word 'sesquipedalian' conveys a lot of information, at least in the structural sense. It should be made clear that the structural sense of information arises from the existence of an ensemble of possible signals which could occur, each having a specifiable probability of occurrence. This is distinct from the connotative sense of information which is that which is signified. For instance the word table signifies an object with a flat surface standing on four legs.

As you, the reader, scan the pages of this book information is transmitted to you by virtue of the fact that there is uncertainty about the spatial distribution of printer's ink, outlining letters and words, which is going to be detected. The different elements of the message, letters, words, and sequences of words, vary in their probability of individual and joint occurrence. The over-all sequence of symbols is, hopefully, unique and therefore totally unpredictable. Thus it is hoped that on the basis of your knowledge of the language and certain concepts referred to, you are able to grasp new concepts and add to your store of information in both the structural and the connotative sense.

Information is implicit in change or discontinuities in space or time. It is to change in the internal or external environment, not to constancy, that the organism must adapt. Thus we find that the nervous system is designed to respond maximally to change in the intensity of pattern or incident stimuli. When a light is turned on, certain neurones in the visual system produce a burst of impulses which die away, although it stays on. Another group of neurones produce a transient response when the light is turned off. Within the retina of the eye the phenomenon or lateral inhibition (discussed in Chapter 10) acts to enhance boundaries between areas of high and low illumination. At the receptors the mechanism of adaptation results in a declining response to a constant stimulus. At higher levels in the nervous system, the response to a monotonously repeated stimulus (thus of high probability) of no import is progressively suppressed by the mechanism of habituation. Thus we can see that the nervous system is tuned to respond to changing patterns of stimulation and low probability events which maximizes the benefits to be gained from the inherent informational richness of an uncertain universe. The concepts of information theory and their relationship to psychology are elegantly presented by Wiener [1950] in his short but seminal book *The human use of human beings.*

Chapter ten

Receiving information

Introduction

We are consciously aware of a world external to ourselves. Sighted individuals are perhaps most acutely aware of a visual world in which solid objects, both stationary and moving are of different colours, have different textures, and are disposed at different distances on the landscape. In addition to seeing objects we may hear the noises they make, feel their hardness and warmth and smell their aroma or odour. These phenomenal qualities of the physical world are not inherent within the objects themselves, but arise from the patterns of electrochemical activity which they generate within our brain. Another facet of these spatio-temporal patterns of activity is our conscious awareness. The physicists description of the material world in terms of atoms, electrons, molecules, and so forth is difficult to reconcile with the world which we see, hear, touch, and smell. However, it is through the translation of selected properties of the physical world into isomorphic neural pulse codes that this world assumes the form in which it enters our conscious awareness.

The objects which surround us reflect electromagnetic radiation emanating from sources such as the sun. This radiation is energy broadcast in the form of waves at 186 000 miles per second, the speed of light. The receptive surfaces in our eyes are sensitive to radiation of this form, with wavelengths in the range 400 nm to 700 nm (nm = nanometre; 1 nanometre = 10^{-9} metres). The visible spectrum is only a tiny portion of the total spectrum of electromagnetic radiation which extends in wavelengths from 10^{-6} nm to more than 10^{12} nm (1 kilometre). Thus it is radiation in this spectrum which gives rise to visual sensation and is defined as light radiation. The concepts of light and the visible spectrum arise from the specific sensitivity of the visual receptor organ. The problem that we are concerned with initially is the basis of the sensitivity of the receptor organs and the basis of coding patterns of incident energy into patterns of nervous activity which represent them.

The basis of receptor sensitivity

Irritability is a basic property of living cells, as we saw in Chapter 1, and receptor cells are cells which have this property enhanced in favour of particular stimuli. The visual receptor cells are 'irritated' by light and are thus known as photoreceptors. Incident light results in the breakdown of photosensitive chemicals peculiar to these cells. By processes which are still not completely understood these chemical reactions result in depolarization of the receptor cells and the consequent appearance of slow potentials, called receptor potentials. These receptor potentials are exactly analogous to the excitatory postsynaptic potentials of neurones, discussed in Chapter 2, and are subsumed under the title of 'generator potentials'. Generator potential is a general term for the graded slow potentials whose summation triggers action potentials within neurones. Many receptor cells, such as those for vision and taste, appear to be incapable of propagating all-or-none action potentials themselves. Therefore impulse activity must be initiated in the sensory neurones which innervate these receptor cells. This must occur either by the direct electrical effort of the receptor potential, causing depolarization of the closely apposed neuronal membrane, or, what is more likely, by the release of chemical transmitter following depolarization of the receptor cell. A receptor cell does not always simply initiate impulse activity in a previously quiescent sensory neurone. The neurone may be spontaneously active and the receptor cell modulate its pattern of activity.

The basis of receptor cell irritability varies from modality to modality. In addition to photoreceptors there are chemoreceptors, mechanoreceptors, and thermoreceptors. The chemoreceptors, which mediate smell and taste and also monitor certain aspects of the internal environment (see Chapters 4 and 5) are differentially receptive to certain chemicals which come into contact with them. The mechanism by which specific chemicals cause depolarization of the cells sensitive to them is not established beyond doubt. The molecules of different chemical substances have different three-dimensional configurations and it is hypothesized that there are receptor sites on the chemoreceptors where the molecules of a specific substance attach themselves on a lock and key principle. This attachment renders the membrane permeable, with consequent depolarization of the receptor cell and the appearance of a receptor potential.

Mechanoreceptors are found, incorporated in different transducer mechanisms in the auditory, orientation, somatosensory, and proprioceptive sense modalities. In each case incident energy results in the mechanical deformation of the membranes of receptor cells. It is hypothesized that this deformation opens the 'pores' in the cell membranes with consequent inflow of sodium ions, depolarization and the appearance of generator potentials.

In audition a complex mechanical system transduces the energy in pressure waves, propagated through the air, into a pattern of mechanical activation of the receptors, which enable them to code the fundamental characteristics of the sound. The orientation sense is based on the mechanical deformation of receptor cells either by weights acted on by gravity or by the inertial properties of a viscous fluid displayed during angular acceleration. The touch and pressure receptors of the somatosensory system are activated much more straightforwardly by the deformation resulting from pressure on the body surface. The mechanoreceptors of the proprioceptive system are activated by the movements of muscles and joints (see Chapter 2.5).

A further type of receptor is the thermoreceptor, whose depolariza- is effected by changes in temperature. These are found both within the body (see Chapter 5) and at the body surface.

One point to appreciate is that the specialization of receptors is not complete. For instance most receptors are sensitive to mechanical deform- ation, whatever their primary specialization. A blow on the head results in us 'seeing stars' due to mechanical stimulation of our photoreceptors. Al- though this example documents incomplete specialization at the receptor organ itself, it does illustrate an important principle operating within the nervous system. The modality of a sensation is not primarily a function of the class of stimulus energy impinging on a particular part of the organism, but is a function of the specific receptor organ stimulated and the destina- tion of its connections to the brain. This principle was first put forward by Muller [1841] as the doctrine of the 'specific energies of nerves'.

Coding at the receptor organs

The doctrine of the specific energies of nerves introduces discussion of the problem of coding at the receptors. The pattern of neural activity set up by an external stimulus must reflect the essential features of the spatial and temporal pattern of energy distribution in that stimulus, if the organism is to benefit from its informational characteristics.

We should first observe the constraints within which this coding system must operate. Firstly, the neurones which transmit information in the different sensory systems are essentially similar in their structure and func- tional characteristics. Secondly, the code used to transmit information in these systems is based on a pattern of simple pulses. All nerve impulses are basically identical in both waveform and amplitude so that they can only represent a single symbol. Thus different features of our environment can- not be coded into different symbols as in a conventional written language. To account for the coding of qualitative and quantitative aspects of environmental stimuli we are compelled to look for different patterns of activation in spatial arrays of neurones and different patterns of activation over time.

It is initially perplexing that a system capable of transmitting only one symbol can code complex information with the speed, efficiency, and accuracy displayed by the nervous system. The doctrine of specific nerve energies gives a clue to the manner in which coding of complex stimulus patterns is handled. In the different sensory systems different categories of stimulus energy are coded into identical neural impulses which travel to different locations in the brain. The different categories of sensation arise because of the different sensory channels used and the different brain locations accessed. The gross coding of sensory modality can thus be characterized as 'place coding'.

The principle of place coding is also found to operate within as well as between sensory modalities. The clearest example of this is in the mapping of the spatial information presented by the visual world. The spatial pattern of light energy presented by the visual world is projected as a 'picture' on the retina of the eye. The retina is a mosaic of minute light sensitive receptors called rods and cones. Each element in this mosaic is thus in a position to code the light value associated with a specific location in the visual field. The total mosaic is thus able to map the visual field in terms of the spatial pattern of output from its array of discrete elements. This 'place coding of place' which takes place at the retina is found to be preserved in its essentials at a macroscopic level in the cortex, where there is 'retinotopic' mapping (see Figure 10.5). 'Place coding' is a very obvious means of coding spatial location but is very uneconomical in terms of the hardware required. It requires that each retinal location has an individual transmission line to its corresponding cortical projection zone. The one million fibres which compose the optic nerve reflect this need for a 'multiplexed' transmission system.

This multiplexed mode of conveying visual information contrasts with the mode used in man-made systems such as television. In a television camera a scanning device codes the spatial pattern of light values, in a visual scene, into a highly complex, temporally patterned electrical signal. This signal is transmitted along a single channel and decoded at the receiver, to reconstruct the picture. This is a materially more economical, but functionally more complex and more vulnerable system.

Coding the frequency dimension

The energy impinging on different receptor systems is distributed on a frequency dimension (alternatively wavelength, which is the speed of propagation of the waves divided by their frequency). The values on this dimension also appear to be complexly place coded despite the apparent lack of compatibility between the signal characteristic and the code.

In the visual system light rays with wavelengths ranging from 400 nm to 700 nm give rise to a correlated spectrum of colours, colour being a subjective stimulus quality, reflecting the wavelength of incident light. Colour vision appears to be based on there being three different types of photoreceptor, each having a peak sensitivity at different points in the visible spectrum. In the carp, for instance, different retinal cones show a maximum response (recorded using microelectrodes) at the red (660 nm), yellow (585 nm) and blue-green (480 nm) regions of the spectrum [Tomita cited by MacNichol, 1966]. The subjective data on colour vision suggests that it is based on just three types of receptor with differential spectral sensitivities, as any spectral colour can be produced by an appropriate mix of the three primary colours, red, yellow, and blue-green mentioned above. Furthermore, it is evident, from unit studies at higher levels in the visual system, that a limited number of different types of pathway carry information about the amounts of energy from different parts of the visible spectrum incident upon the eye [e.g. see De Valois *et al*., 1958; De Valois *et al*., 1964; Wiesel and Hubel, 1966]. In this system for representing wavelength information we can recognize, albeit in a more complex form, the principle of 'place coding' in operation. It is not just the case that activation of a specific channel gives rise to a specific isolated sensation. The fact that any 'mix' of wavelengths gives rise to its own peculiar unitary colour sensation suggests that each discriminable colour sensation is a function of a unique spatio-temporal pattern of activity in the cortical projection zones for the sensory channels coding colour.

In audition the transducer (tympanic membrane or eardrum) responds by vibrating in time to pressure waves propagated through the air, like ripples on a pool, by the vibration of some solid object (e.g. a tuning fork). As there is a visible spectrum of light so there is an audible spectrum of sounds of different frequencies, giving rise to the subjective sensation of a range of different tones. Points on the audible spectrum are expressed as frequencies rather than wavelengths. The understanding of speech is contingent on the resolution of complex sound waves containing many frequency components. In the normal hearing human the auditory spectrum extends from about 15 Hz to 20 000 Hz. In some species, particularly creatures, such as bats which use 'echo location', auditory sensitivity extends up to frequencies of 100 000 Hz.

The most obvious means of coding the frequency of vibration of the transducing tympanic membrane is to produce a train of nerve impulses at the same frequency. It seems that this may happen at the lower end of the auditory range, but as the maximum rate of transmission of nerve impulses is only 1000 Hz, a long way below the 20 000 Hz upper limit of audition, this code cannot be used at all frequencies. Nevertheless, it does seem possible that above 1000 Hz coding by nerve impulse frequency is achieved by groups of neurones firing alternate volleys. However, above 4000 Hz there is insufficient temporal precision in neural activity to code sound wave frequency by any system based on nerve impulse frequency.

The vibrations of the tympanic membrane are transmitted mechanically to an elongated membrane which divides the spiral, liquid filled canal of the cochlea (see Figure 10.7). There is convincing evidence that different regions of the basilar membrane are maximally displaced by different sound frequencies [Bekesy and Rosenblith, 1951]. At all regions of the basilar membrane displacement deforms the receptor 'hair cells' which are connected to it, consequently producing a generator potential. Therefore, there is a clear basis for the 'place coding' of sound frequency as different cells are going to be maximally stimulated by different sound frequencies. Studies of unit responses at higher levels in the auditory system support a place coding hypothesis. At threshold intensities of sound different groups of neurones respond only to specific narrow frequency bands. This 'tuning' of cells in the auditory system becomes less sharp as sound intensity is increased, the frequency specific cells responding to a broader range of frequencies [Katsuki *et al*., 1959].

When the basilar membrane is displaced by a sound of a specific frequency, while it is maximally displaced at a location associated with that frequency, there is also some displacement, proportional to the distance from the critical location, along a large segment of the membrane's length.

This is likely to result in different degrees of activation of many receptor cells. We are therefore led to doubt that a specific frequency is coded by one frequency specific channel alone. As with the coding of colour in the visual system it seems most probable that a specific frequency produces different levels of activity in many different channels so that it is coded by a unique spatio-temporal pattern of activity across those different channels. Again it is more than place coding.

Intensity coding

Another vital stimulus dimension which must be coded is intensity, the brightness of a light or loudness of a sound for instance. Surprisingly three different coding principles appear to operate in this domaine. The most important is a 'pulse density' code in which stimulus intensity is signalled by the rate at which impulses are generated in the sensory nerve, higher impulse rates being generated by more intense stimuli. Expressed as a ratio of the threshold intensity (minimum detectable) the rang of intensities over which a sense organ can make differential responses is enormous. For instance in the auditory system it is 10^{12}. Therefore, in the nervous system, in which the impulse frequency range only extends up to 1000 Hz, it is not surprising to find that as absolute stimulus intensity increases so greater differences in intensity are required to produce a discriminable difference in impulse frequency. This is reflected in the fact that impulse frequency increases linearly when it is plotted against the logarithm of stimulus intensity. A logarithmic scale contracts a ratio scale, the contraction being greater the higher the values on the ratio scale. The relationship between impulse frequency in sensory neurones and stimulus intensity is reflected in the psychophysical relationship between subjective judgements of stimulus intensity and actual intensity. As long ago as 1860 Fechner proposed that sensation was proportional to the logarithm of the stimulus.

In addition to impulse frequency, intensity is also coded by the number of sensory fibres activated. Low intensity stimuli activate just a few low threshold neurones. Increasing intensity recruits progressively greater numbers of neurones as higher firing thresholds are reached. In the auditory system this coding principle appears to operate in a modified form similar to place coding. As intensity increases, while high threshold neurones commence firing, low threshold neurones drop out so that different intensities appear to uniquely activate their own specific channels.

Coding changes in stimulus energy

An important point to remember is that the response characteristics of many sensory neurones do not permit coding of the intensity of a constant stimulus. They adapt rapidly and produce only a transient response to sharp changes in the level of stimulation, either up or down. Thus they are biased to accentuate the neural response to events in the external environment which are informationally important.

Informationally significant sharp changes in stimulus energy not only

Figure 10.1
The principle of lateral inhibition illustrated by showing the firing pattern in a linear array of retinal elements on which a light–dark boundary is projected

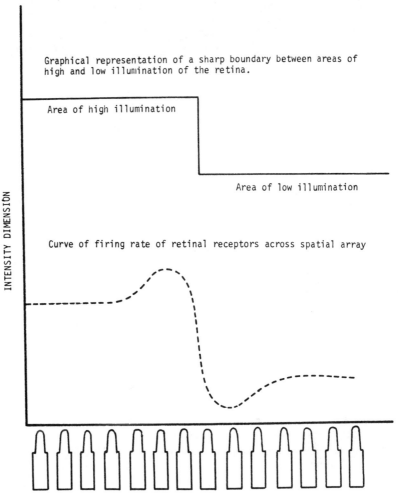

Graphical representation of a sharp boundary between areas of high and low illumination of the retina.

Area of high illumination

Area of low illumination

Curve of firing rate of retinal receptors across spatial array

INTENSITY DIMENSION

Cross section of array of retinal elements

SPATIAL DIMENSION

occur within the temporal dimension, as when a light goes 'on' or 'off', but also in the spatial dimension. A prime example is a sharp boundary between a light and dark area in the visual field. A phenomenon known as 'lateral inhibition' [see Kuffler, 1953; Ratliffe and Hartline, 1959] operates to accentuate boundaries in the spatial dimension, just as boundaries in the temporal dimension are emphasized by brief responses of 'on' or 'off' neurones. In the retina, for instance, lateral inhibition implies that active sensory neurones will inhibit the activity of other spatially adjacent sensory neurones (see Figure 10.1). This is achieved by inhibitory cells making horizontal connections between receptors. At the boundary between a light and a dark region, neurones falling on the dark side are subject to powerful lateral inhibition from those on the bright side. Consequently their firing rates are even more depressed than those of cells further into the dark region. Conversely, on the bright side of the boundary the proximity of less active neurones implies that there is less lateral inhibition

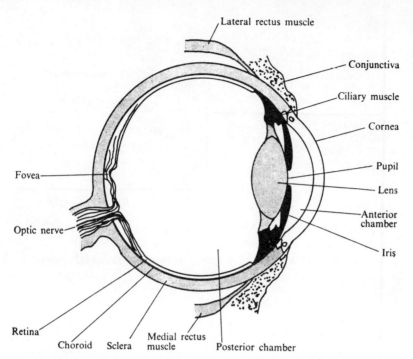

Lateral rectus muscle

Conjunctiva

Ciliary muscle

Cornea

Pupil

Lens

Anterior chamber

Iris

Fovea

Optic nerve

Retina

Choroid   Sclera   Medial rectus muscle   Posterior chamber

Figure 10.2
A cross-sectional drawing of the eye to show its principle anatomical features.

From Duke-Elder, S. (1932), *Textbook of ophthalmology*. Reproduced by permission of Henry Kimpton, publishers

than further into the bright region. Consequently there is a band of sensory neurones with augmented firing rates at the bright 'edge'. Thus the boundary is marked by adjacent bands of depressed and augmented sensory neurone activity (see Figure 10.1). In some circumstances human subjects will actually experience the illusion of bands of lighter and darker colour at a boundary between uniform light and dark areas, reflecting the operation of lateral inhibition.

Lateral inhibition is not peculiar to the enhancement of spatial boundaries within the retina. Mutual inhibitory influences probably occur in other sensory systems, and at a variety of different levels. In the auditory system lateral inhibition is probably responsible for the sharpening of the response of frequency specific pathways as one ascends through the system. An inhibitory influence of more active pathways on less active pathways, at successive levels in the system, predicts that the activity in the latter will be progressively suppressed, while activity in the former will be progressively facilitated by rebound release of inhibition. This would be evident in progressive reduction, with ascent of the system, in the activity of units whose central sound frequency is remote from the frequency of a sound stimulus currently being presented, and which are therefore subject to the inhibitory influence of more active pathways.

In the visual system there is yet a further mechanism for maintaining the salience of boundaries. This is to counteract the rapid adaptation of receptors to constant levels of stimulation, a device which normally accentuates temporal boundaries. A constant minute tremor of the eye [150 Hz, amplitude 0.5 minutes of arc; see Ditchburn *et al.*, 1959] ensures that any boundary is in continual movement back and forth across a band of receptors. This means that they are continually being turned 'on' and 'off' so that the boundary fading effects of adaptation are circumvented. The indispensability of eye tremor for maintaining image intensity is clearly shown by the fact that an image stabilized on the retina, so that no movement occurs, fades and disappears [Ditchburn and Fender, 1955]. Images can be stabilized on the retina either by 'burning' them on with a bright flash or by getting a subject to wear a contact lens with a stalk which has a visual target mounted on the end.

A point to observe about the mechanisms which accentuate sharp temporal or spatial changes in energy level is that they distort the isomorphism between the external environment and the pattern of neural activity which codes its features. In a sense this represents a distortion of reality, but its utility is to enhance the probability of detecting signals which are important to survival.

The appearance of the mechanisms which have just been discussed at the receptor level emphasizes that the mechanisms for selection and analysis of information cannot be uniquely isolated at the cortical end of the sensory systems. Selection and analysis of incoming data is a process which commences at the receptor organs and is accomplished progressively as higher levels in the system are traversed.

Having looked at some of the general principles involved in the reception and coding of information we should now look at the receptor organs in a little more detail.

Vision

Our visual system gives us a 'wide angled' view of a three-dimensional world and enables us to distinguish details of near and far objects. The acute discriminative powers of mammalian visual systems require more than the simple light sensitive surface found in more primitive organisms. The eye (Figure 10.2) is in the form of a hollow sphere with its light sensitive surface within it. Light enters the eye through a variable aperture called the pupil. The aperture is adjusted by muscular operation of an opaque membrane called the iris which is analogous to the variable diaphragm of a camera. When a light is shone into the eye of a fellow human or animal, in darkness, the pupil can be seen to reflexly constrict to limit the amount of light entering the eye and prevent overstimulation of the photoreceptors. Prior to passing through the pupil light passes through a curved 'window' called the cornea, which crudely focuses an image on the retina.

Beyond the pupil light passes through the crystalline lens. The lens can be reflexly bulged or stretched by the ciliary muscles which surround it, modifying its curvature and thus its focal length. This enables us to make precise adjustments, by which we can bring objects at any distance into sharp focus on the retina. Weaknesses in the ciliary muscles may lead to difficulty in bringing either near or far objects into focus. Man-made lenses in the form of spectacles or contact lenses may then be required to correct these defects. It should be noted that, as with a camera, the depth of field within which objects are in focus is greater as the pupil becomes more constricted by brighter light conditions.

In diurnal creatures, such as ourselves, the interior of the eye is coated

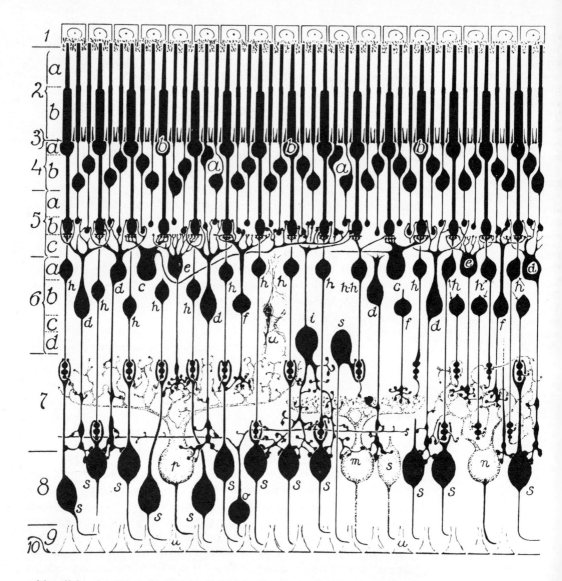

with a light absorbing choroid layer which, like the matt black interior of a camera, reduces the degradation of the image by reflected and scattered light. At the back of the eyeball, and extending approximately 100° around the visual axis (a line passing through the centre of the lens, at right angles to its plane), is the retina, with its dense mosaic of light sensitive rods and cones (Figure 10.3). These receptor units are differentiated by their shape and functional characteristics, as will be seen. The retinal zone directly in line with the axis of vision is called the macula and its centre is a small depression called the fovea, fovea centralis or foveal pit.

The receptor cells in the area of the fovea are almost exclusively slender cones about 1.5 μm (1 μm = 10^{-6} m) in diameter. As one moves out from the fovea the proportion of rods increases until it reaches a maximum at 20°, and then declines towards the edge of the retina. There are about 6.5 million cones and 125 million rods in the human eye.

The image of the object at the centre of vision is formed on the fovea.

It is here that transcription of an image is accomplished with the finest detail, as on a fine grain film, giving maximum visual acuity. This is because there is virtually no convergence in the visual pathways from the foveal cones to the brain. Each cone has its own individual line. In contrast there is a great deal of convergence in the pathways emanating from cones and more particularly rods, away from the fovea. This leads to greater sensitivity to light, so that in dim light an object is seen better when it is not directly in the line of sight. However, the integration of receptor activity over an area, which is achieved by convergence, degrades image detail. The degree of convergence in the visual system is indicated by the fact that the excitation from 6.5 million cones and 125 million rods is carried in only 1 million fibres in the optic nerve.

The cones appear to mediate colour vision. Animals without cones have no colour vision and in humans colour sensitivity decreases away from the fovea. More recently, electrical recording has indicated that different cones are maximally sensitive to different zones of the visible spectrum [Tomita cited by MacNichol, 1966]. Cones only mediate day, or photopic vision. They show some adaptation, by increasing their sensitivity to decreased illumination, but are insufficiently sensitive for night vision. The photic sensitivity of the cones appears to stem from the action of light in decomposing visual pigments, such as iodopsin, into their protein and retinene (a vitamin A derivative) components. It is thought that the protein opsin is the active substance which influences the membrane potential [Wald, 1959].

In bright light the purple pigment rhodopsin, which is the basis of photic sensitivity in the rods, is bleached to colourless vitamin A. Consequently the rods are totally insensitive in these conditions. In the dark rhodopsin is reconstituted from vitamin A, or the intermediate substance retinene, and the protein opsin to give the rods the high photic sensitivity which is the basis of dark, or scotopic vision. When the increasing sensitivity to light of a dark adapting subject is plotted, a scalloped curve is found (see Figure 10.4), reflecting the initial rapid and relatively slight adaptation of the cones, followed by the slower more profound adaptation of the rods. As an individual switches from cone to rod vision the peak sensitivity in the visual spectrum shifts from the red end (wavelength 600 nm) to the blue-

Figure 10.3
cross-sectional drawing of the retina of the eye. The rods and cones at the top of the drawing are innervated by the bipolar cell in the middle section. Horizontal cells in this section make connections across the retina. The bipolar cells make connections with the ganglion cells whose fibres go to make the optic nerve.

From Polyack, S. L., *The retina*. Copyright © 1941 University of Chicago Press. Reproduced by permission of the publisher

Figure 10.4
The dark adaptation curve. The first small scallop represents the adaptation of the cones, the second, deeper scallop represents the adaptation of the rods which are the sole agents of vision at low light intensities.

From Hecht, S. (1934). In C. Murchison (Ed.), *A handbook of general experimental psychology*. Reproduced by permission of Clark University Press

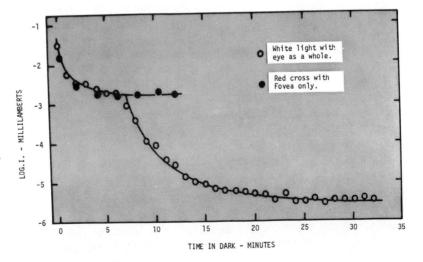

green end (wavelength 500 nm), a phenomenon known as the Purkinje shift.

Rather surprisingly, the rods and cones are orientated away from the light entering the eye, and are behind the layers of sensory neurones which innervate them. Thus light incident upon the retina must pass through these layers. In direct communication with the receptors are a layer of bipolar cells. Foveal cones each have individual bipolar cells, while more peripherally, groups of both rods and cones may be innervated by a single diffuse bipolar cell. This convergence of a number of rods on a single bipolar cell is a further contribution to the very high sensitivity of rod vision, as it forms a basis for the spatial and temporal summation of minimal depolarization initiated by a few receptors in low light conditions. The bipolar cells are, in turn, innervated by ganglion cells which may take their input from single bipolar cells in the foveal region or, as the basis for further convergence, from several bipolar cells in other regions.

It appears that until the ganglion cells are reached information is transmitted through the few hundred micrometres (μm: $1\,\mu m = 10^{-6}$ m) of the receptor and bipolar cell layers by the electrotonic conduction of graded generator or postsynaptic potentials (passive decremental conduction through the cellular medium rather than the generation of action potentials). These potentials may control the liberation of transmitter substances which are only able to initiate action potentials when the ganglion cells are reached.

The axons of the ganglion cells all converge at the optic disc, about 10° away from the fovea, where they are highly compressed and exit from the eye to form the optic nerve. As there are no receptors at this exit it forms a blind spot in the eye, although we are not aware of it in normal circumstances.

A great deal of elegant experimental work has been done on information processing at the retina in the areas of both colour vision and form perception. We have already seen that it has proved possible to isolate single cones with peak electrical responses in different zones of the visible spectrum. In complementary work Brown and Wald [1964] found that cones separated into three groups which absorbed light in different regions of the visible spectrum at 445 nm (violet), 525–535 nm (yellowish green) and 555 or 570 nm (yellow or greenish yellow). Granit [1943, 1955] recorded from ganglion cells in the retina and found units he called dominators which responded to light over the whole visible spectrum. These might be supposed to code intensity. In addition he found cells responding to narrower ranges of wavelength, with peaks at different parts of the spectrum, which he called modulators and supposed were the basis of colour coding.

An alternative to the trichromacy theory of colour vision, postulating three types of receptor, is Hering's 'opponent process' hypothesis. He suggested that there were three types of receptor but that each gave a different type of output according to which of two opponent colours stimulated them. Thus, one receptor signalled either blue or yellow, another red or green, and a third, black or white. Recent evidence suggests that colour information may be coded, according to the opponent process principle, in the neural networks innervating the receptors, so that both theories have some validity. MacNichol and Svaetichin [1958] and Motokawa et al. [1957] recorded generator potentials from horizontal cells in fish retinas and found units which were hyperpolarized (and thus inhibited from firing) at one wavelength (e.g. green) but hypopolarized (facilitating firing) at another wavelength (e.g. violet). Michael [1966] found that in the ground squirrel optic nerve fibres which were fired by green or yellow light were inhibited by blue light. Other fibres had the reverse characteristics. De Valois *et al*. [1964] made similar findings at the level of the lateral geniculate nucleus.

Retinal coding of form

We have already observed that there are units in the sensory nerves which respond specifically to stimulus 'on' or stimulus 'off'. Hartline [1938] was the first to make this observation when recording from individual fibres in the optic nerve of the frog. In more detailed investigations of single gang-lion cell responses Kuffler [1953] moved very small spots of light (100 μm in diameter) about the retina and found that very small changes in position of the light resulted in 'on' cells becoming 'off' cells, and vice versa. Using this technique Kuffler was able to map the 'receptive fields' of ganglion cells. Receptive fields are areas of the retina from which neural pathways project to a single neurone. Thus activation of the receptors in any part of a receptive field will cause that neurone to fire. The receptive fields of ganglion cells take the form of concentric rings. Typically, inner zones might respond to a light stimulus being turned 'on', intermediate zones to it being switched 'on' or 'off' and inner zones to it being switched 'off'. Mapping of the receptive fields of units has become a classical means of investigating information processing as the visual system is ascended. Kuffler [1953] was also able to investigate the interaction between adjacent regions of the retina by using two spots of light. When one spot illuminated the centre of an 'on' region for a unit, the illumination of a nearby region (0.5 mm away) by the second beam of light, inhibited the unit's response to the first spot, thus demonstrating the operation of lateral inhibition. By moving 'edges', separating dark and bright zones, or bright-ness 'ramps' (gradual transitions between two areas of different brightness), across the retina of the limulus (horseshoe crab), Ratliffe and Hartline [1959] were able to demonstrate the augmentation of unit responses on the bright side and depression on the dark side of a boundary, arising from the operation of lateral inhibition, and serving to enhance the neural representation of spatial contours.

Research on creatures higher up the phylogenetic scale than limulus indicates that more complex information processing can take place at the retina. In classical work on the visual system of the frog Maturana *et al*. [1960] found optic nerve fibres which responded variously to sharp 'edges', small dark spots in movement, moving edges or dimming of the light. The first type were named 'boundary detectors' and the second 'bug detectors', the latter because of their probable importance in detecting bugs which the frogs catch and eat. Work on higher animals has revealed units with even more complex receptive field characteristics. The close study of the retina and its immediate neural connections reveals a system which does not simply produce an output mapping the pattern of incident light energy. Even at this level the visual input is processed to extract

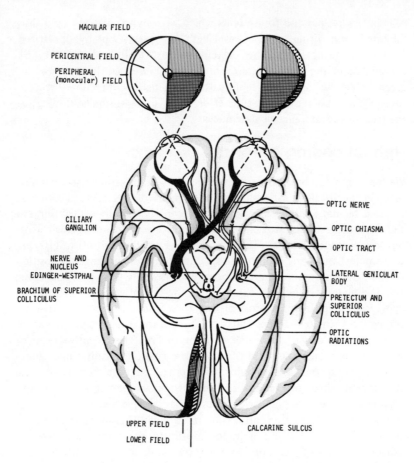

MACULAR FIELD

PERICENTRAL FIELD

PERIPHERAL
(monocular) FIELD

CILIARY
GANGLION

NERVE AND
NUCLEUS
EDINGER-WESTPHAL

BRACHIUM OF SUPERIOR
COLLICULUS

UPPER FIELD

LOWER FIELD

OPTIC NERVE

OPTIC CHIASMA

OPTIC TRACT

LATERAL GENICULAT
BODY

PRETECTUM AND
SUPERIOR
COLLICULUS

OPTIC
RADIATIONS

CALCARINE SULCUS

Figure 10.5
The visual system including the mapping of the retina on the visual projection area of the occipital cortex.

From Noback, C. R., and Demarest, R. J. (1972) *The nervous system.* Copyright © 1972 McGraw-Hill Inc. Reproduced by permission of the publishers

features, including wavelength and form information, for transmission down their own specific pathways.

The visual pathways

Before leaving the visual system we should briefly describe the pathways from the retina to the brain (Figure 10.5). The optic nerves from the two eyes converge at the optic chiasma, beneath the hypothalamus. In primates, fibres from the nasal hemiretinas (half retinas adjacent to the nose) cross to the opposite side, while fibres from the temporal hemiretinas continue on the same side. The reversal of the retinal image by the lens implies that the left visual field is projected on to the nasal hemiretina of the left eye and the temporal hemiretina of the right eye, so that the reorganization at the optic chiasma merges the fibres from corresponding visual fields.

Beyond the optic chiasma the reorganized pathways are called the optic tracts and they continue round the hypothalamus to synapse in the lateral geniculate nucleus of the thalamus. A residue of small fibres continue into the mesencephalon to terminate in the superior colliculi. This is the archaic visual projection area, identified as the optic tectum in lower creatures, such as reptiles. From the lateral geniculate nucleus the thalamic neurones project to the visual cortex at the extremity of the occipital lobe (Brodmann's area 17). Six layers of neurones in the lateral geniculate carry information from each eye alternately so that convergence of information from the corresponding fields in the two eyes does not occur until the cortex is reached.

It has been implied that visual sensation is a function of the activation of specific neural networks in the brain by the optic tract neurones project- to them. However, there is some evidence that following destruction of the visual cortex there is still residual visual function. Primates still show some capacity for discriminating brightness differences [Kluver, 1936] and even movement [Weiskrantz, 1963]. Rats were still able to learn brightness discriminations [Lashley, 1930,1935] and cats still able to perceive depth, indicating some pattern vision [Meyer, 1963]. It may be that while the visual cortex is necessary for the discrimination of fine detail in pattern vision, the discrimination of brightness and rudimentary pattern can be accomplished by the archaic optic tectum (identified as the superior colli- culus in highly evolved creatures). Disruption of the connections to the su- perior colliculus prevented rats from relearning a brightness discrimination.

From studies of brain damaged humans it is still not possible to draw unequivocal conclusions about the indispensability of the visual cortex to all visual sensation. There has probably never been a case of a clearly de- fined loss of the whole of the visual cortex and no other region. Loss of portions of the visual cortex result in scotomata, loss of segments of the visual field. Scotomata, which also occur in migraine, are difficult to map because of the phenomenon of completion by which patients 'fill in' their blind spots. This is presumably a function of the remaining cortex and diminishes the patient's awareness of his defect. This may lead to curious effects. A patient who has lost half of his visual field and is asked to fixate on the nose of an examiner will report that he can see all of the examiner's face, although half is in his blind area. The patient will continue to report seeing a whole face, even if the examiner covers the half of his face, on the patient's blind side, with a card. Only when he moves his eyes is the patient very surprised to find that half of the examiner's face is obscured. Because of the completion effect it is difficult to determine whether the loss of vision, following damage to the visual cortex, is a loss of all vision or a loss of pattern vision with the retention of some capacity to detect the presence or absence of light. Information processing at higher levels in the visual system is pursued at greater depth in Chapter 12 on analysing information.

The auditory system

The external aspect of the auditory system (Figure 10.6) is the pinna which probably deflects extraneous noise from behind and focuses the sound to which it is orientated during attention to a particular source. The pinna funnels the sound waves into a tube called the external auditory meatus. At the end of this tube they impinge on the tympanic membrane or eardrum, in which they set up a resonant vibration. The vibrations of the tympanic membrane operate three bones or ossicles, the malleus, incus, and stapes, of the middle ear. These act as a system of levers which mech- anically transmit the movement of the tympanic membrane to a much smaller membrane, called the oval window. This seals one end of the coiled

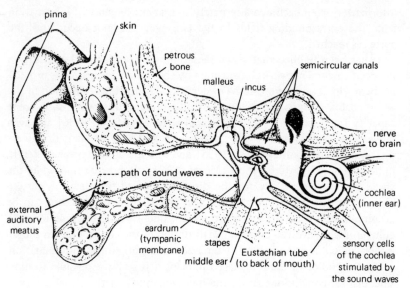

pinna

skin

petrous
bone

malleus
incus

semicircular canals

nerve
to brain

cochlea
(inner ear)

path of sound waves

external
auditory
meatus

eardrum
(tympanic
membrane)

stapes

middle ear

Eustachian tube
(to back of mouth)

sensory cells
of the cochlea
stimulated by
the sound waves

Figure 10.6
The auditory apparatus
including the cochlea,
and the semicircular
canals.

Reproduced by
arrangement with Holt,
Rinehart, and Winston,
New York, from
Hearing and deafness,
by H. Davis and R. S.
Silverman © 1970

tube of the cochlea, the central organ of hearing. The function of the ossicles is to amplify the effective force exerted by the eardrum so that there is sufficient to activate the receptor organ. There is an amplification factor of about 22 between the tympanic membrane and the oval window. There are two small muscles in the middle ear, the tensor tympani and stapedius, which regulate the relative position of the ossicles and thus the degree to which movement of the eardrum is amplified. Their function is analogous to that of the iris of the eye, as they consequently have the capacity to protect the delicate organs of the inner ear from the damaging effects of very loud sounds, by reflexly damping their impact at the oval window.

The receptor organ is a spiral tube called the cochlea (see Figure 10.7) which is divided lengthways into three ducts by two membranes. There is an outer duct called the scala vestibuli, filled with the fluid perilymph, which is bounded by Reissner's membrane. A middle duct, called the scala media, which is filled with endolymph is on the other side of Reisner's membrane and is then separated from the other outer duct by the basilar membrane. This duct, called the scala tympani, is filled with perilymph and communicates with the scala vestibuli via a small hole, called the helicotrema at the apex of the basilar membrane.

The oval window seals the vestibule which is at the basal end of the scala vestibuli. An inward movement of the oval window imparts momentum to the endolymph, which is incompressible, so that it causes Reisner's membrane, and in turn the basilar membrane, to bulge. The fluid displaced on the scala tympani side of the basilar membrane is initially accommodated by the elastic properties of the oval window, which seals this duct from the middle ear. Adjacent to the basilar membrane, in the scala media is a relatively rigid membrane of gelatinous tissue, called the tectorial membrane. This serves as a base for a single row of inner hair cells and a triple row of outer hair cells.. The hair cells stand upon the basilar membrane. Its displacement by sound waves moves these cells so that their

Figure 10.7
A cross-section of the cochlea of the guinea pig showing the receptor apparatus of the organ of Corti.

Reproduced by arrangement with Holt, Rinehart, and Winston, New York, from *Hearing and Deafness*, by H. Davis and R. S. Silverman © 1970

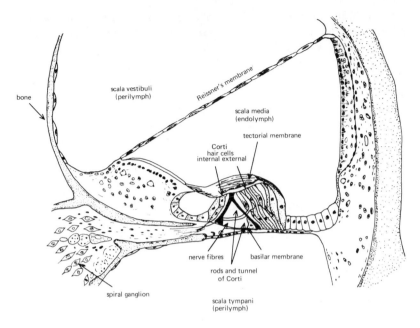

hairs, embedded in the stationary tectorial membrane, are pulled, or bent. The consequent deformation of the cells is supposed to give rise to the generator potentials. With electrodes in the scale media it is possible to pick up potentials with the same waveform as the impinging sound. These are called cochlear microphonics and are thought to be the summed generator potentials of the highly sensitive inner row of outer hair cells [Davis, 1961].

The receptor organ comprising the basilar membrane, tectorial membrane and hair cells (see Figure 10.7) is called the organ of Corti. The hair cells are innervated by dendritic processes from bipolar neurones of the spiral ganglion, which runs up the middle of the cochlea. The axons of the bipolar cells constitute the short acoustic branch of the eighth cranial nerve. This enters the cochlea nucleus in the brainstem just below the pons and at the lateral extremity of the floor of the fourth ventricle. Man's auditory nerve contains about 25 000 fibres.

The peculiar form of the auditory receiving apparatus is designed to permit the place coding of frequency, necessary because of the impossibility of using any other form of coding system with such a restricted alphabet of signals and frequency of impulse transmission. The basilar membrane is wedge shaped, widening from about 40 μm at the base to 500 μm at the apex. As the apex is approached it becomes thinner and more flexible. At one time it was thought that the basilar membrane was under tension, like an array of piano wires, and that different notes set up resonant vibrations in different segments of the membrane. It has since been shown that the membrane is relatively flaccid, but that its physical properties determine that different notes cause maximum displacement at different locations. This was first observed in extraordinarily elegant experiments performed by Bekesy [see Bekesy and Rosenblith, 1951; Bekesy, 1957]. He observed the movement of the basilar membrane through a microscope, at minute 'windows' drilled in the cochlea. By illumination of fine particles of silver on the membrane, using a stroboscope flashing in synchronism with a test sound signal, Bekesy was able to 'freeze' the membrane at the extremes of its displacement, and measure its extent.

At very low frequencies leakage of perilymph through the helicotrema dissipates the sluggish momentum imparted to the fluid so that no movement of the basilar membrane takes place. As the frequency of the pressure waves enters the audible range, perilymph cannot leak through the helicotrema fast enough and the resulting pressure produces a travelling wave which bulges the basilar membrane maximally at its more flexible apical end. As frequency rises the increasing acceleration imparted to the perilymph gives rise to increasing degrees of back pressure from the apical end. This compels the basilar membrane to yield to the greatest extent, to the resultant pressure of the fluid, progressively nearer to its narrower, stiffer basal end. Any note displaces a large proportion of the basilar membrane, but, as we have seen in the sections on frequency coding and lateral inhibition, peak displacements at different locations, by different notes, give a basis for complex place coding of frequency. This supplements the impulse frequency coding which appears to take place at the lower end of the auditory spectrum.

The pathways of the auditory system are complex and will not be explored in detail here. After the cochlea nuclei they travel up through the brainstem in the lateral lemnisci and then synapse successively in the inferior colliculus and medial geniculate nucleus of the thalamus. The thalamic neurones of the auditory system project to the superior gyrus of the temporal lobe.

The vestibular system

The cochlea is part of a multifaceted system called the labyrinth because it forms a complex of fluid filled canals and compartments. The outer 'bony' labyrinth, embedded in the dense petrous (stony) part of the temporal bone contains perilymph which cushions an inner membranous labyrinth containing endolymph. Adjacent to the cochlea are structures called the utricle, saccule and semicircular canals (Figure 10.8) which act as transducers for information about orientation with respect to gravity and angular acceleration of the head.

Within the compartments called the utricle and saccule is a sensitive region called the macula. This consists of hair cells with their hairs embedded in a gelatinous mass, loaded with calcium carbonate crystals, called otoliths. The macula in the utricle is horizontal while that in the saccule is almost vertical. The weight of the otoliths deforms the hairs, according to the direction of the gravitational forces acting upon them. Thus when an organism is in a normal upright orientation, there is a steady flow of impulses along the nerve from the saccule, where the vertical otolith exercises a continuous tension on the hair cells. Conversely there is little output from the utricle with its horizontal otolith. As orientation alters with respect to the pull of gravity the relative output from the two otolith organs changes to reflect this change.

Figure 10.8
The vestibular
apparatus: the
semicircular canals.

From *Gray's Anatomy*
1973, 35th edn.).
Reproduced by
permission of Churchill
Livingstone Ltd

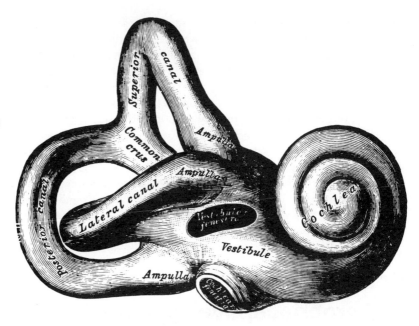

In higher vertebrates vision and receptors in the muscles and joints appear to give us sufficient information to determine our position in space, making the saccule and utricle largely redundant. Individuals with congenital absence of these organs appear to have little difficulty in assessing their orientation, or maintaining balance and posture. The otolith organs may be of greater value to birds in flight, particularly in poor visibility conditions when there are no other cues to orientation.

The labyrinthine organs which appear to be more essential for normal functioning are the semicircular canals. By signalling angular accelerations of the head in different planes they enable us to make reflex compensatory movements of the eyes which maintain the stability of the visual world. Because of these reflex eye movements our visual scene does not joggle up and down when we are walking or running. The semicircular canals radiate from the utricular space like a series of loops. One is in a horizontal plane. The other two are in vertical planes at right angles to each other, intersecting so that they form a 'V' configuration pointing to the centre of the head (see Figure 10.8). The receptors in the semicircular canals are called the crista and are located in small enlargements called ampulae, which occur just before they join the utricular space. In the crista the hairs of hair cells are embedded in a gelatinous cupola, which fits tightly across the ampulla like a valve. When there is an angular acceleration of the head the fluid endolymph lags behind the movement of the canal, because of its inertia, and consequently deflects the cupola. This deforms the hair cells and initiates vestibular nerve activity which signals the movement. When head movements are slow the elastic properties of the cupola enable it to resist the reduced inertial forces of the endolymph and it does not move. The absence of signals in these conditions is probably to allow us to track moving objects by moving head and eyes in the same direction without any disruptive reflex counter movements of the eyes.

When we rotate rapidly at a constant speed or ride on a roundabout, the endolymph will catch up with the speed of the walls of the semi-circular canals and the cupola will slowly return to its normal position. When movement ceases by a process of angular deceleration, the inertia of the endolymph will cause it to lag behind the walls of the semicircular canals so that the cupola is deflected in the opposite direction, falsely signalling a counter rotation. The disparity between vestibular signals that we are moving and visual and probably proprioceptive signals that we are stationary is responsible for postrotational vertigo (dizziness). It appears to be this type of sensory conflict, in which the data from different senses is not correlated in the way we expect, which is responsible for motion sickness [see Reason and Brand, 1974]. When we are on a ship which is pitching heavily, vestibular signals that we are making angular movements are contradicted by visual evidence that we are stationary with respect to the deck of the ship.

Somatosensory and proprioceptive systems

The somatosensory system mediates sensations in the submodalities of touch (possibly subdividing into light touch and pressure), warmth, cold, and pain on the body surface. The proprioceptive system mediates sensation from muscles and joints which provides information about the position of the limbs. The transducers for both touch and proprioception are mechano-receptors. Sensations of warmth and cold must obviously be mediated by thermoreceptors. Pain, which is poorly understood, can probably arise from intense stimulation of any of these receptive systems. In the mechanoreceptors deformation of the end organs of the sensory nerves by touch, pressure, or stretch initiates the processes of depolarization, genera-tion of a receptor potential and subsequently the propagation of action potentials.

In the last century it was thought that Muller's doctrine of specific nerve energies would apply to the submodalities of skin sensation, imply-ing that each submodality had its own receptors and specific pathways to the brain. The histological observation that nerve endings in the skin took a specific number of different forms and that different points on the skin seemed to be responsive to only one submodality seemed to support this hypothesis [Blix, 1884]. Frey [1895] attempted to identify the different morphological types of nerve ending associated with different cutaneous sensations. He concluded that touch was mediated by Paccinian (Figure 10.9 (i)) and Meisner's corpuscles, warmth by Ruffini corpuscles, cold by Krause end bulbs and pain by fine nerve endings. Unfortunately this straightforward scheme has been challenged by the finding that all of the submodalities of body sensation can be elicited by stimulation of the cornea, despite the fact that it only has free nerve endings [Lele and Weddell, 1956]. In addition it has not proved possible to find any special-ized endings in hairy skin, despite the fact that it is sensitive to all types of stimulation [Hagen *et al.*, 1953]. It has even been suggested that morpho-logical differences in cutaneous nerve endings are associated with

Figure 10.9
The somatosensory
system:

(i) The pacinian
corpuscle: a
somatosensory
receptor organ.

From Quilliam, T. A.,
and Sato, M. (1955)
The distribution of
myelin on nerve fibres
from pacinian
corpuscles. *J. Physiol.*,
129, 167–176.
Reproduced by
permission of *Journal
of Physiology*.

(ii) The spinal pathways
and cortical
projections of the
somatosensory
system.

From Noback, C. R.,
and Demarest, R. J.
(1972) *The nervous
system.* Copyright ©
1972 McGraw-Hill Inc.
Reproduced by
permission of the
publishers

(i)

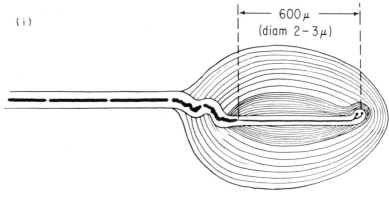

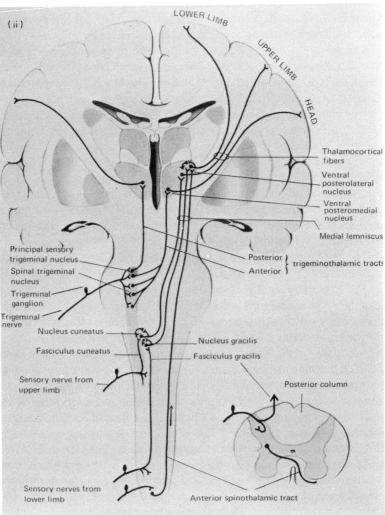

degeneration or regeneration of the nerve fibres. [Oppenheimer *et al.*,
1958]. Despite these objections it is difficult to escape from the conclusion
that submodalities must have specific receptors over large areas of the
body as punctate areas of the skin convey different sensations and, at

higher levels in the somatosensory system, the submodalities of sensation appear to be represented in separate and distinct pathways. It may be that there is not always clear morphological differentiation of receptors sub-serving different submodalities. In areas where morphological differentia-tion does exist there is also evidence for associated functional differentia-tion. The paccinian corpuscle, in which the nerve fibre is surrounded by multiple layers of connective tissue, like an onion, has been shown to be exquisitely sensitive to mechanical displacement (=pressure) but insensitive to thermal stimuli [Gray and Malcolm, 1950]. Other receptors are primarily sensitive to heat or cold, others to both thermal and mechanical stimuli, and still others to all types of stimuli. Thus there is some complexity which a simple specific pathway model cannot account for.

There is less uncertainty about the identity of the proprioceptive organs. The annulospiral endings in the muscle spindles, and golgi tendon organs, signal the degree of extension of the muscles (see Chapter 2).

The sensory nerves have been classified into three groups, types A, B, and C according to their size and speed of conduction. Type A fibres, which are myelinated, are the largest and most rapidly conducting and type C, which are unmyelinated, the smallest and slowest. This differentiation may be important in coding submodalities of sensation, particularly pain.

The pathways from the somatosensory receptors to the brain are complex (see Figure 10.9 (ii)) and only a simplified account of them can be given. The system roughly divides into two functional subdivisions, originally proposed by Head. One mediates 'epicritic' sensation, giving precisely localized information about light touch and pressure. The other mediates more primitive and diffuse protopathic sensation of touch, pain, and temperature. The epicritic system is identified anatomically with the lemniscal system of sensory nerve tracts which traverse the spinal cord and brainstem and terminate in the ventrobasal complex of nuclei in the thalamus.

The large myelinated A fibres from the receptor organ in both the skin and the muscles enter the spinal cord through the medial branch of the dorsal nerve root. Each segment of the spinal cord innervates a band of skin which encircles the body and is called a dermatome. Each dermatome is overlapped by the innervation of the adjacent dermatome so that every point on the body surface is doubly represented in the sensory nerve tracts.

At the level of entry into the spinal cord some sensory neurones synapse, either directly, or via interneurones, with motor neurones, forming the basis for a spinal reflex arc (see Chapter 2). Other fibres turn upwards, without synapsing, and ascend the spinal cord via nerve tracts known as the dorsal columns or gracilis and cuneate funiculi. They terminate in the gracilis and cuneate nuclei in the lower medulla of the brainstem, from which second order neurones cross the midline and converge to form the medial lemnisci (which give their name to the system), flat bundles of fibres close to the midline. The lemnisci ascend through the mesencephalon and terminate in the ventrobasal complex of the posterior thalamus. Thalamic cells project to the first and second somatosensory areas of the cerebral cortex.

A further, phylogenetically older, component of the lemniscal system (sometimes called the spinocervical tract or tract of Morin) is composed of

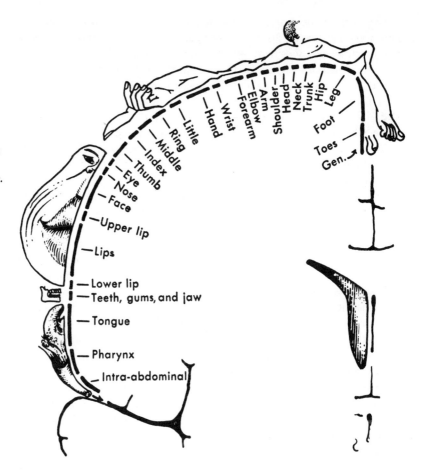

Figure 10.10
A sensory homunculus showing the proportionate representation of different areas of the body at the somatosensory projection cortex.

From Penfield, W., and Rasmussen, T. (1950) *Cerebral cortex of man.* Reproduced by permission of the Macmillan Publishing Co. Ltd

second order neurones originating from synapses in the dorsal horn and ascending the spinal cord in the dorsal portion of the lateral column. It relays in the cervical nucleus in the upper cord, just below the medulla, from which third order neurones emerge to cross and join the medial lemniscus.

Yet another component of the lemniscal system, called the neospino-thalamic pathway, originates from synapses made by collaterals from the cutaneous A fibres entering the dorsal horn. Axons cross the cord and turn to ascend in the ventrolateral tracts of the contralateral sides of the cord, from which they exit, in the medulla, to join directly the other components of the system in the medial lemniscus.

The properties of the lemniscal system in coding the qualities of sensation and its location have been investigated by microelectrode studies of the thalamus and somatosensory cortex [e.g. Mountcastle and Henneman, 1952; Poggio and Mountcastle, 1963; Mountcastle *et al.*, 1963]. Within the ventrobasal region of the thalamus blocks of cells have been shown to respond to stimulation of localized zones of the body, the total body surface being somatotopically mapped in a three-dimensional structure made up of these blocks. Within each block of cells smaller blocks have been shown to be responsive to different submodalities of stimulation; light touch, deep pressure, and joint movement.

The receptive field of any thalamic unit varies in area from 0.2 cm² on the fingers and toes to 20 cm² on the back, reflecting the relative importance of cutaneous sensitivity on different areas of the body. Cells in the thalamus which are responsive to movement code the movement rather precisely in terms of the frequency of spike discharge.

At the somatosensory cortex the mapping of the body surface is translated back into two-dimensions consistent with the cortex's sheet-like nature. The layout of the map and proportionate representation of different areas of the body is shown in the sensory 'homunculus' in Figure 10.10.

The anatomical substrate of the phylogenetically old, diffuse, protopathic sensory system conveying pain, temperature, and diffuse touch is the spinothalamic or extralemniscal system. This system is fed by both myelinated and unmyelinated small fibres which enter the cord in Lissauer's tract at the tip of the dorsal horn, and bifurcate into short ascending and descending branches. Collaterals from these branches pass into a mass of small cells and dendrites at the tip of the dorsal horn called the substantia gelatinosa, which has extensive interconnections to the same and opposite sides of the cord. The ascending pathways from the sensory neurones are a multisynaptic chain of neurones which course through either the tract of Morin or the ventrolateral tract, on either side of the cord, to synapse with the multisynaptic neural networks of the brainstem and midbrain reticular formation. By this route they eventually access the non-specific nuclei of the thalamus, principally the centre median and parafasciculus. The role of this system in mediating diffuse sensation is reflected in the wide and undifferentiated receptive fields (sometimes extending over the whole body surface) of units in the system and also the lack of somatotopic representation at different levels in the system. Some cells only respond to stimuli which actually damage tissue and must presumably be associated with pain.

Pain and its neural basis is poorly understood. Pain sensitivity varies enormously from individual to individual and is also a function of the psychological state of the individual. Soldiers seriously wounded in battle may feel no pain immediately. Melzack and Wall [1965] have presented a 'gate control' theory of pain (see Figure 10.11) which postulates an interaction between collaterals of large A and small C fibres at the bodies of substantia gelatinosa cells. It is supposed that innocuous tactile stimulation primarily activates large A fibres whose collaterals excite substantia gelatinosa cells, whose inhibitory influence limits the firing rate of dorsal horn cells of the spinothalamic system, where the main branch of the A fibres synapse. With more intense stimulation proportionately more C fibres become active, whose collaterals inhibit the substantia gelatinosa cells, which, in turn, attenuates their inhibitory influence on the dorsal horn cells. This opens the 'gate' for the main branches of both A and C axons to initiate a powerful barrage of impulses in the dorsal horn cells which activates, in turn, the central mechanisms of pain. This theory explains the puzzling increase in pain sensitivity which occurs when damage or oxygen lack reduces the innervation of an area by A fibres relative to C fibres [Weddell, 1941, 1961]. It is supposed that the activity of the substantia gelatinosa cells, which control the gate, is also controlled by descending corticofugal neurones. This would help to explain the susceptibility of pain phenomena to psychological factors.

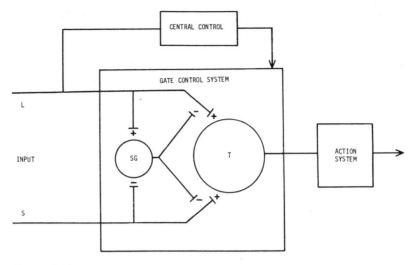

Figure 10.11
Schematic illustration of Melzack and Wall's gate control theory of pain. The
substantia gelatinosa (SG) cells exercise an inhibitory influence at the afferent
terminals of central transmission cells (T), transmitting up the spinal cord. This is the
gate. The gate is opened when the SG cells are themselves inhibited. The SG cells
are inhibited by collaterals from small diameter sensory fibres (S), but excited by the
large diameter sensory fibres (L). The opening of the gate is thus a function of the
balance of activity in the small and large diameter fibre systems.

From Melzack, R., and Wall, P. D. (1965). Pain mechanisms: a new theory. *Science*,
150, 971–979. Reproduced by permission of the authors and the American
Association for the Advancement of Science

Finally mention should be made of spinocerebellar tracts, originating
from medially placed dorsal horn cells, which receive collaterals from the
large myelinated A neurones. These tracts terminate at the cerebellar
cortex where they somatotopically map the body. This system does not
appear to be associated with conscious sensation of bodily stimulation and
presumably subserves the fine control and co-ordination of movement
effected by the cerebellum.

Summary

The organism receives information from the environment by a series of
transducers which respond to the intensity and spatial and temporal
distribution of different classes of energy. Transduction is achieved by
receptors which are specialized to respond to either light (causing a photo-
chemical reaction), specific chemicals, mechanical deformation or temperature change. Receptors respond to their specific stimulus by depolarizing and producing a receptor or generator potential which triggers an
action potential in either themselves or the sensory neurones which
innervate them. The all-or-none nerve impulse constitutes a too limited
alphabet to code complex environmental information in one channel.

Impulse rate codes sound frequency in the lower segment of the auditory spectrum and also partially codes stimulus intensity in all of the sensory systems.

Information about spatial location in both the visual and somatosensory systems is coded on a 'mosaic' basis by individual channels carrying information about incident energy at specific locations, so that retinotopic or somatotopic mapping can be observed in the cortical projections of these systems.

In the visual and auditory systems information about stimulus frequency, experienced as colour and tone respectively, is coded by a series of spatially separated channels which are selectively responsive to different parts of their respective frequency spectrums. The uniqueness of each colour or sound appears to be a function of a specific spatiotemporal pattern of activation across channels, rather than the activation of a single channel.

Processes at the sense organs extend beyond purely coding stimulus patterns into isomorphic patterns of neural activity. Properties of the receptor systems such as adaptation and lateral inhibition enhance the response to sudden changes in energy level in the temporal or spatial dimensions. In addition processing of information appears to occur in which gross stimulus features are coded by activation of specific channels.

The receptor organs of the eye and the ear require elaborate accessory structures to translate the impinging energy into a suitable form for transduction into a neural pulse code. The eye comprises an optical system, with muscular control of aperture and lens curvature, which focuses spatial patterns of light energy on to a small photoreceptive zone called the retina. In the ear a mechanical system of vibrating membranes and levers translates pressure waves in the air into pressure waves in the cochlea fluid which displace the basilar membrane and activate the attached mechanoreceptor hair cells by the shearing force applied.

In the vestibular system mechanoreceptive cells are activated by either the gravitational forces acting on the heavy otoliths, or the inertial properties of the fluid in the semicircular canals under angular acceleration.

The mechanoreceptors of the somatosensory and proprioceptive systems are activated much more simply by the deformation produced by stretch or pressure. There appears to be specialization in the somatosensory system, both to code the submodalities of touch, heat, cold, and pain, and to produce either precisely localized or diffuse sensations.

The sense organs are the origins and instigators of spatiotemporal patterns of activity within our brain which give rise to our conscious experience of the external world. It must be appreciated that the reality of the world which we experience is subjective as our apprehension of this external world as reality is primarily a function of neural processes. The reality of the external world can alternatively be characterized in descriptions, such as those of the physicist, which seem alien to the way we see, hear, and feel it.

Chapter eleven

The selection of information

Introduction: psychological theories of selective attention

Higher animals have seven sensory systems, each receptive to a different class of environmental information, and each transmitting information to the brain in an encoded form. Within any sense modality many different signals may be received simultaneously. This potential profusion of incoming information implies a massive demand on central processing mechanisms which must determine when to initiate an adaptive response.

Much of the information picked up by an animal's sense receptors has no relevance to its adaptive needs; it signifies neither food nor danger. It is therefore more economical on central information processing capacity if information irrelevant to a creature's needs can be screened out by a device which selects or rejects information on the basis of a preliminary analysis. Biological information processing systems which can focus on appropriate environmental stimuli or signal sources as a basis for action are highly adaptive. Inability to select from incident information may lead to paralysis due to overloading of the central processor.

The ability of human beings to focus on specific environmental stimuli, while excluding others, was recognized by early psychologists from their introspections. The terms which have been used to describe this phenomenon have been 'attention' and latterly, and more precisely 'selective attention' or 'focal attention'. James [1890] defined attention as 'the taking possession by the mind in clear and vivid form, of one out of what seems several simultaneous possible objects or trains of thought...It implies withdrawal from some things in order to deal more effectively with others.'

Despite this early discussion of the topic by James, interest in attention lapsed. This was probably due, on the one hand to the ascendancy of the gestalt psychologists. They emphasized the gestalt laws of organization as determinants of our percepts, which seemed to preclude the study of attention as a separate subject. On the other hand the concept of attention was too mentalistic for the early behaviourists with their rigid insistence on restricting their studies to overt and measurable behavioural responses.

Experimental interest in the study of attention was reawakened in the 1950s. There was rejection of the doctrinaire rigidity of the older schools of psychology and a more flexible 'cognitive' approach gathered momentum.

The 'cocktail party phenomenon' is widely cited as inspiration for much of the experimental work on selective attention. In the hubbub of a cocktail party we are able to focus our attention on one conversation which interests us. We can apparently exclude the content of other equally loud conversations nearby from consciousness, although aware of a noise. This situation has been simulated experimentally in studies of dichotic listening. This paradigm was devised by Cherry [1953] and later used notably by Broadbent, Treisman, and Moray [see Broadbent, 1958; Kahneman, 1973; Moray, 1969; Treisman, 1964a, for reviews]. Different messages are delivered to each of a subject's ears by headphones while the subject has to focus his attention on the message to one ear only. If the subject is asked to repeat back the message delivered to one ear as it occurs, a task known as 'shadowing', then at the conclusion of the task he is usually found to be totally ignorant of the content of the unattended message and unaware of such events as a change to a foreign language or the introduction of reverse speech [Cherry, 1953]. Only gross changes in pitch or loudness are noticed. Similar findings have been made in a visual shadowing task in which lines of a prose passage to be shadowed were alternated with lines of an irrelevant passage [Neisser, 1969]. These findings suggested that unattended messages or 'channels' were blocked before all but the crudest analysis had taken place, or that they were held in a short term memory store where decay was very rapid.

Broadbent [1954] conducted the classic 'split span' experiment, in which a different sequence of three digits was presented to each ear simultaneously. When reporting the digits the subject would never alternate between ears, but invariably reported all of the digits delivered to one ear, before reporting those presented to the other. This result led Broadbent [1958] to formulate a theory in which there was both a 'sensory buffer store', briefly holding all incoming information in an unanalysed form, and beyond this a 'selective filter' capable of blocking information arriving on an unattended channel (see Figure 11.1). Broadbent suggested that the filter sorted simultaneous stimuli according to obvious physical characteristics defining the relevant channel. These might be spatial position, voice quality or, in the visual modality, colour.

The existence of the sensory buffer store implied that information arriving on an unattended channel could be forwarded for further analysis if the filter switched to this channel before the information decayed from the store. In the split span experiment cited above the three digits which were reported second were supposedly held in the buffer store while the first three digits were being analysed in a 'single channel processor'. Following report of the first three digits the filter switched to the channel defined by the ear of arrival of the other three digits, and extracted them

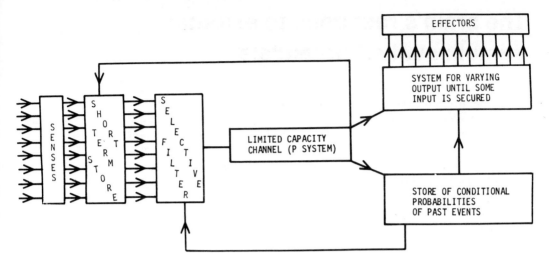

Figure 11.1
Schematic illustration of Broadbent's selective filter theory of selective attention.

From Broadbent, D. E. (1961) *Perception and communication.* London, Scientific Book Guild. Reproduced by permission of London Express News and Feature Services

from the buffer store for analysis and report. The real life example of this system in operation is the occasion when one is spoken to when not attending to the speaker and only realizes what has been said, after a brief delay, when one is actually asking for a repetition of the message. The message is presumed to be captured from the sensory store by switching attention before decay occurs.

Whereas Broadbent [1958] originally supposed that unattended messages were totally blocked by the selective filter, some later experiments on speech shadowing have shown that some of the content of the unattended channel is analysed. Moray [1959] has shown that if the subject's own name prefaces an instruction given to the unattended ear it is detected. Treisman [1954a, b] has observed that bilingual subjects will notice when the message delivered to the unattended ear is identical in content to that delivered to the attended ear, even if the message to the unattended ear is a translation of the other into the alternative language of the subject. These findings imply that the information arriving on unattended channels is subject to quite a high level of analysis. This has led Treisman [1954a, b] to formulate a theory in which unattended messages are attenuated rather than completely blocked. The possibility of unattended messages arriving in consciousness is preserved because some of an array of analyser devices or 'dictionary units', which give rise to perception when activated, have lowered thresholds, so that even highly attenuated signals can trigger them. The thresholds for high priority signals, such as one's name, are likely to be permanently lowered. The thresholds of other dictionary units may be temporarily lowered when their importance is enhanced by context.

Having become acquainted with the basic psychological phenomena exemplifying the operation of selective attention we should now discuss how we might investigate the brain mechanisms underlying it.

The brain's response to external stimuli: evoked potentials

The sense organs translate environmental information into coded patterns of impulses which traverse the sensory nerve pathways and initiate activity in the brain. Electrophysiological techniques have been developed whereby these responses of the nervous system can be recorded graphically as fluctuations of voltage over time (see Chapter 3). Responses of individual neurones can be recorded from microelectrodes while gross evoked potentials (EP), the massed responses of groups of neurones, can be recorded from macroelectrodes located either inside the active tissue or outside it, on such locations as the scalp (see Figure 11.2). The recording of potential fluctuations is usually between an active electrode located over cortical tissue and an indifferent electrode at a location such as the mastoid process (behind the ear) where no potential changes are to be expected. The recording of massed neural responses has the advantage that a better overall picture can be gained of the pattern of activity generated by sensory

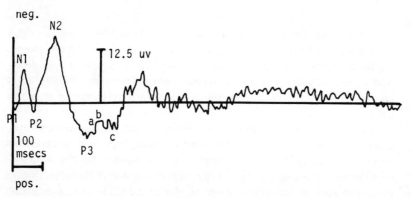

Auditory Evoked Potential.

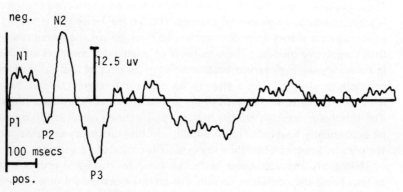

Visual Evoked Potential.

Figure 11.2
Scalp recorded averaged evoked potentials produced by auditory and visual stimuli. Electrode derivation: vertex to left mastoid. Approximately the first 80 ms of the auditory and 100 ms of the visual EP represent a primary response. The following sequence of waves represents a secondary response produced by a diffusely projecting system from the thalamus. It is suggested in the text that the secondary response is associated with conscious perception

information carried by many nerve fibres. Also recording can be achieved without the need for anaesthetic or surgical intervention which may complicate the interpretation of results.

Evoked potentials obtained by averaging

When recording from the scalp, cortical evoked potentials to single stimuli are usually buried in 'noise' arising from the continuous background electrical activity of the brain. To obtain a clear recording the EP to a number of stimulus presentations must be averaged by a computer to improve the signal to noise ratio. To achieve this brief samples of the EEG (the electroencephalogram; the record of the electrical activity of the brain recorded from the scalp) usually in the range of 200 ms to 1 s long, are suitably encoded and stored in the computer. These EEG samples are summed in such a way that a 'net' voltage is obtained for each point in time following a stimulus occurrence, over all the samples. As the background EEG is randomly distributed in time with respect to the evoking stimulus there will be an equal probability of a positive or negative voltage at any point in time following the stimulus and the net voltage will tend to sum to zero as successive EEG samples are summed. On the other hand the peaks and troughs of the potential fluctuations specifically evoked by the stimulus will tend to occur at fixed points in time following each stimulus occurrence. Therefore these fluctuations will tend to be accentuated relative to the background activity because the net voltage will tend to be the sum of voltages with the same sign. An averaged EP is obtained from the summed EP by dividing by the number of EEG samples contributing to the sum.

Whereas averaging has the great benefit of improving the signal to noise ratio there is loss of information about variation in the EP across individual trials, from which we might infer any changes in the state of the brain over time.

Evoked potentials and cortical information processing

The interpretation of gross evoked potentials recorded from the scalp is problematical as it has been shown, by simultaneous recording of unit discharges and gross EP, that the latter do not appear to represent the summed effect of many individual neurone discharges. They are the record of slow changes in potential across neural membranes, synchronized in many cortical cells, and reflecting fluctuations in their excitability [see reviews by Purpura, 1959; Chang, 1959; Bergamini and Bergamasco, 1967].

Fortunately there is some evidence that EPs accurately reflect the pattern and intensity of the neural impulse activity evoked by the external stimulus (see Figure 11.3), which might be supposed to be the physical

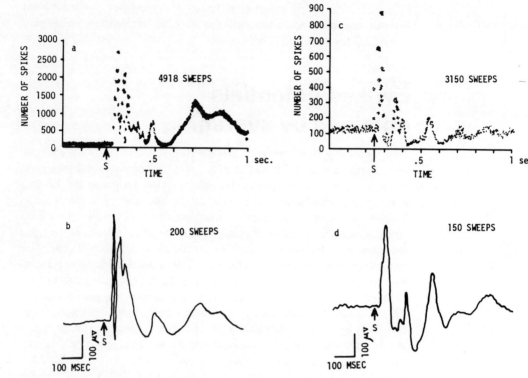

Figure 11.3
Graphs showing the
similarity between
evoked potential
waveshapes (b and d)
and the spike discharge
frequency distributions
(a and c) of single cells
in the visual cortex,
plotted over the same
time period following
a flash stimulus.

From Fox, S. S., and
O'Brien, J. H. (1965)
Duplication of evoked
potential waveform
by curve of probability
of firing of a single cell.
Science, 147, 888–890.
Reproduced by
permission of the
authors and the
American Association
for the Advancement of
Science

basis of cortical information processing [see John, 1967, Chapters 11 and 15; John, 1972 for reviews; Bergamini and Bergamasco, 1967; Fox and O'Brien, 1965 which presents the most direct evidence of the relationship]. Amassian *et al*. [1964] expressed scepticism about the relationship postulated above as EPs can be recorded at a depth of anaesthesia which abolishes all impulse activity. However, such highly abnormal circumstances do not necessarily preclude a correlation between EP wave shapes and the envelopes of unit impulse activity in normal instances.

The foregoing discussion suggests that the amplitude of EPs reflects the number of units active, and therefore presumably the intensity of the input signal and the amount of information processing. If this is so then the EP is potentially an important index in investigating how the nervous system achieves selective processing of incoming information. For instance one could test predictions from the filter theories advanced by Broadbent and Treisman (see above). Blocking or attenuation of incoming messages remote from the focus of attention should be reflected in the abolition or reduction in amplitude of EP at the level in the sensory pathway where the filter is located.

Sensory filtering

Hernandez-Peon *et al*. [1956] claimed to have found a sensory filter at a very peripheral location in the auditory pathway. Using cats as subjects and repeated auditory clicks as stimuli, they recorded EPs from the cochlear nucleus, the first relay in the complex auditory pathway. At various times they presented distracting stimuli, such as mice in a jar or the odour of fish. At such times they observed that the cochlear nucleus EPs to the clicks were very much reduced in amplitude, despite the fact that the stimulus intensity remained constant. EP amplitudes were restored to their former values, either when the cat lost interest in the distracting stimulus, or when it was removed. Hernandez-Peon therefore maintained that the auditory pathway has a filter mechanism immediately adjacent to the sense organ, which has the capacity to block auditory input when attention is focussed in other sense modalities. Hernandez-Peon supposed that decisions about what class of information to block were made centrally. They were put into effect by corticofugal pathways conducting control signals from the brain to the first sensory relay where they activated the filter mechanism. There is considerable evidence of both an anatomical and electrophysiological nature for pathways emanating from the brain to the sensory relays which are able to exercise an inhibitory control over sensory input [see reviews by Livingston, 1960; Hernandez-Peon, 1965]. Hernandez-Peon and his group extended their work and found evidence for peripheral blocking of sensory input in both the visual system and the somatosensory system, when attention was focussed in another sensory modality [see Hernandez-Peon, 1965].

In contrast to these experiments on intermodality selective attention the psychological experiments discussed were concerned with selective attention within a modality. Hernandez-Peon was aware of the importance of selection within a modality and found that EPs recorded from the brainstem relay of the facial somatosensory pathway following electric shocks to the face were greatly diminished in amplitude when a train of more intense shocks were applied to the hand. In a similar vein Palestini et al. [1959] demonstrated that optic tract EPs produced by light flashes were greatly reduced in amplitude when white rats were presented to the cats used as subjects. Hernandez-Peon [1965] considered that these experiments showed that even intramodality selective attention was achieved by selective blocking of information in the sensory pathways peripheral to the brain.

Hernandez-Peon also found that sensory tract EPs to tactile stimuli were highly attenuated in cases of hypnotically induced anaesthesia and hysterical anaesthesia where absence of sensation had no obvious organic basis, suggesting that in these cases the same peripheral blocking mechanism was operating.

The observations and inferences of Hernandez-Peon's group have an elegant simplicity. However, their experiments have latterly attracted a considerable amount of adverse criticism because of inadequate experimental controls. Worden [1966] has laid these out clearly.

In Hernandez-Peon's original experiment attenuation of the cochlea nucleus response to clicks during distraction could have been due to changes in the position of the ears relative to the roof speaker sound source (reducing the effective signal intensity at the ear). Also changes in the tension of the middle ear muscles might have reduced the sensitivity of the sound transducer mechanism. Worden [1966] claimed that when clicks were delivered to a cat through headphones, so that there was a constant relationship between the sound source and the ears, no attenuation of the cochlear nucleus EP occurred when a distracting stimulus was presented to the cat. Evidence for the influence of the middle ear muscles on auditory EPs is contradictory. Studies by Hugelin et al. [1960] and Galambos [1960] support the assertion that they have some influence. However, Moushegian et al. [1961] claimed that cutting the middle ear muscles had no effect on variations in EP amplitude observed during habituation, conditioning, and distraction.

The point is well made in emphasizing the role of prereceptor adjustments of posture and sense organ orientation and sensitivity in contributing to the achievement of selective attention. The experiments by Hernandez-Peon's group on the visual system and the somatosensory system are also open to the criticism that there was no control for prereceptor adjustments, such as pupil dilation. They were thus confounded with any modulation of the input achieved within the nervous system [see review of criticism by Moray, 1969, Chapter 9]. Moray [1969] has also conjectured that the corticofugal afferents which Hernandez-Peon supposed effected the control of the peripheral gating mechanism may rather be concerned with adjusting the 'dynamic range' of sensory systems to cope with prevailing conditions, in much the same way that pupillary adjustments keep the range of light intensities entering the eye within the limits of the retina's capacity to respond. It is clear that better controlled experiments than those carried out by Hernandez-Peon's group are required to establish conclusively whether the nervous system has the capacity to attenuate its own input, and if so, at what location.

A cortical filter

A close analogy to Hernandez-Peon's original experiment but with better controls, has recently been carried out on human subjects by Picton et al. [1971]. They recorded both the cochlear nerve response (at the external auditory meatus) and the scalp evoked potential produced by clicks delivered through headphones. In one condition the subject's attention was focussed on the clicks by requiring them to detect occasional faint clicks, as in a vigilance task, while in the other condition subjects were asked to read a book and ignore the clicks. Hernandez-Peon's earlier finding and 'peripheral gating' hypothesis were not supported. No difference was found between the amplitudes of cochlear nerve EPs to attended and unattended clicks. However, there was a highly significant attenuation of amplitude in the EP to clicks recorded from the scalp when attention was focussed on reading rather than on the clicks. This finding suggested that there was nevertheless some form of gating or filter mechanism putting differential emphasis on inputs, even if higher up the sensory pathways than Hernandez-Peon had suggested, and perhaps in the brain itself.

In a further experiment reported by Picton et al. [1971] evoked potential recording was added to the dichotic listening situation much favoured by psychologists investigating selective attention. They found that the cortical (scalp recorded) EPs produced by clicks to the attended ear, at which subjects had to monitor a sequence of single and double clicks, were significantly larger than EPs produced by clicks of the same intensity delivered to the ignored ear. This suggests that the attenuation, which Treisman [1960] and Broadbent [1958] postulated as the fate of unattended stimuli, is translated into physical reality in the operation of the nervous system. However, it should be noted that Treisman was equivocal about whether the attenuation of unattended signals was of signal intensity or, more nebulously, of information.

The experiment by Picton *et al.* [1971] described above is a good example from among a number of experiments in which amplitude attenuation of cortical EPs to unattended stimuli has been demonstrated [e.g. Chapman, 1966; Davis, 1964; Donchin and Cohen, 1967; Garcia-Austt *et al.*, 1964; Gross *et al.*, 1965; Ohman and Lader, 1972; Picton and Hillyard, 1974; Satterfield, 1965; Smith *et al.*, 1970b; Spong *et al.*, 1965; Haider *et al.*, 1964]. However, before further documentation, analysis, and interpretation can proceed we should look more carefully at the nature of the evoked potentials which are the basis for our hypotheses.

The components of cortical evoked potentials

The evoked potentials which Hernandez-Peon *et al.* [1956] and Picton *et al.* [1971] recorded from the auditory pathway were a brief series of fluctuations in potential lasting only about 5 ms, and thus fairly unequivocally the immediate response of the sensory system to information input. On the other hand the averaged evoked potentials recorded from the scalp are more complex in morphology and have a much longer duration of 400–500 ms or more. Furthermore, there seems to be a clear differentiation between the early components of the EP occurring within 60–100 ms, and the late components following this. In EPs produced by all modalities of stimulation the early components are relatively localized on the scalp and appear to be the specific response of the sensory projection area. They are mediated by the classical sensory projection systems coursing through the specific sensory nuclei of the thalamus. The later components of the EP, on the other hand, are widely diffused over the cortex and recorded with maximum amplitude at the vertex. They are attributed to the diffuse thalamic projection system emanating from the non-specific thalamic nuclei [for detailed review see Goff, 1969]. From the hypothesis that selective attention is achieved by the gating of sensory input at some level in the sensory pathways, we would predict that the amplitude of the early components of the EP would vary according to whether the evoking stimulus was the focus of attention. In fact the scalp EP components which Picton *et al.* [1971] found to vary with attention were not the early primary components but the late secondary components as in all of the other studies cited in the previous section. A number of studies have shown that the early specific components of the EP are relatively invariant across a variety of behavioural and pharmacological manipulations and even during sleep [see Goff, 1969]. It has even been observed that when the activity of the reticular activating system in the brainstem is thoroughly blocked by anaesthetic agents the primary component of the sensory EP may be actually enhanced in amplitude. Also habituation, the diminution of the response to monotonously repeated stimuli, is abolished.

The findings enumerated above rather convincingly refute the idea that unattended messages are blocked or attenuated in the specific sensory pathways. Furthermore, considerable doubt is thrown on the idea that unattended messages are blocked before they are analysed. Both unit studies [Hubel and Weisel, 1962] and evoked potential studies [Campbell and Maffei, 1970; see Regan, 1975 for review] convincingly suggest that stimulus patterns are analysed into their components at the primary projection cortex, in the visual modality at least (see fuller discussion in Chapter 12). Picton and Hillyard [1974] discriminated between early and late components of the EP during manipulation of selective attention to clicks and echoed this view that the stability of the early components of the EP indicates that auditory information is analysed in the primary auditory system whether it is attended to or not. A revision of our ideas is called for.

Secondary components of the EP and perception

It has been found [see review by Goff, 1969] that the primary EP component emanating from the sensory projection area is unattenuated, even if the subject is deeply unconscious. This indicates that the arrival of a message at the sensory projection area, and even its analysis, does not necessarily mean that the subject will become consciously aware of it (make a perceptual response). Goff [1969] observes that it is the secondary non-specific segment of the EP whose amplitude is correlated with the presence and intensity of conscious awareness, and which is abolished when a subject is unconscious; asleep or anaesthetized. We have already seen that variation in the amplitude of late EP component occurs with the manipulation of attention in the work of Picton and Hillyard's group [Picton et al., 1971; Picton and Hillyard, 1974]. It therefore appears that a perceptual response to environmental stimuli is contingent on the activation of this diffuse system mediating the secondary components of the EP, in addition to accessing the specific sensory projection areas. Goff [1969], citing Jasper [1966], suggests that these late components of the cortical EP might reflect the activity of an 'anatomically distinct neuronal system with widespread functional connections to all parts of the brain. It is involved in the selection of the ever changing momentary patterns of neuronal activity producing perceptual awareness. It contrasts with those systems constantly engaged in the unconscious processing of information and in the execution of automatic movements'.

The hypothesis above presupposes that the secondary EP components reflect the information processing giving rise to conscious awareness.

While we have already seen that 'feature analysis' of input signals appears to occur in the sensory projection areas it cannot logically be excluded that this is an intermediate stage of information processing preceding some more centrally achieved synthesis giving rise to integrated percepts. Penfield and Roberts [1959] attributed this function to their subcortically located 'centrencephalic integrating system'.

A more problematical objection to attributing informational significance to the late components of the evoked potentials is that they appear to be mediated by a system classically thought to modulate cortical arousal rather than handle information. The diffuse thalamic nuclei comprise the cephalic portion of the reticular activating system. The fact that the response of this system does not appear to discriminate between sense modalities in its source or pattern seems to preclude the possibility of it carrying detailed information. Naatanen [1967] and Karlin [1970] have attempted to reinterpret the variation of EP amplitude with attention in terms of change in the level of non-specific arousal, rather than in terms of selective attenuation of unattended information (see below).

The reticular arousal system is classically thought to receive its inputs from collateral fibres branching from the ascending sensory systems at the level of the brainstem reticular formation, and to course its way to the cortex independently of the specific sensory systems [Lindsley, 1960]. Goff [1969] reviews evidence from human patients with damage to the specific sensory systems at high levels in the brain. In these cases the absence of the primary components of sensory EPs to external stimuli has invariably been accompanied by absence of the secondary components, despite the intactness of the sensory system up to the level of the reticular formation and the diffuse thalamic projection system. These results suggest a more complex interaction between the specific and non-specific systems (see Chapter 12) which makes an 'information processing' interpretation of the late waves more plausible. Other findings suggesting that the late components of the scalp recorded evoked potential reflect information processing rather than purely the activity of an arousal system are discussed in Chapter 12.

Psychological evidence for the analysis of unattended messages

The accumulation of neurophysiological evidence suggesting that unattended messages are nevertheless analysed at the level of the cortical projection area for the sensory system involved has been paralleled by the collection of behavioural evidence that unattended messages are subject to analysis in some detail even if they are not consciously perceived. The ability of bilingual subjects participating in dichotic listening experiments to detect when a prose passage to the unattended ear is identical in content, although in a different language, to the message to the shadowed ear [Treisman, 1964a, b] is a case in point. Subjects have been conditioned to produce a galvanic skin response (a sign of emotional arousal recorded as a decrease in skin resistance on the palm of the hand) upon presentation of a particular word, by repeatedly pairing it with electric shocks. They will subsequently display the GSR when the critical word is presented to the unattended ear during dichotic listening even though it is not consciously recognized

[Corteen and Wood, 1972]. Oswald [1962] has even demonstrated that messages presented to a subject while asleep must be subject to analysis. When a tape recording of a list of names is played to a subject when asleep the uttering of his own name among them elicits distinct behavioural and EEG responses ('K' complexes).

Lewis [1970] has shown that synonyms of a shadowed word presented on the unattended ear increase the shadowing latency of that word, further evidence for the analysis of unattended messages.

The filter theories of Treisman and Broadbent have some difficulty in coping with the evidence for analysis of unattended stimuli. The theories of Deutsch and Deutsch [1963] and Norman [1968] on the other hand suppose that all signals are analysed by a 'recognizer'. The output of the recognizer is proportional to the importance of the signal to the organism and the strength of this output determines whether the signal reaches a higher level where it enters conscious awareness. This 'higher level' could be the locus of interaction of the signals from the sensory projection areas and the diffuse thalamic projection system, where Goff [1969] has implied conscious awareness arises.

Neisser's [1967] theory of selective attention is more difficult to translate into neurophysiological terms. He maintains that there is no attenuation of the intensity of unattended messages in the input channels, but that their content is not perceived. This is because they are not subjected to the process of 'analysis by synthesis' by which he asserts we arrive at conscious precepts. In analysis by synthesis a probable percept is constructed, based on the input data and stored information, and is then matched against the input to check its veracity. Perhaps the processes underlying 'analysis by synthesis' are reflected in the secondary components of the evoked potential. However, even unattended stimuli produce EPs with secondary components even if these components are amplitude attenuated. These joint facts cannot be reconciled with Neisser's ideas that unattended signals, while unattenuated in amplitude are excluded from the process of analysis by synthesis.

Kahneman's capacity sharing theory of selective attention

Like Deutsch and Deutsch [1963] and Norman [1968], Kahneman [1973, Chapter 5] supposes that recognition of inputs precedes 'perceptual interpretation' (see Figure 11.4), again paralleling the distinction which we have observed between the specific and non-specific sensory systems accessing the cerebral cortex. Furthermore Kahneman [1973, p. 70] emphasizes that, not only may unattended messages be analysed, but that they may have behavioural consequences despite incomplete awareness. A possible example of this is when a person conversing while driving a car is unable to remember any details of the journey, despite the fact that many stimuli must have elicited appropriate responses during its course. Boddy [1972] has presented evidence that simple responses to undifferentiated stimuli may be organized without recourse to the mechanism of 'perceptual interpretation'.

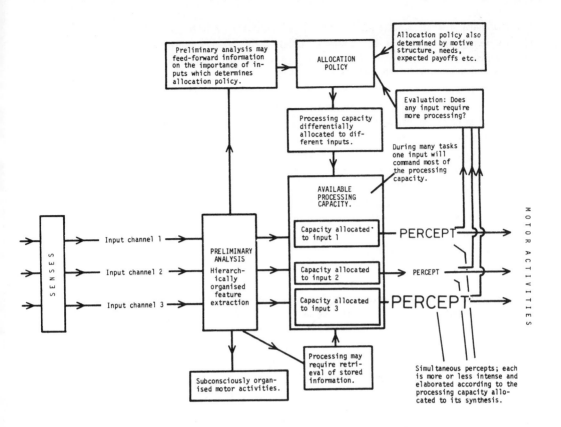

Figure 11.4
Tentative schema for
the human information
processing system
incorporating
multichannel processing
and differential
allocation of processing
capacity. It is largely
based on the theories of
Kahneman (1973) and
summarizes ideas
discussed in this and
the next chapter
(Chapter 12)

In other respects Kahneman introduces a more flexible theory of selective attention in which he escapes from the influential idea, developed by Broadbent [1958] and others [e.g. Davis, 1956, 1957, 1958, 1962, 1965] that selective attention serves a single channel central processor. For instance, as evidence against the single channel hypothesis, Kahneman [1973, p. 147] cites an experiment by his student Levy [1971] in which, following dichotic presentation of word lists, different words which were presented to both ears simultaneously were both selected from among distractors in a recognition list. This was taken as evidence that more than one input channel can be processed simultaneously. Also Allport *et al.* [1972] have confounded the single channel theory with the finding that subjects can shadow speech and sight read music simultaneously without any serious performance decrement on either task. Kahneman takes the view that selective attention is a matter of the differential allocation of processing capacity to different channels carrying simultaneous inputs. This idea is consistent with the evoked potential results, as the secondary EP amplitude differences between attended and unattended stimuli might reasonably be expected to be a function of the number of neural elements activated. This, in turn, should logically be correlated with the neural processing capacity allocated to a particular signal.

Furthermore, it is the case that while secondary EP components vary considerably in their amplitude their latencies are very stable [see Wilkinson, 1967]. Broadbent's single channel processor theory predicted that information arriving on an unattended channel coincident with information already being processed, as in Cherry's [1953] 'split span' experiment cited previously, would have to queue in a sensory buffer store before being processed itself. If EPs reflect cortical information processing then the EPs produced by such stimuli whose processing is delayed, should themselves be delayed with respect to the evoking stimuli.

A series of experiments which are classically supposed to have supported the single channel processor theory are those on the so called 'psychological refractory period' [for the originals see: Telford, 1931; Craik, 1947, 1948; recent reviews: Bertelson, 1966; Smith, 1967]. When a second signal occurs within approximately 400 ms of a first then the reaction time to that second signal is delayed relative to the RT to the first stimulus, or to single stimuli separated by several seconds in a control series. This delay appears if the first signal commands a response, and even if it does not [Davis, 1958, 1965]. The delay in response to the second signal was attributed to the second signal having to queue before entering a single channel central processor. However, Boddy [1972] found that when EPs were recorded in such an experiment, that although highly attenuated in amplitude, there was no delay in the appearance of the secondary components of the EP to the second signal, that might have reflected delayed entry to a central processor. Furthermore, analysis of RT data from twelve subjects in Boddy's experiment showed that subjects responding relatively slowly to the first signal responded relatively quickly to the second, and vice versa [this negative correlation is also reported by Triggs, 1968 and quoted by Kahneman, 1973, p. 175 in support of his theory]. These findings suggested that the two closely succeeding signals were processed in parallel and that there was inter-individual variation in the amount of processing capacity allocated to the first and second signals. The small number of subjects used in earlier experiments may have appeared to operate in a single channel mode because of the constraints imposed by the experimenter rather than because of an intrinsic lack of facility for processing information in parallel.*

Further experiments on evoked potentials and selective attention

We should now consolidate our supposition that the secondary components of EPs vary in amplitude according to the processing capacity allocated to the eliciting stimulus in the focussing of attention.

While Picton *et al.* [1971] showed that secondary EP component amplitudes reflected selectivity between ears within the auditory modality, Donchin and Cohen [1967] have nicely demonstrated that EP amplitudes may reflect selectivity within the visual modality. They used a tachistoscope to present sequences with two different types of stimuli. These were triangular test flashes, presented at intervals varying randomly between two and three seconds, and alternations between a circle and a square (or concentric circle and a star in some trials), drawn in black indian ink on white cards, presented at intervals varying randomly between 3 and 4 s.

*Hink *et al.* (1977) have reported a dichotic listening experiment in which subjects had to respond to signal stimuli to either just one ear (focused attention) or both ears (divided attention). The finding that secondary EPs to stimuli on either ear in the divided attention condition were intermediate in amplitude between EPs to attended ear stimuli and EPs to ignored ear stimuli in the focused attention condition was consistent with the capacity sharing model of attention.

The sequence of intervals for flashes and figure alternations were independent so that the subject should have been unable to build up any expectations about the time of occurrence of the stimuli. In one condition subjects had to depress a switch (recording RT), each time a flash occurred and ignore figure alternations, and in the other condition depress a switch each time a figure alternation occurred and ignore flashes. It was found that the amplitude of the secondary components of the EPs to both flashes and figure alternations were enhanced when they were attended to compared with when they were ignored. This result supports the notion that there is selective perceptual enhancement of attended stimuli (or selective attenuation of unattended stimuli) within the visual modality and is a gross analogue of the experiment by Neisser [1969] in which subjects reading a prose passage showed very limited awareness of the content of an irrelevant message contained in alternate lines of print.

Attention and signal to noise ratio

Donchin and Cohen's results are important as they supply a conclusive answer to critical points made by Horn [1960, 1965] and Moray [1969]. Horn and Moray have questioned whether the amplitude of cortical evoked potentials is necessarily a measure of effective signal strength in neural information processing systems. Horn observes that the level of background activity, or 'noise' in the nervous system varies, and that therefore adjustments in the nervous system which reduce both the noise level and EP amplitudes could also be consistent with improving effective signal strength by improving the signal to noise ratio. Moray [1969] argued that the distribution of an EP over time might be as important an index of effective signal strength as the amplitude of particular components. However, this idea does not appear very plausible as such a temporal diffusion would seem likely to impair the resolution of stimuli patterned in time, such as those in the auditory modality.

Horn [1960] presented to cats regularly repeated flashes, illuminating the whole of the front of their cage. He found that the cortical EPs to the flashes were attenuated when a distracting visual stimulus, such as a mouse, was interposed between the cat and the flashes. In interpreting this result Horn made the psychologically naive presupposition that attention can only be switched between sensory modalities and that therefore visual attention to the interposed mouse was necessarily accompanied by enhanced attention to the flashes. It followed from this premise that evoked potentials were being reduced rather than enhanced when their eliciting stimulus was the focus of attention. Horn would have predicted that EPs to the mouse, were they recordable, would also have been attenuated when the cat was attending to it. Donchin and Cohen's finding that flash evoked potentials were attenuated during attention to figure alternations clearly invalidates Horn's interpretation of his results and indicates that Horn's cats were most probably focusing their attention within the visual modality, so that the EPs to the flashes were attenuated because the cat's attention was focused on the mouse [see also experiment by Palestini *et al.*, 1959, discussed earlier]. In the previously cited experiment by Picton *et al.* [1971] selectively attending to a message to one ear, while ignoring that to the other, was reflected in the EP secondary component amplitudes. This also demonstrates the capacity to select within a modality which Horn did not visualize.

Experiments incorporating behavioural measures of attention

Most experiments on the evoked potential correlates of selective attention assume that the subject has focussed his attention as directed by the experimenter's instruction, without making any effort to verify this assumption by independent behavioural measures of the efficiency of attention. This omission represents a serious neglect of the capricious nature of live experimental subjects.

Haider *et al.* [1964] used detection efficiency in a vigilance task as a behavioural measure of attention to serve as a basis for selecting EEG samples when deriving averaged EPs. Subjects had to depress a key when they detected occasional dim flashes (signal stimuli) randomly interspersed among regularly occurring bright flashes. Loss of attention, was indicated by the decline in detection efficiency over the 80–100 min of the experimental trials. It was reflected in diminished amplitude of EPs to non-signal stimuli. The detection of signal stimuli during attention and the failure to detect them during loss of attention was reflected in greater EP amplitudes to detected than undetected signal stimuli. However, although the percentage of detected signal stimuli decreased as the experiment progressed, the amplitudes of EPs to stimuli which were detected remained constant. This suggested that declining efficiency of signal detection was the result of a decline in the percentage time in which attention was focussed on the task, rather than a decline in general arousal. Broadbent [1958] came to a similar conclusion from purely psychological studies.

The same group [Spong *et al.*, 1965] performed a further experiment in which, during either an auditory or a visual vigilance task, such as that described above, stimuli in the alternative modality were presented alternately with signals in the task modality. Focus of attention within either the visual or the auditory modality was reflected in enhanced secondary components of the evoked potentials.

Another behavioural measure considered to be an index of attention is reaction time. Wilkinson and Morlock [1967], Morrell and Morrell [1966], and Donchin and Lindsley [1966] have all found negative correlations between RT and the amplitude of secondary components of EPs [see review by Wilkinson, 1967]. These have normally been found, either over very long trials, or where variations in RT have been induced by varying the subject's incentive to respond fast. In both of these circumstances variations in performance might be expected to be a function of fluctuations in attention.

Boddy [1972] found that RTs were faster when a warning signal preceded an RT signal by 0.5–1.25 s. In contrast to previous results the RT signal EP was of a much smaller amplitude in the warning signal condition, producing fast RTs, than in the no warning signal condition producing slower RTs. However, within the warning signal condition it was found that faster RTs to more effective warning signals were reflected in relatively greater amplitudes of the RT signal EP. It was considered that the attenuation of RT signal EPs following warning signals was a function of long lasting physiological refractoriness of late EP components [observed by Davis *et al.*, 1966]. Further, it was conjectured that these late EPs reflected the operation of a 'conscious evaluation subroutine', which was superfluous to the organization of ungraded responses to undifferentiated stimuli, and which occurred at lower levels in the system. This echoes Kahneman's idea [1973; see earlier] that stimuli may produce behavioural consequences without perceptual interpretation.

Selective attention
and non-specific activation

The experiments described so far have been interpreted as showing that the nervous system differentiates between attended and unattended stimuli in terms of the amplitude of the secondary components of the cortical EPs which these stimuli produce. Naatanen [1967, 1970] and Karlin [1970] have reinterpreted the data cited. They suggest that the enhancement of EPs observed during attention to relevant stimuli is due to 'non-specific activation' or 'generalized arousal', occurring just prior to the evoking stimulus, rather than differential enhancement of signals from the attended source.

Naatanen [1967, 1970] recorded EPs to clicks which occurred either within an interval between a warning flash and an imperative flash (requiring an RT response), or outside this interval. He claimed that the enhanced amplitude of click EPs within the warning interval, compared with outside it, occurred because the warning flash produced general arousal. This supposedly rendered the NS more sensitive to all incoming stimuli. An alternative interpretation of these results [see Karlin, 1970] is that clicks within the warning interval are focally attended to as an aid to preparation for the signal flash. It has been shown that a click can be a more effective warning for a visual RT signal than a signal in the same modality [Karlin and Mordkoff, 1967; Boddy, 1973]. It is not logically inconceivable that focal attention can be set for a range of stimuli which is circumscribed, but which encompasses more than one sensory modality. This may be particularly likely when, as in the instance above, stimuli in different modalities are both sudden, brief, and undifferentiated step changes in energy level.

In another experiment Naatanen [1967] used a signal detection paradigm. He claimed that when the time and modality of stimuli were unpredictable EP amplitudes did not differentiate between relevant and irrelevant stimuli. When stimuli were predictable, however, relevant stimuli produced the larger EP amplitudes. EP amplitudes appear to reflect non-specific activation which can be produced differentially to anticipate predicted relevant stimuli. When the relevance of stimuli is unpredictable the mean level of activation is the same for relevant and irrelevant stimuli.

Both Naatanen's hypothesis and his results are contested by Donchin and Cohen's observations [1967; outlined earlier in the chapter] that secondary EPs to attended visual stimuli were enhanced relative to EPs to non-attended visual stimuli, in sequences in which relevant and irrelevant stimuli were unpredictable. However, Karlin [1970] maintained that the statistical properties of Donchin and Cohen's sequences did not entirely eliminate the possibility of differential preparation based on probabilistic predictions of quite a high level of accuracy.

Hillyard *et al.* [1973] took great care to exclude the possibility that subjects could predict the occurrence of relevant tone pips (relevance being defined by ear of delivery), either precisely or probabilistically, in a signal detection experiment. It was nevertheless found that relevant tone pips generated EPs of greater amplitude than irrelevant, contradicting Naatanen's findings and supporting a selective attention interpretation.

Eason *et al.* [1969] claim to have modulated EP amplitude with manipulation of both general arousal level and selective attention. However, it is an unproven assumption that their threat of an electric shock for slow RT responses to relevant stimuli (relevance being defined by eye of delivery) raised general arousal rather than improved focal attention to the task relevant channel.

Naatanen's hypothesis that differences in secondary EP amplitude reflect only differences in non-specific arousal must be considered unproven. It still seems possible that they reflect selective responsiveness of the brain to attended stimuli. More experiments are needed, using a wider range of stimuli designated as relevant and irrelevant, both intermodality and intramodality, before we can have confidence in the validity of one or even both hypotheses as explanations of variation in EP amplitude.

Expectancy

Further evidence adduced by Naatanen [1967, 1970] and Karlin [1970] in support of their non-specific activation hypothesis is the fact that when a subject is awaiting an expected imperative stimulus (one requiring a response), usually after a warning signal, the EEG displays a marked negative deviation which is terminated by an abrupt positive deflection, part of the EP, when the imperative stimulus occurs (see Figure 11.5). This phenomenon, named the contingent negative variation (CNV for short) or expectancy wave [first described by Walter *et al.*, 1964. For reviews see Walter, 1964, 1967; Tecce, 1972] is taken by Naatanen and Karlin to be a sign of increasing non-specific arousal during preparation for an expected stimulus. It has been shown by several experimenters that its amplitude is correlated with reaction time and motivation [see Tecce, 1972]. However, these results do not exclude the possibility that the CNV is rather a sign of the focussing of attention as it has not been shown that the subject is equally prepared for all stimuli when the CNV reaches its peak as should be predicted by the non-specific arousal hypothesis. Tecce [1972] cites experiments in which distracting stimuli occurring during the development of the CNV result in a reduction of its amplitude, while other indices of general arousal (e.g. heart rate) increase. From this and other evidence

Figure 11.5
A contingent negative variation (CNV) or expectancy wave. The negative going wave commences after the evoked potential produced by a warning click and terminates when the imperative flashes occur.

Tecce concludes that the CNV is a sign of directed attention rather than general arousal. Thus the recourse to the CNV phenomenon for support by Naatanen and Karlin tends to boomerang when given more careful consideration.

The segregation of channels in selective attention

The basis for segregating messages on attended and unattended channels did not appear to be too much of a problem at the cocktail party or in its experimental analogue, dichotic listening. Messages came from sources with different spatial locations and as man is well equipped to detect differences in spatial location (because of the spatial segregation of his two ears) this was supposed to be the basis for segregating attended and unattended messages [Broadbent, 1958]. Broadbent [1958] suggested that physical characteristics such as voice qualities may also be a basis for segregation. Treisman [1964a] found that bilingual subjects could not separate a prose message in English from a simultaneous prose message in French if both messages were spoken in the same voice and presented to both ears (i.e. they both appeared to emanate from the same sound source). Also Sperling [1960] found that subjects could not focus solely on digits in a mixed array of letters and digits in the same typeface. These experiments emphasized that simultaneous messages can only be separated if one has physical characteristics clearly differentiating it from the other.

In experiments on selective attention the experimenter usually determines the characteristics which are supposed to distinguish the attended from the unattended message and assumes that these are the ones used by his subjects. However, Treisman [1960] found that when subjects were required to shadow one ear and the prose messages to the attended and unattended ears were suddenly switched without warning then subjects would follow the prose message they had been shadowing to the 'unattended' ear for a few words before returning to the ear which they were supposed to be shadowing. This finding suggested that the 'context' of the shadowed prose message may have gained ascendancy over the spatial location which was supposed by the experimenter to be the basis for selection of the attended message.

It appears likely that this problem of the subject's criterion for selection differing from that assumed by the experimenter, may have confounded the interpretation of an experiment on evoked potentials during selective

From McCallum, W. C. (1969) In T. Mulholland and C. R. Evans, *Attention in neurophysiology*. Reproduced by permission of the author and Butterworths, publishers

50%

20μV

1 second

Click

Flashes terminated by button

binaural listening by Smith *et al.* [1970b]. In this experiment three classes of stimuli were presented to each ear, digits at the rate of one per second, letters at the rate of one every 15 seconds and clicks at the rate of one every five seconds. EPs to clicks were recorded in conditions where subjects had to report either the randomly interspersed letters or the more frequently occurring randomly interspersed clicks, in each case one ear was designated the attended ear. It was found that the secondary components of EPs to clicks were of greater amplitude when clicks were being reported than when letters were being reported, very much in line with the other findings discussed in this chapter. On the other hand it was found that in neither condition were EPs to clicks at the attended ear of greater amplitude than those at the unattended ear. This is quite contrary to the finding of Picton *et al.* [1971] and may be a reflection of the criteria of selection. In Picton *et al.*'s experiment (see earlier discussion) clicks were the only stimuli used so that ear of delivery was the only criterion which could be used for selection. In the experiment by Smith's group clicks did not only have to be selected from the designated ear but also from among letters and digits. Subjects may well have been limiting themselves to using class of stimuli as a basis for selection, as reflected in the fact that click EPs were greater in amplitude when reporting clicks than when reporting letters, and neglecting to use ear of delivery. Clearly a great deal of care is required in the interpretation of experiments on selective attention when there is the possibility of subjects using a different criterion for selection than that intended and assumed by the experimenter.

Summary

We can only present a provisional and qualified scheme for the mechanisms in the nervous system which mediate selective attention. Considerable doubt has been thrown on the early evidence that input to an unattended sensory modality is blocked at the first sensory relay. It appears that all sensory input reaches the cortex via the classical specific projection pathways and there is subject to analysis at a reasonably high level. The primary components of the evoked potential, supposed to be generated at the sensory projection area are relatively constant in amplitude across all conditions from deep sleep to full attention. However, conscious perception of stimuli appears to be dependent on the activation of a diffuse cortical projection system emanating from the non-specific thalamic nuclei and apparently responsible for producing the later secondary components of cortical evoked potentials. The abolished or diminished awareness of unattended stimuli appears to be reflected in the reduced amplitude of these EP components, which, in turn, seems likely to be a sign that reduced information processing capacity is being devoted to them. The process of focussing attention during which this 'conscious awareness' system is set-up for the preferential processing of a particular class of stimuli appears to be reflected in the development of a long lasting negative wave in the EEG when a relevant stimulus is expected.

Central processing of information and conscious perception

Introduction

The previous two chapters have focused on the reception and selection of information, yet both, of necessity, have dealt with some aspects of the processing of information. A number of different operations are subsumed under processing information. A pattern of stimulation from the external world is translated into an approximately isomorphic spatio-temporal pattern of activity in the nervous system. This pattern may be translated into related forms. It may be analysed into a series of component features. Some information may be selected for perceptual analysis, while other information is discarded. Input patterns may be compared with stored representations of previous inputs. This sequence of operations commences at the sense receptors themselves.

The phenomena of lateral inhibition and adaptation (see Chapter 10) effect transformations of the input which enhance spatial and temporal boundaries and thus constitute processing information. The coding strategies employed by the sensory systems involve the activation of separate channels according to the presence or absence of specific features in the input. Again we have seen in Chapter 10 that some of the evidence for a process of feature extraction comes from studies of single neurone activity at different levels in the sensory system. For instance in the visual system different channels are selectively responsive to different wavelengths of light (colours) or to different features of the visual environment. The latter is illustrated by the 'bug detectors', cells responding to dark spots moving across the retina, and other feature specific cells, which Maturana *et al.* [1960] found in the frog. Also we have seen that in the auditory system different channels code the amount of activity in different sound frequency bands in the audible range.

The selection of information, implied by selective attention to relevant signal sources, appears to involve the attenuation of the nervous system's response to irrelevant stimulus patterns and amplification of its response to attended channels. We have already examined the arguments about whether the selection process is peripheral or central. The fact that the defining characteristics of a 'channel' can be highly complex, such as when attending to one individual's voice and rejecting another's, implies that some kind of preliminary analysing and matching process takes place as a basis for selection. In the last chapter it was conjectured that a preliminary analysis of input was accomplished at the sensory projection areas, before selected information was forwarded to a more general mechanism which gave rise to conscious perception. Its activation was reflected in the secondary components of averaged cortical evoked potentials.

In this chapter it is proposed to concentrate on evidence concerning the nature of information processing at a cortical level, which can be inferred from recordings of, either individual neurones, or large aggregates of neurones. In many cases recordings at a cortical level do not reflect information processing just at the cortex itself, but the end result of progressive sorting of the data as it ascends a sensory system. This is seen in the visual system, on which we are concentrating, where single neurones respond to increasingly complex features of a visual pattern as the system is ascended from the retina, via the lateral geniculate nucleus of the thalamus, to the visual cortex. The nature of the information processing which occurs specifically at the cortex can be inferred from that which is known about information processing at lower levels in the system, or in some cases, from the deficits which appear when the cortical projection zone of a sensory system is damaged.

At one time it seemed that, at least as far as simple sensation and perception were concerned, there was a simple principle of place coding which accounted for such information processing as occurred. For instance, in the visual system the retinal mosaic was supposedly mapped in a straightforward manner on the visual cortex, so that a simple spatial pattern of excitation in this area was the basis for our perception of spatially organized visual patterns. It was as if a cine projector at the back of the eye was projecting an image of our visual world to the back of our head. Recent studies by Hubel and Wiesel [1962], which have quickly come to be considered classical have indicated that this conception is far from the truth. Their evidence, from individual cell responses in the visual cortex of cats, indicates that any pattern of visual stimulation is analysed into the different features which it contains. Whereas retinotopic mapping occurs at a gross level, at a local level, particularly in the central area of the retina, features such as slits of light at different orientations, or moving in particular directions, are all analysed out by separate channels. Cortical neurones can be found that will respond to the presence of one particular feature in the visual field and one only.

Hubel and Wiesel found that the visual cortex of the cat performed an analysis of the features of the visual field which in the phylogenetically less developed frog was found to be accomplished at the retinal level [Maturana et al., 1960]. Furthermore, the cat's visual cortex analysed out more complex features of the visual stimulus, reflecting its higher phylogenetic status.

The finding [by Maturana et al., 1960] that at the retinal level in the frog there are channels, such as those specifically sensitive to 'bugs' (i.e. small dark spots in movement), or to 'dimming' of the level of illumination (likely to be associated with the arrival of a large predator), suggests that there is a simple and elegant solution to the problem of perception in this creature. The structural and functional organization of the frog's retina is such that environmental features which are important to it produce activation of specific channels. These presumably have access to motor mechanisms producing suitably adaptive reactions such as catching or escape responses. The frog's responses are based on a simple switching system whose properties are innately determined. Thus discussion of mechanisms of perceptual learning, recognition or conscious perception at a higher level are precluded.

In the cat, and presumably in other higher animals, processing of visual input occurs at all levels in the visual system and perhaps principally at the cortex. The input is analysed into features, which can be quite numerous in a complex visual pattern, each feature extracted being registered by the discharge of a channel selectively sensitive to its defining characteristics. It is unlikely that a specific response or response pattern is very often triggered by a single feature in the way that a bug catching response is triggered by the frog's bug detectors. Also cats are able to learn new response patterns to novel combinations of features. It must therefore be supposed that, in the cat, a perceptual response arises from the activation of a combination of feature analysing cells in the visual cortex. However, the paradox exists that, although a complex pattern produces excitation of the multiple, segregated channels of a feature analysis system, it is nevertheless responded to as if it were a unitary entity. Thus, in higher animals the pursuit of an understanding of the neurophysiological basis of perception poses some formidable problems.

As we will see there is also some evidence from which we might reasonably infer feature analysers in the human brain. Again this presents a paradox as we are aware of our world as an integrated pattern, not as a series of abstracted features. The facts of human perception elaborated by the gestalt psychologists [e.g. see Koffka, 1935] and latterly by the cognitive psychologists [e.g. see Neisser, 1967; Kahneman, 1973] emphasize our capacity to organize or synthesize fragmented sense data into coherent, meaningful patterns, rather than to decompose patterns into their component features. The data on human perception seems to suggest that the activation of feature specific cells in the sensory projection areas of the cerebral cortex are not the terminal events, consequent on sensory input, which give rise to our conscious percepts. The unitary nature of our percepts suggests that the feature analysers transmit excitation to a higher level mechanism, which produces some kind of synthesis from this input and also stored data accessed by it. This mechanism gives rise to conscious perception and, when the pattern of activation conforms to a stored specification, generates an output leading to motor activity. It has already been suggested, in the last chapter, that the postulated mechanism is a diffusely projecting system, radiating to widespread cortical locations, from the non-specific zones of the thalamus. Its operation is reflected in the secondary components of cortical evoked potentials.

Cortical analysis of features

In attempting to convey a provisional over-all picture of information processing this chapter has run ahead of itself. The different facets of information processing must be explored in more detail and first we must return to the epoch making work on feature analysis in the visual cortex. This research, to which the major contributors are Hubel and Wiesel [1962], is a logical extension of the work on the receptive fields of retinal ganglion cells [Kuffler, 1953] and optic nerve fibres [Hartline, 1938]. The receptive field of a neurone is the retinal zone within which a stimulus will produce a discharge of that neurone. The optimum stimulus may be illumination of an area of the retina which exactly coincides with the receptive field. Alternatively a receptive field may have no specific retinal location. A neurone in the visual cortex may be activated by a particular stimulus form irrespective of retinal location, and possibly specifically when it is moving in a particular direction.

First Hubel and Wiesel [1961] plotted the receptive fields of single neurones at the level of the lateral geniculate nucleus. They found these to be circular and concentric. Either illumination of the centre produced an 'on' response, and of the surround an 'off' response, or vice versa. They were similar to the ganglion cell receptive fields plotted by Kuffler [1953], but without the intermediate 'on–off' zones.

Later work by Hubel and Wiesel [1962] involved microelectrode recording of spike discharges from single cells, or small groups of cells, in the visual cortex of cats (see Figure 12.1). They found evidence that a great deal of data processing occurred in the visual system beyond the lateral geniculate body, most of it appearing to take place within the cortex itself. The simple concentric receptive fields of neurones of the lateral geniculate body are transformed, at the visual cortex, into receptive fields with a great variety of configurations and response characteristics, often of a complex nature.

Hubel and Wiesel [1962] classified cortical receptive fields as either simple or complex, supposing that the latter represented a higher order of integration. Typically simple receptive fields (see Figure 12.2) were elongated and thus responded maximally to 'slits' of light projected on to restricted regions of the retina. These receptive fields could take configurations which included an excitatory central region with inhibitory flanks, or vice versa. The flanks might be symmetrical or asymmetrical in width, and could be wide or narrow relative to the centre. Alternatively a receptive field could consist simply of an excitatory region and an inhibitory region side-by-side. This type of receptive field responded most effectively to a sharp light–dark boundary falling exactly on the line separating the excitatory and inhibitory regions and therefore represents an 'edge' detector. Perhaps the most significant discovery was that different cortical units responded to slits of light, or edges, at very specific orientations on the retina. A shift of orientation of a slit of more than 5–10° from the optimum was sufficient to greatly reduce or abolish the response of an orientation specific cortical neurone. There appeared to be receptive fields representing all of the possible orientations of slits of light on the retina, so that there is strong evidence that any patterned visual stimulus is analysed into

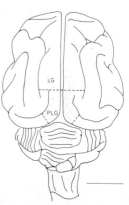

Figure 12.1
Dorsal aspect of a cat's brain showing the entry point of 43 microelectrode penetrations.

From Hubel, D. H., and Wiesel, T. N. (1962) Receptive fields, binocular interaction and functional cytoarchitecture in the cat's visual cortex. *J. Physiol.*, **160**, 106–154. Reproduced by permission of the authors and *Journal of Physiology*

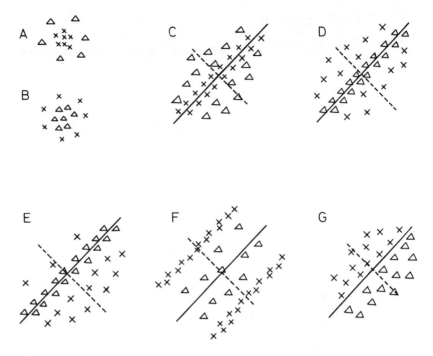

Figure 12.2
Simple receptive fields found in the lateral geniculate body and visual cortex of the
cat. A is an 'on' centre geniculate receptive field and B is an 'off' centre field. C-G
are various arrangements of simple cortical receptive fields, x areas giving 'on'
responses and △ areas giving 'off' responses. The receptive field axes are indicated by
continuous lines. All are oblique in this figure, but each receptive field arrangement
can occur in all orientations.

From Hubel, D. H., and Wiesel, T. N. (1962) Receptive fields, binocular interaction
and functional cytoarchitecture in the cat's visual cortex. *J. Physiol.*, **160**, 106-154.
Reproduced by permission of the authors and *Journal of Physiology*

component contours at different orientations. Examples of different
simple receptive fields are shown in Figure 12.2.

Hubel and Wiesel [1962] have speculated that the elongated receptive
fields of cortical cells arise because of a convergence of fibres from a series
of lateral geniculate cells, with small circular receptive fields, arranged in a
line. A variety of patterns of convergence account for the comprehensive
range of orientations of cortical cell receptive fields.

In addition to these cells with simple receptive fields there are cells
with complex receptive fields (see Figure 12.3) which are suggestive of the
neurophysiological basis of some of the more sophisticated properties of
mammalian perceptual systems, including the abstraction of form irrespective of retinal location, and the perception of movement.

In contrast to cells with simple receptive fields, which have a fixed
location on the retina, cells with complex receptive fields may respond to
slits of light, irrespective of location, within a defined area of the retina.
These cells are nevertheless highly specific in their response to both the
width and the orientation of the slits of light, and will not fire to either
a wider rectangle projected on the area over which the narrow slit elicits a

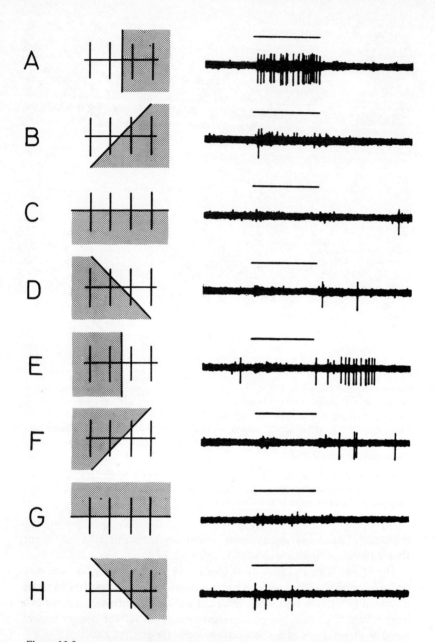

Figure 12.3
The responses of a cell with a large (8 × 16°) complex receptive field found by
Hubel and Wiesel (1962). On the left of the diagram are a series of dark edges (A–H),
at various orientations, projected on to a cat's retina. On the right are records of
discharges in a single ipsilateral cortical cell at the onset and offset of the stimulus
(stimulus 'on' is represented by a horizontal line). It can be seen that a vertical edge
with the dark area to the right (at A) produces a strong response for the duration of
the stimulus. A vertical edge with the dark area to the left (at E) produces an 'off'
response. Edges at other orientations produce either only slight responses or no
response at all.

From Hubel, D. H., and Wiesel, T. N. (1962) Receptive fields, binocular interaction
and functional cytoarchitecture in the cat's visual cortex. *J. Physiol.*, **160**, 106–154.
Reproduced by permission of the authors and *Journal of Physiology*

response, or to a change in orientation. Some complex field cells respond maximally to a moving slit of light, the orientation being critical once again, and the direction of movement being at right angles to the slit. In addition to slits of light some units respond to edges (separating light and dark areas) at specific orientations, again irrespective of retinal location. The cell might show a response to the stimulus being turned 'on' when the light area was to the right of the dark, and to stimulus 'off' when it was to the left. Yet another type of complex field unit responded to dark rectangles against a bright background, once again with orientation being critical, but location not. Movement in a particular direction could also evoke discharges in these cells. Their response is similar to that of the inhibitory region of a simple field cell but it is not confined to a single location.

Hubel and Wiesel [1962] have argued that because complex field cells are excited by such features as slits at specific orientations, irrespective of retinal location, and moving stimuli, each complex cell must receive inputs from many simple cells, each having fields with the same orientation but at different retinal locations. Thus the complex field cells represent a higher order of integration.

More recently Hubel and Wiesel [1965] have recorded from neurones in visual areas II and III [Brodman's areas 18 and 19]. There appear to be three cortical areas on which the retina is topographically mapped in an orderly fashion, area II being lateral to the primary visual area I, and area III, in turn, being lateral to area II. While in area II most cells could be classified as complex, those in area III have even more complex receptive fields and appeared to represent even higher levels of integration, arising from the convergence of connections from complex field cells. Hubel and Wiesel [1965] characterized these cells as lower and higher order hypercomplex. Different cells with hypercomplex fields (see Figure 12.4) responded with a high degree of specificity to a wide range of stimulus forms including two light–dark edges intersecting at right angles, 'stepped' edges of critical dimensions, edges 'stopped' at both ends to give an optimum length and dark tongues of critical width. In each case the response was orientation specific. These experiments indicate that there are feature analysers for a wide range of visual forms, including corners, rectangles etc.

We can see that the plotting of receptive fields of cortical cells yields information which powerfully suggests that visual stimuli are analysed into their component features. Each feature present is registered by the firing of groups of cortical cells. These cells are fired by a specific feature because of the logic of the pattern of connections in the pathways which project to them. Feature analysis cells are able to extract features irrespective of their retinal location and in some cases specifically if they are in movement across the retina. From this information we can begin to conceptualize how the functional organization of the information processing networks gives rise to our elaborated perceptual abilities, enabling us to recognize forms irrespective of retinal location or of retinal image size.

However, conspicuously absent from the catalogue of receptive field configurations is a curved edge. Hubel and Wiesel [1965] conjecture that curved edges may be analysed by several channels, each responding to a segment of the curve over which the tangent does not change its orientation

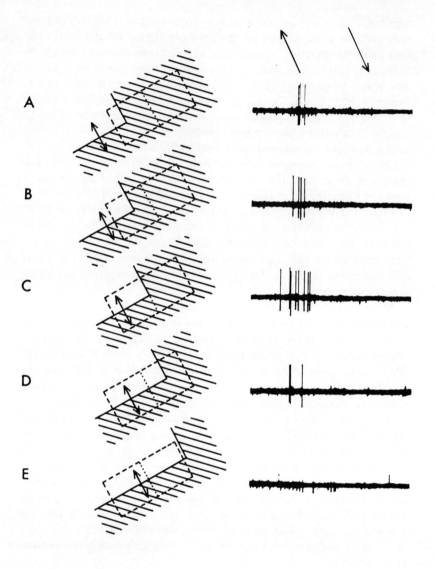

Figure 12.4
A hypercomplex receptive field in visual area II of the cat.

(i) Records from a cell with a hypercomplex receptive field in visual area II of a cat. On the left (A–C) a stimulus consisting of two dark edges intersecting at 90° is moved up and down across varying amounts of the activating zone of the receptive field (left hand side of dotted rectangle). In D and E the stimulus is moved across all of the activating portion and varying amounts of the right hand antagonistic portion of the field. The cell discharge patterns appear on the right.

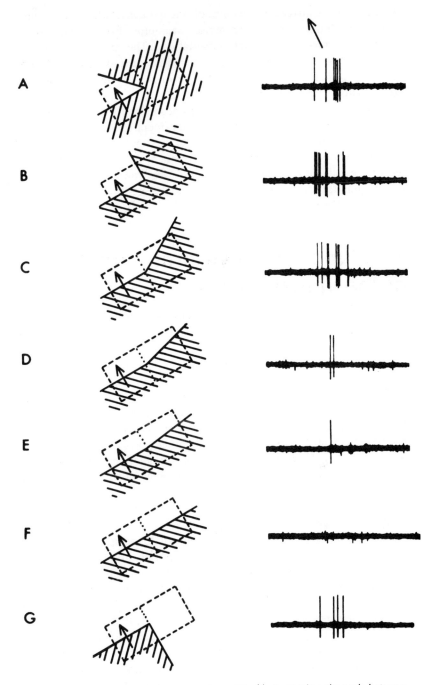

(ii) Further records from the hypercomplex cell in (i) above when the angle between
the two intersecting edges is varied. It can be seen that inhibition is maximum at
F when the antagonistic right hand side of the field is stimulated by an edge having
the same orientation as the optimum for the left activating half.

From Hubel, D. H., and Wiesel, T. N. (1965) Receptive fields and functional
architecture in two non-striate visual areas (18 and 19) of the cat. *J. Neurophysiol.*,
28, 229–289. Reproduced by permission of the authors and American Physiological
Society

sufficiently to be outside of the range of orientations to which the channel is sensitive. Thus a curve would give rise to an output from each of a series of edge detectors with different orientations. The radius of curvature might be measured by hypercomplex cells responding to stopped edges of varying lengths. The tighter the radius of curvature, the shorter the activating segments of fields whose cells respond.

Hubel and Wiesel's [1962] work also documented the convergence of transmission lines from the two eyes. They found units whose maximal response, or even sole response, was elicited by stimulation of corresponding areas of the two retinas with a slit in the same orientation. In fact very few of the cells they recorded from were driven from one eye alone. This finding appears to identify the neurophysiological basis of binocular fusion of the images on the two retinas.

The functional cytoarchitecture of the visual cortex

The functional cytoarchitecture of the visual cortex is the distribution and arrangement of cells according to function, whose description was an important aspect of Hubel and Wiesel's work. They made single and multiple recordings from successively deeper cells as their microelectrodes made vertical penetrations of the cortex (Figure 12.5). They found that all of the cells encountered tended to respond to a slit of light (or any other linear stimuli) with the same axis orientation. If an oblique penetration of the cortex is made the axis orientation of the cell fields changes as the microelectrode progresses (Figure 12.5). In other words it appears that cells whose receptive fields have common axis orientations are grouped in columns perpendicular to the cortical surface, adjacent columns containing cells with different orientations.

different receptive fields is to investigate the mapping of the retina on the visual cortex. Earlier work by Minkowski [1913] and Talbot and Marshall [1941] had indicated that there was systematic topographical mapping of the retina on the visual cortex. Data which Hubel and Wiesel [1962] collected from cortical areas representing peripheral zones of the retina were consistent with these findings. Most of the data which Hubel and Wiesel collected were from cells with receptive fields in the area of central vision and its surround, an area about 8° in diameter. Reflecting its importance in vision, this area has a very large cortical representation which is reflected in the very slow change in receptive field location as an electrode is advanced obliquely through the cortex. At the microscopic level, within this area, there is a breakdown of the topographical representation which is normally observed. For a start receptive fields vary in dimensions from 0.125-8° in width and 3-20° in length, so that they may be larger than the area centralis itself. Vertical penetrations through the cortex yield unit records from a succession of cells with fields whose axes of orientation are identical but whose size varies in an apparently unsystematic manner. Hubel and Wiesel [1962] argue from their data that at the microscopic level topographical representation of the retina at the visual cortex breaks

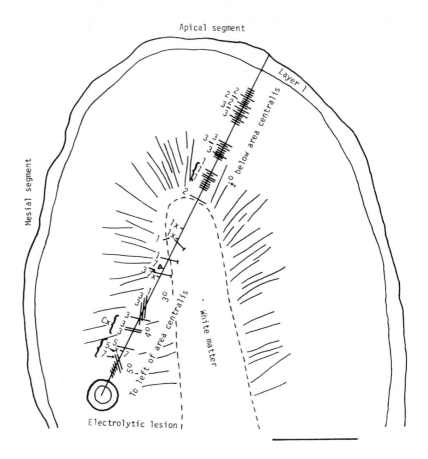

Figure 12.5
Reconstruction of a microelectrode penetration through the lateral gyrus of the cat's visual cortex. Locations where recordings were made from the axons of cortical cells are indicated by cross bars on the long line of the microelectrode penetration. The angles of the cross bars reflect the orientation of the receptive field axes. It can be seen that when the microelectrode progressed at right angles to the cortical surface all the receptive fields had the same orientation. When the course of the electrode was oblique, as at the bottom right, the field orientations change.

From Hubel, D. H., and Wiesel, T. N. (1962). Receptive fields, binocular interaction and functional cytoarchitecture in the cat's visual cortex. *J. Physiol.*, **160**, 106–154. Reproduced by permission of the authors and *Journal of Physiology*

down. Within localized cortical areas each retinal zone has multiple representation in many columns of cells covering the range of features which the system is capable of extracting.

Another feature investigated by Hubel and Wiesel [1962] was the distribution of cells with simple and complex fields through the six different layers of the cortex. The relative concentration of simple field cells in the deeper cortical layers and of complex cells in the more superficial layers was consistent with Hubel and Wiesel's hypothesis that complex cells represented a higher order of integration arising from the convergence of inputs from several simple cortical cells.

The generally systematic structure of the feature analysis system in the cat suggests that its properties are a function of an innately determined pattern of interconnections within the nervous system. In Chapter 7 of this book evidence is reviewed suggesting that although there is some truth in this assertion, appropriate patterns of experience are required, during critical periods of development, to prime this system to respond in its characteristic manner. Also the type of experience during development can modulate the responsiveness of the system so that some features of the environment are responded to more powerfully than others.

Evidence for the existence of feature analysers in man

Hubel and Wiesel's [1959, 1961, 1962, 1965, 1968] work tantalizingly suggests that the understanding of the neurophysiological basis of perception is just around the corner. It has stimulated a lot of research attempting to fill out their findings, and theorizing about the basis of perception to which their findings give crucial support.

Hubel and Wiesel [1968] have themselves extended their work from cats to monkeys and found similar receptive field phenomena. In addition a number of investigators have sought evidence that a comparable feature analysing system exists in man. We might expect that his more highly developed perceptual abilities would be reflected in the existence of analyser cells responding to a larger and more complex array of features.

As it is not possible to record directly from single cells in the human visual cortex, some ingenious psychophysical and electrophysiological techniques have been devised to tease out differential responses, which might indicate the existence of feature detectors. A stimulus pattern which has been widely used in these investigations is the 'grating', rather than slits of light, dark bars or edges used by Hubel and Wiesel [1962]. A 'grating' is a series of alternate light and dark striations of equal width. A number of parameters can be varied; the orientation about the axis of vision, the spatial frequency (number of striations per unit visual angle expressed as cycles per degree), the contrast between the light and dark striations and the luminance profiles (e.g. square wave, sine wave, expressing the sharpness of the boundary between the light and dark regions). These grating patterns are usually generated on an oscilloscope screen.

In a series of experiments by Campbell and Maffei [1970] 'steady state' evoked potentials (EPs) were recorded from the occipital region in human subjects, while they were repetitively stimulated by 180° phase shifts of a grating pattern, occurring at a rate of $8 \, s^{-1}$. The 180° phase shift means that the subject sees fluctuations in which the dark and bright zones replace each other. Campbell and Maffei found that when the contrast of the grating pattern was varied, there was a linear relationship between the amplitude of the evoked potentials (which were manifest as a sinusoidal wave) and the logarithm of the contrast. For a series of different spatial frequencies they found that extrapolation back to the point of zero evoked potential amplitude coincided with the psychophysical contrast threshold (the contrast threshold at which the grating becomes just visible). The electrophysiological data indicated that the linear relationship between the logarithm of stimulus intensity and size of neural response reflected the Weber-Fechner law, postulating a linear relationship between subjective sensation and logarithm of stimulus intensity.

To test the predictions implied by the existence of feature analysers Campbell and Maffei investigated the interaction between gratings set at 90° to each other. A vertical grating presented to the right eye or a horizontal grating presented to the left, singly produced mean regression lines, expressing the relationship between evoked potential amplitude and logarithm grating contrast, which had identical slopes. When the two orthogonal gratings were presented simultaneously, one to each eye, the slope of the regression line relating evoked potential amplitude and the logarithm of grating contrast, increased by a factor of two. This increase in the slope of the regression line is consistent with the summing of potentials from two independent populations of neurones, one sensitive to a vertical orientation, the other to a horizontal orientation. If the same populations of neurones responded to both the vertical and horizontal gratings there should be no summing effect from the two patterns, as the fluctuations of the grating, which serve as the stimulus, involve no change in the spatially average luminance.

Another phenomenon which Campbell and Maffei [1970] exploited, to substantiate the existence of orientation specific channels, was the adaptation to a high contrast grating (with 12 cycles degree^{-1}) which takes place when it is presented for 10–15 s. Psychophysical measurements had shown that this adaptation resulted in an increase in the contrast threshold for detection of a subsequently presented test grating. In addition the adaptation effect progressively diminished as the angle of tilt between the adaptation and test grating was increased (half the effect at 6.75°) [Blakemore and Campbell, 1969; Blakemore and Nachmias, 1971]. Campbell and Maffei [1970] demonstrated that, coincident with the psychophysical measures of adaptation, there was attenuation of cortical potentials evoked by fluctuation of a low contrast test grating. This attenuation was only observed when the adaptation grating had the same orientation as the test grating. It was reduced as the orientation of the adaptation grating moved away from that of the test grating until, at a displacemnt of 15–20°, there was no effect (Figure 12.6). This finding suggests that the adaptation effect is specific to neuronal populations sensitive to a particular orientation and does not affect units tuned to other orientations.

Campbell and Maffei [1970] also investigated selectivity for spatial frequencies. They found that simultaneous stimulation with two or three spatial frequencies produced summing effects in the evoked potential amplitude which could be attributed to the activation of independent channels sensitive to different spatial frequencies.

There have been other investigations in which human psychophysical data has corroborated the neurophysiological evidence for cortical detector cells sensitive to lines, edges, and gratings of different spatial dimensions and orientation [e.g. see Kulikowski et al., 1973; Kulikowski and King-Smith, 1973]. Kulikowski [1969] observed that the threshold contrast for

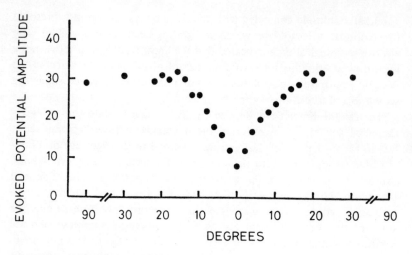

Figure 12.6
Graph showing the relationship between the evoked potential amplitude produced by a fluctuating vertical grating and the angle to this test grating of previously presented high contrast adaptation gratings (see text).

From Campbell, F. W., and Maffei, L. (1970). Electrophysiological evidence for the existence of orientation and size detectors in the human visual system. *J. Physiol.,* 207, 635–652.. Reproduced by permission of the authors and *Journal of Physiology*

detection of a fine dark line, was reduced by superimposing it on a dark striation of a subthreshold grating (which was thus invisible) with a spatial frequency of 5 cycles degree^{-1}. It was increased by a similar amount when placed on a light striation. However, when the spatial frequency of the subthreshold background grating was increased to 20 cycles degree^{-1}, no change was observed in the contrast threshold. This finding was interpreted to mean that in the first instance there was summation of excitation in detectors sensitive to both a fine line and a 5 cycles degree^{-1} grating, whereas in the second instance no summation occurred, because the fine line and the 20 cycles degree^{-1} grating excited different sets of detectors.

Kulikowski and King-Smith [1973] found that when the contrast threshold of a test dark line was plotted against different contrast values of a subthreshold background grating there was a linear relationship. This further substantiated the hypothesis that there was linear summation of excitation when a line–grating detector was activated by two sources simultaneously.

Kulikowski and King-Smith [1973] also made a number of measures of sensitivity to lines superimposed, at different locations, on subthreshold grating patterns, or a pattern comprising two spatially separated, subthreshold parallel lines. They obtained sensitivity functions consistent with the mathematically derived predictions of a multichannel model of the visual system (i.e. a model in which functionally separate channels are selectively activated by different features in the visual environment). They were also able to show that the psychophysically inferred spatial properties of fine line detectors corresponded with the spatial properties of receptive fields having excitatory centres and inhibitory borders, which were mapped by Hubel and Wiesel [1962]. A full account of this work by Kulikowski and his coworkers is beyond the scope of this book.

In other investigations by Kulikowski *et al.* [1973] subthreshold background gratings were tilted at different angles to a superimposed test grating of the same spatial frequency. It was found that the summing effect of the background grating with the test grating diminished rapidly with angle of tilt, being reduced to a half at 3°. Thus there is also psychophysical documentation of orientation specificity of grating detectors.

Models for recognition

While lines and edges at different angles are clearly fundamental components of our visual world, grating patterns do not appear, at first sight, to be typical features of this world. Therefore it might be doubted whether the concentration on the detection of grating patterns is research likely to contribute greatly to our understanding of the processing of information from a highly complex visual world. Only more sophisticated analysis suggests the possible importance of grating detectors. A grating is a pattern which regularly repeats itself in the spatial dimension. Gibson [1950] has pointed out that virtually all of the surfaces in our visual world are textured. Surface irregularities give rise to repetitive patterns of light and shade whose form and spatial frequency vary. Wood, concrete, textiles, and brick walls are all examples of materials with distinctive visually textured surfaces. Grating detectors, and possibly analogous detectors of other spatially repeating patterns, may be important in the identification of objects by surface texture, and the assessment of orientation in three-dimensions (as the contrast in a visual texture varies with the angle of illumination of the object). In particular Gibson asserted that gradients in visual texture (progressive changes from low to high spatial frequency) which arise when a textured surface extends from a near to a far point, are vitally important for structuring our percepts in three-dimensions. The pattern of activation of a series of detectors for different spatial frequencies might be basic to our constructing a three-dimensional internal representation of the environment.

Pollen and associates [1971] have presented a more sophisticated model of visual perception in which detectors sensitive to different spatial frequencies and different orientations play a central part. They suggest that the array of spatial frequency detectors (effectively a bank of filters, each tuned to a different frequency) perform a Fourier analysis of any spatial pattern. This implies that every detector activated gives an output proportional to the amount of its frequency (a combined function of contrast and spatial extent) present in the pattern being analysed. The attractiveness of this hypothesis arises from the fact that the output profile from the spatial frequency analysers activated is invariant for a particular pattern, irrespective of retinal image size. Thus this mode of analysis of incoming data suggests a basis for our capacity to recognize objects independent of their retinal image size.

The models for recognition which we have discussed fail to explain a remarkable and pre-eminent property of our perceptual system. This is our capacity to recognize objects or patterns, not only across a range of transformations in size, but also across transformations in shape of the retinal image they form, as they are viewed from different distances and angles. In this capacity the human brain is vastly superior to the computer, which has proved extremely difficult to programme to recognize patterns in a range of transformations. Models for pattern recognition include the theories of Pitts and McCulloch [1947] and Wiener [1961, pp. 135–143] suggesting that the α-rhythm of the EEG (see Chapter 3) is the manifestation of a scanning mechanism which takes any input pattern through a wide range of transformations. In Pitts and McCulloch's model the transformations were used for computation of an 'average value' which was the basis for recognition. In Wiener's model each transformation was matched against a standard pattern as a basis for identification. Although there was some circumstantial evidence for these models no critical test has been formulated, some inconsistent data has been produced and there has been a loss of experimental interest in them. Furthermore, Hubel and Wiesel's findings cannot easily be reconciled with a scanning theory and its implications for functional activity in the cerebral cortex.

The notion that the visual system is composed of multiple channels coding the different features of the visual scene has been extended beyond spatial patterns. We have already seen in Chapter 11 that different channels are activated by different wavelengths of light (colours) incident on the eye. It is also the case that in the auditory system sounds are segregated into different wavelength components by multiple channels. Regan [1972, 1975] has recorded evoked potentials to stimuli comprising either, instantaneous fluctuations of a uniform colour field between two different hues, or instantaneous interchange of the elements in a red and green checkerboard pattern, no luminance change occurring in either case. He claimed that the appearance of these evoked potentials is evidence that there is segregation of information about wavelength up to the most peripheral pattern sensitive neurones in the brain. Butler [1972] has recorded auditory evoked potentials to tones of different frequencies presented singly and simultaneously. When two tones are sufficiently separated in frequency the summation apparent in the amplitude of the $N1$–$P2$ component of the EP to simultaneously presented tones was taken as evidence that separate populations of neurones were being activated by the different tones. It was also claimed that this supported the idea that there was tonotopic organization in the auditory cortex.

There appears to be a general principle operating in the sensory systems that a temporally or spatially patterned stimulus is represented in multiple channels which decompose the pattern into its component features, defined in various spatial and temporal dimensions.

The substrate
of conscious perception

The data showing that the pattern of connections in the sensory systems culminates in columns of simple and complex feature detecting units in the cortical projection areas, is fascinating in its own right, particularly to those people who derive intellectual satisfaction from exploring the analogies between biological systems and man-made computer systems. These discoveries represent a surprising and dramatic deviation from the earlier expectations that the representation of external reality in the cerebral cortex would be by spatio-temporal patterns of activity much more closely isomorphic with that reality. Initial investigations of the representation of retinal locations in the cortex indicated retinotopic mapping consistent with this expectation [Minkowski, 1913; Talbot and Marsall, 1941].

While the idea of a feature analysis system is conceptually elegant, the notion of isomorphic representation in a cortical zone on which the retina is systematically mapped, seems more consistent with the phenomenology of perception. Our primary or focal awareness of items in our visual world is of holistically apprehended patterns. We are only subsidiarily aware of their component features [see interesting philosophical discussion of focal and subsidiary awareness in Polyani, 1965]. The approaches to the psychology of perception which have been most successful and enduring have been those of the gestalt psychologists [e.g. see Koffka, 1935] and latterly the cognitive psychologists [see particularly Neisser, 1966] who have emphasized the essential unity of our percepts. On a superficial analysis it is difficult to reconcile this unity at the phenomenological level with the dissection of patterns into their constituent elements which takes place at the physiological level. A tentative resolution of this contradiction becomes apparent when we consider further data at both the neurophysiological and psychological levels.

Evoked potentials and conscious perception

In the preceding discussion there has been an implicit assumption that the spatio-temporal pattern of activity engendered by external stimuli in the sensory projection areas of the cortex is the sole and immediate substrate of our conscious percepts. The assumption has already been challenged by the data on scalp recorded evoked potentials discussed extensively in the previous chapter.

Evoked potentials appear to reflect the pattern and intensity of neural discharge in underlying cortical tissue (see Figure 11.3). Furthermore, early components of the EP can be distinguished from later components according to several criteria, including different distribution on the scalp and different responses to behavioural and pharmacological manipulations. The two segments of the EP appear to be generated by the activity of two different neural systems projecting to the cortex.

The early components of the EP, which occur within 60–100 ms, appear to be largely a specific response of the cortical projection area as a barrage of impulses arrive along the classical sensory projection pathways. Regan [1972, Chapter 2] has implied that these responses represent the sum of the responses of the feature analysing cells in the cortex. The work of Campbell and Maffei [1970], discussed earlier, on potentials evoked by simple features also supports this suggestion. A number of observations must be considered alongside the hypothesis that the early components of sensory EPs reflect the firing of feature analysers. A general observation is that they hardly vary in amplitude over a wide range of behavioural and pharmacological manipulations [see Goff, 1969]. The original work of Hubel and Wiesel [1962] on the receptive fields of cells in the cat's cortex was performed on creatures under thiopental sodium anaesthesia and therefore unconscious. Goff [1969] observed that the early (primary) components of EPs are unattenuated, and may even be augmented, in amplitude, in an animal deeply unconscious under an anaesthetic. Furthermore, the primary components of sensory EPs are unattenuated by the focussing of attention away from the evoking stimulus. It appears that the amplitude of the primary EP does not discriminate between states in which a stimulus is consciously perceived and states in which it is not. It is therefore very difficult to identify the primary EP, and thus the discharge of the cortical feature analysers, with the conscious perception of stimulus patterns.

It could be argued that identification of the neural processes underlying conscious perception should be possible from a knowledge of their time course, relative to that of perception itself. If we take the example of simple visual reaction time, which is typically around 180–200 ms, then it is just conceivable that the EP components occurring within 100 ms of the stimulus could reflect the neural processes underlying perception of the stimulus. The additional 80–100 ms could be the time taken to access the command centre in the motor cortex, transmit, via the motor neurone pools, to the muscles and activate the neuromuscular junction. However, when a naive subject starts a reaction time experiment their latencies are typically 400–500 ms. Also when choice reaction time to uncertain alternative stimuli, or recognition time to more complex verbal stimuli, is measured then response latencies are well into the 300–500 ms range.* In these situations the perceptual response to the stimulus takes much longer than the 100 ms of the primary EP as 'motor time' could not conceivably be as long as 200–400 ms. Also evidence has been cited in Chapter 11 that rapid, gross or highly practised responses to simple undifferentiated stimuli may be organized and executed before there is conscious perception of these stimuli [Boddy, 1972; Kahneman, 1973, p. 70]. Kahneman [1968] has presented suggestive evidence that the latency of conscious perception is about the same as the latency of the motor response in a simple reaction time task, which seems to preclude conscious perception prior to the response. Subjectively, if we make an emergency braking response while driving a car, it seems to occur before we are fully consciously aware of the brake lights of the car in front. Thus, if we accept that some special categories of motor response occur prior to and/or independent of the conscious perception of the eliciting stimulus, then the duration of underlying cortical events when conscious perception is an unequivocal intermediary between stimulus and response must be much longer than the primary EP components.

Following the primary components of the evoked potential, the secondary components last for a further 300–400 ms, a time course which suggests that they could reflect at least part of the processes underlying perception. Evidence reviewed in the last chapter more clearly identifies the secondary components of the EP with conscious perception. They are abolished or attenuated in amplitude when conscious perception is absent or dim in anaesthesia or inattention. They are augmented in amplitude when the evoking stimulus is the focus of attention and clearly perceived.

Unlike the primary components of the EP, which are recorded with their greatest amplitude from the projection area for the modality of the evoking stimulus, the secondary components are recorded with their greatest amplitude at the vertex. They appear to reflect widespread activation

*Kutas et al. (1977) have reported a choice reaction time experiment, using verbal stimuli, in which it was found that, when accuracy was emphasized, the latency of a late positive component (called P300) in the signal stimulus EPs correlated 0.66 with RT. Also correct responses almost invariably occurred later than the P300 peak (range 300–800 ms). This result is taken to support the hypothesis that P300 reflects processing underlying stimulus evaluation.

of cortical neurones, stemming from a diffusely projecting system of fibres which emanates from the non-specific thalamic nuclei. Therefore, we cannot identify the secondary EP components with activity of cortical feature analysing cells. It would appear that conscious perception only occurs as a result of activity in a widely diffused system, which includes cortical and subcortical structures, after the feature analysers have responded. Goff [1969] has shown that despite the apparent independence of the cortical projection systems mediating the primary and secondary components of the evoked potential, the secondary components cannot occur unless the sensory projection system for the evoking stimulus is intact. He was unable to evoke secondary EPs in human patients with lesions in the classical projection pathways, beyond the thalamus, despite the fact that the non-specific pathways were intact. This suggested that the secondary EPs arise as a result of interaction between the classical and diffusely projecting cortical systems. This could occur via transverse connections at the cortex. However, if this is the case then lesions of the sensory pathways should still not abolish secondary EP components. The more likely possibility is that non-specific areas of the thalamus are excited by corticofugal fibres from the sensory projection areas. In other words it appears that the occurrence of secondary EPs underlying conscious perception is partially dependent on output from the multiple feature analysing channels of the sensory projection areas. It is a more diffused pattern of neural events subsequent to those representing feature analysis which give rise to our conscious percepts. Perhaps these neural events represent a reintegration or synthesis, constructed from the multiple outputs of the feature analysers, which is responsible for the phenomenological coherence and unity of our percepts.

Perception as a synthetic process

The notion that perception is a synthetic process is far from being new within classical perceptual psychology. One of the most fundamental observations codified and proclaimed by perceptual psychologists is that our percepts represent a constructed subjective reality which need not correspond to objective external reality, and which may go beyond it. The separation of figure from ground, for instance, appears to be a constructive process whose enhancement of certain bounded areas of the visual field extends beyond that achieved by the objectively delineated boundaries. This is simply illustrated by Rubin's figure (see Figure 12.7) which is seen alternately as two silhouetted faces looking at each other, or as a white vase against a black background. The fact that two quite different percepts, both very compelling, but competing for dominance, arise from the same external data argues forcibly that constructive processes must underlie those percepts.

Neisser [1967, Chapter 4] has hypothesized that perception is a process of 'analysis by synthesis' in which data from the external world is combined with stored data to construct an internal representation of the external stimulus pattern. Stored data contributing to the synthetic process may be

Figure 12.7
Rubin's vase-faces
figure.

From Gregory, R. L.
(1970), *The intelligent
eye.* © R. L. Gregory.
Reproduced by
permission of
Weidenfeld and
Nicolson Ltd.,
publishers

accessed as a result of expectancy of what will be perceived. If we are expecting to meet a friend in a crowded street, strangers with some similar features may be momentarily perceived as the expected person. Segments of the input data may access probability stores to produce a complete percept, a probable source of many errors in perception. If an approximation of a familiar word (e.g. toble) is flashed briefly on to a screen an observer may perceive the word which it closely resembles (table), on the basis that the four correct letters in sequence, t, b, l, e, establish a high probability that the second letter will be a.

The maintenance of constancy in the perceived size of objects, irrespective of distance, is a phenomenon in which the percept is a function of stored probabilities associated with particular cues. This is emphasized in the instance of Ames room (see Figure 12.8), in which size constancy breaks down. A person in the left-hand corner appears to be a dwarf compared with the person in the right-hand corner, rather than appearing farther away as she really is. Although the room is highly distorted so that the left-hand person is much farther away than the one on the right, it nevertheless projects a retinal image with all of the cues normally received from a rectangular room. These cues access probability stores which determine that the left-hand figure is perceived as being small rather than distant. In the synthesis of the percept there is a failure to 'scale up' the figure to compensate for distance.

The evoked potential correlates
of perceptual synthesis

The purpose of evoking the concept of analysis by synthesis is to speculate on its neurophysiological basis. It is tentatively suggested that the secondary components of the evoked potential reflect the neural activity mediating synthetic procedures. The analysing channels in the sensory projection areas decompose a stimulus pattern into its component elements. This system might also provide a basis for different features, or combinations of features accessing relevant store locations, possibly by the operation of a template matching principle. The output from the feature analysing channels is transmitted to a more diffusely localized synthesis mechanism which, in the case of vision, reconstructs the visual world from the received and retrieved stored data.

It might appear unlikely that data could be found to substantiate the ambitious hypothesis which has been presented. However, we have already discussed the observations of Donchin and Cohen [1967] (see Chapter 11) that an attended circle square alternation, with no luminance change, will evoke a secondary potential of greater amplitude than an unattended bright flash. The association of intense transient neural activity with changing percepts which are independent of over-all changes in stimulus energy level is quite consistent with an endogenously generated synthetic or constructive process underlying those percepts. John *et al.* [1967] claimed that the wave shapes of visual evoked potentials reliably discriminated

Figure 12.8
Ames room: an example of a false percept constructed on the basis of misleading cues.

From Gregory, R. L. (1966), *Eye and brain.* © R. L. Gregory. Reproduced by permission of Weidenfeld and Nicolson Ltd., publishers

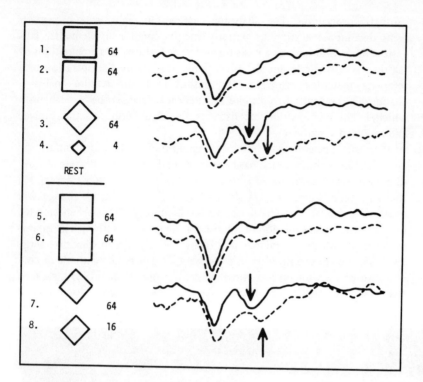

Figure 12.9
Different evoked poten-
tial waveshapes produc-
ed by different geo-
metrical forms. All re-
sponses were recorded
from the same sub-
ject in two sessions
separated by 30 min
rest. The responses
were averaged from
100 stimulus repetit-
ions using a 500 ms
epoch. The evoking
forms are shown on the
left with the stimulus
area, in square inches,
following.

From John, E. R.,
Herrington, R. N., and
Sutton, S. (1967)
Effects of visual form
on the evoked response.
Science, 115, 1439-
1442. Reproduced by
permission of the
author and the Ameri-
can Association for
the Advancement of
Science

between different geometrical forms, independent of stimulus area (see Figure 12.9). Also evoked potentials elicited by presentation of the name assumed similar wave shapes to those evoked by the geometrical forms themselves. Clynes and Kohn [1967] published evidence that there was differentiation between colours and between different field structures (dots, lines, circles, radial lines) in the spatio-temporal pattern of evoked potentials. Thus spatio-temporal patterns of activity which could reflect synthetic processes, differentiate between percepts but are invariant across size transformations of the eliciting stimulus. We might note in passing that these invariant wave shapes are consistent with Pollen and coworker's [1971] model for reconstruction of the visual world, in which a Fourier analysis of the spatial frequency components in a pattern, by multiple filters, provides an output profile which is invariant across size transformations of the pattern.

Evoked potentials
to misperceived stimuli

We have seen that there are instances in which stimuli are misperceived. The subjective percept differs from the physical percept which initiates its formation. In this case the hypothesis that secondary EPs reflect perceptual synthesis generates a complex prediction. The wave shape of the secondary EP elicited by a misperceived stimulus should be identical to that obtained if the reported stimulus were really there, and different from that obtained if the stimulus is correctly perceived. It would appear selfevident that the neural discharge pattern underlying conscious perception will not be correlated with the external stimulus pattern when the percept and the external stimulus pattern are not identical. When they are not identical (i.e. when there is a misperception) then the assumption is made that perceptual synthesis is based on the extraction of inappropriate information from store. This is on the basis that some elements in the external stimulus pattern generate the probabilistic inference that a particular complete pattern is present, when this inference is incorrect in the particular instance. At first sight it might seem excessively optimistic to hope that EP wave shapes will discriminate between true and false perceptions of stimulus patterns, especially when spatially patterned visual stimuli are represented by temporally patterned EPs. However, Ruchkin and John [1966] appear to have found a paradigm which leads to confirmation of the prediction.

Ruchkin and John [1966] used temporally patterned stimuli, flashing lights running at different frequencies. In a frequency range distributed around 10 Hz flashing light stimuli evoke synchronous discharges in subcortical (thalamic) and cortical structures, a response having an obvious isomorphism with the eliciting stimulus. The experimenters trained cats, with chronically implanted electrodes, to depress a lever within 15 s after presentation of a 10 Hz flashing light, in order to avoid receiving an electric shock. After training, a generalization stimulus at 7 Hz was interspersed with presentations of the training stimulus. It was found that on the occasions when generalization occurred, (i.e. when the 7 Hz stimulus elicited the lever pressing avoidance response), then the EP waves recorded from both the thalamus and cortex had a frequency of 10 Hz, the frequency of the training stimulus. It could be argued that the 10 Hz EP waves reflected the synthetic processes underlying the misperception of a 10 Hz stimulus, when a 7 Hz stimulus was, in fact, presented. When no generalization occurred the EP waves had a frequency of 7 Hz, presumably reflecting correct perception. John and Morgades [1969] have made analogous observations, to the ones cited above, at the single cell level, using chronically implanted microelectrodes. This strengthens the conviction that the EPs can be taken as profiles of the underlying patterns of activity in cortical neurones.

On the basis of a whole series of observations, including those above, John and his coworkers [see John et al., 1973] have suggested that the secondary evoked potential reflects 'neural readout from memory' that is, 'related to cognitive decision about the meaning of an afferent input'. Thus the 10 Hz EP waves evoked by the 7 Hz stimulus during generalization, are seen as activation of the memory trace established by the former stimulus. It is suggested here that a more satisfying account of their findings may be that the evoked potential reflects a process of perceptual synthesis triggered by the external stimulus. The notion of perceptual synthesis elaborated by Neisser [1967, Chapter 4] admits to a contribution to a reconstructive process from stored information. It is at least as plausible to suppose that the 10 Hz EP reflects synthetic processes underlying the misperception of the 7 Hz flashing light as a 10 Hz one. The 7 Hz stimulus has features which are sufficiently similar to a 10 Hz one, which has significance as warning of an impending shock, to extract data from store to synthesize a 10 Hz percept.

In later work John et al. [1973] have explored the characteristics of evoked potentials to misidentified stimuli in a great deal more detail, with many controls to check that the effects which they observed were neither a function of just the specific stimuli which they used, nor of differences in non-specific arousal. In these experiments animals were typically trained on two different tasks, to repetitive visual or auditory stimuli at two different frequencies. They might be trained to lever press to avoid an electric shock, following a 10 Hz stimulus, and to approach a tray for food, following a 4 Hz stimulus. On this occasion John looked at the evoked potentials produced by individual light flashes (or clicks) and found that there were distinctive and reliably reproducible differences between the waveforms of the EPs to the two training stimuli. The differences in waveforms were most marked in the late components of the EP which we have tried to identify with conscious perceptual processes.

Following training, occasional stimuli at an intermediate frequency of 7 Hz were interspersed with the training stimuli. On some occasions this stimulus elicited a shock avoidance response and on others a food approach response. In the former case the 7 Hz stimulus evoked a potential with the waveform of the 10 Hz stimulus, normally associated with the shock avoidance. In the latter case the intermediate stimulus evoked a potential with the waveform of the 4 Hz stimulus, normally associated with the food approach response. John and his colleagues claim that these findings have invariably been confirmed across a range of stimulus frequencies, modalities of stimulation, motivations (reward or punishment) and combinations of motivations. They maintain that in each case it must be a memory readout potential which is being observed. Once again the data is equally well accommodated by the thesis that the EPs reflect the process of perceptual synthesis, and that the identity of wave shapes, when the same response is given to two different stimuli, is a function of the same percept being constructed in each case, and in one case constituting a misperception. The finding which is most difficult to reconcile with the perceptual synthesis hypothesis is that stimuli in two different modalities and eliciting the same behavioural response, will elicit EPs with similar wave shapes. The strong association between the stimuli may be the basis for a 'combined' percept with a large contribution of stored information about the external stimulus which does not occur at any particular stimulus presentation.

It is, of course, the case that within the conceptual framework of cognitive psychology the distinction between perception and memory is not a sharp one. Perception is not viewed as being simply passive registration, and memory is not viewed as being simple reproduction. Both are viewed as being constructive or reconstructive processes by which a coherent whole is built from an assembly of elements, which may be incomplete.

The mechanisms of perceptual synthesis might be conceived of as operating with more or less dependence on input from, and validation by, external stimuli. In normal, familiar surroundings percepts are synthesized which accurately reflect the external stimulus pattern eliciting them. When there are contradictory cues, and/or strong expectations then a misperception may be synthesized (e.g. the 'dwarf' in the Ames room). In the delusional world of the paranoid schizophrenic percepts of menacing and persecutory figures might be synthesized under the biasing influence of disordered neural systems mediating emotional responses. In dreams (see Chapter 8) or the hallucinations of schizophrenics (see Chapters 8 and 15) the synthesizing mechanisms may be triggered internally and operate purely on stored information. Penfield [1952; see also Penfield and Roberts, 1959] was able to elicit 'recollective hallucinations' by electrical stimulation of the temporal lobe of conscious patients during brain surgery (see Chapter 13). These apparent 'replays' of past events in the patients' lives have been attributed by Neisser [1967, pp. 165-170] to activation of the mechanisms of perceptual synthesis.

Evoked potentials and subjective experiences

Dreams, psychotic hallucinations, and electrically evoked memories are all examples of subjective, conscious perceptual experiences occurring in the absence of the usual external stimulus patterns. If they are the product of the mechanisms of perceptual synthesis, normally reflected in secondary EPs, then we would expect that these subjective experiences would themselves be accompanied by endogenously generated EPs. Black and Walter [1965] have precisely confirmed this prediction by recording evoked potentials to hallucinated clicks, heard as a result of hypnotic suggestion. At Walter's laboratory Weinberg et al. [1970] have recorded evoked potentials to 'imaginary' stimuli, expected stimuli which fail to occur, that are identical to those elicited by expected stimuli which do occur. In both experiments late EP components appeared as electrophysiological correlates of perceptual experiences, which were generated without any immediate external cause.

Sutton et al. [1967] found a late positive component (occurring at a latency of around 300 ms and known as $P300$) in the evoked potential which occurred when there was resolution of uncertainty, irrespective of whether there was an external stimulus event. Sequences of click stimuli were presented to human subjects, in which they could not guess whether a single click or a double click was going to occur. It was found that at the precise time when the second of the two clicks was normally expected (there was no temporal uncertainty), a secondary EP occurred, irrespective of whether there was an actual click, or not. The non-occurrence of a click at a known instant in time still supplied information by resolving uncertainty about whether a click was going to occur or not, and this was reflected in cortical electrical events. It is, of course, difficult to ascertain whether the EP reflected merely the mental event of knowing that no stimulus had occurred, or whether it reflected the synthesis of an internal representation of an expected click (subjectively manifest as an image of a click) triggered by a combination of expectation and temporal cues.

Evoked potential amplitude and level of processing

If we are going to maintain that the late components of EPs reflect the operation of the mechanisms of perceptual synthesis then we must also account for their variation in amplitude as the information value of the stimuli is varied. In the last chapter the notion that the secondary components of the evoked potential are the electrophysiological correlates of perceptual awareness was introduced in the context of selective attention. It was observed that the amplitude of these components was augmented when a stimulus was attended to, compared with when it was not. These findings have been validated by correlated behavioural measures such as reaction time and signal detection.

It was suggested in the last chapter that variations in secondary EP amplitudes, which are observed in experiments on selective attention, are a function of differential allocation of processing capacity to different information channels. Direction of attention to a particular signal source involved allocation of a large processing capacity (in both neural and psychological terms) with the consequence that the receiver was focally aware of signals from that source and able to distinguish and evaluate the fine detail in complex stimulus patterns such as speech. Signal sources remote from the focus of attention were allocated limited processing capacity with the result that the receiver was only subsidiarily aware of them and only able to distinguish crude detail (e.g. gross characteristics of voice on the non-attended channel during dichotic listening).

The identification of the processes alluded to above with perceptual synthesis therefore implies that perceptual synthesis is a process which can be more or less elaborated according to the fineness of detail required from any particular stimulus pattern. Processing for fine detail might be expected to include finer resolution of intensity and contrast differences and of complex spatial and temporal patterns.

The evidence from the manipulations which alter EP amplitude suggests that the level of processing is multidetermined by inter-related variables including motivation, expectancy, selective attention, and informational value of the stimulus. In experiments on selective attention the subject is motivated to attend to one signal source and exclude others by manipulation of the reinforcement contingencies (usually secondary rewards, such as experimenter's approval, or secondary punishments, such as experimenter's disapproval).

Sutton et al. [1967] and Tueting et al. [1971] observed that the amplitude of secondary EPs increased as stimulus uncertainty increased. This might be attributed to more elaborated processing of less expected stimuli. Less expected stimuli may be elaborated in more detail by the mechanisms of synthesis in order to be confident that they have been correctly identified. Kahneman [1973, pp. 80–85] advances the idea that stimulus properties, such as novelty or incongruity (both coextensive with high uncertainty), initiate secondary processing of stimuli to yield a more detailed and complete perceptual interpretation than that produced by the initial analysis. He backs this up with evidence from purely psychological experiments. High probability stimuli, which by definition conform to the subject's expectancies, are probably given a cursory treatment by the mechanisms of perceptual synthesis, because they match internal representations of themselves at the feature analysis stage. This is particularly likely to be the case in the experiments mentioned as the stimuli were simple clicks. We have already seen evidence, in this and the previous chapter, that responses to simple or familiar stimuli may be organized with minimal or zero recourse to the mechanisms of conscious awareness, possibly on the basis of matching processes at one of the feature analysis stages. In the experiments mentioned above it was observed that when subjects were informed which stimuli would be presented next, then $P300$ was of small amplitude, irrespective of the over-all probability of stimuli in the sequence. Again this is consistent with the idea that an expected stimulus (for which there must be an internal representation) is minimally processed by the mechanisms of conscious perception.

Signal detection theory and level of processing

Ideas similar to those of signal detection theory may be applicable to a discussion of the level of processing of a stimulus. In signal detection theory [see Green and Swets, 1966] one determinant of whether a signal around the threshold of detection will be reported is a decision criterion which may shift up and down a scale of confidence or certainty as to whether a signal has occurred. If there is a strong negative pay-off (punishment) for a false report when no signal occurs, the subject will set his decision criterion high, requiring a high level of subjective confidence before making a positive report. If there is a strong positive pay-off (reward) for correct reports and little or no negative pay-off for 'false alarms' the decision criterion may be set low, with the corollary that a certain proportion of false positives is tolerated. In the instance where perceptual responses are being made to briefly presented, patterned stimuli the decision criterion for identification may vary according to the pay-off for correct and incorrect responses. In other words a stimulus may only be processed sufficiently to identify it with the level of confidence set by the decision criterion. Furthermore, when stimuli vary in probability the decision criterion for signals of high probability may effectively be set lower than for signals of low probability. Identification based on cursory processing of a stimulus may be acceptable when there is a high probability that the signal will occur anyway and some positive pay-off will follow. When a signal has a low probability of occurrence elaborated processing may be undertaken to increase the subject's level of confidence in his identification, because of its low likelihood of occurrence, and the negative pay-off consequent on misidentification. Kahneman [1973, pp. 87–96] has applied the concepts of signal detection theory to perception, asserting that 'perceptual readiness' modulates the setting of the criterion level. A stimulus for which there is perceptual readiness can alternatively be characterized as one which has a high subjective probability of occurrence.

By definition a subject does not know whether a high or low probability stimulus is going to occur until it has occurred. This poses the problem of how and when the decision is made to process the stimulus information to a high or low level. It is suggested that the failure of an input to match temporarily salient internal representations of highly probable stimuli at the initial feature analysis stage of processing, prompts fuller analysis at the secondary, perceptual synthesis stage. This model bears some resemblance to the one proposed by Sokolov [1963] for the elicitation of the orienting response to novel stimuli. In his model a mismatch of the input with an internal representation at the projection cortex prompts the discharge of corticofugal signals to the brainstem reticular formation, which, in turn, produces general arousal. The model outlined here must presuppose that corticofugal fibres activate the non-specific thalamic structures which appear to initiate the secondary EPs. These EPs reflect the elaborated processing of stimulus patterns; a function which is quite consistent with the purpose of the orienting response. As we have seen, the initiation of elaborated secondary processing by unexpected stimuli, has already been proposed by Kahneman [1973, p. 81]. If we evoke the idea of fuller processing to increase confidence in the identification of a stimulus, the conceptual framework based on signal detection theory accommodates the data on variation of secondary EP amplitude with stimulus probability very well.

Also, Hillyard *et al.* [1971] have recorded EPs during a task of detecting auditory signals from noise. They observed that only detected signals produced a *P*300 (late positive wave at approximately 300 ms); misses, false alarms, and correct rejections producing no detectable EP. An increase in size of *P*300 was associated with an increase in the percentage of correct responses, indicating that the fuller the processing of the stimulus, the greater the probability of correct identification. Furthermore, the greater the *P*300 amplitude, the greater the subject's confidence level that he had made a correct detection. This indicated that a more stringent decision criterion was associated with more processing of the signal. In this instance of a simple undifferentiated signal, more processing must involve merely an amplification of its subjective intensity. The notion of elaborated processing could only be fully tested in a task demanding discrimination between complex, spatially or temporally patterned stimuli.

Boddy [unpublished] has made some tentative explorations using stimuli of this type. He recorded EPs to visually presented words in two different semantic categories. One category was a target category demanding identification of the word, the other a non-target category requiring no response. It was found that the secondary EP amplitudes for correctly identified words were greater than to correctly rejected words in the non-target category. The words in the two categories were approximately equated for mean frequency of occurrence in the language. As there was strong negative feedback associated with false alarms, but no feedback associated with misses the EP findings are consistent with a more stringent decision criterion, and thus more elaborated processing, for target words compared with non-target words. Also the words used in the experiment were grouped into three different frequency bands, according to their frequency of occurrence in the language. It was found that the least frequent (that is the least probable, or the words conveying the highest information) words produced the secondary EPs of highest amplitude. This reflected the necessity of processing low probability stimuli to a high level, in order to have a high level of confidence that they have been correctly identified.

We might expect that increasing the complexity of patterned stimuli presented would itself increase the amount of processing and that this would be reflected in the EP amplitude or waveform. Indirect evidence that increasing complexity in the structure of the visual field demands greater processing capacity has been presented by Lehman and Fender [1968]. They found that as they increased the amount of structure in constantly viewed visual targets presented to one eye, the EP evoked by a simple flash, presented to the other eye, decreased in amplitude. This finding can be interpreted in terms of the structured stimulus competing for processing capacity and appropriating more as structure increases. To fully substantiate the hypothesis that the secondary components of evoked potentials reflect the process of perceptual synthesis, the variation of EP parameters with different objective and subjective structuring of stimulus patterns requires more thorough investigation.

This chapter has examined the neurophysiological basis of information processing which underlies our perception and consciousness. It has presented a tentative model in which a process of feature extraction precedes a process of synthesis or reconstruction, based on the output of the feature analysers and stored information. Even if it approaches the truth, which it may not, we should expect that it will prove to be an oversimplified picture. It is not a comprehensive picture and other aspects and theories of information processing have been neglected. However, we have attempted to provide a conceptual framework which can be modified or added to, as new data is collected.

Summary

Processing of information is accomplished progressively at successive stages in the sensory systems. In the visual system lateral inhibition in the retina enhances boundaries, and in the auditory system lateral inhibition in the sensory pathways sharpens the segregation of frequency information into an array of different channels. In the visual system the pattern of converging and diverging connections segregates information about visual patterns into feature specific channels. This is reflected in the response of single cells in the visual cortex to single features, such as slits of light or dark bars, at specific orientations. Cells responding to a specific feature are grouped into vertically orientated columns in the striate cortex. Adjacent columns contain analysers for different features from the same area of the retina. Thus the topographical mapping of the retina which is observable at a gross level, breaks down at a microscopic level.

The feature analyzing cells in the visual cortex appear to be hierarchically organized into simple, complex, and lower and higher order hypercomplex categories. Whereas simple cells may respond to a specifically orientated slit of light at a single retinal location, a complex cell may respond to a slit of light irrespective of location. While simple cells only respond to stationary slits of light, many complex cells respond to moving slits of light. Hypercomplex cells respond to more complex visual features such as two edges at right angles to each other. Psychophysical and electrophysiological investigations of human responses to grating stimuli, with different spatial frequencies, different contrasts or different orientations, superimposed on each other, yields data consistent with a multichannel model of feature analysis.

While the hierarchy of analysers in the visual cortex appears to decompose any visual pattern into its component features, and must clearly be associated with feature recognition, it does not appear to be the source of conscious perception. The initial primary segment of cortical evoked potentials to sensory stimuli, which appears to reflect the response of the projection area analysing system, seems to occur before conscious perception itself. Also this primary EP is not reduced during sleep or anaesthesia and does not appear to vary as a function of attention. In some circumstances, such as simple reaction time, preconscious analysis appears to lead to a fast behavioural response. The later secondary components of evoked potentials, which are readily modified by behavioural and pharmacological manipulations appear to reflect the processes underlying conscious perception. These components are recorded from widespread cortical locations (maximally at the vertex) and appear to represent the operation of a diffuse system emanating from the non-specific thalamic nuclei.

It is suggested that the secondary components of the EP reflect a process of synthesis by which percepts are constructed from the products of feature analysis and stored information. There is data to suggest that differences in the waveform of the secondary EP may reflect the different spatio-temporal patterns of activity associated with the synthesis of different percepts. There is even evidence that the potential evoked by a stimulus which is misperceived has the waveform normally produced by the pattern falsely seen and not that usually produced by the actual evoking stimulus pattern. It appears that percepts may be synthesized with greater or lesser degrees of elaboration depending on motivation, expectancy and information value of the stimulus.

Chapter thirteen

Storing information

Introduction

Mobile organisms are able to adapt to an inconstant environment by storing information. Information derived from experience may enable a creature to find the food and drink to sustain life or escape from dangers which threaten it. This fundamental capacity for storing information even appears to be possessed by the amoeba, life in its most primitive form. This sluggishly mobile single cell learns to avoid noxious chemicals and to approach nutritive ones.

The majority of adaptive responses made by less evolved forms of life are innate. The 'wiring' of their nervous systems predispose them to produce more or less stereotyped patterns of behaviour ('fixed action patterns') which are triggered 'automatically' by specific environmental stimuli ('sign stimuli'). The stereotypy of their response patterns and the restrictedness of their repertoire of behaviour denies these creatures the versatility to cope with novel environmental conditions affecting their survival. Evolutionary progress has been distinguished by the rejection of the fixed action pattern as a primary mode of adaptation. It has been replaced by increasing emphasis on behavioural flexibility, a property which arises from elaboration of the capacity to store information during an animal's lifetime. As we have seen in Chapter 1, behavioural flexibility implies the production of novel responses to cope with changing environmental circumstances. Perhaps the supreme example of behavioural flexibility ensuring survival in an alien environment is man's construction of space vehicles.

Man, representing the highest point in evolution, is the creature with by far the largest capacity for storing information, and consequently the greatest behavioural flexibility. The value of behavioural flexibility is reflected in man's unique success in adapting to the total range of terrestrial environments. Elaborated capacity for storing information in higher animals, and particularly man, implies a number of concomitant capacities, in addition to flexibility of response, which are interdependent. We have seen in Chapters 7 and 12 that the nature of our subjective perceptual world is determined by the patterns of stimulation which we experience as we develop. Information is stored that enhances our ability to discriminate recurring meaningful patterns. Language is another human ability ultimately dependent on the possession of a large capacity information store to carry both the vocabulary and the rules for generation and interpretation.

Information storage in higher animals is much more than just a modification of the 'switch gear' mediating connections between environmental stimuli and behavioural responses. A central facet of human existence is the capacity to remember events, things and information expressed in symbolic form (e.g. language). Recall of stored information need not involve an overt behavioural response, but merely that an image of the remembered item is the present focus of an individual's conscious awareness.

Storage of information is fundamental to man's conscious existence and sense of identity as well as his physical survival. James [1890] characterized the conscious world of the infant as 'a blooming, buzzing confusion'. By storing the products of experience the individual comes to consciously perceive the world as meaningfully patterned. Memory of past experiences establishes the continuity of both our conscious and our physical existence and this leads to the establishment of a sense of personal identity. The philosophically enigmatic concept of mind arises because an individual's stream of conscious experience, extended in time, appears to emanate from the same source. The existence of a stream of conscious experiences is totally dependent upon the ability to recall experiences which happened in the past. A corollary of this is that awareness of the passage of time is dependent upon both the memory of past events and of their temporal relations. Human patients who have sustained brain damage destroying their capacity to store new information become psychologically 'frozen in time', at the moment when the brain damage is sustained. As they are unable to remember the sequence of events demarcating temporal progression, each successive day is the same day repeated to these unfortunate individuals.

Because of its fundamental importance at all levels of existence a great deal of research effort has been devoted to elucidating the biological basis of information storage. The volume of research publications and variety of theories precludes comprehensive coverage in a book of this nature. An attempt will be made to outline the most important findings and the most fruitful hypotheses. A number of different problems are subsumed under the general rubric of 'storage of information'. The first question which we will address ourselves to is the gross location of the information store within the brain. The study of localization has evolved into a search for separate mechanisms subserving short and long term storage, and the processes of entry into the store and retrieval from it.

There will follow a discussion of the possible structural, and concomitant functional changes at the level of individual neurones, which are the material basis for information storage. Enduring plastic changes in the nervous system must be the ultimate basis for novel patterns of response or the recall of memorized information. We will see that most theories suppose that these plastic changes are the basis of modifications in conductivity at the synaptic junctions between nerve cells. Discussion of this topic establishes a conceptual framework for the topics which follow. These topics include the gross electrophysiological correlates of information storage and their implications for the nature of storage, retrieval, and coding. There is a discussion of the vulnerability of the early memory trace, apparently reflecting a process of consolidation in its transition to the status of a long term memory. Speculation on the precise physical nature of the memory trace inevitably leads into the difficult fields of biochemistry and molecular biology. We will attempt to convey the basic concepts of these subjects which are necessary and to review critically, but intelligibly the evidence concerning the mechanisms of biochemical synthesis which may be the key to the storage of information in biological systems.

The localization of the information store

The first systematic attempts to identify the brain structures in which information is stored were made in the experiments of Lashley [see classic 1950 article]. Typically, Lashley trained monkeys to make visual discriminations or to open boxes fastened by latches, and rats to run mazes for food reward. Following training he made incisions or lesions of varying sizes at different cortical locations and then retested the animal on the preoperatively learned task. His expectation that loss of the learned habit would only follow the severance of specific localized connections, essential for its maintenance, was confounded. He found, for instance, that in lesioned rats the number of errors made in a preoperatively learned maze was a function solely of the percentage of cortical tissue destroyed. It was not at all related to the location of the lesion. This generalization is subject only to the qualification that the sensory projection area necessary for the identification of relevant cues should be intact. Lashley [1950] had to conclude that 'it is not possible to demonstrate the isolated location of a memory trace anywhere within the nervous system. The complexity of the functions involved in reproductive memory implies that every instance of recall requires the activity of literally millions of neurones'.

Although Lashley's work has been qualified in many ways, it has given rise to enduring concepts about the location, and manner of storing information in the brain. It is supposed that many neurones, in widely diffused locations are involved in any individual memory and also that any memory is reduplicated many times in different loci. It is a storage system in which redundancy, arising from an inestimable multiplication of components, acts as a protection against damage to any one part of the mechanism. Thus Lashley's rats retained the ability to learn mazes irrespective of the location of cortical damage, and only showed deficits when damage was very extensive. We should also note that the holding of information in diffuse, interdigitated networks might have implications for the retrieval of memories. Memories with common elements might be expected to have overlap in their neural substrate, facilitating mutual activation. A probable corollary of the diffusion of memory is that any individual neurone is involved in many memories. It is a recognized phenomenon in psychological investigations of human memory that evocation of any specific memory lowers the threshold of other memories with which it has some associative link [e.g. see Baddeley, 1972, pp. 48–54].

Man's approach to the problems of biological information storage may have been constricted by the design of man-made information systems in which redundancy is minimized, in the interests of economy, and functions are strictly localized. Within a computer memory each notional store location has its strictly circumscribed site on a hardware component. A recent technological advance which has made diffused and reduplicated storage more conceptually digestible is holography. It is beyond the scope of this book to describe holography in detail. By use of the technique, a photographic plate not only holds all the details of an object photographed, but holds it in such a way that, using a laser, the entire image can be evoked from any fragment of the plate. The only loss in eliciting the image from a small area of the plate is in definition. The total image is degraded rather than any part of the image being completely lost. Pribram [1969] and Longuet-Higgins [1968] have suggested that the brain's system of storing information is analogous to holography. However, this suggestion has not been elaborated into a hypothesis which can be critically tested.

Despite its powerful influence on ideas about the localization of memory Lashley's work has been criticized for methodological weaknesses. The failure to acquire a conditioned response or learn a maze could arise from deficits other than loss of the memory store. In fact damage to any phase of the information processing system, the sensory pathways, mechanisms of selective attention, feature analysers or perceptual synthesizers could be responsible. Iversen [1973] has presented evidence that loss of ability at discrimination learning in monkeys with posterior temporal lobe lesions is due to deficient perception and not inability to store information (see further discussion later). The list above is not exhaustive as disruption of the systems subserving motivation or emotion, which power behaviour could also appear as a learning deficit. Even if we can rule out these factors it still has to be determined whether a performance deficit attributable to dysfunction of the storage system arises in the acquisition, storage or retrieval stage. These criticisms illuminate general methodological problems in the investigation of the storage function. It is impossible to isolate the contributory subsystems because of their spatial and functional proximity and interdependence. To realize this fact brings home to us the holistic nature of brain function in which the whole is more than the sum of the parts. A purely reductionist approach carries dangers of serious misinterpretation and a distorted perspective.

Because of the criticisms outlined students of memory have not been content to accept Lashley's conclusions as authoritative and have persisted in a search for localization of function at some level.

Level of storage of information in the nervous system

Lashley's work carried the implication that information storage is an exclusively cortical phenomenon. Although there are good *a priori* reasons for associating the expansion of storage capacity with elaboration of the cerebral cortex, this does not mean that all storage must occur at this location. Phylogenetically old structures in the human brain represented the full extent of brain development in our distant ancestors. The worm possessed only a reticular formation and yet was capable of rudimentary learning. Lower structures in the brain may retain the capacity to store simple information in more highly evolved creatures. Indeed neural plasticity, the capacity for an enduring change in function, which must be the basis for information storage, may be a basic property of all neural tissue.

Associative learning has been found to occur in simple and subordinate neural systems. Horridge [1962] demonstrated that a headless cockroach would learn to hold up a leg if allowing it to fall into a saline solution resulted in experience of an electric shock. Hoyle [1965] further showed that the electrophysiological correlate of this conditioning was an increase in the firing rate in the thoracic ganglion, which was presumably the site of the plastic change subserving the learning. However, we cannot reliably extrapolate from ganglionic arthropod nervous systems to the more clearly centralized ones of vertebrates.

Eccles [1964, pp. 206–211; 1965] has demonstrated that even at the spinal level in vertebrates it is possible to induce prolonged changes in the functional relations between individual neurones, of the sort which it is generally supposed must mediate information storage. An intense barrage of impulses initiated in a presynaptic neurone, resulted in post-tetanic potentiation, a long-lasting increase in the amplitude of spikes generated in the postsynaptic neurone.

When we come to consider the reticular formation in vertebrate species there is clearer evidence that we have identified a locus where plastic changes underlying learning may take place. Horn [1965] has recorded from individual neurones in the tectotegmental region of the midbrain during the presentation of novel auditory stimuli interjected in habituation sequences. He found cells which show a vigorous response to novel stimuli, but whose response is rapidly attenuated by repeated presentations of the stimulus with no consequence. This change in intensity of response to a repeated constant stimulus meets the basic criteria of information storage. Habituation of the external signs of the orienting response to an insignificant stimulus repeatedly presented is the apparent behavioural consequence of this induced change in neural function.

The modification of response represented by habituation is a very primitive form of information storage. The complexity of information storage possible has increased as the brain has evolved. Therefore it might reasonably be hypothesized that while simple information is stored in phylogenetically old, subcortical structures, more complex information is stored in the newly evolved cortex. Even using the habituation paradigm, Sharpless and Jasper [1956] have observed that while intact cats show habituation to both simple tones and tonal patterns (a brief series of descending tones), cats with their auditory cortex ablated, only habituated to simple tones. Cortical storage appears to be necessary to discriminate more complex stimuli.

Steele Russell [1971] has reviewed evidence that, while relatively simple Pavlovian conditioning is stored subcortically, instrumental conditioning lays down a cortical engram. Oakley and Steele Russell [1972] were able to classically condition the nictitating membrane (a third eyelid found in some animals) response, using an electric shock as a CS and a light as a UCS, in decorticate rabbits. In this instance storage could only be sub-cortical.

Steele Russell and his coworkers have investigated learning in animals made functionally decorticate by potassium chloride induced, spreading depression (CSD). Steele Russell *et al.* [1969] found that while function-ally decorticate rats were unable to acquire a classically conditioned passive avoidance response, they showed perfect retention of such a response learned prior to the application of the CSD. While the cortex appeared to be necessary to establish the trace, its location and the mechanisms of retrieval appeared to be subcortical. By applying cortical spreading depres-sion to one hemisphere only, Steele Russell's group have investigated whether engrams can be lateralized in one hemisphere. Lateralization is shown to have occurred when, with the originally trained hemisphere depressed and the originally untrained hemisphere functioning normally, the animal shows no sign of the response which it had originally learned. Learned instrumental behaviour, such as escape from an electric shock down a runway, was successfully lateralized [e.g. see Steele Russell, 1969]. This was taken as evidence for cortical storage, as depression of one hemisphere should have made no difference to the activation of a sub-cortical trace. In contrast, Ross and Steele Russell [1967] found that they could not lateralize a shock evoked respiratory response, which they con-ditioned to a light flash. The two experiments demonstrate the differential storage locations for classical conditioning and instrumental learning.

In the first experiment, in which shock avoidance learning was success-fully lateralized, there was also some evidence of parallel classical condition-ing. When animals were placed in the shock chamber with their trained hemispheres depressed, they exhibited behavioural and autonomic signs of conditioned fear, although they were unable to perform the escape response. In a situation in which classical conditioning of fear (the UCS was sight of the shock chamber) and instrumental learning were occurring simul-taneously it appears that the former was stored subcortically and the latter cortically.

Further evidence that complex learning is exclusively localized in the cortex comes from the work of Sperry and his associates on animals in which the two cortical hemispheres, and their corresponding halves of the visual system, are separated by section of the corpus callosum and the optic chiasma. When these animals were trained on visual discrimination tasks with one eye patched, it was found that the memory trace was restricted to the hemisphere which had received visual input. When input to the originally trained hemisphere was occluded, the naive hemisphere could successfully be trained to make a reverse discrimination. As communications between the two sides of the nervous system were intact at a subcortical level, cortical storage of more complex information was clearly indicated.

We can now present our tentative conclusions. Plasticity, implying modification of behavioural responses, is a general property of nervous systems. However, it appears that in mammals, whereas storage of simple information can be accomplished by phylogenetically old subcortical structures, more complex information can only be stored in the more extensive and complex neural networks of the newly evolved cerebral cortex.

Localization of storage functions within the cortex

We can now return to the question of the localization of storage functions within the cortex and immediately adjacent structures. Much of the recent research has been done on primates or even brain damaged humans. Organisms in which the cortex is highly developed are clearly more appropriate subjects for research on this topic than the rats which Lashley used.

Perhaps the most dramatic discoveries have been made during brain operations to relieve severe epileptic conditions, performed on conscious human patients. The Canadian neurosurgeon Penfield [e.g. see Penfield, 1951; Penfield and Roberts, 1959] used this opportunity to electrically stimulate different cortical zones and evoked, in his patients, a vivid consciousness of past events in their life which he called 'recollective hallucinations'. The subject's reports of these experiences were totally under the control of the surgeon's stimulating electrode. They were experiences of events extended in time, and in which time was perceived to pass at its normal rate. This was indicated by the fact that a common recollective hallucination was of specific renditions of a piece of music. For instance, one patient stimulated on the superior surface of the right temporal lobe, 'Heard a specific popular song being played as though by an orchestra. Repeated stimulations reproduced the same music. While the electrode was kept in place she hummed the tune, chorus and verse, thus accompanying the music she heard' [Penfield, 1951].

The phenomena reported by Penfield suggested that his electrodes had accessed the traces left by past experiences and caused them to be replayed through the mechanism of conscious awareness, much as a recorded piece of music or speech can be replayed on a tape recorder. An important concomitant observation was that an extraordinary wealth of detail was reported when these experiences were relived. This detail included experience in all sensory modalities and revival of the emotions associated with the experiences. These observations suggested that a very complete record of our life's experiences are stored. Therefore our normal inability to recall details of past events is due to retrieval failure rather than loss of memory.

Penfield [1951] was only able to evoke recollective hallucinations by stimulation of the temporal lobes. Stimulation of the sensory projection areas produced reports of diffuse and meaningless sensation, and of other areas no experience at all. Penfield was thus able to claim, and with some justification, that memory for events is stored in the temporal lobe.

Penfield's findings have attracted some criticism. It has been suggested that an abnormal brain state, induced by chronic epilepsy, with its associated pervasive abnormalities in electrical activity, may be responsible for the substrate of recollective hallucinations. Also, as we have seen in the last chapter, Neisser [1967, pp. 167–169] has suggested that recollective hallucinations are synthesized experiences rather than perfect reproductions of past experiences. This hypothesis does not exclude the contribution of memory traces from the temporal lobe. However, it could be maintained that the stimulating electrode is activating mechanisms of synthesis which are drawing data from other cortical locations.

One finding of Penfield [1951] was that following excision of an area of temporal cortex from which recollections had previously been evoked, the same recollections could still be evoked from adjacent areas. This indicated that even if the memory bank is localized in the temporal lobe, memories are diffused and reduplicated within this area. Furthermore, the fact that an electrode stimulating one point on the cortical surface, evokes the experience of a train of events, suggests that a spatio-temporal pattern of events is triggered in a neural network extending far beyond the electrode tip.

We might now transfer our attention to lesion studies, in the tradition of Lashley, but with refined methodology and carried out on primates and humans. These studies have failed to reveal the location of engrams with any more precision and certainty, probably because they are diffused in the way which we have already surmised. However, some light has been thrown on structures handling input of information to the memory store and output from it. In a review of these studies Iversen [1973] observed that frontal lesions do not affect conditioned reflexes, discrimination habits, and solution of puzzle box problems (where escape requires operation of a hidden lever). However, such lesions do disrupt performance in tasks involving holding of information during enforced delay of a response for reinforcement and where a task requires alternation between two responses to obtain rewards. An obvious interpretation of these deficits is that they are due to impaired short term memory, while long term memory remains intact. However, Iversen [1973, p. 319] observed that if tasks involving STM are given more structure by distinctive time markings, then both animals and humans with frontal lesions are able to perform better. For instance when monkeys were required, following ready signals, to make alternate right and left hand responses to earn a reward, the performance of frontal animals was greatly improved by introducing alternate short and long time delays between trials. The task was consequently structured as successive left–right response doublets. Iversen concluded that the frontal lobe, and specifically the sulcus principalis, was concerned with 'synthesizing and serializing' information. Thus following damage there was loss of temporal and spatial organization in information retrieval.

Following discussion of the frontal lobe Iversen [1973] turned her attention to the posterior cerebral cortex and temporal lobe. Claims have been made that modality specific memories are stored in association areas adjacent to the various sensory projection areas [e.g. see Arnold, 1970].

Pribram and Barry [1956] have reported that lesions of the inferior edge of the temporal lobe and preoccipital cortex resulted in loss of memory specific to visual discrimination habits. From the same class of evidence Weiskrantz and Mishkin [1958] have associated auditory discrimination habits with the posterior temporal cortex and Wilson [1957] has associated somaesthetic discrimination with the parieto-occipital association area. The difficulty is that deficits in acquisition or retention of a discrimination habit can reasonably be interpreted as due to a perceptual rather than a storage deficit. By refining her behavioural techniques Iversen [1973, pp. 333–336] has shown that failure to learn visual discriminations (e.g. of colour, size, brightness, pattern, or orientation) in monkeys with lesions of the posterior temporal lobe is very likely to be due to a perceptual deficit. Their failure is peculiar to difficult discriminations and they learn simple ones quite easily. In contrast monkeys with anterior temporal lobe lesions proved unable to learn either simple or difficult discriminatiqns. Thus the anterior temporal lobe would appear to have a vital function in the storage of information.

Temporal lobe lesions and memory in man

Penfield's operations, referred to above, for the relief of severe and intractable epilepsy, involved excision of segments of the temporal lobe on one or both sides. These lobes were the sites of the epileptic foci. Following these operations the patients were observed to have a very prominent specific memory deficit; an anterograde amnesia in which they seemed unable to add new items to their memory store. The nature of this deficit has been subject to intensive neuropsychological investigation, most notably by Milner [e.g. Milner, 1970b] and Warrington and Weiskrantz [1973]. The specificity of the deficit is indicated by the absence of other perceptual or intellectual difficulties (IQs are unchanged), retention of knowledge acquired before the operation and normal ability to register new information and hold it in short term memory.

One patient, HM, with severe bilateral damage has been studied over a period of many years. When his parents, who cared for him, moved into a new house he was unable to remember anything about the surroundings of the house, even after six years. He was also unable to remember the names of neighbours who were regular visitors to the house, or to recognize them in the street. In the laboratory this and other patients showed no signs of being able to enter any items into long term memory in any of a number of standard tests. For instance they were administered the Hebb repeated digit series test. A number of supraspan digit series were auditorily presented for immediate recall. Unknown to the subject one series was repeated on every third trial. In normal subjects there is progressive improvement in recall performance on the repeated series as a long-term trace is apparently incremented in strength. The lesioned patients showed no improvement over successive presentations of the repeated series. In other experiments it appeared to be impossible to enter either verbal or non-verbal material into the long term store with even the most intensive practice over many days. Milner [1970b] attributed the deficit which she observed to damage to the hippocampus, an elongated structure, rolled into the temporal lobe and on the floor of the lateral ventricle. She observed that the severity of the storage deficit was a function of the degree of damage to the hippocampus.

Milner's investigations included patients with unilateral as well as bilateral hippocampal damage. She found that loss of the left hippocampus resulted in a specific inability to enter verbal material into store. Patients proved quite capable of recalling complex visual–spatial and auditory patterns. Right hemisphere lesions resulted in contrary deficits so that we can infer that the storage of different types of information is lateralized.

A puzzling aspect of the hippocampal syndrome is that common experimental animals do not appear to exhibit the specific memory disturbance shown by man [e.g. see Iversen, 1973]. Monkeys with medial temporal lesions have been able to learn visual discriminations with little or no more difficulty than normals [Orbach et al., 1960; Butler, 1969]. However, in a more penetrating investigation inferotemporal lesioned monkeys were presented with several different object discrimination problems to learn on each of several successive days. Retention was tested after 15 min or after 24 h. However, in each case another problem was learnt during the retention interval to introduce a possible source of interference with memory for the primary task. In this interference paradigm severe retention deficits appeared, analogous to those shown by human patients [Iversen and Weiskrantz, 1970].

Further investigation of the human medial temporal patient has shown that the memory deficit is not as complete as was originally thought. Warrington and Weiskrantz [1973] have shown that amnesic subjects are able to identify fragmented pictures and words. Subjects were presented with successive versions of the picture, progressing systematically from the most fragmented, to the complete picture, until a correct identification was made. Significant savings were shown by amnesic subjects when they attempted relearning at 24 h intervals. Warrington and Weiskrantz also found evidence of retention of incongruous features in cartoon type drawings. In addition, acoustically and semantically 'clustered' (i.e. acoustically or semantically similar) words, were recalled more easily by amnesic patients when 'cued' by category names. Warrington and Weiskrantz claimed that in all of the tasks where amnesic subjects showed some evidence of retention, circumstances were most favourable for the rejection of incorrect responses. These investigators [Warrington and Weiskrantz, 1968] found that when amnesics attempted to learn different lists of words on successive days, recall tests revealed a very large number of intrusions from previous lists. On the basis of the evidence reviewed, Warrington and Weiskrantz [1973] reject Milner's [1970b] hypothesis that the memory defect resulting from hippocampal damage in humans is simply a loss of ability to enter information into the long term store. They argue that the deficit arises from 'interference phenomena'. Attempts to retrieve specific items from memory are confounded by the intrusion of irrelevant items and there is a failure to inhibit incorrect responses. This interpretation could allow a reconciliation of the data on animals and humans with hippocampal damage as we have previously seen that the retention deficit in lesioned animals is specific to an interference paradigm [Iversen and Weiskrantz, 1970]. It is also consistent with Gray's [1971a] theory of hippocampal function (outlined in Chapter 9). Gray supposes that the hippocampus mediates the inhibition of punished or non-rewarded behaviour and also the inhibition of irrelevant sensory input.

Other research on hippocampal function includes stimulation during and after learning, and during attempted recall, and recording from this structure during entry into or retrieval from the memory store. Kesner and Wilburn [1974] have reviewed studies involving hippocampal stimulation. During training trials it appeared to have no effect on acquisition. Correll [1957] found that stimulation failed to prevent cats from learning to traverse a runway and press a lever for a food reward. However, it has usually been reported that post-trial stimulation of the hippocampus at subseizure intensities produces amnesia for such behaviour as passive avoidance acquired in one trial. The amnesia is more likely to be observed following stimulation of the dorsal than the ventral hippocampus, indicating that there might be differentiation of function within this structure. A peculiar feature of the amnesia produced by post-trial hippocampal stimulation was that it did not appear in an immediately following retention test, but only in a test administered 24 h later. Therefore it must be inferred that hippocampal stimulation has no impact on STM but must, in some way, disrupt entry into LTM. Extrapolating again from Gray's theory [1970; see Chapter 9] it could be that this happens because there is interference with the neural consequences of reinforcement which is vital to the 'fixing' of information in store.

Hippocampal stimulation sufficient to produce an after discharge, administered to human patients, has been found to produce temporary amnesia, varying in extent from 12 min to two weeks prior to the stimulation [see Bickford *et al.*, 1958; Brazier, 1962; Chapman *et al.*, 1967]. The temporary nature of the amnesia indicates that only the capacity for retrieval is disrupted. Kesner and Wilburn [1974] warn us against the immediate inference that the hippocampus is the retrieval mechanism as the seizures induced in this structure may well disrupt other neural systems.

Other experimenters have recorded from individual cells in different hippocampal zones. Olds [1969] reported that neurones in the $CA3$ field of the hippocampus increased their discharge rate in the period between an operant response and the delivery of a food reward. The vigour of the response was a function of the strength of motivation and Olds has suggested that these discharge patterns are internal representations of the food or drink rewards which the animal is expecting. Vinogradova *et al.* [1970] have also reported evidence of neural recall in the hippocampus; the specific firing pattern triggered by a particular input may be repeated at intervals for some time after the input has terminated. These observations are consistent with the retrieval function attributed to the hippocampus by researchers like Brazier [1962], or with the fact that hippocampal stimulation induces amnesia. However, the observation that the retrieval of old memories and even, with adequate cues, of new memories could occur in hippocampectomized patients discounts the possibility that the hippocampus is essential for retrieval. However, the electrophysiological data is not inconsistent with the notion that the hippocampus is necessary for the attainment of precision in retrieving from the memory store; the function which Warrington and Weiskrantz [1973] suggest that it must have in view of the inability of hippocampectomized patients to suppress irrelevant responses.

In addition to considering patients whose brain damage disrupts long term memory Warrington and her associates [Warrington and Weiskrantz, 1973] have examined a patient with a specific short term auditory memory deficit. In this condition, generally associated with a left posterior parietal lesion, patients were unable to repeat more than one or two verbal items (digits, letters, words) immediately after auditory presentation. However, the ability to enter verbal material into long term store, with repeated trials, was within normal limits. In the serial position curve plotted from free recalled verbal material there was a marked attenuation of the usual 'recency effect' (better recall of the most recently presented items) which Glanzer and Cunitz [1966] have attributed to STM. Scores at early and middle positions on the serial position curve, associated with LTM, were normal in these patients. The data from the two types of amnesics not only support the hypothesis that there are separate short and long term stores, but also that they are independent and operate in parallel rather than sequentially. It would appear that information enters the long term store directly, while the short term store handles immediate recall. We will see further evidence for this hypothesis at a later stage.

The conclusion which we draw from this survey of attempts to localize the memory store is that broadly speaking Lashley was right and memory is widely diffused and reduplicated. More detailed investigation of structures, which at first sight looked like the location of memory traces suggested that they are concerned more with the processes of organization, storage or retrieval of information, rather than being the site of the engram itself.

The basis of diffuse storage

John [1967, 1972] has elaborated on the concept of diffuse storage. Early theories of learning were of a simple connectionist nature. Simple conditioning, such as that accomplished by Pavlov, involved the establishment of a new connection between a neutral stimulus, such as a bell, and a reflex response, such as salivation. Investigators interested in the physiological basis of memory took this as a straightforward metaphor for the events in the nervous system mediating this connection. They supposed (or made the implicit assumption) that storing information involved the formation of new connections between specific neurones, and that information retrieval arose when conditioned stimuli initiated transmission across these newly formed pathways. Lashley's [1950] perplexity arose from the failure of his lesions to clearly disrupt specific, clearly defined pathways which he had supposed to exist.

In addition to the evidence reviewed here, John points out that a mass of electrophysiological evidence tends to refute the notion that changes in individual neurones, localized pathways or circumscribed ensembles of neurones are the substrate of memory. He observes that when any stimulus is presented, to which an animal has been trained to respond, individual neurone activity, multiple neurone activity and gross evoked potentials may be recorded from widespread areas of the brain. We have already seen in the previous chapter that John and his coworkers have been able to associate the waveforms of evoked potentials, and thus specific spatio-temporal patterns of activity, with particular stimulus patterns which an animal has been trained to respond to. This has been found both for repetitive visual and auditory stimuli and for geometric patterns.

What is more, on presentation of a conditioning stimulus, both post-stimulus histograms of unit activity and evoked potentials, recorded from widely distributed locations in the brain, have been found to have the same stimulus specific wave shape. However, whereas it has been found that populations of neurones exhibit a reliably reproduceable response pattern to the same stimulus, individual neurones vary in their response from presentation to presentation. Only when the response of an individual neurone is averaged over many presentations of a conditioning stimulus does the averaged pattern resemble that obtained from the population of neurones, of which it is a member, on a single presentation.

John et al. [1973] make the assumption that the specifically patterned neural responses evoked by conditioning stimuli represent 'neural readout from memory'. They suggest that readout can be triggered by the occurrence of any fragment of the original pattern acting as a cue for recall. In the previous chapter we argued that the brain potentials referred to reflected the operation of the mechanisms of perceptual synthesis. However, this did not preclude a strong contribution from information retrieved from store. John's ideas seem to converge with these as he speculates that 'coherent temporal patterns in the average activity of anatomically extensive neural ensembles may constitute the neurophysiological basis of subjective experience' [John, 1972]. John therefore argues that retrieval of a specific memory involves the release of a temporal pattern of neural firing, coherent across widely diffused ensembles of neurones within the brain. Individual neurones involved in the retrieval of any memory conform to the specific firing pattern only in the statistical sense that their averaged pattern resembles the ensemble mean. John thus rejects what he calls 'switchboard theories of learning and memory' in favour of statistical ones.

John's theory assumes, and his experimental results clearly indicate, that ensembles of neurones produce response patterns which they have never produced before. However, he does not attempt to account for the functional changes within the neural populations which must underlie any novel pattern of response. In particular he fails to account for the variability in response of individual neurones on repeated presentations of a CS, although they show statistical conformity to the ensemble pattern. The one hypothesis which he definitely rejects is that changed response patterns are based on new connections formed between neurones. He concedes only that there must be changes in the pattern of transmission between neurones already in synaptic contact. He remains open minded about the basis of any change in 'transfer function' between neurones. Possible bases of such change should now be explored.

The neural basis of storage

Man's world abounds in accessory storage systems external to his own brain. The written word is the oldest and most obvious example. Each of these storage systems involves a process of making a physical change in a storage medium. A pen is used to write symbols on paper. The paper is the storage medium and the ink marks are the physical changes which hold the information. The information is retrieved when the words are read. In a book of many pages specific information may only be retrieved quickly by use of the list of contents or the index. By looking up a 'cue' word listed alphabetically we are directed to a particular page number. Our analysis of this man-made information storage system guides our conceptual thinking and helps us to formulate questions about biological information storing systems.

At this stage in this thesis it is perhaps most valuable to focus our attention on physical changes, at a neural level, which might underlie information storage. Insight into the possible nature of these changes should help us to discipline our thinking about the processes of both writing into memory and reading out from it. We have already evoked the idea that information is stored by the formation of new connections between neurones which permit the transmission of excitation mediating new stimulus response connections. The earliest modern physiological theories of learning supposed that the 'writing' in the brain was neural connections formed by neural growth stimulated during learning [see Grossman, 1967, Chapter 15 for a historical review of physiological theories of learning]. An influential early theory of learning was Kapper's [1917, 1933] theory of 'neurobiotaxis'. He supposed that neurones generate magnetic fields which influence the direction of growth of both axonal and dendritic processes of other neurones. It is implied that the neurobiotaxic attractions exerted by concurrently active neurones is the basis for the new connections underlying learning.

It is a virtually impossible task to demonstrate that new interneuronal connections formed by axonal and/or dendritic growth are the substrate of specific learning. Plasticity in structural features of the cortex which is a function of environmental experience, has certainly been observed. We have already seen in Chapter 7, that the brains of animals deprived of sensory experience are subject to a number of structural alterations. These include reduced length and branching of dendrites [Coleman and Reisen, 1968] and deformation [Globus and Scheibel, 1967] or reduction [Valverde, 1968; Fifkova, 1970] in the number of dendritic spines (the site of the synapse). Fifkova [1970] has observed that restoring visual input to kittens deprived for from 10 to 30 days from birth, leads to restoration of the number of dendritic spines on apical dendrites.

The experiments of the Krech, Rosenzweig, Bennett and Diamond group [Rosenzweig et al., 1968] (see also Chapter 7) have shown that cortical thickness and weight, glial proliferation and acetylcholinesterase activity is a function of 'enrichment' or 'impoverishment' of an animal's environment. Globus et al. [1973] have shown that enrichment of an animal's environment leads to an increase in the number of spines on the basal dendrites of cortical neurones, where the intracortical fibres terminate.

While all of these structural changes are suggestive of changes in connectivity between cortical neurones, they do not specifically demonstrate the formation of new connections. The elaboration of microstructural features of the brain associated with normal or enriched environments, is likely to be correlated with a larger store of information. However, although these developments may be necessary for efficient storage, we cannot presume that they are exclusively the substrate of stored information. We concluded in Chapter 7 that rich and varied patterns of stimulation were necessary both for the development and the maintenance of the structural and functional integrity of the brain necessary for the mediation of complex behaviour. We cannot exclude a complex relationship between stimulation, learning and the structural and functional elaboration of cortical neuronal networks. It is possible that not only do the structural changes induced by varied stimulus patterns represent both the physical substrate (or part of it) of their storage but also the basis of non-specific improvements in discriminative capacity and response flexibility in neural networks.

There are other ways in which the functional relationships between neurones can be modified, apart from by the formation of new connections by growth of neural processes. It is conceivable that structurally existent, but functionally dormant connections could be activated, or that the transfer function of structurally and functionally existing connections could be altered. The former hypothesis is not currently influential. The latter hypothesis is implicit in most contemporary theories of learning.

The issue which usually divides competing theories is the mechanism by which the transfer function is modified. We should explain more carefully what we mean by transfer function. We have already seen an example of this in the post-tetanic potentiation phenomenon reported by Eccles [1964]. The modified transfer function was reflected in the increased amplitude of response of a postsynaptic neurone, following intense stimulation of its presynaptic neighbour. Eccles attributed the potentiation to swelling of the terminal knobs of the presynaptic neurone with a resulting decrease in synaptic resistance, manifest as facilitation of transmission. The exact mechanism of the decrease in synaptic resistance has never been made clear. Eccles [1964] has based a theory of learning on the phenomenon of post-tetanic potentiation, although his observations were only made on spinal neurones. Apart from other criticisms, his theory has the shortcoming that the potentiation of spike amplitude has a lifetime measured in minutes and therefore cannot be a good candidate for long-term storage. More fundamental is the fact that spike amplitude is not a recognized basis for coding information in the nervous system. One would expect that if decrease in synaptic resistance was the basis of storage, then it would be reflected in an increase in either the probability of a spike occurring or the frequency of spikes which do occur as a result of a given level of presynaptic activity.

We can reject the details of Eccles's ideas but retain the basic notion that information storage involves changes in the responsiveness of postsynaptic neurones to input from presynaptic neurones. There are a number of modifications of neural function which could produce the same results. An increase in the amount of transmitter substance released by the presynaptic neurone would produce greater depolarization at the postsynaptic membrane. Alternatively, changes in the postsynaptic membrane could render it more sensitive to the transmitter substance, with a consequent increase in its excitability. Another factor which could modulate trans-synaptic propagation is the level of the enzymes, such as acetylcholinesterase, which degrade the transmitter substance. By destroying the transmitter substance released by each presynaptic impulse, these enzymes allow recovery of the postsynaptic cell after it has fired, and are thus the basis of the conduction of discrete impulses. If the level of these enzymes is reduced, the consequent increase in the level of transmitter substance has the net effect of increasing postsynaptic excitability. The relevance of these observations will shortly become apparent.

Information storage by modification of cholinergic synapses

Deutsch [1973] reported a programme of experiments which suggest that storage of information involves modification of conductivity at cholinergic synapses. In one series of experiments he used the anticholinesterase drug di-isopropyl fluorophosphate (DFP) which inactivates the enzyme cholinesterase. Cholinesterase degrades the transmitter substance acetylcholine at the synapse to allow recovery of the postsynaptic membrane between impulses (see Chapter 2). Thus inactivation of cholinesterase by DFP produces an increase in the concentration of acetylcholine at affected synapses. If emission of acetylcholine from presynaptic terminals is meagre and/or if the sensitivity of the postsynaptic membrane is low this increases the probability of transmission at the synapse. However, at higher levels of acetylcholine activity and membrane sensitivity a critical point is passed beyond which the acetylcholine in the synaptic cleft prevents repolarization of the synaptic membrane. Then transmission is blocked. Thus DFP can either facilitate or block transmission depending on pre-existing conditions at the synapse.

In one experiment rats were given intracerebral injections of DFP in peanut oil at intervals of 30 min and three, five, and 14 days after being trained to go to the lighted branch of a 'Y' maze, to avoid an electric shock in the unlighted branch. In relearning trials after injection the animals showed amnesia for their avoidance training at all intervals except the intermediate one of three days. Control animals injected with peanut oil only, showed retention of the habit at all testing intervals. The results have been confirmed by Biederman [1970] using another anticholinesterase, physostigmine, and a bar pressing response. Also Wiener and Deutsch [1968] have observed the same DFP induced amnesia to occur following training using a reward, thus excluding the possibility that the drug's effect is due to a change in the animal's emotionality. The results suggested that, except during a transitional period at three days, learning increased the level of activity at cholinergic synapses to a point where DFP blocked transmission.

The finding cited supported Deutsch's hypothesis but did not exclude an explanation of the amnesia in terms of a more generalized disruption of cerebral function. Other experiments seem to exclude this. We would expect that relatively weak memory traces would be associated with only slight facilitation of acetylcholine activity at 'storage' synapses. We have seen that the acetylcholinesterase DFP may enhance synaptic transmission at low levels of acetylcholine release. Therefore we might predict that DFP would enhance, rather than block, the retention of a poorly learned habit. Deutsch has made an experimental demonstration of this. Control groups of animals, trained to avoid shock in a 'Y' maze, showed retention at 14 days but had forgotten the response at 28 days. In contrast DFP injected animals showed amnesia at 14 days, but retention at 28 days. When the memory trace was strong DFP blocked its expression. When it had faded the DFP revived it, presumably because acetylcholine activity had decreased. These results have been replicated using an appetitive habit [Weiner and Deutsch, 1968].

Deutsch and his associates have also conducted experiments using scopolamine, which attenuates the action of acetylcholine by blocking receptor sites at the postsynaptic membrane. The graph showing retention (expressed as trials to relearn) of a task following scopolamine injections at 30 min, one, three, seven, and 14 days after training, is a mirror image of that for DFP. There is retention comparable with controls at all intervals except three days, when there was amnesia. From the results of the previous experiment it had seemed that cholinergic synapses were at their least sensitive at three days, and would therefore be expected to be more susceptible to the cholinergic blocking agent. The ineffectiveness of the cholinergic blocker at all other intervals is consistent with the enhanced sensitivity of the cholinergic synapses, which Deutsch considers to be the functional basis of information storage.

Deutsch's results with DFP and scopolamine suggest that there is an intermediate period (at three days) following training, when the sensitivity of the information carrying synapses is reduced. Deutsch cites an experiment in which animals not treated with any drug relearn a partly learned habit faster at seven to ten days than at one to three days. It appears that during the establishment of long term memories there is a period of relative inaccessibility for retrieval. It also appears that the time course for the establishment of a long term memory must be measured at least in terms of days and not hours or minutes.

In further experiments Deutsch showed that, while injections of the anticholinesterase DFP improved retention of a poorly learned brightness discrimination habit, it blocked the retention of a well learned habit. This suggested that the changes underlying learning were cumulative changes at individual synapses, rather than the progressive recruitment of more synapses. As habit strength increased, the facilitation at the synapses mediating the habit passed the critical point where the effect of anticholinesterase changed from facilitation to blocking.

Deutsch's initial experiments do not inform us whether the facilitation at cholinergic synapses is based on increased acetylcholine secretion by the presynaptic neurone, or an increase in sensitivity of the postsynaptic neurone to the transmitter substance. Deutsch attempted to make this differentiation by injecting the drug carbachol, which mimics the action of acetylcholine, but is not destroyed by cholinesterase. He found that, while a three day old habit was unaffected by this drug, one of seven days was blocked by it. This suggested an increase in the sensitivity of the post-synaptic membrane, as otherwise carbachol would have blocked transmission, and thus memory, on both occasions.

Deutsch's hypothesis is rendered highly plausible by his elegant series of experiments. However, criticisms can be made on the grounds that other drugs, such as amphetamines and pentobarbital, produce results indistinguishable from those with scopolamine [Laties and Weiss, 1966]. His results may be confounded by the fact that DFP was injected into the hippocampi of animals while under pentobarbital anaesthesia, which has its own behavioural effects on retention [Weiss and Heller, 1969]. Also Deutsch's experiments were not followed by bioassay to determine global or local level of ACh. concentration in the brain. Nevertheless the over-all pattern of the results, particularly those involving recovery of memory, is impressive. It is difficult to escape from the implication that functional changes at central cholinergic synapses are important in the storage of information.

Changes at cholinergic synapses, with their consequent changes in the transmission properties of neural ensembles could conceivably be the basis of the time coherent patterns of activity in widespread neuronal ensembles which John [1972] envisages may be the neural manifestation of 'readout from memory'.

Establishing the memory trace

The evidence which we have reviewed suggests that the engram for any individual memory is diffusely localized in widespread neural networks, and is based on changes in conductance at cholinergic synapses. There is slight evidence that change in conductance is due to an increase in sensitivity at postsynaptic membranes. The manner in which this change is accomplished, and the nature of the change, remains to be discussed.

Contemporary evidence suggests that the information received by an organism may be entered into more than one store, that different stores have different lifetimes and that the rate of establishment of the memory in different stores is variable. The earliest indications that the registration of information in long term memory was not instantaneous came from clinical evidence of post-traumatic amnesias [e.g. Whitty and Zangwill, 1966; Talland, 1968]. Persons who sustain brain injuries, or even just concussion, from violent head impacts suffer from a retrograde amnesia, which extends for some period before the trauma. There is usually recovery of memory over a period of time, except for events immediately prior to the accident, which are never remembered. A similar phenomenon is observed when depressive patients are administered electroconvulsive therapy (ECT), a brief high voltage electric shock to the brain, which usually relieves their depression, but produces an amnesia which is temporary, except for the period immediately prior to the shock. The vulnerability of new memories to cerebral insults suggested that a period of consolidation was necessary before a memory trace was established in a stable form.

In patients suffering from senile dementia, observers have claimed that deterioration of memory commences with the most recent memories and progresses systematically backwards to earlier ones. One could conclude from this observation that memory consolidation continues throughout life. However, Warrington and Weiskrantz [1973] have systematically investigated memories for different life periods in amnesic and normal individuals and claimed that amnesics had poor memories for events at all periods in their lives.

The global effect of both violent mechanical and electrical insults to the brain is a spreading wave of paroxysmal electrical activity followed by a complete depression of neural firing. As this massive disruption of cortical electrical activity appears to result in irrevocable erasure of recent memories, it has been suggested that they may be electrical in nature. Hebb [1949] produced an influential two phase theory of memory in which an initial 'activity trace' led to the establishment of a long term 'structural trace'. He supposed that the activity trace was the repetitive circulation of neural impulse patterns in 'reverberating circuits' or 'self re-exciting chains'. Synaptic facilitation in neural circuits permitted impulses to circulate after the stimulus initiating them had ceased. If the reverberatory activity was sufficiently intense then enduring anatomical changes were produced in the participating neurones which were the basis of long term memory. Clearly, while the basis of storage is reverberatory activity it is highly vulnerable to electrical interference.

Both anatomical and physiological evidence consistent with the reverberating circuit hypothesis has been presented. Lorente de Nó [1938] observed, in histological studies, that some cortical neurones were organized to form closed loops through which impulses could repeatedly circulate. Furthermore, Burns [1958] recorded self-maintaining impulse activity in slabs of cortex isolated from other neural inputs. This activity outlasted the stimulus administered by the experimenter by some time.

The theories that early memory is electrical and that a period of consolidation is necessary to establish long-term memories has prompted a large volume of research involving the production of amnesia by electroconvulsive shocks to the brain (ECS). Interest has been focused on the duration of the consolidation period, whose investigation requires precision in establishing exactly when information is entered into the storage mechanism. In most tasks on which animals can be trained this is not possible as multiple learning trials are required. Therefore the most popular paradigm has been passive avoidance learning in which a rat is able to learn, in just one trial, not to step down from a raised dais onto the floor below or it will receive an electric shock. The orginal observations were that if a passive avoidance training trial was followed by ECS within a few seconds, then on a subsequent test trial the animal 'forgot' to stay on the dais [review of early work by McGaugh and Petrinovich, 1966].

The forgetting of a passive avoidance response countered the argument of Lewis and Maher [1965] that what appeared to be amnesia, was, in fact, conditioned inhibition produced by the punishing effect of the ECS. If ECS is punishing it should additionally reinforce an animal's tendency to avoid stepping off its dais.

Despite the apparent support given by early ECS studies, the simple notion of a two-stage storage process is having to be abandoned. The effects of ECS turn out to be complex and enigmatic. The interval after training, during which ECS has been found to be effective in inducing amnesia has been found to vary from 10 s [Chorover and Schiller, 1965] to 6 h [Kopp *et al.*, 1966]. It seems unlikely that reverberating activity would persist for as long as 6 h, especially as one would expect interference from subsequent inputs to the nervous system. Hughes *et al.* [1970] found that the amnesia inducing effects of ECS varied when the current strength was varied between 40 and 100 μA. In particular it was found that with the weaker currents, amnesia did not appear immediately after ECS, but only appeared after delays which could be as long as 40 days. McGaugh and Landfield [1970] found that when ECS was applied 20 s after a training trial the appearance of amnesia was delayed for at least 6 h.

If the reverberating circuit theory of early memory was correct then we would expect that any treatment sufficient to disrupt electrical activity in the relevant circuits, would produce an immediate and complete erasure of memory. The graded amnesic effects of varying ECS intensity [and also duration, waveform, and cerebral locus; see Mah and Albert, 1973 for review] and the fact that the development of amnesia might be delayed for some time after ECS clearly contradicts this prediction. On the evidence available any electrical trace can have a lifetime of, at the most, a few seconds. Beyond this the observations cited suggest that a short-term trace of a more durable nature survives ECS, but then decays over its normal short lifespan. The amnesia appears following decay of the short-term trace because ECS has terminated consolidation of a long-term trace.

Recovery from ECS induced amnesia

The story does not end here. One of the intractable problems involved in the investigation of storage mechanisms is that there is never any ultimate proof that forgetting is loss of memory, rather than failure to retrieve memories whose engrams are still essentially present in the brain. A cautionary note should have been sounded by the fact that large components of post-traumatic amnesias are temporary. Memory appears to be lost for a period, but is later recovered. This has turned out to be the case with ECS induced amnesia. A number of studies have shown that if animals with ECS induced amnesia are given 'reminders' they recover their memory to avoid an action which results in an electric shock. These reminders, for passive avoidance situations, include foot shock, not contingent on behaviour [Miller and Springer, 1972], exposure to stimulus cues of the training apparatus without any shock reinforcement [King and Glasser, 1970; Sara, 1973] and recovery from the convulsions induced by the ECS in the training environment [Azmitia *et al.*, 1972].

Perhaps the most dramatic finding is that ECS itself may serve as a reminder. Thompson and Neely [1970] found that if ECS was administered before avoidance training, and then before testing 24 or 48 h later, the habit was retained. Controls given only the first ECS showed amnesia. The observation is reminiscent of the 'state dependent learning' effect reported by Overton [1966] in which responses learned while animals were under the influence of centrally acting drugs (e.g. pentobarbital) could only be recalled at later times when the drug was readministered. The most plausible explanation of the instances of recovery from ECS induced amnesia is based on the proposition that the passive avoidance response is conditioned to the total configuration of stimulus cues present around the time of negative reinforcement. As the ECS drastically modifies the brain state established by the cues in the training apparatus, the ECS becomes incorporated in the total configuration of conditioned cues to which the avoidance response is conditioned. When an ECS treated animal is placed in the training situation, there are insufficient cues to produce the avoidance response, unless the configuration is completed by also repeating the ECS.

Recovery from ECS induced amnesia by exposure to reminder cues other than a reinforced trial, cannot be accounted for by the explanation advanced above. Schneider et al. [1974] have advanced an ingenious explanation of reminder induced recovery from amnesia, based on the assumption that the passive avoidance trial produces both classically conditioned fear and instrumentally learned avoidance. They suggest that ECS produces amnesia only for the instrumental learning. Therefore, when the animal is placed in the avoidance situation the cues presented by the apparatus elicit the classically conditioned fear, when the animal steps down from its dais, although in instrumental, and perhaps conscious terms, it had forgotten that a shock was to be expected. Schneider and his colleagues suggested that the reappearance of the passive avoidance behaviour with repeated unreinforced testing, was, in fact, relearning based on the negative reinforcement of fear induced by leaving the dais. In support of their theory Schneider et al. [1974] found that when steps were taken to reduce the number of conditioned cues, eliminate the fear inducing response, or extinguish conditioned fear, then there was no recovery from ECS induced amnesia. Furthermore they cite observations by Mendoza and Adams [1969] and Hine and Raolino [1970] that although ECS produces amnesia for overt passive avoidance behaviour, autonomic responses (e.g. heart rate) suggest that conditioned fear of the experimental situation has not been lost.

Earlier in this chapter we considered evidence that while instrumental learning is localized in the cortex, classical conditioning has a subcortical locus. If this is true then it is to be expected that ECS, whose disruptive effect is largely confined to the cerebral cortex, should disorganize instrumental learning, but not classical conditioning. We should observe that this dual process theory could comfortably coexist with the previously advanced hypothesis that ECS disrupts instrumental learning by inducing a brain state which distorts the pre-existing cue–response relationship.

A number of other ECS related phenomena require explanation. Meyer [see 1972 review] and Thompson and Grossman [1972] have trained animals on a sequence of three tasks, each involving discrimination between visual patterns, and then administered ECS after the last task. Contrary to the expectation that the earlier the task, the less the amnesic effects of ECS, it was found that amnesia was greatest for the task learnt under the same motivation as the one immediately prior to ECS. In other words, if tasks 1 and 3 were responses for food reward, but task 2 was a response for shock avoidance, there was amnesia for tasks 1 and 3, but not for 2.

ECS produced amnesia for tasks learnt under a similar motivation, irrespective of their time relations to the ECS. Meyer suggested that ECT may be clinically effective in elevating mood by inducing selective amnesia for memories associated with the depressive state under which ECT is administered.

Another phenomenon which has been observed is that if a well established memory is evoked by presentation of cue stimuli and then followed by ECS, amnesia develops [Schneider and Sherman, 1968; Misanin *et al.*, 1968]. The observation cannot be explained in terms of interference with consolidation. However, both ECS induced amnesia for reactivated memories and for memories established under a common motivation may have a similar explanation. In both cases ECS may disorganize an established trace because of a period of heightened vulnerability following reactivation, or partial reactivation (e.g. in the case where traces are established under a common motivation). Reactivation of a memory, which is a recognized means of increasing its strength, probably initiates processes in the neural ensembles involved comparable to those occurring when the information is first entered. We have seen that acquisition of information probably involves changes in synaptic sensitivity, and we will later see that protein synthesis following acquisition seems to be essential for the establishment of an enduring trace in the neurones concerned. Protein synthesis, in particular, is known to be inhibited by ECS, which may be the basis of its disruption of the memory trace.

In the final analysis the early promise of the ECS paradigm for investigation of consolidation has not been fulfilled. Although we cannot rule out reverberatory activity in the first few seconds after an input, it is clear that there are other processes which follow representing either temporary storage and/or consolidation, but which are clearly not primarily electrical. These processes are unlikely to yield their secrets in studies involving crude electrical insults to the brain. In an attempt to gain further understanding of both the process of laying down the trace and the substrate of storage itself, we must now turn again to more subtle aspects of cellular function.

The biochemistry of memory

We are now familiar with the notion that the ultimate basis of information storage in the brain is a modification of synaptic function. Plausible candidates for the cause are increased emission of transmitter chemical by presynaptic cells, or an increase in sensitivity of postsynaptic membranes. This is far from being an exhaustive list of candidates. Furthermore it may be dangerous to suppose that all learning involves synaptic changes producing facilitation of transmission. There is no *a priori* reason for excluding, as a possibility, inhibition of transmission at the synaptic level, especially as much learning involves inhibition of a response (e.g. passive avoidance learning).

In recent years a great deal of interest has focused on the possibility of finding the biochemical mechanisms underlying information storage. This has proved to be an exciting, although sometimes misleading field of

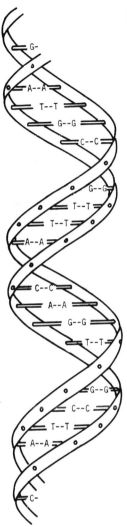

Figure 13.1
The double helix: a schematic representation of the structure of the DNA molecule proposed by Watson and Crick (1953). The two helical ribbons represent the long nucleotide chains. The connecting bars represent the base pairs linked by hydrogen bonds (see text)

research, which makes it worthwhile for a psychologist to take an excursion into the realms of biochemistry.

The opening up of the field of molecular biology in the 1950s provided a major stimulus to research on the molecular basis of memory. Crick and Watson [see Crick, 1963] made the momentous discovery that genetic information was encoded on macromolecules called deoxyribonucleic acid (DNA). This molecule, composed of two long chains of subunits called nucleotides, assumes the structure of a double helix (Figure 13.1). Each nucleotide chain has a backbone of components called bases, which are the sites where the two complementary chains are joined by hydrogen bonds. These bases, adenine, guanine, cytosine, and thymine, are the key to the genetic code. They are an alphabet from which a series of three letter words, or 'codons', are made up in a linear sequence along the nucleotide chains. Each word is an instruction for a particular amino acid to be added to a chain of such acids—a polypeptide chain. Completed polypetide chains are proteins, which are basic components of the body's structure, and in their enzymic form vital contributors to a variety of essential intracellular processes.

Until the discovery of DNA and the breaking of the genetic code, genes were a purely notional entity, inferred from knowledge of the rules of inheritance. DNA molecules are the genes in physical reality and are thus the agents which give an organism its inherited characteristics.

The molecular basis of inheritance has attracted the attention of researchers interested in the biology of memory because the genetic macromolecules carry large amounts of information (a DNA molecule may consist of a chain of many thousands of nucleotides). It would be parsimonious if biological systems utilized the information storing properties of macromolecules for storing both genetic and experiential information. This speculation has generated extensive programmes of research in many countries. Although it now seems unlikely that experiential information is coded directly on to macromolecules, it is almost certain that the total mechanism of protein synthesis, of which DNA is a central determinant, is vital to the establishment and maintenance of memories. Before we proceed to examine the research and associated theories it is necessary to give a simplified outline of the mechanism of expression of genetic information in protein synthesis.

Gene expression and protein synthesis

DNA molecules reside in the nucleus of all the body's cells, while protein synthesis occurs in the surrounding cytoplasm. The information for the manufacture of proteins is therefore carried by an intermediary, which is very similar to DNA, called messenger ribonucleic acid (mRNA). RNA is a long chain of up to 6000 nucleotides. These nucleotides are complexes of the sugar ribose and a phosphate linkage. The bases on the RNA strand are the same as on DNA, with the exception that uracil replaces thymine.

Nuclear DNA serves as a template from which mRNA is transcribed, with the aid of an enzyme called RNA polymerase. RNA polymerase draws free bases from the cytoplasm of the cell and pairs them up with complementary bases on the DNA strand according to the following scheme:

DNA		RNA
	adenine–uracil (U)	
	cytosine–guanine (G)	
	thymine–adenine (A)	
	guanine–cytosine (C)	

An RNA molecule is thus formed on which the base sequence is a systematic translation of the base sequence on a DNA molecule. The segment of a DNA molecule from which an RNA molecule is transcribed is called a cistron.

When mRNA has been formed it migrates from the nucleus to the cytoplasm of the cell where the message which it carries is translated into a protein. This is accomplished by an intracellular structure called a ribosome moving along the RNA strand and progressively adding to a growing chain of amino acids. Each successive codon (base triplet) specifies which amino acid is to be added next. The codons on the messenger RNA actually match with 'anticodons' on another species of RNA called transfer or tRNA. The tRNA molecules collect specified free amino acids from metabolic pools in the cytoplasm of the cell to form a complex called aminoacyl-tRNA. On the basis of the codon–anticodon matching the correct species of amino acid is transferred to the growing peptide chain via the mediation of the ribosome. There appear to be codons on the mRNA to both initiate and terminate translation so that a polypeptide chain of the correct length is produced.

Clearly this is not the whole story of gene expression by protein synthesis. The complexity of an organism and its functions is such that we would not expect transcription to occur from all of the genes all of the time. The expression of individual genes must be turned 'on' and 'off' at appropriate times, in the interest of orderly sequences of events within the cell. There appear to be two types of control system. In one, genes which are normally 'off' are turned 'on', in the other genes which are normally 'on' are turned 'off'. The first system requires the co-ordination of two controlling agents, an apoinducer and a coinducer, to initiate transcription. In the second system transcription is prevented by an aporepressor. However, transcription commences when the aporepressor is itself inhibited by another coinducer. The system for the control of gene transcription should be well noted because it is in the modulation of this mechanism that we have a likely candidate for the basis of information storage.

We must go further and consider the origins of the inducer substances which regulate gene expression. These are themselves proteins, produced by the mechanisms of protein synthesis which we have just described. They are therefore produced by their own genes, called regulator genes. The regulator genes thus control, via the inducer proteins which they produce, the expression of structural genes, which are templates for proteins that are part of the cellular structure. As not only the structural genes, but also the regulator genes are controlled by the proteins which the latter produce, we can see that we are dealing with a system subject to feedback control. It is a principle which we have already seen operating in a variety of biological systems and it is, of course, the principle implied by the concept of homeostasis.

Given that it is subject to feedback control we might infer certain properties of the mechanism of expression of the genes, which should be born in mind for future discussions. In the absence of external influences we might expect that the rate of protein synthesis would be sustained around an equilibrium level because the regulator genes are, by definition, self-regulating via the feedback loop described. Any external influence producing either a temporary increase or decrease in the quantities of active intracellular inducer substances could shift that equilibrium. If the regulator genes were stimulated to produce more of their product, it would lead to an increase in the production of proteins. More importantly, again because of the feedback loop by which the proteins produced influence the regulator genes, the new rate of protein synthesis would be self-perpetuating. As protein synthesis is essential to all cellular processes it would seem likely that any permanent change in the rate of protein synthesis would lead to a corresponding change in the cell's functional properties.

The purpose of this train of throught becomes clear. The activation of a nerve cell by its presynaptic neighbour could be the event which induces a change in the rate of synthesis of certain proteins. The functional properties of the cell modified by this protein synthesis could include permanent changes in excitability and conductivity. These are just the sort of changes which we are looking for as the basis of information storage.

The most popular current theories resemble the one given in outline above. However, we are running ahead in presenting the theory prior to presenting the evidence which has led to its evolution to the present state.

DNA, RNA, and information storage

At first sight the mechanism of gene expression which we have outlined offers a number of possibilities for storage of experiential information. At an early stage in this line of theorizing an attractive candidate was a change in the base sequence in intracellular DNA or RNA molecules. The 'writing in' of each memory would involve a unique configuration of changes in base sequences in the cellular populations involved; the changes being effected by the spatio-temporal pattern of activity initiated by external events. In order to account for extraction of information from memory it had to be supposed that reoccurrence of the original pattern of activity, or some fragment of it, activated the specific storage molecules with consequent synthesis of protein, which in some way facilitated synaptic transmission.

Before going any farther it should be pointed out that DNA is very quickly ruled out as a medium for holding acquired information. This function implies a degree of instability in the structure of the DNA molecule which is inconsistent with its other functions as the substrate of genetic information. This latter role demands ultrastability of the DNA molecule if genetic information is to be handed on from generation to generation without distortion. Structural instability of the DNA molecule would result in catastrophic loss of genetic information and the disappearance of the basis for propagating a species.

The hypothesis that experientially acquired information is stored by alteration of the base sequence on RNA molecules has enjoyed a longer life, although even its original authors now repudiate it. This hypothesis was given credibility by the ingenious experiments of Hydén and his group, in Sweden. Hydén [1959, 1961] devised a technique of measuring both the quantities of RNA and the relative amount of different RNA bases, expressed as base ratios, in individual neurones and their surrounding glia cells. In an initial set of experiments [Hydén and Egyhazí, 1962, 1963] rats were trained in the difficult task of walking up a tightrope wire, set at an angle of 45° to the horizontal, in order to obtain food. Measurements of RNA and DNA base ratios were made on the large Deiter's cells and the surrounding glia cells, in the vestibular nucleus, the first relay in the vestibular system. It was found that in the rats which had learned the experimental task there was an increase in both neuronal RNA and glial RNA, and an increase in the adenine–uracil ratio in the RNA at these sites, compared with untrained control rats. In a further control group, subject to passive stimulation of the vestibular system by rotating them in a centrifuge, while there was a similar increase in nuclear and glial RNA, there was no change in the base ratios.

Hydén's original hypothesis [Hydén, 1961] was that changes in a cell's electrochemical environment produced by impulse patterns, resulted in changes in the base sequences in cellular RNA by detachment of some bases and their replacement by others from a surrounding pool of free bases. A reoccurrence of the impulse pattern which created the new RNA initiated protein manufacture, which led to the explosive release of transmitter substance and the consequent trans-synaptic passage of impulses. The change in base ratios which seemed to be a specific correlate of information storage provided at least circumstantial support for this hypothesis.

It is debatable whether a peripheral nucleus in a sensory system is the right place to search for the substrate of memory. Aware of this criticism, Hydén's group have carried out further research in which the RNA in cortical neurones has been analysed. As each brain carries many memories it might be supposed that isolation of neurones specific to one memory, and determination of their RNA, was totally impossible. To overcome this problem rats were trained to obtain food with their non-preferred paw. It was predicted that the substrate for this learned change in handedness would be limited to the hemisphere controlling the previously non-preferred paw, so that the other hemisphere would therefore act as a control. Consitent with these predictions Hydén and Egyhazí [1964] found that the RNA content significantly increased and the $(G+C)/(A+U)$ ratio decreased in neurones in sensory-motor areas of the non-dominant cortex, when compared with neurones in the contralateral cortex.

In a later experiment, Hydén and Lange [1965] analysed neuronal RNA at early and late stages of the learning process. It was found that RNA increased progressively with improvement in performance, but that a different type of RNA was produced during the early part of learning to that produced when learning was nearly complete. In the former instance the base ratio composition resembled DNA, while in the latter case it resembled ribosomal RNA, which is found concentrated in the cytoplasm of the cell. The species of RNA found early in learning is associated with activation of the gene and thus with protein synthesis. In later experiments Hydén [1970] found that low molecular weight acidic proteins were synthesized in the hippocampus during learning, thus completing the evidence that protein synthesis occurs.

The evidence which accumulated from his own and other research caused Hydén [1970] to discard his original hypothesis that experiential information is stored by changing the base sequences in cellular RNA. Also, unless such changes could only be effected on a special storage RNA, susceptibility to base sequence changes by environmental stimuli would disrupt the normal mechanisms of protein synthesis, with chaotic consequences for cellular metabolism and structural integrity. It appeared to Hydén that storage of information involved activation of genes resulting in the manufacture of specific proteins with the capability of enhancing trans-synaptic conductivity. He observed that the proteins which were synthesized in the hippocampus during learning were of such a small size that they could respond to electrical fields with a very brief latency (10^{-4} s). As a result the molecule could undergo conformational changes, activate transmitters and be incorporated in membranes in a more stable configuration, events consistent with the modification of the functional relationship between nerve cells.

Hydén's initial measurements of RNA levels and base ratios, suggesting that chromosomal (messenger) RNA was produced during the learning process, is of course entirely consistent with his later hypothesis. Chromosomal RNA must be transcribed as an essential preliminary for protein synthesis. Hydén [1970, p. 114] also observes that as only 5–10% of the genes within a cell are active at any one time, there is a large pool of dormant genes available for the synthesis of proteins as a basis for information storage.

Another feature of Hydén's [1970] hypothesis is the importance which he attributes to the glia cells surrounding the neurones. He maintains that they not only support and supply energy to the neurones, but show the same response as neurones during learning. There is a subsequent transfer of acidic proteins and a flow of RNA from the glia to the neurones.

The view that protein synthesis is fundamental to information storage is now quite general among researchers on the biological basis of memory. Booth [1973] observes that as every other function in living organisms is dependent on protein synthesis, it would be surprising if information storage was an exception. Protein synthesis is essential for all metabolic processes within nerve cells and for maintaining cellular structure. The structural or chemical modifications in neurones implied by information strorage thus seem likely to require protein synthesis at some stage.

There are a number of studies, in addition to those by Hydén's group, indicating that increases in RNA and protein synthesis are associated with learning. This has usually been measured by injection of radioactive precursors of RNA or protein and measuring their incorporation in these molecules using radiographic techniques. We can only cite a few representative studies. Evidence of increased RNA production has been found following active avoidance learning in mice [Zemp *et al*., 1966] and spatial discrimination learning (in a 'Y' maze) for a water reward, in rats [Bowman and Stroebel, 1969; Bowman and Kottler, 1970]. Control procedures checked that increased RNA was not simply due to stimulation *per se*, and was not generalized to bodily organs other than the brain. Bateson *et al.* [1972] found evidence of increased RNA synthesis in chicks following imprinting on a blinking light when it was the first visual stimulus seen after hatching.

Turning to protein synthesis, Altman and Das [1964] and Altman *et al.* [1966] have observed that there is increased incorporation of the protein precursor leucine into the brains of rats reared in 'enriched environments', compared with littermates in impoverished environments. In this study it is obviously impossible to separate the effects of stimulation from the effects of learning. Many experiments have attempted to control for the effects of stimulation alone. However, it can be argued that no situation in which an organism is stimulated excludes learning, and that neuronal changes produced by stimulation or learning need not be qualitatively different. Beach *et al.* [1969] and Gaito *et al.* [1968] have found evidence of increased protein in the limbic system following avoidance learning. This complements the findings of Hydén's group, cited previously [e.g. see Hydén and Lange, 1968, 1971, 1972] that there is increased protein synthesis in the hippocampus when rats are trained to respond with their non-dominant paw. When considering the evidence presented, however, we should remember that the biochemical methodology and interpretation are subject to criticisms which are beyond the scope of this book.

Inhibition of protein synthesis and information storage

If protein synthesis is essential to the storage of information, then we would expect that blocking the synthesis of either RNA or protein would prevent the storage of information.

RNA synthesis has been blocked by the antibiotic actinomycin-D, which prevents transcription. In a review of experiments using this agent, Barraco and Stettner [1976] observe that doses producing 95% inhibition in rats at the time of acquisition, produce no observable deficit in learning or in retention up to the time (after a few hours) when irreversible toxicity sets in. When lower doses were used, however, with a consequent reduction in toxic side effects, retention deficits were observed at four hours after learning and beyond. Retention deficits appeared whether actinomycin-D was injected just before or just after learning, and even when inhibition of cerebral RNA synthesis was as low as 18%. This latter finding called into question whether any retention deficit caused by actinomycin-D was a direct effect of its blockage of RNA and protein synthesis. If retention is blocked by inhibition of protein synthesis then the normal acquisition and the delayed development of the amnesia in these experiments suggests that it is the consolidation of memories that is blocked.

Two different antibiotics, puromycin and acetoxycycloheximide, have been used to block protein synthesis. They operate in different ways and different effects have been observed from each. Puromycin, the most widely used, causes the release of incomplete peptide chains from the ribosome during translation, and is bound to these chains to form peptidyl-puromycin fragments. In the earliest experiments by the Flexners and their group [see review by Flexner *et al.*, 1967] intracerebral injections of puromycin were given to mice five hours prior to shock avoidance training to a criterion of nine out of ten trials correct in a 'Y' maze. The correct arm of the maze had to be chosen to avoid shock in either the start box or the incorrect arm of the maze. When the mice were tested by assessing the amount of 'savings' in relearning, there appeared to be a complete amnesia, but this amnesia did not develop until two to three hours after training. Injections of puromycin after learning were found to induce a delayed loss of memory, even up to 43 days after training. The delay could be attributed to the 12–20 hours necessary for protein synthesis inhibition to reach its maximum of 80–90%.

In the period immediately after learning (one to three days) bilateral temporal injections of puromycin were sufficient to induce amnesia, but after five days it could only be produced by injections at three dispersed sites, producing protein synthesis inhibition over the entire cerebrum. This finding suggests that over time an engram becomes diffused to widespread cortical locations.

Puromycin did not invariably produce amnesia. When mice were over-trained (to 60 trials beyond criterion) no amnesia was observed [Flexner *et al.*, 1963]. Also in a study in which goldfish were trained to strike an operandum for a food reward on a variable interval reinforcement schedule, puromycin produced no performance decrement [Golub *et al.*, 1972]. In most other studies on a variety of species negative rather than positive reinforcement has been used. Negative results may have been obtained in the study cited above because the animals were effectively overtrained, especially as a variable interval schedule, implying more training trials, was used.

Barraco and Stettner [1976] have reviewed studies on a variety of species, including rats, mice, chicks, Japanese quail, and goldfish, in which puromycin has produced apparent retention deficits. It has been argued that apparent loss of memory induced by puromycin may be simply a loss of the capacity to perform a task, due to the toxic effects of puromycin. Among studies attempting to control for this possibility Mayor [1969] has shown that puromycin treated Japanese quail learn more quickly than controls to reverse their response on a previously acquired red–green colour discrimination. The reduced interference from previous learning and the fact that learning performance was unimpaired while under the influence of puromycin indicated that this substance produces a specific deficit of information retrieval.

Acetoxycycloheximide has also been used to inhibit protein synthesis, which it does by interfering with the movement of ribosomes along the mRNA strand. From a number of studies it appears that if this drug is injected intracerebrally (or sometimes subcutaneously) five hours before acquisition then there is a transient amnesia, which develops after about three hours, but shows partial recovery after a few days [for review see Barraco and Stettner, 1976]. Under this paradigm protein synthesis is maximal at the time of training. Unlike puromycin, injection of acetoxy-cycloheximide just before or just after training has produced either highly attenuated or undetectable amnesic effects. Also no acetoxycycloheximide induced amnesia has been found when animals have been overtrained.

We have already seen when discussing studies using ECS, that experimenters were too quick to conclude that failure to elicit a learned response was due to erasure of stored information. In recent years it has been shown that many cases of loss of memory are retrieval failure, due to either the blocking of internal mechanisms of retrieval or failure to present the right configuration of cues (e.g. when the ECS has become incorporated in this configuration).

The fact that there is spontaneous recovery from acetoxycycloheximide induced amnesia [Quartermain and McEwen, 1970] indicates that this agent simply blocks retrieval, without interfering with the formation of a permanent memory trace. It has also been shown that behavioural treatments, such as 'reminder' shocks or exposure to the training apparatus [see Quartermain et al., 1972], and physiological treatments, such as administration of amphetamine [Barondes and Cohen, 1968; Cohen and Barondes, 1968] may also recover memories blocked by acetoxycycloheximide. The resemblance between the effects of ECS and acetoxycycloheximide on memory is probably not coincidental. Barraco and Stettner [1976] observe that ECS has a similar effect on cellular metabolism to the glutarimides, and also produces inhibition of cerebral protein synthesis.

It has been shown that recovery from puromycin induced amnesia in mice can be produced simply by administering intracerebral injections of saline solution [Flexner and Flexner, 1967, 1968a, 1968b, 1970]. However, it is not effective when puromycin has been injected within the limits five hours before to eight minutes after acquisition [Flexner and Flexner, 1968a]. Amphetamines have also been found to restore memories blocked by puromycin injections administered one day after 'Y' maze training [Roberts et al., 1970]. The several results are suggestive that puromycin induced inhibition of protein synthesis during, and just after training may produce amnesia by preventing the formation of a long-term memory trace, while at other times it produces an amnesia reflecting only retrieval failure. The delay in the appearance of the amnesia excludes the possibility that puromycin disrupts the initial formation of a short-term trace.

We can begin to ask questions about the mechanism by which protein synthesis inhibitors prevent the formation of a long term trace and block retrieval. It is most difficult to be precise about the mechanism for blocking consolidation, if this is what the administration of puromycin around the time of training achieves. It is impossible to be certain that amnesia represents erasure of memories. If the basis of LTM is a self-perpetuating change in the synthetic rate for gene inducer or derepressor proteins, then inhibition of protein synthesis seems likely to prevent any activation of dormant genes. If puromycin operates on this mechanism then gene activation must occur either parallel with, or subsequent to, other processes underlying the acquisition of information and short-term storage as inhibition of protein synthesis does not interfere with either of these.

We have a better empirical basis for speculating about the mechanism for blocking retrieval. Flexner and Flexner [1969; and see Barraco and Stettner, 1976] have suggested that blockage of retrieval by puromycin occurs because the abnormal peptides (peptidyl-puromycin fragments) which are produced, displace normal peptides involved in neuronal transmission from their receptor sites on the postsynaptic membrane. Thus recall is blocked by prevention of trans-synaptic transmission. The recovery from puromycin induced amnesia by intracerebral saline injections is achieved because the saline solution 'washes' the peptidyl-puromycin fragments off the cell walls.

Memories blocked by puromycin can also be recovered by excitatory drugs such as imiprimine and D-amphetamine, acting at adrenergic synapses [Roberts et al., 1970]. A segment of the puromycin molecule resembles noradrenaline and mescalin-like substances, which could be the basis for peptidyl-puromycin competing for the synaptic receptor sites where these molecules attach.

By injecting radioactive puromycin it has been determined that peptide bound puromycin peaks at 12 hours, decays rapidly for 10–12 days, but persists in detectable amounts for up to 60 days [Flexner and Flexner, 1968b]. This is consistent with the finding that puromycin injections produce disappearance of established memories after a delay of 10–20 h, and that saline injections are effective in recovering memories for up to 60 days.

Another relevant finding is that acetoxycycloheximide actually protects memories from the blocking effect of puromycin injected one day or more after training [Barondes and Cohen, 1967]. This could be attributed to the 70% reduction in peptidyl-puromycin complexes found when the two chemicals are injected together [Gambetti et al., 1968a].

The findings which point to memory block by peptidyl-puromycin fragments conversely support the assertion that a peptide or peptides are intimately involved in the storage and expression of information. Further evidence for the importance of peptides in memory is that pituitary peptides, such as ACTH, are other agents which protect memories from the amnesic effects of puromycin. There is suggestive evidence that peptides may act as carriers of ions across neuronal membranes [Pressman, 1968; Reed and Lardy, 1972; Urry, 1971], a function likely to promote depolarization, and thus consistent with a synaptic facilitation theory of memory.

The retrieval blocking effects of glutarimides (e.g. acetoxycycloheximide) can also be attributed to their effect on neural transmitters, possibly both acetylcholine and noradrenaline. Deutsch [1969] observes that there is a remarkable similarity between the time course of amnesias produced by both anticholinesterases and glutarimides. Serota et al. [1972] observe that during acetoxycycloheximide induced amnesia levels of cerebral noradrenaline are depressed, and that as the noradrenergic system recovers, so does memory. Roberts et al. [1970] have suggested that both cholinergic and adrenergic systems could be involved in memory, as each system has the capacity for modulating the other. We have already examined the evidence presented by Deutsch [1973] that storage of information involves changes in sensitivity at cholinergic synapses. Diverse strands of evidence are beginning to converge.

Memory transfer in brain extracts

The most dramatic and unlikely discovery supporting the thesis that memory has a biochemical basis is the transfer of information from a trained animal to an untrained animal via an injected brain extract from the former. The declaration that this phenomenon could occur, in the early 1960s [for early review see Jacobson, 1966], has since prompted an enormous number of experiments, and although many have produced negative results [see Byrne et al., 1966], there is an accumulation of evidence that, if the conditions are right, a genuine effect can be obtained.

The earliest experiments were conducted on flatworms, called planaria, which could be conditioned to produce a 'wriggle' response to a light after repeated pairing with an electric shock, or even trained to turn left or right in a 'T' maze. McConnell [1962] observed that when trained worms were minced and cannibalized by naive ones, the latter acquired the learning of their devoured fellows. In a subsequent experiment [Jacobson et al., 1967] RNA extracted from trained worms produced savings when recipient worms, injected with the RNA, were conditioned to produce the same response. The possibility that the RNA merely produced increased sensitivity to a light stimulus was tested by using a control group of donors subject to a random sequence of light and shock stimuli (pseudoconditioning). Recipients from this group conditioned at a normal rate.

Planaria are primitive organisms whose nervous system is very different from that of the higher mammals. Thus interest very quickly transferred to common laboratory mammals such as rats and hamsters. A good early example of these experiments is one by Jacobson et al. [1965] in which different donor groups of rats were trained to approach a food cup upon presentation of either a blinking light or an auditory click. It was found that recipients of RNA extracted from the brains of the donors responded only to the stimulus on which their donor had been trained, and not to the other one. The selectivity of the recipients' response indicated that the RNA had transferred a specific response tendency rather than having a general activating effect on behaviour.

Weiss [1970] has transferred passive avoidance of drinking from a tube when a light is on (using rats), thus countering the assertion that brain extracts merely activate behaviour. In other experiments attempting to show that specific information is transferred, donors have been trained to choose one of two responses (e.g. left or right runway, left or right lever) to gain a reward or escape punishment. Fjerdingstad et al. [1965] have obtained transfer of entry into a lighted alley, rather than an unlighted one for water reward. They also transferred learned preferences for pressing right or left hand bars for food reward [Fjerdingstad, 1971]. Positive results have also been obtained by Jacobson et al. [1966], Dyal et al. [1967] and Ungar, 1967. In other comparable experiments negative results have been obtained [Fjerdingstad et al., 1970; Hoffman et al., 1967; Kimble and Kimble, 1966; Luttges et al., 1966]. In an experiment by Nissen et al. [1965] in which donors were trained to choose a lighted alley in preference to an unlighted one, recipients showed tendencies to approach the opposite alley to their donors. Consistent transfer of a light–dark discrimination response has been obtained using a paradigm of Gay and Raphaelson [1970]. Rats placed in the middle of three boxes, joined by a straight runway, were shocked when they entered a black box at one end, in preference to a white box at the other. Recipients of brain extract from the avoidance trained donors spent much less time in the dark box than controls, and showed signs of emotional arousal when entering the dark box.

Cartwright [1970] performed an experiment in which donor rats were trained to turn either left or right, for positive reinforcement, in a maze. While three groups of recipients were injected with extracts from naive, left and right trained animals in the normal way, another three groups of animals were given mixed extracts with amounts from left and right trained animals in the proportions 3:1, 2:2, and 1:3. It was found that rats injected with extract that was 100% or 75% from right trained donors showed a greater tendency to turn right than controls, the strength of this tendency being greater in the 100% than the 75% case. Recipients of extract 75% from left trained donors showed a strong left turning tendency, but the 100% group failed to fulfil the predictions, apparently due to one anomalous subject. While recipients of extract from untrained donors made an equal number of left and right turns in the maze, recipients gaining equal amounts of extract from left and right trained donors showed almost complete suppression of responding. This latter observation is consistent with the extract inducing competing response tendencies of equal strength. In general the experiment indicates the power of a 'trained' brain extract to induce specific behaviours.

A final example of memory transfer which is difficult to explain in any other terms is an experiment by Ungar et al. [1972a]. Goldfish donors were trained, using an electric shock in a shuttle box, to avoid either a blue illuminated compartment in favour of a green one, or vice versa. Brain extracts were injected intracranially. Recipients from blue-avoiding donors showed a strong tendency to escape when placed in the blue end of the shuttle box aquarium, but stayed put when placed in the green end. Recipients from green-avoiding donors exhibited the opposite behaviour. There was evidence that the active agents in the extract were peptides which form dissociable complexes with RNA.

The active agent in memory transfer

The substance injected in transfer experiments has included simply homogenized brain extract and RNA (of questionable purity) derived from the brain extract. In early work [e.g. see Jacobson et al., 1966] RNA was focused on as being the likely transfer agent. However, Rosenblatt et al. [1966] claimed to have obtained positive transfer when the RNA in a brain extract from trained donors was reduced to zero by ribonuclease. Another critical point is that 'trained' RNA brain extracts have usually been injected intraperitoneally. If they genuinely transfer information then it must be supposed that these extracts reach the brain via the bloodstream and there gain entry into neural structures mediating the recognition of stimuli and organization of responses. Unfortunately for the hypothesis, the evidence suggests that RNA cannot pass the blood–brain barrier in an undegraded form [e.g. see Rose, 1968].

Ungar [1970, 1971] has claimed that positive results have been obtained with RNA as the transfer substance because purification procedures have never succeeded in detaching a protein component which forms a complex with RNA, and may be the active agent in transfer. Ungar [1970, 1971] has reported that he and his coworkers have been able to detach a specific peptide from RNA-protein complexes which, if injected into naive animals produces dark avoidance. They even claim to have synthesized this information holding substance which they have called scotophobin [Ungar, 1971; Ungar *et al.*, 1972b]. In earlier work by Ungar and Fjerdingstad [1969] proteolytic enzymes (which degrade peptides) were found to destroy the transfer factor in a brain extract, further evidence that the active agent is a protein (peptide).

If interanimal transfer of information in a chemical brain extract is a genuine phenomenon, as it now appears to be, then there is a lot to explain about the mechanism of such an occurrence. The habits transferred must be mediated by a specific neural substrate. It has to be explained how a chemical which is delivered to the brain via the bloodstream reaches this specific substrate and modifies its functional properties, so that the transferred response is elicited by a training stimulus. A tentative explanation of this phenomenon will be advanced following the discussion of a general theory of the basis of information storage from which it is derived.

Theoretical considerations

It is only possible to present a grossly oversimplified and speculative discussion of the mechanisms of information storage in this work (see Figure 13.2). Several strands of evidence suggest that it involves activation of the genes, with the implied manufacture of peptides or proteins. The peptides produced modify neuronal conductivity in some way.

If a polarizing direct current is applied to a rat's cerebral cortex for five minutes, neuronal conductivity is elevated for up to six hours. This is manifest in increased rates of discharge in cortical neurones. Inhibition of protein synthesis at the time of polarization, by topical application of one of the antibiotics (e.g. cycloheximide, puromycin, 8-azaguanine) blocks the increased discharge rate, indicating that the protein synthesis is necessary for the conductivity change [Gartside, 1968a, 1968b, 1971]. It is not clear whether the peptides produced elevated neuronal conductivity by participating in the production of neurotransmitter, or by modifying the receptivity of cell membranes. The retrieval blocking effects of peptidyl-puromycin, and related phenomena, suggest that the peptides bind to membrane sites where they increase excitability by serving as an ionic transport vehicle. The work of Deutsch [see 1973 review] suggests that membrane receptivity is increased specifically in cholinergic systems. Barraco and Stettner [1976] speculate that storage of information involves activation of cholinergic systems, while retrieval and integration of information involves activation of adrenergic systems, such as appear to be blocked by acetoxycycloheximide.

Peptides are subject to rapid turnover, therefore long term memory requires a system to sustain the level of information holding peptides. This is likely to be achieved by the mechanism of gene induction which we have

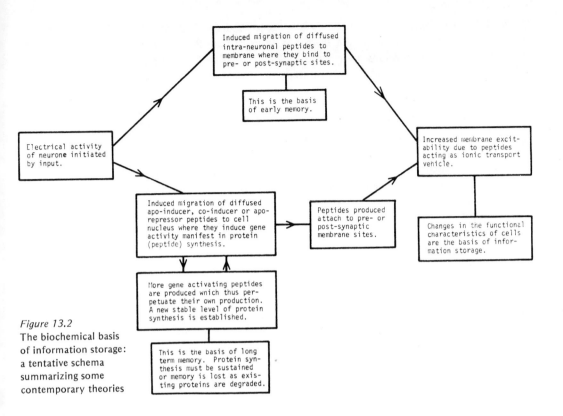

Figure 13.2
The biochemical basis
of information storage:
a tentative schema
summarizing some
contemporary theories

already outlined. The peptides produced during the initial phase of information storage must have a dual role (unless there are two or more peptides
with different functions) of modifying neuronal conductivity and as agents
(apoinducers, coinducers, or aporepressors) inducing gene activity. As such
gene activity leads to the production of more of the same conductivity
modifying, gene inducing agents, the new level of information holding peptides becomes self-perpetuating.

There is a problem in accounting for the initial entry of information.
How are the relevant peptides produced in increased quantities when there
is no initial basis for gene induction? How can information be entered and
held for short periods when protein synthesis is totally inhibited? It might
be supposed that the electrical activation of a neurone, which is the
prelude to information storage, initiates the transport of existing, spatially
diffused peptides to the specific sites, the postsynaptic membrane (or
possibly presynaptic) and the cell nucleus, where they are active in their
different roles. Inhibition of protein synthesis would have no effect on the
change in conductivity produced by this phase, but would block the
mechanism for increasing the level of protein synthesis and replacement of
degraded information proteins, necessary for long-term storage. The fact
that dramatically increased levels of RNA and protein following learning
are short-lived suggests that protein synthesis must peak at an ultrahigh
level before it can attain a new stable level. This might explain why established memories are less vulnerable to inhibition of protein synthesis and
only retrieval is blocked.

We will now consider how our theory can accommodate the discovery that information can be transferred from one animal to another in brain extracts. Further assumptions are necessary. Assuming that the substrate of a memory in a donor animal is distributed in a theoretically specifiable configuration of neurones, no matter how diffuse, then transfer must presuppose that the information carrying chemical reaches the corresponding neural system in the recipient animal. Indeed, the information carrying properties of the transfer agent are inherent in its capacity to selectivity sensitize a specific substrate. The further assumption follows that different elements in the neural storage matrix must themselves have chemical labels which enable the transfer agent to identify them. Byrne [1970] claims to have shown that radioactively labelled brain extracts reach homologous organs in recipients. Other studies, too specialized to discuss in detail here, indicate that groups of nerve cells, or even individual cells have chemical labels which are recognized by either other cells or chemicals [Crain and Peterson, 1963; Mihailovic and Jankovic, 1961; Rosenblatt and Rosen, 1970; Szilard, 1964].

When the transfer chemicals reach the target configuration of neurones they must exhibit the further capacity of modifying their response characteristics as the basis for information storage. In other words they must facilitate synaptic transmission and promote gene expression in the manner described. As the extracts usually injected in transfer experiments are whole brain extracts, we might expect that all of the memories of the donor animal would be transferred, which does not appear to happen. In fact Reinis [1965] has shown that a specific habit can only be transferred in a brain extract if the extract is taken immediately after training of the donor. The extract is only effective when its preparation coincides with the period of peak protein synthesis following training. Probably only then is the relevant peptide present in sufficient concentration to effect synaptic facilitation and induce gene expression in the target neurones of the recipient. We might also observe, in passing, that an exponential decline in the rate of protein synthesis induced by a specific series of learning trials is not inconsistent with the classical graphs of forgetting [e.g. see Woodworth and Schlosberg, 1954, p. 724 et seq.]. Presumably when responses are overlearned, although diminution of the rate of protein synthesis occurs over time, it never falls below that necessary for retrieval to be possible.

The final point which we should make in this discussion of the biological basis of memory is to reiterate that the biochemical changes underlying storage of specific information must occur in many neurones in a widely diffused network. Furthermore they must almost certainly be superimposed on countless prior adjustments of response characteristics in the neurones involved. The persistence of memory must depend on neural ensembles retaining the capacity to reproduce the essentials of time coherent firing patterns, in spite of continuous readjustment of the component neurones by the influx of environmental information. Neural networks within the brain must be organized in such a way that inputs which are irrelevant to their normal function affect the constituent neurones equally so that interneuronal relations are not affected. Information relevant to that which is already stored might modify relationships within the network and perhaps between networks. By this means a basis is established whereby any specific item in store facilitates the retrieval of related items. However, by the same mechanism new information may distort our memories of past events in the same genre.

Summary

Storage of information is the basis for organisms making adaptive modifications of their responses to environmental stimuli. As the phylogenetic scale is ascended there is reduced dependence on innate responses triggered by preordained sign stimuli and greater dependence on acquiring, by information storage, a repertoire of behaviours appropriate for survival in the environment in which an animal matures. In man, elaborated perceptual abilities, language, imagery, concepts of time, personal identity, and mind, all emanate from a highly expanded capacity for storing information.

The ability to store information implies that plastic changes must occur in the segments of the nervous system involved. Plasticity appears to be a general property of nervous tissue, but information of increasing complexity appears to be stored at progressively higher levels in the nervous system and brain. In mammals, for instance, whereas the substrate of classical conditioning appears to be subcortical, that of instrumental discrimination learning appears to be cortical. Within the cortex itself, specific memories do not appear to have a precise spatial localization, but are diffused and reduplicated throughout wide areas. The temporal lobe of the brain seems to be imporant in the storage of experiential information.

In the past, memory deficits associated with frontal lobe damage have suggested that it handles short-term memory. More recent evidence indicates that it is concerned with 'synthesizing and serializing' information. The anterograde amnesia which follows hippocampal destruction suggests a mechanism which enters information into the long-term store. However, another recent interpretation is that it is concerned with the selection of relevant information, and the suppression of irrelevant, in recall.

Electrophysiological data, including gross evoked potentials and unit records supports the assertion that information is stored in neural ensembles diffused through widespread areas of the brain. 'Neural readout from memory', manifest in evoked potentials with information specific waveshapes, arises from time coherent activity in populations of neurones, evoked by some fragment of the original pattern acting as a cue. Individual neurones make a probabilistic contribution to the over-all pattern representing readout. The basis of storage within this theory is modification of the transmission properties within the ensembles of neurones.

Experiments using drugs suggest that, at the neural level, learning involves an increase in sensitivity at cholinergic synapses, which change their transmission properties.

The loss of recently acquired information, following insults to the brain, has suggested that early memory is an activity trace and that long term memory is a structural trace, requiring a period of consolidation. Recent evidence suggests that 'reverberating circuits', if they exist, are very short-lived. However, there is still a period following extinction of any activity trace when memory is vulnerable to disruption. Early experiments with electroconvulsive shock (ECS), in which recent memories appeared to be erased, are now confounded by the finding that reminders, including ECS itself, can revive lost memories. ECS appears either to become an important part of the conditioned stimulus configuration and/or has a disorganizing effect on memory traces. ECS seems to selectively disrupt instrumental learning, leaving autonomic learning intact.

In recent years a great deal of research has been done on the biochemistry of memory. There is considerable evidence that learning involves activation of genes (DNA) with resulting transcription of mRNA and translation into proteins (or peptides). The proteins produced appear to facilitate the retrieval of information by altering the transmission properties of neurones and to sustain the trace by acting as inducers for gene expression. The specificity of the peptide mediating information storage is such that it appears to be possible to transfer information from one animal to another. There are several lines of evidence supporting this theory. It has been shown, both by direct analysis of cellular constituents and by radioactive tracer techniques, that both RNA and protein synthesis increase during learning, and that it is mRNA which is produced. Conversely, drugs which inhibit RNA and protein synthesis have been found to produce amnesia when inhibition is maximal at the time of learning. However, the amnesia has only appeared after a delay, inidicating that entry of information and short term storage can occur without protein synthesis. These functions may be based on the transport of existing peptides to critical sites.

Protein synthesis inhibitors injected after learning appear to block retrieval by secondary effects, such as the formation of abnormal peptides or reduction of neurotransmitters.

The theories presented are tentative and likely to be oversimplified as our knowledge is incomplete and the methodology and interpretation of many experiments is subject to criticism. The biology of memory is a key topic presenting a formidable challenge to the scientist attempting to understand it.

PART 5
CONSCIOUSNESS, CHEMISTRY, AND THE BRAIN

Introduction

This book has primarily considered the brain and nervous system as the mechanism mediating a creature's transactions with the environment in the interests of survival. In this final section it is proposed to focus on the brain as the organ of consciousness and brain chemistry as the determinant of the nature of consciousness. Within this context we will consider brain function in relation to some prominent social concerns, namely mental illness and its treatment, and the uses and abuses of drugs.

It was observed in Chapter 1 that the brain is the substrate of consciousness. As the value which we attach to our existence arises out of our self-awareness, the generation of consciousness might be considered to be the most important property of the brain. The more intensive study of consciousness in scientific laboratories has been precluded by the privacy of conscious content and its consequent inaccessibility to 'respectable' scientific methodology. The individual knows only his own consciousness directly and is reliant on physical signals (e.g. postures, gestures, speech, the EEG record) to infer the state or content of consciousness in others of the same or different species. These inferences are based on the assumption that the physical signals are a language used according to agreed conventions. This assumption arises from the consistency with which correlations between situations, language, and behaviour recur in everyday life. Sad words, sad looks and sad behaviour usually follow sad events.

In some mental illnesses there may be dissociation between verbal and gestural external signs of emotion (e.g. laughing at bereavement, crying at jokes). In these cases normal individuals find it difficult to infer the content of consciousness and the abnormal individual becomes 'disconnected' from his social environment.

The assertions that the brain is the substrate of consciousness and that no consciousness exists independent of underlying brain processes can only be based on inferences about consciousness in different brain states. They cannot be validated by observations of the usually accepted standards of scientific objectivity. Nevertheless there is such consistency across a multitude of observations of modification of consciousness, associated with changes in the structural integrity, pattern of functional activity and biochemistry of the brain, that it is difficult to escape the conclusion that consciousness is a product of a physical system.

Our state of consciousness, whether alert, drowsy or asleep (see Chapter 8), happy or sad, is a function of the prevailing state of the brain. The content of consciousness is determined by the current spatio-temporal pattern of activity. We have seen in Chapter 12 that specific patterns of brain activity seem to be correlated with specific percepts.

The prevailing state of the brain and the current pattern of activity is complexly determined by an immense array of interacting external and internal factors. For instance, we have seen that sleeping and waking is autonomously regulated by an internal biochemical clock. However, during the sleeping phase the clock can be over-ridden by stimuli of sufficient arousing power because of their intensity or motivational significance. During the waking phase such factors as lack of arousing stimuli, lowered atmospheric pressure or reduced oxygen in the air might lead to drowsiness or sleep. In both cases the creature might seek to control its own brain state by moving away from the conditions counteracting the preferred state, sleeping or waking, into which it would currently revert.

External psychological stimuli such as personal disasters (e.g. bereavement, desertion by spouse, loss of a job) might precipitate a state of psychological depression in which consciousness is dominated by feelings of melancholy. This appears to be reflected in a changed balance between biochemically specific systems in the brain, as we will see later. The biochemical balance, and consequently the prevailing mood of the individual can be restored by chemical (antidepressive drugs) or physical (electroconvulsive therapy) manipulation of the person's brain state. The permanence of the cure may then be a function of whether personal adjustments by the individual and changes in external circumstances favour reversion to the depressed state.

In passing we should observe that episodes in an individual's life, which can be characterized as psychological stimuli, are nevertheless received as patterns of physical stimuli impinging on the sense organs and generating a physical pattern of activity in the brain. Their effects on the state of the brain are mediated by subtle processes underlying their interpretation and comparison with stored information. In this sense they differ from gross physical stimuli such as ECT or a blow on the head. Clearly, though, 'psychological' stimuli can have equally momentous effects in terms of the emotions which are aroused and sustained.

When considering the effect of any one factor, particularly the effect of drugs, it is important to remember the fact that the state of the brain, and thus of the mind, is determined by many interacting factors. The precise effects of a drug will depend on the pre-existing mental state of the individual, the biochemical status of his brain, and even the cognitions of the drug taker concerning its likely effects. The 'placebo effect' in which the expected effects of a drug are experienced, even if only a 'dummy' drug is actually administered, is documented many times over [e.g. see Rosenthal, 1966, pp. 132-134]. The writer has observed a control subject, in an experiment on the effects of alcohol on performance, staggering around and giggling uncontrollably. She was drunk solely on tomato juice which she supposed to contain vodka.

Chapter fourteen

Abnormal states of brain and behaviour: mental illness

The dialogue between brain and environment

The imperatives of evolution have directed that the brain should organize responses to the environment which maximize a creature's survival prospects. At a fundamental level simple physical survival is the goal. In addition social animals, such as man, seek, through dialogue between brains, adjustment to their social milieu. Social organization is itself an instrument of survival. Furthermore, from the viewpoint of its own self awareness, the brain seeks subjective feelings of pleasure, well being, and contentment. We have seen in Chapters 4, 5, 7, and 9 that pleasure often is a subjective consequence of consummatory behaviour serving physiological needs. Therefore subjective feelings of pleasure are not dissociated from adaptive behaviour, but reflect the operation of its underlying mechanisms. It will also be readily appreciated that good adjustment to one's social environment is a source of pleasure through the 'positive reinforcement' received from others. Poor social adjustment is a major source of subjective feelings of unhappiness.

In the human species the attainment of subjective states with labels such as pleasure, contentment, fulfilment or happiness is a major preoccupation. This is particularly the case where technological sophistication satisfies physiological needs with a minimum of effort. Whereas the components of transient pleasures are easy to specify, the basis for enduring states of contentment are not. An enormous range of recipes for human happiness have been advanced in a multiplicity of religious, philosophical and, more recently, psychological doctrines. They testify to both the complexity of the determinants of human mental states and the diversity of routes to nirvana. Setbacks and periods of suffering or unhappiness are even seen as necessary milestones on the road to a state of contentment which is 'complete'.

Whereas physical survival is usually fairly easily sustained, at least in industrialized societies, there is often incomplete social adjustment and probably very few people enjoy a permanent state of contentment.

Mental illness

Sometimes the dialogue between the brain and the environment breaks down. At its least severe this may simply result in a chronic state of psychological distress. Deterioration of social adjustment is very likely to be an accompaniment. In more serious cases there may be a failure to perform the actions necessary for survival. Such breakdowns are usually classified as mental illness. It should be understood that there is no clear boundary between normality and mental illness. There is considerable variation both between and within societies in the degree of personal distress and behavioural maladjustment which is considered to qualify for treatment.

Mental illness takes a number of different forms. In neurotic illness there is typically a dysfunction of the mechanisms mediating emotional arousal. Instead of matching their responses to the seriousness of environmental emergencies, they operate continuously, or in response to innocuous stimuli. We saw in Chapter 6 that fearful arousal occurs to facilitate flight from danger. In the anxiety neurotic 'fearful arousal' is the predominant bodily and mental state, consequently producing acute psychological discomfort. The over arousal and anxious preoccupations impair the anxiety neurotic's capacity to conduct normal social relations and to carry out normal domestic and occupational tasks. These consequences tend to generate a positive feedback loop which aggravates the condition.

In phobic conditions extreme fearful arousal may be produced by specific stimuli which are quite innocuous. In such cases as agoraphobia, where a person is afraid of leaving his house, the condition is seriously incapacitating.

Another neurotic illness is reactive depression in which feelings of grief or melancholy, which follow a personal tragedy, persist for an unduly long period, without signs of recovery or to an abnormal degree. There is loss of the capacity to enjoy normally pleasurable experiences and achieve any happiness. In extreme cases the pervasive mood of worthlessness, pointlessness, and despair may over-ride the usually powerful impulse to survive, and the individual may kill himself.

In the neurotic illnesses described there is dysfunction of emotion and mood but not radical loss of contact with reality. The neurotic individual may have good insight into the irrationality of his mental state, but be unable to control it. External reality may only be distorted in the sense that the prevailing mood determines the affective tone of percepts. The depressive views every aspect of his world in gloomy pessimistic terms.

In psychotic illness there is a more radical disturbance of the mechanisms of emotion and information processing, which dramatically dissociates the sufferer from reality. In psychotic depression there is a profound loss of reactivity. In its converse, mania, a mood of intense elation and excitement may generate an incoherent rush of thought and activity. This may make the individual socially impossible, but with a complete lack of insight. An extreme optimism may lead to the initiation of totally unrealistic schemes of a grandiose nature, which may lead to financial or other varieties of disaster.

In schizophrenia there is a radical disturbance of both affect and information processing. Affect may be blunted to the point where the sufferer is unmoved by any disaster. Alternatively it may be quite inappropriate, personal bereavement evoking hilarity, the telling of a joke producing grief. The schizophrenic's perception of the world may be profoundly distorted, quite ordinary scenes and actions by others seeming to be full of menace. All perceived events may be referred to delusional ideas that they are being persecuted. During their waking life schizophrenics may report perceptual experiences, such as voices or body sensations, which have no external existence. These are called hallucinations and appear to represent domination of the mechanisms of conscious perception by internally stored information, such as normally only occurs in dreams (see Chapter 8). In addition there is evidence that the schizophrenic loses the capacity to focus on relevant information and to exclude irrelevant information from the mechanisms of conscious perception. There is failure of the mechanisms of selective attention discussed in Chapter 11. The brain's selective and focussing powers are an important part of its capacity to produce a logical sequence of verbal or behavioural responses. The breakdown of the selective mechanism is apparent in the schizophrenic's incoherent speech, indiscriminate association of ideas and unilateral generation of novel words. In the schizophrenic the disturbances of affect and cognition may be so profound that it becomes impossible to infer their conscious content, and in particular their mood, whether happy or sad. It may be safest to infer that their conscious content is as incoherent as their manifest utterances and behaviour.

This brief and incomplete account of changes in consciousness and behaviour in mental illness is intended to convey some of the ways in which consciousness can be distorted by dysfunction of the physical brain. The discussion of this topic requires that we look more closely at the changes in brain function which may be partly or wholly responsible.

The physical basis of mental illness

Organic illness

Some psychological disturbances result directly from conspicuous organic damage to the brain. We saw in Chapter 12 that bilateral excision of the temporal lobe in severe epileptics resulted in loss of the ability to enter information into long term memory. A similar deficit is seen in the Korsakov syndrome exhibited by some chronic alcholics and senile individuals, and can be attributed to obvious deterioration of the brain tissue, caused by poisoning or occlusion of the blood supply. We saw in Chapter 6 that pathological aggression could be attributed to the activity of a discharging lesion in the temporal lobe; again a clearly observable organic basis.

Sometimes brain function is retarded by more subtle conditions. In phenylketonuria a genetic error results in an individual who lacks a vital enzyme, phenylalanine hydroxylase [Mitoma *et al.*, 1957]. This normally metabolizes the amino acid, phenylalanine, which is plentiful in our diet, into tyrosine. The undegraded phenylalanine in the bloodstream of the sufferer appears to retard the myelination of cortical neurones [see Warburton, 1975, pp. 192-193], with the consequence that an initially normal child exhibits increasing signs of mental defect a few months after birth. This appears to be a clear case of mental capacity being totally determined by inherited characteristics. Thankfully for the sufferer and their parents, if the condition is detected early, as it can be, then the sufferer can be put on a phenylalanine free diet and grow up with normal intelligence. We thus see that even characteristics with quite blatant genetic antecedents can be modulated by the environment.

Sometimes the physical origins of psychological disturbances are insidious and concealed, as in the slow poisoning by toxic substances, such as lead and mercury, which accumulate in the body. Deterioration of psychological functioning may be gradual and may not be detected as clinically significant. One of the costs of the proliferation of motor vehicles in our civilization is pollution of the air with lead, which is added to petrol and expelled with the exhaust fumes. Minute quantities of lead are taken into the body simply by breathing the polluted air, and as heavy metals are not excreted may accumulate until there is sufficient to damage the nervous system. Recent studies have revealed significant rises in the blood lead levels of people living adjacent to busy motorway interchanges [Phillips, 1973]. The threshold for nervous system damage is not clearly established. Other recent investigations have suggested that mental retardation [David *et al.*, 1976] and hyperactivity in children [David *et al.*, 1972] may be associated with lower blood lead levels than were formerly thought to be dangerous. It would be ironic indeed if we were promoting the decay of our civilization by degrading the consciousness and behaviour of its members with our pollutants.

Functional illnesses

The neurotic and psychotic illnesses which we described earlier cannot be attributed to any clear cut organic basis such as injury, infection, occluded blood supply, or poisoning. In neurotic illness the breakdown of a healthy brain-environment dialogue can often be attributed to environmental overloading of the brain's adaptive systems which consequently provokes malfunction. The most blatant examples of this are neurotic collapses precipitated by battle stress. However, prolonged exposure to enemy shellfire is not the only cause of neurosis. In contemporary society stressful situations often arise within the family, the community, or at work which are sufficient to induce neurosis.

In Chapter 9 we discussed the hypothesis that individuals vary in their position on orthogonal personality dimensions of extroversion-introversion and stability-neuroticism. It was inferred that this determined the threshold and type of breakdown of different individuals under stress. Some theorists [e.g. Eysenck, 1967] argue that the functional properties of an individual's nervous system which will determine when and how they will become neurotic are largely genetically inherited. This assertion is disputed by other researchers and in Chapter 9 we also discussed studies indicating that adult pattern of emotional response were determined at least partly by childhood experience. Moderate stress in infancy appeared to enable the adult to match his emotional response to the demands of the situation with much greater precision, and generally to respond more adaptively to stress [Denenberg, 1964; Levine and Mullins, 1966].

Behaviourists account for the genesis of neurosis in terms of maladaptive patterns of learning. These may occur because of both an individual's inherent sensitivities to positive and negative reinforcements and the particular patterns of reinforcement which he receives from his environment. For instance Eysenck [1967] and Gray [1971a] imply that the dysthymic group of disorders (including anxiety neurosis, phobias and reactive depression) arise because of an over sensitivity to negative reinforcement. Negative reinforcement includes both punishment and non-appearance of an expected reward (frustrative non-reward). The sensitive individual will learn to show maladaptive fear, anxiety, or depression if the frequency or intensity of negative reinforcements rise above a very low threshold level (see Chapter 9).

Psychologists and psychotherapists who subscribe to psychoanalytic ideas, maintain that neurosis is determined by patterns of childhood experience which lead to an individual becoming fixated at an intermediate stage of psychosexual development. Emotionally charged experiences are repressed and exercise an influence on behaviour from unconscious areas of the mind. Strictly speaking 'unconscious mind' is a contradiction in terms. However, we observed in Chapter 12 that information could be analysed and even initiate behaviour external to the mechanism generating conscious awareness. Also in Chapter 13 evidence was presented that classical conditioning had its substrate in the brainstem, also external to the thalamocortical mechanism giving rise to consciousness. These and other facts open up the tentative possibility of a reconciliation between psychoanalytical, behaviourist, and psychobiological ideas. Some tentative translations of analytical hypotheses into behavioural terms suggest themselves. 'Fixation at infantile stages of development' could stem from inappropriate positive reinforcement of childish modes of response. Repression of emotionally charged experiences could represent 'passive avoidance' of a recall response. Irrational fears could be the result of early classical conditioning to the phobic stimulus with the trace stored at a subcortical level and thus relatively inaccessible to cortical control.

Whatever the origins of neurosis there is clearly a potentially specifiable physical state in the brain which underlies it. The postulation of hypersensitive reinforcement systems leading to maladaptive passive avoidance learning, or fear conditioning, clearly presupposes a physical substrate. Even Freud supposed that the neurophysiological basis of his psychodynamic mechanisms would eventually be found. However, it appears unlikely that neurosis stems from a clearly definable pathological process within the brain and there is no serious suggestion that it does.

The biochemical basis of affective disorders

Depressive illnesses (affective disorders) can exist in neurotic (reactive) and psychotic (endogenous) forms. In the former instance the illness appears to be precipitated by external events of a tragic nature. In the latter instance there is no obvious external cause. Furthermore the fact that periods of endogenous depression often occur in regular alternation with periods of normality, or even periods of mania, suggests a purely internal, physical cause.

There is now an accumulation of evidence that depression is associated with depletion of the brain amines noradrenaline (NA; also called norepine-phrine or NE), serotonin (5-hydroxytryptamine, or 5-HT) and dopamine (DA), and mania is associated with their elevation. The initial evidence for this was that the drug reserpine, which depletes these biogenic amines, produces a depressive state indistinguishable from naturally occurring depression. Furthermore monoamine oxidase (MAO) inhibitors, which increase functionally available monoamines at central synapses, both reverse reserpine induced depression and lift naturally occurring depression. More direct evidence is that in some (but not all) studies metabolites of NA and 5-HT have been found to be lower in the urine and cerebrospinal fluid of depressives than of normal individuals. NA and 5-HT have also been found to be lower in brain tissue of suicide cases (who were presumably depressed) than in brain tissue of control subjects dying from other causes [see Goodwin and Murphy, 1974 for review]. However, attempts to assay brain amine levels are beset with methodological difficulties which it is beyond the scope of this book to discuss.

Many researchers [e.g. see Warburton, 1975] place emphasis on noradrenaline as the transmitter substance whose depletion at central synapses is the primary immediate cause of depression. There is persuasive evidence that NA is a crucial transmitter in a 'reward system' whose focus is the medial forebrain bundle (MFB). It is asserted that the amount of functionally available NA determines the sensitivity of this system. In experiments in which rats have pressed levers to deliver electrical stimulation directly to the MFB reward area, it has been found that increases in available NA both reduces the threshold current for self stimulation and increases self stimulation rates [Wise and Stein, 1969; Stein and Wise, 1970]. In another experiment Stein and Wise [1969] used a highly sophisticated analysis technique to show that reinforcing electrical brain stimulation produces increases in NA, or its metabolites, in the reward area, while punishing stimulation reduced the production of these substances. This was a nice demonstration that noradrenaline was the transmitter substance used when the reward system was activated. Seligman [1975, pp. 65--74] has reviewed evidence that uncontrollable trauma and inability to obtain reinforcement, in a condition of 'helplessness', leads to a marked depletion of cerebral NA. This evidence is suggestive of the external conditions which are likely to lead to depression.

We will see later that drugs used to treat depression increase the levels of functionally available NA (and other amines) in the brain. Furthermore electroconvulsive therapy (ECT), a powerful treatment for elevating depressed mood, has been shown to produce a massive cerebral discharge of brain amines [Welch *et al.*, 1974].

In recent years some researchers [e.g. Carlsson *et al.*, 1969; Coppen *et al.*, 1972] have argued that serotonin depletion is as important as NA depletion in the genesis of depression. Carlsson *et al.* [1969] have shown that tricyclic antidepressive drugs may act by increasing the amount of functionally available 5-HT at central synapses. Coppen *et al.* [1972] claimed that the 5-HT precursor L-tryptophan was as effective as the tricyclic imipramine in the treatment of a heterogenous group of depressed patients. Contradictory evidence comes from Carroll *et al.* [1970], who were unable to find any antidepressant effect in L-tryptophan.

Holloway [1975] has implicated 5-HT as a transmitter in the brain's reward systems in an experiment using a sophisticated push–pull cannula perfusion assay technique. She found that there was release of both NA and 5-HT from reward areas, including the MFB, which was specific to the delivery of rewarding electrical brain stimulation. Non-rewarding stimulation in other areas inhibited the release of these amines. In contrast Stein *et al.* [1972] have argued that 5-HT is the transmitter in a punishment system having reciprocal relations with the reward system. They imply that potentiation of serotoninergic function reduces sensitivity to reward.

Extrapolating from animal studies, it appears possible that brain amine depletion in reactive depressives may stem, at least partly, from a failure of accustomed reinforcements to appear [e.g. see Seligman, 1975, pp. 65-74]. In endogenous depressives the amine depletion (or functional unavailability) has some unknown internal cause. In both varieties of depressive the amine depletion produces, in turn, insensitivity of the reward system and consequent inability to experience pleasure from the usual sources. The depressive patient is notoriously incapable of extracting enjoyment from any situation. We might speculate that the reward system not only mediates the experience of specific pleasures, but also one's general mood and feeling of wellbeing. Thus depression is due to a reduction of tonic activity in the reward system, as well as insensitivity to transient stimuli, normally experienced as pleasurable.

The mechanisms of schizophrenia

There is a great deal of controversy about the origins of schizophrenia. A recently evolved school of radical psychiatrists suppose that the origins of schizophrenia are almost wholly environmental, stemming from the distorted dynamics of family relationships. Laing [1967, Chapter 5] supposes that individuals subject to 'contradictory and paradoxical pressures, both internally from himself and externally from those around him' invents a special strategy 'in order to live in an unlivable situation'. This involves withdrawal into an 'inner world'. This accounts for the fact that schizophrenics cease to communicate in a meaningful way with normal individuals. Laing [1967, Chapter 5] suggests that schizophrenia is not an illness, but a valid and meaningful experience, an 'exploration of inner space'. Alternatively it is characterized as an escape from an 'insane' outer world to a sane inner world.

These characterizations of schizophrenia ignore the fact that schizo-phrenics have ceased to behave adaptively as far as their social adjustment and physical survival are concerned. They become largely dependent on the care of their fellows for physical survival. One can conceive of a whole society developing pathological behaviour patterns which might earn it the label 'insane'. However, to classify a person exhibiting bizarre behaviour patterns and severely neglecting his physical welfare as normal would seem to devalue the concept of normality.

Many researchers dismiss the idea that the origins of schizophrenia are environmental. There is an accumulation of evidence that a predisposition to schizophrenia may be genetically inherited [see Heston, 1966; Mosher and Feinsilver, 1971; McClearn and De Fries, 1973]. The closer the relationship between two individuals, the higher the probability that if one becomes schizophrenic the other will. In studies of identical twins concord-ance rates (percentage of cases where, if one is schizophrenic, the other is) of between 6% and 86% have been reported. There are many problems in the interpretation of the data however [see Mosher and Feinsilver, 1971].

Most of the protagonists for a mainly physical cause of schizophrenia take the view that it stems from an inborn defect in the metabolism of the amines which act as transmitter substances in the brain. A considerable number of supposedly abnormal metabolites of catecholamines have been found in the urine of schizophrenic patients [see Levitt, 1975, p. 25]. These include adrenochrome, adrenolutin, ceruloplasma, taraxein, and 3,4-dimethoxyphenethylamine. The latter is detected by a pink spot in urine analysis [Hollister and Friedhoff, 1966]. However, in follow-up studies some of these substances have been found in the urine of non-schizophrenic controls. For instance Takesada et al. [1963] recorded 'pink spot' in the urine analysis of 40% of a group of normal subjects. Some researchers have attributed the excretion of abnormal substances by schizophrenics to peculiarities of their drug regime or diet [e.g. see Snyder et al., 1974, p. 1250]. So many substances have now been presented as agents likely to be responsible for the production of schizophrenia that there is understandable scepticism. Schizophrenia is such a large and intractable social problem, and its origins have remained such a mystery, that hints of a solution produce levels of enthusiasm which over-ride the caution normally exercised in the evaluation of scientific research.

Warburton [1975, Chapter 7] has reviewed evidence that schizophrenic hallucinations are produced by abnormal activity in a cholinergic system originating in the reticular formation in the ventral tegmentum of the brainstem, and projecting to the diencephalon and neocortex. He supposes that this system is concerned with selection of relevant stimuli and suppres-sion of responses to irrelevant stimuli. This system is blocked, either by depression of acetylcholine (ACh) activity, or by an increase in ACh to the point where blocking of synaptic transmission occurs because of sustained depolarization of the postsynaptic membrane. In both cases distorted and disordered perception and hallucinations occur, which is consistent with the intrusion of irrelevant external and internal stimuli. These effects resemble the symptoms of schizophrenia and it has been found that intensi-fying cholinergic activity (thus increasing depolarization block) in schizophrenics, exacerbates their symptoms [Rowntree *et al.*, 1950]. On the other hand agents reducing brain cholinergic activity have been found to bring remission of schizophrenic symptoms [Sherwood, 1952; Forrer and Miller, 1958].

Another group of hypotheses concerning the genesis of schizophrenia supposes that the metabolic degradation of adrenalin is anomalous and that an abnormal breakdown product is a hallucinogenic agent. They are called the 'transmethylation hypotheses', because this is the chemical action which it is thought might produce hallucinogenic agents such as the dimethoxyphenylethylamines [Osmond and Smythies, 1952], adrenalutin [Hoffer and Osmond, 1960], 3,4-dimethoxyphenethylamine [Hollister and Friedhoff, 1966]. However, the evidence that these substances are produced and are responsible for schizophrenic symptoms is equivocal [see Warburton, 1975, pp. 131-133].

Another hypothesis is that indoleamine breakdown products of serotonin might be the hallucinogenic agents in schizophrenia [see Warburton, 1975, p. 134]. We saw in Chapter 8 that serotonin was implicated in the genesis of paradoxical sleep, in which the endogenously generated dream images are comparable to hallucinations. Furthermore, prolonged sleep deprivation leads to normal individuals hallucinating and exhibiting other schizophrenic symptoms, presumably in association with a build up of serotonin. In addition, ingestion of the serotonin precursor L-tryptophan intensifies the symptoms in some schizophrenics. Thus there is some evidence that schizophrenia is a correlate of abnormal levels of serotonin in the brain during the waking hours. The breakdown products are the source of the hallucinations.

Yet another recent theory of schizophrenia suggests that schizophrenia arises from abnormal function in two ascending noradrenergic systems [Stein, 1971; Stein and Wise, 1971]. One of these pathways ascending from the ventral brainstem to the hypothalamus and limbic system structures, particularly the MFB, is the same reward system which Stein and Wise [1970] implicated in the genesis of depressive illness. Dysfunction in this pathway is surmised to be responsible for the affective disorders exhibited by some schizophrenics; emotional blandness, failure to respond to rewards or punishments, catatonic stupor. The other noradrenergic pathway courses from the dorsal brainstem up to the cerebral cortex and its dysfunction is thought to be responsible for the thought disorders seen in schizophrenia.

The defective functioning of these noradrenergic systems is thought to be due to a congenital deficiency of the enzyme dopamine-β-hydroxylase, which converts the precursor dopamine to noradrenaline at presynaptic neurone terminals. The excess dopamine present in the presynaptic gap is oxygenated to 6-hydroxydopamine. Transmission at the synapse is then impeded, both by the fact that dopamine and 6-hydroxydopamine are not as effective activators of the postsynaptic membrane as noradrenaline, and by the fact that 6-hydroxydopamine is taken up by the postsynaptic membrane, where it causes damage.

Levitt and Lonorski [1975, pp. 86-87] have reviewed the evidence for the theory outlined above. Administration of 6-hydroxydopamine leads to depletion of brain catecholamines (including NA) and degeneration of nor-adrenergic nerve terminals. It diminishes intracranial self stimulation bar press rates and produces a catatonic-like stupor in rats [Tranzer and Thoenen, 1968]. In monkeys it eliminates expression of emotion and reduces social and self maintenance behaviour [Redmond *et al.*, 1973]. Post-mortem examination of humans has indicated that the concentration of the enzyme dopamine-β-hydroxylase is lower in the brainstem, hypo-thalamus, and amygdala of schizophrenics than in non-schizophrenics [Wise and Stein, 1973]. It is the absence of this enzyme which supposedly leads to the anomalous production of 6-hydroxydopamine.

An obvious flaw in this theory is that it does not distinguish between the basis of schizophrenia and the basis of depression in its account of changes in the reactivity of the reward system. It should be noted however, that the differential diagnosis between schizophrenia and endogenous depression is often difficult, so that dysfunction of the reward system could be a common element.

We should also observe that schizophrenia does not always involve the blunting of affect which supposedly arises from the blocking of reward and possibly punishment systems. In paranoid schizophrenia innocuous stimuli arouse feelings of menace, inappropriate negative affect and in some cases schizophrenics appear to be in a state of bliss [e.g. see Huxley, 1959, p. 45; Snyder *et al.*, 1974] and to see extraordinary beauty and significance in commonplace objects. There would appear to be a complex disturbance of the interaction between the systems mediating affective tone and those mediating perceptual processing.

Another important and influential recent hypothesis concerning the mechanisms of schizophrenia supposes that there are abnormal levels of dopamine activity in dopaminergic systems originating in the brainstem and extending to the limbic forebrain and cerebral cortex [see Snyder *et al.*, 1974; Iversen, 1975]. The evidence for this hypothesis revolves around the dopamine antagonizing effects of the antischizophrenic drugs in the phenothiazine group and is discussed in the section on these drugs in the next chapter.

The schizophrenic's inability to exclude irrelevant information has been documented in psychophysiological investigations [Venables, 1974]. The orienting response, in particular the GSR (galvanic skin response) compon-ent fails to habituate to a monotonously repeated stimulus. Dysfunction of the limbic system and particularly the hippocampus has been implicated in the disturbance of selection and focusing ability [Venables, 1974]. We saw in Chapter 13 that recent views of hippocampal function postulated a role in the selection of information. Hippocampal damage has been found in post-mortem examination of schizophrenics [Venables, 1976]. This could be consistent with the 6-hydroxydopamine hypothesis as this sub-stance has been shown to cause damage to neurone terminals.

Each of the theories of schizophrenia has areas of vagueness and unsup-ported speculation so that it is impossible to be conclusive. Even the identification of the site of action of an effective antischizophrenic drug does not necessarily establish the original cause of the disorder. The drug may correct anomalous synaptic functioning whose cause may arise else-where in the brain or body. The changes in a schizophrenic's behaviour are so radical and so pervasive that we might reasonably suppose that several neural systems are involved. Furthermore there are no *a priori* reasons for excluding the possibility of more than one biochemical anomaly. Also the existence of several different varieties of schizophrenia might be taken to suggest multiple causes. In conclusion the majority of theories of schizophrenia point to a radical alteration of one or more biochemical systems in the brain producing a profound modification of consciousness and behaviour.

Summary

A large and complex array of interacting internal and external factors determine the state and pattern of activity of the brain, which, in turn, determines current consciousness. Normally the brain seeks to initiate behaviour likely to produce reinforcing events serving physiological or social needs, and concomitantly generating subjective feelings of pleasure.

In mental illness the dialogue between brain and environment breaks down. In neurotic illness inappropriate sustained emotional arousal (usually anxiety) and/or loss of the capacity to respond to reinforcement (i.e. in depression) leads to acute psychological distress and disruption of normal adaptive behaviour. There is, however, no radical loss of contact with reality. The genesis of neurotic illness would appear to be a combination of genetic predisposition, faulty learning and environmental stress.

Some psychological disturbance arises from clearly observable organic damage to the brain. Injury, infection, occluded blood supply, tumours, poisoning, and metabolic anomalies may be included among the causes.

There is evidence that depressive illness arises when there is depletion of noradrenaline (NA) and other amines in the reward system focused in the medial forebrain bundle. This may occur because of the failure of accustomed reinforcements to occur or some unknown internal cause (in endogenous depression). The amine depletion results in insensitivity of the reward system so that the depressive loses the capacity to experience normal pleasures and lacks any feeling of well being.

In psychotic illness—schizophrenia or psychotic depression—a radical disturbance of the mechanisms of both emotion and information processing appears to disconnect the sufferer from reality. In schizophrenia hallucinations, distorted perception, disorders of attention, and inappropriate affect are all common symptoms. There is evidence of a genetic component in the genesis of this class of illness and there is evidence of aetiology in a biochemical anomaly of a subtle nature. Alternative hypotheses discussed include those involving variously transmethylation, indoleamine breakdown products of serotonin, dopamine-β-hydroxylase deficiency and abnormal activity in dopamine systems.

Drug modification of consciousness and behaviour

Some general principles in psychopharmacology

The chemical modification of consciousness

In depression and schizophrenia naturally produced alterations in brain chemistry appear to be responsible for serious disturbances of consciousness and adaptive behaviour. It has already been indicated in many studies cited throughout this book that administration of drugs altering brain chemistry, also alter consciousness. We would hardly expect otherwise, having accepted that conscious content is determined by the pattern of activity in a physical system. It is proposed to discuss more fully the different drugs which alter consciousness, the nature of the change in consciousness and the change in neural function which produces it. We will look at drugs which have revolutionized the treatment of the mentally ill by restoring their consciousness and behaviour to something approaching normal. We will look at drugs used by normal people to escape from a tense, oppressive, or dull reality, to reactivate a fatigued mind or to expand and intensify consciousness.

Before proceeding further we should recapitulate on why chemistry is so important in neural function. We saw in Chapter 2 that transmission of information between one neurone and another was dependent on the release of transmitter chemicals into the synaptic cleft. Furthermore we were informed in the chapters on serving basic needs that all brain mechanisms are regulated by chemical agents which modify cellular or synaptic function. Thus hunger was dependent, among other factors on the regulation of firing rates in hypothalamic cells by blood glucose. Sexual arousal is modulated by sex hormones, aggressive arousal by noradrenaline, and sleep by serotonin. We have even seen in Chapter 13 that information storage in memory and learning is probably achieved by some chemically mediated change in the functional properties of synapses. It was speculated that this change occurred through gene activation and consequent modification in the rate of synthesis of transmitter substances. All of these brain mechanisms contribute to the state and content of our consciousness.

Chemically specific systems in the brain

The major known excitatory transmitter chemicals in the brain are acetylcholine (ACh), noradrenaline (NA; also called norepinephrine or NE), dopamine (DA) and serotonin (5-hydroxytryptamine or 5-HT). A further substance, γ-amino-butyric-acid (GABA) is thought to be an inhibitory transmitter substance [Iversen, 1970].

It is possible to distinguish a number of transmitter specific neural systems in the brain. Each of these systems has a relatively specific function. We have already discussed in the previous chapter a cholinergic system concerned with the suppression of responses to irrelevant information and an adrenergic system mediating pleasurable responses to rewarding stimuli and the pervasive mood on a mania–depression dimension. In Chapter 8 we discussed a serotoninergic system which promoted sleep. In addition Fisher and Coury [1962] have plotted a cholinergic system which promotes drinking and Grossman [1962a,b] an adrenergic system initiating eating. These two are parallel systems which are quite widely distributed in the limbic system. Their existence challenges the doctrine implicit in much of Chapter 4, that eating and drinking are handled by discrete, localized centres in the hypothalamus. However, we should observe that a diffused system could nevertheless have a focus in a specific locality so that we should not immediately reject the earlier hypotheses.

A drug acting on the CNS might affect just one of the transmitter specific systems or it might affect two or more. It might have an excitatory action or a depressant action. Clearly the locus and mode of action will determine the effect which the drug has on behaviour and consciousness.

Chemical modification of neural function

Drugs can act on neural function in several different ways, depending on which phase is modified in the sequence of events between the synthesis of transmitter chemicals in the cell body, and the inactivation of transmitter molecules after acting at receptor sites on postsynaptic membranes (see Figure 15.1).

Although there are drugs which modify the rate of synthesis of transmitters, such as α-methyl-dopa, they are not widely used in psychopharmacological research or therapy. Following synthesis transmitter molecules are stored, bound to protein molecules, while they are transported down the axon towards the neurone terminals. The drug reserpine blocks the storage of the biogenic monoamines, serotonin and noradrenaline, with the consequence that they are degraded by the enzyme, monoamine oxidase (MAO), which is present in the neurones. The resulting depletion of monoamines depresses neural activity in their systems, with a consequent depression of behaviour. MAO inhibitors, in contrast, destroy the intra-

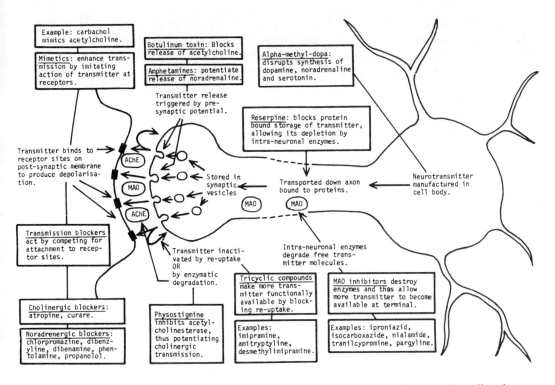

Example: carbachol mimics acetylcholine.

Mimetics: enhance transmission by imitating action of transmitter at receptors.

Botulinum toxin: Blocks release of acetylcholine.

Amphetamines: potentiate release of noradrenaline.

Alpha-methyl-dopa: disrupts synthesis of dopamine, noradrenaline and serotonin.

Transmitter release triggered by presynaptic potential.

Reserpine: blocks protein bound storage of transmitter, allowing its depletion by intra-neuronal enzymes.

Transmitter binds to receptor sites on post-synaptic membrane to produce depolarisation.

Stored in synaptic vesicles

Transported down axon bound to proteins.

Neurotransmitter manufactured in cell body.

Transmission blockers act by competing for attachment to receptor sites.

Transmitter inactivated by re-uptake OR by enzymatic degradation.

Intra-neuronal enzymes degrade free transmitter molecules.

Cholinergic blockers: atropine, curare.

Noradrenergic blockers: chlorpromazine, dibenzyline, dibenamine, phentolamine, propanolol.

Physostigmine inhibits acetylcholinesterase, thus potentiating cholinergic transmission.

Tricyclic compounds make more transmitter functionally available by blocking re-uptake.

Examples: imipramine, amitryptyline, desmethylimipramine.

MAO inhibitors destroy enzymes and thus allow more transmitter to become available at terminal.

Examples: iproniazid, isocarboxazide, nialamide, tranilcypromine, pargyline.

Figure 15.1
Schematic representation of a neurone and synapse to illustrate the mode of action of some common psychoactive drugs

neuronal enzyme, with the consequence that free noradrenaline is no longer degraded. The resulting increase in the functional availability of noradrenaline has a potent excitatory effect on neural function. As NA is a likely transmitter in the MFB reward system which appears to regulate mood, MAO inhibitors, such as iproniazid, have proved to be very valuable antidepressants.

Once transmitters have reached the terminal swellings of the neurones they are stored in synaptic vesicles. There they await the stimulus of an action potential to trigger their release into the synaptic cleft. It is thought that amphetamine, which is a powerful CNS stimulant, enhances the release of noradrenaline, possibly by displacing it from the synaptic vesicles [Levitt and Lonorski, 1975, p. 62].

Following release the transmitter molecules cross the synaptic cleft and bind to receptor sites on the postsynaptic membrane. This alters the permeability of the membrane and is the immediate cause of the depolarization which sets up excitatory postsynaptic potentials (EPSPs). Carbachol is a drug which mimics the depolarizing action of ACh so that if it is introduced into the synaptic zone it potentiates activity at cholinergic synapses. Other drugs compete with transmitters to attach themselves to receptor sites and because they do not produce depolarization, block synaptic transmission. Atropine and curare block cholinergic receptor sites and thus, because ACh is the receptor at the neuromuscular junction, paralyse muscular activity.

The phenothiazines (e.g. chlorpromazine, dibenzyline, dibenamine), phentolamine and propanolol block adrenergic receptor sites. Their capacity to attenuate activity in adrenergic systems has led to their use as tranquillizers and antischizophrenic agents.

After they have performed their primary function the transmitter substances are removed from the synaptic cleft, either by enzymatic degradation, or by reuptake by the presynaptic membrane. This allows recovery of the postsynaptic membrane preparatory for the transmission of the next impulse; it is the basis of discrete transmission. We saw, in Chapter 13 that the drug physostigmine which inactivates the enzyme cholinesterase, either enhances or blocks cholinergic transmission depending on the pre-existing level of cholinergic activity and the dose of the drug. Up to a point the increased cholinergic activity is excitatory. Beyond a critical point excess ACh in the synaptic cleft produces a depolarization block, due to failure of the postsynaptic membrane to recover between impulses. Physostigmine is used extensively in behavioural research.

Between 40 and 60% of transmitter in the synaptic cleft is inactivated by reuptake by the presynaptic terminal. Drugs in the tricyclic group, such as imiprimine and desiprimine block the reuptake of noradrenaline, and because this potentiates noradrenergic activity, have proved to be useful antidepressants. Other drugs which are thought to exercise their excitatory effect, partly through the blocking of reuptake, are amphetamine and cocaine.

The therapeutic use of drugs: a critical approach

Because psychological illnesses stem from the complex malfunction of the body's most complicated organ, their understanding and treatment has lagged behind that of physical illnesses with clearly identifiable pathogenic agents. Since the war the treatment of psychological illnesses has been revolutionized by the development of a range of drugs which have appeared to be the most effective and fastest acting treatments. The alternative treatments by psychoanalysis or psychotherapy were not only long and expensive, but many had begun to question their efficacy [see Eysenck, 1953]. Behaviour therapy or behaviour modification, based on learning theory, has only recently gathered momentum as a potentially effective treatment for certain neurotic disorders such as the phobias. Even then it is likely to be used in conjunction with pharmacotherapy and is only applicable to a limited range of disorders.

The ready availability of powerful psychoactive drugs must appear as a godsend to the busy general practitioner confronted with insomnia and diffuse and incomprehensible neurotic disturbances, and to the overworked psychiatrist confronted with wards full of agitated psychotics. The facility with which drugs can be dispensed enjoins us to look very critically at the use of drugs, from a number of points of view. The question which is most generally asked is about the safety of drugs. The thalidomide disaster, in which pregnant women given this drug as a tranquillizer, subsequently gave birth to severely deformed children, brought this question to the forefront of public consciousness. It emphasizes that the safety testing of drugs must be of the most stringent nature. Many drugs are dangerously toxic if taken in large doses and if taken in combination with other substances. It is quite easy to take a lethal dose of barbiturate which is widely prescribed as a sedative and sleep inducer. It is also very dangerous taken in combination with alcohol. A large number of accidental and deliberate deaths from overdoses of barbiturate have led to severe condemnation of this drug by some critics of modern medical practice.

MAO inhibitors, used in the treatment of depression, reduce the body's ability to metabolize endogenous and exogenous monoamines, such as tyramine, which can produce dangerous levels of adrenergic stimulation. Therefore patients taking MAO inhibitors have to avoid eating fermented foods such as cheese, beer, and wine, which contain tyramine and can prove fatal.

The phenothiazines, used in the treatment of schizophrenia, lower excitation in dopaminergic as well as adrenergic systems. As the dopaminergic systems are concerned with motor control the drug can produce disordered movements, similar to those seen in Parkinson's diseas, as a highly undesirable side effect.

All drugs ingested by the body are excreted through the liver, which thus makes this organ particularly vulnerable to any toxic properties. MAO inhibitors cause liver damage when taken over a long period.

A fundamental question about the use of psychoactive drugs is whether they produce a real and lasting benefit to the patient in the long as well as the short term. Although there is usually a distinctive remission of conspicuous symptoms, which gets a patient out of a doctor's hair, there may be other effects which are not so welcome to the patient. For instance some tranquillizers produce drowsiness which interferes with both perceptual-motor skills and intellectual functioning. This is not much use to an individual who wants to be fully efficient in a demanding occupation.

With the ready availability of drugs for the treatment of symptoms it is too easy to forget that the primary cause of neurotic illness might be environmental stress. If this stress is not removed then the individual is condemned to chronic drug taking, with its attendant danger of addiction or tissue damage. This is not a trivial argument as the level of prescription of sleeping pills and tranquillizers is astronomically high in industrialized societies. The tendency to neglect environmental causes is illustrated in parody by a case known to the author. A doctor who had made his wife anxiety-ridden and sleepless by psychological and physical mistreatment offered her Valium as a palliative. The wife threw the Valium out of the window (literally!) and cured herself by leaving her husband.

It could be argued that the high level of demand for sedatives reflects the proliferation of chronically stressful environments created by our economic and social system. The psychological and physical symptoms produced by the stress of competing in ruthless managerial hierarchies have assumed the status of folklore. In a study of 22 different societies, Rudin [1968] found that high levels of 'achievement motivation' within a society predict high death rates from ulcers and hypertension, complaints likely to have a psychological origin. High achievement motivation indicates an environment, with prizes for success and penalties for failure, which is likely to produce both anxiety and suppressed aggression.

Even shop floor workers are not immune to stress. One can see a sharp irony in a study by Proctor [1962]. Trials of various sedative drugs were conducted on 50 women mill workers suffering from anxiety-tension symptoms with a consequent deterioration of their productivity. It was found that the benzodiazepine, chlordiazepoxide (Librium) relieved the symptoms with the least interference with occupational skills, compared with barbiturate and meprobamate. It led to restoration of production levels. What passed without comment was the fact that the anxiety-tension symptoms were a product of insecurity generated by the piece work system used in the mill. In this sort of context drugs begin to look like a tool for the exploitation of the workers.

Drugs and the dulling of the emotions

It is evident that many of the drugs used to treat psychological disturbances reduce the intensity and clarity of consciousness and dull the emotions. This is certainly the case with many hypnotics and sedatives and also with the tricyclic antidepressants, in the early stages of taking them. While it is true that the express intent is to dull the emotions, when it is a permanent state of emotional arousal which is distressing the patient, we must remember that intense emotion is a normal response to certain events. We saw in Chapter 6 that the aroused emotions had obvious value for physical survival. We might speculate that, in humans, certain emotions, such as grief, have a psychological adaptive function. It is implicit in all psychodynamic doctrines derivative from Freud's analytical psychology, that the emotion generated by intense and disturbing experiences must be fully expressed for psychological equilibrium to be achieved. In behaviourist terms it may be that when an emotion is repeatedly regenerated by a memory image of the events which initially evoked it, there is a process of 'desensitization'. Because the emotion is not reinforced by further external events it tends to 'extinguish' as a response to the repeatedly evoked images. If drugs are used to suppress the emotional response to distressing events there may be a failure to extinguish and memory images may retain their emotion evoking power much later, when drug taking has ceased.

Other arguments against the indiscriminate use of drugs for the treatment of emotional disturbance are of a more metaphysical nature. Vicissitudes of mood and emotion are part of the pattern of every individual's existence. They are claimed to be a part of the process of maturing and becoming wholly human. It may be necessary to have known misery or despair to fully experience the contrasting state of ecstasy. In Chapter 7 we have even seen experimental evidence of a need for contrast and change in our existence.

It is a paradox of our existence that a state or event which can create feelings of extreme happiness, cannot sustain it indefinitely. Human value systems are exceedingly complex and are unlikely to be explained simply in terms of what excites the MFB reward system. For instance we attach a high value to excellence in the graphic, literary, and dramatic arts, yet they often have tragic themes and are judged by the authenticity with which they portray the interplay of strong emotions.

It could also be argued that to know and experience the full range of human emotions is a necessary education for social sensitivity and altruistic responsiveness. From our own experiences we become capable of empathizing with the suffering of others, and thus of responding to them.

If we are persuaded by these arguments, then we might consider that chemical anaesthetization of our emotions is likely to diminish us. We should allow waves of grief or anxiety to fully engulf us and yield to the impact. By progressively working through the emotion and making rational adjustments to a new situation we may emerge feeling wiser, stronger, and more complete. Some individuals in crisis eschew the use of sedatives, which they could easily obtain, because of the subjective validity of the arguments put forward above.

It is important to realize that simply to believe that an emotional crisis can be borne without resort to drugs could make a strong contribution to recovery. This could arise from a placebo effect, such as that associated with belief in the effectiveness of a drug or any other treatment. Also recovery might be aided by a positive feedback effect of each perceived step towards recovery reinforcing the belief that the entire process can be achieved without pharmacological aids.

To express these reservations about the use of drugs in the treatment of emotional distress is not to devalue their usefulness. It is an exhortation to judge carefully whether a neurotic patient is genuinely overwhelmed by his symptoms, and thus unable to alleviate them by changing his attitude and his circumstances. In some crises, where a neurotic's inability to cope with life's demands, and his neurotic symptoms, amplify each other by positive feedback, drugs can help to reverse the process. The calming effect of a sedative drug can facilitate the performance of occupational or domestic tasks, which, in turn, makes a further contribution to the reduction of anxiety. This argument might apply to a student revising for an examination under pressure of time. This presupposes that an effective dose can be found which does not produce drowsiness.

In contemplating the use of drugs for the treatment of psychological distress it is necessary to take a global view of all the additional physical and psychological factors, past, present and future, which bear on the contribution of the drug to promoting a more healthy state of brain and mind.

The major drug groups: their psychological effects and clinical uses

Depressant drugs

Neurotically ill people suffer from a chronic and incapacitating state of mental anguish in which a primary symptom is usually anxiety. Anxiety is a less specific form of fear which is accompanied by the same somatic manifestations, including elevated heart rate and respiration, muscle tension and unpleasant gastrointestinal changes (see Chapter 6). These concomitants of arousal are inconsistent with sleep, so that insomnia is frequently a secondary symptom of neurosis. We saw in Chapter 6 that emotional arousal is mediated by the combined action of the RAS and the limbic system. The former mediates general arousal and the latter, aspects of somatic arousal and expression and behaviour specific to the emotion elicited. The persistent state of emotional arousal and sleeplessness exhibited by the anxiety neurotic is therefore reduced by administering a drug which directly or indirectly depresses neural activity in the structures mentioned.

Alcohol

Wilcox and Levitt [1975] have suggested that the prototype depressant drug is ethanol (ethyl alcohol), which is found in the commonly available alcoholic drinks, beers, wines, and spirits. Alcohol is a product of the fermentation of fruit and vegetables with yeast, which has been used for recreational and medicinal purposes for many centuries and in many cultures. A large proportion of the alcohol ingested in solution in water is delivered to the highly vascularized brain.

Alcohol has a depressant effect at all levels of the CNS, but acts most strongly on the RAS]Gray, 1971a; Guyton, 1971], and depresses the neocortex before the subcortical regions [Wilcox and Levitt, 1975, p. 157]. This latter observation could account for the initial stimulant effect of alcohol, with its release of inhibition of basic drives such as sex and aggression. Neocortical restraint of subcortical drive mechanisms is reduced and according to Arnold [1950] anxiety is reduced by removal of a neocortical excitatory influence on lower emotion centres.

The consumption of alcohol in industrialized societies is enormous and arguably it is the most frequently used medication for tension-anxiety. The felt need for alcohol's soothing effects is indicated by the enormous revenues which governments are able to collect from the high tax on alcohol.

Despite its acceptance by most sectors of society, alcohol is a very harmful drug. As the dose is increased the depressant effect on the nervous system becomes manifest in a deterioration of perceptuomotor and cognitive performance [e.g. see Mardonnes, 1963], which could be fatal when driving a car. With regular consumption of alcohol tolerance develops as the body adjusts and becomes more efficient at metabolizing it. In the regular heavy drinker a rebound effect occurs when alcohol is withdrawn which generates the hangover symptoms of tremor, fatigue, headache, and nausea, and following prolonged heavy drinking can include nightmares and terrifying hallucinations. These highly unpleasant withdrawal symptoms are a strong factor in alcohol addiction. The alcoholic cures his hangover with more alcohol.

Chronic alcohol consumption can have many deleterious effects. Because it is converted to blood sugar, unlike other drugs, it is sometimes relied upon for nutrition with consequent deficiencies due to lack of protein, vitamin and mineral intake. Also there is chronic gastric irritation leading to failure to absorb many nutrients. A frequent complaint following excess alcohol consumption is cirrhosis of the liver (inflammation and hardening), which is probably consequent on nutritional deficits and alcohol's direct toxic effects.

Because it is both highly vascularized and irritable, CNS tssue is particularly sensitive to alcohol's toxic effects. Consequently brain damage is a frequent sequel to alcoholism. Korsakov's syndrome, in which there is loss of ability to store new information, is often observed. Large amounts of alochol taken at one time can easily be lethal, approximately two pints of 100° proof whisky being sufficient to kill a man.

Withdrawal of alcohol after excessive consumption over a period of two weeks or more, in alcoholics or non-alcoholics, can produce delirium tremens (DTs). The progressive adjustment to alcohol's depressant effects cannot be quickly reversed with the consequence that the CNS becomes hyperexcitable as the effects of alcohol wear off. In the worst phase the DT sufferer experiences nightmares, hallucinations, delirium, and convulsions. He is anxious, agitated and in constant movement. He attempts to remove repulsive hallucinated animals, such as snakes, insects, or rodents, from his body or the furniture. He has no comprehension of his surroundings and his clouded consciousness is focused around his drenching sweat, fever, and thumping heart.

We should note that the DTs are not peculiar to alcohol withdrawal, but appear to be a general feature of abstinence from any depressant drug after acquisition of dependence. For instance Isbell *et al*. [1950] observed that symptoms indistinguishable from DTs were exhibited following drug withdrawal from barbiturate addicts.

Barbiturates

Barbiturates are the next category of depressant drug which we will consider. They are really a clinically prescribed alternative to alcohol in pill form. Drugs which depress the brain's arousal systems have progressive effects with increasing dose which are, in turn, anxiety reduction, sleep, anaesthetization, coma, and death. Because of the duration of their effects barbiturates have been used most often to treat insomnia. Additionally they have been used to reduce anxiety and also to reduce the frequency and intensity of convulsions in epilepsy.

Barbiturates, of which more than 2500 have been synthesized, are divided into three groups. These are long acting (one hour to onset, 6-10 h duration; barbital and phenobarbital), intermediate acting (30 min to onset, 5-6 h duration; butabarbital and amobarbital) and short-acting (15 min to onset, 2-3 h duration; pentobarbital and secobarbital).

Barbiturates most powerfully depress the arousal system of the brainstem, the cerebral cortex and the limbic system, consistent with their anxiety reducing and sleep inducing properties. Also, in contrast to their normal depressant effects, there is increased firing from neurones in the sleep promoting inhibitory areas of the medulla and basal ganglia [Wilcox and Levitt, 1975, pp. 168-169]. Furthermore it has been shown that pentobarbital increases the cerebral level of the sleep system transmitter, serotonin [Anderson and Bonnycastle, 1960]. There is argument about whether barbiturates produce normal sleep. Oswald [1968] has reported that barbiturates suppress REM (paradoxical) sleep. However, Meyers *et al*. [1972] have claimed that barbiturates only suppress REM sleep when given in larger doses.

The effects of barbiturates resemble those of alcohol in virtually every respect. A low dose produces an initial excitement and euphoria possibly due to the disinhibition of limbic structures. These effects have led to their recreational use in recent times. The use of barbiturates as a hypnotic are vitiated by the fact that, like alcohol, they produce a hangover whose dizziness, weakness, impaired judgment and motor inco-ordination can persist all day. Where insomnia is not a function of manifest anxiety it may be better to suffer the insomnia than the barbiturate hangover. Long periods on high doses of barbiturates produces dependence on the drug, whose withdrawal results in all the unpleasant symptoms mentioned earlier.

Large doses of barbiturates are extremely toxic and can easily produce depression of the brainstem of such severity that the centres controlling respiration and heart beat cease to function, death thus ensuing. The ease with which a lethal dose of barbiturates (8–10 times the hypnotic dose) can be taken makes them a popular agent for suicide attempts, with a high probability of success. Also the fact that the effects of alcohol and barbiturates are additive has contributed to many accidental deaths. In truth, barbiturates are a highly dangerous drug.

Non-Barbiturate Sedative-Hypnotic Drugs

There are a number of non-barbiturate sedative-hypnotic drugs, although they are chemically related to either the alcohols or the barbiturates. Their behavioural effects, their addictive properties and their toxicity are very similar to the barbiturates. Alcohol related drugs are chloral hydrate, paraldehyde and ethchlorvynol. Chloral hydrate is a rapid onset, short-duration drug, first used in the middle of the last century. It was sometimes used in a mixture with alcohol (known as a 'Mickey Finn') for the sinister purpose of 'knocking out' unsuspecting sailors in order to shanghai them as involuntary recruits to crew sailing ships to distant lands. It is also effective as a quick-acting hypnotic, but has side effects as a gastric irritant. Paraldehyde is an effective and safe CNS depressant which would be in wider use if its taste and smell were not so unpleasant.

The barbiturate related agent glutethimide appeared at first sight to be a safer, less addicitve sedative-hypnotic than the barbiturates, but as cases of acute intoxication, addiction and death were reported with its spreading use, this illusion was dispelled [see Wilcox and Levitt, 1975, p. 177].

A problem in evaluating drugs with therapeutic potential is that the commercial concerns which produce them have a strong vested interest in selectively emphasizing beneficial properties and overlooking undesirable ones. The danger of inadequate publicly observable testing by a commercial concern is particularly well illustrated by the tragic case of thalidomide. This is another barbiturate related sedative-hypnotic which was received with some enthusiasm. After it had been in use for some time it became apparent that it was responsible for an appalling disaster, in which pregnant women who took the drug gave birth to grossly deformed children.

Another long-acting depressant drug is bromide, once thought capable of reducing the sex drive. It is quite effective in suppressing epileptic attacks, but useless as a hypnotic because its toxicity makes it highly irritating to the gastrointestinal tract and difficult to ingest without vomiting.

Depressant tranquillizers

While barbiturates are the most popular drugs prescribed for sleep disorders another group of drugs, the depressant tranquillizers, are most frequently given as a daytime sedative to anxious neurotics. The depressant tranquillizers are very similar in their effect to the other depressants and it is debatable whether their preferential use for the treatment of anxiety has any conclusive empirical basis. It may rather be the result of intense and expensive advertising and marketing campaigns used to promote these drugs. Depressant tranquillizers do have the specific effect of relaxing tense muscles, which is supposed to make a large contribution to their relief of anxiety-tension symptoms. However, the barbiturates are muscle relaxants as well [Iversen and Iversen, 1975, p. 179]. A point in favour of the depressant tranquillizers is that they are much safer than barbiturates because the lethal dose is much higher.

Of a group called the propanediols, meprobamate (Milltown, Equanil) is the most popular tranquillizer used for daytime sedation without producing excessive drowsiness. It has no apparent inhibitory effects on NA, DA, 5-HT or ACh. Its effects on the NS are not well documented, but include a blocking action on the interneurones of the spinal cord, probably responsible for its muscle relaxant effects. It produces slowing of electrical activity in the thalamus, basal ganglia, and limbic structures in cats [Baird et al., 1957], which probably relates to its anxiety relieving effects.

Drugs which a manufacturer is contemplating marketing are initially extensively tested for their behavioural effects and undesirable side effects, on animals. The experimental paradigm used to test anxiety reducing drugs is conditioned suppression. An animal engaging in appetitive activity including eating, drinking, sex, predatory aggression, or responding for intracranial reinforcing stimulation, will suppress this activity when it receives a stimulus which has repeatedly been a warning of imminent electric shock. Conditioned suppression can be interpreted as a fearful response. Antianxiety properties are tentatively inferred in a drug if, like meprobamate, it reduces or eliminates suppression of appetitive behaviour when the conditioning stimulus is presented.

The most popular group of depressant tranquillizers currently prescribed to reduce daytime anxiety are the benzodiazepine compounds, chlordiazepoxide (Librium), diazepam (Valium) and oxazepam (Serax). They also have anticonvulsant properties useful in the treatment of certain types of epilepsy. The production of these drugs has arisen from a drive to find a sedative agent which does not also produce drowsiness and impair intellectual and perceptuomotor performance. Early studies indicated that benzodiazepines may depress limbic structures before depressing the RAS [Schallek and Kuehn, 1965], but more recent studies have shown that they depress neural function in structures ranging from the caudal brainstem to the cortex. Also DiMascio and Barrett [1965] have reported that increasing doses of diazepam produce drowsiness, speech slurring, motor inco-ordination, impairment of intellectual function, and apathy.

The benzodiazepines do appear to produce some behavioural effects specific to themselves. In addition to producing the sedative and muscle relaxant effects of the other depressant drugs they have a very marked taming effect on aggressive behaviour (see also Chapter 6) [Randall et al., 1960]. This has led to their use for calming pathologically hostile psychiatric patients, and in particular reducing combativeness in alcoholics during withdrawal.

In animal experiments using operant conditioning paradigms, the benzodiazepines appear to have an effect which is more specific to fear inducing situations than other depressive drugs. Meprobamate, in addition to producing reduced suppression of responding for reward when conditioned fear is evoked, also increases appetitive responding when there is no punishment. In an illustrative experiment the benzodiazepines reduced suppression of lever pressing for a milk reward during foot shock, following a tone warning, but did not change the rate of response during non-shock periods [Geller et al., 1962]. Whereas other depressant drugs administered in small doses appear to produce a general removal of fore-brain inhibitor influences on drive systems, the benzodiazepines might be hypothesized to selectively depress the medial septum–hippocampus–basal forebrain circuit which Gray [1971a] has argued mediates fear linked passive avoidance learning. This is consistent with a selective ability to reduce anxiety.

Undesirable effects of benzodiazepines include the impairments of awareness and performance mentioned, and physical dependence. However, because of their low toxicity, suicides and accidental deaths are very rare with this drug.

Neuroleptic (antischizophrenic) drugs

There is a further group of drugs, the neuroleptics, which initially sedate by a general depression of neural function, but whose clinical value lies in an additional antipsychotic property. These are the rauwolfia alkaloids, the phenothiazine derivatives, and the butyrophenones.

The prototype rauwolfia alkaloid is reserpine, which occurs naturally in Rauwolfia serpentina, the 'snakeroot plant'. Reserpine exerts its depressive effect by blocking the storage of biogenic amines and thus facilitating their enzymatic degradation. It has a very marked sedative effect and can produce a state of total quiescence and unreactivity in an animal or individual who is still awake. Associated with this it may produce deep psychological depression, which is one of the several undesirable side effects which has led to its discontinuance as a treatment for schizophrenia.

The most widely used neuroleptic drugs are the phenothiazine group, particularly chlorpromazine (CPZ). These are the drugs which have made the greatest contribution to the pharmacological revolution in the treatment of the severely mentally ill. They have the capacity to restore to near normal the disordered thinking, blunted effect and withdrawal, exhibited by the schizophrenic patient. They are the only effective treatments for schizophrenia and have permitted our society to return many patients to a normal existence, who previously would have been condemned to custodial care in a mental hospital for the rest of their lives. It was recently estimated that, up to that time, the staggering total of 250 million people had received one or other of the antischizophrenic drugs, 50 million having received chlorpromazine.

Chlorpromazine has an initial powerful sedating effect to which tolerance rapidly develops. The antischizophrenic effect remains when the drug no longer produces sedation, indicating that the effects are not causally related. The antischizophrenic specificity of CPZ is indicated by the finding that it is most successful in attenuating symptoms considered to be fundamental to schizophrenia; thought disorder, blunted affect, withdrawal and autistic behaviour. It is less successful with supposed accessory symptoms including hallucinations, paranoid ideas, delusions of grandeur, and belligerent behaviour [Klein and Davis, 1969].

Chlorpromazine appears to block the receptor sites for the biogenic amines, being moderately potent in the case of noradrenaline, and most effective in the case of dopamine [e.g. see Iversen and Iversen, 1975, p. 243; Levitt and Lonorski, 1975, p. 87; Iversen, 1975]. However, there is no generally agreed theory as to how this relates to the drug's anti-schizophrenic effects. In the previous chapter we discussed the hypothesis that the effectiveness of CPZ derived from a blocking action on deleterious 6-hydroxydopamine in noradrenergic systems. In contrast Snyder et al. [1974] and Iversen and Iversen [1975] advance well documented arguments that neuroleptic drugs exert their influence by a direct inhibiting effect on a dopaminergic system extending up from the brainstem to areas of the limbic system implicated in emotional behaviour and the cerebral cortex.

There is primary evidence of phenothiazine blockade of dopaminergic receptor sites of a fairly direct nature. It has been observed that administration of different phenothiazine drugs elevate levels of dopamine metabolites in the brain in proportion to their clinical efficacy [see Snyder et al., 1974]. Increased dopamine is associated with blockade of dopamine receptors because of a neuronal feedback mechanism which stimulates dopamine production when none is being received by the receptors. Iversen [1975] has reviewed evidence that antipsychotic drugs inhibit an enzyme, adenykate cyclase, which mediates the action of dopamine at dopaminergic receptor sites.

There are other important classes of evidence. The stimulant drug amphetamine (discussed later in the chapter), best known for its NA potentiating effects, also increases dopaminergic activity. Very large doses of amphetamine produce a psychosis which is indistinguishable from acute schizophrenia. In addition it can produce a worsening of the symptoms in mild schizophrenia or a return of symptoms in a recovered schizophrenic. The patient experiences amphetamine induced psychotic symptoms as identical to his previous schizophrenic symptoms, unlike the instances in which improved or recovered schizophrenics have taken psychotomimetic drugs, such as LSD [Snyder et al., 1974]. The best antitdotes for amphetamine initiated or intensified psychosis are the dopamine blocking anti-schizophrenic phenothiazine and butyrophenone drugs. One of the distinctive psychotic symptoms which high doses of amphetamine produce in man and animals is stereotyped compulsive behaviour including picking, searching, sniffing, and gnawing. Direct injection of DA into the DA pathways of the corpus striatum, nucleus accumbens and olfactory tubercule elicits similar stereotyped behaviour in rats. Conversely lesioning of the same dopamine pathways abolishes amphetamine induced stereotyped compulsive behaviour [Snyder et al., 1974].

The phenothiazines have side effects which are also evidence that they block dopaminergic activity. They produce disorders of the motor system like those seen in Parkinson's disease, which is known to be due to degeneration of DA pathways in the extrapyramidal motor system of the corpus striatum [e.g. see Iversen, 1975]. Recently new phenothiazines (clazapine, thioridazine) have been synthesized which do not produce the highly undesirable extrapyramidal side effects. This appears to occur, not because blockade of DA receptors is reduced, but because there is additional blockade of acetylcholine receptors. It is speculated that this avoids an imbalance between the activity of dopaminergic and cholinergic systems which is responsible for disordered motor system function.

Finally, when considering the mode of action of antischizophrenic drugs we should remember that, as phenothiazines affect virtually all transmitter systems, it may be that observable effects on behaviour stem from a complex modification of the pattern of interaction between more than one system.

Animals do not exhibit any clear analogue of human schizophrenic behaviour. Nevertheless antischizophrenic drugs have been administered to animals behaving in conditioning paradigms to try to make a precise determination of their behavioural effects [for review see Iversen and Iversen, 1975, pp. 246–253]. A general observation has been that CPZ abolishes anticipatory avoidance behaviour, conditioned to a warning stimulus, but leaves escape behaviour, produced by a painful shock, unaffected. CPZ has a greater effect on behavioural control by weak discriminative stimuli than strong ones. Avoidance behaviour triggered by the general environment of an experimental box is more readily abolished by CPZ than that evoked by a specific warning stimulus.

In an experiment in which a fixed ratio (FR) reinforcement schedule (50 lever presses per reinforcement) changed to a fixed interval (FI) schedule (reinforcement of first response after 15 min) CPZ treated rats failed to change their response patterns in the way that controls did. During the FI regime they maintained the high constant rates of lever pressing appropriate to the FR schedule. In a more complicated experiment periods when reinforcement was available were alternated with periods when it was not. Following CPZ administration rats relied less on internal temporal cues about reward availability and made more use of an additional response key which enabled the animal to obtain more precise information (a visual indication of whether or not reinforcement was available) [Cook and Kelleher, 1962]. This experiment clearly indicates that the response decrements usually produced by CPZ are due to diminished ability to discriminate internal and external stimuli and not due to a more generalized depression of drives. This was also shown in a rather different study of the effects of CPZ on social behaviour in rats [Silverman, 1965]. Whereas activity and exploratory behaviour was unchanged by CPZ, social responses elicited by exteroceptive cues were markedly diminished.

Most of the effects of CPZ on animals can be interpreted as a reduction of stimulus control of behaviour, stemming from loss of stimulus salience. A characteristic of human schizophrenic thought disorder is that normally trivial stimuli acquire an undeserved salience. They are perceived with heightened intensity and attributed special significance. This intensified stimulus salience disrupts the mechanisms of attentional control. Either stimuli irrelevant to needs dominate attention at the expense of relevant stimuli, or attention shifts from one irrelevant focus to another. It has been claimed that the intensification of perceptual experience in schizophrenia is similar to that induced by hallucinogenic drugs, such as mescalin or LSD-25. The effects of mescalin have been vividly described by Huxley

[1959]. It may be that the antischizophrenic effects of CPZ derives from a capacity to reduce stimulus salience or perceptual intensity, so that consciousness is no longer distorted, and stimulus control of behaviour conforms to an individual's adaptive needs.

Unlike anxiety reducing drugs, which can only be claimed to ameliorate symptoms produced by the interaction of genetic make-up, past experience and present environment, it can be argued that chlorpromazine actually cures schizophrenia [see Levitt and Krikstone, 1975, p. 120]. It usually brings about a dramatic disappearance of symptoms and it has produced returns to normality so complete and long lasting that 'a basic modification of the psychotic process' is indicated [Longo, 1972, p. 10]. However, we should observe that while neuroleptics might correct a biochemical anomaly in the brain, it is unlikely that they operate on the original cause. Thus it is a cure only in the sense that insulin is a cure for diabetes or a phenylalanine free diet a cure for phenylketonuria.

Stimulant and antidepressant drugs

Exerting an opposite effect on the nervous system to the depressant drugs are the stimulants and antidepressants. These are drugs which increase the level of excitation in one or more of the subsystems of the nervous system. Their main clinical use is to counteract psychological depression, which appears to be characterized by a depression of neural activity in the brain, particularly in the substrates mediating the experience of pleasure (see Chapter 14). In addition, because they induce feelings of well being by increasing alertness and energy, and counteracting drowsiness and fatigue, they invite use for recreational and occupational purposes. This use can have severe dangers.

There are a number of stimulants of great antiquity which are regularly consumed by most members of our society. These include the xanthine derivatives. Theobromine is a weak stimulant found in cocoa and chocolate. Caffeine is a powerful stimulant found in coffee and tea and will be discussed in more detail. Caffeine reaches peak blood levels 30–60 min after oral ingestion. However, the poor solubility of the xanthines in water makes the effects of their oral ingestion variable, due to erratic absorption.

Caffeine has an excitatory effect on the CNS, commencing at the cortex and spreading progressively to the medulla and spinal cord. It produces EEG and behavioural arousal, a more buoyant mood and it retards sleep. In large doses stimulation of medullary centres increases respiration and heart rate. In very large doses an increase in reflex excitability throughout the NS can produce convulsions and death. Caffeine can produce dependence, probably seen in its chronic consumption in tea and coffee by many members of our society. However, withdrawal symptoms, such as mild depression, are slight.

Excess caffeine intake (e.g. more than 10–12 cups of coffee or tea per day) can produce symptoms of poisoning including feverishness, flushing, chilliness, insomnia, irritability, and weight loss. In a case known to the writer a university lecturer was experiencing excessive aggressive feelings and vertigo and a psychiatrist commenced investigation of his background and relations with his wife. It was eventually discovered that stopping his consumption of upwards of 12 cups of tea per day was all that was needed to eliminate his neurotic symptoms.

Another common stimulant is the cholinergic drug nicotine, usually ingested in the smoke from tobacco leaves. Nicotine causes membrane depolarization at the nicotinic receptors of cholinergic synapses. It is such an effective agent that at larger doses its stimulant action on neural function turns to an inhibitory one as it produces depolarization block—the blockage of transmission due to prolonged depolarization. At very large doses the successive excitatory and inhibitory effects can produce heart failure, respiratory paralysis, convulsions, and death.

In low doses (such as obtained by cigarette smoking) nicotine acts on the autonomic ganglia and causes peripheral vasoconstriction, increased blood pressure and release of adrenaline and noradrenaline from the adrenal gland. The latter probably have secondary stimulant effects which increase alertness. Nicotine is an addictive drug. Thus tolerance to its effects develops over time and withdrawal produces drowsiness, headache, cramps, digestive disorders, insomnia, and nervousness. Schachter [1973, 1974] has elegantly shown that heavy smokers regulate their rate of smoking to maintain a constant level of nicotine in their bloodstream. Thus cigarette consumption is increased when the nicotine content of cigarettes is reduced. Also cigarette consumption rises at parties or during periods of intense anxiety, not because of a direct psychological function of smoking, but because emotional arousal results in the more rapid excretion of nicotine.

Cocaine, which is extracted from the coca plant in Peru, is a fast acting CNS stimulant taken by chewing coca leaves, intravenous injection and even by sniffing. It produces cortical arousal, talkativeness, restlessness, excitement and marked mood elevation in humans. It combats fatigue and produces feelings of great muscular strength and increased mental capacity. At low doses it does not appear to produce addiction. Freud, the father of psychoanalysis, used cocaine until he observed a friend, who had taken a toxic dose, hallucinating snakes creeping over the skin. At higher doses tolerance, and thus addiction does develop, withdrawal of the drug producing depression and fatigue.

Another group of drugs which have a powerful stimulant effect on adrenergic pathways are the amphetamines (including benzedrine, dextroamphetamine, and the more potent methamphetamine). Amphetamine increases the excitability of adrenergic synapses by releasing noradrenaline from the synaptic nerve terminals by displacement. Its effect is further enhanced by its preventing the reuptake of NA [see Levitt and Lonorski, 1975, p. 62]. That amphetamine enhances the release of NA is supported by the fact that drugs, such as α-methyl-p-tyrosine, which suppress the biosynthesis of catecholamines, block the stimulant effect of amphetamines on behaviour [see Iversen and Iversen, 1975, p. 169].

Amphetamine is usually taken orally, but can be injected, and produces an intensely pleasurable euphoria and excitement. There is an intense feeling of mental and physical well-being. Thought seems particularly clear and incisive, and there is a feeling of muscular strength and energy. These feelings are well-founded as amphetamine has been found to improve both intellectual and athletic performance [e.g. see Smith and Beecher, 1959,

1960a, 1960b]. Because of this effect amphetamines were widely used by all participants during the Second World War to improve the performance of combatants, particularly when prolonged wakefulness was required. The large stocks of amphetamine accumulated during the war contributed to the epidemics of amphetamine abuse, particularly in America and Japan, which occurred in the years that followed.

As a concomitant to its stimulating effects amphetamine produces an increase in locomotor activity in man and animals. This is an increase in motor activity *per se* and not an increase in exploratory behaviour [Iversen and Iversen, 1975, p. 172]. Amphetamine increases response rates when lever pressing, both for anticipatory shock avoidance and for reward. On an FI reinforcement schedule responding increases more at the beginning of the interval than at the end, just prior to reinforcement. The drug generally has more effect on rates of response when they are low prior to administration than when they are high. When an animal is required to make a 'hold lever down' response to forestall punishment, amphetamine disrupts performance [Lyon and Randrupp, 1972], presumably because the static nature of the response is incompatible with the animal's strong activity drive.

High doses of amphetamines in humans and animals produce 'stereotypy', in which 'fixed response patterns' are repeatedly performed without relevance to environmental stimuli. This is illustrated by the apocryphal story of the student who took heavy doses of amphetamine while preparing for an examination and then, when in the exam, simply wrote his name over and over again. Repeated intravenous injections of amphetamine may produce psychotic symptoms, including paranoid suspicion of those around one and hallucinations of skin parasites which are repeatedly picked at.

Amphetamine can produce quite extreme symptoms of dependence, although it does not produce the severe physical withdrawal symptoms of the classically addicting narcotic drugs, morphine and heroin. After an amphetamine 'binge' the taker 'crashes', with feelings of fatigue and depression. Dependence may be induced by the reinforcing effects of the drug arising from excitation of the MFB reward system. The subjective correlate of the reinforcement is feelings of intense pleasure. There is a close analogy between patterns of amphetamine self-administration and intracranial self-stimulation behaviour (see Chapters 4 and 9). In both instances the behaviour continues frenetically, ignoring hunger, thirst and other drives, until exhaustion intervenes. In addition amphetamines potentiate self-stimulation behaviour [Snyder *et al.*, 1974].

We should also mention the anorexic effects of amphetamine, which has led to its use as an appetite suppressant in obese people. It is thought that this stems from the NA releasing properties of amphetamine, but there is disagreement about the precise mechanism. There is inevitably reservation about using amphetamines for therapeutic purposes because of their potential for producing dependence and abuse.

Antidepressant drugs

Antidepressant drugs are discussed separately from other stimulant drugs because they appear to have mood elevating effects which are specific to depressed patients. Drugs, like amphetamine, which have a stimulant effect on normal individuals, are often ineffective as antidepressants [Goodwin and Murphy, 1974, p. 16], and conversely antidepressant drugs are not stimulant in normals.

Two important classes of drugs, the monoamine oxidase (MAO) inhibitors and the tricyclic compounds, have mood elevating effects which are particularly noticeable in depressives. These two classes of drugs have made an immense contribution to relieving the intense suffering caused by this endemic illness. Individuals who, at different times, have suffered from depression and undergone major abdominal surgery, have expressed a preference for experiencing the intense pain and discomfort of the latter to the misery of depression.

The mood elevating effect of the MAO inhibitor iproniazid was discovered accidentally when the drug was being used to treat tuberculosis sufferers [Delay et al., 1952]. The euphoric effects of the drug were attributed to MAO inhibition [Kline, 1959] and it was introduced into psychiatry to ameliorate the symptoms of depressed patients [see Remmien, 1962].

It is thought that MAO inhibitors, by reducing enzymatic (i.e. by MAO) destruction of the biogenic amines, particularly noradrenaline (NA) and serotonin (5-HT), increase their availability at central synapses in the brain. The evidence includes the observations that MAO inhibitors reverse reserpine induced depression and decrease the levels of metabolites resulting from the enzymatic degradation of brain amines. Also increased biogenic amine levels have been recorded in autopsy observations of terminally ill depressed patients who have been treated with MAO inhibitors [see Biel and Bopp, 1974, pp. 302-309 for review].

MAO inhibitors administered to rats increase their rate of response for intracranial self-stimulation in the MFB and related reward areas. From this observation Stein and Wise [1969] have suggested that MAO inhibitors may lift depression by increasing the sensitivity of the noradrenergic reward systems of the forebrain so that subjectively the patient can once again enjoy experiences which normally elicit pleasure. Iversen and Iversen [1975, pp. 196-198, 204] hesitate to attribute the stimulating effects of MAO inhibitors exclusively to their potentiating effects on noradrenergic systems as both 5-HT and other rarer amines, which could be pharmacologically important, are released (see also the discussion of the biochemistry of depression in the previous chapter).

MAO inhibitors usually have a latency of about two to three weeks before their antidepressant effects are felt. They appear to be most effective in individuals with good premorbid personalities who become neurotically depressed following distressing events in their lives. Accompanying symptoms might be phobic anxiety, concentration difficulty, and disturbed sleep patterns.

MAO inhibitors such as iproniazid, izocarboxazide, and nialamide, which are derivatives of hydrazine, are highly toxic to the liver, making long term use dangerous. This has led to their supplementation by a group of amphetamine derived MAO inhibitors, including tranilcypromine (Parnate) and pargyline (Eutonyl). However, as observed previously patients taking MAO inhibitors must avoid cheese, wines, and beers which contain the adrenergic amine, tyramine. The drug eliminates the detoxification mechanism for this substance which has such a strong stimulant action on the sympathetic nerve endings that it can precipitate cardio-vascular traumas, such as a stroke.

Undesirable psychological effects produced by MAO inhibitors include mania and outward expression of paranoid delusional systems. Also, in the latency period, before the MAO inhibitors have taken their full effect, there may be a danger of the patient committing suicide. This can arise when psychomotor inertia is reduced, while ideas of worthlessness, hope-lessness, and black despair remain. In a case known to the author there was an indication that a death caused by eating cheese, while taking MAO inhibitors, was a suicide.

The tricyclic antidepressants

A further group of antidepressant drugs are derivatives of the previously discussed neuroleptic phenothiazines and are called the tricyclics, because of their chemical structure. They include imipramine (Tofranil), amitripty-line (Elavil), desmethylimipramine (Norpramin), and desmethyl amitripty-line (Aventyl). Like MAO inhibitors, the tricyclic drugs increase the levels of functionally available cerebral biogenic amines at central synapses, but they achieve this by the rather different mechanism of preventing their reuptake at the synapses.

Tricyclics are more enigmatic in their effects than MAO inhibitors. It usually takes at least a week and up to three weeks before their anti-depressant effects are felt. There may be a danger of suicide during this period. When time is given for the tricyclics to work they appear to be very effective in both lifting depression and preventing the relapses to which depressives are prone. In a survey of controlled studies imipramine produced recovery in a mean of 67% of patients in experimental groups of depressives, compared with 19% spontaneous remissions and 40% remis-sions in groups taking placebos [Lehmann, 1966].

During the latency period the action of the tricyclics is more like a sedative. Patients may report the unpleasant feeling that they are psycho-logically numb and remote from their surroundings. In behavioural studies on animals responding both for food and shock avoidance, on both FI and FR schedules, is reduced. This may have occurred because the observations were made before late coming stimulant effects of the drug emerged.

Some clinicians argue that the tricyclic drugs are more effective in the treatment of supposed endogenous depressions, lacking external causes and accompanied by bodily symptoms such as headache, pressure on the chest, weight loss and sleeplessness (caused by early waking). Warburton [1975, pp. 58-60] maintains that a differential response to the two drug groups confirms that reactive (or neurotic) depression and endogenous depression are two distinct clinical entities. He goes on to hypothesize that MAO inhibitors relieve reactive depression by compensating for low rates of synthesis of catecholamines. On the other hand tricyclics are surmised to relieve endogenous depression by compensating for an inadequate mechanism for transmitter release at the presynaptic endings.

With the introduction of the MAO inhibitors and the tricyclic drugs, the intensity and duration of black despair, faced by depressives, have both been dramatically reduced. As with the antischizophrenic drugs it could be argued that these drugs cure depression in the same way that insulin cures diabetes, by correcting a biochemical deficiency. The effectiveness of tricyclics in preventing relapse in depressives even suggests that they may remedy the root cause of the illness in some instances.

In recent years the MAO inhibitors have lost some of their popularity as antidepressants outside of England, largely because of their toxicity for the liver and the dangers associated with transgressing the dietary restrictions. In addition a number of other substances (including the monoamine precursors L-dopa and L-tryptophan, lithium, thyroid hormones and thyrotropin releasing peptides) have been tested for their antidepressant effects with varying degrees of success [for recent review see Biel and Bopp, 1974]. There has been some promise in the use of L-tryptophan. Lithium has been more valuable in the treatment of mania. Thyroid hormones, which cause a rapid increase in noradrenaline turnover, appear to have value in accelerating and enhancing the antidepressant effects of the tricyclic drugs.

The narcotic analgesics

We now come to consider drugs that do not readily fit into the categories of depressive or stimulant and which, in a number of cases are notorious because of their reputation as drugs of abuse. The first class of drugs which we will look at are the opiates or narcotic analgesics. The term 'opiate' derives from the name of the naturally occurring prototype, opium. This is found in the dried juice 'bled' from the seed pod of the poppy, *Papaver somniferum*, in the brief period between loss of the petals and the seed pod bursting. Opium is a drug of great antiquity which the Greek physician Galen described as a panacea for many ills, and which, as recently as the nineteenth century, was an almost invariable ingredient of patent medicines claimed to cure any imaginable disease.

Opium and its more refined derivatives morphine and heroin have their best known and primary effects as analgesics and euphoriants. However, euphoria is only experienced by about 10% of first-time takers who are not in pain [Criswell and Levitt, 1975]. Even addicts report that their first experience of narcotics was unpleasant, and that they had to learn to enjoy the effects. The narcotics have by far their greatest impact when injected intravenously, the route favoured by addicts who call injection 'mainlining'.

The opium derivative morphine has widespread medical application for the relief of pain and, by its euphoriant effects, the anxiety and dread associated with intensely painful injuries and illnesses. Morphine appears to combine excitant and depressive effects. The former is evident in its euphoriant, mentally stimulating effects and the latter in its analgesic, sedative and sleep inducing properties. There is evidence that morphine's analgesic properties arise because it binds to postsynaptic receptor sites in midbrain structures. However, both the analgesic and other effects appear to occur because morphine acts at a variety of other cerebral sites and modifies transmission in the brain's three major neurochemically defined systems; the noradrenergic, serotoninergic, and dopaminergic.

The most dramatic secondary property of the narcotics is the rapid development of tolerance, resulting in the need for increasing doses to produce the same effect. The additional concomitant of tolerance is unpleasant withdrawal symptoms which can only be alleviated by another dose of the drug. The combination of rapidly developing tolerance and abstinence withdrawal symptoms is the major contributory factor to addiction.

Narcotics are addictive drugs *par excellence*. The basis of tolerance is not completely understood, but appears to involve changes in the synthetic rate of neurotransmitters to normalize the effects of foreign neuroactive substances. The nervous system comes to function normally only in the presence of the drug, and absence of the drug leads to abnormal neural activity because the rate of transmitter synthesis cannot rapidly be readjusted [see Warburton, 1975, pp. 136–139]. This abnormal level of activity is responsible for the withdrawal symptoms which compel addiction.

It is suggested that as dependence on a narcotic grows the basis of the compulsion shifts from positively reinforcing euphoria to aversion to negatively reinforcing withdrawal symptoms [Lindesmith, 1970]. The drug becomes merely the basis for maintaining normality. This is shown in narcotic addicted animals, whose pattern of response for morphine injections is merely to escape abstinence symptoms [Weeks, 1964].

Unfortunately recovery from the withdrawal symptoms and a period of abstinence do not cure the addict. In both humans and animals, in which narcotic addiction has been experimentally induced, access to a narcotic after a period of abstinence leads to a rapid resumption of the habit [Nichols, 1963]. The readjustment of the NS to drug free existence does not abolish the powerful acquired reinforcing properties of the drug, presumably represented in some permanent change in the NS.

The extraordinary power of the narcotics as reinforcers may arise because they can both induce intense pleasure and secure escape from intense discomfort. If Gray's [1971a, Chapter 9] theory is correct, that reward and successful escape from pain both activate the same reinforcement mediating system, then narcotics must produce summating effects which imprint them indelibly as reinforcers.

There is evidence that morphine initially increases NA in the MFB reward system, consistent with its reinforcing effect. The depletion of NA as the effects of the drug wear off is consistent with the depression which is one of the withdrawal symptoms. In addition morphine appears to depress activity in the periventricular grey area of the brain (bordering the ventricles), which Stein [1964] has postulated is a punishment area. This action may be the basis of the relief from both physical and psychological pain produced by narcotics [see Criswell and Levitt, 1975, p. 225].

To the addict, his narcotic becomes the only reinforcer which he seeks, all of his other activities being subordinated to obtaining his next supply. As this is expensive and the addict is usually unable to keep a job, he frequently resorts to crime to support his habit. Neglect of other basic physiological needs, particularly for food, often leads to the addict's premature death from malnutrition or illness.

Narcotic addiction is extremely difficult to cure. In some ways the most rational therapy is medically prescribed maintenance doses, which avert withdrawal symptoms and enable the addict to lead a near-normal life. This technique is used in the UK. An alternative is to transfer the addict to maintenance doses of the synthetic narcotic, methadone, which prevents withdrawal symptoms and itself has milder withdrawal symptoms. If narcotic addicts survive into middle age, then there is a chance that they will 'mature out' of the habit on gradually diminishing doses [Ray, 1972]. However, their chances of survival are small. They usually die from one or more causes which include malnutrition, poisoning by impure drugs, infection (often from use of non-sterile needles) and sometimes cardiovascular collapse and pulmonary oedema mysteriously produced by a low dose of heroin [Criswell and Levitt, 1975, p. 229]. It is thought that the latter could be an allergic response.

Consciousness distorting drugs

The last group of drugs to be considered distort consciousness. They distort consciousness in the sense that the taker may perceive any and every aspect of his environment, and even himself, in a way which is new and strange. The precise nature of the distortions, and particularly the drug taker's emotional response to them is highly variable and dependent on such factors as prior mental state, level of anxiety, prior expectations, the surroundings and the presence of companions. This emphasizes that drug effects are a product of interaction of the drug with other factors.

The distorting drugs are popularly termed hallucinogenic and sometimes psychotomimetic. However, they tend to produce distorted perception rather than genuine hallucinations. Also there appear to be distinctive differences between drug induced distortions of consciousness and those of schizophrenic psychosis [Krikstone and Levitt, 1975, p. 256].

Consciousness distorting drugs are not obviously stimulant or depressant, exhibiting both properties at different times. Their mode of action on the NS is not understood and Krikstone and Levitt [1975, p. 257] rather weakly conclude that 'the distorting drugs seem to alter or "distort" transmitter systems in some aberrant manner'. Distorting drugs are rarely used for medical purposes and they are usually taken for pleasure or to attain supposedly higher states of consciousness.

A number of consciousness distorting substances occur naturally and their use has a long history. They include mescalin from the peyote cactus (Figure 15.2) in Mexico; psilocybin from the 'sacred mushrooms', also found in Mexico; ololiqui from the South American morning glory plant; *Amanita muscaria* (fly agaric) mushrooms found in Northern Europe; marijuana, prepared from the hemp plant *Cannabis sativa*. In addition, ergot, a fungus which affects grain, particularly rye, can produce radical disturbances of thinking and consciousness, as well as unpleasant bodily symptoms, such as muscle spasms. Eating of infected rye during periods of famine, produced outbreaks of 'ergotism' in the middle ages.

In recent years a synthetic derivative of ergot, LSD-25 (D-lysergic acid diethylamide) has become the best known of the hallucinogenic drugs. It was discovered in 1943 in Switzerland by Hofmann [see Hofmann, 1968], who took the drug himself and gave the first account of its vision inducing and perception distorting properties. A further powerful synthetic hallucinogen which has been obtainable 'on the street' in America is DOM

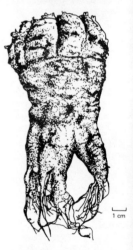

Figure 15.2
The cactus peyote, source of the hallucinogenic drug mescalin.

From Levitt, R. A. (Ed.), *Psychopharmacology: a biological approach.* Reproduced by permission of John Wiley and Sons Ltd., publishers

(2-5-methoxy-4-methylamphetamine). It is also known as STP variously claimed to stand for 'serentity, tranquillity, and peace' or 'scientifically treated petroleum' (after the fuel additive).

It is difficult to produce a strictly scientific account of the effects of consciousness distorting drugs because we are dependent on verbal description of what is an intensely subjective experience. Indeed some devotees of LSD maintain that it can produce an experience so profound and mystical as to be in the realms of the ineffable.

Overt behavioural changes produced by distorting drugs are unsystematic and confusing. Both improvements and decrements have been reported in discrimination task performance by animals under the influence of LSD [see Iversen and Iversen, 1975, pp. 263 *et seq*.). While the enhanced salience of stimuli may aid discrimination in one case, hallucinated stimuli may disrupt it in another. In humans the distorting drugs produce sensory and perceptual experiences of such intensity that the taker is inclined to cease any activity.

It is on consciousness that the distorting drugs have their most profound and important effects. Reliable knowledge of these effects and the variability of these effects can only be gained from an accumulation of verbal accounts in which certain consistencies are apparent.

One of the most vivid and eloquent accounts of changes in consciousness produced by a distorting drug (mescalin) is in Aldous Huxley's *Doors of Perception* [1959]:

'Half an hour after swallowing the drug,' he wrote, 'I became aware of a slow dance of golden lights. A little later there were sumptuous red surfaces, swelling and expanding from bright nodes of energy that vibrated with a continuously changing patterned life.' Speaking of a 'nosegay' of flowers in clashing colours he said: 'I was not looking now at an unusual flower arrangement. I was seeing what Adam had seen on the morning of his creation—the miracle, moment by moment, of naked existence. . .a bunch of flowers shining with their own inner light and all but quivering under the pressure of the significance with which they were charged. . .a transience that was yet eternal life. . .a bundle of minute, unique particulars in which, by some unspeakable and yet self-evident paradox, was to be seen the divine source of all existence.' [Huxley, 1959, p. 17].

The drug experience imbues objects perceived by the taker with a new and profound significance and they seem to generate a sense that ultimate and eternal truths have at last been understood. Huxley continues: 'I continued to look at the flowers, and in their living light I seemed to detect the qualitative equivalent of breathing—but of breathing without return to a starting point, with no recurrent ebbs but only a repeated flow from beauty to heightened beauty, from deeper to ever deeper meaning. Words like Grace and Transfiguration came to my mind' [Huxley, 1959, pp. 17–18].

Huxley discourses extensively on the relationship of the mescalin experience to the artist's perception of the world. He says: 'What the rest of us see only under the influence of mescalin the artist is congenitally equipped to see all the time. His perception is not limited to what is socially or biologically useful. A little of the knowledge belonging to mind at large oozes past the reducing valve of the brain and ego into his consciousness' [Huxley, 1959, p. 21].

Figure 15.3
An artist's impression of how he perceived his own body when under the influence of lysergic acid diethylamide (LSD).

From Levitt, R. A. (Ed.), psychopharmacology: biological approach. Reproduced by permission of John Wiley and Sons Ltd., Publishers

Perceptual changes induced by LSD and other distorting drugs resemble those induced by mescalin. However, LSD is much more powerful than mescalin and is taken in minute quantities. The effects include intensification of all sensory experiences, spontaneous changes in the perceived size of objects, distortions of the taker's body image (see Figure 15.3), feelings of depersonalization and slowing of the perceived passage of time. Another unusual phenomenon is synesthesia in which sensations are experienced in a different modality from that of their origin. For instance sounds may give rise to colour sensations.

It appears that the basis for distorted and intensified sensations may lie partly within the sensory systems themselves. Horn and Mackay [1973] have shown that LSD radically modifies the response of visual receptive field cells in the lateral geniculate nuclei of cats. Sensory and perceptual experience is probably also intensified by an increase in sensitivity of collateral afferent fibres feeding the reticular activating system [Krikstone and Levitt, 1975, p. 262].

The emotional responses to LSD can vary from the euphoria described, to panic. This depends on the taker's prior mental state, expectation and the setting in which they have the drug experience. Panic is most likely to occur when there is little prior knowledge of the drug's effects together with anxiety about what they may be.

Another phenomenon experienced by LSD takers is the 'flashback' in which the effects recur without any further dose of the drug, weeks or months after a 'trip'. Any intense emotional experience can produce a flashback at a later date. Shell shocked soldiers may relive their wartime experiences many years after they occurred. Presumably, like any intense experience, the LSD experience produces a strong 'engram' which is 'replayed' given the right cues.

Instances of LSD trips precipitating frank psychoses have been reported, but these have usually been in individuals with a previous psychiatric history, and in some cases have been caused by impurities or additives in the LSD, such as amphetamine.

Marijuana

Tetrahydrocannabinol, the psychoactive ingredient in marijuana is a powerful distorting drug, but is only absorbed in small amounts when smoked in 'hash' or 'grass'. In small doses it produces effects similar to the 'merry' phase of alcohol intoxication. There is an ebullient mood, loss of psychological and physical tension, loss of inhibition and a tendency to giggle a lot because anything and everything is found amusing. Intensified sensations may lead to a desire to be left alone. There may be a pleasant floating sensation so that walking seems like an effortless transition from one place to another, and the time sense is distorted. Short-term memory is impaired which appears to be the reason why people high on cannabis are unable to sustain a conversation.

It has been observed that the cannabis taker must learn to perceive, control and then enjoy its physiological effects [Becker, 1967]. The first time taker may completely fail to experience a high. It has also been claimed that there is a reverse tolerance effect whereby an individual can get high on less and less of the drug. This may reflect a process of learning to perceive the effects however. In one study chronic marijuana users persistently underestimated the potency of the drug that they were being given, suggesting that tolerance had developed [Jones, 1971]. However, marijuana produces no hangover and no withdrawal symptoms as an obvious physical basis for dependence. In the chronic user any dependence must be 'psychological', based on more subtle factors.

A consequence of chronic marijuana use, in which an individual keeps himself high virtually all of the time, is a profound loss of drive. The user appears quite happy, but is slow in speech and movement, vague, and incoherent in conversation and appears absorbed in a purely passive enjoyment of his own state of consciousness [e.g. Krikstone and Levitt, 1975, p. 297]. As a concomitant he usually neglects educational or occupational ambitions, social obligations and even his own physical well being.

The validity of drug experiences

An account of the consciousness changing effects of the distorting drugs leads to questions about the status of different classes of conscious experience. The LSD taker is clearly experiencing the world and himself in a way which is radically different from those of us in a more normal state of consciousness. The experience may assume the status of a revelation of cosmic significance, both during and after it occurs. It may even resemble a religious conversion experience and change the taker's life, as in the case of the archpriest of LSD, Timothy Leary [see Krikstone and Levitt, 1975, p. 264]. Indeed, in terms of both brain state and conscious content the LSD experience seems to resemble mystical states or religious conversion experiences occurring as the culmination of periods of physical and psychological privation. In both of these cases the subject is utterly convinced that he has had a vision of truth. The 'outsider', who has not had the experience, remains cool and sceptical.

Who therefore is right? Is LSD a sacred chemical, a vehicle through which God enables mere mortals to know his truth directly? It is obviously beyond the scope of this book to consider the wider ramifications of these questions. The power of revelatory experience can only be known to the experiencer, and the only test of its validity is its subjective impact. In other words it is self-validating. However, the psychobiologist can express some reservations about the validity of drug induced changes in consciousness. In the drugged state, as in psychotic illness, the individual perceives the world in a radically different way, and as a consequence his behaviour is radically changed. In extreme cases LSD trippers have experienced delusions of omnipotence which have led to their deaths in such instances as crossing busy roads in the belief that the traffic could not touch them. In less dramatic cases preoccupation with inner experience leads to neglect of vital needs such as food. It is obvious that extensive chemically induced changes in the brain can lead to behaviour which is wholly inconsistent with survival. There is some danger that a drug evoked vision of the divine could lead to a premature departure from this earth to join the gods! Only by denial of the biological imperative of survival and acceptance of a religion which devalues life on this earth could we sustain a belief that drug distorted consciousness had greater validity than more normal states.

Summary

Both consciousness and, concomitantly, behaviour, can be altered by the administration of drugs which modify brain chemistry. The sensitivity of the nervous system to chemical agents arises because transmission at the synapse is achieved by the release of a neurotransmitter chemical from the presynaptic terminal. Drugs which inhibit neural function may do so by blocking the synthesis of neurotransmitter substances, promoting their intra or extraneural enzymatic degradation or by competing for attachment to postsynaptic receptor sites. Drugs enhancing neural function may act by increasing transmitter synthesis, inhibiting the enzymes which inactivate transmitters, increasing transmitter release, blocking the reuptake of transmitter at presynaptic terminals or mimicking the transmitter action at the postsynaptic terminals.

Psychoactive drugs are a powerful tool for the treatment of mental illness, but must be used with great caution. The dangers associated with drug taking include toxic side effects, addiction, and deformation of the foetus in pregnant women. A drug may alleviate conspicuous symtoms but also produce unwelcome dulling of awareness and deterioration of cognitive and perceptuomotor performance. Also treatment of symptoms with drugs may be a too easy alternative to identifying and eliminating the root causes of neurotic disturbance in the sufferer's environment and life style. It can even be argued that drugs may be wrongly used to blunt emotions, which although distressing at the time, are a valid and important part of psychological growth. The prescription of drugs should be in the context of a global view of the total pattern of interacting factors determining an individual's mental state.

Each of the major drug groups and subgroups is discussed. The depressant drugs, including alcohol and the barbiturates selectively or generally depress neural function. They produce progressively loss of inhibitions, sedation, unconsciousness and, in very high doses, death. The depressant tranquillizers, including the propanediols and benzodiazepines, have a milder sedative effect. The neuroleptic drugs, including the rauwolfias and phenothiazines (e.g. chlorpromazine) and butyrophenones have a specific antipsychotic effect which remains when tolerance has developed to their sedative effect. These drugs have revolutionized the treatment of schizophrenia.

The stimulant drugs, including caffein, nicotine, cocaine, and the amphetamines enhance neural function and by so doing elevate mood, improve cognitive and motor performance and increase motor activity levels. High doses of stimulants may produce psychotic episodes or inhibition by depolarization block. There is rebound depression of mood when the effects of the stimulants wear off. Monoamine oxidase (MAO) inhibitors and tricyclic drugs (e.g. imipramine) have strong and specific mood elevating effects which make them very valuable in the treatment of depression. They appear to increase the availability of the biogenic amines, particularly NA and 5-HT (5-hydroxytryptamine) and consequently increase the sensitivity of the MFB reward areas. ·

The narcotic analgesics are not readily classifiable as depressant or stimulant. The opiates (opium, morphine, and heroin) have powerful pain killing and euphoriant effects which make them valuable for the relief of suffering in medical practice. However, tolerance to these drugs develops rapidly. The consequent intensely unpleasant withdrawal symptoms are a major contribution to their powerful addictive properties. Addiction to these drugs is almost impossible to cure.

A final group of drugs, which include mescalin, psylocybin, ololiqui, amanita muscaria, and marijuana distort consciousness by effects on the nervous system which are little understood. The precise subjective and behavioural effects of these drugs are a function of several internal and external factors including expectations and surroundings. The emotional response varies from ecstasy to terror. Perception of commonplace objects is highly intensified and the drug induced experience may seem to be a revelation of profound and often religious significance.

Postscript: The physical brain, human choice, and human survival

It remains to re-emphasize some of the general principles relating brain, behaviour, and consciousness, and to tentatively assess the implications and value of their study for our society in its present state.

All of the evidence in this book supports the principle postulate that all of our conscious content and behaviour is generated by a hypercomplex physical system, namely the nervous system and particularly the brain. An implicit corollary is that this system obeys the laws of physics. This could, of course, include undiscovered laws. The nervous system is in a continuous dialogue with the environment, responding to internal and external physical stimuli. It must be emphasized that even 'psychological' stimuli are reducible to patterns of physical stimuli, albeit complex.

To many people the statement that the brain is simply a physical system is tantamount to saying that it is merely a determined machine. This is rejected on emotional grounds as being quite repugnant, an affront to human dignity and a denial of the autonomy we claim to have. The error in this response is to suppose that it is claimed that man's brain is a machine of similar complexity and scope to man-made machines which are subordinate to man's will and inflexible in their capabilities. The subtlety and complexity of man's brain is infinitely greater than even the most powerful computer. Its internal state and processes are determined by such a multiplicity of complex interacting variables, genetic and environmental, past and present that behavioural biologists despair of ever disentangling them. Although they may be in accordance with the laws of physics, and thus notionally determinable, the causal antecedents of any mental or behavioural event are ultimately infinitely complex. Discernment of the major causes of behaviour may enable behavioural scientists to make some predictions, but they can only be grossly probabilistic in most cases.

Knowledge of the subtlety and complexity of the human brain should enhance rather than diminish human dignity. We know that it represents the culmination of an evolutionary trend towards flexibility, gradually elaborated over countless generations. Plasticity in neural networks and modifiability of behaviour are primary human properties. This permits a wide range of choice of survival strategies, lifestyles and cultural forms. We have a wide ranging intelligence to develop and exercise. To attribute choice to the brain seems to contradict previous assertions that it is a determined physical system. However, when the causal antecedents of a mental event are infinitely extended and complex, and therefore in reality indeterminable, 'choice' reasserts itself as a proper term to describe the subjective state in which alternative courses of action are perceived as being possible.

To know and understand the evolution of the brain and the concomitant emergence of behavioural flexibility creates an important perspective from which to view and criticize human civilization. The utility of behavioural flexibility in satisfying the survival imperative gave a momentum to the evolution of the brain which has enabled it to transcend the mere satisfaction of survival needs. We have the spare capacity to define and satisfy higher needs only tenuously related to our biological ones. At the birth of civilization we entered a new non-biological phase of evolution. By technological evolution we have consolidated and perfected our adaptive abilities, and by social and cultural evolution we have expanded our consciousness. Activities over and above the satisfaction of primary needs, such as philosophy, art and science, are self-validating by the subjective satisfactions which they generate. They may be complexly based on primary drives, particularly the drive for varied stimulus patterns. However, they transcend their roots by virtue of the plasticity and interactive capacity of human brain systems. Human higher activities, for instance the elaboration of social life and cultural forms and the cultivation of fine emotions, are only able to exist in conjunction with a sustained ability to meet survival needs from exertion of a fraction of available energies. The degradation of human social and cultural behaviour when a society cannot meet its survival needs has been vividly described by Turnbull [1973] in his book on the unfortunate African tribe, the Ik.

While accepting that the human brain is the basis of behavioural flexibility in its most highly developed form on this earth, we must remain fully aware of its potential for error. Adaptive mechanisms are selected during biological evolution because they have probabilistic rather than absolute utility for survival. When we are conceiving and choosing adaptive strategies the complexity of the environment and the limitations of human intelligence always carry the possibility of a wrong choice. The history of human civilizations and human technologies contains many disasters testifying to this likelihood.

In the past disaster arising out of the fallibility of man's intelligence were local and did not threaten species survival. In contemporary times strategies are applied on a worldwide scale, with the frightening corollary that an error could lead to worldwide disaster for mankind. We already have warnings that our over exploitation of natural resources and pollution of the environment could lead to ecological collapse. It could be argued that human economic and social organizations have become too centralized for their own safety. Human intelligence has difficulty in grasping the extraordinarily complex interaction between the elements and subsystems making up subcontinental, continental, or supracontinental ecosystems. In evolution the diversity of interacting elements in ecosystems could accommodate to local failures. Also, within species, sexual reproduction with genetic variation allowed for experimentation with diverse adaptive mechanisms within a central theme. It might be argued that, consistent with ecological principles, the human species could enhance its survival prospects by increasing, rather than decreasing, diversity and local autonomy.

It is implicit in the discussion of human futures that human intelligence could, depending on how it is applied, generate patterns of interaction with the environment leading to either catastrophe, or material security and fulfilment of our potential. We should observe the role that positive feedback loops can play in insuring our future. An important example of this is in education, in the broadest sense. The knowledge, skills and attitudes absorbed by the student determines how he interacts with his environment and how he contributes to the educational process, in his turn. If the apparatus of education, particularly educational institutions and the media (i.e. television, newspapers, etc.), can increase man's knowledge of his biological nature and his evolutionary and ecological context, then perhaps a contribution can be made to assisting man to conceive strategies which will enable him both to survive, and to proceed further along a fulfilling and enriching path of technological, social, and cultural evolution.

References

Adametz, J. H. (1959). Rate of recovery of functioning in cats with rostral reticular lesions. *J. Neurosurg.*, **16**, 85-98.

Adolph, E. F. (1947). *Physiology of man in the desert.* New York, Wiley (Interscience).

Adolph, E. F. (1950). Thirst and its inhibition in the stomach. *Amer. J. Physiol.*, **161**, 374-386.

Aghajanian, G. K., Foote, W. E., and Sheard, M. H. (1970). Action of psychotogenic drugs on single midbrain raphe neurones. *J. Pharmac. exp. Ther.*, **171**, 178-187.

Allison, A. C. (1954). Protection afforded by sickle cell trait against subtertian malarial infection. *Brit. Med. J.*, i, 290-292.

Allison, A. C. (1955). Aspects of polymorphism in man. Cold Spring Harbour Symp. *Quart. Biol.*, **20**, 239-255.

Allport, D. A., Antonis, B., and Reynolds, P. (1972). On the division of attention: a disproof of the single channel hypothesis. *Quart. J. Exp. Psychol.*, **24**, 225-235.

Altman, J., and Das, G. D. (1964). Autoradiographic examination of the effects of enriched environment on the rate of glial multiplication in adult rat brain. *Nature*, **204**, 1161-1163.

Altman, J., Das, G. D., and Chang, J. (1966). Behavioural manipulations and protein metabolism of the brain: effects of visual training on the utilization of Leucine-^{3}H. *Physiol. Behav.*, **1**, 111-115.

Amassian, V. E., Waller, H. J., and Macy, J., Jr. (1964). Neural mechanisms of the primary sensory evoked potential. *Annals. N.Y. Acad. Sci.*, **112**, (Art. 1), 5-32.

Anand, B. K. and Brobeck, J. R. (1951a). Hypothalamic control of food intake in rats and cats. *Yale J. Biol. Med.*, **24**, 123-140.

Anand, B. K., and Brobeck, J. R. (1951b). Localization of a 'feeding centre' in the hypothalamus of the rat. *Proc. Soc. Exptl. Biol. Med.*, **77**, 323-324.

Anand, B. K., Dua, S., and Singh, B. (1961). Electrical activity of the hypothalamic feeding centres under the effect of changes in blood chemistry. *Electroenceph. clin. Neurophysiol.*, **13**, 54-59.

Anand, B. K., Chhina, G. S., and Singh, B. (1962). Effect of glucose on the activity of hypothalamic 'feeding centres'. *Science*, **138**, 597-598.

Anderson, E. E. (1938). The interrelationship of drives in the male albino rat: III Interrelations among measures of emotional, sexual and exploratory behaviour. *J. genet Psychol.*, **53**, 335-352.

Anderson, E. G., and Bonnycastle, D. D. (1960). A study of the central depressant action of pentobarbital, phenobarbital and diethyl-ether in relationship to increases in brain serotonin. *J. Pharmacol. Exp. Therap.*, **130**, 138-146.

Anderson, P., and Anderson, S. A. (1968). *Physiological basis of the alpha rhythm.* New York, Appleton.

Andersson, B. (1952). Polydipsia caused by intrahypothalamic injections of hypertonic NaCl solutions. *Experientia*, **8**, 157-158.

Andersson, B., and McCann, S. M. (1955). Drinking, antidiureses and milk ejection from electrical stimulation within the hypothalamus of the goat. *Acta Physiol. Scand.*, **35**, 191-201.

Andersson, B., Grant, R., and Larsson, S. (1956). Central control of heat loss mechanisms in the goat. *Acta Physiol. Scand.*, **37**, 261-280.

Andersson, B., and Larsson, B. (1961). Influence of local temperature changes in the preoptic area and lateral hypothalamus on the regulation of food and water intake. *Acta Physiol. Scand.*, 52, 75–89.

Angeleri, F., Marchesi, G. F., and Quattrini, A. (1969). Effects of chronic thalamic lesions on the electrical activity of the neocortex and on sleep. *Arch. Ital. Biol.*, 107, 633–667.

Annis, R. C. and Frost, B. (1973). Human visual ecology and orientation anistropies in acuity. *Science*, 182, 729–731.

Arnold, M. B. (1950). An excitatory theory of emotion. In M. L. Reymert (Ed.), *The 2nd International Symposium on Feelings and Emotions*. New York, McGraw-Hill, pp. 11–33.

Arnold, M. B. (1970). Brain function in emotion: a phenomenological analysis. In P. Black (Ed.), *Physiological correlates of emotion*. New York and London, Academic Press, pp. 261–286.

Aronson, L. R., and Cooper, M. L. (1966). Seasonal variation in mating behaviour in cats after desensitization of glans penis. *Science*, 152, 226–230.

Aronson, L. R. and Cooper, M. L. (1967). Penile spines of the domestic cat: their endocrine-behaviour relations. *Anat. Rec.*, 157, 71–78.

Aronson, L. R., and Cooper, M. L. (1968). Desensitization of the glans penis and sexual behaviour in cats. In M. Diamond (Ed.), *Perspectives in reproduction and sexual behaviour*. Bloomington, University of Indiana Press.

Aserinsky, E., and Kleitman, N. (1953). Regularly occurring periods of eye motility, and concomitant phenomena during sleep. *Science*, 118, 273–274.

Ax, A. (1953). The physiological differentiation between fear and anger in humans. *Psychosomatic Medicine*, 15, 433.

Azmitia, E. C., Jr., McEwen, B. S., and Quartermain, D. (1972). Prevention of ECS induced amnesia by re-establishing continuity with the training situation. *Physiol. Behav.*, 8, 853–855.

Bacq, Z. (1931). Impotence of the male rodent after sympathetic denervation of the male genital organs. *Amer. J. Physiol.*, 96, 321–330.

Baddeley, A. D. (1972). Human memory. In P. C. Dodwell (Ed.) *New horizons in psychology 2*. Harmondsworth, Penguin Education, pp. 36–61.

Baekeland, F., and Lasky, R. (1966). Exercise and sleep patterns in college athletes. *Percept. Mot. Skills.*, 23, 1203–1207.

Baird, H. W., Szekely, E. G., Wycis, H. T., and Speigel, E. A. (1957). The effect of meprobamate on the basal ganglia. *Annals N.Y. Acad. Sci.*, 67, 873–884.

Ball, J. (1934). Normal sex behaviour in the rat after total extirpation of the vasa deferentia. *Anat. Rec.*, 58, 49.

Ball, J. (1936). Sexual responsiveness in female monkeys after castration and subsequent estrin administration. *Psychol. Bull.*, 33, 811.

Bard, P. (1928). A diencephalic mechanism for the expression of rage with special reference to the sympathetic nervous system. *Amer. Physiol.*, 84, 490–515.

Bard, P., and Mountcastle, V. B. (1948). Some forebrain mechanisms involved in expression of rage with special reference to suppression of angry behaviour. *Res. Publ. Ass. Nerv. Ment. Dis.*, 27, 362–404. Also reprinted in R. L. Isaacson (Ed.) (1964). *Basic readings in neuropsychology*. New York, Harper & Row, pp. 110–158.

Bardier, E. (1911). *Les fonctions digestives*. Paris, O. Doin.

Barlow, H. B., and Pettigrew, J. D. (1971). Lack of specificity of neurones in the visual cortex of young kittens. *J. Physiol.*, 218, 98–101.

Barondes, S. H., and Cohen, H. D. (1967). Comparative effects of cycloheximide and puromycin on cerebral protein synthesis and consolidation of memory in mice. *Brain Res.*, 4, 44–51.

Barondes, S. H., and Cohen, H. D. (1968). Arousal and the conversion of short-term memory to long-term memory. *Proc. Nat. Acad. Sci. U.S.A.*, 61, 923–929.

Barraco, R. A., and Stettner, L. J. (1976). Antibiotics and memory. *Psychol. Bull.*, 83, 242–302.

Bartlett, F. C. (1932). *Remembering: an experimental and social study*. London, Cambridge University Press.

Bateson, P. P. G., Horn, G., and Rose, S. P. R. (1972). Effects of early experience on regional incorporation of precursors into RNA and protein in the chick brain. *Brain. Res.*, 39, 449–465.

Batini, C., Moruzzi, G., Palestini, M., Rossi, G. F., and Zanchetti, A. (1959a). Effects of complete pontine transections on the sleep–wakefulness rhythm: The midpontine pretrigeminal preparation. *Arch. Ital. Biol.*, 97, 1–12.

Batini, C., Palestini, M., Rossi, G. F., and Zanchetti, A. (1959b). EEG activation patterns in the midpontine pretrigeminal cat following sensory deafferentation. *Arch. Ital. Biol.*, 97, 26–32.

Batini, C., Magni, F., Palestini, M., Rossi, G. F., and Zanchetti, A. (1959c). Neural mechanisms underlying the enduring EEG and behavioural activation in the midpontine pretrigeminal cat. *Arch. Ital. Biol.*, 97, 13–25.

Beach, F. A. (1942a). Analysis of the stimuli adequate to elicit mating behaviour in the sexually inexperienced male rat. *J. Comp. Physiol.*, 33, 163–207.

Beach, F. A. (1942b). Effects of testosterone propionate upon the copulatory behaviour of sexually inexperienced male rats. *J. Comp. Psychol.*, 33, 227–247.

Beach, F. A. (1947). A review of physiological and psychological studies of sexual behaviour in mammals. *Physiol. Rev.*, 27, 240–307.

Beach, F. A. (1958). Evolutionary aspects of psycho-endocrinology. In A. Rose and G. G. Simpson (Eds.), *Behaviour and evolution*. New Haven, Yale University Press.

Beach, F. A. (1968). Factors involved in the control of mounting behaviour by female mammals. In M. Diamond (Ed.), *Perspectives in reproduction and sexual behaviour*. Bloomington, Indiana University Press, 83-131.

Beach, F. A. (1970). Coital behaviour in dogs: VI long term effects of castration upon mating in the male. *J. Comp. Physiol. Psychol.*, **70**, 3, Pt. 2.

Beach, F. A., Zitrin, A., and Jaynes, J. (1955). Neural mediation of mating in male cats: II. Contributions of the frontal cortex. *J. Exp. Zoology.*, **130**, 381-402.

Beach, F. A. and Westbrook, W. H. (1968). Dissociation of androgenic effects on sexual morphology and behaviour in male rats. *Endocrinology*, **83**, 395-398.

Beach, G., Emmens, M., Kinble, D. P., and Lickey, M. (1969). Autoradiographic demonstration of bio-chemical changes in the limbic system during avoidance training. *Proc. Nat. Acad. Sci., U.S.A.*, **62**, 692-696.

Becker, H. S. (1967). History, culture and subjective experience: an exploration of the social base of drug induced experiences. *J. Health Soc. Behav.*, **8**, 163-176.

Beeman, E. A. (1947). The effect of male hormone on aggressive behaviour in mice. *Physiol. Zoo.*, **20**, 373-405.

Bekesy, G. (1957, reprinted 1971). The ear. in R. F. Thompson (Ed.), *Physiological psychology*. San Francisco, W. H. Freeman, pp. 232-241.

Bekesy, G. and Rosenblith, W. A. (1951). The mech-anical properties of the ear. In S. S. Stevens (Ed.), *Handbook of experimental psychology*. New York, John Wiley & Sons, pp. 1075-1115.

Bellows, R. T. (1939). Time factors in water drinking in dogs. *Amer. J. Physiol.*, **125**, 87-97.

Benzinger, T. H. (1962). The thermostatic regulation of human heat production and heat loss. *Proc. 22nd Internat. Congress Physiol. Sci.*, **1**, 415-438.

Bennett, E. L., Diamond, M. C., Krech, D., and Rosenzweig, M. R. (1964). Chemical and anatomi-cal plasticity of the brain. *Science*, **146**, 610-619.

Bergamini, L., and Bergamasco, B. (1967). *Cortical evoked potentials in man*. Springfield, Charles Thomas.

Berger, H. (1929). On the electroencephalogram of man. *Archiv für Psychiatrie und Nervenkrankheiten*, **87**, 527-570. Published in translation in P. Gloor (Ed.) (1969) Hans Berger on the Electroencephalo-gram in man. *Electroenceph. clin. Neurophysiol.*, Suppl. 28.

Berger, R. J. (1969). Ochlomotor control: a possible function of REM sleep. *Psychol. Rev.*, **76**, 144-164.

Berlyne, D. E. (1960). *Conflict, arousal and curiosity*. New York, McGraw-Hill.

Bertelson, P. (1966). Central intermittency twenty years later. *Quart. J. Exp. Psychol.*, **18**, 153-163.

Bexton, W. H., Heron, W., and Scott, T. H. (1954). Effects of decreased variation in the sensory environment. *Canad. J. Psychol.*, **8**, 70-76.

Bickford, R., Mulder, D. W., Dodge, H. W., Svien, H. J., and Rome, H. P. (1958). Changes in memory function produced by electrical stimulation of the temporal lobe in man. *Res. Publ. Ass. Res. Ner. Ment. Dis.*, **36**, 227-257.

Biel, J. H., and Bopp, B. (1974). Antidepressant drugs. In M. Gordon (Ed.) *Psychopharmacological agents*. New York, Academic Press, pp. 283-341.

Biederman, G. B. (1970). Forgetting of an operant response: physostigmine produced increases in escape latency in rats as a function of time of in-jection. *Quart. J. Exp. Psychol.*, **22**, 384-388.

Black, S., and Walter, W. G. (1965). Effects on anterior brain responses of variation in the probability of association between stimuli. *J. Psychosomatic Res.*, **9**, 33-43.

Blakemore, C., and Campbell, F. W. (1969). On the existence of neurones in the human visual system selectively sensitive to the orientation and size of retinal images. *J. Physiol.*, **203**, 237-260.

Blakemore, C., and Cooper, G. F. (1970). Development of the brain depends on the visual environment. *Nature*, **228**, 477-478.

Blakemore, C., and Nachmias, J. (1971). The orienta-tion specificity of two visual after effects. *J. Physiol. (Lond.)*, **213**, 157-174.

Blakemore, C., and Mitchell, D. E. (1973). Environ-mental modification of the visual cortex and the neural basis of learning and memory. *Nature*, **241**, 467-468.

Blix, M. (1884). Experimentelle Beiträge zur Lösung der Frage über die specifische Energie der Hautner-ven. *Zeitschrift für Biologie*, **20**, 141-156.

Bloch, G. J., and Davidson, J. M. (1968). Effects of adrenalectomy and experience on post-castration sex behaviour in the rat. *Physiol. Behav.*, **3**, 461-465.

Blumer, D., and Walker, E. (1967). Sexual behaviour in temporal lobe epilepsy. *Arch. Neurol.*, **16**, 37-43.

Blundell, J. E., and Herberg, L. J. (1973). Effectiveness of lateral hypothalamic stimulation. Arousal and food deprivation in the initiation of hoarding be-haviour in naive rats. *Physiol. Behav.*, **10**, 763-767.

Blurton-Jones, N. J. (1967). An ethological study of some aspects of social behaviour of children in nursery school. In D. Morris (Ed.), *Primate ethology*. London, Weidenfeld & Nicolson, pp. 347-368.

Boddy, J. (1972). The psychological refractory period and vertex evoked potentials. *Quart. J. Exp. Psy-chol.*, **24**, 175-192.

Boddy, J. (1973). Evoked potentials in reaction time with a variable foreperiod. *Quart. J. Exp. Psychol.*, **25**, 323-334.

Booth, D. A. (1968). Mechanism of action of nore-pinephrine in eliciting an eating response on injection into the rat hypothalamus. *J. Pharmacol. Exp. Therap.*, **160**, 336-348.

Booth, D. A. (1973). Protein synthesis and memory. In J. A. Deutsch (Ed.), *The physiological basis of memory*. New York and London, Academic Press, pp. 27-58.

Bowlby, J. (1951) *Maternal care and mental health.* Geneva, World Health Organization.

Bowman, R. E., and Kottler, P. D. (1970). Regional brain RNA metabolism as a function of different experiences. In R. E. Bowman and S. P. Datta (Eds.), *Biochemistry of Brain and Behaviour.* New York, Plenum Press, pp. 301–326.

Bowman, R. E., and Stroebel, D. A. (1969). Brain RNA metabolism in the rat during learning. *J. Comp. Physiol. Psychol.,* **67**, 448–456.

Brazier, M. A. B. (1962). Stimulation of the hippocampus in man using implanted electrodes. In M. A. B. Brazier (Ed.). *Brain Function,* Vol. 2, Berkeley, University of California Press, pp. 299–310.

Bremer, F. (1935). Cerveau isolé et physiologie du sommeil. *C.R. Soc. Biol. Paris,* **118**, 1235–1242.

Bremer, F. (1974). Historical development of ideas on sleep. In O. Petre-Quadens, and J. D. Schlag (Eds.), *Basic sleep mechanisms.* New York and London, Academic Press, pp. 3–11.

Bremer, J. (1959). *Asexualization.* New York, Macmillan.

Broadbent, D. (1954). The role of auditory localization and attention in memory span. *J. exp. Psychol.,* **47**, 191–196.

Broadbent, D. E. (1958). *Perception and communication.* London, Pergamon.

Broadhurst, P. L. (1957). Emotionality and the Yerkes–Dodson law. *J. exp. Psychol.,* **54**, 345–352.

Broadhurst, P. L. (1960). Applications of biometrical genetics to the inheritance of behaviour. In H. J. Eysenck (Ed.), *Experiments in personality.* London, Routledge & Kegan Paul, pp. 3–102.

Brobeck, J. R. (1947–8). Food intake as a mechanism of temperature regulation. *Yale J. Biol. Med.,* **20**, 545–552.

Brobeck, J. R. (1960). Regulation of feeding and drinking. In J. Field, H. W. Magoun and V. E. Hall (Eds.), *Handbook of physiology,* Section I. Neurophysiology Vol. II. Baltimore, Williams & Wilkins, pp. 1197–1206.

Brobeck, J. R., Tepperman, J., and Long, C. N. H. (1943). Experimental hypothalamic hyperphagia in the albino rat. *Yale. J. Biol. Med.,* **15**, 831–853.

Bromiley, R. B. (1948). Conditioned responses in a dog after removal of neocortex. *J. Comp. Physiol. Psychol.,* **41**, 102–110.

Brookhart, J. M., Dey, F. L., and Ransom, S. W. (1940). Mating reactions, effect of ovarian hormones and hypothalamic lesions. *Proc. Soc. Exp. Biol. Med.,* **44**, 61–64.

Brookhart, J. M., Dey, F. L., and Ransom, S. W. (1941). The abolition of mating behaviour by hypothalamic lesions in guinea pigs. *Endocrinology,* **28**, 561–565.

Brooks, C. McC. (1937). The role of the cerebral cortex and of various sense organs in the excitation and execution of mating activity in the rabbit. *Amer. J. Physiol.,* **120**, 544–553.

Brossard, M., and Decarie, T. G. (1971). The effects of three kinds of perceptual–social stimulation on the development of institutionalized infants: preliminary report of a longitudinal study. *Early Child Devel. Care,* **1**, 211–230.

Brown, P. K., and Wald, G. (1964). Visual pigments in single rods and cones of the human retina. *Science,* **144**, 45–52.

Brutkowski, S., Fonberg, E., and Mempel, E. (1961). Angry behaviour in dogs following bilateral lesions in the genual portion of the rostral cingulate gyrus. *Acta Biologiae Experimentalis,* **21**, 199–205.

Burns, B. D. (1958). *The mammalian cerebral cortex.* London, Arnold.

Butler, C. (1969). Is there a memory impairment in monkeys after inferior temporal lesions? *Brain Res.,* **13**, 383–396.

Butler, R. A. (1972). Frequency specificity of the auditory evoked response to simultaneous and successively presented stimuli. *Electroenceph. clin. Neurophysiol.,* **33**, 277–282.

Butler, R. A., and Harlow, H. F. (1957). Discrimination learning sets to visual exploration incentives. *J. gen. Psychol.,* **57**, 257–264.

Byrne, W. L. *et al.* (1966). Memory transfer. *Science,* **153**, 658.

Byrne, W. L. (1970). *Molecular approaches to memory and learning.* New York and London, Academic Press, see Introduction, pp. 11–23.

Cabanac, M. (1971). The physiological role of pleasure. *Science,* **173**, 1103–1107.

Cabitto, L. (1923). Sulle cause che provocano il zonno, *Note Riv. Psychiat.,* **11**, 95–114.

Campbell, F. W., and Maffei, L. (1970). Electrophysiological evidence for the existence of orientation and size detectors in the human visual system. *J. Physiol.,* **207**, 635–652.

Cannon, W. B. (1915, 2nd edition 1920). *Bodily changes in pain, hunger, fear and rage: an account of recent researches into fear and emotional excitement.* London, Routledge & Kegan Paul.

Cannon, W. B. (1918). The physiological basis of thirst. *Proc. Royal Soc., Series B,* **90**, 283–301.

Cannon, W. B. (1927). The James–Lange theory of emotion: a critical examination and an alternative. *Amer. J. Psychol.,* **39**, 106–124.

Cannon, W. B. (1932). *The wisdom of the body.* New York, Norton.

Cannon, W. B. (1934). Hunger and thirst. In C. Murchison (Ed.) *Handbook of general and experimental psychology.* Worcester, Mass., Clark University Press, pp. 247–263.

Cannon, W. B., and Washburn, A. L. (1912). An explanation of hunger. *Amer. J. Physiol.,* **29**, 444–454.

Cannon, W. B., and Britton, S. W. (1925). Pseudoaffective meduliadrenal secretion. *Amer. J. Physiol.,* **72**, 283–294.

Carlsson, A., Corrodi, H., Fuxe, K., and Hokfelt, T. (1969). Effect of antidepressant drugs on the depletion of intraneuronal brain 5-hydroxytryptamine stores caused by 4-methyl-o-ethyl-metatyromine. *Eur. J. Pharmacol.*, **5**, 357–366.

Carroll, B. J., Mowbray, R. M., and Davies, B. (1970). Sequential comparison of L-tryptophan with ECT in severe depression. *Lancet*, i, 967–969.

Cartwright, G. M. (1970). Use of a maze habit as a test of the specificity of memory transfer in mice. *J. Biol. Psychol.*, **12**, 53–60.

Casler, L. (1961). Maternal deprivation: a critical review of the literature. *Monogr. Soc. Res. Child Devel.*, **26**, no. 2.

Casler, L. (1968). Perceptual deprivation in institutional settings. In G. Newton, and S. Levine (Eds.), *Early experience and behaviour*. Springfield, Charles C. Thomas.

Chang, H. T. (1959). The evoked potentials. In J. Field, H. W. Magoun, and V. E. Hall (Eds.), *Handbook of physiology*: Section 1. Neurophysiology, Vol. 1. Washington D.C., American Physiology Association, pp. 299–313.

Chapman, L. F., Walter, R. D., Rand, C. H., and Crandall, P. H. (1967). Memory changes induced by stimulation of hippocampus or amygdala in epilepsy patients with implanted electrodes. *Trans. Amer. Neurol. Ass.*, **92**, 50–56.

Chapman, R. M. (1966). Human evoked responses to meaningful stimuli. In *Electrophysiological Correlates of Behaviour. Symposium 6 of the 18th Internat. Congress of Psychol.*, Moscow.

Chapman, R. M., Cavonius, C. R., and Ernest, J. T. (1970). Alpha and kappa electroencephalogram activity in eyeless subjects. *Science*, **171**, 1159–1160.

Cherry, C. (1953). Some experiments on the recognition of speech with one and two ears. *J. Acoust. Soc. Amer.*, **25**, 975–979.

Chomsky, N. (1968). *Language and mind*. New York, Harcourt, Brace & World.

Chorover, S. L., and Schiller, P. H. (1965). Short-term retrograde amnesia in rats. *J. Comp. Physiol. Psychol.*, **59**, 73–78.

Chow, K. C., and Stewart, D. L. (1972). Reversal of structural and functional effects of long term visual deprivation in cats. *Exp. Neurol.*, **34**, 409–433.

Christake, A. (1957). Conditioned emotional stimuli and arousal from sleep. *Amer. Psychol.*, **12**, 405.

Clark, G., and Birch, H. G. (1945). Hormonal modifications of social behaviour; the effect of sex hormone administration on the social status of a male castrate chimpanzee. *Psychosomatic Medicine*, **7**, 321–329.

Clark, T. K., Caggiula, A. R., McConnell, R. A., and Antelman, S. M. (1975). Sexual inhibition is reduced by rostral midbrain lesions in the male rat. *Science*, **190**, 169–171.

Clynes, M., and Kohn, M. (1967). Spatial visual evoked potentials as physiologic language elements for colour and field structure. *Elctroenceph. clin. Neurophysiol.*, Suppl. 26, 82–96.

Cohen, H. D., and Barondes, S. H. (1968). Effect of acetoxycycloheximide on learning and memory of a light–dark discrimination. *Nature*, **218**, 271–273.

Cohen, S. I. (1967). Central nervous system functioning in altered sensory environments. In M. H. Appley and R. Trumbull (Eds.), *Psychological stress*. New York, Appleton-Century Crofts, pp. 77–122.

Coleman, P. D., and Reisen, A. H. (1968). Environmental effects on cortical dendritic fields: I. Rearing in the dark. *J. Anat. (Lond).*, **102**, 363–374.

Commoner, B. (1972). *The closing circle*. London, Jonathan Cape, Chapter 5.

Connolly, K. (1971). The evolution and ontogeny of behaviour. *Bull. Brit. Psychol. Soc.*, **24**, 93–102.

Cook, L., and Kelleher, R. T. (1962). Drug effects on the behaviour of animals. *Annals N.Y. Acad. Sci.*, **96**, 315–335.

Cooper, K. K., and Aronson, L. R. (1974). Effects of castration on neural afferent responses from the penis of the domestic cat. *Physiol. Behav.*, **12**, 93–107.

Coppen, A., Whybrow, P. C., Noguera, R., Maggs, R., and Prange, A. J., Jr. (1972). The comparative antidepressant value of L-tryptophan and imipramine with and without attempted potentiation by liothyronine. *Arch. Gen. Psychiat.*, **26**, 234–241.

Corbit, J. D., and Stellar, E. (1964). Palatability, food intake and obesity in normal and hyperphagic rats. *J. Comp. Physiol. Psychol.*, **58**, 63–67.

Correll, R. E. (1957). The effect of bilateral hippocampal stimulation on the acquisition and extinction of an instrumental response. *J. Comp. Physiol. Psychol.*, **50**, 624–629.

Corteen, R. S., and Wood, B. (1972). Autonomic responses to shock associated words in an unattended channel. *J. exp. Psychol.*, **94**, 308–313.

Craik, K. J. W. (1947). Theory of the human operator in control systems. I. The operator as an engineering system. *Brit. J. Psychol.*, **38**, 56–61.

Craik, K. J. W. (1948). Theory of the human operator in control systems. II. Man as an element in a control system. *Brit. J. Psychol.*, **38**, 142–148.

Crain, S., and Peterson, E. R. (1963). Bioelectric activity in long-term cultures of spinal cord tissue. *Science*, **141**, 427.

Crick, F. H. C. (1963). On the genetic code. *Science*, **141**, 268–269.

Criswell, H. E., and Levitt, R. A. (1975). The narcotic analgesics. In R. A. Levitt (Ed.), *Psychopharmacology*. New York, John Wiley & Sons (Halstead Press), pp. 145–186.

Curtis, H. J., and Cole, K. S. (1942). Membrane resting and action potentials from the squid giant axon. *J. Cell. Comp. Physiol.*, **19**, 135–144.

Dahlstrom, A., and Fuxe, K. (1964). Evidence for the existence of monoamine containing neurones in the central nervous system. *Acta. Physiolog. Scand.*, Suppl. 232, 62.

Dalton, K. (1961). Menstruation and crime. *Brit. Med. J.*, 1752–1753.

Dalton, K. (1964). *The premenstrual syndrome.* Springfield, Charles C. Thomas.

Dana, C. L. (1921). The anatomic seat of the emotions: a discussion of the James–Lange theory. *Arch. Neurol. Psychiatr. (Chicago),* 6, 634–639.

Darwin, C. (1859). *On the origin of species by means of natural selection or the preservation of favoured races in the struggle for life.* London, J. Murray, p. 379.

Dashiell, J. F. (1925). A quantitative demonstration of animal drive. *J. Comp. Psychol.,* 5, 205–208.

David, O. J., Clark, J., and Voeller, K. (1972). Lead and hyperactivity. *Lancet,* ii, 900–903.

David, O., Hoffman, S., McGann, B., Sverd, J., and Clark, J. (1976). Low lead levels and mental retardation. *Lancet,* ii, 1376–1379.

Davidson, J. M. (1969). Effects of estrogen on the sexual behaviour of male rats. *Endocrinol.,* 84, 1365–1372.

Davidson, J. M. (1972). Hormones and reproductive behaviour. In S. Levine, (Ed.), *Hormones and behaviour.* New York and London, Academic Press, pp. 63–103.

Davis, H. (1961). Peripheral coding of auditory information. In W. A. Rosenblith (Ed.), *Sensory communication.* New York, John Wiley & Sons, pp. 119–141.

Davis, H. (1964). Enhancement of cortical evoked potentials in humans related to a task requiring a decision. *Science,* 145, 182–183.

Davis, H., Mast, T., Yoshie, N., and Zerlin, S. (1966). The slow response of the human cortex to auditory stimuli: recovery process. *Electroenceph. clin. Neurophysiol.,* 21, 105–113.

Davis, J. D., Gallagher, R. J., Ladove, R. F., and Turausky, A. J. (1969). Inhibition of food intake by a humoral factor. *J. Comp. Physiol. Psychol.,* 67, 407–414.

Davis, R. (1956). The limits of the 'psychological refractory period'. *Quart. J. Exp. Psychol.,* 8, 24–38.

Davis, R. (1957). The human operator as a single channel information system. *Quart. J. Exp. Psychol.,* 9, 119–129.

Davis, R. (1958). The role of 'attention' in the psychological refractory period. *Quart. J. Exp. Psychol.,* 10, 211–220.

Davis, R. (1962). Choice reaction times and the theory of intermittency in human performance. *Quart. J. Exp. Psychol.,* 14, 157–166.

Davis, R. (1965). Expectancy and intermittency. *Quart. J. Exp. Psychol.,* 17, 75–78.

Delay, J., Laine, B., and Buisson, J. F. (1952). Note concernant l'action de l'isonicotynil hydrazide dans le traitement des états dépressifs. *Annals Med. Psychol. (Paris),* 110, 689.

Dement, W. C. (1969). The biological role of REM sleep (circa 1968). In A. Kales (Ed.), *Sleep: physiology and pathology.* Philadelphia and Toronto, J. B. Lippincott, pp. 245–265.

Dement, W. C., and Kleitman, N. (1957). Cyclic variations in EEG during sleep and their relation to eye movements, body motility and dreaming. *Electroenceph. clin. Neurophysiol.,* 9, 673–690.

Dement, W., Cohen, H., Ferguson, J., and Zarcone, V., (1970). A sleep researcher's odyssey: the function and clinical significance of REM sleep. In L. Madow and L. H. Snow (Eds.), *The psychodynamic implications of the physiological studies of dreams.* Springfield, Charles C. Thomas, pp. 71–123.

De Molina, A. F., and Hunsperger, R. W. (1962). Organization of the subcortical system governing defence and flight reactions in the cat. *J. Physiol.,* 160, 200–213. Reprinted in D. G. Stein and J. J. Rosen, (Eds.) (1974). *Motivation and emotion,* New York, Macmillan, pp. 123–136. Reprinted in E. Gellhorn, (Ed.) (1968). *Biological foundations of emotion.* Illinois, Scott, Foresman & Co., pp. 1–14.

Denenberg, V. H., (1964). Critical periods, stimulus input, and emotional reactivity. *Psychol. Rev.,* 71, 335–357.

Deutsch, J. A. (1960). *The structural basis of behaviour.* Chicago, University of Chicago Press.

Deutsch, J. A. (1969). The physiological basis of memory. *Ann. Rev. Psychol.,* 20, 85–104.

Deutsch, J. A. (1973). The cholinergic synapse and the site of memory. In J. A. Deutsch (Ed.), *The physiological basis of memory.* New York and London, Academic Press, pp. 59–76.

Deutsch, J., and Deutsch, D. (1963). Attention: some theoretical considerations. *Psychol. Rev.,* 70, 80–90.

Deutsch, J. A., and DiCara, L. (1967). Hunger and extinction in intra-cranial self-stimulation. *J. Comp. Physiol. Psychol.,* 63, 344–347.

De Valois, R. L., Jacobs, G. H., and Abramov, I. (1964). Responses of single cells in visual system to shifts in the wavelength of light. *Science,* 146, 1184–1186.

De Valois, R. L., Smith, C. J., Karoly, A. J., and Kitai, S. T. (1958). Electrical responses of primate visual system: I. Different layers of macaque lateral geniculate nucleus. *J. Comp. Physiol. Psychol.,* 51, 662–668.

Dews, P. B., and Wiesel, T. N. (1970). Consequences of monocular deprivation on visual behaviour in kittens. *J. Physiol.,* 206, 437–455.

Dey, F. L., Fisher, C., Berry, C. M., and Ransom, S. W. (1940). Disturbances in reproductive functions caused by hypothalamic lesions in female guinea pigs. *Amer. J. Physiol.,* 129, 39–46.

DiMascio, A., and Barrett, J. (1965). Comparative effects of oxazepam in high and low anxious student volunteers. *Psychosomatics,* 6, 298–305.

Ditchburn, R. W., and Fender, D. H. (1955). The stablized retinal image. *Optica Acta,* 2, 128–133.

Ditchburn, R. W., Fender, D. H., and Mayne, S. (1959). Vision with controlled movements of the retinal image. *J. Physiol.,* 145, 98–107.

Dobzhansky, T. (1950, reprinted 1971). The genetic basis of evolution. In R. F. Thompson (Ed.) *Physiological psychology*. San Francisco, W. H. Freeman, pp. 4-13.

Dobzhansky, T. (1962). *Mankind evolving*. New Haven, Conn., Yale University Press. 2nd edition by Bantam Books in 1970.

Donaldson, H. H. (1890). Anatomical observations on the brain and several sense organs of the blind deaf-mute, Laura Dewey Bridgman. *Amer. J. Psychol.*, 3, 293-342; *Amer. J. Psychol.*, 4, 248-294.

Donchin, E., and Lindsley, D. B. (1966). Averaged evoked potentials and reaction time to visual stimuli. *Electroenceph. clin. Neurophysiol.*, 20, 217-223.

Donchin, E., and Cohen, L. (1967). Averaged evoked potentials and intra-modality selective attention. *Electroenceph. clin. Neurophysiol.*, 22, 537-546.

Dubos, R. (1973). *So human an animal*. London, Sphere Books (Abacus), first published in Britain by Rupert Hart Davis.

Dubuc, P. U., and Reynolds, R. W. (1973). Hypothalamic metallic deposition and the production of experimental obesity. *Physiol. Behav.*, 10, 677-681.

Duffy, E. (1957). The psychological significance of the concept of 'arousal' or 'activation'. *Psychol. Rev.*, 64, 265-275.

Duffy, E. (1962). *Activation and behaviour*. New York, John Wiley & Sons.

Duffy, E. (1972). Activation. In N. S. Greenfield and R. A. Sternbach (Eds.), *Handbook of psychophysiology*. New York, Holt, Rinehart & Winston, pp. 577-622.

Duncan, C. P. (1949). The retroactive effect of electroshock on learning. *J. Comp. Physiol. Psychol.*, 42, 32-44.

Dunn, G. W. (1941). Stilbestrol induced testicular degeneration in hypersexual males. *J. Clin. Endocrinol.*, 1, 643-648.

Dusser de Barenne, J. G. (1920). Récherches experimentales sur les fonctions du système nerveux central, faites en particulier sur deux chats donc le neopallium a été enlevé. *Arch. Neurol. Physiol.*, 4, 31-123.

Dusser de Barenne, J. G., and Koskoff, Y. D. (1932). Flexor rigidity of the hind legs and priapism in the 'secondary' spinal preparation of the male cats. *Amer. J. Physiol.*, 102, 75-86.

Dyal, J. A., Golub, A. M., and Marrone, R. L. (1967). Transfer effects of intraperitoneal injections of brain homogenates. *Nature*, 214, 720-721.

Eason, R. G., Harter, R., and White, C. T. (1969). Effects of attention and arousal on visually evoked cortical potentials and reaction time in man. *Physiol. Behav.*, 4, 283-289.

Ebling, F. J. G., and Highnam, K. C. (1969). *Chemical communication*. London, Edward Arnold.

Eccles, J. C. (1957). *The physiology of nerve cells*. Baltimore, Johns Hopkins Press.

Eccles, J. C. (1964). *The physiology of synapses*. Berlin, Gottingen, and Heidelberg, Springer.

Eccles, J. C. (1965). Possible ways in which synaptic mechanisms participate in learning remembering and forgetting. In D. P. Kimble (Ed.), *Anatomy of memory*. Palo Alto, Calif., Science of Behaviour Books, pp. 12-87.

Eccles, J. C. (1973). *Understanding the brain*. New York, McGraw-Hill.

Edelberg, R. (1972). The electrical activity of the skin. in. N. S. Greenfield and R. A. Sternbach (Eds.), *Handbook of Psychophysiology*. New York, Holt, Rinehart and Winston.

Egger, M. D., and Flynn, J. P. (1963). Effects of electrical stimulation of the amygdala. *J. Neurophysiol.*, 26, 705-720.

Ehrhardt, A. A., Evers, K., and Money, J. (1968). Influence of androgen and some aspects of sexually dimorphic behaviour in women with the late treated adrenogenital syndrome. *Johns Hopkins Med. J.*, 123, 115-122.

Emery, D. E., and Sachs, B. D. (1975). Ejaculatory patterns in female rats without androgen treatment. *Science*, 190, 484-486.

Epstein, A. N. (1960). Reciprocal changes in feeding behaviour 'produced by intra-hypothalamic chemical injections. *Amer. J. Physiol.*, 199, 969-974.

Epstein, A. N. (1967a). Feeding without oropharyngeal sensations. In M. R. Kare and O. Maller (Eds.), *The chemical senses and nutrition*. Baltimore, Johns Hopkins Press. pp. 263-280.

Epstein, A. N. (1967b). Oropharyngeal factors in eating and drinking. In F. Code (Ed.), *Handbook of physiology Section 6: Alimentary Canal*. Washington, D.C., American Physiol. Society, pp. 197-218.

Epstein, A. N. (1971). The lateral hypothalamic syndrome: its implications for the physiological psychology of hunger and thirst. In E. Stellar and J. M. Sprague (Eds.), *Progress in physiological psychology*, Vol. 4. New York and London, Academic Press, pp. 263-317.

Epstein, A. N., and Teitelbaum, P. (1967). Specific loss of the hypoglycemic control of feeding in recovered lateral rats. *Amer. J. Physiol.*, 213, 1159-1167.

Epstein, A. N., and Milestone, R. (1968). Showering as a coolant for rats exposed to heat. *Science*, 160, 895-896.

Epstein, A. N., Fitzsimons, J. T., and Rolls, B. J. (1970). Drinking induced by injection of angiotensin into the brain of the rat. *J. Physiol.*, 210, 457-474.

Ervin, F. R., Mark, V. H., and Stevens, J. (1969). Behavioural and affective responses to brain stimulation in man. In J. Zubin and C. Shagass (Eds.), *Neurobiological aspects of psychopathology*. New York, Grune & Stratton, pp. 54-65.

Evans, C. R. (1968). Dreams: a functional theory. *Electronics and Power*, 14, 323-325.

Evarts, E. V. (1968). Relation of pyramidal tract activity to force exerted during voluntary movement. *J. Neurophysiol.*, **31**, 14–27.

Evarts, E. V. (1967). Representations of movements and muscles by pyramidal tract neurones of the precentral motor cortex. In M. D. Yahr and D. P. Purpura (Eds.), *Neurophysiological basis of normal and abnormal motor activity*. Hewlett, Raven Press, pp. 215–253.

Everitt, B. F., and Herbert, J. (1969). Adrenal glands and sexual receptivity in female rhesus monkeys. *Nature*, **222**, 1065–1066.

Eysenck, H. J. (1953). *Uses and Abuses of Psychology*. Harmondsworth, Pelican.

Eysenck, H. J. (1967). *The biological basis of personality*. Springfield, Charles C. Thomas.

Eysenck, S. B. G., and Eysenck, H. J. (1969). Scores on three personality variables as a function of age, sex, and social class. *Brit. J. Soc. Clin. Psychol.*, **8**, 69–76.

Falk, B., Hillarp, M., Thieme, G., and Torp, A. (1962). Fluorescence of catecholamines and related compounds condensed with formaldehyde. *J. Histochem. Cytochem.*, **10**, 348–364.

Fee, A. R., and Parks, A. S. (1930). Studies on ovulation; effects of vaginal anaesthesia on ovulation in rabbit. *J. Physiol. (Lond.)*, **70**, 385–388.

Fifkova, E. (1967). The influence of unilateral visual deprivation on optic centers. *Brain Res.*, **6**, 763–766.

Fifkova, E. (1968). Changes in the visual cortex of rats after unilateral deprivation. *Nature*, (Lond.), **220**, 379–381.

Fifkova, E. (1970). The effect of unilateral deprivation on visual centres in rats. *J. Comp. Neurol.*, **140**, 431–438.

Finger, F. W., and Mook, D. G. (1971). Basic drives. *Ann. Rev. Psychol.*, **22**, 1–38.

Fisher, A. E. (1956). Maternal and sexual behaviour induced by intracranial chemical stimulation. *Science*, **124**, 228.

Fisher, A. E. (1964). Chemical stimulation of the brain. *Sci. Amer.*, **210**(6), 60–68.

Fisher, A. E., and Coury, J. N. (1962). Cholinergic tracing of central neural circuit underlying the thirst drive. *Science*, **138**, 691–693.

Fisher, C. (1970). Some psychoanalytic implication of recent research on sleeping and dreaming. In L. Madow and L. H. Snow (Eds.), *The psychodynamic implications of the physiological studies of dreams*. Springfield, Charles C. Thomas, pp. 152–167.

Fitzsimons, J. T. (1961). Drinking by rats depleted of body fluid without increase in osmotic pressure. *J. Physiol. (Lond.)*, **159**, 297–309.

Fitzsimons, J. T. (1964). Drinking caused by constriction of the inferior vena cava in the rat. *Nature*, (Lond.), **204**, 479–480.

Fitzsimons, J. T. (1966). Hypovolaemic drinking and renin. *J. Physiol.*, **186**, 130P–131P.

Fitzsimons, J. T. (1969a). The role of a renal thirst factor in drinking induced by extra-cellular stimuli. *J. Physiol.*, **201**, 349–368.

Fitzsimons, J. T. (1969b). Effect of nephrectomy on the additivity of certain stimuli of drinking in the rat. *J. Comp. Physiol. Psychol.*, **68**, 308–314.

Fitzsimons, J. T. (1971). The physiology of thirst: a review of the extraneural aspects of the mechanisms of drinking. In E. Stellar and J. M. Sprague (Eds.), *Progress in physiological psychology*, Vol. 4. New York and London, Academic Press, pp. 119–201.

Fitzsimons, J. T., and Oatley, K. (1968). Additivity of stimuli for drinking in rats. *J. Comp. Physiol. Psychol.*, **66**, 450–455.

Fjerdingstad, E. J. (1971). *Chemical transfer of learned information*. Amsterdam, North Holland Publishing.

Fjerdingstad, E. J., Nissen, T., and Røigaard-Petersen, H. H. (1965). Effect of ribonucleic acid (RNA) extracted from the brain of trained animals on learning in rats. *Scand. J. Psychol.*, **6**, 1–6.

Fjerdingstad, E. J., Byrne, W. L., Nissen, T., and Røigaard-Peterson, H. H. (1970). A comparison of 'transfer' results obtained with two different types of extraction and injection procedures, using identical behavioural techniques. In W. L. Byrne (Ed.), *Molecular approaches to learning and memory*. New York and London, Academic Press, pp. 151–170.

Flexner, J. B., and Flexner, L. B. (1969). Effect on memory of mice when injected with various cations. *Science*, **165**, 1143–1144.

Flexner, J. B., Flexner, L. B., and Stellar, E. (1963). Memory in mice as affected by intracerebral puromycin. *Science*, **141**, 57–59.

Flexner, L. B., and Flexner, J. B. (1968a). Intracerebral saline: effect on memory of trained mice treated with puromycin. *Science*, **159**, 330–331.

Flexner, L. B., and Flexner, J. B. (1968b). Studies on memory: the long survival of peptidyl-puromycin in mouse brain. *Proc. Nat. Acad. Sci., U.S.A.*, **60**, 923–927.

Flexner, L. B., Flexner, J. B., and Roberts, R. B. (1967). Memory in mice analysed with antibiotics. *Science*, **155**, 1377–1383.

Flexner, J. B., and Flexner, L. B. (1970). Further observations on restoration of memory lost after treatment with puromycin. *Yale J. Biol. Med.*, **42**, 235–240.

Flexner, J. B., and Flexner, L. B. (1967). Restoration of expression of memory lost after treatment with puromycin. *Proc. Nat. Acad. Sci., U.S.A.*, **57**, 1651–1654.

Ford, C. S., and Beach, F. A. (1952). *Patterns of sexual behaviour*. New York, Harper and Row. First published in the UK, 1970, London, Methuen.

Forrer, G. R., and Miller, J. J. (1958). Atropine coma: a somatic therapy in psychiatry. *Amer. J. Psychiatr.*, **115**, 455–458.

Forgus, R. H. (1958). The effect of different kinds of

form pre-exposure on form discrimination learning. *J. Comp. Physiol. Psychol.*, 51, 75–81.

Foss, G. L. (1951). The influence of androgens on sexuality in women. *Lancet*, i, 667–669.

Fox, S. S., and O'Brien, J. H. (1965). Duplication of evoked potential waveform by curve of probability of firing of a single cell. *Science*, 147, 888–890.

Francis, S. H. (1971). The effects of own-home and institution rearing on the behavioural development of normal and mongol children. *J. Child Psychol. Psychiatr., Allied Disc.*, 12, 173–190.

Franz, S. I., and Layman, J. D. (1933). Peripheral retinal learning and practice transfer. *Univ. Calif. Los Angeles Publ. in Educ. Philos. Psychol.*, 1(3), 65–136.

Frederichs, C., and Goodman, H. (1969). *Low blood sugar and you*. New York, Constellation International.

Freud, S. (1900). *The interpretation of dreams*. London, Hogarth Press.

Frey, M. (1895). Beitrage zur Sinnesphysiologie der Haut. *Sitzungsberichte sachs Gesamte (Akademische) Wissenchaft Leipzig*, 47, 166.

Fulton, J. F., and Jacobsen, C. F. (1935). The functions of the frontal lobes, a comparative study in monkeys, chimpanzees and man. *Advanc. Med. Biol.*, (Moscow), 4, 113–23. Also in *Abstracts from the second International Neurological Congress*, London, 1935, pp. 70–71.

Funkenstein, D. H. (1955). The physiology of fear and hunger. *Scientific American*, 192 (5), 74–80.

Fuster, J. M. (1958). Effects of stimulation of brain-stem on tachistoscopic perception. *Science*, 127, 150.

Gaito, J., Mottin, J., and Davison, J. H. (1968). Chemical variation in the ventral hippocampus and other brain sites during conditioned avoidance. *Psychon. Sci.*, 13, 259–260.

Galambos, R. (1960). Studies in the auditory system with implanted electrodes. In G. Rasmussen and W. Windle (Eds.), *Neural mechanisms of auditory and vestibular systems*. Springfield, Charles C. Thomas.

Gambetti, P., Gonatas, N. K., and Flexner, L. B. (1968a). Puromycin: action on neuronal mitochondria. *Science*, 161, 900–902.

Gambetti, P., Gonatas, N. K., and Flexner, L. B. (1968b). The fine structure of puromycin induced changes in mouse entorhinal cortex. *J. Cell Biol.*, 36, 379–390.

Garcia, J., Hankins, W. G., and Rusiniak, K. W. (1974). Behavioural regulation of the milieu interne in man and rat. *Science*, 185, 824–831.

Garcia-Ausst, E. J., Bogacz, J., and Vanzulli, A., (1964). Effects of attention and inattention upon visual evoked response. *Electroenceph. Clin. Neurophysiol.*, 17, 136–143.

Gartside, I. B. (1968a). Mechanism of sustained increases of firing rate of neurones in the rat cerebral cortex after polarization: reverberating circuits or modification of synaptic conductance. *Nature*, 220, 382–383.

Gartside, I. B. (1968b). Mechanism of sustained increases of firing rate of neurones in the rat cerebral cortex after polarization: role of protein synthesis. *Nature*, 220, 383–384.

Gartside, I. B. (1971). Is the inhibition by cycloheximide of induced long-term changes in cortical activity due to inhibition of protein synthesis? *Nature*, 232, 47–48.

Gastaut, H., and Collomb, H. (1954). Etude du comportement sexuel chez les epileptiques psychomotor. *Annales Medicopsychologique*, 112, 657–696.

Gauer, O. H., and Henry, J. P. (1963). Circulatory basis of fluid volume control. *Physiol. Rev.*, 43, 423–481.

Gay, R., and Raphaelson, A. C. (1970). A simplified behavioural test of brain extractate transfer effects in rats. In W. L. Byrne (Ed.), *Molecular approaches to learning and memory*. New York and London, Academic Press, pp. 171–178.

Geller, I., Kulak, T., and Seifter, J. (1962). The effects of chlordiazepoxide and chlorpromazine on punishment discrimination. *Psychpharmacologia (Berl.)*, 25, 112–116.

Gellhorn, E. (1968). Attempts at a synthesis: contributions to a theory of emotion. In E. Gellhorn (Ed.), *Biological foundations of emotion*. Illinois, Scott, Foresman & Co., pp. 144–153.

Giachetti, I., MacLeod, P., and Le Magnen, J. (1970). Influence des états de faim et de satieté sur les responses du bulb olfactif chez le rat. *Journal de Psychologie (Paris)*, 62, Suppl. 2, 280–281.

Giantonio, G. W., Lund, N. L., and Gerall, A. A. (1970). Effects of diencephalic and rhinencephalic lesions on the male rat's sexual behaviour. *J. Comp. Physiol. Psychol.*, 73, 38–46.

Gibbs, F. A. (1951). Ictal and non-ictal psychiatric disorders in temporal lobe epilepsy. *J. Nerv. Ment. Dis.*, 113, 522–528.

Gibson, J. J. (1950). *The perception of the visual world*. Boston, Houghton Mifflin.

Gibson, W. E., Reid, L. D., Sakai, M., and Porter, P. B. (1965). Intracranial reinforcement compared with sugar-water reinforcement. *Science*, 148, 1357–1359.

Glanzer, M., and Cunitz, A. R. (1966). Two storage mechanisms in free recall. *J. Verb. Learn. Verb. Behav.*, 5, 351–360.

Globus, A., and Scheibel, A. B. (1967). Effects of visual deprivation on cortical neurones: a Golgi study. *Exp. Neurol.*, 19, 331–345.

Globus, A., Rosenzweig, M. R., Bennett, E. L., and Diamond, M. L. (1973). Effects of differential experience on dendritic spine counts in rat cerebral cortex. *J. Comp. Physiol. Psychol.*, 82, 175–181.

Gloor, P. (1960). Amygdala. In J. Field and H. W. Magoun (Eds.), *American Physiological Society handbook of physiology*, Section I, Neurophysiology Vol. 2. Baltimore, Williams & Wilkins, pp. 1395–1416.

Gloor, P. (1967). Discussion of brain mechanisms related to aggressive behaviour by B. Kaada. In C. D. Clemente and D. B. Lindsley (Eds.), *Aggression and defense: neural mechanisms and social patterns*. Vol. 5. Brain function. Los Angeles, University of California Press.

Gloor, P., Murphy, J. T., and Dreifuss, J. J. (1969). Electrophysiological studies of amygdalo-hypothalamic connections. *Ann. N.Y. Acad. Sci.*, 157, 629–641.

Glusman, M., and Roizin, L. (1960). Role of the hypothalamus in the organization of agonistic behaviour in the cat. *Trans. Amer. Neurol. Ass.*, 85, 177–181.

Goldfarb, W. (1945a). Psychological privation in infancy and subsequent adjustment. *Amer. J. Orthopsychiatr.*, 15, 247–255.

Goldfarb, W. (1945b). Effects of psychological privation in infancy and subsequent stimulation. *Amer. J. Psychiatr.*, 102, 18–23.

Goff, W. R. (1969). Evoked potential correlates of perceptual organization in man. In C. R. Evans and T. B. Mulholland (Eds.), *Attention in neurophysiology*. London, Butterworths, pp. 169–193.

Goltz, F. (1892). Der Hund ohne Grosshirn. *Pflug. Arch. ges. Physiol.*, 51, 570–614.

Golub, M. S., Cheal, M. L., and Davis, R. E. (1972). Effects of electroconvulsive shock and puromycin on operant responding in goldfish. *Physiol. Behav.*, 8, 573–578.

Goodwin, F. K., and Murphy, D. L. (1974). Biological factors in the affective disorders and schizophrenia. In M. Gordon (Ed.), *Psychopharmacological agents*. New York, Academic Press, pp. 9–37.

Graham, D. T. (1972). Psychosomatic medicine. In N. S. Greenfield and R. A. Sternbach (Eds.), *Handbook of psychophysiology*. New York, Holt, Rinehart, Winston, pp. 839–924.

Granit, R. (1943). The spectral properties of the visual receptors of the cat. *Acta Physiologica Scandinavica*, 5, 219–229.

Granit, R. (1955). *Receptors and sensory perception*. New Haven, Conn., Yale University Press.

Grant, E. C. G., and Mears, E. (1967). Mental effects of oral contraceptives. *Lancet*, ii, 945–946.

Gray, J. A. (1970). Sodium amobarbital, the hippocampal theta rhythm and the partial reinforcement extinction effect. *Psychol. Rev.*, 77, 465–480.

Gray, J. A. (1971a). *The psychology of fear and stress*. London, Weidenfeld & Nicolson (World University Library).

Gray, J. A. (1971b). Sex differences in emotional behaviour in mammals including man. *Acta Psychologica*, 35, 29–46.

Gray, J. A. (1972). The psychophysiological nature of introversion–extroversion: a modification of Eysenck's theory. In V. D. Nebylitsyn and J. A. Gray (Eds.), *Biological bases of individual behaviour*.

New York and London, Academic Press, pp. 182–205.

Gray, J. A., and Buffery, A. W. H. (1971). Sex differences in emotional and cognitive behaviour in mammals including man: adaptive and neural bases. *Acta Psychologica*, 35, 89–111.

Gray, J. A. B., and Malcolm, J. L. (1950). The initiation of nerve impulses by mesenteric Pacinian corpuscles. *Proc. Roy. Soc., Series B.*, 137, 96–114.

Green, D. M., and Swets, J. A. (1966). *Signal detection theory and psychophysics*. New York, Wiley.

Green, J. D., Clemente, C. D., and de Groot, J. (1957). Rhinencephalic lesions and behaviour in cats. *J. Compar. Neurol.*, 108, 505–536.

Gregersen, M. I., and Bullock, L. T. (1933). Observations on thirst in man in relation to changes in salivary flow and plasma volume. *Amer. J. Physiol.*, 105, 39–40.

Grinker, R. R., and Serota, H. (1938). Selective electrical activity from deep lying hypothalamic electrodes in man in response to emotional probing. *J. Neurophysiol.*, 1, 573–589.

Gross, L. P. (1968). *Scarcity, unpredictability and eating behaviour in rats*. Unpublished doctoral dissertation. Columbia University.

Gross, M. M., Begleiter, H., Tobin, M., and Kissin, B. (1965). Auditory evoked response comparison during counting clicks and reading. *Electroenceph. clin. Neurophysiol.*, 18, 451–454.

Grossman, M. I., Cummins, G. M., and Ivy, A. C. (1947). The effect of insulin upon food intake after vagotomy and sympathectomy. *Amer. J. Physiol.*, 149, 100.

Grossman, S. P. (1960). Eating or drinking elicited by direct adrenergic or cholinergic stimulation of hypothalamus. *Science*, 132, 301–302.

Grossman, S. P. (1962a). Direct adrenergic and cholinergic stimulation of hypothalamic mechanisms. *Amer. J. Physiol.*, 202, 872–882.

Grossman, S. P. (1962b). Effects of adrenergic and cholinergic agents on hypothalamic mechanisms. *Amer. J. Physiol.*, 202, 1230–1236.

Grossman, S. P. (1967). *A textbook of physiological psychology*. New York, John Wiley & Sons.

Grossman, S. P. (1970). Modification of emotional behaviour by intracranial administration of chemicals. In P. Black (Ed.), *Physiological correlates of emotion*. New York and London, Academic Press, pp. 73–93.

Grossman, S. P., and Rechtschaffen, A. (1967). Variations in brain temperature in relation to food intake. *Physiol. Behav.*, 2, 379–383.

Guyton, A. C. (1971). *Textbook of Medical Physiology* (4th ed.). Philadelphia, Saunders.

Gyllensten, L., Malmfors, T., and Norrlin, M. L. (1965). Effects of visual deprivation on the optic centres of growing and adult mice. *J. Comp. Neurol.*, 124, 149–160.

Gyllensten, L., Malmfors, T., and Norrlin, M. L. (1966). Growth alteration in the auditory cortex of visually deprived mice. *J. Comp. Neurol.*, **126**, 463–469.

Gyllensten, L., Malmfors, T., Norrlin-Grettye, M. L. (1967). Visual and non-visual factors in the centripetal stimulation of postnatal growth of the visual centres in mice. *J. Comp. Neurol.*, **131**, 549–557.

Hagen, E., Knoche, H., Sinclair, D. C., and Wedell, G. (1953). The role of specialized nerve terminals in cutaneous sensibility. *Proc. Royal Soc., Series B*, **141**, 279–287.

Haider, M., Spong, P., and Lindsley, D. B. (1964). Attention, vigilance and cortical evoked potentials in humans. *Science*, **145**, 180–182.

Hall, C. S. (1951). The genetics of behaviour. In S. S. Stevens (Ed.), *Handbook of experimental psychology*. New York, Wiley & Sons, pp. 304–329.

Hamburg, D. A., Moos, R. H., and Yalom, I. D. (1968). Studies of distress in the menstrual cycle and the postpartum period. In R. P. Michael (Ed.), *Endocrinology and human behaviour*. London, Oxford University Press.

Hammel, H. T., Hardy, J. D., and Fusco, M. M. (1960). Thermoregulatory responses to hypothalamic cooling in unanesthetized dogs. *Amer. J. Physiol.*, **198**, 481–486.

Hardy, J. D., Hellon, R. F., and Sutherland, K. (1964). Temperature-sensitive neurones in the dog's hypothalamus. *J. Physiol.*, **185**, 242–253.

Harlow, H. F. (1950). Learning and satiation of response in intrinsically motivated complex puzzle performance by monkeys. *J. Comp. Physiol. Psychol.*, **43**, 289–294.

Harlow, H. F. (1953). Mice, monkeys, men, and motives. *Psychol. Rev.*, **60**, 23–32.

Harlow, H. (1962). Heterosexual affectional system in monkeys. *Amer. Psychol.*, **17**, 1–9.

Harper, R. M., and McGinty, D. J. (1972). A technique for recording single neurones from unrestrained animals. In M. I. Phillips (Ed.), *Brain activity during behaviour*. Iowa, University of Iowa Press.

Harris, G. W., and Levine, S. (1965). Sexual differentiation in the brain and its experimental control. *J. Physiol.*, **181**, 379–400.

Harris, G. W., Michael, R. P., and Scott, P. P. (1958). Neurological site of action of stilboestrol in eliciting sexual behaviour. In *Ciba Foundation symposium on the neurological basis of behaviour*. Boston, Little Brown & Co., pp. 236–254.

Hart, B. L. (1967). Sexual reflexes and mating behaviour in the male dog. *J. Comp. Physiol. Psychol.*, **64**, 388–389.

Hart, B. L. (1968a). Role of prior experience in the effects of castration on sexual behaviour male dogs. *J. Comp. Physiol. Psychol.*, **66**, 719–725.

Hart, B. L. (1968b). Sexual reflexes and mating behaviour in the male rat. *J. Comp. Physiol. Psychol.*, **65**, 453–460.

Hart, B. L. (1974a). Medial preoptic anterior hypothalamic area and sociosexual behaviour of male

dogs: a comparative neuropsychological analysis. *J. Comp. Physiol. Psychol.*, **86**, 328–349.

Hart, B. L. (1974b). Gonadal androgen and sociosexual behaviour of male mammals: a comparative analysis. *Psychol. Bull.*, **81**, 383–400.

Hart, B. L., and Haugen, C. M. (1968). Activation of sexual reflexes in male rats by spinal implantation of testosterone. *Physiol. Behav.*, **3**, 735–738.

Hart, B. L., Haugen, C. M., and Peterson, D. M. (1973). Effects of medial preoptic anterior hypothalamic lesions on mating behaviour of male cats. *Brain Res.*, **54**, 177–191.

Hartline, H. K. (1938). The response of single optic nerve fibres of the vertebrate eye to illumination of the retina. *Amer. J. Physiol.*, **121**, 400–415.

Hartmann, E. (1967). *The biology of dreaming*. Springfield, Charles C. Thomas.

Hawke, C. C. (1950). Castration and sex crimes. *Amer. J. Ment. Defic.*, **55**, 220–226.

Haywood, C. (1967). Experiential factors in intellectual development: the concept of dynamic intelligence. In J. Zubin and G. A. Jervis (Eds.), *Psychopathology of mental development*. New York, Grune & Stratton.

Heath, R. G. (1962). *First Hahnemann symposium on psychosomatic medicine*. Philadelphia, Lea & Febiger, pp. 228–240.

Heath, R. G. (1963). Electrical self-stimulation of the brain in man. *Amer. J. Psychiatr.*, **120**, 571–577.

Hebb, D. O. (1949). *The organization of behaviour*. New York, John Wiley & Sons.

Hebb, D. O. (1955). Drives and the CNS (conceptual nervous system). *Psychol. Rev.*, **62**, 243–254.

Heimburger, R. F., Whitlock, C. C., and Kalsbeck, J. E. (1966). Stereotaxic amygdalotomy for epilepsy with aggressive behaviour. *J. Amer. Med. Ass.*, **198**, 165–169.

Heimer, L., and Larsson, K. (1966). Impairment of mating behaviour in male rats following lesions in the preoptic–anterior hypothalamic continuum. *Brain Res.*, **3**, 248–263.

Held, R. (1965). Plasticity in sensory-motor systems. *Sci. Amer.*, **213**(5), 84–94.

Held, R., and Bossom, J. (1961). Neonatal deprivation and adult re-arrangement: complementary techniques for analysing plastic sensory-motor coordinations. *J. Comp. Physiol. Psychol.*, **54**, 33–37.

Held, R., and Freedman, S. J. (1963). Plasticity in human sensorimotor control. *Science*, **142**, 455–462.

Held, R., and Hein, A. (1963). Movement-produced stimulation in the development of visually guided behaviour. *J. Comp. Physiol. Psychol.*, **56**, 872–876.

Herberg, L. J. (1963). Determinants of extinction in electrical self-stimulation. *J. Comp. Physiol. Psychol.*, **56**, 686–690.

Herbert, J. (1970). Hormones and reproductive behaviour in rhesus and talapoin monkeys. *J. Reproduct. Fertil.*, **Suppl. 11**, 119–140.

Herbert, J. (1973). The role of the dorsal nerves of the

penis in the sexual behaviour of the male rhesus monkey. *Physiol. Behav.*, **10**, 293–300.

Hernandez-Peon, R. (1963). Sleep induced by localised electrical or chemical stimulation of the forebrain. *Electroenceph. clin. Neurophysiol.*, **Suppl. 24**, 188–198.

Hernandez-Peon, R. (1965). Physiological mechanisms in attention. In R. W. Russell (Ed.), *Frontiers in physiological psychology*. New York, Academic Press, pp. 121–147.

Hernandez-Peon, R., Scherrer, H., and Jouvet, M. (1956). Modification of electrical activity in cochlear nucleus during 'attention' in unanesthetized cats. *Science*, **123**, 331–332.

Heron, W., Tait, G., and Smith, G. K. (1972). Effects of prolonged perceptual isolation on the human electroencephalogram. *Brain Res.*, **43**, 280–284.

Hertz, R., Meyer, R. K., and Spielman, M. A. (1937). The specificity of progesterone in inducing receptivity in the ovariectomized guinea pig. *Endocrinology*, **21**, 533–535.

Hess, W. R. (1954). *Diencephalon: autonomic and extrapyramidal functions*. London, William Heineman (also New York, Grune & Stratton).

Heston, L. L. (1966). Psychiatric disorders in foster home children of schizophrenic mothers. *Brit. J. Psychiatr.*, **112**, 819–825.

Hetherington, A. W., and Ransom, S. W. (1940). Hypothalamic lesions and adiposity in the rat. *Anat. Rec.*, **78**, 149.

Hillyard, S. A., Squires, K. C., Bauer, J. W., and Lindsay, P. H. (1971). Evoked potential correlates of auditory signal detection. *Science*, **172**, 1357–1360.

Hillyard, S. A., Hink, R. F., Schwent, V. L., and Picton, T. W. (1973). Electrical signs of selective attention in the human brain. *Science*, **182**, 177–180.

Hine, B., and Paolino, R. M. (1970). Retrograde amnesia: production of skeletal but not cardiac response gradient by electroconvulsive shock. *Science*, **169**, 1224–1226.

Hirsch, H. V. B., and Spinelli, D. N. (1970). Visual experience modifies distribution of horizontally and vertically oriented receptive fields in cats. *Science*, **168**, 869–871.

Hodgkin, A. L., and Huxley, A. F. (1939). Action potentials recorded from inside nerve fibre. *Nature*, **144**, 710–711.

Hoebel, B. G. (1965). Hypothalamic lesions by electrocauterization: disinhibition of feeding and self stimulation. *Science*, **149**, 452–453.

Hoebel, B. G., and Teitelbaum, P. (1962). Hypothalamic control of feeding and self stimulation. *Science*, **135**, 375–376.

Hoebel, B. G., and Thompson, R. D. (1969). Aversion to lateral hypothalamic stimulation caused by intragastric feeding and obesity. *J. Comp. Physiol. Psychol.*, **68**, 536–543.

Hoffer, A., and Osmond, H. (1960). *The chemical basis of clinical psychiatry*. Springfield, Charles C. Thomas.

Hoffman, R. F., Steward, C. N., and Brogavan, H. N. (1967). Failure to transfer a learned response in rats using a brain extract containing RNA. *Psychon. Sci.*, **9**, 151–152.

Hofmann, A. (1968). Psychotomimetic agents. In A. Burger (Ed.), *Drugs affecting the central nervous system*, Vol. 2. New York, Marcel Dekker.

Hollister, L. E., and Friedhoff, A. J. (1966). Effects of 3,4-dimethoxyphenylethylamine in man. *Nature*, **210**, 1377–1378.

Holloway, J. A. (1975). Norepinephrine and serotonin: specificity of release with rewarding electrical stimulation of the brain. *Psychopharmacologia*, **42**, 127–134.

Holman, G. L. (1969). Intragastric reinforcement effect. *J. Comp. Physiol. Psychol.*, **69**, 432–441.

Holmes, J. H., and Gregerson, M. I. (1950a). Observations on drinking induced by hypertonic solutions. *Amer. J. Physiol.*, **162**, 326–337.

Holmes, J. H., and Gregersen, M. I. (1950b). Role of sodium and chloride in thirst. *Amer. J. Physiol.*, **162**, 338–347.

Holmes, J. H., and Cizek, L. J. (1951). Observations on sodium depletion in the dog. *Amer. J. Physiol.*, **164**, 407–414.

Holmes, J. H., and Montgomery, A. V. (1951). Observations on relation of hemorrhage to thirst. *Amer. J. Physiol.*, **167**, 796.

Holmes, J. H., and Montgomery, A. V. (1953). Thirst as a symptom. *Amer. J. Med. Sci.*, **225**, 281–286.

Horn, G. (1960). Electrical activity of the cerebral cortex of the unanaesthetized cat during attentive behaviour. *Brain*, **83**, 57–76.

Horn, G. (1965). Physiological and psychological aspects of selective perception. In D. S. Lehrman, R. A. Hinde and E. Shaw (Eds.), *Advances in the study of behaviour*, Vol. 1. New York, Academic Press, pp. 155–215.

Horn, G., and Mackay, J. M. (1973). Effects of lysergic acid diethylamide on the spontaneous activity and visual receptive fields of cells in the lateral geniculate nucleus of the cat. *Exp. Brain Res.*, **17**, 271–284.

Horne, J. A., and Porter, J. M. (1975). Exercise and human sleep. *Nature*, **256**, 573–575.

Horridge, G. A. (1962). Learning leg position by the ventral nerve cord in headless insects. *Proc. Roy. Soc., Series B*, **157**, 33–52.

Horsley, V., and Clarke, R. H. (1908). The structure and functions of the cerebellum examined by a new method. *Brain*, **31**, 45–124.

Howarth, C. I., and Deutsch, J. A. (1962). Drive decay: the cause of fast 'extinction' of habits learned for brain stimulation. *Science*, **137**, 35–36.

Hoyle, G. (1965). Neurophysiological studies on 'learning' in headless insects. In J. E. Treherne and J. W. L. Beaumont (Eds.), *The physiology of the insect nervous system*. New York, Academic Press, pp. 203–232.

Hubel, D. H., and Wiesel, T. N. (1959). Receptive fields of single neurones in the cat's striate cortex. *J. Physiol.*, **148**, 574–591.

Hubel, D. H., and Wiesel, T. N. (1961). Integrative action in the cat's lateral geniculate body. *J. Physiol.*, **155**, 385–398.

Hubel, D. H., and Wiesel, T. N. (1962). Receptive fields, binocular interaction and functional cytoarchitecture in the cat's visual cortex. *J. Physiol.*, **160**, 106–154.

Hubel, D. H., and Wiesel, T. N. (1965). Receptive fields and functional architecture in two non-striate visual areas (18 and 19) of the cat. *J. Neurophysiol.*, **28**, 229–289.

Hubel, D. H., and Wiesel, T. N. (1968). Receptive fields and functional architecture of monkey striate cortex. *J. Physiol.*, **195**, 215–243.

Hubel, D. H., and Wiesel, T. N. (1970). The period of susceptibility of the physiological effects of unilateral eye closure in kittens. *J. Physiol.*, **206**, 419–436.

Hugelin, A., Dumont, S., and Paillas, N. (1960). Formation reticulaire et transmission des informations auditoires au niveau de l'oreille moyenne et des voies acoustiques centrales. *Electroenceph. clin. neurophysiol.*, **12**, 797–818.

Hughes, R. A., Barrett, R. J., and Ray, O. S. (1970). Retrograde amnesis in rats increases as a function of ECS-test interval and ECS intensity. *Physiol. Behav.*, **5**, 27–30.

Hull, C. L. (1943). *Principles of behaviour.* New York, Appleton-Century-Crofts.

Huxley, A. (1959). *The doors of perception* and *Heaven and hell*, Harmondsworth, Penguin Books. (First published by Chatto & Windus, 1954).

Huxley, H. E. (1965). The mechanism of muscular contraction. *Sci. Amer.*, **213**(6), 18–27.

Hydén, H. (1959). Biochemical changes in nerve cells and glial cells at varying activity. In O. Hoffmann-Ostenhoff (Ed.), *Biochemistry of the central nervous system*, Vol. 3. London, Pergamon.

Hydén, H. (1961). Satellite cells in the nervous system. *Sci. Amer.*, **205**(12), 62–70.

Hydén, H. (1970). The question of a molecular basis for the memory trace. In K. H. Pribram and D. E. Broadbent (Eds.), *Biology of memory.* New York and London, Academic Press, pp. 101–122.

Hydén, H., and Egyhazí, E. (1962). Nuclear RNA changes in nerve cells during a learning experiment in rats. *Proc. Nat. Acad. Sci., U.S.A.*, **48**, 1366–1373.

Hydén, H., and Egyhazí, E. (1963). Glial RNA changes during a learning experiment in rats. *Proc. Nat. Acad. Sci., U.S.A.*, **49**, 618–624.

Hydén, H., and Egyhazí, E. (1964). Changes in RNA content and base composition in cortical neurones of rats in a learning experiment involving transfer of handedness. *Proc. Nat. Acad. Sci., U.S.A.*, **52**, 1030–1035.

Hydén, H., and Lange, P. W. (1965). A differentiation in RNA response in neurones early and late during learning. *Proc. Nat. Acad. Sci., U.S.A.*, **53**, 946–952.

Hydén, H., and Lange, P. W. (1968). Protein synthesis in the hippocampal pyramidal cells of rats during a behavioural test. *Science*, **159**, 1370–1373.

Hydén, H., and Lange, P. W. (1971). Brain cell protein synthesis specifically related to learning. *Proc. Nat. Acad. Sci., U.S.A.*, **65**, 898–904.

Hydén, H., and Lange, P. W. (1972). Protein changes in different brain areas as a function of intermittent training. *Proc. Nat. Acad. Sci., U.S.A.*, **69**, 1980–1984.

Ingram, W. R. (1952). Brainstem mechanisms in behaviour. *Electroenceph. clin. Neurophysiol.*, **4**, 397–406.

Isbell, H., Altschule, S., Kornetsky, C. H., Eisenman, A. J., Flanary, H. G., and Fraser, H. F. (1950). Chronic barbiturate intoxication. *Arch. Neurol. Psychiatr.*, **64**, 1–28.

Iversen, L. L. (1970). Neurotransmitters, neurohormones and other small molecules in neurones. In F. O. Schmitt (Ed.), *The neurosciences: second study program.* New York, Rockefeller University Press.

Iversen, L. L. (1975). Dopamine receptors in the brain. *Science*, **188**, 1084–1089.

Iversen, S. D. (1973). Brain lesions and memory in animals. In J. A. Deutsch (Ed.), *The physiological basis of memory.* New York and London, Academic Press, pp. 305–364.

Iversen, S. D., and Weiskrantz, L. (1970). An investigation of a possible memory defect produced by inferotemporal lesions in the Baboon. *Neuropsychologia.*, **8**, 21–36.

Iversen, S. D., and Iversen, L. L. (1975). *Behavioural pharmacology.* New York and Oxford, Oxford University Press.

Jacobson, A. L. (1966). Chemical transfer of learning. *Discovery*, **27**, 11–16.

Jacobson, A. L., Babich, F. R., Bubash, S., and Jacobson, A. (1965). Differential approach tendencies produced by injections of RNA from trained rats. *Science*, **150**, 636–637.

Jacobson, A. L., Fried, C., and Horowitz, S. D. (1966). Planarians and memory. I. Transfer of learning by injection of ribonucleic acid. *Nature*, **209**, 599–601.

Jacobson, A. L., Fried, C., and Horowitz, S. D. (1967). Classical conditioning, pseudoconditioning, or sensitization in the planarian. *J. Comp. Physiol. Psychol.*, **64**, 73–79.

Jaffe, M. L. (1973). The effects of lesions in the ventromedial nucleus of the hypothalamus on behavioural contrast in rats. *Physiol. Psychol.*, **1**, 191–198.

James, W. (1884). What is emotion. *Mind*, **9**, 188–205.

James, W. (1890). *The principles of psychology.* New York, Dover Press, pp. 402–458.

Janowski, E. S., Gornery, R., and Mandell, A. J.

(1967). The menstrual cycle: psychiatric and ovarian adrenocortical hormone correlates: case study and literature review. *Arch. Gen. Psychiatr.,* **17**, 459–469.

Jasper, H. H. (1966). Brain mechanisms and states of consciousness. In J. C. Eccles (Ed.), *Brain and conscious experience.* Berlin, Springer-Verlag, pp. 256–282.

Jessop, N. M. (1970). *Biosphere: A Study of Life.* Englewood Cliffs, N. J., Prentice-Hall.

Joffe, J. M. (1959). *Pre-natal determinants of behaviour.* Oxford, Pergamon Press.

Johannsen, W. (1911). The genotype conception of heredity. *Amer. Nat.,* **45**, 129–159.

Jones, A. (1969). Stimulus-seeking behaviour. In J. P. Zubek (Ed.), *Sensory deprivation: fifteen years of research.* New York, Appleton-Century-Crofts, pp. 167–206.

Jones, H. S., and Oswald, I. (1968). Two cases of healthy insomnia. *Electroenceph. clin. Neurophysiol.,* **24**, 378–380.

Jones, R. T. (1971). Marijuana induced 'high': influence of expectation, setting and previous drug experience. *Pharmacol. Rev.,* **23**, 359–369.

John, E. R. (1967). *Mechanisms of memory.* New York and London, Academic Press.

John, E. R. (1972). Switchboard versus statistical theories of learning and memory. *Science,* **177**, 850–864.

John, E. R., Herrington, R. N., and Sutton, S. (1967). Effects of visual form on the evoked response. *Science,* **155**, 1439–1442.

John, E. R., and Morgades, P. P. (1969). Patterns and anatomical distribution of evoked potentials and multiple unit activity elicited by conditioned stimuli in trained cats. *Commun. Behav. Biol.,* **3**, 181–207.

John, E. R., Bartlett, F., Shimokochi, M., and Kleinman, D. (1973). Neural readout from memory. *J. Neurophysiol.,* **36**, 893–924.

Jost, A. (1962). Endocrine factors in foetal development. *Triangle,* **5**, 189–194.

Jost, A. D. (1970). Development of sexual characteristics. *Sci. J.,* **6**(6), 67–72.

Jouvet, M. (1962). Récherches sur les structures nerveuses et les mechanismes responsables des different phases du sommeil physiologique. *Arch. Ital. Biol.,* **100**, 125–206.

Jouvet, M. (1965). Paradoxical sleep—a study of its nature and mechanisms. *Progr. Brain Res.,* **1**, 406–424.

Jouvet, M. (1967). Neurophysiology of the states of sleep. *Physiol. Rev.,* **47**, 117–177.

Jouvet, M. (1972). Some monoaminergic mechanisms controlling sleeping and waking. In A. G. Kareczmar and J. C. Eccles (Eds.), *Brain and human behaviour.* Berlin and Heidelberg, Springer-Verlag. Also reprinted in D. G. Stein and J. J. Rosen (Eds.), *Basic structure and function in the central nervous system.* New York and London, Macmillan and Collier-Macmillan, pp. 131–165.

Jouvet, M. (1974). The role of monoaminergic neurones in the regulation and function of sleep. In O. Petre-Quadens and J. D. Schlag (Eds.), *Basic sleep mechanisms.* New York and London, Academic Press, pp. 207–232.

Jouvet, M., and Delorme, F. (1965). Locus coerulus et sommeil paradoxical. *C.R. Soc. Biol.,* **159**, 895–899.

Jung, R. (1972). *Handbook of sensory physiology.* Berlin, Springer.

Jung, R., and Hassler, R. (1960). Extrapyramidal motor system. In J. Field, H. W. Magoun and V. E. Hall (Eds.), *Handbook of physiology,* Section I, Neurophysiology, Vol. II. Washington D.C., American Physiological Society, pp. 863–927.

Kagan, J., and Klein, R. E. (1973). Cross cultural perspectives in early development. *Amer. Psychol.,* **28**, 947–961.

Kahneman, D. (1968). Methods, findings, and theory in studies of visual masking. *Psychol. Bull.,* **70**, 404–425.

Kahneman, D. (1973). *Attention and effort.* Englewood Cliffs, Prentice-Hall.

Kamiya, J., Barber, T. X., Dicara, L. V., Miller, N. E., Shapiro, D., and Stoyva, J. (Eds.) (1971). *Biofeedback and Self-Control.* Chicago, Aldine/Atherton.

Kappers, C. U. A. (1917). Further contributions on neurobiotaxis. *J. Comp. Neurol.,* **27**, 261–298.

Kappers, C. U. A. (1933). Phenomenon of neurobiotaxis in the central nervous system. *Section of anatomy and embryology, Seventeenth International Congress of Medicine, London.* Section 1, part **11**, 109.

Karli, P. (1956). The Norway rats killing response to the white mouse. *Behav.,* **10**, 81–103.

Karlin, L. (1970). Cognition, preparation and sensory evoked potentials. *Psychol. Bull.,* **73**, 122–136.

Karlin, L., and Mordkoff, A. M. (1967). Decreased reaction time produced by discordant warning and reaction stimuli. *Psychon. Sci.,* **9**, 555–556.

Katsuki, Y., Watanabe, T., and Suga, N. (1959). Interaction of auditory neurones in response to two sound stimuli in cat. *J. Neurophysiol.,* **22**, 603–623.

Kellogg, V. (1907). Some silkworm moth reflexes. *Biol. Bull., Woods Hole,* **12**, 152–154.

Kennard, M. A. (1955). Effect of bilateral ablation of cingulate area on behaviour of cats. *J. Neurophysiol.,* **18**, 159–169.

Kendall, S. B., and Thompson, R. F. (1960). Effect of stimulus similarity on sensory preconditioning within a single stimulus dimension. *J. Comp. Physiol. Psychol.,* **53**, 439–442.

Kesner, R. P., and Wilburn, M. W. (1974). A review of electrical stimulation of the brain in the context of learning and retention. *Behav. Biol.,* **10**, 259–293.

Kety, S. S. (1970). Neurochemical aspects of emotional behaviour. In Perry Black (Ed.), *Physiological correlates of emotion.* New York and London, Academic Press, pp. 61–71.

Kimble, D. P., Rogers, L., and Hendrikson, C. W. (1967). Hippocampal lesions disrupt maternal, not sexual behaviour in the albino rat. *J. Comp. Physiol. Psychol.*, **63**, 401–407.

Kimble, R. J., and Kimble, D. P. (1966). Failure to find 'transfer of training' effects via RNA from trained rats injected into naive rats. *Worm Runners Digest*, **8**, 32.

Kinder, E. F. (1927). A study of the nest building activity of the albino rat. *J. Exp. Zoo.*, **47**, 117–161.

King, H. E. (1961). Psychological effects of excitation in the limbic system. In D. E. Sheer (Ed.), *Electrical stimulation of the brain*. Austin, University of Texas Press, pp. 477–486.

King, R. A., and Glasser, R. L. (1970). Duration of electroconvulsive shock-induced retrograde amnesia in rats. *Physiol. Behav.*, **5**, 335–339.

Kinsey, A. C., Pomeroy, W. B., and Martin, C. E. (1948). *Sexual behaviour in the human male*. Philadelphia, W. B. Saunders.

Kinsey, A. C., Pomeroy, W. B., Martin, C. E., and Gebhard, P. H. (1953). *Sexual behaviour in the human female*. Philadelphia, W. B. Saunders.

Klein, D. F., and Davis, J. M. (1969). Diagnosis and drug treatment of psychiatric disorders. Baltimore, Williams & Wilkins.

Kleitman, N. (1963). *Sleep and wakefulness*. Chicago, University of Chicago Press.

Kline, N. S. (1959). *Psychopharmacology frontiers*. Boston, Little Brown.

Kline, N. (1962). Drugs are the greatest practical advance in the history of psychiatry. *New Medical Materia*, **49**.

Kluver, H. (1936). An analysis of the effects of the removal of the occipital lobes in monkeys. *J. Psychol.*, **2**, 49–61.

Kluver, H., and Bucy, P. C. (1939). Preliminary analysis of the function of the temporal lobes in monkeys. *Archives of Neurology and Psychiatry*, **42**, 979–1000. Also reprinted in R. L. Isaacson (Ed.), *Basic readings in neuropsychology*. New York: Harper & Row, 1964.

Kobayashi, T., Lobotsky, J., Lloyd, C. W. (1966). Plasma testosterone and urinary 17-ketosteroids in Japanese and occidentals. *J. Clin. Endocrinol.*, **26**, 610–614.

Koella, W. P. (1974). Neurochemical aspects of sleep. In O. Petre-Quadens and J. D. Schlag (Eds.), *Basic sleep mechanisms*. New York and London, Academic Press, pp. 237–246.

Koffka, K. (1935). *Principles of gestalt psychology*. New York, Harcourt, Brace.

Kogan, A. B. (1969). On physiological mechanisms of sleep inhibition irradiation over the cerebral cortex. In T. Radil-Weiss and H. L. Williams (Eds.), *Interdisciplinary sleep research*. *Activitas Nervosa Superior*, **11-12**, 141–148.

Kopp, R., Bohdanecky, Z., and Jarvick, M. E. (1966). A long temporal gradient of retrograde amnesia for a well discriminated stimulus. *Science*, **153**, 1547–1549.

Krech, D., Rosenzweig, M. R., and Bennett, E. L. (1962). Relations between brain chemistry and problem solving among rats raised in enriched and impoverished environments. *J. Comp. Physiol. Psychol.*, **55**, 801–807.

Krikstone, B. J., and Levitt, R. A. (1975). Distorting drugs. In R. A. Levitt (Ed.), *Psychopharmacology: A Biological Approach*. New York, John Wiley, pp. 255–298.

Kuffler, S. W. (1953). Discharge patterns and functional organization of mammalian retina. *J. Neurophysiol.*, **16**, 37–68.

Kulikowski, J. J. (1969). Limiting conditions of visual perception (in Polish, also English translation). *Prace Instytutu Automatkyi P.A.N., (Warsaw)*. **77**, 1–133.

Kulikowski, J. J., Abadi, R., and King-Smith, P. E. (1973). Orientational selectivity of grating and line detectors in human vision. *Vision Res.*, **13**, 1479–1486.

Kulikowski, J. J., and King-Smith, P. E. (1973). Spatial arrangement of line, edge and grating detectors revealed by subthreshold summation. *Vision Res.*, **13**, 1455–1478.

Lacey, J. I. (1967). Somatic response patterning and stress: some revisions of activation theory. In M. H. Appley and R. Trumbull, *Psychological stress*. New York, Appleton-Century-Crofts, pp. 14–37.

Lacey, J. I., and Lacey, B. C. (1970). Some autonomic-central nervous system inter-relationships. In P. Black (Ed.), *Physiological correlates of emotion*. New York, Academic Press, pp. 205–227.

Laing, R. D. (1967). *The politics of experience*. Harmondsworth, Penguin Books.

Lange, C. G. (1885). Om sindsberaegelser et psyko fysiolog studie. Copenhagen, Krønar.

Larsson, K. (1964). Mating behaviour in male rats after cerebral cortical ablation. II. Effects of lesions in the frontal lobes compared to lesions in the posterior half of the hemispheres. *J. Zoology.*, **155**, 203–214.

Larsson, K. (1962). Mating behaviour in male rats after cerebral cortical ablation. I. Effects of lesions in the dorsolateral and the median cortex. *J. Zoology*, **151**, 167–176.

Larsson, K., and Sodersten, P. (1973). Mating in male rats after section of the dorsal penile nerve. *Physiol. Behav.*, **10**, 567–571.

Larue, C. G., and Le Magnen, J. (1972). The olfactory control of meal patterns in rats. *Physiol. Behav.*, **9**, 817–821.

Lashley, K. S. (1930). The mechanism of vision. II. The influence of cerebral lesions upon the threshold of discrimination for brightness. *J. Genet. Psychol.*, **37**, 461–480.

Lashley, K. S. (1935). The mechanism of vision. XII. Nervous structures concerned in habits based on reactions to light. *Comp. Psychol. Monogr.*, **11**, 43-79.

Lashley, K. S. (1938). The thalamus and emotion. *Psychol. Rev.*, **45**, 42-61.

Lashley, K. S. (1950). In search of the engram. *Symp. Exp. Biol.*, **4**, 454-482.

Laties, V., and Weiss, B. (1966). Influence of drugs on behaviour controlled by internal and external stimuli. *J. Pharmacol. Exp. Therap.*, **152**, 388-396.

Lehmann, H. E. (1966). Depression: categories, mechanisms, and phenomena. In J. O. Cole and J. R. Wittenhorn (Eds.), *Pharmacotherapy of depression.* Springfield, Charles C. Thomas.

Lehman, D., and Fender, D. H. (1968). Component analysis of human averaged evoked potentials: dichoptic stimuli using different target structures. *Electroenceph. clin. Neurophysiol.*, **24**, 542-553.

Leibowitz, H. W., and Pick, H. A. (1973). Cross cultural and educational aspects of the Ponzo perspective illusion. *Percept. Psychophys.*, **12**, 430-432.

Lele, P. P., and Wedell, G. (1956). The relationship between neurohistology and corneal sensibility. *Brain*, **79**, 119-154.

Le Beau, J. (1952). The cingular and precingular areas in psychosurgery (agitated behaviour, obsessive compulsive states, epilepsy). *Acta Psychiatrica et Neurologica Copenhagen*, **27**, 305-316.

Le Magnen, J. (1953). Activité de l'insuline sur la consommation spontanée des solutions sapid. *C. R. Soc. Biol.*, 1753-1757.

Le Magnen, J. (1954). Le processus de discrimination par le rat blanc des stimuli sucres alimentaires et non alimentaires. *J. Physiol. (Paris)*, **46**, 414-418.

Le Magnen, J. (1956). Hyperphagie provoquée chez le rat blanc par alteration du mecanisme de satieté peripherique. *C. R. Soc. Biol.*, **150**, 32.

Le Magnen, J. (1971). Advances in studies on the physiological control and regulation of food intake. In E. Stellar and J. M. Sprague (Eds.), *Progress in physiological psychology*, Vol. 4. New York and London, Academic Press, pp. 204-261.

Le Magnen, J., Davos, M., Gaudilliere, J-P., Sylvestr., J. L., and Tallon, S. (1973). Role of a lipostatic mechanism in regulation by feeding of energy balance in rats. *J. Comp. Physiol. Psychol.*, **84**, 1-23.

Lemaire, L. (1956). Danish experience regarding the castration of sexual offenders. *J. Crim. Law. Criminol.*, **47**, 294-310.

Lester, B. K., Chanes, R. E., and Condit, P. T. (1969). A clinical syndrome and EEG sleep stages associated with amino acid deprivation. *Amer. J. Psychiatr.*, **126**, 185-190.

Levine, S. (1962). The psychophysiological effects of infantile stimulation. In E. L. Bliss (Ed.), *Roots of behaviour.* New York, Harper, pp. 246-253.

Levine, S., and Mullins, R. F. (1966). Hormonal influences on brain organization in infant rats. *Science*, **152**, 1585-1592.

Levitt, R. A. (1975). *Psychopharmacology: a biological approach.* New York, John Wiley & Sons (Halstead Press).

Levitt, R. A., and Krikstone, B. J. (1975). The tranquilizers. In R. A. Levitt (Ed.), *Psychopharmacology.* New York, John Wiley & Sons (Halstead Press), pp. 117-144.

Levitt, R. A., and Lonorski, D. J. (1975). Adrenergic drugs. In R. A. Levitt (Ed.), *Psychopharmacology.* New York, John Wiley & Sons (Halstead Press), pp. 15-50.

Levy, R. (1971). *Recognition of dichotic word lists in focussed and divided attention.* Unpublished M.A. thesis, Hebrew University, Jerusalem (Hebrew).

Lewis, D. J., and Maher, A. (1965). Neural consolidation and ECS. *Psychol. Rev.*, **72**, 225-239.

Lewis, J. L. (1970). Semantic processing of unattended messages using dichotic listening. *J. Exp. Psychol.*, **85**, 225-228.

Lindesmith, A. (1970). Psychology of addiction. In W. G. Clark and J. del Guidice (Eds.), *Principles of psychopharmacology.* New York and London, Academic Press, pp. 471-476.

Lindsley, D. B. (1951). Emotion. In S. S. Stevens (Ed.), *Handbook of experimental psychology.* New York, John Wiley & Sons, pp. 473-516.

Lindsley, D. B. (1960). Attention, consciousness, sleep, and wakefulness. In J. Field, H. W. Magoun, and V. E. Hall (Eds.), *Handbook of physiology* Section I. Neurophysiology, Vol. III. Washington D.C., American Physiological Society, pp. 1553-1593.

Lindsley, D. B. (1970). The role of non-specific reticulo-thalamo-cortical systems in emotion. In P. Black (Ed.), *Physiological correlates of emotion.* New York, Academic Press, pp. 147-188.

Lindsley, D. B., Schreiner, L. H., Knowles, W. B., and Magoun, H. W. (1949). Effect on EEG of acute injury to the brainstem activating system. *Electroenceph. clin. Neurophysiol.*, **1**, 475-486.

Lindsley, D. B., Shreiner, L. H., Knowles, W. B., and Magoun, H. W. (1950). Behavioural and EEG changes following chronic brain stem lesions in the cat. *Electroenceph. clin. Neurophysiol.*, **2**, 483-498.

Lippold, O. (1970). Are alpha waves artefactual? *New Scientist*, **45**, 506-507.

Lisk, R. D. (1962). Diencephalic placement of estradiol and sexual receptivity in the female rat. *Amer. J. Physiol.*, **203**, 493-496.

Lisk, R. D. (1968). Copulatory activity of the male rat following placement of preoptic anterior hypothalamic lesions. *Exp. Brain. Res.*, **5**, 306-313.

Livingston, R. B. (1960). Central control of receptors and sensory transmission systems. In J. Field, H. W. Magoun, and V. E. Hall (Eds.), *Handbook of physiology* Section I. Neurophysiology, Vol. III, Washington D.C., American Physiological Society, pp. 741-760.

Lloyd, C. W. (1968). The influence of hormones on human sexual behaviour. In E. B. Astwood (Ed.), *Clinical endocrinology*, Vol. 2. New York, Grune & Stratton, pp. 665-674.

Longo, V. G. (1972). *Neuropharmacology and behaviour*. San Francisco, Freeman.

Longuet-Higgins, H. C. (1968). Holographic model of temporal recall. *Nature*, **217**, 104.

Loomis, A. L., Harvey, E. N., and Hobart, G. (1937). Cerebral states during sleep as studied by human brain potentials. *J. Exp. Psychol.*, **21**, 127–144.

Loomis, A. L., Harvey, E. N., and Hobart, G. (1938). Distribution of disturbance patterns in the human electroencephalogram, with special reference to sleep. *J. Neurophysiol.*, **1**, 413–430.

Lorente de Nó. Analysis of the activity of the chains of internuncial neurones. *J. Neurophysiol.*, **1**, 207–244.

Lorenz, K. (1952). *King Solomon's Ring*. London, Methuen.

Luttges, M., Johnson, T., Buck, C., Holland, J., and McGaugh, J. (1966). An examination of 'transfer of learning' by nucleic acid. *Science*, **151**, 834–837.

Lynn, R. (1966). *Attention, arousal and the orientation reaction*. Oxford, Pergamon Press.

Lyon, M., and Randrupp, A. (1972). The dose-response effect of amphetamine upon avoidance behaviour in the rat seen as a function of increasing stereotypy. *Psychopharmacologia (Berl.)*, **23**, 334–347.

McCance, R. A. (1936). Experimental sodium chloride deficiency in man. *Proc. Roy. Soc., Series B*, **119**, 245–268.

McCarley, R. W., and Hobson, J. A. (1975). Discharge patterns of cat pontine brain stem neurones during desynchronized sleep. *J. Neurophysiol.*, **38**, 751–766.

MacLean, P. D. (1949). Psychosomatic disease and the visceral brain: recent developments bearing on the Papez theory of emotion. *Psychosomatic Med.*, **11**, 338–353.

MacLean, P. D. and Delgardo, J. M. R. (1953). Electrical and chemical stimulation of frontotemporal portion of limbic system in waking animal. *Electroenceph. clin. Neurophysiol.*, **5**, 91–100.

McClearn, G. E., and De Fries, J. C. (1973). *Introduction to behavioural genetics*. San Francisco, W. H. Freeman.

McConnell, J. V. (1962). Memory transfer through cannibalism in planarians. *J. Neuropsychiatr.*, **Suppl. 1**, 542–548.

McGaugh, J. L., and Petrinovich, L. F. (1966). Neural consolidation and electroconvulsive shock re-examined. *Psychol. Rev.*, **73**, 382–387.

McGaugh, J. L., and Landfield, P. W. (1970). Delayed development of amnesia following electroconvulsive shock. *Physiol. Behav.*, **5**, 1109–1113.

MacNichol, E. F. (1966). Retinal processing of visual data. *Proc. Nat. Acad. Sci., U.S.A.*, **55**, 1331–1344.

MacNichol, E. F., and Svaetichin, G. (1958). Electric responses from isolated retinas of fishes. *Amer. J. Opthalmology.*, **46**, 26–40.

Magendie, F. (1826). *Lehrbuch der Physiologie*. Tubingen, Ostrander.

Magoun, H. W. (1963). *The waking brain*. Springfield, Charles C. Thomas.

Magoun, H. W., Harrison, F., Brobeck, J. R., and Ransom, S. W. (1938). Activation of heat loss mechanisms by local heating of the brain. *J. Neurophysiol.*, **1**, 101–114.

Mah, C. J., and Albert, D. J. (1973). Electroconvulsive shock-induced retrograde amnesia: an analysis of the variation in the length of the amnesia gradient. *Behavioural Biol.*, **9**, 517–540.

Malmo, R. B. (1959). Activation: a neurophysiological dimension. *Psychol. Rev.*, **66**, 367–386.

Malsbury, C. W. (1971). Facilitation of male rat copulatory behaviour by electrical stimulation of the medial preoptic area. *Physiol. and Behav.*, **7**, 797–805.

Maranon, G. (1924). Contribution a l'étude de l'action émotive de l'adrenaline. *Rev. Francaise Endocrinol.*, **2**, 301–325.

Mardones, J. (1963). The alcohols. In W. S. Root and F. G. Hoffman (Eds.), *Physiological pharmacology: a comprehensive treatise*, Vol. 1, Pt. A. New York, Academic Press.

Margules, D. L., and Olds, J. (1962). Identical 'feeding' and 'rewarding' systems in the lateral hypothalamus of rats. *Science*, **135**, 374–375.

Marshall, N. B., Barnett, R. J., and Mayer, J. (1955). Hypothalamic lesions in goldthioglucose injected mice. *Proc. Soc. Exp. Biol. Med.*, **90**, 240.

Mason, J. W. (1958). The central nervous system regulation of ACTH secretion. In H. H. Jaspers *et al.* (Eds.), *Reticular formation of the brain*. Boston, Little Brown, pp. 645–670.

Mason, J. W. (1972). Organization of psychoendocrine mechanisms: a review and reconsideration of research. In N. S. Greenfield and R. A. Sternbach (Eds.), *Handbook of psychophysiology*. New York, Holt, Rinehart & Winston, pp. 3–91.

Masserman, J. H. (1941). Is the hypothalamus a centre of emotion? *Psychosom. Med.*, **3**, 3–25.

Masters, W. H., and Johnson, V. E. (1965). The sexual response cycles of the human male and female: comparative anatomy and physiology. In F. A. Beach (Ed.), *Sex and behaviour*. New York, John Wiley & Sons, pp. 512–534.

Masters, W. H., and Johnson, V. E. (1966). *The human sexual response*. Boston, Little Brown.

Matthews, M. R. (1964). Further observations on transneural degeneration in the lateral geniculate nucleus of the macaque monkey. *J. Anat.*, **98**, 255–263.

Maturana, H. R., Lettvin, J. Y., McCulloch, W. S., and Pitts, W. H. (1960). Anatomy and physiology of vision in the frog (*Rana pipiens*). *J. General Physiol.*, **43**, (Suppl. 2), 129–175.

Mayer, J. (1953). Glucostatic mechanisms of regulation of food intake. *New England J. Med.*, **249**, 13–16.

Mayer-Gross, W., Slater, E. T. C., and Roth, M. (1960). *Clinical psychiatry*. Baltimore, Williams & Wilkins.

Mayor, S. J. (1969). Memory in the Japanese quail: effects of puromycin and acetoxycycloheximide. *Science*, 166, 1165–1167.

Mendel, G. J. (1866). *Experiments in plant hybridization*. Translation of Mendel's original classic paper with commentary and assessment by Sir R. A. Fisher. Edinburgh, Oliver & Boyd (1965).

Mendoza, J. E., and Adams, H. E. (1969). Does electroconvulsive shock produce retrograde amnesia. *Physiol. Behav.*, 4, 307–309.

Melzack, R., and Wall, P. D. (1965). Pain mechanism: a new theory. *Science*, 150, 971–979.

Merton, P. A. (1950). Significance of the 'silent period' of muscles. *Nature*, 166, 733–734.

Merton, P. A. (1951). The silent period in a muscle of the human hand. *J. Physiol.*, 114, 183–198.

Meyer, D. R. (1972). Access to engrams. *Amer. Psychol.*, 27, 124–133.

Meyer, P. M. (1963). Analysis of visual behaviour in cats with extensive neocortical ablations. *J. Comp. Physiol. Psychol.*, 56, 397–401.

Meyers, F. H., Jawetz, E., and Goldfien, A. (1972). *A review of medical pharmacology*, (3rd ed.) Los Altos, Calif., Lange.

Michael, C. R. (1966). Receptive fields of opponent colour units in the optic nerve of the ground squirrel. *Science*, 152, 1095–1097.

Mihailovic, L., and Jankovic, B. D. (1961). Effect of intraventricularly injected anti-m. caudatus antibody on the electrical activity of the cat brain. *Nature*, 192, 665–666.

Miller, N. E. (1955). Shortcomings of food consumption as a measure of hunger; results from other behavioural techniques. *Annals. N.Y. Acad. Sci.*, 63, 141–143.

Miller, N. E., Bailey, C. J., and Stevenson, J. A. F. (1950). Decreased 'hunger' but increased food intake resulting from hypothalamic lesions. *Science*, 112, 256–259.

Miller, R. R., and Springer, A. D. (1971). Temporal course of amnesia in rats after electroconvulsive shock. *Physiol. Behav.*, 6, 229–233.

Miller, R. R., and Springer, A. D. (1972). Induced recovery of memory in rats following electroconvulsive shock. *Physiol. Behav.*, 8, 645–651.

Miller, R. R., Malinowski, B., Puk, G., and Springer, A. D. (1972). State dependent models of ECS-induced amnesia in rats. *J. Comp. Physiol. Psychol.*, 81, 533–540.

Milner, B. (1970b). Memory and the medial temporal regions of the brain. In K. H. Pribram and D. E. Broadbent (Eds.), *Biology of memory*. New York and London, Academic Press, pp. 29–50.

Milner, P. M. (1970a). *Physiological psychology*. New York, Holt, Rinehart & Winston.

Minkowski, M. (1913). Experimentelle Untersuchungen uber die Beziehungen der Grosshirnrinde und der Netzhaut den primaren optischen Zentren, besonders zum Corpus geniculatum externen. *Erb. Hirnanat. Inst. Zurich*, 7, 255–362.

Misanin, J. R., Miller, R., and Lewis, D. J. (1968). Retrograde amnesia produced by electroconvulsive shock after reactivation of a consolidated memory trace. *Science*, 160, 554–555.

Mitoma, C., Auld, R. M., and Udenfriend, S. (1957). On the nature of enzymatic defect in phenylpyruric oligophrenia. *Proc. Soc. Exp. Biol. Med.*, 94, 632–638.

Mize, R. R., and Murphy, E. H. (1973). Selective visual experience fails to modify receptive field properties of rabbit-striate cortex neurones. *Science*, 180, 320–323.

Money, J. (1961a). Sex hormones and other variables in human eroticism. In W. C. Young (Ed.), *Sex and internal secretions*. Baltimore, Williams & Wilkins, pp. 1383–1400.

Money, J. (1961b). Components of eroticism in man. I. The hormones in relation to sexual morphology and sexual desire. *J. Nerv. Ment Dis.*, 132, 239–248.

Money, J. (1965). Influence of hormones on sexual behaviour. *Ann. Rev. Med.*, 16, 67–82.

Money, J. (1970). Sexual dimorphism and homosexual gender identity. *Psychol. Bull.*, 74, 425–440.

Monnier, M., Kalbere, M., and Krupp, P. (1960). Functional antagonism between diffuse reticular and intralaminary recruiting projections in the medial thalamus. *Exp. Neurol.*, 2, 271–289.

Monro, D. H., Horne, H. W., and Paull, D. P. (1948). The effect of injury to the spinal cord and cauda equina on sexual potency in man. *New England. J. Med.*, 239, 903–911.

Monroe, R. R. (1959). Episodic behavioural disorders—schizophrenia or epilepsy. *Arch. Gen. Psychiatr.*, 1, 205–214.

Montgomery, M. F. (1931a). The influence of atropine and pilocarpin on thirst (voluntary ingestion of water). *Amer. J. Physiol.*, 98, 35–41.

Montgomery, M. F. (1931b). The role of the salivary glands in the thirst mechanism. *Amer. J. Physiol.*, 96, 221–227.

Moray, N. (1959). Attention in dichotic listening: affective clues and the influence of instructions. *Quart. J. Exp. Psychol.*, 9, 56–60.

Moray, N. (1969). *Listening and attention*. Harmondsworth, Penguin Books.

Morgan, C. T., and Morgan, J. D. (1940). Studies in hunger. II. The relation of gastric denervation and dietary sugar to the effect of insulin upon food intake in the rat. *J. Gen. Psychol.*, 57, 153–163.

Morgane, P. J. (1961a). Medial forebrain bundle and 'feeding centres' of the hypothalamus. *J. Comp. Neurol.*, 117, 1–26.

Morgane, P. J. (1961b). Distinct 'feeding' and 'hunger' motivating systems in the lateral hypothalamus of the rat. *Science*, 133, 887–888.

Morrell, L. K., and Morrell, F. (1966). Evoked potentials and reaction times: a study of inter-individual variability. *Electroenceph. clin. Neurophysiol.*, 20, 567–575.

Morton, J. H., Addition, H., Addison, R. G., Hunt, L.,

and Sullivan, J. J. (1953). A clinical study of pre-menstrual tension. *Amer. J. Obst. Gynecol.*, **65**, 1182–1191.

Moruzzi, G. (1974). Neural mechanisms of the sleep-ing–waking cycle. In O. Petre-Quadens and J. D. Schlag (Eds.), *Basic sleep mechanisms*. New York and London, Academic Press, pp. 13–31.

Moruzzi, G., and Magoun, H. W. (1949). Brainstem reticular formation and activation of the EEG. *Electroenceph. clin. Neurophysiol.*, **1**, 455–473.

Moses, J. M., Johnson, L. C., Naitoh, P., and Lubin, A. (1975). Sleep stage deprivation and total sleep loss: effects on sleep behaviour. *Psychophysiol.*, **12**, 141–146.

Mosher, L. R., and Feinsilver, D. (1971). *Special report: schizophrenia*. Rockville, Maryland, U.S. Department of Health, Education and Welfare. Publ. No. (HSM) 72-9042.

Motokawa, K., Oikawa, T., and Tasaki, K. (1957). Receptor potential of vertebrate retina. *J. Neuro-physiol.*, **20**, 186–199.

Mountcastle, V. B., and Henneman, E. (1952). The representation of tactile sensibility in the thalamus of the monkey. *J. Comp. Neurol.*, **97**, 409–431.

Mountcastle, V. B., and Poggio, G. F., and Werner, G. (1963). The relation of thalamic cell response to peripheral stimuli varied over an intensive continu-um. *J. Neurophysiol.*, **26**, 807–834.

Moushegian, G., Rupert, A., Marsh, J. J., and Galambos, R. (1961). Evoked cortical potentials in absence of middle ear muscles. *Science*, **133**, 582–583.

Moyer, K. E. (1971). *The physiology of hostility*. Chicago, Markham.

Muir, D. W., and Mitchell, D. E. (1973). Visual resolu-tion and experience. Acuity deficits in cats follow-ing early selective visual deprivation. *Science*, **180**, 420–422.

Muller, J. (1842). *Elements of Physiology*. London, Taylor & Walton.

Myers, T. I. (1969). Tolerance for sensory and percep-tual deprivation. In J. P. Zubeck, (Ed.), *Sensory deprivation: fifteen years of research*. New York, Appleton-Centry-Crofts, pp. 289–331.

Naatanen, R. (1967). Selective attention and evoked potentials. *Annals. Acad. Sci. Fennicae.*, (Annals of the Finnish Academy of Sciences), **151**, 1–226.

Naatanen, R. (1970). Evoked potential, EEG and slow potential correlates of selective attention. *Acta Psychologica.*, **33**, 178–192.

Nakayama, T., Eisenman, J. S., and Hardy, J. D. (1961). Single unit activity of anterior hypothala-mus during local heating. *Science*, **134**, 560–561.

Nakayama, T., Hammel, H. T., Hardy, J. D., and Eisenman, J. S. (1963). Thermal stimulation of electrical activity of single units of the preoptic region. *Amer. J. Physiol.*, **204**, 1122–1126.

Nash, J. (1970). *Developmental psychology: a psycho-biological approach*. Englewood Cliffs, Prentice-Hall.

Neisser, U. (1967). *Cognitive psychology*. New York, Appleton-Century-Crofts.

Neisser, U. (1969). *Selective reading: a method for the study of visual attention*. Presented at the 19th International Congress of Psychology, London.

Netter, F. H. (1953). *The Ciba collection of medical illustrations*, Vol. 1. Nervous System. New York, Ciba.

Neumann, F., and Elger, W. (1966). Permanent changes in gonadal function and sexual behaviour as a result of early feminization of male rats by treat-ment with an antiandrogenic steroid. *Endocrino-logie*, **50**, 209–225.

Nichols, J. R. (1963). A procedure which produces sustained opiate directed behaviour (morphine addiction) in the rat. *Psychol. Rev.*, **13**, 895–904.

Nisbett, R. E. (1972). Hunger, obesity and the ventro-medial hypothalamus. *Psychol. Rev.*, **79**, 433–453.

Nissen, H. W. (1929). The effects of gonadectomy, vasotomy, and injections of placental and orchic extracts on the sex behaviour of the white rat. *Genet. Physiol. Monogr.*, **5**, 451–547.

Nissen, H. W. (1930). A study of exploratory behaviour in the white rat by means of the obstruction method. *J. Genet. Psychol.*, **37**, 361–376.

Nissen, T., Riøgaard Peterson, H. H., and Fjerdingstad, E. J. (1965). Effect of ribonucleic acid (RNA) ex-tracted from the brain of trained animals on learning in rats. II. Dependence of the RNA-effect on training conditions prior to RNA extraction. *Scand. J. Psychol.*, **6**, 265–272.

Noble, G. K., and Aronson, L. R. (1942). The sexual behaviour of anura. I. The normal mating pattern of *Rana pipiens. Bull. Amer. Mus. Nat. Hist.*, **80**, 127–142.

Norman, D. A. (1968). Towards a theory of memory and attention. *Psychol. Rev.*, **75**, 522–536.

Oakley, D. A., and Steele Russell, I. (1972). Neo-cortical lesions and Pavlovian conditioning. *Physiol. Behav.*, **8**, 915–926.

Oatley, K. (1964). Changes of blood volume and osmotic pressure in the production of thirst. *Nature*, **202**, 1341–1342.

Ohman, A., and Lader, M. (1972). Selective attention and 'habituation' of the auditory averaged evoked response in humans. *Physiol. Behav.*, **8**, 79–85.

Ohmer, E., Hayden, M. P., and Segelbaum, R. (1969). Encephalic cycles during sleep and wakefulness: a 24-hour pattern. *Science*, **164**, 447–449.

Okuma, T., Majamura, K., Hayashi, A., and Fujimori, M. (1966). Psychophysiological study on the depth of sleep in normal human subjects. *Electroenceph. clin. Neurophysiol.*, **21**, 140–147.

Olds, J. (1956a). A preliminary mapping of electrical reinforcing effects in the rat brain. *J. Comp. Physiol. Psychol.*, **49**, 281–285.

Olds, J. (1956b). Runway and maze behaviour con-trolled by basomedial forebrain stimulation in the rat. *J. Comp. Physiol. Psychol.*, **49**, 507–512.

Olds, J. (1960). Differentiation of reward systems in the brain by self-stimulation technics. In E. R. Ramey and D. S. O'Doherty (Eds.), *Electrical studies on the unanaesthetized brain*. New York, Hoeber, pp. 17–51.

Olds, J. (1962). Hypothalamic substrates of reward. *Physiol. Rev.*, **42**, 554–604.

Olds, J. (1969). The central nervous system and the reinforcement of behaviour. *Amer. Psychol.*, **24**, 114–132.

Olds, J., and Milner, P. (1954). Positive reinforcement produced by electrical stimulation of septal area and other regions of rat brain. *J. Comp. Physiol. Psychol.*, **47**, 419–427.

Olds, J., and Olds, M. E. (1961). Interference and learning in paleocortical systems. In J. F. Delafresnaye (Ed.), *Brain mechanisms and learning*. Springfield, Charles C. Thomas, pp. 153–183.

Olds, J., and Olds, M. (1965). Drives, rewards and the brain. In F. Barron *et al.* (Eds.), *New directions in psychology*, Vol. 2. New York, Holt, Rinehart & Winston, pp. 329–410.

Oomura, Y., Ooyama, H., Yamamato, T., and Naka, F. (1967). Reciprocal relationship of the lateral and ventromedial hypothalamus in the regulation of food intake. *Physiol. Behav.*, **2**, 97–115.

Oomura, Y., Ono, T., Ooyama, H., and Wayner, M. J. (1969). Glucose and osmosensitive neurones of the rat hypothalamus. *Nature*, **222**, 282–284.

Oparin, A. I. (1938). *The origin of life on earth*. London, Macmillan, (2nd ed., 1957, Academic Press, New York).

Orbach, J., Milner, B., and Rasmussen, T. (1960). Learning and retention in monkeys after amygdala-hippocampus resection. *Arch. Neurol.*, **3**, 230–251.

Oppenheimer, D. R., Palmer, E., and Wedell, G. (1958). Nerve endings in the conjuctiva. *J. Anat.*, **92**, 321–352.

Osmond, H., and Smythies, J. R. (1952). Schizophrenia: a new approach. *J. Ment. Sci.*, **98**, 309–315.

Oswald, I. (1962). *Sleeping and waking*. Amsterdam and New York, Elsevier.

Oswald, I. (1968). Drugs and sleep. *Pharmacol. Rev.*, **20**, 273–297.

Oswald, I. (1969). Human brain protein, drugs, and dreams. *Nature*, **223**, 893–897.

Overton, D. A. (1966). State-dependent learning produced by depressant and atropine like drugs. *Psychopharmacologia (Berlin)*, **10**, 6–31.

Palestini, M., Davidovitch, A., and Hernandez-Peon, R. (1959). Functional significance of centrifugal influences upon the retina. *Acta. Neurol. Latinoamer.*, **5**, 113–131.

Palka, Y. S., and Sawyer, C. H. (1966). Induction of oestrus behaviour in rabbits by hypothalamic implants of testosterone. *Amer. J. Physiol.*, **211**, 225–228.

Panksepp, J. (1971a). Is satiety mediated by the ventromedial hypothalamus? *Physiol. Behav.*, **7**, 381–384.

Panksepp, J. (1971b). A re-examination of the role of the ventromedial hypothalamus in feeding behaviour. *Physiol. Behav.*, **7**, 385–394.

Panksepp, J., and Booth, D. A. (1971). Decreased feeding after injections of amino acids into the hypothalamus. *Nature*, **233**, 341–342.

Papez, J. (1937). A proposed mechanism of emotion. *Arch. Neurol. Psychiatr.*, **38**, 725–744. Also reprinted in R. L. Isaacson (1964). *Basic readings in neuropsychology*. New York, Harper & Row, pp. 87–109.

Parker, M. M. (1939). The inter-relationship of six different situations in the measurement of emotionality in the adult albino rat. *Psychol. Bull.*, **36**, 564–5.

Penfield, W. (1951). Memory mechanisms. *Amer. Neurol. Ass. Trans.*, **76**, 15–39.

Penfield, W. (1952). Memory mechanisms. *Arch. Neurol. Psychiatr.*, **67**, 178–198.

Penfield, W., and Roberts, L. (1959). *Speech and brain mechanisms*. Princeton, Princeton University Press.

Peters, R. H., Senserig, L. D., and Reich, M. J. (1973). Fixed ratio performance following ventromedial hypothalamic lesions in rats. *Physiol. Psychol.*, **1**, 136–138.

Pettigrew, J. D., and Freeman, R. D. (1973). Visual experience without lines: effect on developing cortical neurones. *Science*, **182**, 599–601.

Pettigrew, J. D., Olson, C., and Hirsch, H. V. B. (1973). Cortical effect of selective visual experience: degeneration or reorganisation? *Brain Res.*, **51**, 345–351.

Pfaff, D. (1968). Autoradiographic localization of radioactivity in rat brain after injection of tritiated sex hormones. *Science*, **161**, 1355–1356.

Pfaff, D. W. (1969). Histological differences between ventromedial hypothalamic neurones of well fed and underfed rats. *Nature*, **223**, 77–78.

Phillips, A. G., and Mogenson, G. J. (1968). Effects of unilateral hypothalamic lesions on drinking and self stimulation in the rat. *Psychonom. Sci.*, **10**, 307–308.

Phillips, S. G. (1973). Report by S. G. Phillips, Senior Medical Officer for Environmental Services to Birmingham City Health Committee on the blood lead levels of people living near the spaghetti junction motorway interchange; summarized by Anthony Tucker *The Guardian* 13 July, 1973.

Phoenix, C. H., Goy, R. W., Gerall, A. A., and Young, W. C. (1959). Organising action of prenatally administered testosterone propionate on the tissues mediating mating behaviour in the female guinea pig. *Endocrinol.*, **65**, 369–382.

Phoenix, C. H., Slob, A. K., and Goy, R. W. (1973). Effects of castration and replacement therapy on the sexual behaviour of adult male rhesuses. *J. Comp. Physiol. Psychol.*, **84**, 472–481.

Picton, T. W., Hillyard, S. A., Galambos, R., and Schiff, M. (1971). Human auditory attention: a central or peripheral process? *Science*, **173**, 351–353.

Picton, T. W., and Hillyard, S. A. (1974). Human auditory evoked potentials. II. Effects of attention. *Electroenceph. clin. Neurophysiol.*, **36**, 191–199.

Pitts, W., and McCulloch, W. S., (1947). How we know universals: the perception of auditory and visual forms. *Bull. Maths. Biophysics*, **9**, 127–147.

Pliskoff, S. S., Wright, J. E., and Hawkins, T. D. (1965). Brain stimulation as a reinforcer: intermittent schedules. *J. Exp. Anal. Behav.*, **8**, 75–88.

Poggio, G. F., and Mountcastle, V. B. (1963). The functional properties of ventrobasal thalamic neurones studied in unanaesthetized monkeys. *J. Neurophysiol.*, **26**, 775–806.

Polanyi, M. (1965). Structure of consciousness. *Brain*, **88**, 799–811.

Pollen, D. A., Lee, J. R., and Taylor, J. H. (1971). How does the striate cortex begin the reconstruction of the visual world. *Science*, **173**, 74–77.

Pompeiano, O. (1967). The neurophysiological mechanisms of the postural and motor events during desynchronized sleep. In *Res. Publ. Ass. Res. Nerv. Ment. Dis.*, **45**, *Sleep and altered states of consciousness*. Baltimore, Williams & Wilkins Co., pp. 351–423.

Premack, D. (1970). The education of Sarah. *Psychology Today*. **4**, 54–58.

Pressman, B. C. (1968). Ionophorous antibiotics as models for biological transport. *Fed. Proc.*, **27**, 1283–1288.

Pringle, M. L. K., and Tanner, M. (1958). The effects of early deprivation on speech development. *Lang, Speech*, **1**, 269–287.

Pribram, H. B., and Barry, J. (1956). Further behavioural analysis of parieto-temporo-preoccipital cortex. *J. Neurophysiol.*, **19**, 99–106.

Pribram, K. H. (1969). The neurophysiology of remembering. *Sci. Amer.*, **220**, 73–86.

Proctor, R. C. (1962). Clinical use of chlordiazepoxide. In J. H. Nodine and J. H. Mayer (Eds.), *Psychosomatic medicine*. Philadelphia, Lea & Febiger, pp. 480–488.

Provence, S., and Lipton, R. C. (1962). *Infants in institutions*. New York, International Universities Press.

Purpura, D. P. (1959). Nature of electrocortical potentials and synaptic organizations in cerebral and cerebellar cortex. *Internat. Rev. Neurobiol.*, **1**, 47–163.

Quartermain, D., and McEwen, B. S. (1970). Temporal characteristics of amnesia induced by protein synthesis inhibitor: determination by shock level. *Nature*, **228**, 677–678.

Quartermain, D., McEwen, B. S., and Azmitia, E. C. (1972). Recovery of memory following amnesia in the rat and mouse. *J. Comp. Physiol. Psychol.*, **79**, 360–370.

Quay, W. B., Bennett, E. L., Rosenzweig, M. R., and Krech, D. (1969). Effects of isolation and environmental complexity on brain and pineal organ. *Physiol. Behav.*, **4**, 489–494.

Radford, E. P. (1959). Factors modifying water metabolism in rats fed dry diets. *Amer. J. Physiol.*, **196**, 1098–1108.

Ramon Y Cajal, S. (1909). Histologie du système nerveux de l'homme et des vertébrés (reprinted from original 1909–1911). Madrid, Consejo Superior de Investigaciones Cientificas, 1952–1955.

Ramon Y Cajal, S. (1934). Les preuve objectives de l'unité anatomique des cellules nerveuse. *Trob. Lab. Inest. Biol. Univ. Madr.*, **29**, 1–37.

Ramon Y Cajal, S. (1954). Neurone theory or reticular theory? *Consejo Superior de Investigaciones Cientificas, Madrid*, (English translation).

Rampone, A. J., and Shirasu, M. E. (1964). Temperature changes in the rat in response to feeding. *Science*, **144**, 317–319.

Randall, L. O., Schallek, W., Heise, G. A., Kieth, E. F., and Bagdon, R. E. (1960). The psychosedative properties of methaminodiazepoxide. *J. Pharmacol. Exp. Therap.*, **129**, 163–171.

Ratliffe, F., and Hartline, H. K. (1959). The responses of limulus optic nerve fibres to patterns of illumination on the receptor mosaic. *J. General Physiol.*, **42**, 1241–1255.

Ray, O. S. (1972). *Drugs, society, and human behaviour*. St. Louis, Miss., C. V. Mosby.

Reason, J. T., and Brand, J. J. (1974). *Motion sickness*. London, Academic Press.

Rechtschaffen, A., and Monroe, L. J. (1969). Laboratory studies of insomnia. In A. Kales (Ed.), *Sleep: physiology and pathology*. Philadelphia and Toronto, J. B. Lippincott & Co., pp. 158–170.

Redmond, D. E., Hinriches, R. L., Maas, J. W., and Kling, A. (1973). Behaviour of free ranging macaques after intraventricular 6-hydroxydopamine. *Science*, **181**, 1256–1258.

Reed, P. W., and Lardy, H. A. (1972). A divalent cation ionophore. *J. Biol. Chem.*, **247**, 6970–6977.

Regan, D. (1972). *Evoked potentials in psychology, sensory physiology, and clinical medicine*. London, Chapman and Hall.

Regan, D. (1975). Recent advances in electrical recording from the human brain. *Nature*, **253**, 401–407.

Reinis, S. (1965). The formation of conditioned reflexes in rats after the parenteral administration of brain homogenate. *Activitas Nervosa Superior*, **7**, 167–168.

Reis, D. J., and Fuxe, K. (1969). Brain norepinephrine: evidence that neuronal release is essential for sham rage behaviour following brainstem transection in the cat. *Proc. Nat. Acad. Sci., U.S.A.*, **64**, 108–112.

Reis, D. J., and Gunne, L.-M. (1965). Brain catecholamines: relation to the defence reaction evoked by amygdaloid stimulation in cats. *Science*, **149**, 450–451.

Remmien, E. (1962). *Psychochemotherapy.* Los Angeles, Western Medical Publications.

Reynolds, R. W. (1963). Radio frequency lesions in the ventromedial hypothalamic 'feeding centre'. *J. Comp. Physiol. Psychol.*, **56**, 965–967.

Richter, C. P. (1939). Salt take thresholds of normal and adrenalectomized rats. *Endocrinol.*, **24**, 367–371.

Richter, C. P. (1942–3). Total self-regulatory functions in animals and human beings. *Harvey Lect.*, **38**, 63–103.

Richter, C. P., Holt, L. E., and Barelare, B. (1938). Nutritional requirements for normal growth and reproduction in rats studied by the self-selection method. *Amer. J. Physiol.*, **122**, 734–744.

Riddoch, G. (1917). The reflex functions of the completely divided spinal cord in man, compared with those associated with less severe lesions. *Brain*, **40**, 264–402.

Riesen, A. H. (1961). Stimulation as a requirement for growth and function in behavioural development. In D. W. Fiske and S. R. Maddi (Eds.), *Functions of varied experience.* Homewood, Illinois, Dorsey, pp. 57–80.

Riesen, A. H. (1966). Sensory deprivation. In E. Stellar and J. M. Sprague (Eds.), *Progress in physiological psychology*, Vol. I. New York, Academic Press, pp. 117–147.

Riesen, A. H., and Aarons, L. (1959). Visual movement and intensity discrimination in cats after early deprivation of pattern vision. *J. Comp. Physiol. Psychol.*, **52**, 142–149.

Riess, B. F. (1950). The isolation of factors of learning and native behaviour in field and laboratory studies. *Ann. N.Y. Acad. Sci.*, **51**, 1093–1102.

Roberts, R. B., Flexner, J. B., and Flexner, L. B. (1970). Some evidence for the involvement of adrenergic sites in memory. *Proc. Nat. Acad. Sci., U.S.A.*, **66**, 310–313.

Roberts, W. W. (1958). Rapid escape learning without avoidance learning motivated by hypothalamic stimulation in cats. *J. Comp. Physiol. Psychol.*, **51**, 391–399.

Romaniuk, A. (1965). Representation of aggression and flight reactions in the hypothalamus of the cat. *Acta Biologicae Experimentalis Sinica (Warsaw)*, **25**, 177–186.

Rose, S. P. R. (1968). Biochemical aspects of memory mechanisms. In A. N. Davidson and J. Dobbing (Eds.), *Applied neurochemistry.* Oxford, Blackwell, pp. 356–376.

Rosenberg, P. H. (1966). Management of disturbed adolescents. *Dis. Nerv. Syst.*, **27**, 60–61.

Rosenblatt, F. R., Farrow, J. T., and Herblin, W. F. (1966). Transfer of conditioned responses from trained rats to untrained rats by means of a brain extract. *Nature*, **209**, 46–48.

Rosenblatt, F., and Rosen, S. (1970). Effects of trained brain extracts on behaviour. In *Symposium on biology of memory*. Budapest, Hungarian Academy of Sciences.

Rosenblatt, J. S. (1965). Effects of experience on sexual behaviour in male cats. In F. A. Beach (Ed), *Sex and behaviour*. New York, John Wiley & Sons, pp. 416–439.

Rosenblatt, J. S. (1967). Non-hormonal basis of maternal behaviour in the rat. *Science*, **156**, 1512–1514.

Rosenblatt, J. S., and Aronson, L. R. (1958). The decline of sexual behaviour in male cats after castration with special reference to the role of prior sexual experience. *Behaviour*, **12**, 285–338.

Rosenthal, R. (1966). *Experimenter effects in behavioural research.* New York, Appleton-Century-Crofts.

Rosenzweig, M. R. (1966). Environmental complexity, cerebral change and behaviour. *Amer. Psychol.*, 321–332.

Rosenzweig, M. R. (1970). Evidence for anatomical and chemical changes in the brain during primary learning. In K. H. Pribram and D. E. Broadbent (Eds.), *Biology of memory*. New York and London, Academic Press, pp. 69–86.

Rosenzweig, M. R., Krech, D., Bennett, E. L., and Diamond, M. C. (1968). Modifying brain chemistry and anatomy by enrichment or impoverishment of experience. In G. Newton and S. Levine (Eds.), *Early experience and behaviour*. Springfield, Charles C. Thomas, pp. 258–298.

Rosenzweig, M. R., and Bennett, E. L. (1972). Cerebral changes in rats exposed individually to an enriched environment. *J. Comp. Physiol. Psychol.*, **80**, 304–313.

Rosenzweig, M. R., Bennett, E. L., and Diamond, M. C. (1972). Brain changes in response to experience. *Sci. Amer.*, **226**(2), 22–29.

Ross, R. B., and Steele Russell, I. (1967). Subcortical storage of classical conditioning. *Nature*, **214**, 210–211.

Rossi, A. M. (1969). General methodological considerations. In J. F. Zubeck (Ed.), *Sensory deprivation: fifteen years of research*. New York, Appleton-Century-Crofts, pp. 16–43.

Roth, S. R., Schwartz, M., and Teitelbaum, P. (1969). *Recovered lateral hypothalamic rats fail to learn specific food aversions*. Paper presented at the meeting of the Psychonomic Society, St. Louis, Missouri.

Roth, W. T., Kopell, B. S., and Bertozzi, P. E. (1970). The effect of attention on the averaged evoked response to speech sounds. *Electroenceph. clin. Neurophysiol.*, **29**, 38–46.

Rowland, V. (1957). Differential electroencephalographic response to conditioned auditory stimuli in arousal from sleep. *Electroenceph. clin. Neurophysiol.*, **9**, 585–594.

Rowntree, D. W., Nevin, S., and Wilson, A. (1950). The effects of di-isopropylfluorophosphonate in schizophrenia and manic depressive psychosis. *J. Neurol. Neurosurg. Psychiatr.*, **13**, 47–62.

Ruch, T. C. (1960). The cerebral cortex: its structure and motor functions. In T. C. Ruch and J. F. Fulton (Eds.), *Medical physiology and biophysics.* Philadelphia, Saunders, pp. 249–276.

Ruchkin, D. S., and John, E. R. (1966). Evoked potential correlates of Generalisation. *Science,* **153**, 209–211.

Rudin, S. A. (1968). National motives predict psychogenic death rates 25 years later. *Science,* **160**, 901–903.

Rutter, M. (1972). *Maternal deprivation reassessed.* Harmondsworth, Penguin Education.

Saginor, M., Horton, R. (1968). Reflex release of gonadotrophin and increased plasma testosterone concentration in male rabbits during copulation. *Endocrinol.,* **82**, 627–630.

Salmon, U. J., and Geist, S. H. (1943). Effects of androgens upon libido in women. *J. Clin. Endocrinol.,* **3**, 235–238.

Sandrew, B. B., and Mayer, J. (1973). Hyperphasia induced by Intrahypothalamic implants of mercury thioglucose. *Physiol. Behav.,* **10**, 1061–1066.

Sands, D. E. (1954). Further studies on endocrine treatment in adolescence and early adult life. *J. Ment. Sci.,* **100**, 211–219.

Sar, M., and Stumpf, W. E. (1973). Autoradiographic localization of radioactivity in the rat brain after the injection of $1,2-^3$ H-testosterone. *Endocrinology,* **92**, 251–256.

Sara, S. J. (1973). Recovery from hypoxia and ECS-induced amnesia after a single exposure to training experiment. *Physiol. Behav.,* **10**, 85–89.

Satterfield, J. H. (1965). Evoked cortical response enhancement and attention in man. A study of responses to auditory and shock stimulus. *Electroenceph. clin. Neurophysiol.,* **19**, 470–475.

Sawyer, C. H. (1956). Effects of central nervous system lesions on ovulation in the rabbit. *Anat. Rev.,* **124**, 358.

Sawyer, C. H. (1957). Triggering of the pituitary by the central nervous system. In T. H. Bullock (Ed.), *Physiological triggers.* Washington D.C., American Physiological Society.

Sawyer, C. H., and Robinson, B. (1956). Separate hypothalamic areas controlling pituitary gonadotrophic function and mating behaviour in female cats and rabbits. *J. Clin. Endocrinol.,* **16**, 914.

Schachter, S. (1971). *Emotion, obesity and crime.* New York and London, Academic Press.

Schachter, S. (1972). Cognitive effects on bodily functioning: studies of obesity and eating. In J. F. Lubar (Ed.), *A first reader in physiological psychology.* New York, Harper & Row, pp. 220–235.

Schachter, S. (1973). Nesbett's paradox. In W. L. Dunn (Ed.), *Smoking behaviour: motives and incentives.* Washington D.C., V. H. Winston & Sons.

Schachter, S. (1974). Unpublished observations from a paper delivered at the London Conference of the British Psychological Society in December 1974.

Schachter, S., and Singer, J. E. (1962). Cognitive, social and psychological determinants of emotional state. *Psychol. Rev.,* **69**, 379–399. Also reprinted in C. G. Gross and H. P. Zeigler (1969), *Readings in physiological psychology.* New York, Harper & Row, pp. 296–323.

Schachter, S., and Wheeler, L. (1962). Epinephrine, chlorpromazine and amusement. *J. Abnorm. Soc. Psychol.,* **56**, 121–128.

Schallek, W., and Kuehn, A. (1965). Effects of benzodiazepines on spontaneous EEG and arousal responses of cats. *Progr. Brain Res.,* **18**, 231–238.

Schein, N. W., and Hale, E. B. (1965). Stimuli eliciting sexual behaviour. In F. A. Beach (Ed.), *Sex and behaviour.* Sidney, New York and London, John Wiley & Sons.

Schneider, A. M., and Sherman, W. (1968). Amnesia: a function of the temporal relation of foot shock to electroconvulsive shock. *Science,* **159**, 219–221.

Schneider, A. M., Tyler, J., and Jinich, D. (1974). Recovery from retrograde amnesia: a learning process. *Science,* **184**, 87–88.

Schneiden, H. (1962). Solution drinking in rats after dehydration and after hemorrhage. *Amer. J. Physiol.,* **203**, 560–562.

Schreiner, L., and Kling, A. (1953). Behavioural changes following rhinencephalic injury in cat. *J. Neurphysiol.,* **16**, 643–659. Also reprinted in R. L. Isaacson (1964) *Basic readings in neuropsychology.* New York, Harper & Row, pp. 159–180.

Schultz, D. P. (1965). *Sensory restriction.* New York, Academic Press.

Schwade, E. D., and Geiger, S. C. (1956). Abnormal EEG findings in severe behaviour disorders. *Dis. Nerv. Syst.,* **17**, 307–317.

Schwade, E. D., and Geiger, S. C. (1960). Severe behaviour disorders with abnormal electroencephalograms. *Dis. Nerv. Syst.,* **21**, 616–620.

Segall, M. A., Campbell, T. D., and Herskowitz, M. J. (1963). Cultural differences in the perception of geometric illusions. *Science,* **139**, 769–771.

Seligman, M. E. P. (1975). *Helplessness: on depression, development and death.* San Francisco, W. H. Freeman & Co. (Distributed by Charles Scribner's Sons, New York).

Serota, R. G., Roberts, R. B., and Flexner, L. B. (1972). Acetoxycycloheximide induced transient amnesia: protective effects of adrenergic stimulants. *Proc. Nat. Acad. Sci., U.S.A.,* **69**, 340–342.

Seward, J. P. (1945). Aggressive behaviour in the rat. I. General characteristics, age and sex differences. *J. Comp. Psychol.,* **38**, 175–197.

Sharma, K. N. (1967). Perceptive mechanisms in the alimentary tract: their excitation and functions. In C. F. Code (Ed.), *Handbook of physiology.* Section 6: Alimentary canal. Washington D. C., American Physiology Society, pp. 225–237.

Sharma, K. N., Anand, B. K., Dua, S., and Singh, B.

(1961). Role of stomach in regulation of activities of hypothalamic feeding centre. *Amer. J. Physiol.*, **201**, 593–598.

Sharpless, S., and Jasper, H. H. (1956). Habituation of the arousal reaction. *Brain*, **79**, 655–680.

Shealy, C., and Peele, J. (1957). Studies on amygdaloid nucleus of cat. *J. Neurophysiol.*, **20**, 125–139.

Sheard, M. H., and Flynn, J. P. (1967). Facilitation of attack behaviour by stimulation of the midbrain of cats. *Brain Res.*, **4**, 324–333.

Sheard, M. H., and Flynn, J. P. (1968). Differential effects of electrical stimulation and lesions of the hippocampus and adjacent regions upon attack behaviour in cats. *Brain Res.*, **7**, 252–267.

Sheffield, F. D., and Roby, T. B. (1950). Reward value of non-nutritive sweet taste. *J. Comp. Physiol. Psychol.*, **43**, 471–481.

Sherrington, C. S. (1900). Experiments on the value of vascular and visceral factors for the genesis of emotion. *Proc. Roy. Soc., (Series B)*, **66**, 390–403.

Sherwood, S. L. (1952). Intraventricular medication in catatonic stupor. *Brain*, **75**, 68–75.

Shlaer, R. (1971). Shift in binocular disparity causes compensatory change in the cortical structure of kittens. *Science*, **173**, 638–641.

Sidman, M., Brady, J., Boren, J., Conrad, D. G., and Schulman, A. (1955). Reward schedules and behaviour maintained by intracranial self stimulation. *Science*, **122**, 830–831.

Sigg, E. B. (1969). Relationship of aggressive behaviour to adrenal and gonadol function in male mice. In S. Garattini and E. B. Sigg (Eds.), *Aggressive behaviour*. Amsterdam, John Wiley & Sons, pp. 143–149.

Silverman, A. P. (1965). Ethological and statistical analysis of drug effects on the social behaviour of laboratory rats. *Brit. J. Pharmacol.*, **24**, 579–590.

Smith, D. B. D., Donchin, E., Cohen, L., and Starr, A. (1970b). Auditory averaged evoked potentials in man during selective binaural listening. *Electroenceph. clin. Neurophysiol.*, **28**, 146–152.

Smith, D. E., King, M. B., and Hoebel, B. G. (1970a). Lateral hypothalamic control of killing: evidence for a cholinoceptive mechanism. *Science*, **167**, 900–901.

Smith, D. F., and Stricker, E. M. (1969). The influence of need on the rat's preference for dilute NaCl solutions. *Physiol. Behav.*, **4**, 407–410.

Smith, G. M., and Beecher, H. K. (1959). Amphetamine sulfate and athletic performance. I. Objective effects. *J. Amer. Med. Ass.*, **170**, 542–547.

Smith, G. M., and Beecher, H. K. (1960a). Amphetamine, secobarbital and athletic performance. II. Subjective evaluations of performances, mood states. *J. Amer. Med. Ass.*, **172**, 1502–1514.

Smith, G. M., and Beecher, H. K. (1960b). Amphetamine, secobarbital and athletic performance. III. Quantitative effects on judgement. *J. Amer. Med. Ass.*, **172**, 1623–1629.

Smith, M. C. (1967). Theories of the psychological

refractory period. *Psychol. Bull.*, **67**, 202–213.

Snyder, F., and Scott, J. (1972). The psychophysiology of sleep. In N. S. Greenfield and R. A. Sternbach (Eds.), *Handbook of psychophysiology*. New York, Holt, Rinehart & Winston, pp. 645–708.

Snyder, S. H., Banerjee, S. P., Yamamura, H. I., and Greenberg, D. (1974). Drugs, neurotransmitters and schizophrenia. *Science*, **184**, 1243–1253.

Sokolov, E. N. (1963). Higher nervous functions: the orienting reflex. *Ann. Rev. Physiol.*, **25**, 545–580.

Solomon, P. (1972). Sensory deprivation. In A. M. Freedman and H. I. Kaplan (Eds.), *Human behaviour: biological, psychological, sociological*. New York, Atheneum, pp. 492–497.

Soulairac, A., and Soulairac, M. L. (1956). Effets de lésions hypothalamiques sur le comportement sexuel et le tractus genital du rat male. *Annales d'Endocrinologie*, **17**, 731–735.

Sperling, G. (1960). The information available in brief visual presentations. *Psychol. Monogr.*, **74**, (Whole No. 498).

Spong, P., Haider, M., and Lindsley, D. B. (1965). Selective attentiveness and cortical evoked responses to visual and auditory stimuli. *Science*, **148**, 395–397.

Stamm, J. S. (1955). The function of the median cerebral cortex in maternal behaviour of rats. *J. Comp. Physiol. Psychol.*, **48**, 347–356.

Steele Russell, I. (1969). Cortical mechanisms and learning. In N. S. Sutherland and R. Gilbert (Eds.), *Animal discrimination learning*. London, Academic Press, pp. 335–356.

Steele Russell, I. (1971). Neurological basis of complex learning. *Brit. Med. Bull.*, **27**, 278–285.

Steele Russell, I., Kleinman, D., and Plotkin, H. C. (1969). The role of the cerebral cortex in the acquisition and retention of a classically conditioned passive avoidance response. *Physiol. Behav.*, **4**, 517–525.

Stein, L. (1964). Reciprocal action of reward and punishment mechanisms. In R. G. Heath (Ed.), *The role of pleasure in behaviour*. New York, Harper & Row, pp. 113–139.

Stein, L. (1965). Facilitation of avoidance behaviour by positive brain stimulation. *J. Comp. Physiol. Psychol.*, **60**, 9–16.

Stein, L. (1971). Neurochemistry of reward and punishment: some implications for the aetiology of schizophrenia. *J. Psychiatr. Rev.*, **8**, 345–361.

Stein, L., and Wise, C. D. (1969). Release of norepinephrine from hypothalamus and amygdala by rewarding medial forebrain bundle stimulation and amphetamine. *J. Comp. Physiol. Psychol.*, **67**, 189–198.

Stein, L., and Wise, C. D. (1970). Behavioural pharmacology of central stimulants. In W. G. Clark and J. Del Giudice (Eds.), *Principles of pharmacology*. New York, Academic Press.

Stein, L., and Wise, C. D. (1971). Possible ethology of schizophrenia: progressive damage to the noradrenergic reward system by 6-hydroxydopamine. *Science*, 171, 1032–1036.

Stein, L., Wise, C. D., and Berger, B. D. (1972). Noradrenergic reward mechanisms, recovery of function and schizophrenia. In J. L. McGaugh (Ed.), *The Chemistry of mood, motivation and memory.* New York and London, Plenum Press, pp. 81–103.

Stellar, E. (1954). The physiology of motivation. *Psychol. Rev.*, 61, 522.

Stellar, E. (1959). Drive and motivation. In J. Field, H. W. Magoun and V. E. Hall (Eds.), *Handbook of physiology*. Section 1. Neurophysiology, Vol. III. Washington D.C., American Physiological Society, pp. 1501–1527.

Stellar, E. (1967). Hunger in man: a comparative and phsyiological study. *Amer. Psychol.*, 22, 105–117.

Sterman, M. B., and Clemente, C. D. (1974). Forebrain mechanisms for the onset of sleep. In O. Petre-Quadens and J. D. Schlag (Eds.), *Basic sleep mechanisms.* New York and London, Academic Press, pp. 83–97.

Stone, C. P. (1927). The retention of copulatory ability in male rats following castration. *J. Comp. Psychol.*, 7, 369–387.

Stricker, E. M. (1969). Osmoregulation and volume regulation in rats. Inhibition of hypovolemic thirst by water. *Amer. J. Physiol.*, 217, 98–105.

Stumpf, C. (1965). Drug action on the electrical activity of the hippocampus. *Internat. Rev. Neurobiol.*, 8, 77–138.

Stunkard, A. J., Van Itallie, T. B., and Reis, B. B. (1955). The mechanism of satiety: effect of glucagon on gastric hunger contractions in man. *Proc. Soc. Exper. Biol., Med.*, 89, 258–261.

Suedfeld, P. (1969). Changes in intellectual performance and susceptibility to influence. In J. P. Zubek (Ed.), *Sensory deprivation: fifteen years of research*. New York, Appleton-Century-Crofts, pp. 126–166.

Summers, T. B., and Kaelber, W. W. (1962). Amygdalectomy: effects in cats and a survey of its present status. *Amer. J. Physiol.*, 203, 1117–1119.

Sutton, S., Tueting, P., Zubin, J., and John, E. R. (1967). Information delivery and sensory evoked potentials. *Science*, 155, 1436–1439.

Swanson, P. P., Timson, G. H., and Frazier, E. (1935). Some observation on the physiological adjustment of the albino rat to a diet poor in salts when edestin is the source of dietary protein. *J. Biol. Chem.*, 109, 729–737.

Sweet, W. H., Ervin, E., and Mark, V. H. (1969). The relationship of violent behaviour to focal cerebral disease. In S. Garattini and E. B. Sigg (Eds.), *Aggressive behaviour.* New York, John Wiley, pp. 336–352.

Szilard, L. (1964). On memory and recall. *Proc. Nat. Acad. Sci., U.S.A.*, 51, 1092–1099.

Takesada, M., Kakimoto, Y., Sano, I., and Koneko, Z. (1963). 3,4-dimethoxyphenylethylamine and other amines in the urine of schizophrenic patients. *Nature*, 199, 203.

Talbot, H. S. (1955). The sexual function in paraplegia. *J. Urol.*, 73, 91–100.

Talbot, S. A., and Marshall, W. H. (1941). Physiological studies on neural mechanisms of visual localization and discrimination. *Amer. J. Opthal.*, 24, 1255–1264.

Taleisnik, S., Caligaris, L., and Astrada, J. J. (1966). Effect of copulation on the release of pituitary gonadotrophine in male and female rats. *Endocrinol.*, 79, 49–54.

Talland, G. A. (1968). *Disorders of memory and learning.* Harmondsworth, Penguin Books.

Tecce, J. J. (1972). Contingent negative variation (CNV) and psychological processes in man. *Psychol. Bull.*, 77, 73–108.

Teilhard De Chardin, P. (1955). *Le phénomène humain.* Editions de Seuil. First published in English as 'The phenomenon of man', in 1959 London, William Collins Sons & Co Ltd, and New York, Harper & Row. Issued in Fontana Religious books in 1965.

Teitelbaum, P. (1955). Sensory control of hypothalamic hyperphagia. *J. Comp. Physiol. Psychol.*, 48, 156–165.

Teitelbaum, P. (1961). Disturbances of feeding and drinking behaviour after hypothalamic lesions. In M. R. Jones (Ed.), *Nebraska symposium on motivation*, Lincoln, Nebraska, University of Nebraska Press, pp. 39–65.

Teitelbaum, P. (1971). The encephalization of hunger. In E. Stellar and J. M. Sprague (Eds.), *Progress in physiological psychology*, Vol. 4. New York and London, Academic Press, pp. 319–350.

Teitelbaum, P., and Cytawa, J. (1965). Spreading depression and recovery from lateral hypothalamic damage. *Science*, 147, 61–63.

Teitelbaum, P., and Epstein, A. N. (1962). The lateral hypothalamic syndrome: recovery of feeding and drinking after lateral hypothalamic lesions. *Psychol. Rev.*, 69, 74–90.

Teitelbaum, P., and Stellar, E. (1954). Recovery from failure to eat produced by hypothalamic lesions. *Science*, 120, 894–895.

Telford, C. W. (1931). The refractory phase of voluntary and associative responses. *J. Exp. Psychol.*, 14, 1–36.

Terzian, H., and Dalle Ore, G., (1955). Syndrome of Kluver and Bucy reproduced in man by bilateral removal of the temporal lobes. *Neurology*, 5, 373–380.

Thach, W. T. (1968). Discharge of Purkinje and cerebellar nuclear neurones during rapidly alternating arm movements in the monkey. *J. Neurophysiol.*, 31, 785–797.

Thistlethwaite, P. (1951). An experimental test of a reinforcement interpretation of latent learning. *J. Comp. Physiol. Psychol.*, 44, 431–441.

Thomas, T. R., and Neiman, C. N. (1968). Aspects of copulatory behaviour preventing atrophy in male rats. *Endocrinol.*, **83**, 633-635.

Thompson, C. I., and Grossman, L. B. (1972). Loss and recovery of long term memories after ECS in rats: evidence for state dependent recall. *J. Comp. Physiol. Psychol.*, **78**, 248-254.

Thompson, C. J., and Neely, J. E. (1970). Dissociated learning in rats produced by electroconvulsive shock. *Physiol. Behav.*, **5**, 783-786.

Thompson, W. R. (1957). Influence of prenatal maternal anxiety on emotionality of young rats. *Science*, **125**, 698-699.

Thorndike, E. L. (1913). *The psychology of learning.* New York, Teacher's College.

Tinbergen, N. (1951). *The study of instinct.* London and New York, Oxford University Press.

Tizard, J. (1969). The role of social institutions in the causation, prevention and alleviation of mental retardation. In C. Hayward (Ed.), *Socio-cultural aspects of mental retardation.* New York and London, Academic Press.

Torda, C. (1969). Biochemical and bio-electrical processes related to sleep, paradoxical sleep and arousal. *Psychol. Rep.*, **24**, 807-824.

Tow, P. M., and Whitty, C. W. (1953). Personality changes after operations on the cingulate gyrus in man. *J. Neurol. Neurosurg. Psychiatr.*, **16**, 186-193.

Towbin, E. J. (1949). Gastric distension as a factor in the satiation of thirst in esophagostomized dogs. *Amer. J. Physiol.*, **159**, 533-541.

Tower, S. S. (1935). The dissociation of cortical excitation from cortical inhibition by pyramidal section and the syndrome of that lesion in the cat. *Brain*, **58**, 238-255.

Tower, S. S. (1936). Extrapyramidal action from the cat's cerebral cortex: motor and inhibitory. *Brain*, **59**, 408-444.

Tranzer, J. P., and Thoenen, H. (1968). An electron microscope study of selective, acute degeneration of sympathetic nerve terminals after administration of 6-hydroxydopamine. *Experientia*, **24**, 155-156.

Treffert, D. A. (1964). The psychiatric patient with an EEG temporal lobe focus. *Amer. J. Psychiatr.*, **120**, 765-771.

Treisman, A. (1960). Contextual cues in selective listening. *Quart. J. Exp. Psychol.*, **12**, 242-248.

Treisman, A. (1964a). Verbal cues, language and meaning in attention. *Amer. J. Psychol.*, **77**, 206-214.

Treisman, A. (1964b). The effect of irrelevant material on the efficiency of selective listening. *Amer. J. Psychol.*, **77**, 533-546.

Treisman, A. (1964c). Selection attention in man. *Brit. Med. Bull.*, **20**, 12-16.

Triggs, T. J. (1968). *Capacity sharing and speeded reactions to successive signals.* Technical Report No. 9 (August), University of Michigan, Contract No. AF 49(638)-1736, United States Department of Defense.

Tueting, P., Sutton, S., and Zubin, J. (1971). Quantitative evoked potential correlates of the probability of events. *Psychophysiol.*, **7**, 385-394.

Turnbull, C. (1973). *The mountain people.* London, Pan Books (Picador).

Udry, J. R., and Morris, N. M. (1968). Distribution of coitus in the menstrual cycle. *Nature*, **220**, 593-596.

Ungar, G. (1967). Transfer of learned behaviour by brain extracts. *J. Biol. Psychol.*, **9**, 12-27.

Ungar, G. (1970). Role of proteins and peptides in learning and memory. In G. Ungar (Ed.), *Molecular mechanisms in memory and learning.* New York, Plenum Press, pp. 149-175.

Ungar, G. (1971). Chemical transfer of acquired information. In A. Schwartz (Ed.), *Methods in pharmacology*, Vol. 1. New York, Appleton-Century-Crofts, pp. 479.

Ungar, G., and Fjerdingstad, E. J. (1969). Chemical nature of the transfer factor. RNA or protein? In G. Adam (Ed.), *Biology of Memory.* New York, Plenum Press, pp. 137-143.

Ungar, G., Galvan, L., and Chapouthier, G. (1972a). Evidence for chemical coding of color discrimination in goldfish brain. *Experientia*, **28**(2), 1026-1027.

Ungar, G., Desiderio, D. M., and Parr, W. (1972b). Isolation, identification and synthesis of a specific-behaviour inducing brain peptide. *Nature*, **238**, 198-199.

Urich, J. (1938). The social hierarchy in albino mice. *J. Comp. Psychol.*, **25**, 373-413.

Urry, D. W. (1971). The gramicidin: a transmembrane channel, a proposed II (L,D) helix. *Proc. Nat. Acad. Sci., U.S.A.*, **68**, 672-676.

Valbo, A. B. (1971). Muscle spindle response at the onset of isometric voluntary contractions in man: time difference between fusimotor and skeleto-motor effects. *J. Physiol.*, **218**, 405-431.

Valenstein, E. S. (1965). Independence of approach and escape reactions to electrical stimulation of the brain. *J. Comp. Physiol. Psychol.*, **60**, 20-30.

Valenstein, E. S. (1967). Selection of nutritive and non-nutritive solutions under different conditions of need. *J. Comp. Physiol. Psychol.*, **63**, 429-433.

Valenstein, E. S., Riss, W., and Young, W. C. (1955). Experiential and genetic factors in the organization of sexual behaviour in male guinea pigs. *J. Comp. Physiol. Psychol.*, **48**, 397-403.

Valenstein, E. S., and Young, W. C. (1955). An experiential factor influencing the effectivenss of testosterone propionate in eliciting sexual behaviour in male guinea pigs. *Endocrinol.*, **56**, 173-177.

Valenstein, E. S., Cox, V. C., and Kakolewski, J. W. (1968). Modification of motivated behaviour elicited by electrical stimulation of the hypothalamus. *Science*, **159**, 1119-1121.

Valenstein, E. S., Cox, V. C., and Kakolewski, J. W. (1970). Re-examination of the role of the hypothalamus in motivation. *Psychol. Rev.*, **77**, 16-31.

Valverde, F. (1968). Structural changes in the area striata of the mouse after enucleation. *Exp. Brain Res.*, **5**, 274-292.

Valzelli, L. (1967). Drugs and aggressiveness. *Adv. Pharmacol.*, **5**, 79–108.

van Dis, H., and Larsson, K. (1971). Induction of sexual arousal in the castrated male rat by intracranial stimulation. *Physiol. Behav.*, **6**, 85–86.

Van Lawick-Goodall, J. (1968). The behaviour of free living chimpanzees in the Gombe Stream Reserve. *Animal Behav.*, **1**, 161–311.

Van Sluyters, R. C., and Blakemore, C. (1973). Experimental creation of unusual neuronal properties in visual cortex of kitten. *Nature*, **246**, 506–508.

Vaughan, E., and Fisher, A. E. (1962). Male sexual behaviour induced by intracranial electrical stimulation. *Science*, **137**, 758–760. Also in C. G. Cross and H. P. Zeigler (Eds.) (1969), *Readings in physiological psychology*. London, Harper & Row.

Venables, P. (1974). Psychophysiological aspects of psychiatric investigation. *Excerpta Medica Internat. Congr. Ser. 359, Proc. IX Congr. Colleg. Internat. Neuropsychopharmacol.*, pp. 159–162.

Venables, P. H. (1976). Experimental studies on schizophrenia. Paper delivered at the 10th Postgraduate-Postdoctoral Conference in the Behavioural Sciences held in Manchester.

Verney, E. B. (1947). The antidiuretic hormone and the factors which determine its release. *Proc. Roy. Soc., Series B*, **135**, 25–106.

Von Frisch, K. (1967). *The dance language and orientation of bees*. Cambridge, Mass., Harvard University Press.

Von Senden, M. (1932). *Space and sight: the perception of space and shape in congenitally blind patients, before and after operation*. Leipzig, Barth, (English translation, London, Methuen, 1960).

Vinogradova, O. S., Semyonova, T. P., and Konovalov, V. Ph. (1970). Trace phenomena in single neurones of hippocampus and mammiliary bodies. In K. H. Pribram and D. E. Broadbent (Eds.), *Biology of memory*. New York and London, Academic Press, pp. 191–222.

Wald, G. (1959). The photoreceptor process in vision. In J. Field, H. W. Magoun, and V. E. Hall (Eds.), *Handbook of Physiology*. Section I. Neurophysiology, Vol. I. Washington D.C., American Physiological Society, pp. 671–692.

Waller, W. H. (1940). Progression movements elicited by subthalamic stimulation. *J. Neurophysiol.*, **3**, 300–307.

Walter, W. G. (1964). The convergence and interaction of visual, auditory and tactile responses in human non-specific cortex. *Annals. N.Y. Acad. Sci.*, **112**, 320–361.

Walter, W. G. (1967). Slow potential changes in the human brain associated with expectancy, decision and intention. In W. Cobb and C. Morocutti (Eds.), *The evoked potentials. Electroenceph. clin. Neurophysiol.*, **Suppl. 26**, 123–130.

Walter, W. G., Cooper, R., Aldridge, V. J., McCallum, W. C., and Winter, A. L. (1964). Contingent negative variation: an electric sign of sensori-motor association and expectancy in the human brain. *Nature*, **203**, 380–384.

Wampler, R. S. (1973). Increased motivation in rats with ventromedial hypothalamic lesions. *J. Comp. Physiol. Psychol.*, **84**, 275–285.

Warburton, D. M. (1975). *Brain, behaviour and drugs*. London, John Wiley & Sons.

Warrington, E. K., and Weiskrantz, L. (1968). A study of learning and retention in amnesic patients. *Neuropsychologia*, **6**, 283–291.

Warrington, E. K., and Weiskrantz, L. (1973). Short and long term memory defects in man. In J. A. Deutsch (Ed.), *The physiological basis of memory*. New York and London, Academic Press, pp. 365–396.

Washburn, S. L. (1960). Tools and human evolution. *Sci. Amer.*, **103**(3), 62–75. Reprinted in R. F. Thompson (Ed.), *Physiological psychology*. San Fransisco, W. H. Freeman, pp. 15–27.

Wasman, M., and Flynn, J. P. (1962). Directed attack elicited from hypothalamus. *Arch. Neurol.*, **6**, 220–227.

Watson, J. B. (1919). *Psychology from the standpoint of a behaviourist*. Philadelphia, Lippincott.

Watson, J. D., and Crick, F. H. (1953). Molecular structure of nucleic acids. *Nature*, **171**, 737–738.

Waxenberg, S. E., Drellich, M. G., and Sutherland, A. M. (1959). The role of hormones in human behaviour. I. Changes in female sexuality after adrenalectomy. *J. Clin. Endocrinol.*, **19**, 193–202.

Wayner, M. J., and Carey, R. J. (1973). Basic drives. *Ann. Rev. Psychol.*, **24**, 53–80.

Wayner, M. J., Cott, A., Millner, J., and Tartaglione, R. (1971). Loss of 2-deoxy-D-glucose induced eating in recovered lateral rats. *Physiol. Behav.*, **7**, 881–884.

Webb, W. B. (1971). Sleep behaviour as a biorhythm. In W. P. Colquhoun (Ed.), *Biological rhythms and human performance*. London and New York, Academic Press, pp. 149–177.

Weddell, G., (1941). The pattern of cutaneous innervation in relation to cutaneous sensibility. *J. Anat.*, **75**, 346–367.

Weddell, G. (1961). Receptors for somatic sensation. In M. A. B. Brazier (Ed.), *Brain and behaviour*. Vol. I. Washington D.C., American Institute of Biological Sciences, pp. 13–48.

Weeks, J. R. (1964). Experimental narcotic addiction. *Sci. Amer.*, **211**(3), 46–52.

Weinberg, H., Walter, W. G., and Crow, H. J. (1970). Intracerebral events in humans related to real and imaginery stimuli. *Electroenceph. clin. Neurophysiol.*, **29**, 1–9.

Weiskrantz, L. (1963). Contour discrimination in a young monkey with striate cortex ablation. *Neuropsychologia*, **1**, 145–164.

Weiskrantz, L., and Mishkin, M. (1958). Effects of temporal and frontal cortical lesions on auditory discrimination in monkey. *Brain*, **81**, 406–414.

Weiss, B., and Laties, V. G. (1961). Behavioural thermoregulation. *Science,* 133, 1338-1344.

Weiss, B., and Heller, A. (1969). Methodological problems in evaluating the role of cholinergic mechanisms in behaviour. *Fed. Proc.,* 28, 135-146.

Weiss, K. P. (1970). Measurements of the effects of brain extract on interorganism information transfer. In W. L. Byrne (Ed.), *Molecular approaches to learning and memory.* New York, Academic Press, pp. 325-334.

Welch, B. L., Hendley, E. D., and Turek, I. (1974). Norepinephrine uptake in cerebral cortical synaptosomes after one fight or electroconvulsive shock, *Science,* 183, 220-221.

Welker, W. I. (1961). An analysis of exploratory and play behaviour in animals. In D. W. Fiske and S. R. Maddi (Eds.), *Functions of varied experience.* Homewood, Illinois, Dorsey, pp. 253-277.

Wettendorf, H. (1901). Modifications du sang sous l'influence de la privation d'eau. Contribution a l'étude de la soif. *Traveaux du laboratoire de physiologie. Institute Solvay,* 4, 353-384.

Whalen, R. E. (1963). The initiation of mating in naive female cats. *Animal Behaviour,* 11, 461-463.

Whalen, R. E. (1966). Sexual motivation. *Psychol. Rev.,* 73, 151-163.

Wheatley, M. D. (1944). The hypothalamus and affective behaviour in cats: a study of the effects of experimental lesions with anatomical correlations. *Arch. Neurol. Psychiatr.,* 52, 296-316.

White, J. C. (1940). Autonomic discharge from stimulation of the hypothalamus in man. *Res. Publ. Ass. Res. Nerv. Ment. Dis.,* 38, 62-70.

Whitty, C. W. M., and Zangwill, O. (1966). *Amnesia.* London and Washington D.C., Butterworths.

Wiener, N. (1950). *The human use of human beings.* New York, Houghton Mifflin (Published in 1968 by Sphere Books, London).

Wiener, N. (1961). *Cybernetics, or control and communication in the animal and the machine.* (2nd ed.), Cambridge, Mass., MIT Press.

Wiener, N. I., and Deutsch, J. A. (1968). Temporal aspects of anticholinergic and anticholinesterase induced amnesia for an appetitive habit. *J. Comp. Physiol. Psychol.,* 66, 613-617.

Wiesel, T. N., and Hubel, D. H. (1963). Effects of visual deprivation on morphology and physiology of cells in the cat's lateral geniculate body. *J. Neurophysiol.,* 26, 978-993.

Wiesel, T. N., and Hubel, D. H. (1965a). Comparison of the effects of unilateral and bilateral eye closure on cortical unit responses in kittens. *J. Neurophysiol.,* 28, 1029-1040.

Wiesel, T. N., and Hubel, D. H. (1965b). Extent of recovery from the effects of visual deprivation in kittens. *J. Neurophysiol.,* 28, 1060-1072.

Wiesel, T. N., and Hubel, D. H. (1966). Spatial and chromatic interactions in the lateral geniculate body of the rhesus monkey. *J. Neurophysiol.,* 29, 1115-1156.

Wiesner, B. P., and Mirskaia, L. (1930). On the endocrine basis of mating in the mouse. *Quart. J. Exp. Physiol.,* 20, 274-279.

Wilcox, R. E., and Levitt, R. A. (1975). The depressants. In R. A. Levitt (Ed.), *Psychopharmacology.* New York, John Wiley & Sons (Halstead Press), pp. 145-186.

Wilder, J. (1947). Sugar metabolism in its relation to criminology. In R. M. Linduer and R. V. Seliger (Eds.), *Handbook of correctional psychology.* New York, Philosophical Library.

Wilkinson, R. T. (1967). Evoked response and reaction time. *Acta Psychologica,* 27, 235-245.

Wilkinson, R. T., and Morlock, H. C. (1967). Auditory evoked response and reaction time. *Electroenceph. clin. Neurophysiol.,* 23, 50-56.

Williams, H. C., Hammack, J. T., Daly, R. L., Dement, W. C., and Lubin, A. (1964). Responses to auditory stimulation, sleep loss and the EEG stages of sleep. *Electroenceph. clin. Neurophysiol.,* 16, 269-279.

Williams, H. L., Holloway, F. A., and Griffiths, W. J. (1973). Physiological psychology: sleep. *Ann. Rev. Psychol.,* 24, 279-316.

Williams, H. L., Morlock, H. C., Jr., and Morlock, J. V. (1966). Instrumental behaviour during sleep. *Psychophysiology,* 2, 208-216.

Williams, R. A., and Campbell, B. A. (1961). Weight loss and quinine-milk ingestion as measures of 'hunger' in infant and adult rats. *J. Comp. Physiol. Psychol.,* 54, 220-222.

Wilson, M. (1957). Effects of circumscribed cortical lesions upon somesthetic and visual discrimination in the monkey. *J. Comp. Physiol. Psychol.,* 50, 630-635.

Wise, C. D., and Stein, L. (1969). Facilitation of brain stimulation by central administration of norepinephrine. *Science,* 163, 229-301.

Wise, C. D., and Stein, L. (1973). Dopamine-β-hydroxylase deficits in the brain of schizophrenic patients. *Science,* 181, 344-347.

Wolf, S. (1965). *The stomach.* New York, Oxford University Press.

Wolf, S., and Welsh, J. D. (1972). The gastrointestinal tract as a responsive system. In N. S. Greenfield and R. A. Sternbach, *Handbook of Psychophysiology.* New York, Holt, Rinehart, Winston, pp. 419-456.

Wolf, S., and Wolf, H. G. (1947). *Human Gastric Function: an experimental study of a man and his stomach,* (2nd edn). New York, Oxford University Press.

Wood, C. D. (1958). Behavioural changes following discrete lesions of temporal lobe structures. *Neurology,* 8, 215-220.

Woodworth, R. S., and Schlosberg, H. (1954). *Experimental Psychology.* London, Methuen.

Woodworth, R. S., and Sherrington, C. S. (1904). A pseudoaffective reflex and its spinal path. *J. Physiol. (London),* 31, 234-243.

Woolley, D. W. (1967). Involvement of the hormone serotonin in emotion and mind. In D. C. Glass (Ed.), *Neurophysiology and emotion*. New York, Rockefeller University Press, pp. 108–116.

Worden, F. G. (1966). Attention and auditory electrophysiology. In E. Stellar and J. M. Sprague (Eds.), *Progress in physiological psychology*, Vol. 1. New York and London, Academic Press, pp. 45–116.

Wynne-Edwards, V. C. (1962). *Animal dispersion in relation to social behaviour*. Edinburgh, Oliver & Boyd.

Yamamoto, J., and Seeman, W. (1960). A psychological study of castrated males, *Psychiat. Res. Rep. Amer. Psychiat. Ass.*, **12**, 97.

Yasukochi, G. (1960). Emotional responses elicited by electrical stimulation of the hypothalamus in cat. *Folia Psychiat. Neurol. Jap.*, **14**, 260–267.

Young, P. T. (1940). Reversal of food preference of the white rat through controlled prefeeding. *J. Gen. Psychol.*, **22**, 33–66.

Young, W. C., and Fish, W. R. (1945). The ovarian hormones and spontaneous running activity in the female rat. *Endocrinology*. **36**, 181–189.

Young, W. C. (1961). The hormones and mating behaviour. In W. C. Young (Ed), *Sex and internal secretions*. Baltimore, Williams & Wilkins, pp. 1173–1239.

Young, W. C., Goy, R. W., and Phoenix, C. H. (1964). Hormones and sexual behaviour. *Science*, **143**, 212–218. Also reprinted in Gross, C. G., and Zeigler, H. P., (1969). *Readings in physiological psychology*. London, Harper & Row, pp. 153–167.

Zeigler, H. P. (1964). Displacement activity and motivational theory: a case study in the history of ethology. *Psychol. Bull.*, **61**, 362–376.

Zeitlin, A. B., Cottrell, T. L., and Lloyd, F. A. (1957). Sexology of the paraplegic male. *Fertility and sterility*, **8**, 337–344.

Zemp, J. W., Wilson, J. E., Schlesinger, K., Boggan, W. C., and Glassman, E. (1966). Brain function and macromolecules, I. Incorporation of uridine into RNA of mouse brain during short term training experience. *Proc. Nat. Acad. Sci., U.S.A.*, **55**, 1423–1431.

Zimbarbo, P. G. (1958). The effects of early avoidance training and rearing conditions upon the sexual behaviour of the male rat. *J. Comp. Physiol. Psychol.*, **51**, 764–769.

Zubek, J. P. (1969). Physiological and biochemical effects. In J. P. Zubek (Ed.), *Sensory deprivation: fifteen years of research*. New York, Appleton-Century-Crofts, pp. 254–288.

Zubek, J. P., and Welch, G. (1963). EEG changes after prolonged sensory and perceptual deprivation. *Science*, **139**, 209–210.

Zubek, J. P., Bayer, L. Milstein, S., and Shephard, J. M. (1969). Behavioural and physiological changes during prolonged immobilization plus perceptual deprivation. *J. Abnorm. Psychol.*, **74**(2), 230–236.

Zuckerman, M. (1969a). Hallucinations, reported sensations, and images. In J. P. Zubek (Ed), *Sensory deprivation: fifteen years of research*. New York, Appleton-Century-Crofts, pp. 407–432.

Zuckerman, M. (1969b). Theoretical formulations. I. In J. P. Zubek *Sensory deprivation: fifteen years of research*. New York, Appleton-Century-Crofts, pp. 407–432.

Footnote references

Friedman, M. I., and Stricker, E. M. (1976). The physiological psychology of hunger: a physiological perspective. *Psychol. Rev.*, **83**, 409–431—see pp. 111 and 122.

Hink, R. F., van Voorhis, S. T., and Hillyard, S. A. (1977). The division of attention and the human auditory evoked potential. *Neuropsychologia*, **15**, 597–605—see p. 298.

Kutas, M., McCarthy, G., and Donchin, E. (1977). Augmenting mental chronometry: the P300 as a measure of stimulus evaluation time. *Science*, **197**, 792–794—see p. 322.

Index

visual image ie of the Taj Mahal although not seen

auditory image —

Emotional states results from arousal
results from evaluation re expectations
envy, jelousy — have their own characteristic
tone fear, hate,

Jelousy a whole host of current evaluations
connected with ones own image of self-esteem
                                        (ie paranoia)
Jelousy can arise from a constructed fantasy
as well as evidence
Some people go around looking for rivals —
if nobody is a threat — no interruption.
If everyone is seen as a rival — continuous
interruption from within.
What does your mind tell you to expect
or what does does the world tell you to expect.

The need to possess ∴ everyone can be a rival.
Irrational behaviour — what one thinks + arousal
not necessarily from external effects.

The Theory

interruption - if one expects
a £100 & given £80 - interruption
of expectations
if given £150 = also interruption

Psycopaths / Sociopaths - high characteristically
autonomic arousal systems
often emotionally impoverished - difficult
to find sufficient autonomic arousal

The evidence of our senses overrides
our fantasies most of the time .

autonomic nervous system.

anxiety = I don't know what to do
next plus arousal
(helplessness)

always in some state of arousal ∴.
arousal is always judged against the
state of arousal.

∴ evaluation.
positive evaluation.
negative evaluations.

Mood:-   background of
a continuing ~~state~~ of evaluation + raised
                    level
arousal. (low state of emotion which
persists.

Emotion:-   aroused
People who are ~~aroused~~ will react more
strongly to evaluation
                    +
Appropriate or inappropriate affect.

negative evaluation — more likely to react to
negative stimulus.

Spinal Injuries
The more extensive the injury to the body the more
extensive the loss of affect. The higher the injury
I don't the neck
ie the neck up the less affect. ie less bodily feedback
ie errors of autonomic arousal which are
not presently as good